T0202826

Communications
in Computer and Information Science   **1753**

More information about this series at https://link.springer.com/bookseries/7899

Irena Koprinska · Paolo Mignone ·
Riccardo Guidotti · Szymon Jaroszewicz ·
Holger Fröning · Francesco Gullo ·
Pedro M. Ferreira · Damian Roqueiro et al. (Eds.)

Machine Learning and Principles and Practice of Knowledge Discovery in Databases

International Workshops of ECML PKDD 2022
Grenoble, France, September 19–23, 2022
Proceedings, Part II

 Springer

For the full list of editors *see next page*

ISSN 1865-0929   ISSN 1865-0937 (electronic)
Communications in Computer and Information Science
ISBN 978-3-031-23632-7   ISBN 978-3-031-23633-4 (eBook)
https://doi.org/10.1007/978-3-031-23633-4

This Springer imprint is published by the registered company Springer Nature Switzerland AG
The registered company address is: Gewerbestrasse 11, 6330 Cham, Switzerland

Editors

Irena Koprinska
University of Sydney
Sydney, Australia

Riccardo Guidotti
University of Pisa
Pisa, Italy

Holger Fröning
Heidelberg University
Heidelberg, Germany

Pedro M. Ferreira
University of Lisbon
Lisbon, Portugal

Gaia Ceddia
Barcelona Supercomputing Center
Barcelona, Spain

João Gama
University of Porto
Porto, Portugal

Ricard Gavaldà
UPC BarcelonaTech
Barcelona, Spain

Zbigniew Ras
University of North Carolina
Charlotte, USA

Francesca Naretto
University of Pisa
Pisa, Italy

Przemyslaw Biecek
Warsaw University of Technology
Warszaw, Poland

Gregor Schiele
University of Duisburg-Essen
Essen, Germany

Michaela Blott
AMD
Dublin, Ireland

Ivan Luciano Danesi
UniCredit
Milan, Italy

Paolo Mignone
University of Bari Aldo Moro
Bari, Italy

Szymon Jaroszewicz
Warsaw University of Technology
Warsaw, Poland

Francesco Gullo
UniCredit
Rome, Italy

Damian Roqueiro
Roche
Basel, Switzerland

Slawomir Nowaczyk
Halmstad University
Halmstad, Sweden

Rita Ribeiro
University of Porto
Porto, Portugal

Elio Masciari
University of Naples Federico II
Naples, Italy

Ettore Ritacco
ICAR-CNR
Rende, Italy

Andreas Theissler
Aalen University of Applied Sciences
Aalen, Germany

Wouter Verbeke
KU Leuven
Leuven, Belgium

Franz Pernkopf
Graz University of Technology
Graz, Austria

Ilaria Bordino
UniCredit
Rome, Italy

Giovanni Ponti
National Agency for New Technologies
Rome, Italy

Lorenzo Severini
Unicredit
Rome, Italy

Giuseppina Andresini (iD)
University of Bari Aldo Moro
Bari, Italy

Guilherme Graça (iD)
University of Lisbon
Lisbon, Portugal

Naghmeh Ghazaleh (iD)
Roche
Basel, Switzerland

Diego Saldana
Novartis
Basel, Switzerland

Arif Canakoglu
Fondazione IRCCS Ca' Granda Ospedale
Maggiore Policlinico
Milan, Italy

Pietro Pinoli
Politecnico di Milano
Milan, Italy

Sepideh Pashami (iD)
Halmstad University
Halmstad, Sweden

Annalisa Appice (iD)
University of Bari Aldo Moro
Bari, Italy

Ibéria Medeiros
University of Lisbon
Lisbon, Portugal

Lee Cooper (iD)
Northwestern University
Chicago, USA

Jonas Richiardi (iD)
University of Lausanne
Lausanne, Switzerland

Konstantinos Sechidis (iD)
Novartis
Basel, Switzerland

Sara Pido
Politecnico di Milano
Milan, Italy

Albert Bifet (iD)
University of Waikato
Hamilton, New Zealand

Preface

The European Conference on Machine Learning and Principles and Practice of Knowledge Discovery in Databases (ECML PKDD) is the premier European conference on machine learning and data mining. In 2022, ECML PKDD took place in Grenoble, France during September 19–23.

The program included workshops on specialized topics held during the first and last day of the conference. This two-volume set includes the proceedings of the following workshops:

1. 7th Workshop on Data Science for Social Good (SoGood 2022)
2. 10th Workshop on New Frontiers in Mining Complex Patterns (NFMCP 2022)
3. 4th Workshop on eXplainable Knowledge Discovery in Data Mining (XKDD 2022)
4. 1st Workshop on Uplift Modeling (UMOD 2022)
5. 3rd Workshop on IoT, Edge and Mobile for Embedded Machine Learning (ITEM 2022)
6. 7th Workshop on Mining Data for Financial Application (MIDAS 2022)
7. 4th Workshop on Machine Learning for Cybersecurity (MLCS 2022)
8. 2nd Workshop on Machine Learning for Buildings Energy Management (MLBEM 2022)
9. 3rd Workshop on Machine Learning for Pharma and Healthcare Applications (PharML 2022)
10. 1st Workshop on Data Analysis in Life Science (DALS 2022)
11. 3rd Workshop on IoT Streams for Predictive Maintenance (IoT-PdM 2022)

Each workshop section contains the papers from the workshop and a preface from the organizers.

We would like to thank all participants and invited speakers, the Program Committees and reviewers, and the ECML PKDD conference and workshop chairs – thank you for making the workshops successful events. We are also grateful to Springer for their help in publishing the proceedings.

October 2022

Irena Koprinska
on behalf of the volume editors

Organization

ECML PKDD 2022 Workshop Chairs

Bruno Crémilleux   Université de Caen Normandie, France
Charlotte Laclau   Télécom Paris, France

SoGood 2022 Chairs

João Gama   University of Porto, Portugal
Irena Koprinska   University of Sydney, Australia
Rita P. Ribeiro   University of Porto, Portugal
Ricard Gavaldà   BarcelonaTech, Spain

NFMCP 2022 Chairs

Elio Masciari   University Federico II of Naples, Italy
Paolo Mignone   University of Bari Aldo Moro, Italy
Zbigniew W. Ras   University of North Carolina, USA
Ettore Ritacco   ICAR-CNR, Italy

XKDD 2022 Chairs

Riccardo Guidotti   University of Pisa, Italy
Francesca Naretto   Scuola Normale Superiore, Italy
Andreas Theissler   Aalen University of Applied Sciences, Germany
Przemysław Biecek   Warsaw University of Technology, Poland

UMOD 2022 Chairs

Szymon Jaroszewicz   Polish Academy of Sciences and Warsaw
     University of Technology, Poland
Wouter Verbeke   KU Leuven, Belgium

ITEM 2022 Chairs

Holger Fröning   Heidelberg University, Germany
Gregor Schiele   University of Duisburg-Essen, Germany
Franz Pernkopf   Graz University of Technology, Austria
Michaela Blott   AMD, Dublin, Ireland

MIDAS 2022 Chairs

Ilaria Bordino   UniCredit, Italy
Ivan Luciano Danesi   UniCredit, Italy
Francesco Gullo   UniCredit, Italy
Giovanni Ponti   ENEA, Italy
Lorenzo Severini   UniCredit, Italy

MLCS 2022 Chairs

Pedro M. Ferreira   University of Lisbon, Portugal
Annalisa Appice   University of Bari, Italy
Giuseppina Andresini   University of Bari, Italy
Ibéria Medeiros   University of Lisbon, Portugal

MLBEM 2022 Chairs

Pedro M. Ferreira   University of Lisbon, Portugal
Guilherme Graça   University of Lisbon, Portugal

PharML 2022 Chairs

Damian Roqueiro   Roche, Basel, Switzerland
Lee Cooper   Northwestern University, USA
Naghmeh Ghazaleh   Roche, Basel, Switzerland
Jonas Richiardi   Lausanne University Hospital and University of
                               Lausanne, Switzerland
Diego Saldana   Novartis, Basel, Switzerland
Konstantinos Sechidis   Novartis, Basel, Switzerland

DALS 2022 Chairs

Gaia Ceddia   Barcelona Supercomputing Center, Spain
Arif Canakoglu   Fondazione IRCCS Ca' Granda Ospedale
                               Maggiore Policlinico, Milan, Italy
Sara Pido   Massachusetts Institute of Technology, USA, and
                               Politecnico di Milano, Italy
Pietro Pinoli   Politecnico di Milano, Italy

IoT-PdM 2022 Chairs

Joao Gama   University of Porto, Portugal
Albert Bifet   Telecom-Paris, Paris, France, and University of
                               Waikato, New Zealand
Sławomir Nowaczyk   Halmstad University, Sweden
Sepideh Pashami   Halmstad University, Sweden

Contents – Part II

Workshop on Data Analysis in Life Science (DALS 2022)

**3rd Workshop and Tutorial on Streams for Predictive Maintenance
(IoT-PdM 2022)**

Contents – Part I

Workshop on New Frontiers in Mining Complex Patterns (NFMCP 2022)

Workshop on eXplainable Knowledge Discovery in Data Mining (XKDD 2022)

Workshop on Mining Data for Financial Application (MIDAS 2022)

MIDAS 2022: The 7th Workshop on MIning DAta for financial applicationS

Like the famous King Midas, popularly remembered in Greek mythology for his ability to turn everything he touched with his hand into gold, the wealth of data generated by modern technologies, with widespread presence of computers, users, and media connected by Internet, is a goldmine for tackling a variety of problems in the financial domain.

Nowadays, people's interactions with technological systems provide us with gargantuan amounts of data documenting collective behavior in a previously unimaginable fashion. Recent research has shown that by properly modeling and analyzing these massive datasets, for instance representing them as network structures, it is possible to gain useful insights into the evolution of the systems considered (i.e., trading, disease spreading, political elections). Investigating the impact of data arising from today's application domains on financial decisions is of paramount importance. Knowledge extracted from data can help gather critical information for trading decisions, reveal early signs of impactful events (such as stock market moves), or anticipate catastrophic events (e.g., financial crises) that result from a combination of actions, and affect humans worldwide.

The importance of data-mining tasks in the financial domain has been long recognized. For example, in the Web context, changes in the frequency with which users browse news or look for certain terms on search engines have been correlated with product trends, level of activity in certain given industries, unemployment rates, or car and home sales, as well as stock-market trade volumes and price movements. Other core applications include forecasting the stock market, predicting bank bankruptcies, understanding and managing financial risk, trading futures, credit rating, loan management, and bank customer profiling. Despite its well-recognized relevance and some recent related efforts, data mining in finance is still not stably part of the main stream of data mining conferences. This makes the topic particularly appealing for a workshop proposal, whose small, interactive, and possibly interdisciplinary context provides a unique opportunity to advance research in a stimulating but still quite unexplored field.

The aim of the 7th Workshop on MIning DAta for financial applicationS (MIDAS 2022), held in conjunction with the 2022 European Conference on Machine Learning and Principles and Practice of Knowledge Discovery in Databases (ECML-PKDD 2022), September 19–23, 2022, Grenoble, France, was to discuss challenges, potentialities, and applications of leveraging data-mining and machine-learning tasks to tackle problems in the financial domain. The workshop provided a premier forum for sharing findings, knowledge, insights, experience, and lessons learned from mining data generated in various domains. The intrinsic interdisciplinary nature of the workshop promoted the interaction between computer scientists, physicists, mathematicians, economists, and financial analysts, thus paving the way for an exciting and stimulating environment involving researchers and practitioners from different areas.

Topics of interest included, among others, trading models, discovering market trends, predictive analytics for financial services, network analytics in finance, planning investment strategies, portfolio management, understanding and managing financial risk, customer/investor profiling, identifying expert investors, financial modeling, anomaly detection in financial data, fraud detection, discovering patterns and correlations in financial data, text mining and NLP for financial applications, sentiment analysis for finance, financial network analysis, financial time series analysis, pitfalls identification, financial knowledge graphs, learning paradigms in the financial domain, explainable AI in financial services, quantum computing for finance.

MIDAS 2022 was structured as a full-day workshop. Participation to the workshop followed a "hybrid" modality allowing participants to attend the workshop either in-person or remotely. Most presentations were in-person, only a few (three out of a total of 13, including the invited speaker) were remote. Remote presentations followed a "live" mode, i.e., they happened in real-time, with the speaker remotely joining the event.

We encouraged submissions of regular papers (long or short) and extended abstracts. Regular papers were asked to report on novel, unpublished work, while extended abstracts were required to summarize already published work. All submitted regular papers were peer reviewed by three reviewers from the Program Committee, and selected for presentation at the workshop and inclusion in the proceedings on the basis of these reviews. Extended abstracts were presented at the workshop without peer reviewing, and they were not included in the proceedings. MIDAS 2022 received 13 regular submissions, among which 10 papers were accepted, along with two extended abstracts.

In accordance with the reviewers' scores and comments, and also taking into account the quality of the presentation, the paper entitled "Towards Data-Driven Volatility Modeling with Variational Autoencoders", authored by Thomas Dierckx, Wim Schoutens, and Jesse Davis, and presented by Thomas Dierckx, was selected as the best paper of the workshop. The paper entitled "Multi-Task Learning for Features Extraction in Financial Annual Reports", authored by Syrielle Montariol, Matej Martinc, Andraž Pelicon, Senja Pollak, Boshko Koloski, Igor Lončarski, Aljoša Valentinčič, Katarina Sitar Šuštar, Riste Ichev, and Martin Žnidaršič, and presented by Syrielle Montariol, was recognized as runner up.

The program of the workshop was enriched by an invited speaker: José Antonio Rodríguez-Serrano from Esade Business School, who gave a talk titled "Modernizing Banking and Finance with Machine Learning: Techniques, Successes and Challenges", whose abstract is as follows:

Machine learning (ML) adoption in the banking and fintech industry is accelerating and recently demonstrating success beyond the old-school applications of e.g. risk and fraud. This leads to a modernization of the industry with interesting advances such as more interactive apps, proactive advice, or shift in customer relation models. But adoption still feels slow-paced, opportunistic, and unevenly distributed, not systemic; and the sector is still undergoing a learning process.

This talk will review how ML has the potential to become an horizontal enabling layer in several non-traditional domains of banking and finance (such personalization, personal and corporate customer relations, or process optimization). This will include a review of relevant ML techniques (e.g. forcasting with uncertainty, or graph-based methods), real examples of known success cases, and also discussions of relevant challenges and cultural shifts that need to happen in this industry. The talk will also draw from the speaker's personal experience in research and applied data science in an AI banking lab during the last 7 years.

September 2022

Ilaria Bordino
Ivan Luciano Danesi
Francesco Gullo
Giovanni Ponti
Lorenzo Severini

Organization

Program Chairs

Ilaria Bordino   UniCredit, Italy
Ivan Luciano Danesi   UniCredit, Italy
Francesco Gullo   UniCredit, Italy
Giovanni Ponti   ENEA, Italy
Lorenzo Severini   UniCredit, Italy

Program Committee

Aris Anagnostopoulos	Sapienza University of Rome, Italy
Annalisa Appice	University of Bari, Italy
Argimiro Arratia	Universitat Politécnica de Catalunya, Spain
Davide Azzalini	Politecnico di Milano, Italy
Fabio Azzalini	Politecnico di Milano, Italy
Xiao Bai	Yahoo Research, USA
Luca Barbaglia	JRC - European Commission, Italy
Luigi Bellomarini	Banca d'Italia, Italy
Eric Benhamou	AI for Alpha, France
Livia Blasi	Banca d'Italia, Italy
Ludovico Boratto	University of Cagliari, Italy
Cristian Bravo	Western University, Canada
Jeremy Charlier	National Bank of Canada, Canada
Daniela Cialfi	University of Chieti-Pescara, Italy
Sergio Consoli	JRC - European Commission, Italy
Jacopo De Stefani	TU Delft, The Netherlands
Carlotta Domeniconi	George Mason University, USA
Wouter Duivesteijn	Eindhoven University of Technology, The Netherlands
Edoardo Galimberti	Independent Researcher, Italy
Cuneyt Gurcan Akcora	University of Manitoba, Canada
Roberto Interdonato	CIRAD, France
Anna Krause	University of Würzburg, Germany
Malte Lehna	Fraunhofer IEE, Germany
Domenico Mandaglio	University of Calabria, Italy
Yelena Mejova	ISI Foundation, Italy
Syrielle Montariol	Inria Paris, France
Aldo Nassigh	UniCredit, Italy
Roberta Pappadà	University of Trieste, Italy

Giulia Preti   ISI Foundation, Italy
David Saltiel   AI for Alpha, France
Daniel Schloer   University of Würzburg, Germany
Edoardo Vacchi   Red Hat, Italy
Elaine Wah   BlackRock AI Labs, USA

Multi-task Learning for Features Extraction in Financial Annual Reports

Syrielle Montariol[1](✉), Matej Martinc[1], Andraž Pelicon[1], Senja Pollak[1],
Boshko Koloski[1], Igor Lončarski[2], Aljoša Valentinčič[2], Katarina Sitar Šuštar[2],
Riste Ichev[2], and Martin Žnidaršič[1]

[1] Jožef Stefan Institute, Jamova Cesta 39, 1000 Ljubljana, Slovenia
`syrielle.montariol@gmail.com`
[2] School of Economics and Business, University of Ljubljana, Kardeljeva pl. 17,
1000 Ljubljana, Slovenia

Abstract. For assessing various performance indicators of companies, the focus is shifting from strictly financial (quantitative) publicly disclosed information to qualitative (textual) information. This textual data can provide valuable weak signals, for example through stylistic features, which can complement the quantitative data on financial performance or on Environmental, Social and Governance (ESG) criteria. In this work, we use various multi-task learning methods for financial text classification with the focus on financial sentiment, objectivity, forward-looking sentence prediction and ESG-content detection. We propose different methods to combine the information extracted from training jointly on different tasks; our best-performing method highlights the positive effect of explicitly adding auxiliary task predictions as features for the final target task during the multi-task training. Next, we use these classifiers to extract textual features from annual reports of FTSE350 companies and investigate the link between ESG quantitative scores and these features.

Keywords: Multi-task learning · Financial reports · Corporate social responsibility

1 Introduction

There is a slowly but steadily emerging consensus that qualitative (textual) information, when aiming at analysing a company's past, present and future performance, is equally if not more informative than quantitative (numerical) information. Traditionally, financial experts and economists have used such qualitative information for decision making in a manual way. However, the volume of textual data increased tremendously in the past decades with the progressive dematerialisation and the growing capacity to share and store data [15], making the manual analysis practically infeasible.

Textual information about companies is found mainly in three contexts: mandatory public disclosures, news articles, and social media. Among all these data sources, periodic corporate reporting receives a particularly close attention

I. Koprinska et al. (Eds.): ECML PKDD 2022 Workshops, CCIS 1753, pp. 7–24, 2023.
https://doi.org/10.1007/978-3-031-23633-4_1

from the research community, with an already plentiful literature in the financial domain and a growing one in natural language processing (NLP) [7,18,22]. The reports are made publicly available periodically by all companies above a certain size and market value threshold, as defined by regulatory authorities of each country. The content of these periodical financial reports is also controlled by the regulators, with the goal of disclosing and communicating in great detail the financial situation and practices of the companies to investors [29].

Apart from the strictly quantitative financial information, these reports are rich in qualitative linguistic and structural information. This qualitative data can yield information about various financial aspects of companies at the time of filing, as well as predictions about future events in a company's financial ecosystem, such as future performance, stockholders' reactions, or analysts' forecasts [2,14]. Especially in sections that allow for a more narrative style, there is room for subjectivity and human influence in how financial data and prospects are conveyed. Even though financial disclosures follow a reasonably well-established set of guidelines, there is still a great deal of variation in terms of how the content of these disclosures is expressed. The choice of specific words and tone when framing a disclosure can be indicative of the underlying facts about a company's financial situation that cannot be conveyed through financial indicators alone.

Extraction and processing of this information, however, prove to be much more challenging than for quantitative information. There is a growing body of literature dedicated to the analysis of non-financial information in financial reports, where not only the content, but also stylistic properties of the text in reports are considered (e.g., [21,30]). For example, capturing and understanding the effect of information such as sentiment or subjectivity conveyed in the reports might give indications to predict investor behavior and the impact on supply and demand for financial assets [32].

Here, we study three key stylistic indicators associated with a text sequence: its sentiment, its objectivity, and its forward-looking nature. On top of this, we focus on a specific topic addressed by the annual reports: the Environmental, Social and Governance (ESG) aspects. These are part of the global Corporate Social Responsibility (CSR) framework, which refers to a set of activities and strategies that a company conducts in order to pursue pro-social and environmental objectives besides maximizing profit. Examples of these activities would include minimization of environmental externalities and charity donations.

As CSR is subject to a growing interest from investors, regulators and shareholders in the past few years, companies have become more aware of how their actions and vocals impact the society and environment, prompting them to regularly report on their socio-environmental impact in the annual reports. The first requirements with regards to corporate social responsibility reporting were introduced by EU 2014/95 Directive (so called Non-Financial Reporting Directive or NFRD).[1] One of the proposed measures of CSR are the ESG criteria. The measure covers companies' environmental impact (Environmental), relationships with their stakeholders — e.g. workplace conditions and impact of company's

---

[1] https://ec.europa.eu/info/business-economy-euro/company-reporting-and-auditing/company-reporting/corporate-sustainability-reporting_en.

behaviour on the surrounding community — (Social), and the integrity and diversity of its leadership (Governance), which considers criteria such as the accountability to shareholders and the accuracy and transparency of accounting methods. However, numerical indicators measuring the ESG performance of a company are few and far from being enough to evaluate precisely this concept. Similarly to other non-financial indicators, most ESG analyses are thus performed manually by experts [17].

In this study, we aim at linking stylistic indicators with ESG-related concepts through multi-task learning, by fine-tuning pre-trained language models jointly on several classification tasks. More generally, we aim at proposing methods to extract features from textual reports using signals such as objectivity and forward-looking nature of sentences.

Our contributions are as follows. We highlight the challenges of grasping the concepts of sentiment, objectivity and forward-looking in the context of finance by classifying content inside financial reports according to these categories. We compare several ways of exploiting these features jointly with the concept of ESG, through various multi-task learning systems. We show that we are able to make up for the difficulty of the tasks by training them in a multi-task setting, with a careful task selection. Moreover, we show that our ExGF multi-task learning system, where we Explicitly Give as Feature the predictions of auxiliary tasks for training a target task, beats other classical parameter sharing multi-task systems. Finally, we provide qualitative insight into the link between ESG content, stylistic textual features and ESG numerical scores provided by press agencies. Our code is available at https://gitlab.com/smontariol/multi-task-esg.

2 Related Works

2.1 Annual Reports

The literature on corporate Annual Reports (ARs) analysis is plentiful in the financial research community. From the NLP perspective, research is more scarce and much more recent. One of the most widely studied type of company reports are 10-K filings [10]. These are AR required by the U.S. Securities and Exchange Commission (SEC), and are so diligently studied thank to their format, which is highly standardised and controlled by the SEC. Outside the US, companies periodic reporting is less standardized and more shareholder-oriented. Here, we focus on UK annual reports. Lewis and Young [15] report significant increase in the size and complexity of UK annual report narratives: the median number of words more than doubled between 2003 and 2016[2] while the median number of items in the table of contents also doubled in the same period. In face of these numbers, the automated analysis of financial reporting faces a growing contradiction: on the one hand, the huge increase in volume leads to the increased need for a solution from the NLP community to analyse this unstructured data automatically. On the other hand, more reporting from more companies leads to

---

[2] For a sample of 19,426 PDF annual reports published by 3252 firms listed on the London Stock Exchange.

more diversity in the shape of the documents; this lack of standardization and structure makes the analysis tougher and requires more complex methods [15].

In particular, concepts such as ESG are too recent to be included in any reporting standardization policy from the regulators, leading to very heterogeneous dedicated reporting. Consequently, as stated before, the work on detection of ESG-related content is somewhat scarce. Several works analyse the link between the publication of ESG report by a firm and its market value, without diving into the content of the report [27]. Purver et al. [26] use frequencies to capture semantic change of ESG-related keywords in UK companies' annual reports between 2012 and 2019. They interpret it using contextualised representations. A shared task aiming at classifying sentences as "sustainable" or not was organized in 2022 for the FinNLP workshop.[3] The sentences were extracted from financial and non-financial companies' reports.

Another work closely related to our objective is the one from Armbrust et al. [4]. They underline the limited impact of the quantitative information in US companies annual reports, since detailed financial metrics and key performance indicators are often disclosed by the company before the publishing of the annual reports. Thus, as most of the financial information is redundant to the investors, regulators and shareholders, we turn towards stylistic features.

2.2   Multi-task Learning

In this work, we investigate the methods to make use of various stylistic information to extract features from annual reports. We use pre-trained language models [9] in a supervised multi-task learning (MTL) setting. The idea behind MTL, in which multiple learning tasks are solved in parallel or sequentially, relies on exploiting commonalities and differences across several related tasks in order to improve both training efficiency and performance of task-specific models.

The sequential MTL pre-training approach was formalized by Phang et al. [24] under the denomination STILT (Supplementary Training on Intermediate Labeled-data Tasks), improving the efficiency of a pre-trained language model for a downstream task by proposing a preliminary fine-tuning on an intermediate task. This work is closely followed by Pruksachatkun et al. [25], who perform a survey of intermediate and target task pairs to analyze the usefulness of this intermediary fine-tuning. They find a low correlation between the acquisition of low-level skills and downstream task performance, while tasks that require complex reasoning and high-level semantic abilities, such as common-sense oriented tasks, had a higher benefit. Aghajanyan et al. [1] extend the multi-task training to another level: they proposed "pre-fine-tuning", a large-scale learning step (50 tasks for around 5 million labeled examples) between language model pre-training and fine-tuning. They demonstrate that, when aiming at learning highly-generalizable representations for a wide range of tasks, the amount of tasks is key in multi-task training. Indeed, some tasks may hurt the overall

---

[3] https://sites.google.com/nlg.csie.ntu.edu.tw/finnlp-2022/shared-task-finsim4-esg.

performance of the system; but when performed in a large-scale fashion (e.g. with about 15 tasks), performance improved linearly with the number of tasks.

When it comes to parallel multi-task learning, the studies on this topic are abundant [36]. While the research on the topic pre-dates the deep learning era, it has not been extensively researched until recently, when novel closely related transfer learning and pre-training paradigms [9] proved very successful for a range of NLP problems. At the same time, multiple-task benchmark datasets, such as GLUE [34] and the NLP Decathlon [19] were released, offering new multi-task training opportunities and drastically reduced the effort to evaluate the trained models. Due to these recent developments, several studies research weights sharing across networks and try to identify under which circumstances and for which downstream tasks MTL can significantly outperform single-task solutions [35]. The study by Standley et al. [31] suggested that MTL can be especially useful in a low resource scenario, where the problem of data sparsity can effect the generalization performance of the model. They claim that by learning to jointly solve related problems, the model can learn a more generalized internal representation. The crucial factor that determines the success of MTL is task similarity [6]. To a large extent, the benefit of MTL is directly correlated with the success of knowledge transfer between tasks, which improves with task relatedness. In cases when tasks are not related or only loosely related, MTL can result in inductive bias resulting in actually harming the performance of a classifier. Another factor influencing the success of the MTL performance is the neural architecture and design, e.g., the degree of parameters sharing between tasks [28]. Here, we investigate several MTL architectures and methods and apply them to an annotated dataset of annual reports.

3   Datasets

3.1   FTSE350 Annual Reports and Annotations

The analysis is conducted on the same corpus as [26].[4] It is composed of annual reports from the FTSE350 companies, covering the 2012–2019 time period. Only annual reports for London Stock Exchange companies that were listed on the FTSE350 list on 25th April 2020 are included. Altogether 1,532 reports are collected in the PDF format and converted into raw text.

We use an annotated dataset associated with the FTSE350 corpus. The annotated sentences are extracted from reports covering the period between 2017 and 2019. The annotators were given a sentence and asked to jointly label 5 tasks. In total, 2651 sentences were annotated. Here, we list the task definitions and label distributions.

- **Relevance**: business related text (1768)/general text (883). Indicates whether the sentence is relevant from the perspective of corporate business.
- **Financial sentiment**: positive (1769)/neutral (717)/negative (165). Sentiment from the point of view of the financial domain.

---

[4] Code and details to re-create the dataset are available at osf.io/rqgp4.

- **Objectivity**: objective (2015)/subjective (636). Indicates whether the sentence expresses an opinion (subjectivity) or states the facts (objectivity).
- **Forward looking**: FLS (1561)/non-FLS (1090). Indicates whether the sentence is concerned with or planning for the future.
- **ESG**: ESG related (1889)/not ESG related (762). Indicates whether the sentence relates to sustainability issues or not.

Inter-annotator Agreement. In total, 13 annotators took part in the labeling process, all graduate students of MSc in Quantitative Finance and Actuarial Sciences. Among the annotated sentences, 48 sentences are annotated by all annotators. We use them to compute the inter-annotator agreement. To build the final corpus, we deduplicate the sentences used for inter-rater agreement, performing a majority vote to select the label for each sentence.

We compute three global measures of agreement between all annotators: Krippendorff's α, Fleiss' κ, and the percentage of samples where all annotators agree. As a complement, we compute a pairwise measure: Cohen's κ [8], which we average between all pairs of annotators to obtain a global measure. It is similar to measuring the percentage of agreement, but taking into account the possibility of the agreement between two annotators to occur by chance for each annotated sample. All these measures are indicated in Table 1.

Table 1. Global measures of agreement between the 13 annotators on 48 sentences, for each of the 5 tasks.

	Krippendorff α	Fleiss κ	Cohen κ	Agreement (%)
Relevance	0.09	0.09	0.10	6
Financial sentiment	0.27	0.36	0.37	12
Objectivity	0.26	0.26	0.25	18
Forward looking	0.32	0.32	0.33	12
ESG/not-Esg	0.43	0.42	0.43	28

The agreement measures are consistently low. The tasks with the best inter-annotators agreements are sentiment and ESG. The Cohen κ for ESG indicates a "moderate" agreement according to [8], but it also indicates that less than one third of the annotations are reliable [20]. However, similar studies performing complex or subjective tasks such as sentiment analysis on short sentences also show low agreement values [5].

4 Multi-task Classification Methods

Here, we tackle the classification tasks on the annotated dataset described in Sect. 3.1. We use an encoder-decoder system for the classification tasks. A shared encoder is used to encode each sentence into a representation space, while different decoders are used to perform the classification. Here, we use the term 'decoders' to denote the classification heads, which take as input the sentence representation encoded by the encoder part.

We describe the encoding and decoding systems in the following sections.

4.1   Encoder: Pre-trained Masked Language Model

Transformers-based pre-trained language models are a method to represent language, which establishes state-of-the-art results on a large variety of NLP tasks. Here, we use the RoBERTa model [16]. Its architecture is a multi-layer bidirectional Transformer encoder [33]. The key element to this architecture, the bidirectional training, is enabled by the Masked Language Model training task: 15% of the tokens in each input sequence are selected as training targets, of which 80% are replaced with a [MASK] token. The model is trained to predict the original value of the training targets using the rest of the sequence.

Contextualized language models are mostly used in the literature following the principle of transfer learning proposed by Howard and Ruder [12], where the network is pre-trained as a language model on large corpora in order to learn general contextualised word representations.

In our case, we perform domain adaptation [23] by fine-tuning RoBERTa on the masked language model task on the FTSE350 corpus. Then, we perform a task-specific fine-tuning step for our various sentence classification tasks. To represent the sentences during the fine-tuning, we use the representation of the [CLS] token, which is the first token of every sequence. The final hidden state of the [CLS] token is usually used in sequence classification tasks as the aggregated sequence representation [9].

4.2   Joint Multi-task Learning

In the classical MTL setting, we implement a simple architecture taking as input each sentence's representation encoded by the contextualised language model, and feeding it to several decoders. Each decoder is a classification head associated with one task. The sentence representation is passed through an architecture consisting of linear and dropout layers, before being projected to a representation space of the same dimension as the number of labels associated with the task. As a reminder, the financial sentiment task has three labels while the other ones have two. This final representation is called the *logits*. We use them to compute the loss associated with each classification head.

To train all the decoders jointly with the encoder in an end-to-end fashion, we sum the losses outputted by each decoder, at each step. By optimizing this sum of losses, the model learns jointly on all tasks. In the results section, we denote this method as *Joint*. We experiment with several task combinations to evaluate the positive and negative effects of each task on the performance of the classifier on other tasks.

4.3   Weighting Tasks

Since the relatedness between tasks can vary, we also investigate an approach where weights for each task (i.e., the influence each task has on an average performance of the classifier across all tasks) are derived automatically. We train weights associated with each task jointly with training the classifiers, by adding an additional trainable "weight layer", containing n scalars corresponding to n tasks. These weights are first normalized (i.e. the sum of weights is always one in order to prevent the model to reduce the loss by simply reducing all weights) and then multiplied to the calculated losses obtained for each task during training before summing up all losses and performing back-propagation.

The learned weights can both be used to improve the overall performance, and to "probe" the importance of each task for the overall system.

4.4   Sequential Multi-task Learning

Sequential MTL is an alternative to the joint MTL setting presented in Sect. 4.2. In the sequential setting, we use multi-task learning in an intermediary fashion, as a "pre-fine-tuning" for a given target task. This is close to the concept of STILT [24] and large-scale multi-task pre-fine-tuning presented in the related works section. The model, through a preliminary multi-task training step, is expected to acquire knowledge about all these training tasks and to accumulate it in the weights of the encoder. Then, the encoder is fine-tuned only on the downstream target task.

In this setting, we experiment with various task combinations trained jointly before fine-tuning the encoder on one of the target tasks. We distinguish two sequential settings. First, systematically excluding the target task from the pre-fine-tuning step; for example, when the target task is the ESG classification, we pre-fine-tune the encoder using classification on various combinations of the four other tasks. Second, systematically including the target task; in that case, the encoder has seen the training data for the target task during pre-fine-tuning. In the results section, this method is referred to as *Seq*.

4.5   Explicitly Giving Features for Multi-task Learning (ExGF - MTL)

As explained before, task-specific classification heads output logits for each task. In this approach, we aim at performing multi-task learning by Explicitly Giving the output of the classification heads for "auxiliary tasks" as additional Features for the prediction of the final target task. These features are concatenated, fed into a linear layer (i.e., the "common auxiliary task features' classification head"), and projected into a vector space of the same dimension as the logits of the final target task. The features are then summed with the logits of the ESG task, and this sum is used to compute the loss for the final target task. This final target task loss is then summed with the losses of the four auxiliary tasks (calculated on the logits outputted by the task-specific classification heads for each auxiliary task) and the backpropagation is performed the same way as for the joint MLT system.

4.6 Task-aware Representations of Sentences (TARS)

Task-aware representations [11] were proposed as an alternative method to MTL where one general model can be trained and used for any task while preserving the maximum amount of information across tasks. The method transforms any classification task into a binary "Yes/No" classification task. Informally, for each task, a model is presented with a tuple consisting of a task label and an instance to classify. The task for the model to solve is to classify if the presented label matches with the presented instance or not. We adapt the proposed approach to model all five tasks jointly in a multitask setting. For a task with M classes, M <original label, instance> tuples are generated for each instance in the training set. Each such generated instance is labeled with the generalized label "Yes" if the original label and instance match and with the generalized label "No' otherwise. Original labels are prepended to the instance in order to condition the model both on the task and the instance to classify.

The model is trained jointly on instances for all tasks. Instances are generated in the same way during evaluation phase. As predicted class, we consider the class with the highest probability for the "Yes" generalized label. For example, given the sentence "[...] colleagues were trained to deliver weekly walks targeted at individuals aged over 65." and the task of classifying if this sentence is ESG-related or not, the original label is "ESG". We create two instances and their respective labels:

- "ESG [SEP] *sentence*". Gold label: "Yes". Probability of "Yes": 0.92.
- "Not ESG [SEP] *sentence*". Gold label: "No". Probability of "Yes": 0.37.

The model learns on all examples; at inference, given a similar pair of sentences and their "Yes" probability predicted by the model, we assign to the sentence the label associated with the highest probability of "Yes".

The motivation behind this system is related to the core idea behind multi-task training. All our systems implement a separate decoder for each task, as the task labels are different. Thus, the sharing of weights is only at the encoder-level. By gathering all tasks under a common setting, with the same binary labels, the setting is both more generalizable and fully shares all parameters during training. Recently, this idea of gathering all tasks under the same setting has gained a large popularity in NLP through the sequence-to-sequence paradigm [3].

5 Multi-task Experiments

In this section, we report the performance of the mono-task (used as a baseline) and the various multi-task settings introduced in the previous section.

5.1   Experimental Framework

In all experiments, the metric used to compare the systems is the macro-F1 score. It is the most adapted for classification settings with class imbalance (see Sect. 3.1 for the label distribution for each task), as it computes performance for each label and averages them, without giving more importance to the over-represented ones. We divide the annotated dataset into 3 parts, keeping 20% for development and 20% for test. The test sets sampled from the original corpora are relatively small (531 examples). To increase the robustness of the results, we use five different seeds when fine-tuning the language model on the classification tasks and report the average scores over the five runs.

We tune hyper-parameters for the mono-task setting using the development set (batch size, learning rate, weight decay and number of epochs). The models are trained for 5 epochs and the selected model is the best one out of the 5 epochs in terms of average macro-F1 across all tasks (for joint multi-task learning) or best macro-F1 of the target task (sequential MTL or mono-task training), computed on the development set.

5.2   Results

Using each method for all task combinations, we compute the average macro-F1 score (across the five seeds) on the test set of each task. To compare the numerous methods and task combinations, we compute their rank in terms of performance (i.e. average macro-F1) for each target task. Then, we define the global performance of a method as the average rank of its performance across all target tasks, with a total number of methods and task combinations of 66. Table 2 shows the best-ranked methods and task combinations as well as a few lower-ranked methods for the sake of comparison. Task combinations are indicated by lists of integers; each integers corresponds to a task, and the matching is indicated in the caption. The N/As (Not Available) in the table correspond to the scores for a target task on which the system was not trained nor evaluated, because it is not part of the task combination.[5] The last column of the table shows the rank of the specific method and task combination among all approaches. For the sake of the further analysis and comparison between distinct architectures and task combinations, we include the last 4 lines of the table, which appear lower in the overall systems' ranking.

With a relatively large margin, the best performing method is the ExGF-MTL system, leading to higher individual task scores compared with the mono-task training (in *italic* in the table) for all tasks except financial sentiment. It is especially efficient on the ESG task. In terms of task combinations, the best systems exclude the Objectivity task (task #2) and often the Relevance task (task #0). These tasks have low inter-rater agreement, making them more difficult to tackle for the models. We further investigate their effect on MTL in the next table.

---

[5] Note that the N/As can only appear in the joint and weighted settings, where there is no explicit final target task.

The last 4 lines of the table show systems with lower rankings. They allow us to compare the weighted MTL system trained on all task combinations, with the unweighted one; and the sequential and joint systems for the best task combinations. Except for the best task combination (i.e. 0-1-3-4, where sequential MTL beats joint MLT in terms of ranking (but by a low margin), the joint training seems overall better than the sequential one in the rankings. We further investigate this distinction in Table 3.

Table 2. Performance of all tested approaches according to the macro-F1 score arranged according to the average rank across tasks, i.e. the ranking of a row is the average of the five column-wise rankings, ignoring missing values (N/As). The task combinations are indicated as a list of integers with the following matching: 0 = Relevance; 1 = Financial-sentiment; 2 = Objectivity; 3 = Forward-looking; 4 = ESG. *Mono* corresponds to the baseline classification results without multi-task learning.

Method	Tasks	Relevance	Fin-sentiment	Objectivity	Fwd-looking	ESG	Rank
ExGF	all	51.67	58.67	**68.94**	68.59	**69.14**	1
seq	0-1-3-4	50.26	53.13	66.28	69.66	60.64	2
joint	0-1-3-4	49.09	50.37	N/A	**70.07**	64.07	3
mono		*50.13*	*63.11*	*64.29*	*64.24*	*64.52*	4
weighted	all	**54.70**	48.29	61.64	68.67	61.42	5
joint	1-3-4	N/A	50.94	N/A	64.77	61.06	6
joint	1–3	N/A	49.56	N/A	67.32	N/A	7
joint	all	48.80	48.34	63.53	66.00	55.31	19
TARS	all	49.48	46.42	59.62	66.49	59.86	24
seq	1-3-4	48.30	47.43	59.20	60.13	52.69	39
seq	all	46.12	48.15	59.03	57.05	51.01	43

The last comparison is performed between weighted multi-task joint training (rank #5) and non-weighted (rank #19) training on all tasks; the joint method is outperformed by the weighted method on all tasks but one, the Objectivity task. The task importance according to the weights obtained during the weighted training are as follows: {Relevance: -0.64; Fin-sentiment: 1.83; Objectivity: -1.42; Fwd-looking: 1.6; ESG: -1.37}.

For the sake of clarity, instead of showing the raw weights, we report the difference between the learned weights and the default uniform weights used in the other multi-task settings. Higher weights are given to the financial sentiment and the forward-looking tasks, while lower weights are given to the other three. Note that among the three tasks with the lower weights, two of them – relevance and objectivity – have the lowest inter-rater agreement (see Table 1).

To compare the various methods from a more global point of view, we average the scores of all task combinations for each method. Additionally, we also report on results for averages across all tasks but tasks #0 (Relevance) and #2 (Objectivity), the two tasks with the worst inter-annotator agreement, to further analyse the impact of removing low-performance tasks out of the MTL framework. The results are reported in Table 3[6].

Removing the Objectivity and Relevance tasks leads to a small improvement in several cases, particularly for the joint training, where the weights are more directly impacted by the MTL system. The positive effect is less visible for the sequential training. It shows that for a small amount of tasks, or when a limited amount of data is available, more is often better.

The results also show that on average, regardless of the task combination, joint MTL tends to lead to better performance. Moreover, as expected, including the target task in the pre-fine-tuning step of the sequential training is highly beneficial, as it allows the model to learn interactions between this task and the auxiliary ones. However, note that this tactic is not in line with the initial idea behind large-scale pre-fine-tuning, which is to allow the model to be able to generalize to *unseen* tasks (i.e. it is assumed that the target task data is not available during the preliminary step).

Table 3. Macro-F1 average score over the 5 seeds and over all tasks combinations for the multi-task systems, *except* some selected tasks when indicated in the second column. Seq-INCL means sequential training WITH the target task being already part of the pre-fine-tuning step.

Method	Except	Relevance	Fin-sentiment	Objectivity	Fwd-looking	ESG
joint		47.9	48.78	57.38	66.18	56.80
joint	0	N/A	48.56	60.32	67.41	57.82
joint	2	49.33	48.41	N/A	67.17	54.88
seq		42.95	40.7	57.23	55.37	49.88
seq	0	N/A	38.59	56.78	54.57	49.44
seq	2	44.41	37.24	N/A	55.95	51.35
seq-INCL		47.46	46.17	58.13	59.23	51.13

6   Linking ESG Ratings with Textual Features

In the previous section, we identified ExGF-MTL as the best method to optimally exploit the information from all five tasks to improve the overall performance. We use this method to extract features from the annual reports, for all target tasks. Our aim is to investigate, on the large corpus of entire FTSE350 reports (i.e. not just on the manually labeled sentences extracted from these reports), the correlation between our extracted features and real-world numerical measures of ESG performance, obtained from Reuters, associated with each report.

---

[6] Note that the results for each method reported in Table 3 are lower than the results reported in Table 2, since here we report the average method's performance across all task combinations, while in Table 2 we only report results for the best ranked task combinations for each specific method.

6.1   Inference on Reports

Pre-processing the Corpus. We filter sentences in the corpus according to several conditions; these conditions are mainly related to the noise induced by the transformation from pdf to text, and to the corpus artefacts inherent to the format of the annual reports. We filter sentences depending on the proportion of upper-cased words and the proportion of non-letter characters in the sentence. We also filter short sentences not containing enough characters and words due to corpus artefacts such as the presence of split words into space-separated letters. Finally, we keep only sentences starting with a capital letter and ending with a punctuation sign. Following the pre-processing, we obtain an average number of around 1900 sentences by report.

Feature Extraction. Using the ExGF-MTL models trained in the previous section, we perform inference on the full FTSE350 annual reports corpus. Thus, for each sentence, we predict its label associated to each task. We extract the following five features from each annual report: first, the proportion of ESG sentences. Then, among ESG sentences, the proportion of positive, negative, forward-looking, and objective sentences. Note that the Financial sentiment task is divided into two features to only get a set of binary features to compute the Spearman correlation.

6.2   Correlation Analysis

We use ESG scores from the financial press agency Reuters; for each company of the FTSE350 index and for each year, one score per ESG pillar (Environment, Governance and Social) and one Global ESG score are provided. They range from 0 to 100. They are inferred by financial analysts through careful reading of the financial reports of these companies.

We correlate these scores, using the Spearman correlation, with the five textual features extracted from the reports using the classification models. We also correlated the textual features with the year of the report, as an ordinal variable. We perform the correlation analysis by grouping companies by ICB industry code (11 industries) and by extracting the 5 highest correlations between the two groups of features (numerical an text-extracted) in Table 4.

First, we note that the pillar score (Environment, Governance or Social) most correlated with the textual features is often related to the industry of the company (e.g. the Environment pillar for the Energy industry, the Governance pillar for the Financial industry). Among the most correlated text features with the ESG scores, the proportion of ESG sentences is often the highest, meaning that writing more about ESG in the reports is often linked with having good ESG scores. Following closely in terms of Spearman correlation, is the percentage of negative and objective ESG sentences. We also note that the year is often correlated with the proportion of ESG sentences, meaning that ESG is increasingly discussed in the recent years. The proportion of forward-looking sentences is seldom correlated with the ESG scores; a notable correlation is the one between the

20   S. Montariol et al.

Table 4. Top 5 highest pairwise Spearman correlations between textual features (proportion of positive, negative, objective ESG sentences & proportion of ESG sentences in the full report), Reuters ESG scores (Global, Env., Social and Gov.) and year, by industry. Only Spearman correlations higher than 0.18 are displayed.

Industry	Reuters Scores (%)	Textual Features (%)	ρ
Energy	Environment	Objective	0.49
	Social	Objective	0.45
	Environment	ESG	0.43
	Social	ESG	0.42
	Global	Objective	0.42
Consumer Staples	Global	ESG	0.43
	Social	ESG	0.42
	Governance	ESG	0.33
	Environment	ESG	0.33
	Environment	Negative	0.30
Industrials	Social	Objective	0.41
	Global	Objective	0.38
	Environment	Objective	0.32
	year	Objective	0.26
	year	ESG	0.17
Telecommunication	year	ESG	0.44
	Environment	ESG	0.41
	year	Positive	0.41
	year	Objective	0.38
	Environment	Fwd-looking	0.32
Real Estate	year	ESG	0.32
	Environment	Negative	0.28
	Social	ESG	0.26
	year	Objective	0.23
	Global	ESG	0.23
Basic Materials	Governance	Fwd-looking	0.22
	year	Objective	0.18

Industry	Reuters Scores (%)	Textual Features (%)	ρ
Utilities	Social	ESG	0.55
	Global	Negative	0.39
	Social	Objective	0.33
	Governance	Negative	0.31
	year	ESG	0.29
Financials	Governance	Fwd-looking	0.29
	Governance	Negative	0.28
	Governance	ESG	0.25
	Global	Objective	0.24
	year	Objective	0.22
Consumer Discretionary	Environment	Negative	0.31
	Environment	Objective	0.30
	Global	Objective	0.26
	year	Objective	0.21
	Social	Fwd-looking	0.20
Technology	Governance	ESG	0.54
	Environment	Objective	0.42
	Global	ESG	0.39
	Governance	Negative	0.35
	Social	Negative	0.34
Health Care	Social	Objective	0.29
	year	Positive	0.29
	year	Objective	0.25
	Global	Objective	0.24
	Governance	Objective	0.20

forward-looking proportion and Governance Pillar score in the financial industry, which indicates a specific writing style about governance in this industry.

7   Conclusion

The focus of this study was the joint use of stylistic features – financial sentiment, objectivity and forward-looking – and ESG classification. We turned towards ESG because it is a challenging concept to quantify and evaluate, partly because few numerical metrics exist to characterize it, and because it is a recent concept that is still not perfectly defined and structured. But our experimental framework and MTL methods are generic and can be applied to any other topic of interest, for investigating the correlation between financial and textual data.

Methodologically, we showed that the best way to combine information from related tasks is to explicitly provide the predictions of auxiliary tasks as features for the prediction of a target task. This system is even efficient for tasks made very challenging by a very low inter-rater agreement. Note that in the majority of the literature, MTL is performed using different datasets for each task, while in our case, all the tasks are included in a single dataset, each instance having a label for each task. However, the proposed best approach, ExGF-MTL, can easily be applied to the multi-dataset multi-task learning; the only difference being the data loading implementation and encoder-decoder interactions. We also showed the importance of task selection when performing multi-task learning with a low number of tasks. We posit that a higher number of tasks would allow the system to compensate for low-performance tasks. When identifying low-performance tasks that harm the MTL system, we highlighted the link between performance and annotation quality. Finally, following recent trends for large-scale NLP multi-task learning, we compared sequential and joint fine-tuning, and experimented with MTL using a unique decoder for all tasks (TARS). However, we could not show any positive effect of this latter method. A better way to use a unique decoder for MTL while making the most out of large pre-trained language models would be to adopt the sequence-to-sequence paradigm for all tasks [3].

Qualitatively, we showed that our method allows us to extract meaningful features from annual reports that correlate with numerical features provided by press agencies, on the topic on corporate social responsibility. In future work, we plan to extend our method to perform causal discovery and causal inference between textual features, ESG scores and various financial performance indicators for companies [13].

Acknowledgements. This work was supported by the Slovenian Research Agency (ARRS) grants for the core programme Knowledge technologies (P2-0103) and the project quantitative and qualitative analysis of the unregulated corporate financial reporting (J5-2554). We also want to thank the students of the SBE for their effort in data annotation.

References

1. Aghajanyan, A., Gupta, A., Shrivastava, A., Chen, X., Zettlemoyer, L., Gupta, S.: Muppet: massive multi-task representations with pre-finetuning. arXiv preprint arXiv:2101.11038 (2021)
2. Amir, E., Lev, B.: Value-relevance of nonfinancial information: the wireless communications industry. J. Account. Econ. **22**(1), 3–30 (1996). https://doi.org/10.1016/S0165-4101(96)00430-2
3. Aribandi, V., et al.: Ext5: towards extreme multi-task scaling for transfer learning. arXiv preprint arXiv:2111.10952 (2021)

4. Armbrust, F., Schäfer, H., Klinger, R.: A computational analysis of financial and environmental narratives within financial reports and its value for investors. In: Proceedings of the 1st Joint Workshop on Financial Narrative Processing and MultiLing Financial Summarisation, pp. 181–194, COLING, Barcelona, Spain, December 2020. https://aclanthology.org/2020.fnp-1.31
5. Bobicev, V., Sokolova, M.: Inter-annotator agreement in sentiment analysis: machine learning perspective. In: Proceedings of the International Conference Recent Advances in Natural Language Processing, RANLP 2017, pp. 97–102, INCOMA Ltd., Varna, Bulgaria, September 2017. https://doi.org/10.26615/978-954-452-049-6_015
6. Caruana, R.: Multitask learning. Mach. Learn. **28**(1), 41–75 (1997)
7. Chen, C.C., Huang, H.H., Takamura, H., Chen, H.H.: An overview of financial technology innovation (2022)
8. Cohen, J.: A coefficient of agreement for nominal scales. Educ. Psychol. Measure. **20**(1), 37–46 (1960). https://doi.org/10.1177/001316446002000104
9. Devlin, J., Chang, M.W., Lee, K., Toutanova, K.: BERT: pre-training of deep bidirectional transformers for language understanding. In: Proceedings of the 2019 Conference of the North American Chapter of the Association for Computational Linguistics: Human Language Technologies, Volume 1 (Long and Short Papers), pp. 4171–4186, Minneapolis, Minnesota, June 2019
10. Dyer, T., Lang, M., Stice-Lawrence, L.: The evolution of 10-k textual disclosure: evidence from latent dirichlet allocation. J. Account. Econ. **64**(2), 221–245 (2017). https://EconPapers.repec.org/RePEc:eee:jaecon:v:64:y:2017:i:2:p:221-245
11. Halder, K., Akbik, A., Krapac, J., Vollgraf, R.: Task-aware representation of sentences for generic text classification. In: Proceedings of the 28th International Conference on Computational Linguistics, pp. 3202–3213 (2020)
12. Howard, J., Ruder, S.: Universal language model fine-tuning for text classification. In: Proceedings of the 56th Annual Meeting of the Association for Computational Linguistics (Volume 1: Long Papers), pp. 328–339, Melbourne, Australia, July 2018
13. Keith, K., Jensen, D., O'Connor, B.: Text and causal inference: a review of using text to remove confounding from causal estimates. In: Proceedings of the 58th Annual Meeting of the Association for Computational Linguistics, pp. 5332–5344, Association for Computational Linguistics, July 2020. https://doi.org/10.18653/v1/2020.acl-main.474, https://aclanthology.org/2020.acl-main.474
14. Lev, B., Thiagarajan, S.R.: Fundamental information analysis. J. Account. Res. **31**(2), 190–215 (1993). https://doi.org/10.2307/2491270, http://dx.doi.org/10.2307/2491270
15. Lewis, C., Young, S.: Fad or future? automated analysis of financial text and its implications for corporate reporting. Account. Bus. Res. **49**(5), 587–615 (2019). https://doi.org/10.1080/00014788.2019.1611730
16. Liu, Y., et al.: Roberta: a robustly optimized bert pretraining approach. arXiv preprint arXiv:1907.11692 (2019)
17. Lydenberg, S., Rogers, J., Wood, D.: From transparency to performance: Industry-based sustainability reporting on key issues. Technical Report, Hauser Center for Nonprofit Organizations at Harvard University (2010). https://iri.hks.harvard.edu/links/transparency-performance-industry-based-sustainability-reporting-key-issues
18. Masson, C., Montariol, S.: Detecting omissions of risk factors in company annual reports. In: Proceedings of the Second Workshop on Financial Technology and Natural Language Processing, pp. 15–21 (2020)

19. McCann, B., Keskar, N.S., Xiong, C., Socher, R.: The natural language decathlon: multitask learning as question answering. arXiv preprint arXiv:1806.08730 (2018)
20. McHugh, M.L.: Interrater reliability: the kappa statistic. Biochemia medica **22**(3), 276–282 (2012)
21. Merkl-Davies, D.M., Brennan, N.M., McLeay, S.J.: Impression management and retrospective sense-making in corporate narratives: a social psychology perspective. Account. Audit. Account. J. **24**(3), 315–344 (2011), https://doi.org/10.1108/09513571111124036
22. Montariol, S., Allauzen, A., Kitamoto, A.: Variations in word usage for the financial domain. In: Proceedings of the Second Workshop on Financial Technology and Natural Language Processing, pp. 8–14, Kyoto, Japan, 5 January 2020. https://aclanthology.org/2020.finnlp-1.2
23. Peng, B., Chersoni, E., Hsu, Y.Y., Huang, C.R.: Is domain adaptation worth your investment? comparing BERT and FinBERT on financial tasks. In: Proceedings of the Third Workshop on Economics and Natural Language Processing, pp. 37–44, Association for Computational Linguistics, Punta Cana, Dominican Republic, November 2021. https://doi.org/10.18653/v1/2021.econlp-1.5, https://aclanthology.org/2021.econlp-1.5
24. Phang, J., Févry, T., Bowman, S.R.: Sentence encoders on stilts: supplementary training on intermediate labeled-data tasks. arXiv preprint arXiv:1811.01088 (2018)
25. Pruksachatkun, Y., et al.: Intermediate-task transfer learning with pretrained language models: When and why does it work? In: Proceedings of the 58th Annual Meeting of the Association for Computational Linguistics, pp. 5231–5247, Association for Computational Linguistics, July 2020. https://doi.org/10.18653/v1/2020.acl-main.467, https://aclanthology.org/2020.acl-main.467
26. Purver, M., et al.: Tracking changes in ESG representation: initial investigations in UK annual reports. In: LREC 2022 Workshop Language Resources and Evaluation Conference 20–25 June 2022, pp. 9–14 (2022)
27. Reverte, C.: Corporate social responsibility disclosure and market valuation: evidence from Spanish listed firms. Rev. Manage. Sci. **10**(2), 411–435 (2016)
28. Ruder, S.: An overview of multi-task learning in deep neural networks. arXiv preprint arXiv:1706.05098 (2017)
29. SEC: Securities exchange act of 1934. Securities Exchange Act of 1934 (2012)
30. Slattery, D.: The power of language in corporate financial reports. Commun. Lang. Work **3**(3), 53–63 (2014). https://doi.org/10.7146/claw.v1i3.16555
31. Standley, T., Zamir, A., Chen, D., Guibas, L., Malik, J., Savarese, S.: Which tasks should be learned together in multi-task learning? In: International Conference on Machine Learning, pp. 9120–9132, PMLR (2020)
32. Stepišnik-Perdih, T., Pelicon, A., Škrlj, B., Žnidaršič, M., Lončarski, I., Pollak, S.: Sentiment classification by incorporating background knowledge from financial ontologies. In: Proceedings of the 4th FNP Workshop, 2022, to appear
33. Vaswani, A., et al.: Attention is all you need. In: Advances in Neural Information Processing Systems, vol. 30 (2017)
34. Wang, A., Singh, A., Michael, J., Hill, F., Levy, O., Bowman, S.: GLUE: a multitask benchmark and analysis platform for natural language understanding. In: Proceedings of the 2018 EMNLP Workshop BlackboxNLP: analyzing and interpreting Neural Networks for NLP, pp. 353–355, Association for Computational Linguistics, Brussels, Belgium, November 2018. https://doi.org/10.18653/v1/W18-5446, https://aclanthology.org/W18-5446

35. Worsham, J., Kalita, J.: Multi-task learning for natural language processing in the 2020s: where are we going? Pattern Recogn. Lett. **136**, 120–126 (2020)
36. Zhang, Y., Yang, Q.: A survey on multi-task learning. IEEE Trans. Knowl. Data Eng. **01**, 1 (2021)

What to Do with Your Sentiments in Finance

Argimiro Arratia[(✉)] [iD]

Soft Computing Research Group (SOCO) at Intelligent Data Science and Artificial
Intelligence Research Center, Department of Computer Sciences,
Universitat Politècnica de Catalunya, Barcelona, Spain
argimiro@cs.upc.edu

Abstract. This paper presents some practical ideas for making use of
financial news-based sentiment indicators in trading, portfolio selection,
assets' industry classification and risk management.

Keywords: Sentiment analysis · Algorithmic trading · Portfolio
selection · Factor models

1 Introduction

Acuity Trading[1] produces a variety of news-based sentiment indicators for many
markets' assets conveying different emotions, with the collaboration of a research
team lead by the author from the Polytechnical University of Catalonia.

This alternative data can be used in many ways in the financial business, and
the purpose of this note is to give some ideas to practitioners in the industry,
and consumers of this sentimental data, on how to make use of these sentiment
indicators in their investment decisions. We focus on ideas for the construction
of algorithmic trading rules, portfolio selection, and sentimental factor models,
which are useful in forecasting, assets' return covariance estimation and assets'
industry classification. Hence, this is a survey paper of methods for exploiting
the news-based sentimental information on markets' assets, intended for hedge
fund managers, traders and practitioners in the financial industry in general.

1.1 Sentiment Analysis in Finance

Several existing studies in behavioural finance have shown evidence to the fact
that investors do react to news. Usually, they show greater propensity for making an investment move based on bad news rather than on good news (e.g. as
a general trait of human psychology [4,15], or due to specific investors trading attitudes [6]). Li [10] and Davis, Piger, and Sedor [5], analyse the tone of
qualitative information using term-specific word counts from corporate annual
reports and earnings press releases, respectively. Tetlock, Saar-Tsechansky and

---

[1] https://acuitytrading.com/.

© The Author(s), under exclusive license to Springer Nature Switzerland AG 2023
I. Koprinska et al. (Eds.): ECML PKDD 2022 Workshops, CCIS 1753, pp. 25–37, 2023.
https://doi.org/10.1007/978-3-031-23633-4_2

Macskassy [18] examine qualitative information in news stories at daily horizons, and find that the fraction of negative words in firm-specific news stories forecasts low firm earnings. Loughran and McDonald [12] worked out particular lists of words specific to finance, extracted from 10-K filings, and tested whether these lists actually gauge tone. The authors found significant relations between their lists of words and returns, trading volume, subsequent return volatility, and unexpected earnings. The important corollary of these works is that the selection of documents from where to build a basic lexicon has major influence on the accuracy of the final forecasting model, as sentiment varies according to context, and lists of words extracted from popular newspapers or social networks convey emotions differently than words from financial texts. Being aware of this, the sentimental lexicons used in this study are built from financial documents provided by *Dow Jones Newswires*, and in a way similar to [12].

Once a sound sentiment lexicon is built (and as stated before much the soundness relies on the choice of appropriate news sources), we build sentiment indicators quantifying, on a daily basis (usually), the mood of the public towards a financial entity. Ways of building sentiment indicators are well explained in [11]. Then financial modelling based on these sentiment indicators is done basically from two perspectives: either use the sentiment indicators as exogenous features in econometric or machine learning forecasting models, and test their relevance in forecasting price movements, returns of price or other statistics of the price; or use them as external advisors for ranking the subjects (target-entities) of the news (e.g. exchange market stocks) and create a portfolio. A few selected examples from the vast amount of published research on the subject of forecasting and portfolio management with sentiment data are [9,12,18,19], and further review of econometric models that include text as data can be found in [8].

1.2   The Sentiment Indicators

Acuity trading tracks news for more than 90K companies worldwide, and produces news-based entity sentiment indicators for each one of these. The sentiment indicators are based on proprietary lexicons, from which Acuity is able to extract up to nine different emotions pertaining to a given entity. This article focus on 6 of these sentiment types, which can be grouped into Bullish and Bearish emotions. In the Bullish emotions group we have indicators for (the terminology is from Acuity):
Positivity, Certainty, FinancialUp;
and in the Bearish emotions group we have
Negativity, Uncertainty, FinancialDown.

We can make the following aggregations of the different sentiment indicators exposed above to build general Bull/Bear signals:

- $BULL = 0.33 \cdot (Positivity + Certainty + FinancialUP)$; that is, at each time step consider the arithmetic average of bullish emotion scores. Likewise, consider

- $BEAR = 0.33 \cdot (Negativity + Uncertainty + FinancialDown)$;
- $BBr = 100 \cdot BULL/(BULL + BEAR)$;
- $PNlog = 0.5 \cdot \ln((Positivity + 1)/(Negativity + 1))$.

The BBr has been inspired by the well-known Bull-Bear ratio of Technical Analysis [1], which in the pre-internet era was concocted from market professionals opinion polls. In the sentiment data it may well be that for particular stocks, and for particular timestamps, all bullish and bearish sentiment scores are 0. In this case we interpolate the non-existent (or NA) BBr score by leftmost and rightmost non-NA values. The $PNlog$ is of similar nature as BBr [3].

For readers who are new to sentiment analysis, and its particular application to Finance, a good book to start is [11], and survey papers [2,3]. In particular [3] gives details of the construction of the sentiment indicators presented above. In the following sections I shall describe different ideas for using Acuity's entity sentiment indicators in your investment decisions.

2   Technical Trading with Sentiment

The general idea is to take your favorite trading rule from Technical Analysis (the book by Achelis [1] presents a large list of these trading rules), and instead of using the price of the stock in the rule substitute this by a sentiment indicator. To illustrate this idea consider the **Dual Moving Average Crossover** rule. This consist on computing two moving averages on the Closing price, one a short term over s days, named $MA(s)$, and the other a long term over m days, $MA(m)$, up to day t. The trading rule states to go long on the next day $t + 1$ if $MA(s) > MA(m)$, or short otherwise. An example of parameters values is $s = 12$, $m = 50$, but of course these can be tuned from data.

I applied this trading rule separately to each sentiment indicator Positivity, Negativity, Bull, Bear, and BBr, in place of the price, for the JP Morgan Chase & Co. stock (JPM:NYSE) from Jannuary 2, 2018 to May 22, 2020, an epoch that reflects both bull and bear market conditions. Thus, I feed the sentiment time series to the technical indicator, take position in the stock according to the signal and hold it until the next signal. My main measure of performance is the cumulative excess return given by the strategy with respect to buy-and-hold, but I will also consider the strategy annualized return, annualized volatility, its win-rate, maximum drawdown and Sharpe ratio (considering a risk-free interest rate of 1%). There are other important performance measures that one may consider, but the subset I propose give a fair idea of the health of the strategy with respect to benefits and risk.

I repeated the experiment with different values for s and m (in fact, $(s, m) \in \{5, 10, 15, 20\} \times \{25, 50, 100\}$), considered long-only and long-short trading, and applied a rolling window analysis with window sizes of 254 d (a year) and 127 d (6 months), both with 1 day increments. The results obtained showed that 96 out of the 240 variants of the MA strategy yielded positive excess return. All results are plotted in Fig. 1, where a code of diamond shape of different sizes and various shades of blue represent the combinations of pair values for (s, m); right boxes show long-only trading whilst left boxes show long-short trades; upper boxes show results of rolling window analysis with window size 127 (6 months), whilst lower boxes contains results of rolling analysis with window size 254 (a year). We readily observed that the best performing strategy (with respect to excess return) was based on the $BULL$ sentiment indicator, with $s = 10$, $m = 25$, window size of a year and allowing long and short positions. This strategy yielded 33.9% excess return and a Sharpe ratio of 1.74; its annualized volatility is 23.9% and maximum drawdown of –15.9%. For a more conservative strategy with volatility 14% and maximum drawdown of –9%, and a reasonable excess return of 10.6%, whilst offering a Sharpe ratio of 1.34, we have the BBr strategy with $s = 15$, $m = 25$, trading long only and window size of a year. Table 1 exhibits a count of successful strategies per sentiment. We can see there that the BEAR and Negativity sentiments give the greater number of successful variants of the MA strategy (i.e. with positive excess returns, ER).

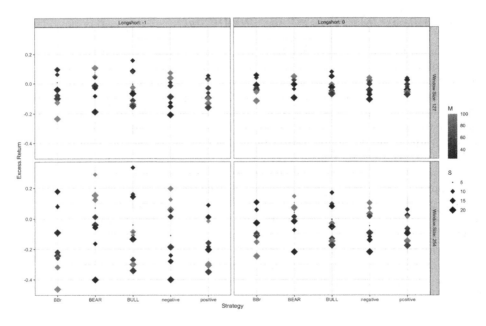

Fig. 1. All combinations of MA trading strategy with the five sentiment indicators and their performance with respect to excess return.

3   Sentiment Driven Portfolio Selection

The next idea is to use the sentiment indicators to rank stocks and use this ranking in the popular heuristic of quintile portfolio weighting. Subsequently,

Table 1. Count of successful strategies per sentiment.

Sentiment	# MA with $ER > 0$	% of total
BEAR	28	29.2%
Negative	26	27.1%
Positive	15	15.6%
BBr	14	14.5%
BULL	13	13.5%

a backtesting approach is implemented to compare these sentiment-based quintile portfolio selection with other popular portfolio selection and rebalancing strategies, and across the trading performance measures already mentioned in Sect. 2.

The quintile portfolio selection strategy is a popular simple strategy in financial investment. This consists on first sort the stocks according to some characteristics (e.g. in our case, this will be done with respect to the sentiment scores), and then the strategy equally longs the top 20% (i.e., top quintile) and possibly shorts the bottom 20% (i.e., bottom quintile). In my experiments I will restrict trading to long positions only. Despite its simplicity, the quintile portfolio strategy has shown great advantage over more sophisticated portfolios in terms of stable performance and easy deployment. Moreover, a recent paper [20] gives a mathematical interpretation of quintile portfolios as solutions of robust portfolio designs, with respect to some uncertainty sets for the expected returns.

In this study, I make use of the various functionalities of the R package `portfolioBacktest` [14], which allows to automate the performance analysis of backtests on a list of portfolios over multiple datasets on a rolling-window basis. By performing a rolling-window analysis one can cover many of the performance weakness of a single backtest and obtain more realistic results.

3.1   The Experiments and Results

The dataset consists of a set of 16 stocks from different sectors including the technological, oil, pharmaceutical, banking and financial services, and entertainment. This includes the following companies (listed by their market ticker): AAPL, ABBV, AMZN, DB, DIS, FB, GOOG, GRFS, HAL, HSBC, JPM, KO, MCD, MSFT, PFE, XOM. Their price history is taken on a daily basis from January 1, 2015 to June 9, 2020.

Several types of portfolios are constructed on the basis of different approaches for weighting the different stocks in the portfolio. As benchmarks, I use both the Global Minimum Variance Portfolio (GMVP) and the classical Mean-Variance (MV) portfolio due to Markowitz [13], which is the tangency portfolio constructed from the "efficient frontier" of optimal portfolios offering the maximum possible expected return for a given level of risk. I also include a simple portfolio in which the same weight is assigned to each stock (the uniform or equal weighted portfolio), as well as a quintile portfolio built simply on the basis of estimated expected returns. I use these portfolios as reference points for comparison with the sentiment-based portfolios, the Quintile-BBr and the Quintile-PNLog, which are constructed using the sentiment indicators BBr and PNLog, respectively, as the key input used for selecting stocks in a quintile portfolio strategy. I apply a look-back rolling window of length 252, and optimize the portfolio every 20 (i.e. perform a selection of stocks roughly every month according to strategy). For comparison purposes among the different portfolio selection strategies I do not consider transaction costs. However, I have made a simulation of the quintile portfolio with BBr selection considering transaction costs. Results are summarized below. Table 2 exhibits the performance of the six different portfolio selection strategies under the different measures considered (where Sharpe ratio is abbreviated as Sharpe, Maximum Drawdown as Max-DD, Annualized return as A_return, and Annualized volatility as A_volat).

Table 2. Performance of the six different portfolio selection strategies.

Strategy	Perform.			
	Sharpe	Max-DD	A_return	A_volat
Quintile	0.7106	0.2769	0.1743	0.2453
GMVP	0.3826	0.3359	0.0679	0.1774
MV	0.3339	0.3660	0.1077	0.3226
Quintile-BBr	0.9352	0.3139	0.1979	0.2116
Quintile-PNlog	0.6533	0.3282	0.1469	0.2248
Uniform	0.6078	0.3644	0.1216	0.2002

Performance can be also viewed in the plots below of cumulative returns and bar-plots of the drawdown and Sharpe ratio (Figs. 2 and 3). It can be observed that the quintile portfolio with BBr sentiment selection constructs relatively more successful portfolios in terms of Sharpe ratio and annual return. Moreover, all methods result in an approximately similar maximum drawdown. Additionally, it is remarkable that the uniform approach to assign weights performs comparably to other more sophisticated methods such as the Markowitz and the GMVP. This is consistent with the literature on portfolio management and highlights the key flaw in general Markowitz mean-variance optimization, as it demonstrates that a large degree of instability in the covariance matrix makes implementation of Markowitz not especially fruitful in practice (more on this in Sect. 4).

Finally, I simulate the Quintile-BBr portfolio selection strategy with transaction costs set at 15 bps, and compare to the same strategy without transaction costs. It can be observed that both strategies performed quite similarly (Fig. 4).

Cumulative Return

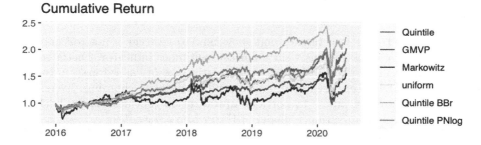

Fig. 2. Cumulative returns of the six portfolio's strategies.

Performance of portfolios

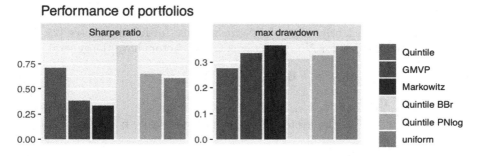

Fig. 3. Sharpe ratio and Maximum Drawdown of the six portfolio's strategies.

Wealth

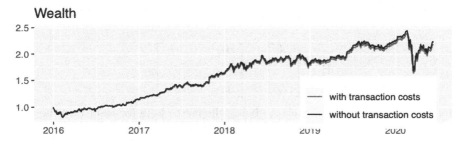

Fig. 4. Performance Quintile-BBr strategy with transaction costs set at 15 bps (red) and without (black). (Color figure online)

Overall, this study indicates that incorporation of sentiment analysis to portfolio selection has the potential to enhance risk-adjusted returns when compared with many of the standard portfolio choice frameworks. In particular, the Bull-Bear sentiment scoring used as the criteria for sorting in the quintile portfolio selection strategy performed substantially better than the reference portfolios, and the PNlog-Quintile portfolio performed slightly better than the best reference portfolio (the equal-weighted portfolio).

4 Sentiment Factor Model of Returns

In this section I go a step further and show how to leverage a macroeconomic factor model for stock returns with a market sentiment indicator. Factor models are used to make good estimates of the covariance of capital asset returns. Covariance matrices of asset returns are fundamental for choosing diversified portfolios and are key inputs to portfolio optimization routines, dating back to the now classical mean-variance model of Harry Markowitz [13].

The use of factor models to estimate large covariance matrices of asset returns dates back to William Sharpe [16]. The most well known factor models for capital assets are the capital asset pricing model, which uses excess market returns as the only factor (Sharpe [17]), and the Fama-French 3-factor model (Fama and French [7]).

Let us begin with a brief review of factor models (for full details see [21, Ch. 15]). Multifactor models for N asset returns and K factors have the general form

$$\mathbf{R}_t = \alpha + \mathbf{B} \cdot \mathbf{f}_t + \epsilon_t, \qquad t = 1, \dots, T \tag{1}$$

where $\mathbf{R}_t = \begin{bmatrix} R_{1t} \\ \vdots \\ R_{Nt} \end{bmatrix}$ is the vector of N assets log-returns, $\mathbf{f}_t = \begin{bmatrix} f_{1t}, \dots, f_{Kt} \end{bmatrix}$ is the vector of K factors, $\epsilon_t = \begin{bmatrix} \epsilon_{1t}, \dots, \epsilon_{Nt} \end{bmatrix}$ is the vector of N assets *specific factors*, $\alpha = \begin{bmatrix} \alpha_1, \dots, \alpha_N \end{bmatrix}$ is the vector of N assets alpha (which in a macroeconomic model corresponds to the excess return or abnormal rate of return), and

$$\mathbf{B} = \begin{bmatrix} \beta_1' \\ \vdots \\ \beta_N' \end{bmatrix} = \begin{bmatrix} \beta_{11} & \cdots & \beta_{1K} \\ \vdots & \ddots & \vdots \\ \beta_{N1} & \cdots & \beta_{NK} \end{bmatrix}$$

is matrix of factor loadings (each β_{ki} being the factor beta for asset i on the k-th factor).

In the multifactor model it is assumed that the factor realizations are independent with unconditional moments, and that the asset specific error terms are uncorrelated with each of the common factors, and are serially uncorrelated and contemporaneously uncorrelated across assets:

$$cov(\epsilon_{it}, \epsilon_{js}) = \sigma_i^2 \quad \text{for all} \quad i = j \quad \text{and} \quad t = s, \quad \text{or} \quad 0 \text{ otherwise}$$

Under these assumptions the covariance matrix of asset returns has the form

$$cov(\mathbf{R}_t) = \Sigma = \mathbf{B}cov(\mathbf{f}_t)\mathbf{B}' + \mathbf{D} \tag{2}$$

where $\mathbf{D} = cov(\epsilon_t) = E[\epsilon_t \epsilon_t' | \mathbf{f}_t]$ a diagonal matrix. From Eq. (2) we have that the variance of each asset is given by

$$var(R_{it}) = \beta_i' cov(\mathbf{f}_t)\beta_i + \sigma_i^2 \tag{3}$$

and the assets' pairwise covariance is fully determined by the covariance of the market factors:

$$cov(R_{it}, R_{jt}) = \beta_i' cov(\mathbf{f}_t)\beta_j \tag{4}$$

4.1 Sentiment Factor Models for the US Market

I shall consider the following five factor models for stocks of companies trading in the New York Stock Exchange:

1. macroeconomic 1-factor model based on the SP500 returns (factor name: SP500)
2. macroeconomic 1-factor model based on a Sentiment index (factor name: Sentiment)
3. fundamental 3-factor Fama-French model (factors: SMB, HML, Mkt.RF)
4. fundamental 4-factor Fama-French and Sentiment index model (factors: SMB, HML, Mkt.RF, Sentiment)
5. macroeconomic 2-factor model based on SP500 and Sentiment index (factors: SP500, Sentiment).

The Fama-French factors are constructed using 6 value-weight portfolios formed on size and book-to-market. SMB (Small Minus Big market capitalization) is the average return on the three small portfolios minus the average return on the three big portfolios; HML (High Minus Low book-to-market ratio) is the average return on the two value portfolios minus the average return on the two growth portfolios; Mkt.RF is the excess return on the market, value-weight return of all CRSP firms incorporated in the US and listed on the NYSE, AMEX, or NASDAQ. These factors are compiled and kept up to date by Professor French in his web page at the University of Dartmouth. The Sentiment factor will be Acuity's PNlog described above.

I consider the set of stocks from NYSE, with the following tickers: AAPL, ABBV, AMZN, DB, DIS, FB, GOOG, HAL, HSBC, JPM, KO, MCD, MSFT, PFE, XOM, and sample their prices from 1-1-2015 to 31-12-2019, a bullish period for the American stock market. Let S be the set containing the log-returns of these stocks in the aforementioned period. I construct all our five factors (Mkt.RF, SMB, HML, SP500, Sentiment) in the same period.

It is instructive to see first how the factors we are considering correlate to each other. Table 3 shows the correlation between these factors.

Table 3. Correlation matrix of factors

	Mkt.RF	SMB	HML	SP500	Sentiment
Mkt.RF	1	0.1429	−0.034	0.929	0.0174
SMB	0.149	1	−0.0491	0.0819	0.0139
HML	−0.034	−0.0491	1	−0.0386	−0.0572
SP500	0.929	0.0819	−0.0386	1	0.0169
Sentiment	0.0174	0.0139	−0.0572	0.0169	1

We can observe that none of the correlations are statistically significant (except of course between Mkt.RF and SP500 which are both quantifying basically the same statistic: Mkt.RF is the American's markets joint excess return while the other is the SP500 return). One can conclude from this correlation analysis that the Sentiment index does provide different information on the stocks from the market.

Next, I fit a 1-factor model based on Sentiment to the log-returns of portfolio S, and estimate the covariance matrix of the residuals of this factor model fit. I apply a hierarchical clustering algorithm using as similarity metric the correlation of these residuals. Figure 5 shows the covariance matrix of residuals and in rectangular boxes the clusters obtained by correlation on these residuals.

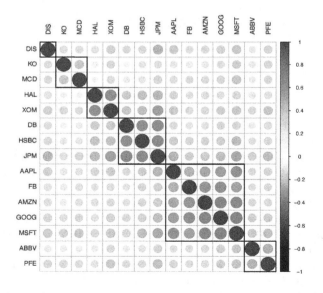

Fig. 5. Covariance of sentiment factor model and clustering.

We can see that the clustering performed on residuals (or asset's sentiment-specific factor) correctly identifies the sector of each stock: ABBV, PFE (pharmaceuticals); AAPL, FB, AMZN, GOOG, MSFT (technologicals); DB, HSBC, JPM (financials); HAL, XOM (oil); KD,MCD (consumption); DIS (entertainment).

4.2   Comparison of Returns Covariance Matrix Estimation via Different Factor Models

For further reference I will denote by $SP500$ the 1-factor model based on the SP500 returns; by *Sentiment* the 1-factor model based on Sentiment index (PNlog); by FF the 3-factor model due to Fama and French; by $FFwSent$ the 4-factor Fama-French and Sentiment index model; and by $SPwSent$ the 2-factor model based on SP500 and Sentiment index.

I fit each one of these factor models to the log-returns of our considered portfolio (the set S), and estimate for each the returns covariance matrix according to Eq. (2). I will estimate the models during a training phase (first half of the period considered) and then I will compare how well the estimated covariance matrices do compared to the sample covariance matrix of the test phase (second half of the period considered), and do this for different length periods to assess the impact of the length of sample data on the estimations. The estimation error will be evaluated in terms of the Frobenius norm $||\Sigma - \Sigma_{true}||_F^2$ as well as the PRIAL (PeRcentage Improvement in Average Loss):

$$PRIAL(\Sigma) = 100 \times \frac{||\Sigma_{scm} - \Sigma_{true}||_F^2 - ||\Sigma - \Sigma_{true}||_F^2}{||\Sigma_{scm} - \Sigma_{true}||_F^2}$$

which goes to 0 when the estimation Σ tends to the sample covariance matrix Σ_{scm} and goes to 100 when the estimation Σ tends to the true covariance matrix Σ_{true} (the sample covariance matrix of the test phase). Since one can not expect perfect uncorrelated residuals across assets, nor with the factors, the PRIAL can be negative when the sample covariance is very close to the true covariance and the factor model estimation of the covariance is not as good. This can (and surely) happen for example when taking large samples, which improves the asymptotic convergence of the sample covariance to the true covariance, but makes for a bad covariance matrix for portfolio management.

Tables 4 and 5 present the covariance estimation error and the PRIAL for each one of the five considered factor models on a selection of different periods varying their lengths and beginning date.

We can observe that in the period 2015-01-01/2017-12-31, the Sentiment-factor model by itself beat all other models in covariance estimation. In the periods where separately the SP500 and Sentiment factors have similar estimation accuracy (marked in bold), their joint model (the 2-factor model of SP500 and Sentiment) remarkably improves the error in the covariance estimation to the level of the Fama and French model. Considering a large sampling period (2015-01-01/ 2019-12-20) improves notably the accuracy of the sample covariance estimation (SCM), but deteriorates the estimation by all factor models,

Table 4. Frobenius-norm error in covariance estimation by the different factor models in different sampling periods

Period	SCM	SP500	Sentiment	FF	FFwSent	SPwSent
2015-01-01/2017-12-31	0.00134	0.00137	**0.00096**	0.00134	0.00134	0.00136
2017-01-01/2019-12-20	0.00079	**0.00148**	**0.00148**	0.00083	0.00083	**0.00085**
2018-01-01/2019-12-20	0.00106	**0.00131**	**0.00130**	0.00108	0.00108	0.00110
2015-01-01/2019-12-20	0.00055	0.00063	0.00126	0.00059	0.00059	0.00062

Table 5. PRIAL in covariance estimation by the different factor models in different sampling periods

Period	SCM	SP500	Sentiment	FF	FFwSent	SPwSent
2015-01-01/2017-12-31	0	−4.4299	**48.9348**	−1.1015	−1.0675	−4.6621
2017-01-01/2019-12-20	0	**−253.537**	**−253.008**	−10.328	−10.217	**−16.737**
2018-01-01/2019-12-20	0	**−53.127**	**−50.766**	−3.380	−3.351	−7.613
2015-01-01/2019-12-20	0	−30.798	−433.022	−17.173	−17.203	−30.937

most notably that of the Sentiment factor model, as one may expect since old news is no news.

To end, as it has been shown financial news sentiment is largely uncorrelated to other well-known financial factors and, in consequence, it does give complementary information about the market. The assets' sentiment-specific residuals from the Sentiment factor model of log-returns can help identify assets with similar risk, and the classification based on these residuals coincide with their sector classification. Using sentiment as a factor on its own can often give good estimations of assets' returns covariance matrix, and in combination with the SP500 returns series make a 2-factor model as comparatively as good as the Fama-French 3-factor model.

Acknowledgement. Research partially funded by *Programa Estatal de I+D+i Orientado a los Retos de la Sociedad de la AEI* (Ref.: PID2019-104551RB-I00).

References

1. Achelis, S.: Technical Analysis from A to Z, Mc Graw-Hill, New York (2001)
2. Algaba, A., ArdIa, D., Bluteau, K., Borms, S., Boudt, K.: Econometrics meets sentiment: an overview of methodology and applications. J. Econ. Surv. **34**(3), 512–547 (2020)
3. Arratia, A., Avalos, G., Cabaña, A., Duarte-López, A., Renedo-Mirambell, M.: Sentiment analysis of financial news: mechanics and statistics. In: Consoli, S., Reforgiato Recupero, D., Saisana, M. (eds.) Data Science for Economics and Finance, pp. 195–216. Springer, Cham (2021). https://doi.org/10.1007/978-3-030-66891-4_9
4. Baumeister, R.F., Bratslavsky, E., Finkenauer, C., Vohs, K.D.: Bad is stronger than good. Rev. Gener. Psychol. **5**(4), 323–370 (2001)

5. Davis, A.K., Piger, J.M., Sedor, L.M.: Beyond the numbers: measuring the information content of earnings press release language. Contemp. Acc. Res. **29**(3), 845–868 (2012)
6. Engelberg, J.E., Reed, A.V., Ringgenberg, M.C.: How are shorts informed?: Short sellers, news, and information processing. J. Finan. Econ. **105**(2), 260–278 (2012)
7. Fama, E., French, K.: The cross-section of expected stock returns. J. Finan. **47**(2), 427–465 (1992)
8. Gentzkow, M., Kelly, B., Taddy, M.: Text as data. J. Econ. Lit. **57**(3), 535–574 (2019)
9. Heston, S.L., Sinha, N.R.: News vs. sentiment: Predicting stock returns from news stories. Finan. Anal. J. **73**(3), 67–83 (2017)
10. Li, F.: Do stock market investors understand the risk sentiment of corporate annual re- ports?. SSRN 898181 (2006). http://www.greyfoxinvestors.com/wp-content/uploads/2015/06/ssrn-id898181.pdf
11. Liu, B.: Sentiment Analysis: Mining Opinions, Sentiments, and Emotions. Cambridge University Press, Cambridge (2015)
12. Loughran, T., McDonald, B.: Textual analysis in accounting and finance: a survey. J. Account. Res. **54**(4), 1187–1230 (2016)
13. Markowitz, H.: Portfolio selection. J. Finan. **7**(1), 77–91 (1952)
14. Palomar, D., Zhou, R.: PortfolioBacktest: Automated Backtesting of Portfolios over Multiple Datasets. R package v. 0.2.1 (2019)
15. Rozin, P., Royzman, E.B.: Negativity bias, negativity dominance, and contagion. Pers. Soc. Psychol. Rev. **5**(4), 296–320 (2001)
16. Sharpe, W.F.: A simplified model for portfolio analysis. Manage. Sci. **9**(2), 277–293 (1963)
17. Sharpe, W.: Capital asset prices: a theory of market equilibrium under conditions of risk. J. Finan. **19**(3), 425–442 (1964)
18. Tetlock, P.C., Saar-Tsechansky, M., Macskassy, S.: More than words: Quantifying language to measure firms fundamentals. J. Financ. **63**(3), 1437–1467 (2008)
19. Uhl, M.W., Pedersen, M., Malitius, O.: What?s in the news? using news sentiment momentum for tactical asset allocation. J. Portfolio Manage. **41**(2), 100–112 (2015)
20. Zhou, R., Palomar, D.: Understanding the quintile portfolio. IEEE Trans. Sig. Process. **68**, 4030–4040 (2020)
21. Zivot, E., Wang, J.: Modeling Financial Time Series with S-plus, 2nd edn. Springer, New York (2006). https://doi.org/10.1007/978-0-387-21763-5

On the Development of a European Tracker of Societal Issues and Economic Activities Using Alternative Data

Sergio Consoli[(⊠)], Marco Colagrossi, Francesco Panella, and Luca Barbaglia

European Commission, Joint Research Centre (DG JRC), Ispra, VA, Italy
{sergio.consoli,marco.colagrossi,francesco.panella,
luca.barbaglia}@ec.europa.eu

Abstract. We provide an overview on the development of a tracker of economic activities and societal issues across EU member states mining alternative data sources, that can be used to complement official statistics. Considered alternative datasets include Google Searches, Dow Jones Data, News and Analytics (DNA), and the Global Dataset of Events, Language and Tone (GDELT). After providing an overview on the methodology under current development, some preliminary findings are also given.

Keywords: Alternative (big) datasets · Economy and society · Social media

1 Introduction

A number of novel big data sources have the potential to be useful for socio-economic analyses [9]. These alternative sources of information include, for example, administrative data (e.g., tax and hospital records), commercial data sets (e.g., consumer panels, credit or debit card transactions), and textual data (e.g., social media, web searches, news data). In some cases, these data sets are structured and ready for analysis, while in other cases, for instance text, the data is unstructured and requires some preliminary steps to extract and organize the relevant information [2]. These unconventional data sources have been particularly relevant during the COVID-19 pandemic [14,24], when this information has been used to integrate and augment the official statistics produced by national and international statistical agencies [4]. In general, the evolution of this field is contributing to the development of various decision-making instruments that help policymakers in designing policy interventions with the potential of fostering economic growth and societal well-being. These trends are inspiring the research activities at the European Commission's Competence Center on Composite Indicators and Scoreboards (COIN)[1] at the European Commission, Joint Research Centre (JRC)[2]. This contribution

---

[1] European Commission's Competence Center on Composite Indicators and Scoreboards (COIN): https://composite-indicators.jrc.ec.europa.eu/.

[2] The Joint Research Centre (JRC) of the European Commission (EC): https://ec.europa.eu/info/departments/joint-research-centre_en.

I. Koprinska et al. (Eds.): ECML PKDD 2022 Workshops, CCIS 1753, pp. 38–43, 2023.
https://doi.org/10.1007/978-3-031-23633-4_3

describes our currently on-going research work, aimed at developing a tracker of economic activities and societal issues by obtaining policy-relevant insights from data sets which are considered unconventional in social sciences as well as stimulating the adoption of cutting hedge modeling technologies in the EU intuitions.

2   Google Search Data

Beginning with the work in [7], Google Search data have been used as a proxy of a variety of economic measures, especially in those contexts in which official statistics are not easily available. The JRC has studied the effects of Google Searches in monitoring the interests of European citizens in three main fields related to the pandemic crisis: health, economy and social isolation.[3] Web searches heavily depend on their link with the underlying phenomenon. As a result, scientists are required to be able to find the most relevant set of queries in each language and institutional environment. This task is especially difficult in a cross-country context, since locating the relevant queries is either time-consuming or even impossible (due to language barriers). To overcome this issue, authors in [5, 6, 23] recently exploited Google Trends topics, that are language-independent aggregations of various queries belonging to the same concept from a semantic perspective, enabling cross-country studies. Through the Google Trends API[4], it is possible to get access to Google Search data by the Search Volume Index (SVI) of both queries and topics, normalized to query time and location. Each data point filtered by time range (either daily, weekly or monthly) and geography (either country or ISO 3166-2), is divided by the total number of searches to get a measure of relative popularity. The figures are based on a uniformly distributed random sample of Google Searches updated once per day from 2004, thus there may be some difference between similar requests. Google also displays when possible the top-25 searches and topics linked to any particular topic or query. Top queries and topics are the most frequently searched queries (or topics) by users in the same session at any particular time and location.

3   DNA: Dow Jones Data, News and Analytics

We consider also newspaper articles as an alternative dataset. Several papers have tried to understand the predictive value of news for measuring financial and economic activities, such as GDP, stock returns, unemployment, or inflation [3, 15, 20–22]. In particular, many works have used the sentiment extracted from news as a useful addition to the toll-set of predictors that are commonly used to monitor and forecast the business cycle [1, 8, 11–13]. For this task, we rely on a commercial dataset of economic news obtained from the Dow Jones Data, News and Analytics (DNA) platform.[5] We use in particular the articles published by

---

[3] See   https://knowledge4policy.ec.europa.eu/projects-activities/tracking-eu-citizens %E2%80%99-concerns-using-google-search-data_en.

[4] https://trends.google.com/trends/.

[5] DNA platform: https://www.dowjones.com/dna/.

Thomson Reuters News consisting of several million news texts, full-text, since 1988. The content is about a wide set of topics, ranging from financial matters, to macro-economic announcements or political implications on national economies. We use this news data set to build a set of real-time economic sentiment indicators for the EU27 countries and the UK, focusing on a number of topics of interest [3, 10]. The sentiment indicators are: (i) fine-grained, i.e. they are bound in the [−1, +1] interval; (ii) aspect-based, meaning that they are computed only about the specific topic of interest [3, 10]. Sentiment indicators are computed for the different European countries by filtering directly on a direct mention in the text of the articles. Along with this extracted *sentiment* signal, for each filtered topic and country we also report the *volume* time-series, that is the number of sentences dealing about that specific topic-country under analysis, representing a measure of the popularity of the specific topic in the selected country. For each time-series, daily averages of *sentiment* and *volume* scores are calculated. Lower-frequency aggregations at monthly or quarterly frequencies, are also allowed.

4 GDELT: Global Dataset of Events, Language and Tone

GDELT[6] is the global database of events, locations and tone that is maintained by Google [17, 18]. It is an open big data platform of news collected at worldwide level, containing structured data mined from broadcast, print and web sources in more than 65 languages. It connects people, organizations, quotes, locations, themes, and emotions associated with events happening across the world. It describes societal behavior through eye of the media, making it an ideal data source for measuring social factors. The data set starts in February 2015 and is freely available to users via REST APIs.[7] GDELT processes over 88 million articles a year and more than 150,000 news outlets, updating the output every 15 min.[8] We use GDELT themes to filter out news related to certain social or economic topics (e.g., "industrial production", "unemployment", "cultural activities", etc.), limiting only to the news of the European country we are interested about. After this processing, we compute as output the (i) *Article Tone*, that is, a score between −1 and +1 expressing whether a certain message conveys a positive or negative sentiment with respect to a certain topic[9]; (ii) *Topic Popularity* rate, that is, the number of articles referred to the searched topic normalized by the total number of articles in the period.

In our application, we first select a list of representative keywords for the topic of interest along with the country to focus on and the period of extraction. The list of curated keywords is further extended programmatically by means of synonyms, which are computed using the Sense2Vec python library[10]. By using

---

[6] GDELT website: https://blog.gdeltproject.org/.

[7] See https://blog.gdeltproject.org/gdelt-2-0-our-global-world-in-realtime/.

[8] See http://data.gdeltproject.org/gdeltv2/lastupdate.txt for the English data, while http://data.gdeltproject.org/gdeltv2/lastupdate-translation.txt for the translated data.

[9] https://blog.gdeltproject.org/vader-sentiment-lexicon-now-available-in-gcam/.

[10] Sense2Vec library: https://pypi.org/project/sense2vec/.

the Word Embeddings [16] from the pre-trained GloVe model [19], we select only the articles from GDELT such that the topics are related to one of the selected themes of interest. Once collected the relevant news data, we are then able to calculate the *Articles Tone* score and the *Topic Popularity* rate by averaging the obtained measures from GDELT for the selected articles by the period of extraction.

5   Data Visualization and Analytics

We construct alternative indicators using the described datasets on various social and economic topics, representing broad categories of variables, such as: "economy", "industrial production", "unemployment", "inflation", "capital market", "cultural activities", "housing market", "international trade", "monetary policy" or "loneliness". We are building a number of services in order to provide access to the processed data along with intuitive and user-friendly visualizations. We rely on Business Intelligence (BI) and construct an interactive dashboard by means of the Microsoft Power BI infrastructure.[11] The dashboard allows users to choose which data to visualise by filtering the country, topic and time, and is available at https://knowledge4policy.ec.europa.eu/composite-indicators/socioeconomic-tracker_en.

We are also running a number of empirical exercises to analyse the relationships between the information extracted from our unconventional datasets and official releases of social and economic variables. We are particularly interested in nowcasting social and economic variables, that is, forecast the value of a variable during period t when the official release of the value will occur only in period t^*, with $t^* > t$. For European countries the typical delay in the release of official statistics ranges from 30 to 45 days. The goal of our studies consists then in nowcasting the value of the economic or social variable in real-time and before the official release of the statistical agencies. We use standard forecasting models augmented by the alternative indicators as additional regressors and compare their performance relative to the models without them. Timely and reliable forecasts for these signals play a relevant role in planning policies in support to the most vulnerable [6]. Given the delay and infrequent publication of official figures from statistical agencies, the importance of reliable unconventional indicators is even more prominent in times of high uncertainty, as also emphasized by the recent COVID-19 pandemic. Our early results, that we plan to extensively report in the form of an extended paper, show that our unconventional variables are relevant predictors in various nowcasting applications.

6   Conclusions and Future Work

We present our work-in-progress related to the development of alternative economic and social indicators from various unconventional data sets, including GDELT, Google Search, and newspaper articles. The currently on-going project

---

[11] Microsoft Power BI: https://powerbi.microsoft.com/.

aims to provide intuitive and user-friendly access to the data analysed by using an interactive BI dashboard, as well as producing improved nowcasting and forecasting methods to analyse various socio-economic measures for countries in the EU. When mature, we will discuss the results of our nowcasting applications by producing an extended version of this work which we plan to submit to a scientific outlet.

We are in particular aiming at a specific case with the goal of nowcasting inflation in different EU countries. In particular, at this purpose we intend to use advanced neural forecasting methods using deep learning[12] to obtain improved performance over classical forecasting approaches. The obtained preliminaries results seem to show that the information extracted from the considered alternative datasets have a predicting power for the inflation indicator in several EU countries. A thorough statistical analysis of these results needs however to be performed before we can release any robust conclusion on the subject.

References

1. Barbaglia, L., Consoli, S., Manzan, S.: Forecasting GDP in Europe with textual data. Available at SSRN, 3898680:1–38 (2021)
2. Barbaglia, L., Consoli, S., Manzan, S., Reforgiato Recupero, D., Saisana, M., Tiozzo Pezzoli, L.: Data science technologies in economics and finance: a gentle walk-in. In: Consoli, S., Reforgiato Recupero, D., Saisana, M. (eds.) Data Science for Economics and Finance, pp. 1–17. Springer, Cham (2021). https://doi.org/10.1007/978-3-030-66891-4_1
3. Barbaglia, L., Consoli, S., Manzan, S.: Forecasting with economic news. J. Bus. Econ. Stat. 1–12 (2022). (in press). https://doi.org/10.1080/07350015.2022.2060988
4. Barbaglia, L., Frattarolo, L., Onorante, L., Pericoli, F., Ratto, M., Tiozzo Pezzoli, L.: Testing big data in a big crisis: nowcasting under COVID-19. working paper available at SSRN, 4066479:1–38 (2022)
5. Brodeur, A., Clark, A.E., Flèche, S., Powdthavee, N.: COVID-19, lockdowns and well-being: evidence from google trends. J. Public Econ. **193**, 104346 (2021)
6. Caperna, G., Colagrossi, M., Geraci, A., Mazzarella, G.: A babel of web-searches: Googling unemployment during the pandemic. Labour Econ. **74**, 102097 (2022)
7. Choi, H., Varian, H.: Predicting the present with google trends. Econ. Record **88**, 2–9 (2012)
8. Consoli, S., Pezzoli, L., Tosetti, E.: Emotions in macroeconomic news and their impact on the European bond market. J. Int. Money Finan. **118**, 102472 (2021)
9. Consoli, S., Reforgiato Recupero, D., Saisana, M. (eds.): Data Science for Economics and Finance. Springer, Cham (2021). https://doi.org/10.1007/978-3-030-66891-4
10. Consoli, S., Barbaglia, S., Manzan, S.: Fine-grained, aspect-based sentiment analysis on economic and financial lexicon. Knowl.-Based Syst. 247:108781, 2022 ISSN 0950-7051. https://doi.org/10.1016/j.knosys.2022.108781
11. Consoli, L., Pezzoli, T., Tosetti, E.: Neural forecasting of the Italian sovereign bond market with economic news. J. Royal Stat. Soc. Ser. A Stat. Soc. 1–28 (2022). (in press)

---

[12] https://docs.aws.amazon.com/sagemaker/latest/dg/deepar.html.

12. Dridi, A., Atzeni, M., Reforgiato Recupero, D.: FineNews: fine-grained semantic sentiment analysis on financial microblogs and news. Int. J. Mach. Learn. Cybern. **10**(8), 2199–2207 (2018). https://doi.org/10.1007/s13042-018-0805-x
13. Gentzkow, M., Kelly, B., Taddy, M.: Text as data. J. Econ. Lit. **57**(3), 535–74 (2019)
14. Goodell, J.W.: Covid-19 and finance: agendas for future research. Financ. Res. Lett. **35**, 101512 (2020)
15. Hansen, S., McMahon, M.: Shocking language: understanding the macroeconomic effects of central bank communication. J. Int. Econ. **99**, S114–S133 (2016)
16. Kusner, M., Sun, Y., Kolkin, N., Weinberger, K.: From word embeddings to document distances. In: 32nd International Conference on Machine Learning (ICML 2015), vol. 2, pp. 957–966, United States, ACM (2015)
17. Kwak, H., An, J.: A first look at global news coverage of disasters by using the GDELT dataset. In: Aiello, L.M., McFarland, D. (eds.) SocInfo 2014. LNCS, vol. 8851, pp. 300–308. Springer, Cham (2014). https://doi.org/10.1007/978-3-319-13734-6_22
18. Leetaru, K., Schrodt, P.A.: GDELT: global data on events, Location and Tone. Technical report, KOF Working Papers, pp. 1979–2012 (2013)
19. Pennington, J., Socher, R., Manning, C.: GloVe: global vectors for word representation. In: EMNLP 2014–2014 Conference on Empirical Methods in Natural Language Processing, Proceedings of the Conference, pp. 1532–1543, United States, ACL (2014)
20. Shapiro, A.H., Sudhof, M., Wilson, D.: Measuring news sentiment. Federal Reserve Bank of San Francisco Working Paper (2018)
21. Tetlock, P.C.: Giving content to investor sentiment: the role of media in the stock market. J. Financ. **62**(3), 1139–1168 (2007)
22. Thorsrud, L.A.: Words are the new numbers: a newsy coincident index of the business cycle. J. Bus. Econ. Stat. **38**(2), 1–17 (2018)
23. Alberti, V.: Tracking EU Citizens? Interest in EC Priorities Using Online Search Data - The European Green Deal. Publications Office of the European Union, Luxembourg (Luxembourg) (2021)
24. Zhang, D., Hu, M., Ji, Q.: Financial markets under the global pandemic of COVID-19. Financ. Res. Lett. **36**, 101528 (2020)

Privacy-Preserving Machine Learning in Life Insurance Risk Prediction

Klismam Pereira[1,2]([⊠]) [iD], João Vinagre[1,2] [iD], Ana Nunes Alonso[1,3] [iD],
Fábio Coelho[1,3] [iD], and Melânia Carvalho[4] [iD]

[1] INESC TEC, Porto, Portugal
{klismam.f.pereira,jnsilva,ana.n.alonso,fabio.a.coelho}@inesctec.pt
[2] University of Porto, Porto, Portugal
[3] University of Minho, Braga, Portugal
[4] NAU21, Porto, Portugal
melania.carvalho@nau-21.com

Abstract. The application of machine learning to insurance risk prediction requires learning from sensitive data. This raises multiple ethical and legal issues. One of the most relevant ones is privacy. However, privacy-preserving methods can potentially hinder the predictive potential of machine learning models. In this paper, we present preliminary experiments with life insurance data using two privacy-preserving techniques: discretization and encryption. Our objective with this work is to assess the impact of such privacy preservation techniques in the accuracy of ML models. We instantiate the problem in three general, but plausible Use Cases involving the prediction of insurance claims within a 1-year horizon. Our preliminary experiments suggest that discretization and encryption have negligible impact in the accuracy of ML models.

Keywords: Machine learning · Privacy · Insurance risk prediction

1 Introduction

Machine learning (ML) models require large volumes of training data to achieve good performance. This prerequisite often limits the potential usage of data-driven applications in significant real-life problems, as several domains contain privacy-sensitive data. In this context, there is a recent increase in research on privacy-preserving ML (PPML) solutions, either by devising new ML approaches or by assimilating well-accepted anonymization methods to the ML pipeline. However, there is no single solution to privacy issues, and often a trade-off is present. E.g. computation overhead can be an issue when applying modern cryptosystems to sensitive data, and differential privacy (DP) usually comes with model utility loss [6,13].

This paper reports the first results of ongoing work evaluating the impact of two privacy-preserving techniques on ML models for risk prediction in life insurance: discretization and cryptography. We instantiate three Use Cases where the application of these techniques can be used to avoid certain types of attacks.

I. Koprinska et al. (Eds.): ECML PKDD 2022 Workshops, CCIS 1753, pp. 44–52, 2023.
https://doi.org/10.1007/978-3-031-23633-4_4

We aim to quantify the impact of each technique on the model's utility. Our main contribution is a set of experiments using real-world data from an insurance company. The insights provided by our results clearly show the potential impact of privacy-preserving methods on traditional ML tasks.

The remainder of this paper is organized as follows. Section 2 identifies related work. In Sect. 3 we describe the privacy-preserving techniques. We describe three application scenarios in Sect. 4, followed by experiments and results in Sect. 5. We conclude in Sect. 6.

2 Related Work

Most works on assessing life insurance risk through machine learning do not examine privacy issues. The primary concern is evaluating the performance of supervised models. We argue that there is a shortcoming in evaluating models' efficiency and cost savings without considering privacy concerns.

Boodhun & Jayabalan [4] applied ML techniques to a real-world publicly available dataset to predict the risk level of applicants. Data contains more than a hundred anonymized attributes from around fifty nine thousand applications. Nonetheless, the work by Narayanan & Shmatikov [1] demonstrates that an adversary can circumvent anonymization with background knowledge.

Maier et al. [8] developed a mortality model and a risk assessment indicator. A life insurance company provided data collected during fifteen years. It contains almost a million applicants' health, behaviour, and financial attributes. The model is regularly updated with new applicants' and clients' data. Concerns about transparency and fairness are made, but privacy is not addressed.

Levantesi et al. [10] reviews the usage of ML in longevity risk management. The reviewed contributions do not use individual-level data. Nevertheless, Dwork & Naor [2] show that even aggregate data can leak individual sensitive information.

There is also a great effort in recent research on privacy-preserving solutions. Liu et al. [5] survey security threats and defense techniques of ML. Kenthapadi et al. [7] concisely underline recent privacy breaches, lessons learned, and present case studies in which privacy-preserving techniques were applied. Kaisis et al. [9] present an overview of methods for federated, secure and privacy-preserving artificial intelligence on medical imaging applications. Majeed et al. [12] survey anonymization techniques for privacy-preserving data publishing. Liu et al. [11] review the literature on privacy concerns and solutions in the context of ML.

3 Privacy Methods

The three most common categories of privacy preservation techniques rely on (i) data obfuscation, (ii) data encryption, or (iii) differential privacy. This paper reports results in the first two.

3.1   Data Types

In a typical supervised machine learning problem, the data consists of a table with multiple columns. Each line is a data example represented by a vector with N attributes, i.e. the predictor variables/fields, and a label y, i.e. the target variable. Each of these variables can contain numerical data (e.g. numbers, dates), categorical data (e.g. marital status, postcode), or unstructured text such as names and addresses. Specific techniques can be applied to different types of variables. It is also relevant that the columns typically have a label that helps identify what information is in that field. In this paper, we work exclusively with numerical and categorical variables.

3.2   Obfuscation Methods

Obfuscation through aggregation is the most straightforward type of data manipulation that can be performed to improve privacy. The main idea is to reduce the granularity of the information so that the original values are harder to retrieve. In this paper, we experiment with the discretization – or *binning* – of values. The variable is divided into a relatively low number of intervals. Then it can be represented as a one-hot encoding scheme, or the original values are replaced with some value in that interval (i.e. mean, mode, median or even a random value within the interval). In our experiments in Sect. 5, we apply binning to the *age* field of a life insurance customer database.

3.3   Encryption Methods

Encryption is a widely used tool in privacy-preserving techniques. Essentially, it achieves the replacement of values with data that is unreadable by humans or machines in a way that is extremely hard to recover the original data. The most commonly used types of encryption on privacy-preserving machine learning are the following:

- *Hashing* passes values through a one-way function, that typically outputs a fixed-size unreadable string;
- *Order-preserving encryption (OPE)* performs a similar operation to hashing, but in a way that order between values is maintained before and after encryption – i.e. it is possible to reliably sort the encrypted items;
- *Homomorphic encryption* relies on an encryption function that is interchangeable with other functions applied to data. The result of applying an operation over an encrypted value, is the same as encrypting the result of the same operation over the unencrypted value. This property allows computations over data to be performed by potentially untrusted parties, since, in principle, only the entity that encrypts the data is able to make sense of the result of such computations.

Our experiments use hashing with categorical variables and OPE with numerical variables (see Sect. 5).

3.4   Differential Privacy

While encryption aims to enclose private information fully, differential privacy provides a mechanism to avoid individual identification of records, even if the data itself is readable. The idea is to introduce a certain level of noise such that it becomes impossible to reconstruct the original data, even with full access to the model. Using differential privacy techniques, we can prevent an attacker from i) inferring whether an individual record is in the dataset used to train the model and ii) reconstructing data from individuals by querying the model.

4   Proposed Scenarios

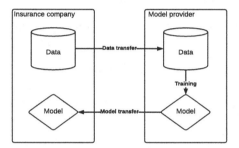

Fig. 1. Use Case 1: External model training

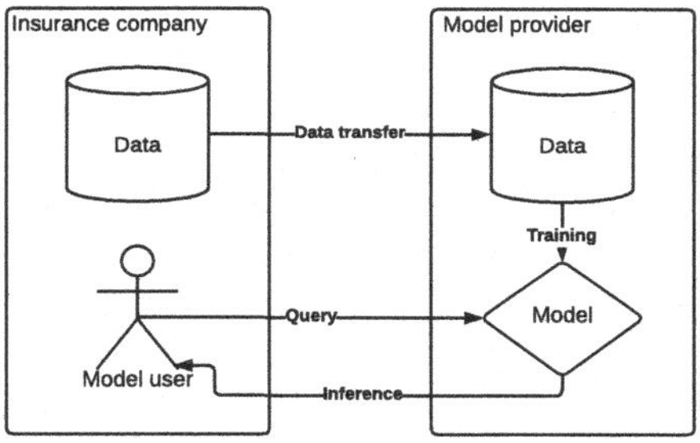

Fig. 2. Use Case 2: External model training and hosting

Since privacy is mostly application-dependent, for this study we devised generalizeable real-world scenarios, with particular focus on risk prediction in life insurance. Thus, we devise three Use Cases where an insurance company holds data containing sensitive customer data. We assume customers have given permission to the insurance company to process their data but not to share their data in clear text with third parties, even if it is anonymized or pseudonymized.

In all cases, the underlying task is to produce an ML model to predict the risk of a certain contract. We divide this in two complementary tasks:

- Task 1: predict if a contract will receive a claim within a 1-year horizon;
- Task 2: predict which type of claim is more likely to occur.

Figure 1 depicts the first Use Case. In this case, the life insurance company wishes to delegate the training of the ML model to a third party – e.g. an IT contractor specialized in AI. The third-party will train ML models for the two tasks described above. After models are trained, they are transferred back to the insurance company, which may integrate them into their IT infrastructure.

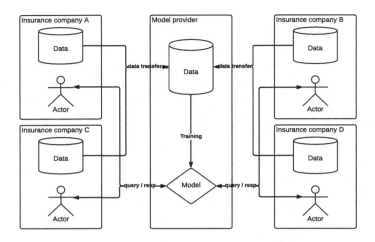

Fig. 3. Use Case 3: External model with collaborative network

The second Use Case, depicted in Fig. 2, is similar to the first; however, in this case, the model never leaves the realm of the entity that trains it. Instead, this entity provides a hosting service that allows the insurance company to query the model remotely – e.g. using a web service.

Finally, the third Use Case (Fig. 3) involves a series of insurance companies and other interested entities that rely on a central entity responsible for building a model using data from all parties (e.g. authorities, regulators, complementary service providers, or customer associations). This scenario allows all participating parties to take advantage of each other's data without accessing it.

Privacy leak risks mostly reside in two interactions: data transfer from the insurance company to an external entity (all Use Cases) and the querying of the model (Use Cases 2 and 3). Table 1 summarizes the potential usefulness of each of the techniques – discretization, encryption, and differential privacy – in each of the presented use cases, both at the data transfer and model query stages. In the case of data transfer, the effective solutions rely on (weak) aggregation methods, or (strong) encryption methods. Discretization can obfuscate specific numeric

Table 1. Applicability of privacy strategies

Use Case	Risk	Discretization	Encryption	Differential privacy
1	Data transfer	Yes	Yes	No
	Model query	No	Yes	No
2	Data transfer	Yes	Yes	No
	Model query	Yes	Yes	No
3	Data transfer	Yes	Yes	Yes
	Model query	Yes	Yes	Yes

fields essentially by reducing the numerical resolution. This can be applied if privacy requirements for the database fields in question are not high. Encryption is an obvious solution to protect data privacy when these requirements increase. Differential privacy is mostly useful in Use Case 3, where multiple parties contribute with their data. In this case, the model can leak information of the data it was trained on and be vulnerable to the attacks identified in Sect. 3.4.

5 Experiments and Results

5.1 Dataset

The dataset comprises about 540 thousand cases of individual life insurance registers. It was provided by a private life insurance company. It contains insured individuals' information such as *gender, age, marital status, profession, city of residence*, and other variables related to their contract. The dataset also contains the date on which an incident has occurred and its type. Incident types were aggregated into a binary variable that denotes the occurrence of an incident. Incident types and their binary aggregation were used as target variables for model training. As the dataset is imbalanced only results for the minority class are reported - incidents represent around 1% of examples.

5.2 Experimental Methodology

The performance of Random Forests models is evaluated in two classification tasks: for the next year, 1) binary classification predicting incident occurrences, and 2) multi-class classification predicting the type of incident of positive cases. A test set with all incidents that occurred in the last year of the dataset is held. Non-incident cases were randomly transferred from the training to the test set until it contained 20% of examples (108252 cases). The performance impact of privacy-preserving techniques was assessed for features individually.

Discretization of features was applied in two experiments. In the first experiment, the feature *age* was discretized into 5, 10, and 20 bins. Each bin has the same number of samples. In the second experiment, values in each bin are substituted by the median of the interval.

Hashing was applied with the SHA256 algorithm to categorical variables related to *profession, location, gender*, and *marital status*. An OPE implementation based on [3] was applied to *age*.

Experiments were run on a machine with a sixteen cores 2.20 GHz processor and 7.7 Gb RAM.

5.3 Results

The test performance of the baseline model in the binary classification task can be seen in Table 2. The results of the multi-class task are omitted. The baseline model for the multi-class task presents a high f1-score of 0.89 in the majority class - 78% of covered incident cases belong to the class *deceased*. However, the support of the remaining incident types is inferior to eighteen examples; therefore, the performance is not representative of the model's generalization capability. Attempts to circumvent the issue were made by applying over and undersampling techniques, but without success.

Table 2. Test performance scores of the binary baseline model in the minority class (i.e. positive incident). Precision shows almost half of the positive predictions are correct, while recall indicates a quarter of positive cases are identified.

Model	Auc	f1-score	Precision	Recall	Support
Baseline	0.83	0.33	0.47	0.25	852.0

Results for *age* discretization experiments can be seen in Fig. 4. Binning experiments are represented on the horizontal axis. The vertical axis presents delta - the relative difference between the experiments' scores and the baseline scores shown in Table 2. Metrics are represented by coloured bars.

In both experiments, decreasing the number of bins is associated with performance reduction across metrics. Using fewer bins reduces data variability, which may be seen as a trade-off between available information and privacy. AUC is slightly improved in the discretization with 20 and 10 bins when using the median. We argue that the delta observed for AUC across experiments is inferior to 1% in absolute terms; thus, the improvement could be spurious.

Binning with and without the median present similar performances across metrics; excluding AUC, these range between $[-2\%, -4.5\%]$ for twenty bins, $[-4\%, -6\%]$ for ten bins, and $[-7\%, -10\%]$ for five bins. In this sense, using bins without the median information might be more beneficial concerning privacy.

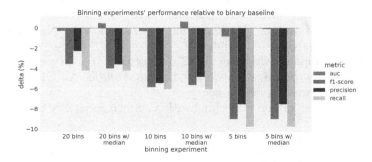

Fig. 4. Binning experiments. Each experiment is named on the horizontal axis. The vertical axis shows delta - the relative difference between the test scores of experiments and the baseline model. From left to right, overall performance diminishes with fewer bins. Using the median did not improve results.

Performance for the hashing experiments were identical to the baseline in all metrics. This result is expected as each categorical label is mapped to a unique string object; thus, the information contained in each feature is preserved.

Applying OPE to *age* resulted in a relative difference in performance inferior to 1% across metrics. The result suggests privacy can be enhanced by using OPE without sacrificing performance. Nonetheless, using OPE had a pre-processing time overhead of eleven minutes, close to 20000% more than the baseline.

5.4 Discussion

The privacy-preserving techniques did not alter the performance of the baseline model by more than 10%, while obfuscation with five bins had the most negative impact. Techniques did not result in training and inference time overhead.

Using the median in conjunction with the bin aggregation of *age* proved to be an unnecessary addition of information, as the experiments' performances were very similar. The number of bins might be adjusted based on the privacy and performance requirements and the characteristics of the numeric variable.

Hashing categorical features did not affect performance. Data uniqueness is preserved, while the original labels' context is lost. It had a negligible effect on the pre-processing time.

The model trained with OPE applied to *age* performs similarly to the baseline as metrics did not vary more than 1%, indicating its usefulness in providing computable encrypted data. OPE significantly increased pre-processing time.

6 Conclusions

This paper presents a set of experiments measuring the impact of privacy-preserving techniques in life insurance risk prediction with machine learning models. We present three Use Cases and identify where each technique holds relevant privacy gains. Our experiments with each technique show that discretization and encryption have minimal impact on the accuracy of ML models, which suggests that they are viable techniques. In our ongoing work, we are experimenting with differentially private machine learning. In the future, we will study more advanced encryption schemes (e.g. homomorphic encryption), and further develop our framework to apply multiple techniques in conjunction.

Acknowledgements. This work is financed by National Funds through the Portuguese funding agency, FCT - Fundação para a Ciência e a Tecnologia, within project LA/P/0063/2020, and by the ERDF - European Regional Development Fund through the North Portugal Regional Operational Programme (NORTE 2020), under the POR-TUGAL 2020 Partnership Agreement within project SIS˜1 (NORTE-01-0247-FEDER-45355).

References

1. Narayanan, A., Shmatikov, V.: Robust de-anonymization of large sparse datasets. In: 2008 IEEE Symposium on Security and Privacy (SP 2008), pp. 111–125 (2008)
2. Dwork, C., Naor, M.: On the difficulties of disclosure prevention in statistical databases or the case for differential privacy. J. Priv. Confidentiality **2** (2010)
3. Boldyreva, A., Chenette, N., Lee, Y., O'Neill, A.: Order-preserving symmetric encryption. In: IACR Cryptol. ePrint Arch. (2012)
4. Boodhun, N., Jayabalan, M.: Risk prediction in life insurance industry using supervised learning algorithms. Complex Intell. Syst. **4**(2), 145–154 (2018). https://doi.org/10.1007/s40747-018-0072-1
5. Liu, Q., Li, P., Zhao, W., Cai, W., Yu, S., Leung, V.C.M.: A survey on security threats and defensive techniques of machine learning: a data driven view. IEEE Access **6**, 12 103–12 117 (2018)
6. Papernot, N., Mcdaniel, P., Sinha, A., Wellman, M.P.: SOK: security and privacy in machine learning. In: 2018 IEEE European Symposium on Security and Privacy (EuroS&P), pp. 399–414 (2018)
7. Kenthapadi, K., Mironov, I., Thakurta, A.: Privacy-preserving data mining in industry. In: Companion Proceedings of the 2019 World Wide Web Conference (2019)
8. Maier, M.E., Carlotto, H., Sanchez, F., Balogun, S., Merritt, S.A.: Transforming underwriting in the life insurance industry. In: AAAI (2019)
9. Kaissis, G., Makowski, M.R., Rückert, D., Braren, R.F.: Secure, privacy-preserving and federated machine learning in medical imaging. Nat. Mach. Intell. **2**, 305–311 (2020)
10. Levantesi, S., Nigri, A., Piscopo, G.: Longevity risk management through machine learning: state of the art (2020)
11. Liu, B., Ding, M., Shaham, S., Rahayu, W., Farokhi, F., Lin, Z.: When machine learning meets privacy. ACM Comput. Surv. (CSUR) **54**, 1–36 (2021)
12. Majeed, A., Lee, S.: Anonymization techniques for privacy preserving data publishing: a comprehensive survey. IEEE Access **9**, 8512–8545 (2021)
13. Xu, R., Baracaldo, N., Joshi, J.: Privacy-preserving machine learning: methods, challenges and directions, ArXiv, vol. abs/2108.04417 (2021)

Financial Distress Model Prediction Using Machine Learning: A Case Study on Indonesia's Consumers Cyclical Companies

Niken Prasasti Martono[✉] and Hayato Ohwada

Department of Industrial Administration, Faculty of Science and Technology, Tokyo University of Science, Tokyo, Japan
{niken,ohwada}@rs.tus.ac.jp

Abstract. Machine learning has been gradually introduced into corporate financial distress prediction and several prediction models have been developed. Financial distress affects the sustainability of a company's operations and undermines the rights and interests of its stakeholders, also harming the national economy and society. Therefore, we developed an accurate predictive model for financial distress. Using 17 financial attributes obtained from the financial statements of Indonesia's consumer cyclical companies, we developed a machine learning model for predicting financial distress using decision tree, logistic regression, LightGBM, and the k-nearest neighbor algorithms. The overall accuracy of the proposed model ranged from 0.60 to 0.87, which improved on using the one-year prior growth data of financial attributes.

Keywords: Financial distress · Machine learning · Corporate finance · Consumer cyclical

1 Introduction

Financial distress refers to when a company or individual cannot generate sufficient revenue or income because it cannot meet its financial obligations. This is generally due to the high fixed costs, illiquid assets, or revenues that are sensitive to economic downturns. A company experiencing financial distress exhibits the following characteristics: problematic operating cash flow, high loan interest, default, increasing creditor or debtor days, and decreasing company margins. Some financial attributes related to financial distress conditions are ratios related to profitability, solvency, liquidity, activity, and valuation [4]. Several previous studies used classical statistical methods, such as logistic regression, to develop financial distress prediction models [4,7,11]. Some have shown that the profitability ratios of the return on assets and equity, solvency ratio (debt-to-asset ratio), and the valuation ratio (price-to-earnings ratio) influence financial distress.

Financial distress is also related to economic uncertainty, wherein the economy experiences a long-lasting downturn. Indonesia, as an example, has experienced significant economic recession. For instance, the trade war between the

I. Koprinska et al. (Eds.): ECML PKDD 2022 Workshops, CCIS 1753, pp. 53–61, 2023.
https://doi.org/10.1007/978-3-031-23633-4_5

United States and China as well as the economic recession due to the COVID-19 pandemic that was still ongoing during this research affected various industrial sectors in Indonesia. Some of the highly affected sectors include hotels and tourism, air transportation services, restaurants, entertainment, retail, consumer electronics, and automobiles. These sectors belong to the consumer cyclical sector, also referred to as the consumer discretionary sector, which is closely related to economic conditions and has a greater chance of experiencing financial distress.

This study focused on creating a precise prediction model for financial distress with such limited data. The main contribution of this preliminary study was that we used the value of growth of each financial attribute data, instead of using yearly raw financial attribute data. The remainder of this study is organized as follows. The next section describes related works on financial distress and its prediction models, as well as the machine learning algorithms considered for the study. Section 3 presents the data, experimental setup, and results. Finally, Sect. 4 presents the conclusions and outlines future directions for this work.

2   Related Works

Previous studies defined the term financial distress differently, with some providing contradicting definitions. In general, financial distress is the point when cash flows are lower than a firm's current obligations. Companies with financial distress have a negative operating cash flow from investing and financing activities. Due to insufficient cash flow, they also default on loan payments and start to enter the liquidation phase or file for bankruptcy [4]. Financial distress captures a dynamic process of corporate failure.

In the Indonesian context, financial distress is also defined as companies that are classified under some special notation, an additional letter (notation) given to the Listed Company when the company meets certain conditions, as referred to in Indonesian Circular Letter Number SE-00017/BEI/07-2021 concerning the Addition of Information Display of Special Notation to the Listed Company Code. This special notation is a warning provided by the Indonesian Stock Exchange to investors regarding the company's condition. Indirectly, this special notation also functions as an indicator to help investors determine whether the company is facing financial difficulties. Although data on these specific notations are available, in this study, we used the operating cash flow amount as the target for the prediction model because of the small sample representing these notations.

Altman in 1968 [1] considered multivariate discriminant analysis (MDA) to quantify the critical value of Z-score and proposed Z-score model in order to check financial health of a company. Ohlson in 1980 [8] improved the bankruptcy prediction model and used logistic regression (LR) to estimate the bankruptcy probability of enterprises, avoiding common problems related to MDA. Some basic linear processes are impractical for developing real-time prediction models because they are overly simplistic. With developing information technology, several financial distress prediction models have been built based on artificial intelligence approaches, from simple to complex, transitioning from statistical methods. To better predict financial distress, several methods, such as machine learning and data mining techniques, such as logistic regression [7,11], support vector machines [6], and survival analysis models [5], and deep learning models are widely used for predicting financial distress [3,13,14].

3 Experimental Settings

3.1 Data Set

This study used a purposive sampling method to sample on the condition that the financial ratio data are available. Data sources for both the dependent and independent variables were obtained from the SP Capital IQ website and the Indonesia Stock Exchange website (https://www.idx.co.id/). This preliminary step used data on Indonesian companies in the consumer cyclical sector. The consumer cyclical sector includes companies that produce or distribute products and services that are generally sold to consumers; however, the demand for cyclical or secondary goods and services is directly proportional to economic growth. This industry includes companies that manufacture passenger cars and their components, durable household goods, clothing, shoes, textile goods, sports goods, and goods related to hobbies. This industry also includes companies providing tourism, recreation, education, consumer support services, media, advertising, entertainment providers, and secondary goods retail companies.

This article determined whether or not a company may be classified as being in financial distress. For preprocessing, incomplete samples, missing data, and null values were removed. Data from 117 companies were available; however, after pre-processing, we excluded a few companies having incomplete data, leaving us with data from 87 companies. The operating cash flow of the companies in 2019 was used as the target variable. When the operating cash flow value is negative, the company will be categorized as having financial distress (class 1, positive sample), and if the value is positive; the company will be categorized as having non-financial distress (class 0, negative sample). The predictor variable was determined by 17 variables: Quick Ratio (x_1), Current Ratio (x_2), Cash Ratio (x_3), Debt Ratio (x_4), Debt to Equity Ratio (x_5), Long Term Debt to Equity Ratio (x_6), Receivables Turnover (x_7), Inventory Turnover (x_8), Fixed Asset Turnover (x_9), Asset Turnover (x_{10}), Gross Profit Margin (x_{11}), Operating Profit Margin (x_{12}), Net Profit Margin (x_{13}), Return on Equity (x_{14}), Earning per Share (x_{15}), Return on Asset (x_{16}), and Operating Cash Flow Margin (x_{17}).

A new variable x_{2i} was defined to calculate the growth rate of each variable s_{1i} from 2017 (two years before financial distress) and 2018 (one year before financial distress). We used two scenarios to develop the model: Scenario 1 utilized the data of the current year (x_1 to x_{17}) and one-year growth rate of financial attributes (x_{1_1} to $x_{1_{17}}$) as predictor variables, and Scenario 2 utilized the data of the current year (x_1 to x_{17}) and two-year growth rate of financial attributes (x_{2_1} to $x_{2_{17}}$) as predictor variables.

Table 1. Description of data set used in the modeling

Property	Value
Country	Indonesia
Businesses type	Consumer cyclical
Selection procedure	Purposive random sampling
Business number	87 (22 financial distress, 65 non financial distress)
Duration	2017–2019

3.2 Methodology

To estimate financial distress, we evaluated the default probability of a company. Each company is described by a set of variables (predictors) x (the financial attributes mentioned previously) and its class or target y that can be either y = 0 ('non-financial distress') or y = 1 ('financial distress'). Initially, an unknown classifier function $f : x \rightarrow y$ is estimated on a training set of companies $(x_i, y_i), i = 1, ..., n$. The training set represents data for companies that are known to have survived financial distress or have gone into financial distress in 2019. This study developed four machine learning models (decision tree, logistic regression, LightGBM, and K-nearest neighbor). The optimal hyper-parameters for each machine learning model were obtained using the grid search method and five-fold cross-validation. Since the data experienced imbalance in negative and positive classes as shown in Table 1, we employed synthetic minority oversampling technique (SMOTE) to overcome the overfitting in learning process. After SMOTE is performed, we execute each of the following algorithm.

Decision Trees Classification. Decision trees, or classification trees, are a non-parametric machine learning technique. The trees are built by a recursive process of splitting data when moving from higher-to-lower levels [5]. Decision trees are superior in their ability to illustrate the splitting rules that describe how data are split. For instance, in financial distress, one example of a decision we can expect is as follows:

– Financial Distress if a financial attribute ≤ some value, or
– Non Financial Distress if a financial attribute > some value.

Logistic Regression Model. The subject variable of the study is the financial distress of a company; it takes the value of 1 in the case of financial distress, and 0 otherwise. Based on this, we chose a logistic regression model to predict the probability of occurrence of a distressing event. This binary model estimate the probability P_i of the occurrence of the event $y_i = 1$ (distress). The decision threshold (probability of P) most adopted by previous research and by the software is 50%. Therefore, the decision rule can be written as follows:

$$y_i = 1 \quad \text{if} \quad \beta_i x_i + \epsilon_i > 0 \text{ financial distress}$$

$$y_i = 0 \quad \text{if} \quad \beta_i x_i + \epsilon_i \leq 0 \text{ non-financial distress}$$

LightGBM. LightGBM is an adaptive gradient boosting model, which is an efficient implementation form of gradient boosting trees. To improve the algorithm's computing power and prediction accuracy, LightGBM primarily uses the histogram algorithm and other algorithms [10]. While other tree-based algorithms grow trees horizontally, Light GBM grows leaves-wise, or simply vertically. Leaves with the greatest loss in delta will be chosen for growth. This helps reduce the loss of Delta in subsequent iterations. This method results in much better accuracy than existing gradient boosting algorithms.

K-Nearest Neighbor. k-nearest neighbor (KNN) is a simple classification algorithm often used as a benchmark for more complex classifiers. The KNN classifier is a non-parametric method, such as decision trees, which does not rely on assumptions regarding the probability distribution of the input. It is based on the Euclidean distance between a test sample and specified training samples. The basic idea of the KNN algorithm is that as new data are collected, the k-nearest neighbors of the current point are chosen to predict its value. The prediction of the new point can be obtained by averaging the values of its k-nearest neighbors.

3.3 Classification Performance Evaluation

Correct classification or misclassification was quantified using four metrics: true positive (TP), true negative (TN), false positive (FP), and false negative (FN). The classification results were analyzed using evaluation metrics, including precision, recall, F1-score, and accuracy, based on the formula shown below.

$$Accuracy = \frac{TP + TN}{TP + TN + FP + FN}$$

$$Precision = \frac{TP}{TP + FP}$$

$$Recall = \frac{TP}{TP + FN}$$

$$F1 = \frac{2 * TP}{2 * TP + FP + FN}$$

4 Experimental Results

Using all the sample data mentioned in the previous section, we used the proposed method to classify financial distress in a cyclical consumer company using financial attribute data. Table 2 shows the evaluation performance of each algorithm using five-fold cross-validation. The overall accuracy ranged from 0.60 to 0.87. Using the dataset in Scenario 1 with one-year prior growth data of financial attributes resulted in better prediction performance. Among the four algorithms used in model building, LightGBM was superior in accuracy score for both Scenarios 1 and 2, with a prediction accuracy score of over 80 (Table 3).

Table 2. Performance measurement using 5-fold cross validation

Scenario	Method	Precision	Recall	Accuracy	F-1 score
1	Decision Tree	0.65	0.85	0.77	0.73
	LR	0.75	0.81	0.80	0.77
	LightGBM	0.79	0.78	0.87	0.78
	KNN	0.6	0.63	0.70	0.61
2	Decision Tree	0.70	0.85	0.77	0.76
	LR	0.80	0.77	0.79	0.78
	LightGBM	0.74	0.78	0.83	0.75
	KNN	0.66	0.60	0.60	0.62

Table 3. Example of rules obtained from Decision Tree

```
|--- feature_assetturnovergrowth <= -0.88
|    |--- class: 1
|--- feature_assetturnovergrowth >  -0.88
|    |--- feature_longtermdebttoequityratio <= 0.03
|    |    |--- feature_cashratio <= 0.02
|    |    |    |--- class: 1
|    |    |--- feature_cashratio >  0.02
|    |    |    |--- class: 0
|    |--- feature_longtermdebttoequityratio >  0.03
|    |    |--- feature_debttoequityratio <= 0.09
|    |    |    |--- class: 0
|    |    |--- feature_debttoequityratio >  0.09
|    |    |    |--- class: 0
```

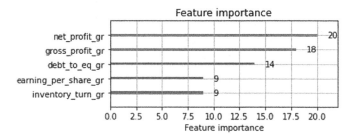

Fig. 1. Feature importance by LightGBM

4.1 Decision Tree Rules Interpretation

As previously mentioned, one of the advantages of using a decision tree is that it generates interpretable and understandable rules. For example, these rules were obtained from Scenario 1 using one year of prior growth data. From these rules, one can understand that the model will predict a company to be in financial distress if the following conditions are met:

- The value of asset turn over growth in a year is lower than −0.88, or
- Long term debt to equity is smaller or equal to 0.03 and cash ratio value is less than 0.02.

By definition, the asset turnover ratio is the ratio of the value of a company's sales or revenues to the value of its assets. This is an indicator of the efficiency with which a company deploys its assets to produce revenue. With a growth rate worse than 0.88, the model predicts the company status to be in financial distress. In addition, if the long-term debt-to-equity score is below or equal to 0.03, and the cash ratio is less than or equal to 0.02, the company is predicted to be in financial distress. Otherwise, the company is not experiencing financial distress. This is supported by previous work results that indicated that lower debt-to-equity ratio is better because it implies that the company is in less debt and is less risky for lenders and investors [12].

4.2   Feature Importance by LightGBM

Along with developing prediction models, LightGBM can rank features according to their importance in predicting financial distress. Figure 1 shows that in developing the prediction model using Scenario 1 (better performance), the highest ranked features based on importance (from the first to the third rank) are the growth rate of net profit, growth rate of gross profit, and growth rate of debt-to-equity ratio, which is also in line with previous works [2, 6, 9].

5   Conclusion and Future Works

Difficulty in financing is a major hindrance to business development. Investors want to invest money into creditworthy firms; thus, accurately predicting a company's financial difficulties is crucial for both companies and investors. Based on the predicted financial distress, a company can enhance the operation of the business and boost its risk-resistance capacity, and based on the predicted financing risk of each company, investors can target investments in companies with low risk. This study proposed a prediction model based on several machine learning algorithms to forecast financial distress in the customer cyclical sector. Four machine learning algorithms were implemented: decision tree, logistic regression, LightGBM, and k-nearest neighbor.

The prediction accuracies of the proposed model ranged from 0.60 to 0.87, with LightGBM leading in the accuracy score. As for the dataset, using the one-year prior growth rate resulted in better performance compared to the two-year prior growth rate. The decision tree and LightGBM algorithms provided the following interpretable results: (1) asset turnover growth rate, long-term debt-to-equity ratio, and debt-to-equity ratio are variables that represent decisions of financial distress of a company, and (2) growth rate of net profit, growth rate of gross profit, and growth rate of debt-to-equity ratio are variables with the highest importance in predicting financial distress using LightGBM.

This study had certain limitations that must be addressed. First, the limited sample size can be improved by using more samples from other sectors or companies. In addition, the results of this study can be improved by introducing unsupervised learning, such as cluster analysis, to further analyze the types of companies that suffer from financial distress. It would also be interesting to integrate macroeconomic variables into a larger sample that includes all sectors of Indonesian companies.

References

1. Altman, E.I.: Financial ratios, discriminant analysis and the prediction of corporate bankruptcy. J. Financ. **23**(4), 589–609 (1968)
2. Brîndescu-Olariu, D.: Bankruptcy prediction based on the debt ratio. Theoret. Appl. Econ. **XXIII**, 145–156 (2016). www.levier.ro
3. Chen, Y.S., Lin, C.K., Lo, C.M., Chen, S.F., Liao, Q.J.: Comparable studies of financial bankruptcy prediction using advanced hybrid intelligent classification models to provide early warning in the electronics industry. Mathematics **9** (2021). https://doi.org/10.3390/math9202622
4. Fawzi, N.S., Kamaluddin, A., Sanusi, Z.M.: Monitoring distressed companies through cash flow analysis. Procedia Econ. Finance **28**, 136–144 (2015). https://doi.org/10.1016/s2212-5671(15)01092-8
5. Gepp, A., Kumar, K.: Predicting financial distress: a comparison of survival analysis and decision tree techniques, vol. 54, pp. 396–404. Elsevier (2015). https://doi.org/10.1016/j.procs.2015.06.046
6. Härdle, W., Moro, R.A., Schäfer, D.: Predicting bankruptcy with support vector machines. http://sfb649.wiwi.hu-berlin.de
7. Mraihi, F.: Distressed company prediction using logistic regression: Tunisian's case. Q. J. Bus. Stud. **2**, 34–54 (2015). Type: Double Blind Peer Reviewed International Research Journal Publisher: Global Journals Inc 15
8. Ohlson, J.A.: Financial ratios and the probabilistic prediction of bankruptcy. J. Account. Res. **18**(1), 109–131 (1980)
9. Van, M.G., Şehribanoğlu, S., Van, M.H.: Finansal başarısızlık ve İflası etkileyen faktörlerin genelleştirilmiş sıralı logit modeli ile analizi. Int. J. Manage. Econ. Bus. **17**, 63–78 (3 2021). https://doi.org/10.17130/ijmeb.803957
10. Wang, D., Li, L., Zhao, D.: Corporate finance risk prediction based on lightGBM. Inf. Sci. **602**, 259–268 (2022). https://doi.org/10.1016/j.ins.2022.04.058
11. Xu, K., Zhao, Q., Bao, X.: Study on early warning of enterprise financial distress - based on partial least-squares logistic regression, vol. 65, pp. 3–16. Akademiai Kiado Rt., December 2015. https://doi.org/10.1556/032.65.2015.S2.2
12. Xu, P., et al.: Debt structure and bankruptcy of financially distressed small businesses tsuruta daisuke national graduate institute for policy studies/CRD association debt structure and bankruptcy of financially distressed small businesses * (2007). http://www.rieti.go.jp/en/

13. Zeng, S., Li, Y., Yang, W., Li, Y.: A financial distress prediction model based on sparse algorithm and support vector machine. Math. Probl. Eng. **2020** (2020). https://doi.org/10.1155/2020/5625271
14. Zhang, X.: A model combining lightgbm and neural network for high-frequency realized volatility forecasting (2022)

Improve Default Prediction in Highly Unbalanced Context

Stefano Piersanti[1,2(✉)]

[1] Sapienza University of Rome, Rome, Italy
`piersanti@diag.uniroma1.it`
[2] Bank of Italy - Statistical Data Collection and Processing Directorate,
Rome, Italy
`stefano.piersanti@bancaditalia.it`

Abstract. Finding a model to predict the default of a firm is a well-known topic over the financial and data science community.

Bankruptcy prediction has been studied in the literature for more than fifty years. Of course, despite the plethora of studies, predicting the failure of a company remain a hard task.

We dedicated a special effort to the analysis of the highly unbalanced context that characterizes bankruptcy prediction. Imbalanced classes are a common problem in machine learning classification that typically is addressed by removing the imbalance in the training set. We conjecture that it is not always the best choice and propose the use of a slightly unbalanced training set, showing that this approach contributes to improve the performance.

1 Introduction

Bankruptcy prediction of a company is, not surprisingly, a topic that has attracted a lot of research in the past decades by multiple disciplines [2,4–6,10–13,15–17,21,22,26,27]. The importance of such research is closely connected with financial stability since it stemming from its financial applications in bank lending, investment, governmental support and bank supervisory activity.

In particular, default prediction is one of the most challenging activities for managing credit risk. In fact, banks need to predict the possibility of default of a potential counterpart before they extend or renew a loan. An effective predictive system can lead to a sounder and profitable lending decisions leading to significant savings for the banks and the companies and to a stable financial banking system. This relevant topic has been studied in the literature for more than fifty years and several techniques for predicting bankruptcy have been developed over the years. Statistical techniques and Machine Learning (ML) approaches are the two broad categories used to predict bankruptcy [4,5,15,27]. Of course, despite the plethora of studies over the past fifty years, predicting the failure of a company remain a hard task. The need of an improvement in default prediction is common to the main interested stakeholders which, in our opinion, fall into

I. Koprinska et al. (Eds.): ECML PKDD 2022 Workshops, CCIS 1753, pp. 62–78, 2023.
https://doi.org/10.1007/978-3-031-23633-4_6

three main categories: 1) Private banks, 2) Supervisory Authorities, 3) Central Governments (when, for example, they provide public guarantees to companies).

In this paper we face the problem of bankruptcy prediction of companies, using ML techniques and historical data for predicting whether a company will enter in default within the following year. We base our analysis on the use of a very large dataset based both on credit data and balance sheet data. More in particular, we try to analyze in detail the specific highly unbalanced scenario that characterize our reference context, in order to obtain an improvement in prediction performance.

Contributions. The main contributions of our paper are: (i) we analyze default prediction in highly unbalanced context, using a very large dataset based on both credit data and balance sheet data; (ii) we conjecture that the use of AuROC like performance indicator may not represents the best choice in an unbalanced context; (iii) we show that the use of a fully balanced training set (which maximizes the AuROC and Recall) does not represent the best approach in general, when we work in a highly unbalanced context and we propose the use of a slightly unbalanced training set.

Roadmap. In Sect. 2 we present some related work. In Sect. 3 we describe our dataset and methods, while in Sect. 4 we provide our analysis related to prediction in an unbalanced scenario; some conclusion are reported in Sect. 5.

2   Related Work

There has been an enormous amount of work on bankruptcy prediction. In order to give a flavor of how the literature that concerns bankruptcy prediction models has evolved, we briefly review the most influential previous studies below.

Initially, scholars focused on making a linear distinction between healthy companies and the ones that will eventually default. Among the most influencing pioneers in this field we can distinguish Altman [2] and Ohlson [22], both of whom made a traditional probabilistic econometric analysis. Altman, essentially defined a score, the Z discriminant score, which depends on several financial ratios to asses the financial condition of a company. Ohlson on the other side, used a linear regression (LR) logit model that estimates the probability of failure of a company and identifies the main factors that affect that probability. Some papers criticize these methods as unable to classify companies as viable or non-viable [6]. However, both approaches are used, in the majority of the literature, as a benchmark to evaluate more sophisticated methods.

Since these early works there has been a large number of works based on Machine learning (ML) techniques [18,20,24]. The most successful have been based on decision trees [14,17,19,28] and neural networks [4,8,13,21,27]. Typically, all these works use different datasets and different sets of features, depending on the dataset. There exists a wide range of classification methods included in the category of decision trees. Lee [16] by making a comparison of three of them using a dataset of Taiwan listed electronic companies concludes that the most efficient is the Generic Programming decision tree classifier. Zhou and Wang [28] on the other side, starting from the traditional Random forest, propose the assignment of weights to each of the decision trees created, which are retrieved from each tree's past performance (out-of-bag errors in training method). Chakraborty and Joseph (2017) [9] train a set of models to predict distress in financial institutions based on balance sheet items, finding that ML approaches generally outperform statistical models based on logistic regression.

In a recent very important study, Barboza et al. [5] compare such techniques with Support vector machines and ensemble methods showing that ensemble methods and Random forests perform the best. Recently, Andini et al. [3] have used data from Italian Central Credit Register to assess the creditworthiness of companies in order to propose an improvement in the effectiveness of the assignment policies of the public guarantee programs.

Regarding the prediction in an unbalanced context, in [25] an accurate analysis about the performance of predictions is carried out, considering also a dynamic variation of the training set. In that paper, a proposal of cost function in order to measure the prediction results is also introduced. We try to use this paper as a reference point in our following analysis. The problem of prediction in highly unbalanced contexts has been addressed in recent years also in other works (see, for example [23]). Some well-known techniques aim to rebalancing the training set using sophisticated algorithms, including for example SMOTE (see [7]).

3   Dataset and Methods

In this paper we use a very large dataset which we now describe. The dataset combine credit information of companies from the Italian Central credit register (CCR) with balance sheet data of a large subsample of medium-large Italian firms. In the following we enter more in the details.

The Italian Central credit register is an information system on the debt of the customers of the banks and financial companies supervised by the Bank of Italy. It collects information on customers' borrowings from the banks and notifies the financial companies of the risk position of each customer towards the entire banking system. In this paper we use a large dataset obtained from Central credit register data that contains data related to almost 800K firms for each quarter from 2014 to 2020. For each company and each quarter in this period, the dataset contains about 20 different variables. On the other hand, our balance sheet dataset consists of financial data for more than 500K Italian firms (generally medium and large companies) and contains about 15 attributes. In our study we use balance sheet information for the years from 2014 to 2020, in combination with the credit dataset. The overall dataset (CCR + balance sheet data) that we use in order to predict the default of companies contains information related to over 300,000 Italian firms. In Table 1 we can observe the main features of our dataset.

Table 1. Main attributes for CCR dataset (on the left) and Balance sheet dataset (on the right).

ID	(1) CCR data	ID	(2) Balance sheet data
C1	Granted amount of loans	B1	Rating
C2	Used amount of loans	B2	Revenues
C3	Banks classification of firms	B3	Return on equity (ROE)
C4	Average amount of used loans	B4	Return on asset (ROA)
C5	Overdraft	B5	Total turnover
C6	Margins	B6	Total assets
C7	Past due (loans not returned)	B7	Financial charges/operating margin
C8	Amount of problematic loans	B8	EBITDA
C9	Amount of non-performing loans		

Measurement of prediction results will play a key role in our work. We use a variety of evaluation measures to assess the effectiveness of our prediction, which we briefly define. As usually, in a binary classification context, we use the confusion matrix and the related standard concept: **True Positive (TP)** equivalent with "hit" (a positive successful classification); **True Negative (TN)** equivalent with "correct rejection" (a negative successful classification); **False Positive (FP)** equivalent with "false alarm" (a positive wrong classification, Type I error); **False Negative (FN)** equivalent with "miss" (a negative wrong classification, Type II error).

Our analysis will take into consideration some important performance indicators, connected with the elementary components of the confusion matrix. We report in the table below the most important that we will use in the following.

Precision: $\mathbf{Pr} = \dfrac{\mathbf{TP}}{\mathbf{TP + FP}}$	Recall: $\mathbf{Re} = \dfrac{\mathbf{TP}}{\mathbf{TP + FN}}$	F1-score: $\mathbf{F1} = 2 \cdot \dfrac{\mathbf{Pr \cdot Re}}{\mathbf{Pr + Re}}$
AuROC: *The ROC curve shows the TPR value at various levels of TNR, and AuROC is the area under this curve.*		
$\mathbf{MCC} = \dfrac{\mathbf{TP * TN - FP * FN}}{\sqrt{\mathbf{(TP + FP) * (TP + FN) * (TN + FP) * (TN + FN)}}}$ (Matthews correlation coefficient)		

A firms that has a good financial situation (no default) at time T and will be in default at time T+1 year represents our target variable. In the following we better explain the concept of default we use for predictions. In general, default is the failure to pay interest or principal on a loan or security when due. In this paper we consider the classification of *adjusted default status* (in line with [1]), which is a classification that the Italian Central bank (Bank of Italy) gives to a company that has a problematic debt situation towards the entire banking system. According to this definition, a borrower is defined in default if its credit exposure has became significantly negative. More in detail, to asses the status of adjusted default, Bank of Italy considers three types of negative exposures. They are the following, in decreasing order of severity: (1) a bad (performing) loan is the most negative classification; (2) an unlikely to pay (UTP) loan is a loan for which the bank has high probability to loose money; (3) a loan is past due if it is not returned after a significant period past the deadline. Bank of Italy classifies a company in adjusted default if it has a total amount of loans belonging to the aforementioned three categories exceeding certain pre-established proportionality thresholds. If a company enters into an adjusted default status then it is typically unable to obtain new loans.

Regarding the classifiers used in default prediction (Sect. 4), our study represents an extension of the work done in [1], in which we showed the superiority of some tree-based ML techniques. Here, in particular, we perform the classification using LGBM (Light gradient boosting) classifier, that show remarkable performance in prediction, also in comparison with other well-known boosting techniques. But, as we will see better later, in this analysis our goal is not the comparison between classifiers but rather between different training set configurations and the evaluation of different performance indicators. In our experiments we use Python scikit implementation of the classifier with the default parameters. We split the datasets to training, performing a random stratified split of the full training data into train set (80%) and validation set (20%). The algorithm that we use in order to vary the imbalance of the training set (see again Sect. 4) perform a gradual reduction of the majority class, starting from the natural imbalance of the dataset until a perfect balance of the two, thus implementing a procedure of undersampling.

4   Prediction Performance Analysis in an Unbalanced Scenario

In general, in default prediction experiments the main objective is to reach the best possible performance (see, for example Aliaj et al. [1]). Typically, it is possible to obtain the best possible result using a balanced training set and measuring performance using the AuROC. Moreover, this represents a choice widely shared by the most important literature on the subject, in which generally we can observe a tendency to maximize the Recall (TPR) and try to minimize Type-1 and Type-2 errors (see for example [5]). This result is typically achieved using a perfectly balanced training set, which guarantees a high Recall value but at the expense of a lower Precision. Furthermore, also the choice of the performance indicator can be relevant in the evaluation of the results. In [25] an accurate analysis about the performance of predictions is carried out in an unbalanced context, considering also a dynamic variation of the training set. In that paper, a proposal of cost function in order to better measure the results is also introduced. The proposed function takes into account the gain deriving from correct predictions of the minority class and the losses arising from errors in classification. The main finding in that paper show that the balanced training set is not always the optimal choice, but only if the gain for a correct prediction (on the minority class) is much greater than the loss for an incorrect prediction (always on the minority class). We try to use this paper as a reference point in our following analysis. In particular, in Sect. 4.3 we will extend the approach in [25], however, suggesting a new proposal of linear gain function that takes into account both the results obtained on the minority class and those relating to the majority class. In other word, our gain function take into account all the four component of the confusion matrix: TP (True Positive), TN (True Negative), FP (False Positive) and FN (False Negative).

Our goal will be to identify a structured framework to apply to default prediction that helps to maximize the performance.

4.1   Prediction in a Highly Unbalanced Context: Which Performance Measure is Best to Use?

In this section we try to discuss to what extent the use of AuROC represents always a good choice when we consider a highly unbalanced scenario and even if it is the best choice to use a perfectly balanced training set. First of all, we observe that very different classification performances can match to the same value of AuROC. For example, we can consider a binary classification over a simple dataset of 1000 total elements (960 negative and 40 positive elements). In the Table 1 we show two cases that have the same AuROC value. But we observe that they represents two really different classification results (19 True Positive for case 1 versus 40 True Positive for case 2, while 946 True Negative for case 1 versus 441 for case 2: what is better?). In addition, we can mention that the two cases obtain very different F1-score values and also very different MCC values.

What is the best performance? The reply to this question is not always simple. It depends in a significant manner on whether we are interested in predicting the minority class only or whether we are also interested in predicting the majority class. If we are mainly interested in the correct identification of the minority class, the case 2 could be the best option. In this case we obtain the correct identification of all elements in the minority class: 40 True Positive classifications over 40 of total positive elements. On the other hand we have identified less than half of the majority class: only 441 compared to a total of 960 elements. Observing the performance indicators in Fig. 1, we can observe that F1-score more rewards a balanced stance between Precision and Recall, while AuROC rewards more the correct prediction of the minority class (and therefore a high Recall).

In the following, we continue to consider our example of a sample of 1000 elements strongly unbalanced at 4%. In particular, here we want to analyze the differences and the relationships between some widely used performance indicators. In the Fig. 2 we considered all the possible values for the confusion matrix (i.e. $960 * 40$ different combinations) and we calculated the correspondent performance indicators. In the bottom right chart, we show the relation between F1-score and AuROC for all the possible classification combinations. We can observe that exists a large interval of F1-values in correspondence with a single

	TP	TN	FP	FN	REC	PRE	F1-score	MCC	TPR	TNR	AuROC
case 1	19	946	14	21	0.48	0.58	0.52	0.51	0.48	0.99	0.73
case 2	40	441	519	0	1.00	0.07	0.13	0.18	1.00	0.46	0.73

Fig. 1. Comparison between two different binary classifications. We have considered a sample of 1000 total elements highly unbalanced (960 negative and 40 positive). We can observe that the two cases have the same AuROC but show very different values for F1-score and MCC.

value of AuROC. This means that they exist a lot of cases for which we obtain the same AuROC value but we obtain at the same time significantly different F1-score values (like in the case 1 and case 2, in Fig. 1). This fact is particularly true for high value of AuROC (from 0.6 upwards). Moreover, to a lesser extent, the opposite situation is also true: we observe classification points that have the same F1-score values but different values for the AuROC. In the other charts we report scatter plots between some pairs of performance indicators. Moreover, in these experiments we consider two different scenarios for each couple of indicators: a balanced dataset (on the left of each of the figures) and an unbalanced scenario (on the right). We can observe that F1-score and MCC show a similar behaviour when we consider an unbalanced dataset (Fig. 2 on the right) while AuROC and MCC have a good correspondence in balanced scenario. Instead, in the other cases there are many classification points in which we observe the same phenomenon described above, with many cases in which one indicator achieve the same performance result in correspondence of very different performances values for the other performance indicator we are comparing. To summarize, we can assert that the choice of the performance indicator is certainly not irrelevant in measuring the results.

4.2   Which Training Set Should We Use?

Here we are interested to evaluate what kind of training set should we use in order to maximize the prediction performance. In particular, we analyze some experiments that involve two cases with a different degree of imbalance. In both cases, we perform the prediction as the training set varies, starting from a completely balanced scenario (training set with $ratio = 1$ between defaulted firms and healthy firms). Then, gradually move to an increasingly unbalanced training set up to the natural imbalance of the overall dataset, that is equivalent to the imbalance of the test set.

We can observe the results in Fig. 3: AuROC is maximum for a completely balanced training set and it decrease as the imbalance of the training set increases. More precisely, Recall is maximum when the training set is balanced and decreases significantly as the train set imbalance increases. Instead, F1-score shows a maximum point corresponding to the imbalance for which Precision and Recall assume the same value. Our results regarding the dynamic of Precision, Recall and F1-score are absolutely in line with those reported in [25].

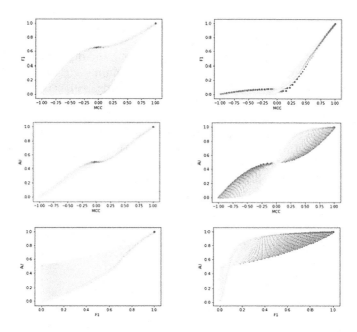

Fig. 2. Scatter plot between some couples of performance indicators. On the left we can observe the results for a balanced dataset of 1000 elements with 489 positive, while on the right a highly unbalanced dataset of 1000 elements with 40 positive elements.

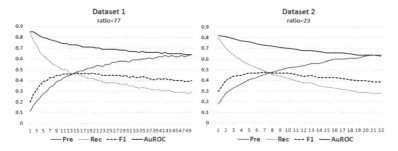

Fig. 3. Variations of some performance indicators as a function of the imbalance of the training set. The numbers reported on the x-axes represent the imbalance of the training set. We consider two different cases: Dataset 1 (default prediction in 2019) and Dataset 2 (default prediction in 2014) that have two different degree of imbalance.

However, we perform the prediction using two different dataset with a different degree of unbalance (77 versus 23). In particular, we try to predict bank default for 2019 and for 2014. The percentage of default firms in these two years are significantly different since in 2014 we observe a higher firms default rate in Italy, respect to 2019. So, we can add the observation that the degree of imbalance of the training set for which F1-score reaches its maximum seems to depend on the overall imbalance of the dataset. That is, in other words, equals to the imbalance of the test set we used. In fact, we can see on the left in Fig. 3 that the point at which Precision and Recall assume the same value falls in correspondence with an imbalance equal to about 15 (ratio between majority class and minority class in the training set). In this case the imbalance of the test set is equal to 77. On the other hand, when the imbalance of the test set is equal to 23 (on the right of Fig. 3) the point at which Precision and Recall assume the same value falls in correspondence with an imbalance equal to 7.

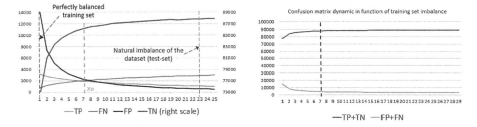

Fig. 4. Confusion matrix in function of the imbalance of the training set. The numbers reported on the x-axes represent the ratio between majority class and minority class.

In Fig. 4 we show the variation of the confusion matrix in function of the training set imbalance, for the least unbalanced scenario (ratio equal to 23). But we clarify that the results we obtained are the same also for the more unbalanced dataset, in terms of dynamic of the several components of the confusion matrix.

We can observe (figure on the left) that the number of True positive (TP) is maximum using a balanced training set but it decrease sharply if we increase the training set imbalance. On the contrary the number of True Negative (TN) shows an exactly opposite dynamic, even in terms of absolute numbers they are very different, since the negative class represents the majority one. The slopes of growth [decrease] of FN [of TP] are reduced only slightly instead as the imbalance of the training set increases. It is interesting to note that there is a value of the training set imbalance for which the TN [FP] growth [decrease] slope is drastically reduced. Therefore, to the left of this point on the graph, increasing the training set imbalance results in much more TN and much less FP; to the right of this point an increase in imbalance will impact these variations much less. This can be relevant in the research for an optimal prediction performance which depends on how relevant we consider to have more TN at the expense of less TP.

According to the observed trend of the confusion matrix as the imbalance of the training set varies, we can assert that the overall correct predictions (TP+TN) are lower using a completely balanced training set, while the overall prediction errors (FP+FN) are larger. This result (highlighted in Fig. 4, on the right) arise as a consequence of the different slope of the TP and TN curves (and correspondingly FP and FN curves) as we reduce the imbalance of the training set and tend towards a perfectly balanced training set scenario. We conclude this section highlighting the fact that all the performance indicators we used until now take into account only information contained in the confusion matrix that result from the classification procedures. In the next section we try to consider also another point of view, given that our prediction needs arise from an important business problem. The attempt will be to incorporate in the evaluation of the results also a business point of view.

4.3   A Model to Maximize the Value of Predictions

In this section we propose a linear gain function (Total Gain, GT) that take into account all the four components of the confusion matrix. We define the total gain function GT according to the following formula:

$$GT = \alpha * TP + \beta * TN - \gamma * FP - \delta * FN \tag{1}$$

where $\alpha, \beta, \gamma, \delta$ are positive values that we can use in order to determine the relevance of each of the components of the confusion matrix.

This proposal extends the gain function introduced in [25], in which are considered only TP and FP. Therefore, in that paper the author suggest exclusive relevance only to the prediction results relating to the minority class. This approach is reasonable but it implies the risk of excessively rewarding the achievement of correct positive classification (TP). But we observe (Fig. 4) that when we tend towards a balanced training set we obtain an increase of TP but at the same time a greater reduction (in absolute number) of TN. Hence our choice to consider all the four different components of the confusion matrix in our gain function GT. Taking into account that: $P = TP + FN$ (total positive) and $N = TN + FP$ (total negative), we can rewrite the Eq. (1) using a dependence from only two of the confusion matrix components:

$$GT = (\alpha + \delta) * TP - (\beta + \gamma) * FP + \beta * N - \delta * P \tag{2}$$

But, in (2) we can observe that, given our generalization, the coefficient of TP take into account both the value that we assign to a correct positive classification (TP) and the loss that we consider respect to a FN classification.

It is also interesting to analyze the dynamic of GT function when we modify the imbalance of the training set. In particular we refer to Fig. 4 and consider a variation in the imbalance of the training set, that means a different point on the x-axes in the graph. The correspondent variation ΔGT of the gain function is:

$$\Delta GT = (\alpha + \delta) * \Delta TP - (\beta + \gamma) * \Delta FP \tag{3}$$

This means that if we go to the left in the graph, towards a balanced training set, the total gain GT will increase only if:

$$(\alpha + \delta) * \Delta TP > (\beta + \gamma) * \Delta FP \tag{4}$$

But, as we saw in Fig. 4, the ratio $(\Delta FP / \Delta TP)$ is very high in the left part on the graph. So, we can write that:

$$\Delta GT > 0 \leftrightarrow \frac{(\beta + \gamma) * \Delta FP}{(\alpha + \delta) * \Delta TP} < 1 \tag{5}$$

Since $\frac{\Delta FP}{\Delta TP} \gg 1$, our conclusion is that it is convenient to use a fully balanced training set if and only if the following condition holds:

$$(\alpha + \delta) \gg (\beta + \gamma) \tag{6}$$

This appear a really residual scenario. In the other cases we conclude that it is useful to increase the imbalance of the training set in order to improve the performance of the prediction. Moreover, we can observe immediately that the previous scenario coincides with the case: $\alpha \gg \gamma$, if we assume that $\delta \simeq \beta$.

This conclusion is perfectly in line with the results in [25] in which, in fact, they are not considered the relevance of prediction about the majority class. But, as we anticipate before, we think that it is not an effective approach to consider irrelevant the contribution of the correct negative classification (TN) and the negative impact of the False negative (FN) attribution (that is the same as saying $\delta = \beta \simeq 0$). In addition, we consider that the condition reported in (6) could be represent in many case a too strong requirement. For example, in the case of a bank that would increase its credit portfolio or in a case in which a Public Authorities would support the economy by issuing guarantees to firms in order to obtain a new loan.

4.4   Some Case Studies

In this section we try to draw some more general consideration about the measurement of prediction performance in a highly unbalanced context. A relevant question could be: "Are we only interested in performance on the correct classification of the minority class?" In Sect. 4.3 we try to deal with issues introducing a gain function GT that take into account both minority and majority class (and both in terms of correct classification and errors). In the following, we report four case studies, that represent different examples relating to our reference context concerning the business failures. The choices we made in setting the parameters of the gain functions GT (and the relative business justifications) are absolutely questionable. But the main objective of our exercise is to show, however, how the business-side evaluation related to the convenience of the prediction can significantly change the final gain obtained from them. In fact, we think that the more effective way to measure a prediction performance framework should take into account the business assessments of the stakeholders involved in the predictions and should reflect their needs. In addition, our practical cases will confirm the conjecture that to use a perfectly balanced training set is not necessarily the best choice, even it leads to predict a much higher number of positive cases.

Example 1: Point of view of a private bank that gives a new loan.

- $\alpha = 0$: to identify correctly a future default implies that the bank do not extend a new loan
- $\beta = 10$: to identify correctly a no-default determine a gain (we assume 10%) for the bank that extend a new loan of 100
- $\gamma = 10$: to have a FP determine a miss gain (10%) for the bank that does not give a loan of 100
- $\delta = 100$: to have a FN implies a loss for the bank that gives a loan to 100 to a future default firm.

If we use a fully balanced training set we obtain a lower total gain (Fig. 5).

Example 2: Point of view of a private bank that manages its loan portfolio.

- $\alpha = 50$: to identify correctly a future default implies that the bank can act some measure in order to reduce losses, let's assume 25% of the total portfolio
- $\beta = 10$: to identify correctly a no-default determine a gain for the bank that can extend new loan to its client
- $\gamma = 20$: to have a FP determine a miss gain for the bank that act measure to contain the risk and does not give a new loan to its client
- $\delta = 100$: to have a FN implies a loss for the bank that can loss all the asset due to the default of the firm.

Also in this case (Fig. 5) it isn't convenient to use a fully balanced training set.

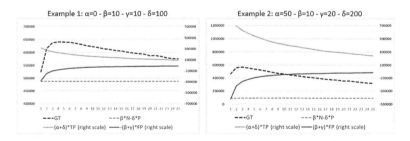

Fig. 5. Example 1 (left): Point of view of a bank that gives a new loan. Example 2 (right): Point of view of a bank that manages its loan portfolio. In this two examples we consider the dynamic of gain function GT and its component in Eq. 1.

Example 3: Point of view of bank Supervisory Authority.

- $\alpha = 100$: to identify correctly a future default implies that the supervisor can act measure to mitigate bank's risk obtaining a gain in ensuring overall financial stability
- $\beta = 0$: to identify correctly a no-default does not implies a gain for the supervisor perspective
- $\gamma = 0$: to have a FP determine a not necessary measure imposed on the bank (for example additional capital)
- $\delta = 150$: to have a FN implies a case for which supervisor does not take into account the individual risk of the bank by exposing the entire system to serious risks.

In this case a balanced training set assure the maximum total gain GT.

Example 4: Point of view of bank Supervisory Authority (with a little integration).

- $\alpha = 100$: to identify correctly a future default implies that the supervisor can act measure to mitigate bank's risk obtaining a gain in ensuring overall financial stability
- $\beta = 0$: to identify correctly a no-default does not implies a gain for the supervisor
- $\gamma = 30$: to have a FP determine a not necessary measure imposed on the bank (for example additional capital). But we can assume that this measure represent a loss for the bank profitability and can also involve risks for the entire system
- $\delta = 150$: to have a FN implies a case for which supervisor it does not take into account the individual risk of the bank by exposing the entire financial system to serious risks.

A little integration in the treatment of FP coefficient (compared to the previous case) determines it is no longer convenient to use a fully balanced training set.

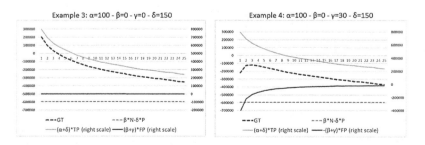

Fig. 6. Example 3 (left): Point of view of Supervisory Authority. Example 4 (right): Again the point of view of Supervisory Authority but with a little integration.

As we can see in the previous case studies, only one time the gain function (GT, dashed black line in the figures) reach its maximum value in correspondence of a fully balanced training set scenario (Example 3, on the left in Fig. 6). In fact, we can note that in this case we met the conditions indicated in the formula (6). In other words, in this scenario we are giving mainly relevance to correct positive classification and to avoid false negative classification. This means that we consider more important in GT function (formula 1) the values of α and δ. But this approach pay also a cost in terms of less number of True negative (TN) and a major number of False positive (FP). In particular, for each single correct classification in the minority class (TP) that we gain, we pay a high cost that means to obtain a higher number of errors (FP). But, if we let's take it to the extremes, we may be tempted to classify every case as positive in this particular situation. In fact, in this case we would have the maximum of TP and no occurrence of FN. In this case, since we are considering only α and δ as relevant parameters in our GT function, we could claim to have achieved a greatest result; but, obviously this is not what we are looking for. It is interesting to note that if we use AuROC as performance indicator we obtain the maximum results with a balanced training set, because AuROC particularly rewards a high Recall and therefore the high number of TP. But, if we are interested also in Precision we will instead be penalized by the increase in FP that derives from a training set more balanced. In this case the use of F1-score (or MCC) as performance indicator can represent a better choice. Finally, in the previous case studies we found that also some gain functions set taking into account the needs of some stakeholders would indicate that a fully balanced training set is not always the best choice.

To conclude, we can assert that the convenience in the use of a more balanced training set is highly dependent from the different slopes of the curve TP and TN and from the relative values that we attribute to have each one of the four element of the confusion matrix. We try to illustrate this evidence with some figures that report the variation of AuROC, F1-score and our GT function we used in the first use case. In particular, we calculate the dynamic of this performance indicators in function of the variation of TP and TN over the dataset composed of 1000 elements (of which only 40 positive). We can observe in Fig. 7 that AuROC is more sensible to the variation long the TP axis respect, for example, to the GT function. Also the dynamic of the F1-score indicator seems

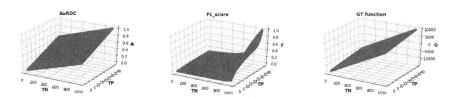

Fig. 7. The figure show the dynamic of the AuROC, F1-score and GT, in function of TP and TN. In this case the coefficient of GT are $\alpha = 0$, $\beta = 10$, $\gamma = 10$, $\delta = 100$.

less sensible to the variation of TP. This evidence motivate the convenience to use a more balanced training set (that improve the number of TP) when we measure the performance using AuROC.

5   Conclusion

Business-failure prediction is a very important topic of study for economic analysis and the regular functioning of the financial system. In our study, we try to predict the default of Italian companies using Machine Learning techniques, in line with a large part of the relevant recent literature. But our work is specifically dedicated in developing a framework to maximize the performance of predictions, taking into account the specific highly unbalanced scenario that characterize our reference context. We conjecture that the use of a perfectly balanced training set does not represent in many cases the right choice. We perform an in-depth analysis and we propose a total gain function in order to establish a sound framework for evaluating the performance of default predictions. With this regard, we propose the following conclusions: (1) we show that the use of a fully balanced training set (which maximizes the AuROC and the Recall) does not represent the best approach in general, when we work in a highly unbalanced context and, at the same time, the use of AuROC as performance indicator does not represents the best solution; (2) we conjecture that exist a well defined range in the training set imbalance in which we can determine the optimal configuration and this specific range depends to the imbalance of the dataset (and the test set) we are considering; (3) we show that performance evaluation task is highly dependent on the specific metrics that we use but also on the specific stakeholders needs and we hypothesize that a gain function (that have to take into account all the four components of the confusion matrix) could represent the best way to evaluate results.

Finally, our analysis leads further to assert that in our specific scenario we can obtain the best prediction results using a slightly unbalanced training set (in particular, a ratio between majority class and minority class between 3 and 5 in the case considered in Fig. 3) and we conjecture that, among the best known performance indicators, F1-score and MCC are the two metrics that appear best suited to measure the results in such unbalanced scenario.

References

1. Aliaj, T., Anagnostopoulos, A., Piersanti, S.: Firms default prediction with machine learning. In: Bitetta, V., Bordino, I., Ferretti, A., Gullo, F., Pascolutti, S., Ponti, G. (eds.) MIDAS 2019. LNCS (LNAI), vol. 11985, pp. 47–59. Springer, Cham (2020). https://doi.org/10.1007/978-3-030-37720-5_4
2. Altman, E.: Predicting financial distress of companies: revisiting the z-score and zeta. In: Handbook of Research Methods and Applications in Empirical Finance 5 (2000)

3. Andini, M., Boldrini, M., Ciani, E., de Blasio, G., D'Ignazio, A., Paladini, A.: Machine learning in the service of policy targeting: the case of public credit guarantees (1206) (2019). https://www.bancaditalia.it/pubblicazioni/temi-discussione/2019/2019-1206/en_tema_1206.pdf
4. Atiya, A.: Bankruptcy prediction for credit risk using neural networks: a survey and new results. IEEE Trans. Neural Netw. **12**, 929–935 (2001). https://doi.org/10.1109/72.935101
5. Barboza, F., Kimura, H., Altman, E.: Machine learning models and bankruptcy prediction. Expert Syst. Appl. **83**(C), 405–417 (2017). https://doi.org/10.1016/j.eswa.2017.04.006
6. Begley, J., Ming, J., Watts, S.: Bankruptcy classification errors in the 1980s: an empirical analysis of Altman's and Ohlson's models. Rev. Acc. Stud. **1**, 267–284 (1996)
7. Blagus, R., Lusa, L.: Smote for high-dimensional class-imbalanced data. BMC Bioinform. (2013). https://doi.org/10.1186/1471-2105-14-106
8. Boritz, J., Kennedy, D., Albuquerque, A.d.M.e.: Predicting corporate failure using a neural network approach. Intell. Syst. Account. Finance Manage. **4**(2), 95–111 (1995). https://onlinelibrary.wiley.com/doi/abs/10.1002/j.1099-1174.1995.tb00083.x
9. Chakraborty, C., Joseph, A.: Machine learning at central banks (september 1, 2017) Bank of England Working Paper No. 674 (2017). https://doi.org/10.2139/ssrn.3031796. https://ssrn.com/abstract=3031796
10. Chen, M.Y.: Bankruptcy prediction in firms with statistical and intelligent techniques and a comparison of evolutionary computation approaches. Comput. Math. Appl. **62**(12), 4514–4524 (2011). https://doi.org/10.1016/j.camwa.2011.10.030
11. Cho, S., Hong, H., Ha, B.C.: A hybrid approach based on the combination of variable selection using decision trees and case-based reasoning using the mahalanobis distance: for bankruptcy prediction. Expert Syst. Appl. **37**(4), 3482–3488 (2010). http://www.sciencedirect.com/science/article/pii/S0957417409009063
12. Erdogan, B.: Prediction of bankruptcy using support vector machines: an application to bank bankruptcy. J. Stat. Comput. Sim. **83**, 1–13 (2012)
13. Fernandez, E., Olmeda, I.: Bankruptcy prediction with artificial neural networks. In: Proceedings of the 2018 2nd International Conference on Inventive Systems and Control (ICISC 2018), vol. 930, pp. 1142–1146 (1995)
14. Gepp, A., Kumar, K.: Predicting financial distress: a comparison of survival analysis and decision tree techniques. Procedia Comput. Sci. **54**, 396–404 (2015)
15. Kumar, P.R., Ravi, V.: Bankruptcy prediction in banks and firms via statistical and intelligent techniques - a review. Eur. J. Oper. Res. **180**(1), 1–28 (2007). https://doi.org/10.1016/j.ejor.2006.08.043
16. Lee, S., Choi, W.S.: A multi-industry bankruptcy prediction model using back-propagation neural network and multivariate discriminant analysis. Expert Syst. Appl. **40**(8), 2941–2946 (2013). https://doi.org/10.1016/j.eswa.2012.12.009
17. Lee, W.C.: Genetic programming decision tree for bankruptcy prediction. In: 9th Joint International Conference on Information Sciences (JCIS 2006). Atlantis Press (2006)
18. Lin, W.Y., Hu, Y.H., Tsai, C.F.: Machine learning in financial crisis prediction: a survey. IEEE Trans. Syst. Man Cybernet. TSMC **42**, 421–436 (2012). https://doi.org/10.1109/TSMCC.2011.2170420
19. Martinelli, E., de Carvalho, A., Rezende, S., Matias, A.: Rules extractions from banks' bankrupt data using connectionist and symbolic learning algorithms. In: Proceedings of the Computational Finance Conference (1999)

20. Nanni, L., Lumini, A.: An experimental comparison of ensemble of classifiers for bankruptcy prediction and credit scoring. Expert Syst. Appl. **36**(2), 3028–3033 (2009). https://doi.org/10.1016/j.eswa.2008.01.018
21. Odom, M., Sharda, R.: A neural network model for bankruptcy prediction. In: Proceedings of the 1990 IJCNN International Joint Conference on Neural Networks, vol. 2, pp. 163–168 (1990)
22. Ohlson, J.A.: Financial ratios and the probabilistic prediction of bankruptcy. J. Account. Res. **18–1**, 109–131 (1980)
23. Branco, P., Torgo, L., Ribeiro, R.P.: A survey of predictive modeling on imbalanced domains. ACM Comput. Surv. **49** (2017). https://doi.org/10.1145/2907070
24. Sarojini Devi, S., Radhika, Y.: A survey on machine learning and statistical techniques in bankruptcy prediction. Int. J. Mach. Learn. Comput. **8**, 133–139 (2018). https://doi.org/10.18178/ijmlc.2018.8.2.676
25. Sophia Daskalaki, I.K., Avouris, N.: Evaluation of classifiers for an uneven class distribution problem. Appl. Artif. Intell. **20:5**, 381–417 (2006). https://doi.org/10.1080/08839510500313653
26. Wang, G., Ma, J., Yang, S.: An improved boosting based on feature selection for corporate bankruptcy prediction. Expert Syst. Appl. **41**(5), 2353–2361 (2014). http://www.sciencedirect.com/science/article/pii/S0957417413007872
27. Wang, N.: Bankruptcy prediction using machine learning. J. Math. Finance **07**, 908–918 (2017). https://doi.org/10.4236/jmf.2017.74049
28. Zhou, L., Wang, H.: Loan default prediction on large imbalanced data using random forests. TELKOMNIKA Indones. J. Electr. Eng. **10**, 1519–1525 (2012)

Towards Explainable Occupational Fraud Detection

Julian Tritscher[✉], Daniel Schlör, Fabian Gwinner, Anna Krause,
and Andreas Hotho

University of Würzburg, Am Hubland, 97074 Würzburg, Germany
{tritscher,schloer,anna.krause,hotho}@informatik.uni-wuerzburg.de,
fabian.gwinner@uni-wuerzburg.de

Abstract. Occupational fraud within companies currently causes losses of around 5% of company revenue each year. While enterprise resource planning systems can enable automated detection of occupational fraud through recording large amounts of company data, the use of state-of-the-art machine learning approaches in this domain is limited by their untraceable decision process. In this study, we evaluate whether machine learning combined with explainable artificial intelligence can provide both strong performance and decision traceability in occupational fraud detection. We construct an evaluation setting that assesses the comprehensibility of machine learning-based occupational fraud detection approaches, and evaluate both performance and comprehensibility of multiple approaches with explainable artificial intelligence. Our study finds that high detection performance does not necessarily indicate good explanation quality, but specific approaches provide both satisfactory performance and decision traceability, highlighting the suitability of machine learning for practical application in occupational fraud detection and the importance of research evaluating both performance and comprehensibility together.

Keywords: Fraud detection · Anomaly detection · XAI · ERP

1 Introduction

As a study by the Association of Certified Fraud Examiners shows, occupational fraud, such as theft of materials or abuse of permissions by employees, is estimated to cause average losses of around 5% of an organization's revenue each year [1]. Digitization of business operation, for example in Enterprise Resource Planning (ERP) systems, unifies business processes and provides a standardized data base, which also opens up new possibilities for automated occupational fraud detection with Machine Learning (ML) [37,38,47].

To qualify for practical use, fraud detection systems must, on the one hand, accurately detect fraud and, on the other hand, provide comprehensible suggestions and decisions [19]. Consequently, prior studies on ML-based fraud detection name explainability explicitly as requirement [10,14] and future research

I. Koprinska et al. (Eds.): ECML PKDD 2022 Workshops, CCIS 1753, pp. 79–96, 2023.
https://doi.org/10.1007/978-3-031-23633-4_7

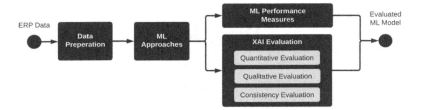

Fig. 1. Experimental setup for the evaluation of explainable occupational fraud detection in ERP system data.

[20]. However, for many state-of-the-art ML techniques, especially newly popular deep learning approaches, their high precision is attributed to a non-linear decision function that makes explaining their decision process non-trivial and turns them into a non-transparent black-box. This black-box nature is problematic for detecting fraud in ERP systems, where applying algorithms that do not act on reasonable fraudulent characteristics can introduce major consequences for potential wrongly suspected persons, in addition to ethical and legal requirements regarding privacy, transparency, and antidiscrimination [13,18].

The research discipline of eXplainable Artificial Intelligence (XAI) has developed several approaches towards explaining a model's decision and finally gaining insight into the decision process of black box models [4]. The question of whether ML approaches provide strong performance in detecting occupational fraud in ERP systems while maintaining a comprehensible decision process when used in combination with XAI, however, has not yet been answered in current research to the best of our knowledge.

We therefore construct a three-fold evaluation setting to assess the explainability of ML based occupational fraud detection approaches on ERP data based on quantitative, qualitative and consistency criteria. We then conduct extensive experiments on the detection performance and explainability of different fraud detection approaches, as outlined in our experimental setup depicted in Fig. 1: We combine five different ML-based fraud detection approaches, two classical anomaly detection approaches (One-Class SVM [36] and Isolation Forest [21]), a linear approach (Principle Component Analysis based Anomaly Detection [40]), and two task specific Deep Learning based approaches (Autoencoder [15] and improved Neural Arithmetic Logic Units [34]), with a state-of-the-art XAI component (Shapley Additive exPlanations [22]) providing explanations for the underlying decision process of each ML model. We evaluate the ML performance and the explanations generated from each fraud detection approach based on our three-tier XAI evaluation on ERP system data that includes fraudulent transactions with labeled explanations. As datasets with labeled explanations are rare and costly to obtain, we conduct an additional experiment investigating whether our measured detection performance and explanation quality are transferable to other datasets without the need for repeating hyperparameter studies that may require expensive labeling procedures in practice.

Our experiments identify ML-based fraud detection approaches that are capable of strong fraud detection performance on ERP system data, while also acting upon reasonable fraudulent characteristics. However, our experiments also show that strong detection performance does not automatically result in good explanation quality, suggesting that joint evaluation of model performance and explainability is essential in applications that require comprehensible decisions.

Our contributions can be summarized as follows:

- We construct a three-fold evaluation setting for the explainability of occupational fraud detection.
- We evaluate multiple ML approaches with respect to their detection performance and explainability through our evaluation scheme.[1]
- We assess whether our results obtained transfer to new datasets without the need for expensive labeling procedures.

The remaining paper is structured as follows: Sect. 2 gives an overview on occupational fraud detection and ML explainability. Section 3 introduces data preparation, ML approaches, and ML evaluation measures used in this study. Section 4 describes the constructed XAI evaluation setting. Section 5 presents our experiments and discusses results, while Sect. 6 concludes the paper.

2   Related Work

2.1   Fraud Detection

In the field of financial fraud detection, traditional ML, deep learning, and anomaly detection methods, as well as approaches relying on expert knowledge and auditors' views, have been subject to studies on both synthetic and real-world datasets. There are several surveys summarizing findings specifically from the financial domain [44] or from the broader field of anomaly detection, including financial fraud detection as an application domain [8,9]. While many of these works utilize machine learning to detect frauds such as credit card misuse [23,32], there are also works that focus on detecting occupational fraud within ERP system data.

Earlier work on fraud detection in ERP systems leverages statistical, visual, or clustering based approaches to detect frauds in database logs and transactional data [26,30,41–43]. Process mining, sometimes extended with filtering and rule based approaches, is another promising approach [5,12,24,33]. Instead of transactional data, process mining uses event logs as main data source, which introduces further layers of abstraction with the creation of process graphs.

Since the rise of neural networks, an increasing number of publications directly utilize ERP data. Multiple works proposed autoencoder neural network architectures for fraud detection directly on transactional data [37,38,47], or conducted case studies that provide empirical evidence for the practical application of autoencoder architectures on real data [25,39]. These approaches either

---

[1] Our code is available under https://professor-x.de/xai-erp-fraud.

limit the ERP tables to few discriminative attributes used in their approach, or directly rely on feature engineering to create audit-relevant aspects of entries through domain knowledge. In contrast, our approach does not rely on explicit modeling of domain knowledge or process mining. Instead, we focus on raw ERP data without extensive feature selection or feature engineering.

2.2 Explainable Artificial Intelligence

With the rise of deep learning, assessing the decision process of non-transparent black-box models has become a core field of research in the ML community, which has been categorized by Arrieta et al. [4].

In the domain of fraud detection, multiple works have focused on detecting and explaining fraud caused by malicious credit card transactions. In addition to work proposing inherently explainable network architectures [48], multiple works investigate the use of popular post hoc feature relevance XAI approaches [22,29] in detecting credit card fraud [3,28]. Post hoc feature relevance XAI explains an already trained ML model by finding the impact of each input feature toward the model's final decision. This allows insight into the reasoning behind single model decisions, which has been identified in prior studies as desirable property for ML-based fraud detection in general [10] and in occupational fraud detection on ERP system data [14]. Due to their promising results in the related domain of credit card fraud detection, we follow Antwarg et al. [3] and Psychoula et al. [28] in utilizing a post hoc feature relevance approach to obtain explanations, but propose a different XAI evaluation scheme: Rather than performing XAI evaluations on artificial data [3] and comparing them to simple linear models [28], we construct an evaluation on expert-labeled ground truth and derive requirements for consistent XAI decisions in ERP system data. To our knowledge, we are the first to investigate the performance of feature relevance XAI in the domain of occupational fraud detection in ERP system data.

3   Machine Learning Methodology

This section introduces the data preprocessing schemes, ML approaches, and ML performance metrics used in our study.

3.1 Data Preprocessing

With transactions in ERP systems that contain sparse information in many columns, manual feature extraction in combination with the feedback of business experts may seem like a promising approach for detecting common and known fraud cases. However, we argue that in a live setting, attackers can continuously create new and previously unseen frauds, which can only be detectable through additional information contained in sparse columns of the ERP system. This makes the ability of monitoring all available data appealing for a fraud detection system in a realistic setting. Therefore, we utilize established preprocessing techniques that largely retain the information contained in the ERP dataset and do not require vast amounts of manual feature engineering.

Categorical Columns are transformed by one-hot encoding. We further add a column for empty values, retaining the information of a column within the ERP data being left empty and allowing us to distinguish between empty columns and column entries that have not been observed during training time.

Numerical Columns can cause problems for many ML approaches due to large value ranges, which is problematic in a domain where monetary amounts or quantities vary from single digits to figures in millions. We test multiple established scaling techniques on numerical ERP system data, implementing z-score and minmax scaling [27], as well as quantization which transforms numerical values into categorical buckets. To highlight outliers within the data, we adapt the quantization technique to first choose two buckets that include the 1% highest and lowest numerical values and then choose buckets that equally distribute the remaining data. This allows the data representation to highlight unusually high or low values that may indicate fraudulent abuse of the system.

In our experiments, all preprocessing schemes are fitted purely on the training data and applied without fitting to both evaluation and test data. For the quantization scheme, we use 5 buckets since we observed decreasing performance with larger bucket sizes in preliminary testing.

3.2 ML Approaches

Common difficulties in the training and application of anomaly detection algorithms are the unavailability of anomalies during training time, and the diverse characteristics of potential anomalies [9]. These issues are further fortified in occupational fraud detection by a very high ratio of normal to anomalous datapoints and the motivation of fraudsters to create frauds that are highly diverse, novel, and difficult to detect. In this work, we therefore employ ML algorithms that exclusively train with normal data and are designed to detect anomalous datapoints that show deviating behavior. For our study, we investigate established deep learning approaches, classical anomaly detection approaches, and a linear model, which we introduce with the abbreviations and references used in Table 1. To unify the approaches, we make the following adjustments:

Table 1. Utilized ML algorithms.

Approach	Description	Source
AE	Autoencoder neural network architecture with ReLU activation	[15]
iNALU	AE with ReLU and improved neural arithmetic logic unit activation	[34]
IF	Isolation Forest	[21]
OC-SVM	One-Class Support Vector Machine using rbf kernel	[36]
PCA	Anomaly detection using Principle Component Analysis	[40]

iNALU is used in an autoencoder setup with linear layers at the beginning and end and intermediate mixed layers that contain an even number of ReLU and improved neural arithmetic logic unit activations [35]. While IF and PCA have a direct anomaly scoring function, we use reconstruction loss to detect anomalies with AE and iNALU. For the OC-SVM, we utilize the signed distance from the datapoint to the hyperplane in feature space as our anomaly score.

3.3 ML Evaluation

Classification metrics such as precision, recall, and f-score are widely used in ML applications to assess model performance [6] but require a direct classification of transactions into normal or fraudulent datapoints. This, in turn, requires a fixed threshold value on the anomaly scores of our ML approaches. Since the optimal threshold choice depends on task, data, use case, ML approach, and possibly even the ML model's parameters used during training, setting this threshold is non-trivial and requires striking a balance between detection rate and the number of anomalies detected [7]. Area-Under-the-Curve (AUC) scores omit a threshold by calculating scores over varying threshold values. A popular choice for AUC scores, the well-known AUC Receiver-Operating-Characteristic (ROC) score is sensitive to class imbalance, which skews its results in highly unbalanced settings such as fraud detection. Therefore, we base our evaluation on the AUC Precision-Recall (PR) score which addresses this issue [11].

Furthermore, we report the rank of the least suspicious fraud r_{min}, which corresponds to the practical question of how many transactions would have to be inspected until all frauds are found. Mathematically, the rank of the least suspicious fraud of all frauds $F \subseteq X$ of dataset X is given as

$$r_{min} = |\{x \in X : score(x) \geq \min_{f \in F} score(f)\}| \tag{1}$$

where $score$ denotes the anomaly scoring function of the detection approach that yields high values for anomalous samples.

4   XAI Methodology

To assess the decision process of different ML approaches during occupational fraud detection, we construct a three-fold evaluation process based on quantitative evaluation, qualitative inspection, and consistency testing.

4.1   XAI Approach

In previous work, the post hoc feature relevance approach Shapley Additive exPlanations (SHAP) [22] has been identified as XAI approach providing good comprehensibility both in the related area of credit card fraud detection [3, 28] and on categorical tabular data [45], which encompass a large number of columns within ERP system data. We therefore employ SHAP on individual model predictions to find which features are most relevant for the model's decision. SHAP utilizes game theory to find feature relevance by switching feature combinations with background data and assessing the resulting behavior of the model. SHAP is model-agnostic and can be employed on any ML model. In this work, we employ SHAP's KernelSHAP method that generates background data through the centroids of k-means clustering with $k = 20$ clusters.

4.2   Quantitative XAI Evaluation

To measure the quality of the feature relevance explanations generated by SHAP, a quantitative evaluation measure is required. Samek et al. [31] propose a quantitative evaluation procedure which assumes that perturbing relevant feature entries leads to different model decisions. This evaluation may prove problematic in heavily unbalanced domains such as anomaly or fraud detection, as finding replacement values that form valid, non-anomalous datapoints is non-trivial. While Hooker et al. [17] extend this approach by proposing to retrain the entire model from scratch after perturbing the training data, their resulting scheme requires repeating extensive training steps and potential repetition of entire hyperparameter studies, which limits its use in practice.

To quantitatively evaluate XAI explanations in our occupational fraud detection scenario, we therefore propose an evaluation scheme based on suspicious data entries of fraud cases: In the evaluation, we focus on fraudulent datapoints, where feature entries that deviate from the normal business process can be seen as indicative of the fraud case. For a given fraud, this requires identification of indicative feature entries by auditing experts, which then serve as ground truth for quantitatively evaluating feature relevance explanations, where indicative feature entries should be rated as more relevant than normal features.

For the evaluation of explanation heatmaps through ground truth on image data, Hägele et al. [16] proposes an evaluation scheme based on ROC scores. We adopt this evaluation scheme for our tabular data, ranking the quality of single datapoint explanations through ROC score against our ground truth. For one datapoint, this results in a ranking score that increases when deviating data entries are given higher feature relevance within the explanation. Additionally, the ROC score is scale-invariant, focusing only on whether deviating entries are found before normal entries. For all fraud cases, we aggregate the individual ROC scores for each datapoint into an average ROC score and use this metric as a quantitative measure that represents how highly features with information concerning the fraud case rank in the given explanation.

4.3   Qualitative XAI Evaluation

Beyond examining individual metrics, we use qualitative inspection of explanations as a more in-depth assessment of XAI explanation quality. To qualitatively assess explanations, feature relevance of single datapoints may be visualized using SHAP's force plots, as seen in Fig. 2a. Here, feature names are listed at the bottom of their corresponding bar, with a larger bar width corresponding to a feature's greater impact on the (negative) anomaly score shown above the bars (e.g. feature f0 showing a greater impact than the features f1 or f2).

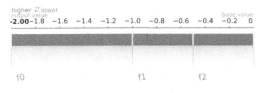
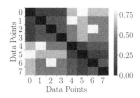

(a) Exemplary SHAP force plot [22]   (b) Exemplary explanation heatmap

Fig. 2. Demonstration plots of explanations for single datapoints (2a) and heatmaps to compare datapoint explanations (2b).

4.4 XAI Consistency Evaluation

Cirqueira, Helfert, and Bezbradica [10] discover that auditors check previously detected frauds and their explanations to assess new frauds, and define a requirement for XAI in fraud detection to allow comparison of frauds based on previous explanation patterns. To evaluate new cases with explanations based on historical patterns, similar frauds need to be consistent in their explanations.

Approaches that assess the consistency of explanations are currently limited to the robustness of XAI methods against adversarial attacks [2] and analyze whether minimal changes to a *single* datapoint maintain a similar explanation. In contrast, we propose an evaluation that focuses on the consistency of explanations of *similar* frauds. We construct a heatmap for fraud datapoints that can be used both to evaluate explanation similarity between different fraud cases and to find similar anomalies for currently evaluated fraud cases during the application.

Consider a feature relevance explanation $y \in \mathbb{R}^d$ for a fraudulent datapoint $x \in F$ within the fraudulent subset $F \subseteq X$ of dataset X with data dimensionality d. We first binarize y by applying a threshold of 25% of the highest relevance value, to focus our evaluation on highly relevant features and reduce noise.

$$\hat{y}_i = \begin{cases} 1 \,, \ y_i > 0.25 \cdot \max(y) \\ 0 \,, \ y_i \le 0.25 \cdot \max(y) \end{cases} \tag{2}$$

We apply this transformation to the explanations of all fraudulent datapoints and compute the Manhattan distance pairwise as a measure of explanation similarity through $dist(\hat{y}, \hat{y}') = \|\hat{y} - \hat{y}'\|_1$ for a pair of binarized explanations $\hat{y}$ and $\hat{y}'$. We then arrange explanations so that similar frauds are grouped together and visualize the pairwise similarity of explanations in a heatmap. Therefore, consistent explanations for similar frauds are expected to form a block-like structure around the diagonal, as shown in Fig. 2b for the datapoints 0-3 and 4-7, which features all similar fraud cases within one block of low pairwise distances.

5   Experiments

Using our XAI evaluation setting introduced in Sect. 4, we now evaluate multiple ML approaches introduced in Sect. 3 with respect to performance and comprehensibility when detecting occupational fraud in ERP system data.

Table 2. Total datapoints and fraud cases within the used ERP system data [46].

Group	Dataset	Transactions	Frauds	IK1	IK2	L1	L2	L3	L4	CI
Group 1	Normal 1	54677	0	0	0	0	0	0	0	0
Group 1	Fraud 1	39430	24	4	0	2	4	0	0	14
Group 2	Normal 2	32337	0	0	0	0	0	0	0	0
Group 2	Fraud 2	36778	50	6	18	2	4	10	6	4
Group 2	Fraud 3	37407	86	24	6	8	10	26	4	8

L = Larceny, IK = Invoice Kickback, CI = Corporate Injury

5.1 ERP System Data

For our experiments, we use publicly available ERP system data that contains both normal business documents and fraudulent activities [46]. The data contains five distinct datasets obtained from data generation of a simulated production company with two participant groups, with two datasets consisting of completely normal operation and three datasets including different fraud cases within the normal business process. Frauds include different scenarios of material theft (larceny), bribery in material procurement (invoice kickback), and cause of malicious damage to the company (corporate injury), with details on specific fraud cases introduced in the original paper [46]. Table 2 gives a brief overview of the distribution of normal and fraudulent transactions within the data. Beyond the separation of transactions into normal or fraudulent behavior, these datasets also contain expert annotations of individual fraud cases. As all fraudulent transactions have marked column entries that correspond to the entries that are indicative of the underlying fraud, these annotations are used as ground truth for our quantitative XAI evaluation of Sect. 4.2.

5.2 Experiment 1: Explainable Occupational Fraud Detection

Prior research into fraud detection has found both high performance and comprehensibility to be desirable properties of detection approaches [10,14,19]. In our first experiment, we therefore evaluate multiple established ML approaches on occupational fraud detection in ERP system data. We conduct a hyperparameter study encompassing more than 1500 cpu core hours to assess the detection performance of the algorithms studied. We further generate explanations for these approaches through SHAP as described in Sect. 4.1, and analyze explanation quality through our XAI evaluation setting from Sect. 4 to discover approaches that deliver both high performance and satisfactory explanations.

Experimental Setup. In this experiment, we focus on the ERP datasets generated by the second participant group (normal 2, fraud 2, fraud 3), as introduced in Sect. 5.1. We choose these datasets as they contain a larger amount and broader spectrum of fraud cases, and additionally offer two fraudulent datasets

Table 3. Best results of each approach on evaluation (1) and test (2) set.

Approach	$PR^{(1)}$	$PR^{(2)}$	$ROC^{(1)}$	$ROC^{(2)}$	$r_{min}^{(1)}$	$r_{min}^{(2)}$
OC-SVM	0.34	0.73	0.99	1.00	1201.0	740.0
iNALU[†]	0.34	0.52	0.99	1.00	1769.0	1022.4
AE[†]	0.31	0.69	0.99	1.00	1615.0	825.0
IF[†]	0.19	0.49	0.99	0.99	2232.0	1046.0
PCA	0.08	0.12	0.82	0.91	36778.0	37407.0

[†]Non-deterministic: averaged over 5 seeds to mitigate statistical fluctuation

that can be used as separate validation and test datasets. As training data, we use the dataset normal 2, which only contains normal data and simulates training on records that have previously been audited. While training of our ML algorithms only requires normal data, all algorithms have additional hyperparameters that influence the detection rate. Therefore, an audited dataset containing fraudulent samples is required as evaluation dataset, which is potentially not available in practice. The necessity of this dataset will be assessed in the subsequent experiment in Sect. 5.3. In Experiment 1, the partially fraudulent dataset fraud 2 is used as evaluation set to select hyperparameters and the overall performance is evaluated on dataset fraud 3 as test set. This separation allows for tuning ML hyperparameters on an evaluation dataset with fraudulent transactions, while retaining an unseen test dataset for the evaluation of the resulting algorithms.

Parameter Search and Performance Results. To assess detection performance, we utilize the metrics introduced in Sect. 3.3. To select the best performing hyperparameters, we rank architectures by PR score on the evaluation set. Table 3 shows the best results of each approach for both evaluation set (1) and test set (2), where we also report ROC and r_{min} denoting how many transactions would have to be audited to find all frauds using the detectors. We make the tested hyperparameters and results of individual runs available online for reproducibility[2]. Our findings can be summarized as follows:

For the linear PCA we find no parameter setting capable of reliably detecting fraudulent transactions, with even the best hyperparameters yielding poor detection results on all metrics. Although IF is capable of detecting fraud cases, it performs considerably worse than the remaining approaches in PR score. AE and OC-SVM both show very strong detection performance, with OC-SVM highlighting all fraud cases within 1201 and 740 suspected datapoints for the evaluation and test set, respectively. iNALU performs on par with AE and OC-SVM on the evaluation data, but detects fraud cases considerably later on the test set. Upon closer inspection, all well-performing approaches highlight the Larceny 4 and Corporate Injury frauds within the first anomalous transactions. Lowered scores are caused mainly by Larceny 3 and Invoice Kickback 1 frauds. This may be explained by the subtle and well-hidden nature of the two frauds. For Larceny

---

[2] Supplementary material under https://professor-x.de/xai-erp-fraud-supplementary.

Table 4. Quantitative explanation evaluation for Experiment 1 (see Sect. 4.2).

Approach	$\text{ROC}^{(1)}_{XAI}$	$\text{ROC}^{(2)}_{XAI}$
OC-SVM	0.542	0.579
iNALU	**0.642**	**0.794**
AE	0.603	0.658

3 only a small portion of materials is stolen and for Invoice Kickback 1 prices are increased only by a small percentage that may well be within the range of normal price fluctuations. As a result, while the approaches manage to find the frauds, detection occurs later than on cases with clearly identifiable characteristics such as items that have never been purchased before in Larceny 4.

Overall, we observe high performance for OC-SVM, iNALU and AE when detecting occupational fraud in ERP data.

Model Explanation Results. To evaluate, whether well performing detection systems can also provide a satisfactory decision process, we generate post hoc feature relevance explanations for the best performing OC-SVM, iNALU and AE approaches through the XAI approach SHAP as outlined in Sect. 3.3 and evaluate the resulting explanations through our XAI evaluation setting.

Quantitative Evaluation. To quantitatively assess the explanation quality of our trained models, we evaluate the explanations of fraudulent datapoints with ground truth as described in Sect. 4.2. Table 4 shows the quality of the explanation measured in the evaluation set (1) and the test set (2). The explanations for OC-SVM show the smallest similarity to the ground truth, in spite of its strong detection rate in our performance evaluation. While AE displays higher explanation quality, iNALU explanations produce the highest ROC scores.

Qualitative Evaluation. To discover the reasons for this behavior, we qualitatively evaluate SHAP plots across all frauds from the test data. To illustrate the fraud visualization process, we show a non-cherry-picked explanation visualization of a fraud case from the test set fraud 3 in Fig. 3.

In the Larceny 1 case shown in Fig. 3, only iNALU focuses on the anomalous entry that marks the transaction as blocked by the ERP system (blocking reason quantity). While AE focuses on suspiciously small quantities ordered and in stock, OC-SVM highlights many features that are not related to fraud. Approaches also show sensitivity towards columns, such as G/L account, valuation class, or transaction, that describe the general transaction type (e.g. material entry, withdrawal). This may be caused by value combinations that are anomalous for the given transaction, but characteristic of another transaction type, causing the transaction type to be seen as anomalous. OC-SVM is particularly sensitive to this behavior and highlights many transaction-type features that are not indicative of fraud. This pattern is also noticeable in other larceny frauds.

On invoice kickback frauds, where the fraudster's activity causes atypically high unit prices, both iNALU and AE highlight the amounts and quantities

90   J. Tritscher et al.

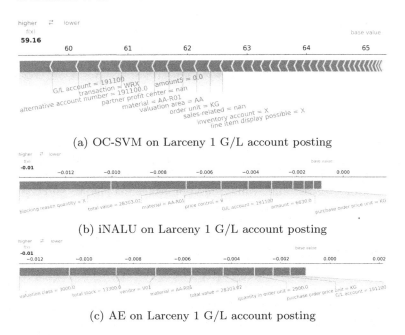

(a) OC-SVM on Larceny 1 G/L account posting

(b) iNALU on Larceny 1 G/L account posting

(c) AE on Larceny 1 G/L account posting

Fig. 3. SHAP explanations on a fraudulent Larceny 1 transaction, showing feature influence through bar width. iNALU and AE focus on anomalous quantities and amounts, while OC-SVM reacts to a variety of features.

required for inference. While OC-SVM is sensitive to some amount columns, they carry only small influence over columns that are not related to fraud.

In the corporate injury scenario, fraudulent purchase activities result in high purchase amounts and purchase quantities. Here, iNALU is strongly sensitive to anomalous quantities and amounts, while AE additionally focuses on some not directly relevant columns such as vendor or material entries, and OC-SVM focuses on many columns that do not directly indicate fraudulent activities.

Overall, the qualitative observations are consistent with the quantitative results, indicating that AE and iNALU consistently show sensitivity to columns that are sufficient to explain and detect fraudulent transactions, with iNALU providing the best explanations. OC-SVM, despite its slightly stronger detection performance observed in Table 3, produces explanations that are noisy and difficult to interpret, potentially limiting its use in practice, when insights into the decision process or justifications are required.

Explanation Consistency. To evaluate the consistency of trained approaches when explaining similar anomalies, we create heatmap plots as described in Sect. 4.4. For both iNALU and AE, Fig. 4 shows clear similarities between the explanation of transactions from the same fraud scenarios, indicating that both approaches react to fraud cases in a consistent way. While iNALU is capable of producing slightly sharper contrasts between similar and dissimilar fraud cases

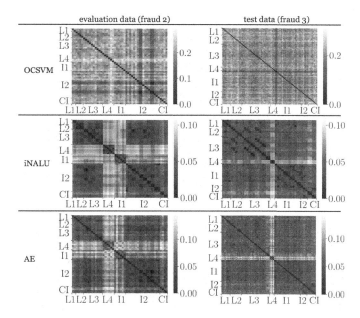

Fig. 4. Manhattan distance of SHAP explanations for larceny frauds (L1, L2, L3, L4), invoice kickback (I1, I2), and corporate injury (CI), ordered by type and time of occurrence. Plots show consistent explanations for iNALU and AE.

in comparison to AE, OC-SVM focuses on very different features even when considering very similar fraudulent data samples. Overall, both iNALU and AE show consistency in their decisions, which may be used to compare explanations with historical patterns of fraud cases.

5.3   Experiment 2: Performance After Retraining

Through the conducted hyperparameter study and evaluation of explanation quality, Experiment 1 has produced models and hyperparameter configurations that can explain fraud cases precisely and comprehensibly on the used dataset. For practical applications, however, annotated data for selecting models and parameters is usually not readily available. In particular, if the normal behavior within a company shifts (for example, due to changing employees or operational changes), the model must also be retrained on the new normal data to adopt for the changes. If an additional annotated dataset is necessary in these cases to re-evaluate the model and parameter selection, this would be associated with considerable costs that may prove prohibitive in practical applications. In this experiment, we therefore evaluate to what extent previously found optimal model parameters can also be transferred to a new dataset with changed business circumstances and different employees, investigating how stable the respective models are with regard to their hyperparameter selection on different datasets.

Experimental Setup. We use the normal (normal 1) and fraudulent (fraud 1) game runs introduced in Sect. 5.1 that originate from different ERP system users than data from Experiment 1 and retrain our models with the hyperparameters that showed the best performance during our first experiment in Sect. 5.2. To gain further insights into whether re-evaluation of the approaches would have allowed for choosing a better performing set of hyperparameters for each approach, we also repeat our first experiment on the new dataset entirely. This allows us to rank our previously best performing parameter configurations in comparison to all other parameter settings that could have been chosen through reevaluation with regard to each of our evaluation metrics.

Stability Results. For all the ML approaches evaluated, we report both the performance metrics, as well as the ranking of the hyperparameters of Experiment 1 compared to the optimal hyperparameter configurations in Table 5. We further use the feature-level fraud annotations within the dataset to repeat our quantitative explanation evaluation on the previously best performing detection systems. Although the linear PCA initially shows strong performance through a high PR score, the r_{min} metric reveals that the approach detected few frauds very early at the expense of completely failing to detect other fraud cases, resulting in a high PR score that is sensitive to this behavior. As all other approaches are detecting all fraud cases within a small number of audited datapoints, as shown in their r_{min} scores, PCA remains a non-desirable detection approach for this scenario. IF remains behind the three approaches that have been best performing previously on the r_{min} metric. The previously best performing AE and OC-SVM drop considerably in performance, with multiple better performing hyperparameter configurations as seen in both r_{min}_rank and PR$\_rank$, which would require costly re-evaluation with an annotated evaluation dataset. iNALU, on the other hand, is capable of maintaining its performance on the dataset with a highly stable PR score and a very strong r_{min} score. Furthermore, there are only a few parameter configurations for iNALU that improve over the previous best parameter set on the r_{min} metric, with the lower rank on the PR score being caused by the sensitive PR score behavior discussed above.

Table 5. Results for retraining the best models found in Experiment 1. The rankings compare performance with other hyperparameter settings.

Approach	PR	ROC	r_{min}	PR$\_rank$	ROC$\_rank$	r_{min}_rank	ROC$_{XAI}$
OC-SVM	0.16	1.00	228.00	50	10	17	0.582
iNALU[†]	0.34	1.00	146.60	46	5	6	0.859
AE[†]	0.21	1.00	253.20	36	34	19	0.820
IF[†]	0.22	1.00	366.40	187	66	31	0.783
PCA	0.44	0.95	19432.00	16	1	18	0.517

[†]Non-deterministic: averaged over 5 seeds to mitigate statistical fluctuation

Overall, this study highlights iNALU as an approach that, while showing slightly lower performance compared to AE and OC-SVM in Experiment 1, is capable of providing satisfactory decision traceability and additionally proving stable towards model retraining, making it a strong model choice within the domain of occupational fraud detection.

6   Conclusion

In this study, we investigated whether different ML approaches could provide strong performance and a satisfactory decision process in occupational fraud detection. We first constructed an evaluation setting for the explanations of occupational fraud detection approaches based on quantitative, qualitative, and consistency criteria. We then conducted extensive experiments on multiple fraud detection approaches combined with post hoc XAI, finding highly performing detection approaches through a hyperparameter study and assessing the quality of their decision process through the XAI evaluation setting. Further, we assessed whether ML approaches are capable of maintaining their performance and explanation quality on company data with changed underlying characteristics, by retraining and re-evaluating the approaches on an additional ERP dataset.

Our results indicate that high detection performance does not necessarily come with good explanation quality, as the OC-SVM approach displays a strong detection rate with poorly performing explanations. However, the AE and iNALU approaches provide satisfactory performance and decision traceability. Despite its lower detection performance compared to the AE, our second experiment reveals that iNALU is the more stable detection approach, managing to best retain its performance after retraining. Our findings demonstrate a possible strong performance and explanation quality of ML-based occupational fraud detection approaches and motivate the use of the investigated deep learning approaches for detecting occupational fraud in ERP system data.

In this work, we conducted a first broad evaluation on established ML-based detection approaches covering deep learning, anomaly detection, and linear models. With the promising results of our experiments, we plan to systematically extend our research to further detection architectures. Similarly, our explanation experiments conducted with an established and proven XAI algorithm could be extended to other types of explanations to provide additional comprehensibility in occupational fraud detection. With this study, we took a first step towards explainable ML-based occupational fraud detection systems on ERP system data, and encourage future research by highlighting the need to investigate detection performance and explainability in a joint fashion.

Acknowledgement. The authors acknowledge the financial support from the German Federal Ministry of Education and Research as part of the DeepScan project (01IS18045A).

References

1. ACFE: Occupational Fraud 2022: a report to the nations. In: Report To the nations (2022). [Online 01 Jun 2022]. URL:https://legacy.acfe.com/report-to-the-nations/2022/
2. Melis, D.A., Jaakkola, T.: Towards robust interpretability with self-explaining neural networks. In: Advances in neural information processing systems 31 (2018)
3. Antwarg, L., et al.: Explaining anomalies detected by autoencoders using SHAP. In: arXiv preprint arXiv:1903.02407 (2019)
4. Arrieta, A.B., et al.: Explainable Artificial Intelligence (XAI): concepts, taxonomies, opportunities and challenges toward responsible AI. In: Information Fusion 58, pp. 82–115 (2020)
5. Baader, G., Krcmar, H.: Reducing false positives in fraud detection: combining the red flag approach with process mining. Int. J. Account. Inf. Syst. **31**, 1–16 (2018)
6. Buczak, A.L., Guven, E.: A survey of data mining and machine learning methods for cyber security intrusion detection. In: IEEE Communications surveys & tutorials 18.2, pp. 1153–1176 (2015)
7. Callegari, C., et al.: When randomness improves the anomaly detection performance. In: 2010 3rd International Symposium on Applied Sciences in Biomedical and Communication Technologies (ISABEL 2010), pp. 1–5. IEEE (2010)
8. Chalapathy, R., Chawla, S.: Deep learning for anomaly detection: a survey. In: arXiv preprint arXiv:1901.03407 (2019)
9. Chandola, V., Banerjee, A., Kumar, V.: Anomaly detection: a survey. In: ACM Computing Surveys (CSUR) 41.3, pp. 1–58 (2009)
10. Cirqueira, D., Helfert, M., Bezbradica, M.: Towards design principles for user-centric explainable AI in fraud detection. In: Artificial Intelligence in HCI. Springer International Publishing, pp. 21–40 (2021). ISBN: 978-3-030-77772-2. https://doi.org/10.1007/978-3-030-77772-2_2
11. Davis, J., Goadrich, M.: The relationship between Precision-Recall and ROC curves. In: Proceedings of the 23rd International Conference on Machine learning, pp. 233–240 (2006)
12. Febriyanti, K.D., Sarno, R., Effendi, Y.A.: Fraud detection on event logs using fuzzy association rule learning. In: 2017 11th International Conference on Information & Communication Technology and System (ICTS), pp. 149–154. IEEE (2017). https://doi.org/10.1109/ICTS.2017.8265661
13. Felzmann, H., et al.: Transparency you can trust: transparency requirements for artificial intelligence between legal norms and contextual concerns. In: Big Data & Society 6.1, p. 2053951719860542 (2019). https://doi.org/10.1177/2053951719860542
14. Fuchs, A., et al.: A meta-model for real-time fraud detection in ERP systems. In: Proceedings of the 54th Hawaii International Conference on System Sciences, p. 7112 (2021)
15. Goodfellow, I., Bengio, Y., Courville., A.: Deep Learning, http://www.deeplearningbook.org. MIT Press (2016)
16. Hägele, M., et al.: Resolving challenges in deep learning-based analyses of histopathological images using explanation methods. In: Scientific reports 10.1, pp. 1–12 (2020)
17. Hooker, S., et al.: A benchmark for interpretability methods in deep neural networks. In: Advances in Neural Information Processing Systems 32 (2019)

18. Kamarinou, D., Millard, C., Singh, J.: Machine learning with personal data. In: Queen Mary School of Law Legal Studies Research Paper 247 (2016)
19. Krieger, F., Drews, P., Velte, P.: Explaining the (non-) adoption of advanced data analytics in auditing: a process theory. In: International Journal of Accounting Information Systems 41, p. 100511 (2021). ISSN: 1467–0895. https://doi.org/10. 1016/j.accinf.2021.100511
20. Lahann, J., Scheid, M., Fettke, P.: Utilizing machine learning techniques to reveal vat compliance violations in accounting data. In: 2019 IEEE 21st Conference on Business Informatics (CBI), vol. 1, pp. 1–10 . IEEE (2019)
21. Liu, F.T., Ting, K.M., Zhou, Z.-H.: Isolation forest. In: 2008 Eighth IEEE International Conference on Data Mining, pp. 413–422. IEEE (2008)
22. Lundberg, S.M., Lee, S.-I.: A unified approach to interpreting model predictions. In: Advances in Neural Information Processing Systems 30 (2017)
23. Mishra, S.P., Kumari, P.: Analysis of techniques for credit card fraud detection: a data mining perspective. In: Patnaik, S., Ip, A.W.H., Tavana, M., Jain, V. (eds.) New Paradigm in Decision Science and Management. AISC, vol. 1005, pp. 89–98. Springer, Singapore (2020). https://doi.org/10.1007/978-981-13-9330-3_9
24. Naufal, M.F.: Fraud detection using Process mining and analytical hierarchy process with verification rules on ERP business process. In: International Conference on Informatics, Technology, and Engineering (InCITE)-2nd (2019)
25. Nonnenmacher, J., et al.: Using autoencoders for data-driven analysis in internal auditing. In: Proceedings of the 54th Hawaii International Conference on System Sciences (2021)
26. Oliverio, W.F.M., Silva, A.B., Rigo, S.J., da Costa, R.L.B.: A hybrid model for fraud detection on purchase orders. In: Yin, H., Camacho, D., Tino, P., Tallón-Ballesteros, A.J., Menezes, R., Allmendinger, R. (eds.) IDEAL 2019. LNCS, vol. 11871, pp. 110–120. Springer, Cham (2019). https://doi.org/10.1007/978-3-030-33607-3_13
27. Patro, S., Sahu, K.K.: Normalization: a preprocessing stage. In: arXiv preprint arXiv:1503.06462 (2015)
28. Psychoula, I., et al.: Explainable machine learning for fraud detection. In: Computer 54.10, pp. 49–59 (2021)
29. Ribeiro, M.T., Singh, S., Guestrin, C.: Why should i trust you?: Explaining the predictions of any classifier. In: 22nd ACM SIGKDD International Conference on Knowledge Discovery and Data mining, pp. 1135–1144. ACM (2016)
30. Sabau, A.S.: Survey of clustering based financial fraud detection research. In: Informatica Economica 16.1, p. 110 (2012)
31. Samek, W., et al.: Evaluating the visualization of what a deep neural network has learned. In: IEEE transactions on neural networks and learning systems 28.11, pp. 2660–2673 (2016)
32. Sánchez-Aguayo, M., Urquiza-Aguiar, L., Estrada-Jiménez, J.: Fraud detection using the fraud triangle theory and data mining techniques: a literature review". In: Computers 10.10, p. 121 (2021)
33. Sarno, R., et al.: Hybrid association rule learning and process mining for fraud detection. In: IAENG International Journal of Computer Science 42.2 (2015)
34. Schlör, D., Ring, M., Hotho, A.: iNALU: improved neural arithmetic logic unit. In: Frontiers in Artificial Intelligence 3, p. 71 (2020). ISSN: 2624–8212. https://doi. org/10.3389/frai.2020.00071
35. Schlör, D., et al.: Financial fraud detection with improved neural arithmetic logic units. In: Volume Fifth Workshop on mining data for financial applications (2020)

36. Schölkopf, B., et al.: Estimating the support of a high-dimensional distribution. In: Neural Computation 13.7, pp. 1443–1471 (2001)
37. Schreyer, M., et al.: Detection of accounting anomalies in the latent space using adversarial autoencoder neural networks. In: 2nd KDD Workshop on Anomaly Detection in Finance. ACM (2019)
38. Schreyer, M., et al.: Detection of anomalies in large scale accounting data using deep autoencoder networks. arXiv preprint arXiv:1709.05254 (2017)
39. Schultz, M., Tropmann-Frick, M.: Autoencoder neural networks versus external auditors: detecting unusual journal entries in financial statement audits. In: Proceedings of the 53rd Hawaii International Conference on System Sciences (2020)
40. Shyu, M.-L., et al.: A novel anomaly detection scheme based on principal component classifier. Tech. Rep. Coral Gables, Florida: Miami Univ. Dept. of Electrical and Computer Engineering (2003)
41. Singh, K., Best, P.: Interactive visual analysis of anomalous accounts payable transactions in SAP enterprise systems. In: Managerial Auditing Journal (2016)
42. Singh, K., Best, P., Mula, J.: Automating vendor fraud detection in enterprise systems. In: Journal of Digital Forensics, Security and Law 8.2, p. 1 (2013)
43. Singh, K., Best, P., Mula, J.M.: Proactive fraud detection in enterprise systems. In: Proceedings of the 2nd International Conference on Business and Information: Steering Excellence of Business Knowledge (ICBI 2011). University of Kelaniya, Faculty of Commerce and Management Studies (2011)
44. Singla, J., et al.: A survey of deep learning based online transactions fraud detection systems. In: 2020 International Conference on Intelligent Engineering and Management (ICIEM), pp. 130–136. IEEE (2020)
45. Tritscher, J., et al.: Evaluation of post-hoc XAI approaches through synthetic tabular data. In: 25th International Symposium on Methodologies for Intelligent Systems ISMIS (2020)
46. Tritscher, J., et al.: Open ERP system data for occupational fraud detection. arXiv preprint arXiv:2206.04460 (2022)
47. Yu, J., et al.: Unusual insider behaviour detection framework on enterprise resource planning systems using adversarial recurrent autoencoder. In: IEEE Transactions on Industrial Informatics (2021)
48. Zhu, Y., et al.: Modeling users' behavior sequences with hierarchical explainable network for cross-domain fraud detection. In: Proceedings of The Web Conference 2020, pp. 928–938 (2020)

Towards Data-Driven Volatility Modeling with Variational Autoencoders

Thomas Dierckx[1,2](✉) ⓘ, Jesse Davis[2] ⓘ, and Wim Schoutens[1] ⓘ

[1] Department of Statistics and Risk, KU Leuven, Leuven, Belgium
{thomas.dierckx,wim.schoutens}@kuleuven.be
[2] Department of Computer Science, KU Leuven, Leuven, Belgium
jesse.davis@kuleuven.be

Abstract. In this study, we show how S&P 500 Index volatility surfaces can be modeled in a purely data-driven way using variational autoencoders. The approach autonomously learns concepts such as the volatility level, smile, and term structure without leaning on hypotheses from traditional volatility modeling techniques. In addition to introducing notable improvements to an existing variational autoencoder approach for the reconstruction of both complete and incomplete volatility surfaces, we showcase three practical use cases to highlight the relevance of this approach to the financial industry. First, we show how the latent space learned by the variational autoencoder can be used to produce synthetic yet realistic volatility surfaces. Second, we demonstrate how entire sequences of synthetic volatility surfaces can be generated to stress test and analyze an options portfolio. Third and last, we detect anomalous surfaces in our options dataset and pinpoint exactly which subareas are divergent.

Keywords: Volatility modeling · Variational autoencoder · Synthetic data · Market simulation · Anomaly detection · Portfolio stress testing

1 Introduction

The price of an option contract is mainly determined by the expected future volatility of its underlying asset. When the market anticipates high (low) volatility, option prices rise (fall), and vice versa. Therefore, the prices of these derivatives imply an expected volatility. This implied volatility is often used synonymously with trade price and its value varies across different contract strikes and maturities. This in turn leads to the concept of a volatility surface, a three-dimensional surface that expresses implied volatility in function of strike and maturity for a given day and asset. This surface can take on a variety of shapes depending on the state of the market. Well-documented phenomena include the volatility smile (or skew), the volatility term structure, and volatility persistence.

In practice, volatility surfaces are produced by calibrating and fitting volatility models on observed market prices. Examples of such models are the Variance-

I. Koprinska et al. (Eds.): ECML PKDD 2022 Workshops, CCIS 1753, pp. 97–111, 2023.
https://doi.org/10.1007/978-3-031-23633-4_8

Gamma model [13], Heston model [9], local volatility models [7], and arbitrage-free SVI parameterization [8]. Each technique employs a different set of underlying assumptions on concepts such as the stochastic process driving the underlying asset and the shape of the volatility surface. These models are not perfect and their underlying hypotheses often contribute to the varying degrees of success they achieve in practice.

In recent years, researchers have explored machine learning techniques to improve volatility modeling. For example, neural networks have been used to correct estimation errors made by existing volatility models [2], or as standalone models where the loss function is altered to include existing concepts such as the Dupire formula [7] and no-arbitrage conditions [4]. However, these approaches continue to hinge on traditional assumptions. Other work takes this one step further through the use of variational autoencoders [10]. Here, a purely data-driven approach was investigated, leaving it up to the model to learn the shapes of FX volatility surfaces without an explicit bias towards hypotheses from the traditional approaches [3]. They showed that their approach beat the Heston model in reconstructing both complete and incomplete volatility surfaces. In addition, because these are generative models, they can be used to generate synthetic volatility surfaces.

The authors proposed a point-wise approach for reconstructing volatility surfaces. Here, the encoder first maps a surface to its smaller, latent representation. The decoder then uses this surface representation, together with the strike price and time to maturity of an option contract, to reconstruct a single point on the surface. This process is repeated for each point on the surface. Note that this is in contrast with a more conventional grid-wise approach where the decoder reconstructs the entire surface in one go, and only relies on the latent representation for reconstruction. The authors argue that the point-wise approach is more expressive as surfaces of different granularity can be produced. This is in contrast with the grid-wise approach, where the generated surfaces are limited to the dimension of the input surface. The authors did not compare the reconstruction accuracy of the two different approaches.

In this work, we initially set out to replicate the results from [3] on US equity indices. However, we ran into the problem of posterior collapse [12] using their proposed point-wise architecture. This phenomenon is a well-known complication for variational autoencoders in which the learned latent space becomes uninformative. A common culprit is a decoder that relies too heavily on input features other than the latent ones. We hypothesize that the given architecture is sub-optimal for learning a proper latent space and suggest an alternative method using two separate steps. First, we learn the latent space using a traditional grid-wise approach and obtain the latent representations of the surfaces. This way, the decoder can only rely on latent variables during training. Afterward, a separate point-wise decoder model then uses these latent representations, together with the moneyness and time to maturity of an option contract, to reconstruct individual points on the surface. In doing so, the learning of latent space and the point-wise reconstruction of the surface is effectively decoupled, and we obtain a more informative latent space without sacrificing the expressivity of the original point-wise approach. Another advantage is that, instead of neural networks, any suitable machine learning technique can serve as the separate decoder model, which may improve results even further.

The contribution of this chapter is three-fold. First, we replicate the FX volatility surface approach from [3] on S&P500 Index options (SPX). We identify posterior collapse and suggest a decoupling approach that bypasses this problem and beats the original method on all hyper-parameter settings. Second, we suggest additional adjustments that further improve the reconstruction error. We show that a better latent space can be learned using convolutional layers instead of regular feed-forward ones, and that gradient boosted trees [5] make better point-wise decoder models than neural networks. Third and last, to highlight the impact of generative modeling with variational autoencoders on the financial industry, we provide three concrete use case examples. Namely, we show that our best approach learns latent factors that correspond to the volatility smile, term structure, and level, and that these factors can be used to generate synthetic yet realistic volatility surfaces. We then demonstrate how synthetic volatility surfaces can be used to stress test an options portfolio. Lastly, we show how the built model can be used to detect anomalous volatility surfaces in a dataset.

2   Background on Variational Autoencoders for Volatility Surfaces

Variational autoencoders belong to the family of generative models. Here, patterns in input data are automatically learned and summarized such that the trained model can produce new instances that are (ideally) indistinguishable from observed instances. This is in contrast with discriminative modeling, where models learn what differentiates instances and how to optimally assign labels to them. For example, a generative model could generate new realistic pictures of fruit, whereas a discriminitative model could identify whether a picture contains either an apple or an orange.

The architecture of a variational autoencoder (VAE) [10] is closely aligned to that of a regular autoencoder (AE). Here, a neural network (encoder) encodes input into a smaller, latent representation. At the same time, a second neural network (decoder) learns how to decode this latent representation into the original input. In contrast to the AE, the encoding of a VAE is not deterministic. Instead, latent representations are obtained by sampling from a (multivariate) distribution parameterized by the encoder. The architecture of a standard VAE is presented in Fig. 1 (a). The objective function $\mathcal{L}$ for training such model breaks down into two components: a reconstruction error and the Kullback-Leibler (KL) divergence [11] between the parameterized distribution and a prior distribution, which is typically a multivariate standard normal distribution. More specifically, the loss is computed by:

$$\text{MSE} = \frac{1}{N} \sum_{i=1}^{N} (y_i - x_i)^2 \tag{1}$$

$$\text{KL} = \frac{1}{2} \sum_{k=1}^{K} (-1 - \log \sigma_k^2 + \sigma_k^2 + \mu_k^2) \tag{2}$$

$$\mathcal{L} = \text{MSE} + \beta * \text{KL} \tag{3}$$

where N is the dimensionality of the input and output, y_i is the ith input value, x_i the ith output value produced by the decoder, and μ_k and σ_k are the mean and standard deviation of the kth latent variable.

Combining the reconstruction error with the KL divergence leads to a latent space that is both continuous and complete. Indeed, points sampled from the same distribution should produce similar output. Note that the KL-loss can be weighted using hyper-parameter β and that a higher weight will force the VAE to align the learned posterior distribution closer to that of the prior.

Two different VAE approaches can be used to reconstruct volatility surfaces [3]. The grid-wise approach takes as input a volatility surface and reconstructs the surface in its entirety based on the latent encoding. The point-wise approach is equal in input, but only outputs one specific point on the surface. Moreover, the decoder takes two additional input variables: the moneyness K and time to maturity (in days) T of the relevant option contract. Note that the point-wise approach requires the reconstruction procedure to be repeated for each point on the grid. The architectures are visually laid out in Fig. 1.

3   Methodology

We tackle four objectives in this study:

1. Can we replicate and improve the point-wise approach taken by the authors in [3]?
2. Can our approach generate realistic synthetic volatility surfaces?
3. Can our approach produce synthetic scenarios to backtest options portfolios?
4. Can our approach detect anomalous volatility surfaces in an options market dataset?

In what follows, we explain the data we used, which architectures we investigated to improve the original approach, and how they can be used to reconstruct (partial) volatility surfaces.

3.1   Data

We used end-of-day market data of SPX call options from January 1st, 2010 to May 1st, 2019 for our study. The data was obtained from IVolatility and contains

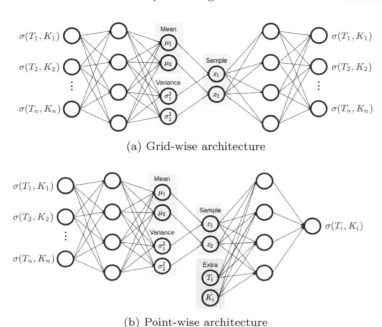

(a) Grid-wise architecture

(b) Point-wise architecture

Fig. 1. This figure shows two different VAE architectures to reconstruct volatility surfaces: the grid-wise architecture (a), and the point-wise architecture (b). Note that $\sigma(T_i, K_i)$ denotes the implied volatility for a given option contract with moneyness K and maturity T.

daily information on all available option contracts including trade price, implied volatility derived from the Black-Scholes model, and the Greeks. We considered volatility surfaces comprised of 30 gridpoints, made from five deltas (0.1, 0.25, 0.5, 0.75, 0.9) and six maturities (30, 60, 90, 180, 270, 365 calendar days). This follows the decisions made by the authors in [3].

The data was partitioned into a training, validation, and test set. The training and validation set were obtained by randomly sampling dates from January 1st, 2010 to December 31st, 2017. Their proportions were respectively 85% and 15% of this period. The test set was comprised of data from January 1st, 2018 to May 1st, 2019. All data was normalized so that values fall between zero and one. This was done using training set statistics to prevent data leakage.

3.2 Model Architectures

We evaluated a total of five different variational autoencoder approaches.

First, VAE_p is a replication of the point-wise model proposed by previous work in [3]. The model uses a neural network architecture comprised of two layers with 32 nodes for both the encoder and decoder. The encoder takes as input a volatility surface represented as a 1-dimensional vector of dimension

30×1 and outputs Z latent variables. The decoder takes as input Z latent variables and two additional input variables delta (K) and time to maturity (T), and produces a single scalar that represents the implied volatility of one option contract. We used the ReLU activation function on each layer and varied the size of the encoded space $z \in \{2, 3, 4\}$ and weighting of the KL-divergence loss term $\beta \in \{0.01, 0.1, 1, 2\}$. The neural networks were built using the Python package Tensorflow [1].

Second, VAE_g is an implementation of the grid-wise model. Its architecture is largely the same as that of VAE_p. However, the decoder only takes Z latent variables as input, and outputs a complete volatility surface represented by a 1-dimensional vector of dimension 30×1.

Third, VAE_d combines the previous two approaches in a two-step process. First, VAE_g is fit on the data after which its encoder is used to transform said data into a feature matrix of dimension $T \times Z$ where each row denotes the Z-dimensional latent representation of the volatility surface on day t. After, a separate decoder sharing the same architecture as the one from VAE_p is trained on this feature matrix to replicate the point-wise approach. Note that in contrast to VAE_p, we now have decoupled the process of learning a latent representation and the estimation of individual gridpoints.

Fourth, VAE_d^{xgb} copies the approach of VAE_d but uses a different decoder model in the second step. Here, we hypothesize that gradient boosted trees may learn more accurate pricing maps as demonstrated in earlier studies [6]. To this end, gradient boosted trees are fit on the feature matrix $T \times Z$ containing the latent representations of the volatility surfaces obtained by VAE_g. We used the Python package XGBoost [5] to built these models and tried different values for $n\_estimators \in \{25, 50, 100, 200\}$, $max\_depth \in \{3, 5, 7\}$, $learning\_rate \in \{0.01, 0.1\}$, $subsample \in \{0.5, 0.75, 1\}$, and $colsample\_bytree \in \{0.5, 1\}$. The optimal hyper-parameter configuration was selected based on the best root mean squared error obtained on the validation set.

Fifth and last, VAE_{cnn}^{xgb} combines the approach of both VAE_g and VAE_d^{xgb}. First, the latent representations are learned following the grid-wise approach of VAE_g using convolutional neural networks instead of regular ones. We believe that explicitly exploiting surface locality this way will improve accuracy as neighboring option contracts likely have stronger relationships. More specific, the encoder consists of two convolutional layers with a kernel size of three and ReLU as activation function. The decoder shares the same structure, but naturally uses transposed convolutional layers. Both input and output of this encoder-decoder architecture are now two-dimensional with dimension 6×5 $(K \times T)$ as they directly a two. After, gradient boosted trees are fit on the feature matrix $T \times Z$ to replicate the point-wise approach similar to the approach of VAE_d^{xgb}.

Note that all proposed methods ultimately reconstruct surfaces in a point-wise fashion, except for VAE_g which uses the grid-wise approach.

3.3   Volatility Surface Reconstruction and Completion

There are two possible approaches for volatility surface reconstruction. In the first approach, the volatility surface is fed into the encoder, after which the obtained latent variables are used by the decoder to reconstruct the original volatility surface (encoder approach). Note that this approach cannot be used (as is) to complete volatility surfaces with missing gridpoints as the encoder cannot handle missing input values.

In the second approach, an optimization algorithm is used to find the optimal latent variables to feed into the decoder to reconstruct the original surface (calibration approach). This method bypasses the encoder and is therefore suitable to complete volatility surfaces with missing gridpoints. In this case, latent variables are tried until a surface is found that minimizes the error between the produced surface and the known gridpoints. We used the L-BFGS-B optimization algorithm [18], combined with a basin-hopping approach which prevents local minima [17], to complete (partial) volatility surfaces with 5, 10, 20, and 30 (all) known gridpoints. All reconstruction approaches were compared to the Heston model [9] and the reconstruction error was measured using the mean absolute error (MAE). The known gridpoints (chosen randomly) were kept the same throughout the experiments.

Note that both the grid-wise and point-wise architecture can be used in these reconstruction methods. However, the grid-wise approach can only produce volatility surfaces of the same dimension as the input, whereas the point-wise approach is more flexible and can produce volatility surfaces of any arbitrary dimension $K \times T$.

4   Results and Applications

4.1   Reconstructing Volatility Surfaces

We first look at the results obtained using the encoder approach to reconstruct complete volatility surfaces. After, we select our best performing architecture and use the calibration approach to reconstruct incomplete surfaces. Here, we compare it to both Heston and the original point-wise architecture [3]. The encoder-based reconstruction errors obtained on the test set for all architectures and hyper-parameters are presented in Table 1.

We notice several interesting outcomes. First, the point-wise architecture VAE_p beat the grid-wise architecture VAE_g for all settings. This suggests that the additional input variables K and T add value. However, looking at the KL-loss in Table 2, it seems that the point-wise approach suffers from posterior collapse for $\beta >= 1$. This might also explain why there seems to be little difference in performance for $\beta \geq 1$, as the decoder solely relies on the additional input variables K and T. The grid-wise approach VAE_g does not seem to suffer from posterior collapse. Second, our decoupled approach VAE_d consistently beat VAE_p. This suggests that first learning the latent space using a grid-wise architecture, and then training a point-wise decoder is indeed a sound approach. Although

Table 1. Reconstruction error for different approaches expressed in mean absolute error (basis points) on the test set ranging from January 1st, 2018 to May 1st, 2019. The best performance for each hyper-parameter configuration is bold-faced.

β	z	VAE_p	VAE_g	VAE_d	VAE_d^{xgb}	VAE_{cnn}^{xgb}
0.01	2	175.0	241.6	165.7	154.2	**136.3**
	3	164.9	211.2	152.2	147.4	**134.9**
	4	165.1	216.2	147.7	141.5	**131.1**
0.1	2	269.6	343.0	236.5	210.5	**158.8**
	3	273.7	341.9	227.0	207.0	**143.8**
	4	261.3	332.2	218.4	202.9	**135.7**
1	2	451.1	630.0	368.8	355.6	**175.3**
	3	455.0	659.1	375.0	360.5	**182.4**
	4	468.7	642.0	372.9	359.1	**182.2**
2	2	446.7	740.0	451.4	421.3	**191.6**
	3	463.6	744.8	429.9	424.5	**201.1**
	4	456.5	740.6	464.4	421.1	**201.3**

Table 2. The KL-loss obtained on the training set for architectures VAE_p and VAE_g using a three-dimensional latent space. Bold-faced entries indicate posterior collapse.

	$\beta = 0.01$	$\beta = 0.1$	$\beta = 1$	$\beta = 2$
VAE_p	2.88	0.66	**0.00**	**0.00**
VAE_g	4.56	1.28	0.41	0.19

K and T seem valuable input variables, they seem to hinder the encoder in optimally learning a latent space. Third, VAE_d^{xgb} further improves the results and shows that gradient boosted trees might be better point-wise decoders than neural networks. Fourth and last, using both a decoupled approach with convolutional layers instead of feed-forward ones, and gradient boosted trees as point-wise decoder during the second step, yields a significantly better reconstruction for all settings. Note that reconstruction errors are smaller for lower values of β for all architectures. This makes sense as the latent space is less constrained during training. However, this comes at the cost of reduced space continuity. Although there does not seem to be a clear pattern for an optimal value of z, scenarios with lower values for β seem to favor larger latent dimensions.

Next, Table 3 outlines the reconstruction results using the calibration method for completing partial volatility surfaces. We compare both the original approach VAE_p and Heston to our best approach VAE_{cnn}^{xgb}. For the sake of brevity, we only compare the hyper-parameter settings for which the methods achieved their best result.

Table 3. Reconstruction error expressed in mean absolute error (basis points) using the L-BFGS-B optimization method to find the optimal (latent) input variables to reconstruct incomplete volatility surfaces with different number of known points.

	5	10	20	30
Heston	-	-	-	510.3
$VAE_p(\beta = 0.1, z = 3)$	361.2	283.6	247.3	238.4
$VAE_{cnn}^{xgb}(\beta = 1, z = 3)$	199.5	156.7	141.01	138.0

We find that both VAE approaches beat the Heston model, and that our approach VAE_{cnn}^{xgb} consistently outperformed the original one. Remarkably, both VAE approaches were able to outperform Heston using a complete surface with only partial surfaces. For this reason, we did not further investigate the Heston model on incomplete surfaces. Note that the reconstruction accuracy naturally drops when fewer points are known, and that a three-dimensional latent space seems optimal for both approaches. This is in contrast with work in [3] that found a four-dimensional latent space to be optimal. This might be due to fundamental differences between FX and equity volatility surfaces. Lastly, it seems that the optimal value for β is larger in this exercise than the one suggested by results found in Table 1. We hypothesize that lower values for β produce latent spaces with less favorable loss landscapes for the L-BFGS-B optimization algorithm.

4.2   Use Case One: Synthetic Volatility Surfaces

The prime benefit of generative models is that they can produce new instances with similar statistical properties as those found in the training dataset. In this case, the learned n-dimensional latent spaces can be used to generate synthetic volatility surfaces by feeding the decoder n-dimensional vectors drawn from the prior distribution. In order to investigate the learned latent space of our three-dimensional VAE_{cnn}^{xgb} with $\beta = 1$, we sampled twice from each separate coordinate axis while keeping the others constant. The results can be seen in Fig. 2, where each column shows two samples from one specific axis.

These results seem to suggest that our model has cleverly learned the term structure (axis one), volatility smile/skew (axis two), and volatility level (axis three). Note that the effect shifts from one extreme to the other when sampling

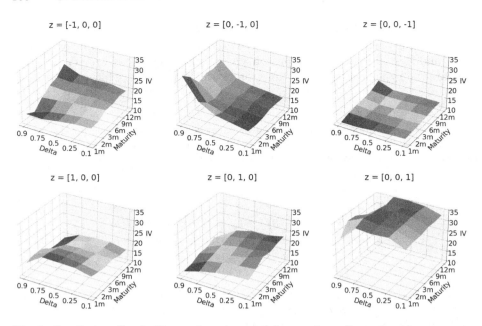

Fig. 2. Synthetic call volatility surfaces sampled from a three-dimensional latent space learned by VAE$_{cnn}$ with $\beta = 1$. Implied volatility (z-axis) and maturity (y-axis) are denoted using percentages and months. Each column displays two samples from one specific coordinate axis. The vector that was fed into the decoder is shown above each subplot. The plots seem to suggest that the three axes respectively encode the volatility term structure, smile and level.

along the same axis. For example, sampling from -1 to 1 on the first coordinate axis seems to gradually increase the price of option contracts with shorter maturities, and decrease the price of those with longer maturities (term structure). This ability to produce new realistic volatility surfaces using interpretable latent factors is interesting for practitioners. Indeed, synthetic samples can be produced to create additional what-if scenarios to make trading strategies and risk management practices more robust.

4.3   Use Case Two: Stress Testing Options Portfolios

Options portfolios can be analyzed and stress tested using the interpretable latent factors learned by a variational autoencoder. For instance, by generating sequences of synthetic volatility surfaces through time, practitioners can backtest their strategies on alternative what-if scenarios to gain more confidence in their approach. Because the latent factors correspond to real concepts such as the volatility level, smile, and term structure, we have more control over what kind of artificial scenarios we want to create. This is in contrast with existing methods such as portfolio bootstrapping and Monte Carlo simulation that do not offer this type of flexibility.

As an example, we backtest a random options portfolio that implements a short volatility strategy during the period of January 1st, 2018 to May 1st, 2019 on both a real and artificial scenario. We measure the strategy by its volatility performance approximated on each day by $\text{pnl}_t = \text{vega}_{t-1} * (\sigma_t - \sigma_{t-1})$ where vega is the net volatility exposure of our portfolio measured by the options greek vega, and σ_t is the implied volatility on day t. The synthetic data is generated as follows. First, we fit $\text{VAE}_{cnn}^{xgb}(\beta = 1, z = 3)$ on the real volatility surface sequence during the given time period. In doing so, we obtain daily values for each of the three latent factors. Second, we sample new paths for each latent variable (i.e. using Monte Carlo). These are then used by the decoder to generate a new and synthetic sequence of volatility surfaces, which in turn can be used to backtest the portfolio. Figure 3 (a) shows the latent factors through time obtained by $\text{VAE}_{cnn}^{xgb}(\beta = 1, z = 3)$ applied to real options market data (left), and the cumulative volatility pnl of the options portfolio (right). Figure 3 (b) shows the resampled latent variables (left) and the cumulative volatility pnl of the options portfolio (right) achieved on the synthetic data.

Unsurprisingly, the alternative scenario yields a different equity curve for the portfolio. We can measure the sensitivity of the example portfolio to the latent variables learned by the model. By using simple correlation, we find that the portfolio is particularly sensitive to factor two (volatility level) and suffers when the volatility level goes up (correlation of -50%). It is also sensitive to the term structure (factor 0) and volatility smile/skew (factor 1), but to a smaller extent (correlation of -20%). Note that practitioners can construct new paths for the latent variables using any technique they see fit. An especially interesting case is where shocks are introduced to one or more latent variables to assess the performance of the portfolio.

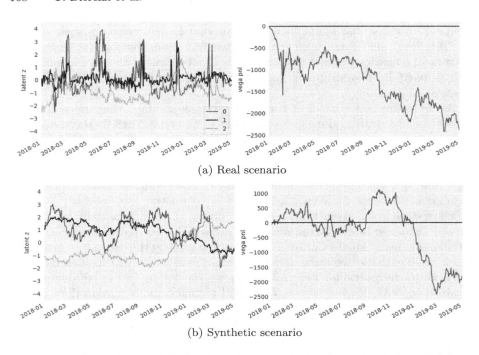

(a) Real scenario

(b) Synthetic scenario

Fig. 3. This figure shows two different backtest scenarios that each involve a different sequence of volatility surfaces. The latent variables that produce the surfaces are displayed on the left, and the volatility performance of the options portfolio backtested on those sequences is displayed on the right. The latent variables of the real scenario (a) were obtained using $\mathrm{VAE}_{cnn}^{xgb}(\beta = 1, z = 3)$ on real options data, whereas those of the synthetic scenario were taken from a Monte Carlo simulation. Note that the latent factors encode the term structure (0), smile (1), and level (2)

4.4   Use Case Three: Detecting Anomalies

Variational autoencoders can be used to detect data anomalies. First, the reconstruction errors are obtained on a given set of samples. After, a threshold is chosen that defines when an error is too large and thus considered an outlier, or anomaly.

We collected the reconstruction errors made by VAE_{cnn}^{xgb} on the test set which ranges from January 1st, 2018 to May 1st, 2019. We considered errors that fall above the 95th percentile as anomalies. Note that this cutoff point was chosen arbitrarily for the sake of example. In reality, the threshold is usually carefully selected based on domain expertise. The reconstruction errors are plotted through time in Fig. 4 (left), where anomalies lie above the red horizontal line. To further explore what type of anomalous volatility surfaces our model detects, we computed the point-by-point reconstruction error to see what part of the surface is divergent. The median point-by-point reconstruction error on detected anomalies is shown in Fig. 4 (right).

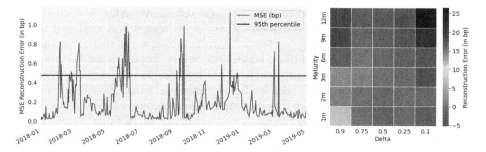

Fig. 4. This figure shows the reconstruction error obtained on the test set through time (left), and the median point-by-point reconstruction error on all anomalous volatility surfaces (right). All errors are expressed in basis points.

These results show a clear pattern in divergence with long-term deep in-the-money options (top right) being consistently over-estimated, and long-term deep out-the-money contracts (top left) being consistently under-estimated. The error seems significantly larger for the long-term deep out-the-money option contracts. A closer look at the actual options data revealed that the anomalies correspond to erroneous data provided by IVolatility.

Identifying anomalous volatility surfaces can be a useful exercise in practice. First, in the case of real options market datasets, erroneous volatility surfaces can be filtered out to not negatively affect downstream tasks. Moreover, diverging subareas not caused by data errors might offer fruitful trading opportunities. Second, the approach can be used as a sanity check for surfaces produced by traditional volatility models. This way, practitioners can detect when their models output surfaces that are not in line with expectations.

5   Conclusion

In this study, we successfully modeled SPX volatility surfaces using variational autoencoders in a purely data-driven way. We showed that the approach is autonomously able to learn concepts such as the volatility level, smile, and term structure without leaning on hypotheses from traditional volatility modeling techniques. We introduced an array of modifications to the original approach [3] that drastically improve the reconstruction of both complete and incomplete volatility surfaces. First, we showed that the original approach suffers from posterior collapse, a phenomenon in which the learned latent space becomes uninformative. We overcame this problem using our decoupled approach that separates the learning of latent space and point-wise reconstruction of the surface. Moreover, we demonstrated that convolutional networks learn more informative latent spaces by explicitly modeling surface locality, and that gradient boosted trees reconstruct volatility surfaces better.

We also showed three applications that follow from this modeling approach. First, we established that the learned latent space can be interpreted, and that random samples produce synthetic yet realistic volatility surfaces. Second, we demonstrated how an options portfolio can be stress tested and analyzed using synthetic sequences of volatility surfaces. Third and last, we detected anomalies in our options dataset and pinpointed exactly which subareas on the flagged volatility surfaces were divergent.

We list a few interesting tracks for future research. First, this study would benefit from an extensive analysis on multiple assets instead of SPX alone. Second, we did not verify whether the produced volatility surfaces were arbitrage-free. Although the authors using the point-wise variational autoencoder method in [3] claim the majority of surfaces did not exhibit arbitrage, they did not show concrete results. Third, more work is needed to determine the best machine learning model to serve as the separate decoder. We chose gradient boosted trees due to their incredible performance showcased in multiple domains, but better options may exist. Fourth, there are multiple other generative models that might do a better task than variational autoencoders. Examples include models such as normalizing flows [15], and the more recent SurVAE [14]. Lastly, the use of conditional variational autoencoders [16] or additional decoder input features might improve reconstruction results even further.

References

1. Abadi, M., et al.: Tensorflow: a system for large-scale machine learning. In: 12th {USENIX} Symposium on Operating Systems Design and Implementation ({OSDI} 16), pp. 265–283 (2016)
2. Ackerer, D., Tagasovska, N., Vatter, T.: Deep smoothing of the implied volatility surface. Tech. rep., arXiv.org (2020)
3. Bergeron, M., Fung, N., Hull, J., Poulos, Z.: Variational Autoencoders: a hands-off approach to volatility. arXiv:2102.03945 (2021)
4. Chataigner, M., Crépey, S., Dixon, M.: Deep local volatility. Risks 8(3) (2020). https://doi.org/10.3390/risks8030082
5. Chen, T., Guestrin, C.: XGBoost: A scalable tree boosting system. In: Proceedings of the 22nd ACM SIGKDD International Conference on Knowledge Discovery and Data Mining, pp. 785–794. KDD '16, ACM, New York, NY, USA (2016). https://doi.org/10.1145/2939672.2939785
6. Davis, J., Devos, L., Reyners, S., Schoutens, W.: Gradient boosting for quantitative finance. J. Comput. Finance 24(4), 1–40 (2021). https://doi.org/10.21314/JCF.2020.403
7. Dupire, B.: Pricing with a smile. Risk Magazine, pp. 18–20 (1994)
8. Gatheral, J., Jacquier, A.: Arbitrage-free SVI volatility surfaces. Quant. Finance 14(1), 59–71 (2014). https://doi.org/10.1080/14697688.2013.819986
9. Heston, S.: A closed-form solution for options with stochastic volatility with applications to bond and currency options. Rev. Finan. Stud. 6, 327–343 (1993)
10. Kingma, D.P., Welling, M.: Auto-encoding variational bayes (2013). https://doi.org/10.48550/ARXIV.1312.6114
11. Kullback, S., Leibler, R.A.: On information and sufficiency. Ann. Math. Stat. 22(1), 79–86 (1951). https://doi.org/10.1214/aoms/1177729694
12. Lucas, J., Tucker, G., Grosse, R.B., Norouzi, M.: Don't blame the ELBO! a linear VAE perspective on posterior collapse. In: NeurIPS (2019)

13. Madan, D., Carr, P., Stanley, M., Chang, E.: The variance gamma process and option pricing. Rev. Finance 2 (1999). https://doi.org/10.1023/A:1009703431535
14. Nielsen, D., Jaini, P., Hoogeboom, E., Winther, O., Welling, M.: Survae flows: surjections to bridge the gap between VAEs and flows. In: NeurIPS (2020)
15. Rezende, D.J., Mohamed, S.: Variational inference with normalizing flows. In: Proceedings of the 32nd International Conference on International Conference on Machine Learning - Volume 37, pp. 1530–1538. ICML'15, JMLR.org (2015)
16. Sohn, K., Lee, H., Yan, X.: Learning structured output representation using deep conditional generative models. In: NIPS (2015)
17. Wales, D., Doye, J.: Global optimization by basin-hopping and the lowest energy structures of lennard-jones clusters containing up to 110 atoms. The Journal of Physical Chemistry A 101 (1998). https://doi.org/10.1021/jp970984n
18. Zhu, C., Byrd, R.H., Lu, P., Nocedal, J.: Algorithm 778: L-BFGS-B: fortran subroutines for large-scale bound-constrained optimization. ACM Trans. Math. Softw. **23**(4), 550–560 (1997). https://doi.org/10.1145/279232.279236

Auto-clustering of Financial Reports Based on Formatting Style and Author's Fingerprint

Braulio C. Blanco Lambruschini[1]([⊠])[iD], Mats Brorsson[1][iD], and Maciej Zurad[2]

[1] SNT - University of Luxembourg, Esch-sur-Alzette, Luxembourg
{braulio.blanco,mats.brorsson}@uni.lu
[2] Yoba S.A., Esch-sur-Alzette, Luxembourg
maciej.zurad@yoba.com

Abstract. We present a new clustering algorithm of financial reports that is based on the reports' formatting and style. The algorithm uses layout and content information to automatically generate as many clusters as needed. This allows us to reduce the effort of labeling the reports in order to train text-based machine learning models for extracting person or company names, addresses, financial categories, etc. In addition, the algorithm also produces a set of sub-clusters inside each cluster, where each sub-cluster corresponds to a set of reports made by the same author (person or firm). The information about sub-clusters allows us to evaluate the change in the author over time.

We have applied the algorithm to a dataset with over 38,000 financial reports (last Annual Account presented by a company) from the Luxembourg Business Registers (LBR) and found 2,165 clusters between 2 and 850 documents with a median of 4 and an average of 14. When adding 2,500 new documents to the existing cluster set (previous annual accounts presented by companies), we found that 67.3% of the financial reports were placed in the correct cluster and sub-cluster. From the remaining documents, 65% were placed in a different subcluster because the company changed the formatting style, which is expected and correct behavior. Finally, labeling 11% of the entire dataset, we can replicate these labels up to 72% of the dataset, keeping a high feature coverage.

Keywords: Clustering · NLP · Machine learning · Unstructured data · Financial reports

1 Introduction

In many countries, public companies are required to submit and disclose financial reports promoting transparency and security of business trading. The most commonly required type of document is the Annual Accounts where the company

This work has been partly funded by the Luxembourg National Research Fund (FNR) under contract number 15403349.

I. Koprinska et al. (Eds.): ECML PKDD 2022 Workshops, CCIS 1753, pp. 112–127, 2023.
https://doi.org/10.1007/978-3-031-23633-4_9

publishes the results of the business performance during one fiscal year[1]. The annual account of a company consists of a *balance sheet* and an *annex*. The balance sheet is formal and follows the same style and format for all companies as it is filled electronically. The annex, however, describes the company's operation in natural text and can differ significantly from company to company depending on the person or firm drafting the reports. Nevertheless, the information in the annexes contains valuable information that we would like to analyze.

In order to be able to use the annexes in supervised learning algorithms, we need to label the data. Unfortunately, dataset labeling requires a huge effort and we need to find ways to reduce it.

We propose in this paper an automatic clustering method grouping documents (the annual account annexes) in clusters with the same sections/subsections and similar content so that it would be enough to label meaningful information in just a very small subset inside each cluster and then simply replicate automatically these labels in each single document for each cluster. For example, some labels can help us to identify person or company names, addresses, positions or roles, workforce information, financial/accounting categories/subcategories, phrases denoting uncertainty or financial risk, etc. We found that with this methodology if we do manual labeling of 11% of the dataset, we could automatically replicate these labels in 72% of the complete dataset, reducing significantly the labeling effort, covering 92% of the subtitles features.

Furthermore, inside each cluster of reports we do sub-clustering to group even more similar reports (sharing the same document template). This similarity represents the *author's fingerprint* and implies that in a sub-cluster we find all the reports made of a single author to multiple companies. This use case is a common practice in financial reports. The author can here represent a person or an accounting firm and we have confirm that they tend to use the same document template and writing style in all of their reports for different companies.

Our methodology builds upon a *clustering algorithm* fed by format- and content-based features extracted from the annual account annexes that creates as many clusters and sub-clusters as needed depending on the threshold parameters.

We are using public annual accounts submitted to the Luxembourg Business Registers and are able to use both digital native documents as well as the ones where the PDF documents contain scanned pages.

Our work contributes insights on how to learn the similarity of the financial reports based on the formatting style and author's fingerprint and how to cluster them together. Most of the uses cases for applying this algorithm in Financial reports are directly or indirectly related to Internal and External Risk Analysis business processes. This clustering information can allow us to:

- reduce and simplify the labeling effort for training supervised Deep Neural Networks (DNN),
- identify authors (accounting firms) that attend to multiple companies; for external risk analysis like analysis of possible fraudulent behavior,

---

[1] We are here describing the situation in Luxembourg but similar structures exist in many other countries.

- train machine learning models that can discard all the common phrases among the documents in a sub-cluster and identify the meaningful information, and to
- analyze the behavior of a company with respect to their accountant (changes over time) for internal risk analysis.

The algorithm is used in a larger project where the aim is to build an automated credit risk platform for small and medium sized enterprises (SME). The algorithm is not limited to be applied to Financial Reports but these documents fit perfectly in the main scenario: thousands of templates and thousands of hidden authors using similar terms for reporting (detailing them with their own writing style). Also considering that different companies can share the same hidden author. It can, however, be generalized and used in any application where it would be useful to find similarities (and differences) in form and content between documents and cluster the documents based on these similarities.

2   Related Work

We have concentrated our research on Document Analysis, which in turn is focused on processing whole documents in contrast to short-text processing. In a longer document you typically find the use of many typesetting features such as different text sizes, various styles such as bold, italics, underline, etc., and whether or not the document will have features such as cover page or table of contents. The position, and style of page numbers, logos, text footers and so on also provide a *Document Class-Specific Knowledge* [2] and constitute a fingerprint of the author of the document as the same author tends to use the same style of writing for all documents of the same kind.

Existing approaches for document clustering like k-means, and k-medoids, all need the number of clusters in advance, therefore they are not applicable for us as we cannot know this beforehand. Other approaches more oriented to Natural Language Processing were proposed like Latent Dirichlet Allocation (LDA) [4], and Document-Term Matrix (DTM) [16]. However, these methods mostly suffer from the same issue. Even though DBSCAN [7] does not require to know the number of clusters in advance; but for this case, the number of features could be infinite (features are generated based on the content and format that can have huge amounts of variations according to the template used by the company and the modifications made by the author). In addition to that, for checking dense regions[2] we need to compare each document with the whole dataset, having a cubic complexity (comparison also at feature level).

The algorithm Hierarchical Agglomerative Clustering (HAC) [5] is a good option for similar clustering tasks, but the main problem is that each new document is added to the closest document (edge growing) and at the end the distance of two edge documents can be big; or if we grow vertically, the resulting dendrogram can be too complex to understand the results.

---

[2] A dense region is a big group of elements that were plotted together in all dimensions.

Xu et al. [16] performed document clustering by using Non-Negative Matrix Factorization (NMF) of the document-term matrix. The algorithm assigns one of the k topics to a document. Here the authors are filtering out stop words and applying stemming. In our case, we are only replacing numeric and date information with the [NUMBER] and [DATE] tags.

Most of the current algorithms are focused only on the evaluation of the content for topic analysis. As we are dealing with clustering within a single topic, we need to consider format features additionally to the content ones.

The use of graphs is another approach proposed by some authors. Hamza et al. [9] use graph-matching in order to cluster administrative documents. Unlike other approaches, they create as many clusters as required and is not topic-clustering oriented. This algorithm uses content and relative position of each document to create a set of features. They use graph-probing distance to evaluate if a document is going to be added to an existing cluster or if it will create its own cluster. It is also important to mention that this algorithm adopts incremental learning, hence, there is no need for retraining. Inspired by this approach, our algorithm also compares a document with a set of existing clusters based on a list of text-oriented features. Compared to Hamza et al. [9], we added three posterior phases, which allow us to work with large datasets, to remove insignificant features and to perform a second clustering step inside each cluster. Our algorithm considers that each feature can contribute distinctively, depending on how many documents shares each feature. Each time a cluster accepts a new document, it becomes more robust because of the shared features.

The selection of a distance function or similarity score is one of the most important aspects of any clustering algorithm. Common distance functions are Manhattan, Euclidean, Cosine, Mahalanobis, etc. These functions need numeric values for calculation. In our case, the comparison of features are text-based features, consequently, these functions are not suitable for us. Transforming the features into embeddings or to do a one-hot enconding are also not feasible as the number of features can be infinite. The graph-probing distance proposed by Hamza et al. [9] computes the distance between two graphs based on the frequency (freq) of the edges between the nodes of each cluster. Our approach uses a similar metric that is the feature-set similarity score, which considers the contribution of each feature according to a confidence score. This confidence score highlights the feature's importance (which is automatically updated by the algorithm during the process). See Sect. 4.1 for more information.

As the first evaluation method, we are going to check a small part of the dataset and manually assign the corresponding cluster and sub-cluster. Once we have the labeled dataset, we need to specify the metrics to be used for evaluation, as shown by Palacio-Niño & Berzal [13], the commonly used distance metrics are Jaccard, Recall, Precision, Accuracy, Hubert statistics and Rand Index [15]. We use Rand Index (RI) because it measures the correct assignment of an element into a cluster as shown in Eq. 1, where a is the number of pairs of elements belonging to the same cluster, and b is the number of pairs of elements belonging to different clusters, according to the training dataset (T) and labeled dataset (L) with a total of n elements. The second evaluation method consists in adding more reports from existing companies (previous years) and analyze the true-positive ratio of the clustering.

$$RI(T, L) = \frac{a + b}{n(n - 1)/2} \tag{1}$$

3   Dataset

Our data was obtained from the Luxembourg Business Registers[3], which is a public database for company data in Luxembourg. The information available at the LBR contains annual accounts and their modifications, court orders (like bankruptcy, judicial dissolution, temporal administration assignation, etc.), registration and so on.

As mentioned before. the Annual Accounts consists of structured or table-oriented financial statements like balance sheets and profit and loss statements, but also include an annex in free-form text that is not subject to a specific document template. The annexes can be submitted in French, German or English where French is the most common consisting of about 85% of the documents. Examples of annexes are shown in Fig. 1 and Fig. 2.

The format of the annexes can be quite different. However, we have empirically found that some of the annexes are more similar than others and we conclude that they are prepared by the same author or accounting firm which uses a template for all (or several) or their customers. A clustering algorithm can group similar annexes, this allows us to label a small sub-set of documents in a cluster and then replicate these labels to the entire cluster.

We have downloaded 53,210 Annual Accounts from 2015 on-wards from LBR. In Table 1 we can see some statistics about our dataset. The total of working pages is obtained removing empty pages and financial statements pages from our dataset.

Table 1. Full dataset statistics.

	Full dataset	Last year dataset
Number of business types	452	452
Number of companies	38,644	37,999
Number of reports	53,210	38,455
* Number of reports in French	46,191 (86.8%)	32,943 (85.7%)
* Number of reports in German	4,214 (7.9%)	3,209 (9.3%)
* Number of report in English	2,805 (5.2%)	2,303 (6.0%)
Total of pages	375,544	277,798
Total working pages	195,546 (52.1%)	144,895 (52.1%)

---

[3] https://www.lbr.lu.

The *last year dataset* is considering only the most recent Annual Accounts presented by a company. A company can present two Annual accounts the same year in case there is a need for a rectification.

For validating our algorithm's performance we need to work with a labeled dataset. There are many labeled datasets available for Document Analysis, like DocBank [11], PubLayNet [18], DSSE-200 [17], ICDAR2015 [3], DocVQA [12], Web Document dataset [14], TDT2 [8], TTC-3600 [10], and Reuters-21578 [1]. More datasets can be found in UCI Machine Learning repository [6]. These datasets could be used for different kinds of tasks like text extraction and labeling [3,11,17,18]; for question answering based on images [12]; for document clustering [1,8,14] and so on. Most of them only have the text available and not the document itself.

None of the previous datasets can be used to identify clusters based on the formatting style and/or author's fingerprint. For this reason, we have labeled a small part of our dataset in a semiautomatic way (explained in the *Evaluation* section). This labeled test dataset is composed of 1,000 documents and more details are given in Table 2.

Table 2. Test dataset statistics.

Number of documents	1,000
* Number of documents in French	905 (90.5%)
* Number of documents in German	91 (9.1%)
* Number of documents in English	4 (0.4%)
Number of business types	193

4   Auto-clustering Algorithm

Our algorithm is a *two-level auto-clustering algorithm* for financial reports. The first level is a template-oriented clustering and the second level is an author's fingerprint-oriented clustering.

There is no need to specify the number of clusters but a few threshold parameters needs to be specified, see Table 3. The code for the clustering algorithm and associated tools are publicly available in github[4].

Table 3. Threshold parameters used in the algorithm.

Threshold parameter	Notation	Explanation
Clustering	κ_c	Min similarity for appending a document into a cluster
Merging	κ_m	Min similarity for considering merging two similar clusters
Sub-clustering	κ_s	Min similarity for appending a document into a sub-cluster

---

[4] https://github.com/Script-2020/autoclusteringFinReports.

118 B. C. Blanco Lambruschini et al.

Algorithm 1. Main autoclustering algorithm.

---

function MAIN_CLUSTERING(D, S_c, S_m, S_s)   ▷ D:List of documents,κ_c: clustering threshold,κ_m: merging threshold,κ_s: sub-clustering threshold
   $C, Id_{max} \leftarrow \{\}, 0$ ▷ Phase I: Generation of candidates
   for each $d \in \mathcal{D}$ **do**   ▷ Can be done in parallel
      $C, Id_{max} \leftarrow add\_document\_to\_cluster(d, C, \kappa_c, Id_{max})$
   end for
   $C \leftarrow do\_feature\_cleaning(C)$ ▷ Phase II: Feature Cleaning
   $C \leftarrow merge\_clusters(C, \kappa_m)$ ▷ Phase III: Cluster Merging
   for each $c \in \mathcal{C}$ **do**   ▷ Phase IV: Sub-clustering
      $Sc, Sc_{idmax} \leftarrow \{\}, 0$
      for each $d \in c.documents$ **do**
         $Sc, Sc_{idmax} \leftarrow add\_document\_to\_cluster(d, Sc, \kappa_s, Sc_{idmax})$
         $c.subclusters.add(Sc)$
      end for
   end for
   return C
end function

Preprocessing. For each document, the algorithm needs the extracted text and some meta-data for each page. We have used a tool we developed for this process[5] which uses PyTesseract[6] to extract text from PDF documents (including PDFs based on scanned pages) and most of the meta-data.

Our algorithm consists of four phases: (I) Generation of cluster candidates, (II) Cluster feature cleaning, (III) Cluster merging and, (IV) Sub-clustering.

Algorithm 1 shows in detail how these phases are sequenced.

4.1 Phase I: Generation of Cluster Candidates

The algorithm to generate cluster candidates uses a set of format-based features and a set of content-based features. Our OCR extractor tool provide us the language, page orientation, text bounding box and the text. The format-based features are:

- Language (French, German or English).
- Page orientation (portrait or landscape).
- Horizontal position of each line (frequency ≥ 2).
- Text line width and height (frequency ≥ 2).
- Enumerator patterns (e.g. 1. [arabic point], I) [roman parenthesis], etc.).

We include only format features for lines that have at least two values being the same (frequency ≥ 2). Language and Page orientation features are used for clustering while position, text width and height are used for sub-clustering.

---

[5] FDExt: Available in the repository.
[6] https://pypi.org/project/pytesseract/.

Algorithm 2. Add a document into a existing cluster or create a new cluster

function ADD_DOCUMENT_TO_CLUSTER$(d, C, \kappa_c, max_{id})$ ▷ d:document, C: Map
of clusters, κ_c: clustering threshold, max_{id}: Max id in the map C
 $f_d \leftarrow get\_features(d)$
 $found \leftarrow False$
 for each $c \in C$ **do**
  $f_c \leftarrow c.features$
  $\chi \leftarrow calculate\_similarity(f_d, f_c)$
  if $\chi \leq \kappa_c$ **then**
   $c.features \leftarrow merge\_features(f_d, f_c)$
   $c.confidence \leftarrow update\_confidence(c)$
   $c.documents.add(d)$
   $found \leftarrow True$
  end if
 end for
 if $\neg found$ **then**
  $max_{id} \leftarrow max_{id} + 1$
  $C[max_{id}].features \leftarrow f_d$
  $Cmax_{id}.documents.add(d)$
 end if
 return C, max_{id}
end function

For enumerated text lines, we replace the enumerators with their correspond-ing pattern (e.g. arabic, cardinal, letter). The enumerators are extracted using regular expressions to identify alphanumeric, roman or mixed sequences and its corresponding separators like dots, colons, dashes, or parenthesis. Enumerators patters are used for clustering.

For the *content-based feature set*, the algorithm adds subtitles as features. A text line is identified as a subtitle if it starts with an enumerator pattern. The next consecutive line following a sub-title is added also as a text-line feature. Sub-titles are used for clustering while text-line features are used for sub-clustering.

The algorithm begins iterating document by document, to assign a proper cluster or create a new one if the document does not fit into any existing cluster (Algorithm 2). At first, as there are no clusters, the first document creates a cluster of one document (itself), the document's features are copied to the cluster. The iteration continue with the following document.

The candidate document is going to iterate through the existing clusters and the document's features are going to be compared with the cluster's features. If the feature-set similarity score (χ) of both set of features is bigger than the clustering threshold (κ_c), the document is included into the cluster and the cluster's features are updated by merging in the features of the document.

The feature merging (method *merge_features* in Algorithm 2) consists of adding the new document's features to the cluster's features and update the *con-fidence score* of each cluster's feature. When the cluster is created, each feature has a confidence score equal to 1 (transferred directly from the single document).

When a new feature is added to the cluster, this confidence score is updated. For example, if a cluster of one document has a initial confidence score of 1, and the new document also has the same feature, the confidence score will remain 1, but in case the new document does not have this feature, the new confidence score is equals to 0.5. For a bigger cluster, the feature's confidence score before merging is equals to 0.2 in a cluster of 20 documents (this means that 4 of these documents share the feature). In case the document is including an unseen feature to this cluster, the feature's confidence score is 0.048 (1/21). The feature's confidence score (σ) is part of the similarity score (χ). The feature's confidence score allows the cluster to focus in the most important features that are more common to most of the documents.

Our similarity metric is the *feature-set similarity score* (χ). Is based on the graph-probing distance but considering the feature's confidence score (σ). The *feature-set similarity score* (χ) is shown in Eqs. 2 and 3. χ is used for comparing the similarity of one cluster with a document (phase I) or between two clusters (phase III).

$$avg_{features}(A, B) = (|f_{(A)}| + |f_{(B)}|)/2 \qquad (2)$$

$$\chi(A, B) = \sum_{i=0}^{|f_{(A \cup B)}|} \begin{cases} \sigma_i/avg_{features} & , \exists f_i \varepsilon A \wedge f_i \varepsilon B \\ 0 & , \text{otherwise.} \end{cases} \qquad (3)$$

where $|f(A)|$ is the number of features in the cluster A, $|f(B)|$ is the number of features in the document or cluster B; σ_i is the confidence score of the ith feature in $f_{(A \cup B)}$ (the union of features of A and B).

When a new document is added to the cluster, the features are merged and the confidence score of each feature is updated as shown in Eq. 4.

$$\sigma_{(f_{t+1})} = (\sigma_{(f_t)} * n_t + 1)/n_{t+1} \qquad (4)$$

The new confidence score for each feature in the cluster $\sigma_{(f_{t+1})}$ is calculated by multiplying the current confidence score $\sigma_{(f_t)}$ with the current number of documents (n_t) plus 1, all divided by the number of new documents (n_{t+1}).

Additionally, the sparsity measure of the cluster is calculated. This metric is the cluster confidence (τ_c) and as shown in Eq. 5, is the average of all its features' confidence score (σ).

$$\tau = \sum_{i=0}^{n} (\sigma_{(f_i)})/n \qquad (5)$$

4.2   Phase II: Cluster's Features Cleaning

In this phase, each cluster is analyzed and the less confident cluster's features are pruned. Only features with a confidence score $\sigma_{(f)}$ less than a forgetting threshold (κ_f) are kept. κ_f allows to remove features that are only in one or two documents inside the cluster. This cleaning phase is applied only in clusters with more than 4 documents. We empirically found that setting $\kappa_f = 1/n_{docs}$

Algorithm 3. Cluster merging

```
processed_pairs ← {}
function MERGE_CLUSTERS(d, C, κm)                          ▷ d:document, C: Map of clusters
    adj_matrix ← get_similarity_matrix(C, κm)
    high_confident_pairs ← get_highconfident_pairs(adj_matrix)
    for each pair ∈ high_confident_pairs do
        if pair ∉ processed_pairs then
            recursive_pairs ← get_recursive_pairs(high_confident_pairs, pair[1])
            for each pair_r ∈ recursive_pairs do
                if pair_r ∉ processed_pairs then
                    C[pair[0]].features ← merge_features(pair[0].features, pair[1].features)
                    C[pair[0]].confidence ← update_confidence(C[pair[0]])
                    C[pair[0]].documents.extend(C[pair[1]].documents)
                    C[pair_r[1]] = Null
                    processed_pairs.add(pair_r)
                end if
                processed_pairs.add(pair)
            end for
        end if
    end for
    return C
end function
```

for clusters with 10 documents or less and $\kappa_f = 2/n_{docs}$ otherwise, provided good results. As some features could be removed in this process, the cluster's confidence (τ_c) is recalculated.

4.3 Phase III: Cluster Merging

In this phase we improve on the candidate clusters from phase I, merging similar clusters. Documents that are similar to other documents but were placed in other clusters because of the parallel processing are merged together into a single cluster. For doing this instead of comparing the features of one document with one cluster, features are compared between two clusters and the merging threshold (κ_m) is used as parameter.

In this phase we are creating k_m groups of clusters to be distributed. Each group with N clusters is going to create a $N \times N$ similarity matrix, where each cell is the feature-set similarity score (χ) between a pair of clusters. Then all the high-confident pairs are retrieved ($\tau_c \leq \kappa_m$). Then, each pair is analyzed, and per each pair, all its high-confident clusters are also retrieved in a recursive way. This allow us to get a chain of similar clusters to merge. Afterwards, we merge all the chain of clusters, merging their features and the corresponding cluster confidence (τ_c). We use Eq. 4 but instead of adding one, should be the product of the feature's confidence of the second cluster times the number of documents in that cluster.

4.4 Phase IV: Sub-clustering

In this phase we repeat the algorithm used for the generation of candidates, but this time is done cluster by cluster and only considering the documents inside the cluster. The parameter is the sub-clustering threshold (κ_s).

5 Evaluation

The clustering task usually falls under the unsupervised Machine Learning category, but in this case, for our first evaluation method, we are going to use a subset of the data to evaluate the performance of the clustering algorithm and measure the success of the algorithm. For doing this we need to label a test dataset as mentioned before.

Our labeling method consists of running our algorithm with lower threshold parameters (κ_c & κ_m) in order to get similar documents together and then do manual check. This labeling was done manually by a single person to achieve consistency. The cluster and sub-cluster are assigned to each document (the assigned sub-cluster number is subjective because is not too strict, allowing for certain differences between documents). The main rules for considering to put two documents into the same cluster are: i) if both are using the same document template, and ii) they use the same words in the subtitles, left alignment and so on.

Two documents in the same cluster are not going to be in the same sub-cluster if they do not share the same format features such as: the same cover page, table of contents, size, and location of the text etc. Some details can vary if it is clear for the labeler that the same person/company used that template. To make this labeling effort easier, we generate a report of cluster's similarity, where we include for each cluster the list of cluster which were not so similar to be merged but the similarity is around 50% (not merged clusters with κ_m less than 0.50), this allow us to check manually clusters discarded by the algorithm that should be merged. This manual assignation is going to be considered as our *ground truth*.

The final labeled dataset has 1,000 documents divided into 77 clusters and 175 sub-clusters in total. The biggest cluster contains 86 documents divided into 19 sub-clusters. The biggest sub-cluster has 27 documents. On average each cluster has 12 documents. 66% of the sub-cluster contains less than 6 documents and 13% of the sub-clusters contains more than 10 documents. 50 clusters with only one sub-cluster with an average of 8 documents each. Other metrics are shown in Table 4.

Table 4. Metrics for ground truth labeled dataset.

Measure	Max	Min	Average	Median	Mode
Clusters (doc/cluster)	87	4	12.7	8	5 (14)
Sub-clusters (doc/sub-cluster)	27	1	5.6	4	1 (45)

The Rand coefficient or Rand Index is the metric used for comparing similarity of correct classified pairs over the total of pairs, and this can be used to compare the ground truth with the results of our algorithm.

For our second evaluation method, we are going to train the model considering only the Annual Accounts presented by the company in the last year (Last year dataset) and then order by cluster size and do a manual checking of the first 1,500 documents. The results of this evaluation is the true-positive ratio for clustering. Later, we are going to append documents to the existing model, which contains previous reports presented by the company (remaining reports from the Full dataset) and then check if all the documents from one company are in the cluster and sub-cluster. This is also measured as true-positive ratio for sub-clustering or author's fingerprint.

For labeling purposes, based on the final results, we define the number of documents to be labeled (n_{lab}), and the *feature_coverage*] (in total how many features can be labeled with respect to the total of features). The selection of documents to be labeled is first done by selecting the document that contains most of the shared subtitle features. The next selected document in the cluster is the next one which contains most of the remaining features. This iteration continues until all of the features were covered or a minimum threshold (*min_feature_coverage_ratio*) has been reached or a maximum number of iterations were done (*max_iterations*). Only are considered clusters with more than a minimum number of documents (*min_docs_threshold*).

The *feature_coverage* formula is shown in Eq. 6. It is calculated as the average of the number of labeled features divided by the total number of features in all clusters that has equals or more documents than *min_docs_threshold*.

$$feature\_coverage = n\_labeled\_features \div n\_features \qquad (6)$$

6   Experiment and Results

We ran the algorithm with our dataset with 38,455 reports. The following values were used as threshold parameters: κ_c (clustering) = 0.20, κ_m (merging) = 0.30, κ_s (sub-clustering) = 0.17.

Different threshold values were tested, these were the best comparing the 1,000 reports in our test dataset and the Rand Index (RI). As shown in Table 5, the best Rand Index for clustering was 87% and 55% for sub-clustering. The lower RI for sub-clustering is mainly because some documents should be placed in the same sub-cluster according to the labeler because it looks like the same, but in terms of content there are some mistypos or more additional information.

Table 5. Rand Index (RI) results

Metric	Clustering	Sub-clustering
Rand Index	87%	55%

As shown in Table 6, 6,119 clusters were found, 35.4% corresponds to clusters with 2 documents or more, representing 81.3% of the dataset. 10.3% creates a cluster of one (itself) and 8.4% documents were discarded because they have less than 5 features (usually scanned documents with few lines of readable text). If we consider only clusters with a cluster confidence τ_c bigger than 0.85, we got that 66.9% of the documents were clustered with a high confidence.

Table 6. Auto-clustering Results

Total clusters	One document	More than 2 docs		discarded	High confident clusters	
		Clusters	Documents		Clusters	Documents
6,119	3,953	2,165	31,264	3,238	2,070	25,735
	10.2%		81.3%	8.4%		66.9%

It is important to notice that because of the content features and language features, all the documents within a cluster are the in same language. At this point and for our goals, there is no need to translate into a single language and then process it, even more because our main language is french and the current tools are not well developed in French.

In Fig. 1 we see an example of two reports that belongs to the same cluster but in different sub-cluster. The information in the two documents is quite similar, but there are some differences. Also for this specific example, the first document has a cover page and the second one does not.

Fig. 1. Two reports from the same cluster but different sub-cluster.

On the other hand, in Fig. 2, we can see that all the reports belongs to the same cluster and the same sub-cluster, this is the author's fingerprint. Basically what is changing is some part of the content (different specific company-related information), but the layout and words to present the information is quite the same.

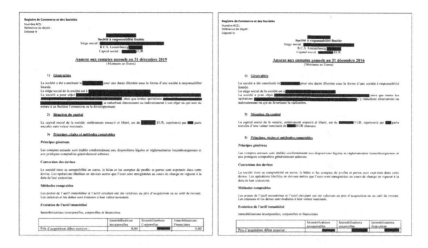

Fig. 2. Two reports from the same sub-cluster: author's fingerprint.

Checking only the clustering level, we have checked manually 1,322 reports distributed into 37 clusters where the biggest cluster has 850 reports and the smallest cluster has only 4 reports. We found that only 9 reports were placed in the wrong cluster, having a true-positive ratio of 99.3%

We have checked manually, at a cluster and sub-cluster level, 502 reports where we found 122 sub-clusters with an average of 4 reports per each sub-cluster. The algorithm could place correctly 378 reports in its corresponding sub-cluster, reaching a true-positive ratio of 75.3%. We identified that in some cases two sub-clusters had to be considered in the same sub-cluster because analyzing the report visually, looks alike, but usually one of the groups does not change the format but increase the financial concepts to be described, when this changes overpasses the threshold value, it splits into two different sub-clusters.

Considering the dataset which includes only the last presented report (38,455 documents), we use different threshold parameters for obtaining the documents to be labeled. The results are shown in Table 7. We specified $max\_iterations = 10$, but none of the clusters need more than 4 documents to be labeled.

In consequence labeling $n_{lab} = 4,190$ documents (10.90%) will allow us replicate up to 27,799 documents, that represents (72.29% of the entire dataset), having a very good feature coverage (92.80%).

Finally we append to the existing model 2,500 new documents from 799 companies. One document from each of these companies were fed into the model during the training phase. From all these new documents, 67.3% of the financial reports where placed in the right subcluster. For the remaining documents, we

Table 7. Number of documents to be labeled

min_docs_threshold	2 (81.3% of the dataset)				3 (72.29% of the dataset)			
min_feature_coverage_ratio	0.0	0.1	0.2	0.3	0.0	0.1	0.2	0.3
n_{lab}	7,694	6,556	5,902	5,749	6,360	5,091	4,365	4,190
% dataset (38,455)	(20.01%)	(17.05%)	(15.35%)	(14.95%)	(16.54%)	(13.24%)	(11.35%)	(10.90%)
feature_coverage	99.34%	97.51%	95.65%	95.03%	99.04%	96.39%	93.70%	92.80%

analyzed manually 100 reports chosen randomly, and we found that 65% of them were placed in a different subcluster because the company had changed the formatting style over the time.

For analyzing the contribution of each phase in the model's outcomes, we kept only the first phase and remove a phase for each test case. Removing the cleaning phase does not change too much the results, only affects the quality of the features, removing noisy features(15%). Removing the cluster merging phase we end up with 3.3 times more clusters. The contribution is significantly but can be removed if the first phase is not distributed, in this sense the contribution of this phase is zero because the number of clusters are almost the same[7]. Removing the sub-clustering phase does not have any impact in the clustering because it operates inside each cluster. The contribution at template-level clustering is zero but very high for author's fingerprint-level clustering.

7   Conclusions and Following Steps

We have demonstrated that our algorithm, using content and layout features, is able to cluster different financial documents and even to identify the author's fingerprint. There is no need to define the number of clusters.

With a semi-manual labelling of about 11% of the dataset, we can use the clusters from the algorithm to replicate them up to 72% of the dataset, effectively reducing the labeling effort.

The sub-clustering results when a company has different documents in different clusters can be later analyzed the whole dataset with a Temporal Machine Learning Model to classify if the author has changed the formatting style or if the company has changed of author.

This algorithm can be generalized to other domains differentiating the content-based features with the format-based features, where the first group should have a bigger weight. This allows to cluster documents focused on the text more than the format. For example, applying in internal documents provided for the different departments in a company, to cluster documents interdepartmental documents to label for training machine learning models. Similarly can be applied to reports from external consultants to look for hidden patterns between them.

---

[7] This test was done only in a small dataset because it requires more memory resources, for larger datasets the contribution of the phase is very high.

References

1. UCI Machine Learning Repository: Reuters-21578, Distribution 1.0, Text Categorization Collection Data Set, https://archive.ics.uci.edu/ml/datasets/reuters-21578+text+categorization+collection
2. Aiello, M., Monz, C., Todoran, L., Worring, M.: Document Understanding for a Broad Class of Documents 5(1). https://doi.org/10.1007/s10032-002-0080-x
3. Antonacopoulos, A., Clausner, C., Papadopoulos, C., Pletschacher, S.: ICDAR2015 competition on recognition of documents with complex layouts - RDCL2015. https://doi.org/10.1109/ICDAR.2015.7333941
4. Blei, D.M., Ng, A.Y., Jordan, M.I.: Latent dirichlet allocation. J. Mach. Learn. Res. **3**, 993–1022 (2003)
5. Manning, C.D., Raghavan, P., Schutze, H.: Introduction to information retrieval. In: kdd, vol. 1 (2008)
6. Dua, D., Graff, C.: UCI machine learning repository. http://archive.ics.uci.edu/ml
7. Ester, M., Kriegel, H.P., Sander, J., Xu, X., et al.: A density-based algorithm for discovering clusters in large spatial databases with noise. In: kdd, vol. 96, pp. 226–231 (1996)
8. Fiscus, J.G., Doddington, G.R.: Topic detection and tracking evaluation overview. In: Topic detection and tracking, pp. 17–31. Springer (2002) https://doi.org/10.1007/978-1-4615-0933-2_2
9. Hamza, H., Belaid, Y., Belaid, A., Chaudhuri, B.B.: An end-to-end administrative document analysis system. In: 2008 The Eighth IAPR International Workshop on Document Analysis Systems, pp. 175–182
10. Kılınç, D., Özçift, A., Bozyigit, F., Yıldırım, P., Yücalar, F., Borandag, E.: TTC-3600: A new benchmark dataset for Turkish text categorization **43**(2), 174–185
11. Li, M., et al.: DocBank: A Benchmark Dataset for Document Layout Analysis. http://arxiv.org/abs/2006.01038
12. Mathew, M., Karatzas, D., Jawahar, C.V.: DocVQA: A Dataset for VQA on Document Images. http://arxiv.org/abs/2007.00398
13. Palacio-Niño, J.O., Berzal, F.: Evaluation Metrics for Unsupervised Learning Algorithms. http://arxiv.org/abs/1905.05667
14. Sinka, M., Corne, D.: A Large Benchmark Dataset for Web Document Clustering
15. William M. Rand: Objective criteria for the evaluation of clustering methods, vol. 66(336), pp. 846–850. https://doi.org/10.1080/01621459.1971.10482356
16. Xu, W., Liu, X., Gong, Y.: Document clustering based on non-negative matrix factorization. In: Proceedings of the 26th Annual International ACM SIGIR Conference on Research and Development in Informaion Retrieval, SIGIR 2003, pp. 267–273. Association for Computing Machinery
17. Yang, X., Yumer, E., Asente, P., Kraley, M., Kifer, D., Giles, C.L.: Learning to Extract Semantic Structure from Documents Using Multimodal Fully Convolutional Neural Network. http://arxiv.org/abs/1706.02337
18. Zhong, X., Tang, J., Yepes, A.J.: PubLayNet: Largest dataset ever for document layout analysis. http://arxiv.org/abs/1908.07836

InFi-BERT 1.0: Transformer-Based Language Model for Indian Financial Volatility Prediction

Sravani Sasubilli[1] and Mridula Verma[2(✉)]

[1] University of Hyderabad, Hyderabad, India
[2] Institute for Development and Research in Banking Technology, Hyderabad, India
vmridula@idrbt.ac.in

Abstract. In recent years, BERT-like pretrained neural language models have been successfully developed and utilized for multiple financial domain-specific tasks. These domain-specific pre-trained models are effective enough to learn the specialized language used in financial context. In this paper, we consider the task of textual regression for the purpose of forecasting financial volatility from financial texts, and designed *Infi-BERT* (*In*dian *Fi*nancial *BERT*), a transformer-based pre-trained language model using domain-adaptive pre-training approach, which effectively learns linguistic-context from annual financial reports from Indian financial texts. In addition, we present the first Indian financial corpus for the task of volatility prediction. With detailed experimentation and result analysis, we demonstrated that our model outperforms the base model as well as the previous domain-specific models for financial volatility forecasting task.

Keywords: Financial volatility prediction · Textual regression · Indian financial corpus · Transformer-based models · Domain-adaptive Pre-training

Financial NLP is a relatively new research direction emerged in the past decade due to the growing maturity of NLP techniques and resources in the landscape of financial domain. Recently, there has been a growing interest in exploiting the contextual embeddings using transformer-based language models, such as BERT [8], and RoBERTa [14] for different Financial NLP tasks, e.g., volatility forecasting [4,24], financial sentiment analysis [1,15,25], structure boundary detection in financial documents [3], document causality detection [17], document summarization [26] and many more. These models are able to exploit the linguistic-understandings from professional periodicals, aggregated financial news, message boards, social media, financial reports and corporate disclosure,

Supported by Ministry of Electronics and Information Technology (MeiTy), Government of India and IIT Bhilai Innovation and Technology Foundation (IBITF) under the project entitled "Blockchain and Machine Learning Powered Unified Video KYC Framework".

I. Koprinska et al. (Eds.): ECML PKDD 2022 Workshops, CCIS 1753, pp. 128–138, 2023.
https://doi.org/10.1007/978-3-031-23633-4_10

and showing better performance in comparison to traditional machine learning-based NLP algorithms.

Most of the traditional approaches for volatility prediction tasks use time series models for historical pricing data [11]. Recently, deep learning models such as CNN [7], and RNN [13] have been utilized for volatility prediction using financial text. Predicting the financial volatility from the annual reports has been defined by Kogan et al. (2009) [10] as a text regression task, which refers to the task of predicting a continuous quantity by analysing the textual information related to the quantity. Stock pricing is influenced by many uncertainties and exhibits a strong nonlinear characteristics and linguistic characteristics, which makes traditional analytical methods ineffective. Pre-trained models, such as BERT [8] are trained on very large corpora and initialised with weights learned from the language modeling task, which helps them to represent the semantic information. However, using these BERT-based general purpose language model straight away would not be effective, since the financial reports and news articles have a specialized language-semantics. Moreover, these model may not be able to reflect the national financial context.

Following the recent trend, we have considered using the method of transfer learning [20], as it has the ability of extending the applicability of pretrained transformer-based language models to new domains. Previous works in this direction [4,5] utilized the BERT model for the purpose of generating the contextualized embeddings only, whereas we have created a whole new financial pretrained model with the help of domain-adaptive pre-training approach [9]. More specifically, our principal research interest is to come up with a domain-specific pretrained model for Indian finance domain, which has knowledge of contextual semantic relations of the Indian financial domain. For this purpose, we considered the domain-adaptive pre-training the base BERT model with the Indian Financial dataset, and then fine-tuned the model for the task of prediction of volatility of a company based on their financial annual reports. To the best of our knowledge, this is the first attempt (thus, InFi-BERT **1.0**) to design pretrained Indian financial corpus and pre-trained model available for the tasks of volatility forecasting, which can be further explored for multiple Indian Financial NLP tasks. The main contributions of this paper are as follows:

- An Indian Financial corpus for volatility prediction task containing the annual reports and volatility of top Nifty 50 companies for the years 2010–2021.
- InFi-BERT 1.0 model - the first transformer-based pre-trained language model for Indian Financial Domain.
- Detailed comparative study of InFi-BERT 1.0 with the base transformer-based models for the task of volatility prediction.

1   Background

1.1   Pretrained Language Models

We employed pretrained transformer-based language models, that independently learn semantic and syntactic meaning from a large amount of training data and are generally available for other related/extended purposes. Specifically, these models provide contextual word embeddings with the help of stacked attention models. For an instance, BERT model [8] is trained on the BooksCorpus (800M words) and English Wikipedia (2,500M words), for two unsupervised tasks, namely Masked Language Model and Next Sentence Prediction to train the model. RoBERTa [14], a variant of BERT, has similar architecture as BERT which is pretrained only on Masked Language Model task on $BERT_{LARGE}$ architecture with larger batch sizes and sequences to achieve optimised training over BERT. Another variant, ALBERT [12], uses factorization of the embedding matrix and cross-layer parameter sharing and inter sentence coherence prediction to achieve improved results over BERT.

1.2   Financial Language Models

Domain-specific language models refer to models which are pretrained using a domain specific corpora to achieve better performance on domain specific tasks, keeping the model architecture similar. A number of Financial-BERTs or Fin-BERTs are proposed by different research groups by following different pre-training approaches. The first FinBERT was proposed in [1], which pre-trained the based BERT model further on the financial data of Reuters TRC2 corpus. With the help of extensive experiments it outperformed all the previous LSTM-like models, as well as the base BERT. The second FinBERT [25] trained the model following both the approaches: (1) further pre-training a BERT Base model on three different corpora, and (2) training afresh. A good comparative study of these two models is provided in [18]. Another FinBERT was proposed in [16], which is trained in multi-task self-supervised training approach with six new tasks.

1.3   Stock Volatility Prediction

Stock volatility prediction helps in indicating the financial risk of a company, which is a great interest to anyone who invests money in stocks [10]. Studies have shown that financial reports and news articles have affected the stock volatility to a great extent. Predicting stock volatility from financial reports is another NLFF task, where the financial reports from an organization are analysed to make predictions of the stock volatility, which in turn benefit the organization as well as the investors or shareholders in making valuable decisions. Stock Volatility is characterized as the rate at which the cost of a stock increments or diminishes over a given time period.

It can also be defined as standard deviation of the closing prices of the stock over the period. Stock return volatility [7,19,22] for τ days is given as,

$$v_{[t-\tau,t]} = \sum_{i=0}^{\tau} \frac{(R_{t-i} - R_t)^2}{\tau} \tag{1}$$

where R_t is the stock return of the day which is calculated as $R_t = \frac{S_t}{S_{t-1}} - 1$ and S_t is the adjusted closing stock price for the day t. Higher volatility indicates the higher chance for the security to be at risk.

2   Preparation of Indian Financial Corpus

In India, all publicly-traded companies produce annual reports, which contain details about the history and organization of the company, cash flow statements and other financial information. These reports are available at public domain and on the website of Bombay Stock Exchange[1]. We have collected 550 such reports published over the period of 2010-2021 of top NIFTY 50 companies. The monthly stock prices are collected from money control website[2]. The dataset is available here[3]. The volatility of a company for a year is calculated using these monthly aggregated stock prices. If considered a annual report for year 2010, we are trying to predict the volatility for the following year 2011.

For corpus preparation, each annual report is converted into a text document using an online OCR tool[4]. The text documents are further pre-processed by removing special characters, numerical data and continuous tab spaces and then all the documents are copied into a single file, where each document is separated by two new line characters, and the sentences in each document are separated by a single new line character. New vocabulary has been created by using WordPiece tokenizer [23] and Byte-Pair Encoding (BPE) [21], as the existing pretrained tokenizers are unable to tokenize the Indian financial keywords.

3   InFi-BERT 1.0

In this section, we present our proposed models for the Indian financial domain. Motivated from FinBERT [25], we have incorporated BERT pre-training language model. We also experimented with its variant, RoBERTa. Likewise the ALBERT can also be extended. The architecture and the process of pre-training and fine-tuning are shown in Fig. 1 and Fig. 2 respectively. The fine-tuning of the model involves adding additional layers to the pretrained model, namely, a global max pooling layer followed by fully connected neural network layers.

We propose InFi-BERT model, which is a uncased version of pretrained BERT model on Indian Financial dataset. Our model is pretrained on two unsupervised tasks, Masked Language Model (MLM) and Next Sentence Prediction (NSP) similarly to BERT. The model is built with similar configuration of $BERT_{BASE}$ with 12 hidden layers and maximum sequence length of 128. The model has been trained for 3 epochs with batch size being 32 and learning rate being 3e-5. The new vocabulary is obtained by training a WordPiece tokenizer with a size of 30,522. The pretrained model is further fine tuned by adding a global max pooling layer followed by linear layers for volatility prediction task. We also experimented with the RoBERTa model by pre-training it on our Indian Financial corpus (InFi-RoBERTa). The architecture used is RobertaFor-MaskedLM, which uses dynamic masked language modelling for the pre-training

---

[1] https://www.bseindia.com/.
[2] https://www.moneycontrol.com/.
[3] https://github.com/MridulaVerma/Indian-financial-Corpus.
[4] https://www.pdf2go.com/pdf-to-text.

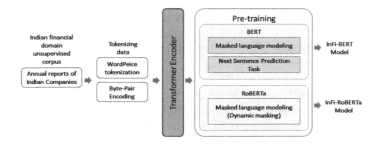

Fig. 1. Domain adaptive Pre-training of the proposed models

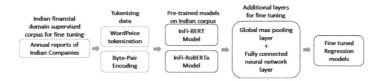

Fig. 2. Fine-tuning of the proposed models

process. The model has been trained with 6 hidden layers for 5 epochs with a batch size of 32 and block size of 128. The newly created vocabulary uses The Byte-Pair Encoding (BPE) and created a vocabulary of length 52,000. Similarly to InFi-BERT, this model was also fine tuned further by adding additional layers at the end to predict the volatility. Total number of parameters are approx. 100 million for InfiBERT, and 800 million for InfiRoBERTa.

From Table 1, it is observed that financial keywords like depository is not considered as a single token by general purpose models (BERT, ALBERT, RoBERTa). These general purpose models have split the words, where the ## token means it is a suffix word when a word is split into prefix and suffix. But financial domain models (FinBERT, InFi-BERT, InFi-RoBERTa) have properly tokenized it as a single word. We have also observed that financial name-entities which are specific to Indian financial domain like demat, SEBI (Securities and Exchange Board of India), NECS (National Electronic Clearing Service) are being tokenized properly only by the newly proposed models, InFi-BERT and InFi-RoBERTa.

Table 1. Comparison of Words encoding for different pretrained models.

Word	BERT	AlBERT	RoBERTa	FinBERT	InFi-BERT	InFi-RoBERTa
shareholders	shareholders	shareholders	shareholders	shareholders	shareholders	shareholders
disclosures	disclosure,##s	disclosure s	disclosures	disclosures	disclosures	disclosures
depository	deposit, ##ory	deposit,ory	dep,ository	depository	depository	depository
demat	dem,##at	de,mat	dem,at	dem,##at	demat	demat
sebi	se, ##bi	se, bi	se,bi	seb,##i	sebi	sebi
necs	nec,##s	nec,s	ne,cs	nec,##s	necs	necs

4   Experimental Details

The experiments have been conducted to evaluate the performance of the proposed models, InFi-BERT, and InFi-RoBERTa, and to compare their performances with the following pretrained models: BERT, RoBERTa, ALBERT, and FinBERT [25] for the task of volatility prediction. We are considering only one FinBERT, since in this work, our objective is to investigate the domain-adaption pre-training. For the purpose of comparison of performances for the task of financial text regression, traditional deep learning models - CNN [7] and RNN (with single layer LSTM) [13] are also implemented. For the CNN model [7] is implemented for the 10K dataset only, as the available word embeddings are trained only for 10K dataset. This embedding is created by using word2vec with a dimension of 200 which only considers the semantic meaning. The maximum length of document is fixed to 20,000 and truncated if processed text had words more than 20,000. The 3 channels has different filter size as 3, 4, 5. The result from all the 3 max pooling layers is then concatenated and dropout is applied and flattened. The training has been done keeping the embedding layer to be further fine tuned for the task of predicting the postreturn volatility. Similar to CNN architecture, RNN was also implemented using the same word embedding and is implemented only for the 10K dataset. The RNN architecture consists a layer of LSTM with 64 nodes and a fully connected neural network layer with single node to predict the output value.

BERT model was implemented for 10K dataset where the input tokenised text is processed in 2 different ways (1) applying BERT summarizer to bring down the length of the tokenized documents to 512 words (2) to truncate the documents whose length is more than 512. This resulted text data is tokenized using the BertTokenizer which are pretrained from the "bert-base-uncased" architecture. RoBERTa is also fine tuned for predicting the stock volatility for the 10 K dataset and Indian Financial domain. The input data is tokenised using Roberta-Tokenizer which is the pretrained architecture of "roberta-base". The pretrained models are available in the transformers library[5]. InFi-BERT took 24 h for training where each epoch took 8 h approximately, whereas, InFi-RoBERT took 18 h for training. We used Mean Square Error (MSE) as the evaluation metric, which is calculated as

$$MSE = \frac{1}{n} \sum_{i=1}^{n} (y_i - \hat{y}_i)^2 \tag{2}$$

Targeting to the financial text regression task, we have conducted experiments on 10K dataset from [22] and our own Indian Financial dataset. The 10K dataset[6] contains tokenized text documents. As part of tokenization, punctuation are deleted, numerical values replaced with # and text has been lowercased. The reports are directly used as input for the pretrained models to create the embedding. The dataset contains forecasting four different output values. We have considered only post-event return volatility as the output parameter.

---

[5] https://huggingface.co/transformers/v2.9.1/model_doc/roberta.html.
[6] https://clip.csie.org/10K/data.

These output values have been normalised using Minmax normalisation. All the experiments are performed on two GeForce RTX 2080 GPUs each of 8 GB Memory.

For 10K dataset, the pretrained models have been applied by adding a dense layer and applied dropout and flattening followed by the addition of a single node dense layer. Adam optimiser has been used and models are trained for 10 epochs. All the results reported are after performing 5 fold cross-validation and are the average of multiple experiments. Fine tuning is performed only on the dense layers. The pretrained models have been applied with a learning rate of 0.01 and batch size of 32. The maximum sequence length used for the models is 512. The documents have been summarised using BERT summarizer. The target volatility values are the log of volatility because the publishers [22] found it convenient to work in the logarithmic domain for the predicted variable. We have used inverse logarithm to get the values of the volatility.

For the experimentation with the Indian dataset, the pretrained models were applied as to the 10K dataset, except here all the documents were summarised before applying tokenization. To predict the volatility of a specific year the previous 3 years dataset is used for training. Authors of [7] have mentioned that including financial reports which are four years older than the test year does not help and might even produce noise.

5   Results and Analysis

The experiments have been conducted on the two datasets and the performance of the models are compared based on the MSE error rates obtained by the model for each year. Table 2 shows MSE scores for 10K dataset for the years 2009 to 2013. Table 3 shows MSE scores for Indian dataset for the years 2015 to 2019 and the average score throughout the years. Boldface indicates best results out of all pretrained models for the corresponding years. Models which are suffixed with "_summ" represent that in the pre-processing, the text has been summarised using BERT summarizer and others mean that the text has been truncated.

For Indian dataset, it can be observed from Table 3 that on average InFi-BERT has performed better over all the other models. The proposed model is trained on a comparatively smaller dataset, but has still performed better over the models, which have been trained on larger corpus. It can also be observed that the general purpose model RoBERTa has performed better over the Fin-BERT model on Indian corpus. That is why, we chose to fine-tune the standard BERT as well as RoBERT models for our purpose. For 10K dataset, FinBERT produces better results over all the pretrained models. This might be because the FinBERT training corpus includes the 10K dataset Reports.

The word tokens are inputs to the pretrained models. In order to understand how the tokenization varies over the pretrained models, we have performed the vocabulary similarity check [2] among all the models (shown in Table 4). It can be observed from the table that the vocabulary of InFi-BERT and InFi-RoBERTa are the most similar. Also the vocabulary is very dissimilar with existing models.

Table 2. MSE scores for volatility prediction for 10K dataset

Model	2009	2010	2011	2012	2013	Average
CNN	0.2414	0.3688	0.2583	0.3841	0.3392	0.3183
RNN	0.0483	0.0556	0.0540	0.0496	0.0410	0.0497
BERT	0.0461	0.0566	0.0567	0.0561	0.0514	0.0533
BERT$_{summ}$	0.0465	0.0621	0.0524	0.0501	0.0396	0.0501
AlBERT	0.0525	0.0536	0.0504	0.0515	0.0435	0.0503
ALBERT$_{summ}$	0.0487	0.0619	0.0598	0.0509	0.0436	0.0529
RoBERTa	0.0482	0.0543	0.0509	0.0497	0.0413	0.0488
RoBERTa$_{summ}$	0.0470	0.0607	0.0526	0.0475	0.0395	0.0494
FinBERT [25]	**0.0446**	**0.0476**	**0.0441**	**0.0443**	0.0391	**0.0439**
FinBERT$_{summ}$	0.0495	0.0822	0.0511	0.0454	0.0413	0.0539
InFi-BERT	0.0532	0.0538	0.0550	0.0505	0.0486	0.0522
InFi-BERT$_{summ}$	0.0506	0.0604	0.0566	0.0496	0.0466	0.0527
InFi-RoBERTa	0.0494	0.0677	0.0607	0.0640	**0.0386**	0.0560
InFi-RoBERTa$_{summ}$	0.0629	0.0546	0.0707	0.0575	0.0423	0.0576

Table 3. MSE scores for volatility prediction for Indian Dataset

Models	2015	2016	2017	2018	2019	Average
BERT$_{summ}$	0.0541	0.0257	0.0435	0.0536	0.0594	0.0517
AlBERT$_{summ}$	0.0854	0.0319	0.1111	0.0343	0.0993	0.0775
RoBERTa$_{summ}$	0.0136	0.0113	**0.0114**	0.0207	0.0371	0.0172
FinBERT$_{summ}$ [25]	0.0247	0.0411	0.0575	0.0378	0.0175	0.0277
InFi-BERT$_{summ}$	**0.0067**	0.0230	0.0139	**0.0087**	**0.0069**	**0.0144**
InFi-RoBERTa$_{summ}$	0.0338	**0.0086**	0.0233	0.0148	0.0490	0.0274

Table 4. Vocabulary overlap comparison of pre-trained models

Similarity	BERT	RoBERTa	FinBERT [25]	InFi-BERT	InFi-RoBERTa
BERT	1.0	0.61	0.41	0.41	0.49
RoBERTa	0.41	1.0	0.28	0.32	0.38
FinBERT	0.41	0.42	1.0	0.40	0.45
InFi-BERT	0.41	0.47	0.40	1.0	**0.94**
InFi-RoBERTa	0.33	0.38	0.31	**0.65**	1.0

This also proves the need of Indian financial domain specific model. Vocabulary similarity of the models is calculated by taking vocabulary of the models and removing the special character used for suffix words and then getting a count of the matching tokens and then divide it by vocabulary length of the model as vocabulary length varies for each model.

6   Conclusion and Future Scope

In this paper, we have proposed domain-adaptive transformer-based pretrained models for Indian Financial sector for the task of financial volatility prediction. The two models are compared with other pretrained base as well as domain-specific language models. With the help of extensive experimentation, we observe that the proposed models outperform the previous models for the task of Indian financial volatility prediction, and conclude that, domain-adaptive pretrained models perform well over general purpose models. In future, we aim to perform deeper analysis in terms of effects of different volatility proxies [6].

References

1. Araci, D.: Finbert: Financial sentiment analysis with pre-trained language models. CoRR abs/ arXiv: 1908.10063 (2019)
2. Arslan, Y., et al.: A comparison of pre-trained language models for multi-class text classification in the financial domain. In: Companion Proceedings of the Web Conference 2021, WWW 2021, pp. 260–268. Association for Computing Machinery, New York (2021). https://doi.org/10.1145/3442442.3451375
3. Au, W., Ait-Azzi, A., Kang, J.: Finsbd-2021: The 3rd shared task on structure boundary detection in unstructured text in the financial domain. In: Companion Proceedings of the Web Conference 2021, pp. 276–279 (2021)
4. Barbaglia, L., Consoli, S., Wang, S.: Financial forecasting with word embeddings extracted from news: A preliminary analysis. In: Kamp, M., et al. (eds.) Machine Learning and Principles and Practice of Knowledge Discovery in Databases, pp. 179–188. Springer International Publishing, Cham (2021). https://doi.org/10.1007/978-3-030-93733-1_12
5. Chen, Q.: Stock movement prediction with financial news using contextualized embedding from bert. arXiv preprint arXiv:2107.08721 (2021)
6. De Stefani, J., Caelen, O., Hattab, D., Bontempi, G.: Machine learning for multi-step ahead forecasting of volatility proxies. In: MIDAS@ PKDD/ECML, pp. 17–28 (2017)
7. Dereli, N., Saraclar, M.: Convolutional neural networks for financial text regression. In: Proceedings of the 57th Annual Meeting of the Association for Computational Linguistics: Student Research Workshop, pp. 331–337. Association for Computational Linguistics, Florence, Italy (Jul 2019). https://doi.org/10.18653/v1/P19-2046, https://www.aclweb.org/anthology/P19-2046
8. Devlin, J., Chang, M., Lee, K., Toutanova, K.: BERT: pre-training of deep bidirectional transformers for language understanding. CoRR abs/ arXiv: 1810.04805 (2018)
9. Gururangan, S., et al.: Don't stop pretraining: adapt language models to domains and tasks. arXiv preprint arXiv:2004.10964 (2020)
10. Kogan, S., Levin, D., Routledge, B.R., Sagi, J.S., Smith, N.A.: Predicting risk from financial reports with regression. In: Proceedings of Human Language Technologies: The 2009 Annual Conference of the North American Chapter of the Association for Computational Linguistics, pp. 272–280. Association for Computational Linguistics, Boulder, Colorado (Jun 2009), https://www.aclweb.org/anthology/N09-1031

11. Kristjanpoller, W., Fadic, A., Minutolo, M.C.: Volatility forecast using hybrid neural network models. Expert Syst. Appli. 41(5), 2437–2442 (2014). https://doi.org/10.1016/j.eswa.2013.09.043, https://www.sciencedirect.com/science/article/pii/S0957417413007975

12. Lan, Z., Chen, M., Goodman, S., Gimpel, K., Sharma, P., Soricut, R.: ALBERT: A lite BERT for self-supervised learning of language representations. CoRR abs/arXiv: 1909.11942 (2019)

13. Lin, P., Mo, X., Lin, G., Ling, L., Wei, T., Luo, W.: A news-driven recurrent neural network for market volatility prediction. In: 2017 4th IAPR Asian Conference on Pattern Recognition (ACPR), pp. 776–781 (2017). https://doi.org/10.1109/ACPR.2017.35

14. Liu, Y., et al.: Roberta: A robustly optimized BERT pretraining approach. CoRR abs/ arXiv: 1907.11692 (2019)

15. Liu, Z., Huang, D., Huang, K., Li, Z., Zhao, J.: Finbert: A pre-trained financial language representation model for financial text mining. In: Bessiere, C. (ed.) Proceedings of the Twenty-Ninth International Joint Conference on Artificial Intelligence, IJCAI 2020, pp. 4513–4519. International Joint Conferences on Artificial Intelligence Organization (7 2020), special Track on AI in FinTech

16. Liu, Z., Huang, D., Huang, K., Li, Z., Zhao, J.: Finbert: A pre-trained financial language representation model for financial text mining. In: Proceedings of the Twenty-Ninth International Conference on International Joint Conferences on Artificial Intelligence, pp. 4513–4519 (2021)

17. Mariko, D., Labidurie, E., Ozturk, Y., Akl, H.A., de Mazancourt, H.: Data processing and annotation schemes for fincausal shared task. arXiv preprint arXiv:2012.02498 (2020)

18. Peng, B., Chersoni, E., Hsu, Y.Y., Huang, C.R.: Is domain adaptation worth your investment? comparing bert and finbert on financial tasks. In: Proceedings of the Third Workshop on Economics and Natural Language Processing, pp. 37–44 (2021)

19. Rekabsaz, N., Lupu, M., Baklanov, A., Dür, A., Andersson, L., Hanbury, A.: Volatility prediction using financial disclosures sentiments with word embedding-based IR models. In: Proceedings of the 55th Annual Meeting of the Association for Computational Linguistics (Volume 1: Long Papers), pp. 1712–1721. Association for Computational Linguistics, Vancouver, Canada (Jul 2017). https://doi.org/10.18653/v1/P17-1157, https://www.aclweb.org/anthology/P17-1157

20. Ruder, S., Peters, M.E., Swayamdipta, S., Wolf, T.: Transfer learning in natural language processing. In: Proceedings of the 2019 Conference of the North American Chapter of the Association for Computational Linguistics: Tutorials, pp. 15–18. Association for Computational Linguistics, Minneapolis, Minnesota (Jun 2019). https://doi.org/10.18653/v1/N19-5004, https://aclanthology.org/N19-5004

21. Sennrich, R., Haddow, B., Birch, A.: Neural machine translation of rare words with subword units. In: Proceedings of the 54th Annual Meeting of the Association for Computational Linguistics (vol.1: Long Papers), pp. 1715–1725. Association for Computational Linguistics, Berlin, Germany (Aug 2016). https://doi.org/10.18653/v1/P16-1162, https://aclanthology.org/P16-1162

22. Tsai, M., Wang, C.: Financial keyword expansion via continuous word vector representations. In: Moschitti, A., Pang, B., Daelemans, W. (eds.) Proceedings of the 2014 Conference on Empirical Methods in Natural Language Processing, EMNLP 2014, 25–29 Oct 2014, Doha, Qatar, A meeting of SIGDAT, a Special Interest Group of the ACL, pp. 1453–1458. ACL (2014). https://doi.org/10.3115/v1/d14-1152

23. Wu, Y., et al.: Google's neural machine translation system: Bridging the gap between human and machine translation. CoRR abs arXiv: 1609.08144 (2016)

24. Yang, L., Ng, T.L.J., Smyth, B., Dong, R.: Html: Hierarchical transformer-based multi-task learning for volatility prediction. In: Proceedings of The Web Conference 2020, pp. 441–451 (2020)

25. Yang, Y., Uy, M.C.S., Huang, A.: Finbert: A pretrained language model for financial communications. CoRR abs/ arXiv: 2006.08097 (2020)

26. Zheng, S., Lu, A., Cardie, C.: Sumsum@ fns-2020 shared task. In: Proceedings of the 1st Joint Workshop on Financial Narrative Processing and MultiLing Financial Summarisation, pp. 148–152 (2020)

Workshop on Machine Learning for Cybersecurity (MLCS 2022)

Machine Learning for CyberSecurity (MLCS 2022)

Cybersecurity research has been gaining attention and interest from both academia and industry as current estimates project the cost of cybercrime to be up to 1 percent of global GDP. The number, frequency, and sophistication of threats will only increase and will become more targeted in nature. Furthermore, today's computing systems operate under increasing scales and dynamic environments, ingesting and generating more and more functional and non-functional data.

The capability to detect, analyze, and defend against threats in (near) real-time conditions is not possible without employing machine learning techniques and big data infrastructure. This gives rise to cyber threat intelligence and analytic solutions, such as (informed) machine learning on big data and open-source intelligence, to perceive, reason, learn, and act against cyber adversary techniques and actions. Moreover, organizations – security analysts have to manage and protect these systems and deal with the privacy and security of all personal and institutional data under their control. This calls for tools and solutions combining the latest advances in areas such as data science, visualization, and machine learning. We strongly believe that the significant advance of the state of the art in machine learning over the last years has not been fully exploited to harness the potential of available data, for the benefit of systems-and-data security and privacy.

In fact, while machine learning algorithms have been already proven beneficial for the cybersecurity industry, they have also highlighted a number of shortcomings. Traditional machine algorithms are often vulnerable to attacks, known as adversarial learning attacks, which can cause the algorithms to misbehave or reveal information about their inner workings. As machine learning-based capabilities become incorporated into cyber assets, the need to understand adversarial learning and address it becomes clear. On the other hand, when a significant amount of data is collected from or generated by different security monitoring solutions, big-data analytical techniques are necessary to mine, interpret, and extract knowledge of these big data.

This workshop aims to provide researchers with a forum to exchange and discuss scientific contributions, open challenges, and recent achievements in machine learning and their role in the development of secure systems. The ethics guidelines for trustworthy artificial intelligence authored by the European Commission's Independent High Level Expert Group on Artifificial Intelligence in April 2019 have highlighted that machine learning-based artificial intelligence developments in various fields, including cybersecurity, are improving the quality of our lives every day, that AI systems should be resilient to attacks and security, and that they should consider security-by-design principles.

This year's workshop followed the success of the three previous editions (MLCS 2019, MLCS 2020, and MLCS 2021) co-located with ECML-PKDD. In all the previous editions the workshop gained strong interest, with attendance of between 20 and 30 participants, lively discussions after the talks, amazing invited talks in all the editions, and a vibrant panel discussion in both 2019 and 2021 editions.

As in its previous iterations, MLCS 2022 aimed at providing researchers with a forum to exchange and discuss scientific contributions and open challenges, both theoretical and practical, related to the use of machine-learning approaches in cybersecurity. We wanted to foster joint work and knowledge exchange between the cybersecurity community, and researchers and practitioners from the machine learning area, and its intersection with big data, data science, and visualization. The workshop provided a forum for discussing novel trends and achievements in machine learning and their role in the development of secure systems. It aimed to highlight the latest research trends in machine learning, privacy of data, big data, deep learning, incremental and stream learning, and adversarial learning. In particular, it aimed to promote the application of these emerging techniques to cybersecurity and measure the success of these less traditional algorithms. MLCS 2022 received 16 submissions which were reviewed in a single-blind process, with each submission receiving at least 3 reviews. In total, 4 full papers and 2 short-papers were selected for presentation at the workshop. We hope that the workshop contributed to identifying new application areas as well as open and future research problems related to the application of machine-learning in the cybersecurity field.

Annalisa Appice
Giuseppina Andresini
Ibéria Medeiros
Pedro M. Ferreira

Organization

MLCS 2022 Chairs

Annalisa Appice	Universitíà degli Studi di Bari, Italy
Giuseppina Andresini	Università degli Studi di Bari, Italy
Ibéria Medeiros	Universidade de Lisboa, Portugal
Pedro M. Ferreira	Universidade de Lisboa, Portugal

Web and Publication Chairs

Nuno Dionísio	Universidade de Lisboa, Portugal
Samaneh Shafee	Universidade de Lisboa, Portugal

Program Committee

Antonio Pecchia	University of Sannio, Italy
Davide Maiorca	University of Cagliari, Italy
Donato Malerba	University of Bari Aldo Moro, Italy
Feargus Pendlebury	King's College London, UK
Gianluigi Folino	National Research Council of Italy, Italy
Giovanni Apruzzese	University of Liechtenstein, Liechtenstein
Leonardo Aniello	University of Southampton, UK
Luca Demetrio	University of Cagliari, Italy
Marc Dacier	Eurecom, France
Marco Vieira	University of Coimbra, Portugal
Miguel Correia	University of Lisbon, Portugal
Tommaso Zoppi	University of Florence, Italy

Intrusion Detection Using Ensemble Models

Tina Yazdizadeh[1], Shabnam Hassani[2], and Paula Branco[2(✉)] [ID]

[1] Carleton University, Ottawa, ON, Canada
`tinayazdizadeh@cmail.carleton.ca`
[2] EECS, University of Ottawa, Ottawa, ON, Canada
`{shass126,pbranco}@uottawa.ca`

Abstract. A massive amount of work has been carried out in the field of Intrusion Detection Systems (IDS). Predictive models are used to identify various attacks on the network traffic. Several machine learning approaches have been used to prevent malware attacks or network intrusions. However, single classifiers have several limitations which cause low performance in the classification between normal traffic and attacks. In other words, they are not strong enough to be used in practical settings. This is the reason why researchers seek to find more robust and high-performing models. Examples of these stronger models are ensemble models which are able to take advantage of the characteristics of different base models combining them. The main goal of using ensemble classifiers is to achieve higher performance.

In this paper, we propose two novel ensemble solutions for a network intrusion problem. We use pairs of strong and weak learners based on five different classifiers and combine them using weights derived through a Particle Swarm Optimization algorithm. We propose a voting and a stacking scheme to obtain the final predictions. We show the overwhelming advantage of using our proposed stacking solution in the context of an intrusion detection problem for multiple performance assessment metrics including F1-Score, AUCROC and G-Mean, a rare outcome in this type of problems. Another interesting outcome of this work concerns the finding that the majority voting scheme is not competitive in the studied scenario.

Keywords: Ensemble classifier · Intrusion detection · NSL-KDD dataset

1 Introduction

In recent days, financial losses and crippled services continue to increase due to the development of more sophisticated cyber-attacks. As a result, the traditional firewalls and Intrusion Detection Systems (IDS) layers are not enough to protect networks against intrusions. However, Machine Learning (ML) and Artificial Intelligence (AI) can leverage Intrusion Detection Systems (IDS) along with firewalls to provide an improved security against intrusions. The recent

I. Koprinska et al. (Eds.): ECML PKDD 2022 Workshops, CCIS 1753, pp. 143–158, 2023.
https://doi.org/10.1007/978-3-031-23633-4_11

advancements in ML and AI have helped to identify with high accuracy any type of network intrusion (e.g. [3,14]). Among Machine Learning algorithms, single classifiers have been used extensively as a solution for intrusion detection problems. Nevertheless, single classifiers might not fully provide the expected performance due to their inherent weaknesses when compared against, for instance, ensembles. Thus, more recent works have been taking advantage of combining different classifiers as base learners in order to achieve lower False Alarm Rate (FAR) and better accuracy in terms of finding intrusions.

In this paper, we explore the use of five classifiers which are categorized as weak and strong according to their performance. A novel ensemble approach is implemented by pairing weak and strong base learners to increase the predictive performance. We use the Particle Swarm Optimization (PSO) for weighting the base learners and inject these weights into the ensemble classifiers. Moreover, we explore the use of two different combination schemes for obtaining the final predictions. Namely, we apply both majority voting and stacking and show that stacking provides an advantage when considering multiple performance metrics for the intrusion detection problem selected. Our main contributions are as follows: (i) we present a novel algorithm that uses 5 base classifiers which are combined through weights derived from PSO; (ii) we use majority voting and stacking to obtain the final predictions; and (iii) we provide an extensive experimental evaluation using the well-known NSL-KDD dataset that shows the advantage of our solution.

This paper is organized as follows. Section 2 provides a literature review on intrusion detection solutions using ensemble methods. In Sect. 3 we present our framework for building an ensemble. In Sect. 4 an extensive experimental evaluation using the NSL-KDD dataset is carried out and Sect. 5 concludes this paper and presents future research directions.

2   Related Work

The main strengths and weaknesses of using an ensemble-based approach rather than using an individual learner have been pointed out by Sagi et al. [12]. The authors mentioned how an ensemble-based approach can overcome the overfitting by averaging different hypotheses which in turn reduces the risk of choosing an incorrect hypothesis. In addition, they highlighted various unique advantages that ensembles have when compared against single learners and clearly mentioned how these ensemble learners can tackle the problem of class imbalance, concept drift and curse of dimensionality.

Given their advantages, multiple ensemble algorithms have been presented in the intrusion detection context. For instance, Seth et al. [14] proposed a new approach for multiclass attack detection using the ensemble algorithms. The approach ranked the detection ability of different base classifiers for identifying different types of attacks and rankings are based on the final F1-Score of each classifier for their predictions. They used seven most famous base learners and based on the performance of each classifier, a rank matrix was calculated. According to this matrix the results of the best classifier were used for the final prediction. The reason behind using F1-Score is related to the fact that some classifiers can have high recall but low precision, like Random Forest. The proposed method obtained 100% for detecting Bots and DDoS attacks. Bhati and Rai [3] proposed an ensemble-based approach without any optimization for intrusion detection using extra tree classifiers. They combined the results of different classifiers to increase the power of the classifier. The proposed algorithm achieved 99.97% accuracy on the KDD-cup99 dataset and 99.32% on the NSL-KDD dataset. In a tentative to improve the performance of an IDS, Pham et al. [11] used hybrid methods and feature selection. The authors applied Bagging and Boosting, which are the most popular ensemble techniques, using tree-based classifiers. The tree-based algorithms used can eliminate the irrelevant features as well as feature selection because of the use of the best variable in each split of the tree. The authors selected several tree-based algorithms: J48, RandomTree, REPTree, Random Forest. Leave-One-Out was their selected feature extraction method for extracting 25 features and the Gain Ration was used for extracting 35 features. The experiments carried out on the NSL-KDD dataset showed that in the 25 features set, although Bagging with REPTree increased the accuracy, it did not reduce the FAR. In this subset, the J48 had the lowest FAR. However, in the 35 features subset, the authors achieved the goal of having a higher accuracy with less FAR by using Bagging with J48. Yousef Nezhad et al. [18] used eight versions of SVM and KNN (with different hyperparameters) in the feature selection phase in addition to ensemble classification. The used kernels for SVM were RBF and Hermit Kernel with different degrees for increasing the classification speed. The number of neighbors for KNN are 3, 5, 8, and 10 for adding diversity. The output of SVM and KNN were converted to probable values using a sigmoid function. This method can integrate the numerical, signals, and multidimensional data. Based on their results, using the Dempster-Shafer as an integrating module helped them in increasing the performance. Another way to improve the performance is using the feature selection optimizers. Zhou et al. [20] proposed an ensemble approach on the basis of the modified adaptive boosting with the area under the curve (M-AdaBoost-A) algorithm so that network intrusions will be identified. The authors combined many M-AdaBoost-A-based classifiers to provide an ensemble classifier by employing various strategies such as simple majority voting (SMV) and PSO. The proposed approach, M-AdaBoost-A algorithm, takes into account the area under the curve into the boosting process to be able to address class imbalance issue in network intrusion detection. The PSO algorithm and SVM were used to combine multiple M-AdaBoost-A-based classifiers into an ensemble for achieving improvements in network intrusion detection; thus, this system can be considered as a multiple-boosting-fused ensemble. Several other works (e.g. [7,10]) study ensembles in the context of cybersecurity predictive problems.

The problem of huge network traffic data and the invisibility patterns have posed a great challenge in the domain of intrusion detection. Zainal et al. [19] proposed a way to address these challenges. The authors employed two strategies: (i) selecting the appropriate important features which represent the patterns of traffic, and (ii) forming an ensemble classifier model by engineering multiple classifiers with different learning paradigms. This study formed a 2-tier selection process, by utilizing a hybrid approach where Rough Set Technique and Binary Particle Swarm Optimization (BPSO) were hierarchically structured. In this case, each class had one specific feature set since features were obtained based on class-specific characteristics. Moreover, Rough Set techniques were used to remove the redundant features and rank the top 15 features for each class of traffic. These significant features are termed as reducts. Regarding the classification of the network connection, ensemble machine learning techniques with different learning paradigms, such as, Linear Genetic Programming (LGP), Adaptive Neural Fuzzy Inference System (ANFIS) and Random Forest (RF) were used and the decision function was determined based on the individual performances when considering the overall accuracy and the true positive rates. The experimental results showed an improvement in the detection accuracy for all classes of network traffic.

Our research is inspired by the work of Aburomman et al. [1], extending it to consider: other alternative ensemble combinations, multiple base learners, and considering pairs of weak and strong base learners.

3 Our Proposed Ensemble for Intrusion Detection

Figure 1 provides an overview of our proposed method, which builds on top of the work proposed by Aburomman et al. [1]. After the data preprocessing and the feature extraction steps, five different machine learning algorithms are chosen and trained on the dataset. After training, the performance is inspected and used to classify them into either weak or strong learners. The initial achieved performance is used to manually build the weak/strong classification. On the next step, by using PSO, an average weight for the base learners is obtained. The following step takes advantage of two ensemble models namely, stacking and majority voting. The following sections provide a description of the data pre-processing and feature selection steps, the base learners and the ensemble models. Then, the procedure of using PSO is explained in detail.

3.1 Data Pre-processing

As a very first step of each machine learning process, data pre-processing should be done in an effective way. Typically, this step involves converting categorical data into numerical data in order to have better results in the predictions. We selected one hot encoding method for this procedure. Another standard pre-processing step concerns the data normalization.

3.2 Feature Selection

The second step of the methodology is feature selection. The feature selection refers to techniques that make a subset of most relevant and important features of a dataset. Having fewer features allows the machine learning algorithm to occupy less space while simultaneously running faster, an important characteristic of

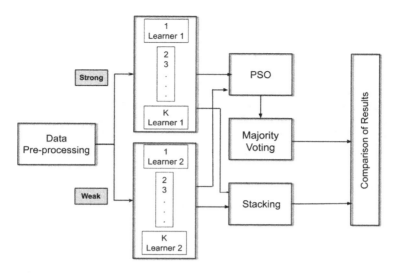

Fig. 1. The overview of proposed method

systems dealing with network intrusion detection problems. We selected an embedded method, the feature importance ranking of Random Forests as a method for extracting the most relevant features. The motivation for this selection is related to the fact that these methods are highly accurate and interpretable. In the random forest, each tree of the random forest is a decision tree and can calculate the importance of feature based on the feature's ability in increasing the pureness of the leaves. Then we used Recursive Feature Elimination (RFE) as a wrapper-based feature selection. The idea of the RFE is to select features by recursively considering the smaller and smaller sets of features. This method has two main steps which are: first, an estimator will be trained on a set of features and calculate the importance of each feature, and second step is to prune the least important features from the current set of features. In this paper, the core machine learning algorithm is Random Forest as mentioned before.

3.3   Base Learners

The third step in our proposed method is to select and train 5 base learners. We used Support Vector Machine, Naïve Bayes, K-nearest Neighbor, Decision Tree, and Logistic Regression for our base learners. This selection of base learners is based on the literature study and by taking into account the strengths and weaknesses of each particular classifier.

Support Vector Machines. The motivation for selecting Support Vector Machines (SVMs) is related to the fact that this classifier is able to address space complexity. Moreover, SVMs can handle non-linearity and are least impacted by possible outliers in the data. In this paper, we use SVM with probability estimates enabled, we set Gamma to 1/(number of features) and we used a radial basis function kernel. We considered the following values for the parameter C of the SVM: 5, 2, 1, 0.5, 0.2, 0.1.

Naïve Bayes. The goal of selecting Naïve Bayes (NB) classifier is to include one of the most simple algorithms. Although having strong assumption on the data, it is easy and fast to obtain the predictions. This is a probabilistic classifier which exhibits an overall good performance when compared to other algorithms such as logistic regression when the assumption of the independence among the features is verified. In particular, we used the Gaussian Naïve Bayes classifier due to its suitability to be applied in an online learning setting, which is a possible future research direction we are considering.

K-nearest Neighbor. The K-Nearest Neighbor (KNN) is a well-known lazy learner. We used the Euclidean distance and varied the number of k of neighbors being considered in the different models generated. In particular, we used 1, 3, 5, 7, 9, and 11 as the number of neighbors.

Decision Tree. We selected to use a Decision Tree (DT) algorithm due to its ability to observe information and identify critical features that demonstrate the malicious activities like the intrusions. In this paper, we considered the following values for the max depth in the ensemble part: 2, 4, 6, 8, 10, and 12.

Logistic Regression. Logistic Regression (LR) is an efficient algorithm that adds diversity to the learners we have selected. We used the Logistic regression with the maximum number of iterations set to 100. For the parameter C, on the ensemble part, we used the following values: 100, 10, 1, 0.1, 0.01, and 0.001.

3.4   Ensemble Models

An ensemble classifier is a method which uses or combines several classifiers to develop robustness of a system as well as to improve the performance when compared against any of the base classifiers used. Based on Schapire [13] and Dong et al. [17], ensemble methods have the advantage of being able to adapt to any changes in the monitored data stream more accurately than single model techniques. As an important parameter for the success of an ensemble approach is the diversity in the individual classifiers with respect to the misclassified instances. Dietterich [6] reports three main reasons why an ensemble classifier is usually significantly better than a single classifier: (i) the training data does not always deliver enough information for selecting a single accurate hypothesis; (ii) the learning process of the weak classifier may be imperfect; and (iii) the hypothesis space being searched may not contain the true target function while an ensemble classifier may be able to provide a good estimation. There are three main types of ensembles: bagging, boosting, and stacking. Bagging and boosting are alternatives to voting methods. In this paper, after training the base learners, we used two different ensembles: Majority Voting and Stacking. The motivation for this selection is associated to a previous successful use of the first one [1] and the exploration of the second one as a different and possibly more robust alternative.

Particle Swarm Optimization. Particle swarm optimization (PSO) is a population-based iterative optimization algorithm, formulated by Kennedy and Eberhart [9]. PSO is derivative-free, zero-order method. This means that PSO does not need to calculate gradients, so it can be applied to a variety of problems, including those with discontinuous, non-convex or multimodal problems. The algorithm starts out with a set of agents, called particles, in random positions in the problem space. Each is also assigned a random velocity. A fitness function is defined on a particle's location. The optimization problem to be solved is to find the best position, i.e. the position that minimizes the fitness function. Through each iteration, the algorithm evaluates each particle's fitness. Then, its velocity is updated and a new position is computed. A particle's new velocity is a function of its current velocity, its distance from its best position known and its distance from the population best position so far. The weights obtained from PSO are used as the weights for the base learners, i.e., PSO is only used to derive each base learner weights.

Majority Voting. A drawback of Voting Classifier is that it assumes that all models in the ensemble are equally effective. This may not be the case as some models may be better than others especially when different machine learning algorithms are used to train each base model of the ensemble. An alternative to voting is to assume that the base models are not all equally capable and instead some models may be better and thus should have more votes when making a prediction. This motivates the use of the weighted average ensemble method. Weighted average ensembles weight the contribution of each base model proportionally to the trust or performance of the model on a holdout dataset. If we need to predict a class label, the prediction is obtained through the mode of the models predictions. If we need to predict a class probability, then the prediction is obtained through the argmax of the summed probabilities for each class label. To ensure greater diversity in the classifiers and to maximize their use, each one of the 5 classifiers selected is trained with 6 different parameters and then combined with another classifier with 6 different parameters to utilize the full potential of these classifiers. For example, in case of KNN-Logistic Regression ensemble model, 6 KNN models with different values of K are combined with 6 logistic regression models with 6 different values of C for each model. Similarly, all models are trained and tested with this novel ensemble method. Figure 2 shows the flow chart of the weighted ensemble models inspired by the proposal in [1].

Stacking. Stacking [16] is a different technique of combining multiple classifiers. Unlike bagging and boosting, stacking is usually used to combine various classifiers, such as decision tree, neural network, naïve bayes, or logistic regression, where the learning process consists of two levels: base learning and meta-learning. In the base learning, the initial (base) learners are trained with training data set in order to create a new dataset for the next step which is the meta-learning. The meta-learner is then trained with new training data set. The trained meta-learner is used to classify the test set. A crucial part in stacking is the selection of the most suitable base learners. In this paper, we choose the base algorithms

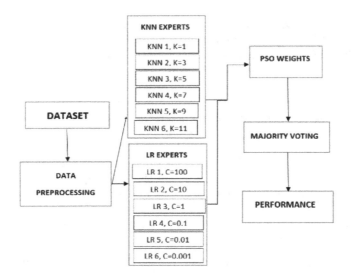

Fig. 2. The flow chart for ensemble models [1]

which are frequently used in the literature review for intrusion detection and then classified them into weak and strong based on their performance. The final estimator in all stacking models, i.e., in the meta-learning stage, is the Logistic Regression. We must highlight the novelty of using pairs of strong and weak learners integrated with the stacking ensemble method. As far as we know, this configuration has never been tried.

4   Experimental Evaluation

This section provides the details of our experiments. We begin by presenting the dataset we selected, then we describe the performance metrics used and we provide the results and a discussion. Finally we analyse the performance of the competitor methods and we discuss the limitations and advantages of the two ensembles tested.

4.1   Dataset and Experimental Settings

NSL-KDD [15] is a dataset that was proposed as an improved version of the well-known KDD'99 dataset solving some of its issues. The NSL-KDD dataset contains records of internet traffic that can be used for an intrusion detection task. It is comprised of two general sub datasets: KDD_Train+ and KDD_Test+. In this paper, we used KDD_Train+ because it prevents the overfitting of the model. The reasons behind using this dataset are first the fact that during most of the previous studies mentioned this dataset was used as it contains complete information about intrusions inside the internet traffic. Moreover, this dataset does not have redundant records in the train data, so the classifier will not provide any biased results during prediction.

The NSL-KDD dataset consists of 41 features that correspond to the network traffic input and a last column containing the target class label. The features can be categorized into four categories such as Intrinsic, Content, Host-based, and Time-based. Intrinsic features which are columns 1 to 9, contain the packet information and can be derived from the header of the packet. Content features which are columns 10 to 22, contain original packets information which can be used by the system to access the payload. Time-based features which are columns 23 to 31, contain the information about how many connections it attempted to make to the same host over two-second windows. Host-based features which are columns 32 to 41, contain information about the number of requests made to the same host over a certain number of connections. Also, the feature types in this dataset can be broken down into 4 types which are categorical, binary, discrete, and continuous. The distribution of the data types is as follow: 3 Categorical, 6 Binary, 23 Discrete, and 10 Continuous. We converted the categorical values into numerical values using one hot encoding. We applied this method to columns Protocol Type, Service and Flag. We also encoded the target label column into 0 and 1, where 1 represents an anomaly and 0 represents normal cases. In addition to encoding the categorical data, since there are different values in the dataset, we applied data normalization for increasing the cohesion of the dataset.

The final step consists of splitting the dataset into 70% for train and 30% for test. Regarding the PSO settings we have set the number of particles to the number of cases in the test set and the number of dimensions was set to the number of columns. The remaining PSO hyperparameters were set as follows: 'c1' = 0.8, 'c2' = 0.6, 'w' = 0.9, 'number of iterations' = 1000. We used five base learners in our experiments: DT, LR, SVM, NB and KNN. The parameters of these learners are provided in Sect. 3.3.

4.2 Performance Metrics

We selected different evaluation metrics for this work. The main goal is to have both an overall view of the performance, and a detailed view of the performance on the anomalous and under-represented cases. For this reason, we use Accuracy (as a standard reference metric), but also Precision, Recall, F1-Score, Specificity, Geometric Mean (G-Mean) and Area Under the Curve ROC (AUCROC) as recommended in [5]. These metrics assume the positive class or the minority class is the class of interest and the most relevant to the end user. In our case, the positive class is the anomalous class, while the negative (majority) class is the normal class. We observe the performance on multiple metrics suitable for tasks suffering from the class imbalance problem as suggested in [8]. We selected the F1-Score, G-Mean and AUCROC to base our final analysis and conclusions.

Precision is the ratio between the True Positives and all the observed Positive predictions. Recall quantifies the number of positive class predictions made out of all positive examples in the data set. The F1-Score considers both precision and recall metrics as being equally good indicators of how the model performs specially when there is a minority class present in the dataset. The F1-Score is the harmonic mean of the precision and recall metrics. Accuracy is the fraction of predictions that the model got right since it is calculated as the ratio of all true predictions to all the possible predictions. Specificity is defined as the proportion of actual negatives, which got predicted as the negative (or true negative).

The Receiver Operator Characteristic (ROC) curve is an evaluation metric used for binary imbalanced classification problems that depends on two metrics: the True Positive Rate (TPR) and the False Positive Rate (FPR). The TPR is the proportion of correctly predicted positive values out of all positive values present, while the FPR represents the ration between the false positive (values predicted as positive that are actual negative) and the actual negative cases present in the data. The ROC curve plots the TPR against the FPR at different threshold values and essentially separates the 'signal' from the 'noise'. The AUCROC provides a numeric summary of the ROC curve. The higher the AUCROC, the better the performance of the model at distinguishing between the positive and negative classes. The G-Mean is the squared root of the product of the recall of each class (positive and negative). By considering both recall values of the problem classes, this metric provides more insights regarding the performance on both classes giving a different perspective of the performance when compared against, for instance, the F1-Score.

4.3   Results and Discussion

Table 1 shows the results of all our base learners. From these results we observe that the Decision Tree is the best performing model for the vast majority of the performance metrics. This algorithm achieved an F1-Score of 0.984, a G-Mean of 0.982. However, for the AUCROC metric, the best performing algorithm was the SVM with 0.995. The Decision Tree is closely followed by SVM, K-Nearest Neighbor, Logistic Regression and Naïve Bayes. Among all these algorithms, Naïve Bayes is the worst performing model in terms of F1-Score, G-Mean and AUCROC, exhibiting a score of 0.912, 0.904 and 0.949 respectively.

Table 1. Base learners results across all the performance metrics.

Measure	Decision Tree	SVM	LR	Naive Bayes	KNN
Accuracy	**0.98255**	0.96792	0.95801	0.90686	0.973536
Precision	**0.9835**	0.95983	0.94544	0.96384	0.974895
Recall	**0.98557**	0.98426	0.98216	0.86723	0.978221
F1-Score	**0.98454**	0.97189	0.96345	0.91298	0.976555
Specificity	**0.97867**	0.94683	0.92685	0.95801	0.967491
G-Mean	**0.98241**	0.96936	0.96048	0.90421	0.973331
AUCROC	0.98262	**0.99536**	0.98207	0.94987	0.993251

Table 2. The overall results of the majority voting ensemble method on NSL-KDD dataset.

Measure	(LR, DT)	(LR, KNN)	(DT, KNN)	(SVM, KNN)	(SVM, DT)	(SVM, LR)
Accuracy	**0.965**	0.944	0.960	0.946	0.961	0.962
Precision	**0.961**	0.941	0.957	0.957	0.954	0.956
Recall	0.978	0.961	0.972	**0.981**	0.979	0.979
F1-Score	**0.969**	0.951	0.954	**0.969**	0.966	0.967
Specificity	**0.949**	0.922	0.944	0.942	0.932	0.941
G-Mean	**0.966**	0.945	0.960	**0.966**	0.963	0.963
AUCROC	**0.991**	0.966	0.983	0.99	0.981	0.983

Table 3. The overall results of stacking ensemble method on NSL-KDD dataset.

Measure	(LR, DT)	(LR, KNN)	(DT, KNN)	(SVM, KNN)	(SVM, DT)	(SVM, LR)
Accuracy	0.973	**0.984**	0.972	0.983	0.973	**0.984**
Precision	0.977	0.983	0.971	0.979	0.975	**0.985**
Recall	0.976	0.989	0.979	**0.992**	0.977	0.986
F1-Score	0.976	**0.986**	0.975	0.985	0.976	**0.986**
Specificity	0.970	0.978	0.962	0.972	0.967	**0.981**
G-Mean	0.973	**0.984**	0.972	**0.984**	0.972	**0.984**
AUCROC	0.997	0.998	0.995	0.997	0.997	**0.999**

After assessing the performance of base classifiers we proceeded with their categorization into strong and weak classifiers. Then, we built the two proposed ensemble models through voting and stacking. Table 2 displays the performance of various ensembles models that are built using the majority voting method, while Table 3 displays the performance of the ensembles built using the stacking method.

From Table 2, we observe that the pair (LR, DT) is the best performing ensemble model followed by (SVM, KNN) when considering all the results on the 7 performance metrics analysed. The remaining pairs of algorithms all perform worst than pairs (LR, DT) and (SVM, KNN). Furthermore, we also observe that the overall performance of the ensemble models using the majority voting scheme is worse than that of the baseline models. This is an interesting result that indicates that the majority voting with pairs of weak and strong learners is not effective in the intrusion detection context.

Our next step was to build ensembles using stacking and assess the performance of the resulting models. Similarly to the previous evaluation, we present the results of multiple metrics and focus our attention on the F1-Score, G-Mean and AUCROC as the base metrics given the imbalance present between the two classes of the problem.

From the results in Table 3, we can observe that the pair (SVM, LR) provides the best results in 6 out of the 7 performance metrics calculated. The next

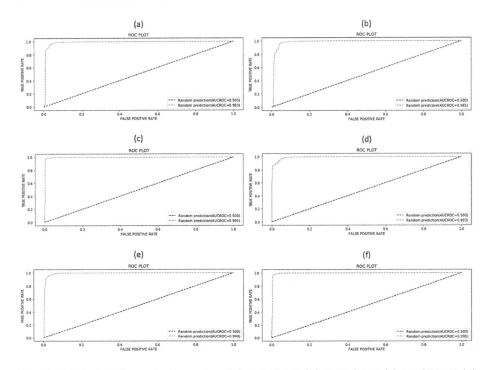

Fig. 3. ROC plots for majority voting; (a) SVM&LR (b) SVM&DT (c) DT&KNN (d) KNN&LR (e) SVM&KNN (f) DT&LR

pairs with the best results are (LR, KNN) and (SVM, KNN) wining in 3 and 2 out of 7 metrics, respectively. We must highlight that the use of the stacking scheme provided enhanced results when compared to the base learners. This is the opposite that we verified when compared to the use of the majority voting scheme. Stacking provided the best overall results while majority voting provided the worst ones. When considering the F1-Score we observe that the best results of 0.986 are achieved with the stacking scheme on the pairs (SVM, LR) and (LR, KNN), while the best base learner achieved 0.98454. The G-Mean results show the same trend with 0.984 obtained on 3 stacking scheme ensemble pairs and 0.98241 obtained on the best base learner. Finally, for AUCROC we notice that all stacking pairs provide a results higher than the best base learner. In this case the SVM provides a resulting AUCROC of 0.99536 while all the stacking-based ensemble pairs proposed achieve an AUCROC value higher or equal to 0.995, with the best result being 0.999.

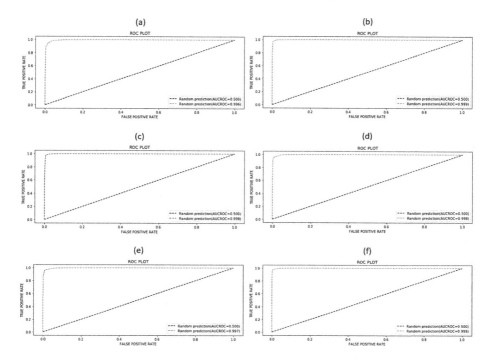

Fig. 4. ROC plots for stacking ensembles; (a) SVM&LR (b) SVM&DT (c) LR&DT(d) SVM&KNN (e) LR&KNN (f) DT&KNN

This shows the clear advantage of applying the stacking-based ensemble proposed in this paper for the different performance assessment metrics considered. We hypothesize that a possible reason for this trend could related to the fact that stacking allows to use the strength of each individual estimator by using their output as input of final estimator whereas voting classifier takes the most common output to be the output of final estimator. Figures 3 and 4 show the ROC curves obtained for the pairs of models when voting and stacking are applied.

4.4 Competitor Method Analysis

This section presents a comparison and analysis between the results from the literature survey and our proposed methodology.

Table 4. Results comparison between proposed methods and previous solutions. (Best result in bold and second best result underlined.)

Research Papers	Dataset used	Model used	F1-Score (%)	Accuracy (%)	Precision (%)
[20]	NSL-KDD	M-AdaBoost using PSO	91.64	**99.89**	88.34
[3]	NSL-KDD	Ensemble Trees Classifier	<u>97.8</u>	<u>99.32</u>	**99**
[2]	NSL-KDD	Majority voting	87	92	–
Proposed Model	NSL-KDD	Majority voting with PSO	96.9	96.5	96.1
Proposed Model	NSL-KDD	Stacking method	**98.6**	98.4	<u>98.3</u>

Table 4 shows all the results of the different performance metrics of our proposed ensemble methods and previously proposed solutions. We observe that, compared to all previous solutions, the proposed method using the stacking method performed better in terms of F1-Score, is the second best in terms of Precision and the third best in terms of accuracy. Moreover, we must also highlight that our proposed ensemble of majority voting with PSO has scores close to the top overall scores achieving a competitive performance. Primarily, our models were trained and tested using the best hyper-parameters for each ensemble learning. So, a greater diversity is obtained and the use of each classifier in the ensemble model is maximized by using the approach of combining 6 LRs and 6 KNNs in our approach.

4.5   Limitations and Advantages

In the case of real-world intrusions, the number of false alarms is a problematic aspect of these decision support systems. High false alarm rates may prevent these solutions to be put in practice. Although we used a clean dataset, as a limitation in the intrusion detection system, we can mention the presence of noise in the dataset. The bad packet generated from different sources like software bugs can severely limit the effectiveness of these systems. Moreover, the hyper parameter tuning of SVM model was time-consuming and more powerful hardware setup was required especially while training large datasets.

The fact that not always a combination of strong base learners would perform better than other combinations, for instance including weak learners, is another important lesson from this work. Finally, we think that more attention should be given to the imbalance problem present in this dataset. Other works have shown that the use of resampling methods can be effective for this problem [4]. However, our solution does not take into account any of these techniques, thus we consider this to be a limitation of our solution. This means that, by combining our stacking-based solution with resampling methods we could potentially obtain an even more robust algorithm. We plan to explore this aspect as our future work.

5   Conclusions and Future Work

In this paper, we tackled the intrusion detection problem through the proposal of two new stacking-based and majority voting-based ensemble methods. We used

5 different base learners to form pairs of weak and strong classifiers and then, by using these pairs, we performed classification with two ensemble learning models: Majority Voting and Stacking. Moreover, we used PSO as a mean for optimizing the weights of the ensemble models. Based on the results obtained in the NSL-KDD dataset, we show that the stacking-based ensemble outperformed the voting-based ensemble and the baseline models. Furthermore, out of all the models tested, our stacking-based ensemble model using SVM and LR provided the best overall performance across multiple metrics achieving an F1-Score of 0.986, a G-Mean of 0.984 and an AUCROC of 0.999. The fact that this solution provides consistently better results than the competitors across a high diversity of performance metrics is outstanding. On the other hand, the majority voting-based ensemble provided the worst overall results leading to the conclusion that this model is not the most suitable for the intrusion detection task.

For our future work, we will consider the extension of our work to more base learners and datasets and will analyse the statistical significance of the results. We also plan to study online ensemble learning and adapt the ensemble model proposed to a data stream context while considering the concept drift problem. Another interesting avenue regards the integration of resampling methods into our stacking-based ensemble in order to deal with the class imbalance problem.

References

1. Aburomman, A.A., Reaz, M.B.I.: A novel SVM-KNN-PSO ensemble method for intrusion detection system. Appl. Soft Comput. **38**, 360–372 (2016)
2. Bamhdi, A.M., Abrar, I., Masoodi, F.: An ensemble based approach for effective intrusion detection using majority voting. Telkomnika **19**(2), 664–671 (2021)
3. Bhati, B.S., Rai, C.S.: Ensemble based approach for intrusion detection using extra tree classifier. In: Solanki, V.K., Hoang, M.K., Lu, Z.J., Pattnaik, P.K. (eds.) Intelligent Computing in Engineering. AISC, vol. 1125, pp. 213–220. Springer, Singapore (2020). https://doi.org/10.1007/978-981-15-2780-7_25
4. Branco, P.: Exploring the impact of resampling methods for malware detection. In: 2020 IEEE International Conference on Big Data (Big Data), pp. 3961–3968. IEEE (2020)
5. Branco, P., Torgo, L., Ribeiro, R.P.: A survey of predictive modeling on imbalanced domains. ACM Comput. Surv. (CSUR) **49**(2), 1–50 (2016)
6. Dietterich, T.G.: Machine-learning research. AI Mag. **18**(4), 97–97 (1997)
7. Folino, G., Pisani, F.S.: Evolving meta-ensemble of classifiers for handling incomplete and unbalanced datasets in the cyber security domain. Appl. Soft Comput. **47**, 179–190 (2016)
8. Gaudreault, J.-G., Branco, P., Gama, J.: An analysis of performance metrics for imbalanced classification. In: Soares, C., Torgo, L. (eds.) DS 2021. LNCS (LNAI), vol. 12986, pp. 67–77. Springer, Cham (2021). https://doi.org/10.1007/978-3-030-88942-5_6
9. Kennedy, J., Eberhart, R.: Particle swarm optimization. In: Proceedings of ICNN 1995-International Conference on Neural Networks, vol. 4, pp. 1942–1948. IEEE (1995)

10. Leevy, J.L., Hancock, J., Zuech, R., Khoshgoftaar, T.M.: Detecting cybersecurity attacks using different network features with LightGBM and XGBoost learners. In: 2020 IEEE Second International Conference on Cognitive Machine Intelligence (CogMI), pp. 190–197. IEEE (2020)
11. Pham, N.T., Foo, E., Suriadi, S., Jeffrey, H., Lahza, H.F.M.: Improving performance of intrusion detection system using ensemble methods and feature selection. In: Proceedings of the Australasian Computer Science Week Multiconference, pp. 1–6. ACM, Brisband Queensland Australia, January 2018. https://doi.org/10.1145/3167918.3167951
12. Sagi, O., Rokach, L.: Ensemble learning: a survey. WIREs Data Mining Knowl. Discov. **8**(4), e1249 (2018). https://doi.org/10.1002/widm.1249
13. Schapire, R.E.: The boosting approach to machine learning: an overview. In: Bickel, P., et al. (eds.) Nonlinear Estimation and Classification. Lecture Notes in Statistics, vol. 171, pp. 149–171. Springer, New York (2003). https://doi.org/10.1007/978-0-387-21579-2_9
14. Seth, S., Chahal, K.K., Singh, G.: A novel ensemble framework for an intelligent intrusion detection system. IEEE Access **9**, 138451–138467 (2021). https://doi.org/10.1109/ACCESS.2021.3116219
15. Tavallaee, M., Bagheri, E., Lu, W., Ghorbani, A.A.: A detailed analysis of the KDD cup 99 data set. In: 2009 IEEE Symposium on Computational Intelligence for Security and Defense Applications, pp. 1–6. IEEE (2009)
16. Wolpert, D.H.: Stacked generalization. Neural Netw. **5**(2), 241–259 (1992)
17. Dong, Y.-S., Han, K.-S.: A comparison of several ensemble methods for text categorization. In: IEEE International Conference on Services Computing, 2004, (SCC 2004), Proceedings, pp. 419–422. IEEE, Shanghai, China (2004). https://doi.org/10.1109/SCC.2004.1358033
18. Yousefnezhad, M., Hamidzadeh, J., Aliannejadi, M.: Ensemble classification for intrusion detection via feature extraction based on deep Learning. Soft. Comput. **25**(20), 12667–12683 (2021). https://doi.org/10.1007/s00500-021-06067-8
19. Zainal, A., Maarof, M.A., Shamsuddin, S.M., et al.: Ensemble classifiers for network intrusion detection system. J. Inf. Assur. Secur. **4**(3), 217–225 (2009)
20. Zhou, Y., Mazzuchi, T.A., Sarkani, S.: M-AdaBoost-A based ensemble system for network intrusion detection. Expert Syst. Appl. **162**, 113864 (2020). https://doi.org/10.1016/j.eswa.2020.113864

Domain Adaptation with Maximum Margin Criterion with Application to Network Traffic Classification

Zahra Taghiyarrenani[1][(✉)] and Hamed Farsi[2]

[1] Center for Applied Intelligence Systems Research, Halmstad University,
Halmstad, Sweden
`zahra.taghiyarrenani@hh.se`
[2] Qamcom Research and Technology, Gothenburg, Sweden
`hamed.farsi@2550.engineering`

Abstract. A fundamental assumption in machine learning is that training and test samples follow the same distribution. Therefore, for training a machine learning-based network traffic classifier, it is necessary to use samples obtained from the desired network. Collecting enough training data, however, can be challenging in many cases. Domain adaptation allows samples from other networks to be utilized. In order to satisfy the aforementioned assumption, domain adaptation reduces the distance between the distribution of the samples in the desired network and that of the available samples in other networks. However, it is important to note that the applications in two different networks can differ considerably. Taking this into account, in this paper, we present a new domain adaptation method for classifying network traffic. Thus, we use the labeled samples from a network and adapt them to the few labeled samples from the desired network; In other words, we adapt shared applications while preserving the information about non-shared applications. In order to demonstrate the efficacy of our method, we construct five different cross-network datasets using the Brazil dataset. These results indicate the effectiveness of adapting samples between different domains using the proposed method.

Keywords: Traffic classification · Domain adaptation · Transfer learning

1 Introduction

Recently, machine learning (ML) has gained increasing attention in the field of internet network security for various applications, including network traffic classification. The emergence of machine learning-based traffic classification is a consequence of the inefficiencies of traditional approaches such as port-based and signature-based methods; dynamic port numbers and data encryption are among the reasons for the inefficiency of traditional methods [2]. In order to resolve these issues, ML methods employ and analyze flow level statistical properties rather than port numbers or the content of flow data.

I. Koprinska et al. (Eds.): ECML PKDD 2022 Workshops, CCIS 1753, pp. 159–169, 2023.
https://doi.org/10.1007/978-3-031-23633-4_12

Numerous ML-based approaches have been presented in the literature to classify the traffic in a network [13,14]. These methods employ information, namely training samples, to learn a classification model. In ML, there is a core assumption which holds that the training and test samples should be distributed independently and identically (IID assumption) [16]. Intuitively, the training and test samples should, therefore, be produced under the same condition. According to this assumption, for a ML-based network traffic classification model, the training samples should be updated and extracted from the desired network [13,14].

However, in practice when we want to construct a model specific to a network, collecting enough samples from that network may be challenging. We may access to outdated information from the desired network or related information from other networks. Authors in [7], however, mentioned the problem of temporal and spatial decays in network traffic classification; which mean how the performance of a classification model get affected if training and test data are not from the same network. They addressed these two issues using data gathered at different times and from different sites so that the gathered data follow different distributions.

Domain Adaptation (DA) is a machine learning technique that makes use of samples that are generated from a different but related environment to the desired environment [8,15,20]. To be more precise, DA reduces the difference (distribution shift) between two different datasets by adapting the datasets. Typically, the training dataset is referred to as the source, while the test dataset is referred to as the target. Similarly, we refer to a network with available labeled data as the source network and to the desired network as the target network.

Data from two different networks may include different types of traffic. Therefore, an appropriate DA should only adapt the shared types of traffic without destroying the information about other types of traffic (which are not shared between two networks).

In this paper, we propose a Domain Adaptation method for network traffic classification. Our proposed method adapt two different datasets which may include different applications, although they have some shared applications. To this end we uses a small percentage of the labeled data in the desired network as well as samples from other networks or outdated samples. we perform experiments on 5 cross-network scenarios to evaluate the proposed method.

2   Related Works

In the last decades, machine learning methods have increasingly received attention for solving network security tasks, including network traffic classification [13]. Some of these methods are Support Vector Machine [17], Neural Networks [3,10], Bayesian Techniques [12]. In all of the mentioned methods, because of the IID assumption of machine learning methods, the training and test datasets are from one network.

Authors in [18] proposed utilizing samples from different datasets for intrusion detection purposes. Following the mentioned paper, authors in [9] proposed incrementally constructing a model using samples from different datasets.

A cross-domain network traffic classification is proposed in [5] to solve the problem in case the source and target networks are same but the samples are collected in different times. This paper constructs a new latent space in which the distribution of source and target samples are minimized. On top of this space, a classifier trained with samples from source network is generalized to target network.

An application-level traffic identification is proposed in [19] using data from a small-scale and a large-scale network. In this method a classifier is trained with small-scale network data; After that, using domain adaptation, this network is adapted to a large-scale network data.

In last two mentioned methods, the label set (applications) of source and target networks are identical. However, authors in [4] proposed a cross-domain method that assume source and target network traffics are totally different in terms of applications; the label set of source and target are different; tCLD-Net, at first, is trained with samples from from source network. After that the last layers of the network, which are task specific, are removed and replaced by new layers. Theses new layers are retrained using the target samples. In such methods, however, we need enough target training samples for retraining the network.

In this paper, we assume there are some shared applications between the source and target networks. We employ domain adaptation to adapt shared applications as well as keeping information from non-shared applications. In other words, our method is capable to transfer knowledge for non-shared applications between source to target networks.

3   Background

3.1   Domain Adaptation

Let $D_s = (x_i, y_i)_{i=1}^{n}$ is the source dataset consisting of n samples. D_s is drawn from the distribution $P_s(X, Y)$. Similarly, $D_t = (x_j, y_j)_{j=1}^{m}$ is the target dataset consisting of m samples and is drawn from distribution $P_t(X, Y)$ so that $P_s(X, Y) \neq P_t(X, Y)$. Domain Adaptation aims to adapt source and target domains so that $P_s(X, Y) = P_t(X, Y)$ to use D_s as training samples to construct a model that is generalizable to target domain; to predict the labels of the target samples D_t.

3.2   Maximum Mean Discrepancy (MMD)

Maximum Mean Discrepancy (MMD) is a non parametric distribution distance estimation criterion [1]. MMD measure the difference between source and target domains as follow:

$$Dist(D_s, D_t) = \| \frac{1}{n} \sum_{i=1}^{n} \phi(x_s^i) - \frac{1}{m} \sum_{j=1}^{m} \phi(x_t^j) \|^2 \tag{1}$$

where $\phi(x) : X \rightarrow \mathcal{H}$ and $\mathcal{H}$ is a universal Reproducing Kernel Hilbert Space (RKHS).

3.3   Maximum Margin Criterion

One of the most popular feature extraction methods with the classification goal is Fisher Linear Discriminant Analysis (FLDA) [11]. To project samples into a new space, FLDA finds a projection vector w by maximizing the following objective function:

$$J_F(w) = \frac{w^T S_b w}{w^T S_w w} \qquad (2)$$

where S_b is between class scatter and S_w is within class scatter. Accordingly, FLDA minimizes the distance between samples that share the same class and maximizes the distance between samples with different classes.

To maximize Eq. 2, the transformation matrix w must be constituted by the largest eigenvectors of $S_w^{-1} S_b$. However, when within_class scatter matrix is singular, the FLDA cannot be used. To overcome this problem, [6] proposed *Maximum Margin Criterion* (MMC) criterion that optimizes the following objective function:

$$J(w) = tr(w^T(S_b - S_w)w) \qquad (3)$$

4   Methodology

4.1   Problem Formulation

We propose a method to solve the cross-domain network traffic classification problem with the following assumptions:

– There is only one source network and one target network.
– The applications are not the same for the source and target networks; There are some applications in either source network or target network.
– Source and target networks have some common applications.
– Samples from the source network are labeled.
– A small percentage of samples from the target network are labeled and correspond to all the applications in the target network.

More formally, we state the mentioned assumptions and the problem as follows.

Assume X as $d - dimensional$ input space and Y an output spaces. $D_s = \{x_s^i, y_s^i\}_{i=1}^n$ is source traffic samples, $D_t = D_t^l \cup D_t^u$ is target traffic samples where $D_t^l = \{x_t^i, y_t^i\}_{i=1}^{m_l}$ is labeled, $D_t^u = \{x_t^i\}_{i=1}^{m_u}$ is unlabeled target traffic samples; $m = m_l + m_u$ is the total number of target samples; so that $x \in X$ and $y \in Y$. D_s is drawn from distribution $P_s(X, Y)$, D_t^l and D_t^u are drawn from distribution $P_t(X, Y)$, where $P_s(x, y) \neq P_t(x, y)$.

There are Cc common applications in source and target networks. The number of the total set of applications in source and target is C.

$w \in \mathbb{R}^{d \times D}$ is a projection matrix that maps $x \in X$ to $\mathbf{x} \in \mathbf{X}$, where $\mathbf{X}$ is a $D - dimensional$ new shared feature space for both source and target traffic domains.

$\mathbf{C} : \mathbf{X} \rightarrow Y$ is a classifier that is trained on top of the new shared feature representation.

We aim to construct the new shared space ($\mathbf{X}$) so that a trained classifier on top of that ($\mathbf{C}$) generalizes to the target domain.

In the rest of the paper we refer to the new space with bold letters.

4.2 Proposed Method

In this subsection, we present a criterion for cross-domain feature extraction for network traffic classification. To this end, we construct a new feature space in which: (1) the distribution distance between the source and target network traffics with the same applications are minimized, (2) the within-class sample distances for both source and target samples are minimized (3) the between-class sample distances of both source and target samples are maximized. Accordingly, we use the following criterion:

$$J = \sum_{c=1}^{Cc} Dist(\mathbf{D_s}^{(c)}, \mathbf{D_t}^{(c)}) + \sum_{c=1}^{C} S(c) - \frac{1}{2} \sum_{c_1=1}^{C} \sum_{c_2=1, c_1 \neq c_2}^{C} diff(c_1, c_2) \quad (4)$$

where $Dist(., .)$ calculates the distance between two distributions. In fact, using $Dist(., .)$, we align the source and target networks samples. However, since the assumption is that some domain-specific applications may exist, if we align all samples from the source to all samples from the target domain without considering the applications, the application misalignment will happen. For this reason, we only minimize the distribution distance between shared applications. Since there are Cc common applications, we calculate Cc distribution distance. $\mathbf{D_s}^{(c)}$ and $\mathbf{D_t}^{(c)}$ are the projected source and target samples in the new space with class c. By minimizing this distance, we unify the distribution of the shared application of source and target networks.

$S(c)$ is within-class scatter of samples with application c, regardless of the samples' domain. The second term in Eq. 4 calculates the amount of scattering of each application. To prepare the new space for classification, we are interested in minimizing this scatter.

The third term in Eq. 4 calculates the distance between different applications. By maximizing this difference, we force different applications in the new space to be separated from each other and, consequently, easily classified. Besides, maximizing this distance helps prevent application misalignment.

In continue, we will describe how we calculate each part of the Eq. 4 for a linear feature extractor. The embedding of the samples in the new space is calculated as $\mathbf{x} = w^T x$.

Distribution Distance Calculation: We utilize the MMD criterion to calculate $Dist(.,)$ for unifying the distribution distance between source and target samples with the common applications.

$$\sum_{c=1}^{Cc} Dist(\mathbf{D_s}^{(c)}, \mathbf{D_t}^{(c)}) =$$

$$\sum_{c=1}^{Cc} \| \frac{1}{n_s^{(c)}} \sum_{x_s \in D_s^{(c)}} w^T x_s^{(c)} - \frac{1}{n_t^{(c)}} \sum_{x_t \in D_t^{t(c)}} w^T x_t^{(c)} \|^2 = \qquad (5)$$

$$\sum_{c=1}^{Cc} tr(w^T x L^{(c)} x^T w) = w^T x L x^T w$$

for $x \in D^{(c)} = [D_s^{(c)}, D_t^{l(c)}]$ where,

$$L_{ij}^{(c)} = \begin{cases} \frac{1}{n_s^{(c)} n_s^{(c)}} & x_i, x_j \in D_s^{(c)} \\ \frac{1}{n_t^{(c)} n_t^{(c)}} & x_i, x_j \in D_t^{(c)} \\ \frac{-1}{n_s^{(c)} n_t^{(c)}} & \text{otherwise} \end{cases} \quad \text{and}, L = \sum_{c=1}^{Cc} L^c. \qquad (6)$$

Within Scatter Matrix Calculation. Assuming $\mathbf{S_c}$ as covariance matrix which is calculated by the samples of application c and $tr(\mathbf{S_c})$ as overall variance, we calculate the second term in the Eq. 4 as follows:

$$\sum_{c=1}^{C} S(c) = \sum_{i=1}^{C} tr(w^T \mathbf{S}_c w) = tr(\sum_{i=1}^{C} w^T \mathbf{S}_c w) = w^T tr(\sum_{i=1}^{C} \mathbf{S}_c)w = w^T s_w w \qquad (7)$$

where s_w is within scatter matrix. We calculate the within scatter matrix for $x \in D = [D_s, D_t^l]$.

Between Scatter Matrix Calculation. To calculate the difference between samples with different applications, we calculate the distance between the mean of the samples of different applications. Assuming $\mu^{(}c)$ as the mean of samples with application c in the new space, we calculate the third term in Eq. 4 as follows:

$$\frac{1}{2} \sum_{c1=1}^{C} \sum_{c2=1}^{C} diff(c1, c2) = tr(\frac{1}{2} \sum_{c1=1}^{C} \sum_{c2=1}^{C} w^T (\mu^{c1} - \mu^{c2})^T (\mu^{c1} - \mu^{c2})w)$$

$$= w^T tr(\frac{1}{2} \sum_{c1=1}^{C} \sum_{c2=1}^{C} (\mu^{c1} - \mu^{c2})^T (\mu^{c1} - \mu^{c2}))w = w^T s_b w \qquad (8)$$

where s_b is the between scatter matrix. We calculate the within scatter matrix for $x \in D = [D_s, D_t^l]$.·

According to Eqs. 5, 7 and 8, the objective function in Eq. 4 is:

$$J(w) = w^T (x^T L x + s_w - s_b)w. \qquad (9)$$

We aim to find the best transformation matrix by minimizing the Eq. 9.

Let $w = [w_1, w_2, .., w_d]$. ; To avoid the trivial solution $w = 0$, we add the constraint to the optimization problem:

$$min \qquad \sum_{k=1}^{d} w_k^T (x^T L x + s_w - s_b) w_k \tag{10}$$
$$s.t. \qquad w_k^T w_k = I \qquad k = 1, 2, ..., d$$

To solve the optimization problem in Eq. 10, we define $\lambda = diag(\lambda_1, \lambda_2, ..., \lambda_d)$ as the Lagrange multiplier; Then we introduce a Lagrangian as follow:

$$L(w_k, \lambda_k) = \sum_{k=1}^{d} w_k^T (x L^{(c)} x - S_b + S_w) w_k \tag{11}$$
$$+ \lambda_k (I - w_k^T w_k)$$

The Lagrangian L must be minimized with respect to λ_k and w_k. Setting $\dfrac{\partial L(w_k, \lambda_k)}{w_k} = 0$, leads to

$$(x L^{(c)} x - S_b + S_w) w_k = \lambda_k w_k \tag{12}$$
$$k = 1, 2, ..., d$$

which means that the λ_ks are the eigenvalues of $(x L^{(c)} x - S_b + S_w)$ and the w_ks are the corresponding eigenvectors. Therefore, the criterion is minimized when w is composed of the first d smallest eigenvectors of $(x L^{(c)} x - S_b + S_w)$.

5 Experiments

5.1 Experimental Setup

Dataset: We carry out several experiments on the Brasil datasets [7] to examine the effectiveness of our proposed method.

Brasil datasets are recorded from two communication networks, SiteA and SiteB, which are research-centric networks. What differentiates SiteA and SiteB is they are located in different countries; In addition, research in various disciplines is carried out there. SiteA consists of three day-long sub-datasets denoted as Day1, Day2, and Day3. These datasets are taken on three weekdays in 2003, 2004, and 2006. As shown in Table 1, we construct five cross-domain datasets using these four available sub-datasets(Day1, Day2, Day3, SiteB) to investigate the effect of the domain adaptation between different networks. Two first cross-domain datasets correspond to the spatial problem in which data are collected from two different networks. The last three cross-domain correspond to temporal decay in which data are from the same network but at different times;

In all datasets, each sample corresponds to a flow and is defined by 12 features; the details about the features can be found in [7]. The features are

Table 1. Source and target datasets

Problem	Source network	Target network
Spatial	Day3	SiteB
	SiteB	Day3
Temporal	Day1	Day2
	Day2	Day3
	Day1	Day3

extracted from UDP, TCP, and IP headers of packets. For this paper, however, we use TCP traffics to perform our experiments.

Assuming TP as true positives, FN as false negatives, FP as false positives, and TN as true negatives, we calculate the overall accuracy as $Accuracy = \dfrac{TP + TN}{TP + TN + FP + FN}$. In addition we calculate F-measure as $F\_measure = \dfrac{2 * (Recall * Precision)}{Recall + Precision}$ where $Recall = \dfrac{TP}{TP + FN}$ and $Precision = \dfrac{TP}{TP + FP}$.

In order to validate the effectiveness of the proposed method, we carry out two sets of experiments: 1) With_DA 2) Without_DA. In the first case, we first apply the proposed method to construct a new shared feature space. We then train an SVM classifier on top of the constructed space using available labeled source and target samples. In the second case, we simply train an SVM classifier in the original space using available labeled source and target samples. We report the prediction results on the unlabeled target samples in both cases.

For all experiments, we use 10 percent of the labeled samples from the target network and the labeled samples from the source network. Although by adjusting weights for s_w, s_b and L in Eq. 11, we can improve the results, for simplicity, we ignore it.

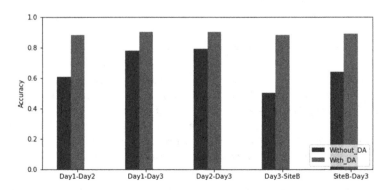

Fig. 1. Accuracy of traffic prediction in 5 cross-network datasets.

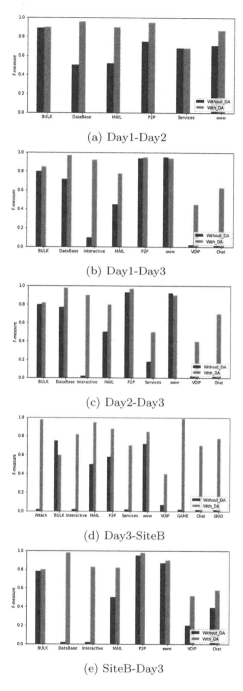

(a) Day1-Day2

(b) Day1-Day3

(c) Day2-Day3

(d) Day3-SiteB

(e) SiteB-Day3

Fig. 2. For 5 cross-domain scenarios the results are shown in terms of F-measure per application in target network. The captions of sub-figures show the source and target networks.

5.2   Results

Figure 1 shows the overall accuracy on the target domains in five cross-domain scenarios. This figure has five sets of bars, each corresponding to one cross-domain scenario. The label of each set of bars shows the source and target networks. For example, in the first one, Day1 is used as the source and Day2 as the target. The provided results are the accuracy of traffic prediction in target networks. For all cross-domain scenarios, we show the results With_DA and Without_DA. Comparing With_DA and Without_DA confirms the effect of using our proposed DA in prediction and turns out that DA has succeeded in improving the overall accuracy for all cross-network scenarios.

In addition, for each cross-domain scenario, we show the results in terms of the F-measure per application in Fig. 2. The results of the Day1-Day3 scenario are shown in the Fig. 2b. In this case, we don't have any sample from VOIP and Chat applications from the source domain, i.e., Day1 network. However, our method is able to detect them. This is also the case for the Day2-Day3 scenario shown in the Fig. 2c. In these two scenarios (Day1-Day3 and Day2-Day3), we can see a significant difference between the results of Without_DA and With_DA for Interactive applications. The reason behind this difference is that the datasets are imbalanced for this specific application; There are not enough samples for this application, neither in source nor target networks. However, our method can overcome this problem, resulting in a high F-measure. In the case of the Day3-SiteB scenario also, the source and target datasets are highly imbalanced. We can see the impact of our method in adapting the domains and overcoming this issue in Fig. 2d.

6   Conclusion

In this paper, we propose a new domain adaptation method for the purpose of network traffic classification. Since there may be different applications in source and target networks, we propose to adapt only the shared applications while retaining information about non-shared applications. As a result, the final constructed model will be applicable to all applications. This is achieved by minimizing the distribution distance between shared applications using the MMD criterion. Additionally, regardless of the domain of the samples, we minimize the distance between samples of each application and maximize the distance between different applications. We construct five cross-network datasets in order to evaluate our method. In three cases, the source and target samples come from the same network but are collected at different times; In two other cases, the source and target networks are totally different. Results show that our proposed method for ML-based network traffic classification is effective.

References

1. Borgwardt, K.M., Gretton, A., Rasch, M.J., Kriegel, H.P., Schölkopf, B., Smola, A.J.: Integrating structured biological data by kernel maximum mean discrepancy. Bioinformatics **22**(14), 49–57 (2006)

2. Callado, A., et al.: A survey on internet traffic identification. IEEE Commun. Surv. Tutorials **11**(3), 37–52 (2009)
3. CireAan, D., Meier, U., Masci, J., Schmidhuber, J.: Multi-column deep neural network for traffic sign classification. Neural Netw. **32**, 333–338 (2012)
4. Hu, X., Gu, C., Chen, Y., Wei, F.: TCLD-net: a transfer learning internet encrypted traffic classification scheme based on convolution neural network and long short-term memory network. In: 2021 International Conference on Communications, Computing, Cybersecurity, and Informatics (CCCI), pp. 1–5. IEEE (2021)
5. Li, D., Yuan, Q., Li, T., Chen, S., Yang, J.: Cross-domain network traffic classification using unsupervised domain adaptation. In: 2020 International Conference on Information Networking (ICOIN), pp. 245–250. IEEE (2020)
6. Li, H., Jiang, T., Zhang, K.: Efficient and robust feature extraction by maximum margin criterion. In: Advances in Neural Information Processing Systems 16 (2003)
7. Li, W., Canini, M., Moore, A.W., Bolla, R.: Efficient application identification and the temporal and spatial stability of classification schema. Comput. Netw. **53**(6), 790–809 (2009)
8. Lu, J., Behbood, V., Hao, P., Zuo, H., Xue, S., Zhang, G.: Transfer learning using computational intelligence: a survey. Knowl.-Based Syst. **80**, 14–23 (2015)
9. Mahdavi, E., Fanian, A., Mirzaei, A., Taghiyarrenani, Z.: ITL-IDS: Incremental transfer learning for intrusion detection systems. Knowl.-Based Syst. **253**(1), 109542 (2022). https://doi.org/10.1016/j.knosys.2022.109542
10. Michael, A.K.J., Valla, E., Neggatu, N.S., Moore, A.W.: Network traffic classification via neural networks. University of Cambridge, Computer Laboratory, Tech. rep. (2017)
11. Mika, S., Ratsch, G., Weston, J., Scholkopf, B., Mullers, K.R.: Fisher discriminant analysis with kernels. In: Neural networks for signal processing IX: Proceedings of the 1999 IEEE Signal Processing Society Workshop (cat. no. 98th8468), pp. 41–48. IEEE (1999)
12. Moore, A.W., Zuev, D.: Internet traffic classification using Bayesian analysis techniques. In: Proceedings of the 2005 ACM SIGMETRICS International Conference on Measurement and Modeling of Computer Systems, pp. 50–60 (2005)
13. Nguyen, T.T., Armitage, G.: A survey of techniques for internet traffic classification using machine learning. IEEE Commun. Surv. Tutorials **10**(4), 56–76 (2008)
14. Pacheco, F., Exposito, E., Gineste, M., Baudoin, C., Aguilar, J.: Towards the deployment of machine learning solutions in network traffic classification: a systematic survey. IEEE Commun. Surv. Tutorials **21**(2), 1988–2014 (2018)
15. Redko, I., Morvant, E., Habrard, A., Sebban, M., Bennani, Y.: A survey on domain adaptation theory: learning bounds and theoretical guarantees. arXiv preprint arXiv:2004.11829 (2020)
16. Sugiyama, M.: Introduction to statistical machine learning. Morgan Kaufmann (2015)
17. Sun, G., Chen, T., Su, Y., Li, C.: Internet traffic classification based on incremental support vector machines. Mob. Netw. Appl. **23**(4), 789–796 (2018)
18. Taghiyarrenani, Z., Fanian, A., Mahdavi, E., Mirzaei, A., Farsi, H.: Transfer learning based intrusion detection. In: 2018 8th International Conference on Computer and Knowledge Engineering (ICCKE), pp. 92–97. IEEE (2018)
19. Tobiyama, S., Hu, B., Kamiya, K., Takahashi, K.: Large-scale network-traffic-identification method with domain adaptation. In: Companion Proceedings of the Web Conference 2020, pp. 109–110 (2020)
20. Weiss, K., Khoshgoftaar, T.M., Wang, D.D.: A survey of transfer learning. J. Big Data **3**(1), 1–40 (2016). https://doi.org/10.1186/s40537-016-0043-6

Evaluation of the Limit of Detection in Network Dataset Quality Assessment with PerQoDA

Katarzyna Wasielewska[1]([✉])[iD], Dominik Soukup[2][iD], Tomáš Čejka[3][iD], and José Camacho[1][iD]

[1] Signal Theory, Networking and Communications Department, University of Granada, Granada, Spain
{k.wasielewska,josecamacho}@ugr.es
[2] Faculty of Information Technology, Czech Technical University in Prague, Prague, Czech Republic
soukudom@fit.cvut.cz
[3] CESNET a.l.e, Prague, Czech Republic
cejkat@cesnet.cz

Abstract. Machine learning is recognised as a relevant approach to detect attacks and other anomalies in network traffic. However, there are still no suitable network datasets that would enable effective detection. On the other hand, the preparation of a network dataset is not easy due to privacy reasons but also due to the lack of tools for assessing their quality. In a previous paper, we proposed a new method for data quality assessment based on permutation testing. This paper presents a parallel study on the limits of detection of such an approach. We focus on the problem of network flow classification and use well-known machine learning techniques. The experiments were performed using publicly available network datasets.

Keywords: Dataset quality assessment · Permutation testing · Network dataset · Network security · Attack detection · Machine learning · Classification

1 Introduction

Network security is a key research area today. Development in the field of the Internet goes hand in hand with increasing threats. Machine learning (ML) systems play a critical role in this field. However, ML techniques suffer of the "garbage-in-garbage-out" (GIGO) problem, meaning they can only be as good as the data they are trained on [26]. This is a fact that has serious consequences because, despite its high performance, the model may be ineffective when trained on a dataset that does not represent the real environment. This situation can easily happen if the ML model is moved to another network or there is a drift in input data.

I. Koprinska et al. (Eds.): ECML PKDD 2022 Workshops, CCIS 1753, pp. 170–185, 2023.
https://doi.org/10.1007/978-3-031-23633-4_13

Although the network traffic can be easily captured from the network, many papers noticed the lack of the high-quality network datasets [9, 27] and the problem of assessing the quality of datasets is overlooked. Scientists and practitioners tend to focus their efforts on optimizing ML models rather than on the quality of the datasets [7], and the research area related to assessing the quality of the dataset is overlooked. Dataset cleaning fixes well-known bugs in data but does not fix the problem of the quality. After removing duplicates, outliers, and errors resulting from technical problems or human activity, there are still problems with the completeness of the dataset, its accuracy, consistency, or uniqueness of the data, and these characteristics still remain difficult to assess [7]. In addition, problems such as class imbalance [25], class overlapping [12], noisy data [15], incorrect labels [10], or non-stationarity [33] are often unnoticed.

In this paper, we focus on the dataset quality assessment problem. In previous work, we presented how to use permutation testing for this task [8]. Our approach allows us to check whether the dataset contains enough information to predict a specific labeling, i.e., assignation of traffic units to the legitimate or attack class. We showed that the proposed methodology is able to effectively assess the quality of a network dataset by checking the relationship between the observations and labels. In this article, we highlight the problem of the sensitivity of this method to partial mislabeling, that is, the incorrect assignation of a subset of traffic units to the normal/attack classes, and demonstrate how to use our approach to capture even a small inconsistency.

The advantage of permutation testing [22, 23] is that the permutation tests create a null distribution that allows us to test the statistical significance of the performance results of a given ML classifier or set of classifiers. Moreover, as already shown in [21], permutation testing can be a useful tool to evaluate the impact of noisy data on the model performance.

In this paper, our contributions are as follows:

- We describe challenges for dataset quality assessment which are crucial for the effectiveness of machine learning-based network systems;
- We emphasize that a small problem in the network data may affect ML results;
- We experimentally investigate the limit of detection in our dataset quality assessment method based on permutation testing (PerQoDA) presented in [8, 32] and propose the change in our original methodology;
- We show how by permuting (even extremely) a small number of labels, we can detect small mislabeling problems in the dataset. These are important research results because, to the best of our knowledge, there are no methods that can detect mislabeling at such a high level of sensitivity.

The rest of the paper is organized as follows. Section 2 discusses related work in the literature. Section 3 provides an introduction to permutation testing, the details of the permutation-based methodology for assessing the quality of the dataset, and how to interpret the results. Section 4 describes the problem of the limit of detection in our method. Section 5 lists the results of the experiments carried out on real network datasets. Finally, Sect. 6 concludes the paper and discusses future work.

2 Related Work

Dataset quality evaluation is key in the analysis and modeling of big data [4], and it is of interest when developing new benchmarking datasets, critical for network security. Evaluating the dataset quality is challenging and must be done prior to any data modeling. While there are metrics that evaluate some important properties of a dataset (accuracy, completeness, consistency, timeliness, and others), these metrics often overlap [16]. Also, these metrics are more focused on the quality of data, and there is a lack of complete and proven methodologies for assessing the quality of datasets from a general perspective [30]. Soukup et al. [28] proposed general dataset quality definitions and an evaluation methodology of dataset quality based on selected performance measures between several versions of the dataset. Statistical methods were used to compare their results. However, no methods for overall evaluation were proposed.

Current research is mainly focused on data cleaning and optimization that can indirectly improve the dataset's quality. Taleb et al. [30] proposed quality evaluation scheme that analyzes the entire dataset and seeks to improve it. More metrics and proposals are part of future work. Another method is crowdsourcing, where experts perform small tasks to address difficult problems. There are many applications of this approach, for example, a query-oriented system for data cleaning with oracle crowds [5] or a technique that improves the quality of labels by repeatedly labeling each sample and creating integrated labels [34]. Another technique is metamorphic testing, originally developed to evaluate software quality and verify relations among a group of test outputs with corresponding test inputs [36]. Auer et al. [3] proposed to use this method to assess the quality of data expressing data as functions and defining metamorphic relations on these functions. Ding et al. [11] showed another application of metamorphic tests that were used to assess the fidelity, diversity, and validity of datasets on a large scale. The authors of [31] proposed a black-box technique that uses metamorphic tests to find mislabeled observations for which there is a probability that the metamorphic transformations will cause an error. Erroneous labels are found using entropy analysis, which leverages information about the output uncertainty. Additional options for dataset optimization are transfer learning [24] and knowledge graphs [6] that were used to detect information gaps and semantic problems. There is also an approach using reinforcement learning [35]. This meta learning framework explores how likely it is that each training sample will be used in training the predictive model.

Apruzzese et al. [2] proposed semisupervised methods within the framework of active learning. This is very beneficial to improve the current dataset but it cannot be used to evaluate quality. Moreover, Joyce et al. [17] is focused on the unlabeled part of the dataset. The proposed solution can detect problematic traits of dataset that can lead to over-fitting. However, the quality measure is missing, and domain knowledge is required. Engelen et al. [14] is focused on dataset quality assessment, however, the dataset is analyzed manually based on deep domain knowledge.

In the paper [8], we proposed a permutation-based assessment methodology that allows the analyst to conveniently check whether the information contained in the dataset is rich enough to classify observations precisely. Our method can detect inconsistencies in the relationships between observations and labels in multidimensional datasets. We also proposed a scalar metric allowing us to compare two versions of a dataset (e.g., after some differential preprocessing) in terms of quality [32]. We focus on supervised binary classification problems and estimate dataset quality without input data or hyperparameters optimization.

In this article, we explore the detection limits of our approach and show how to detect small imperfections in large datasets.

3   Background

In this section, we describe the permutation testing method, introduce an approach that uses permutation tests to assess the quality of a dataset, and explain how to interpret the results.

3.1   Permutation Testing

Permutation tests are a form of statistical inference which does not rely on assumptions about the data distribution [23]. Thanks to this approach, we can test if there is a significant relationship between the content of a traffic dataset and its corresponding labeling. For that, we define the so-called null hypothesis that the association of the traffic and the labeling is mild enough so that it could be the result of randomness, and we test whether this hypothesis could be rejected.

Permutation testing relies on random sampling. We repeatedly shuffle (i.e., permute) the selected data and check if the unpermitted (real) data comes from the same population as the resamples. To compute the p-value, we typically take the number of test statistics computed after permutations that are greater than the initial test statistic and divide it by the number of permutations. If the p-value is less than or equal to the selected significance level, we can reject the null hypothesis and accept the alternative hypothesis, which reflects that the relationship between traffic and labels is statistically significant.

3.2   Dataset Quality Assessment Based on the Permutation Testing

In short, our method presented in [8] is to calculate the model performance after each permutation and see how many times that performance was better than the model performance on the original data (true results). If this happens many times, it would mean that our dataset is so random that it does not allow classifiers to learn an accurate classification model. Since we want to assess the quality of the dataset and not the quality of a specific ML classification strategy, our approach is based on a pool of classifiers (from the simplest to complex and from traditional to the state-of-the-art). In our method, we only permute labels and examine the relationship between observations and labels. For each classifier, after P permutations, we obtain P performance results. Then we compare each result with the true performance result and compute a p-value. The obtained p-value table allows us to evaluate the quality of the dataset.

Let M be the model performance[1] calculated from the original dataset and M^* the model performance computed after permutation. The p-value can be defined as follows [1]:

$$\text{p-value} = \frac{\text{No. of } (M^* \geq M) + 1}{\text{Total no. of } M^* + 1} \tag{1}$$

In our method, we set the significance level to 0.01, and we define the null hypothesis as that the association between observations and labels in the dataset is the simple result of chance. This means that if the p-value > 0.01, the null hypothesis cannot be rejected. Therefore the dataset has a weak relationship between observations and labels. On the other hand, if the p-value ≤ 0.01, we can reject the null hypothesis and conclude that the relationship is significantly strong.

We assess the statistical significance of the performance results permuting a selected part of the dataset, not just the whole dataset. We run permutation tests for different label percentages (for example, 50%, 25%, 10%, 5%, 1%). By taking an increasing number of labels into the permutation, we are able to identify different levels of quality in the data, that is, of association between data and labels. Note these set of tests are incremental and as such we did not apply corrections on the significance level (e.g., Bonferroni corrections).

Let $(\mathbf{X}, \mathbf{y})$ be a dataset, where $\mathbf{X}$ is the set of observations and $\mathbf{y}$ is the set of labels. To evaluate the quality of the dataset, we perform the following steps:

1. Train a pool of classifiers using the original dataset $(\mathbf{X}, \mathbf{y})$
2. Evaluate each model using the selected metric
3. Permute selected percentage of the labels $\mathbf{y}$ to get new labels $\mathbf{y_p}$ and new dataset $(\mathbf{X}, \mathbf{y_p})$
4. Train the pool of classifiers on the dataset $(\mathbf{X}, \mathbf{y_p})$
5. Evaluate each model with the selected performance metric
6. For y_p and y, compute the correlation coefficient
7. Repeat the steps 3 through 6, P times
8. Calculate p-value according to Eq. (1)
9. Repeat the steps 7 and 8 for each value of percentage

The proposed approach works for both balanced and imbalanced datasets because it is finding trends in permutations [32].

3.3   Visualisation and Interpretation

After the procedure described in Sect. 3.2, we get a pool of performance results after permutations and a p-value table. To assess the performance results, we

---

[1] We can choose any performance metric such as accuracy, precision, recall, etc.

combine a permutation chart and a p-value table. If at least one classifier shows statistical significance in all permutation percentages, we can deem the dataset as *good*. The reason is that we can find at least one ML method that can identify the relationship between data and labels. If no ML method shows significant results at any permutation level, the data should be considered of *bad* quality. Any result in between these two extreme outputs reflect a partial level of quality, which grows with the number of permutation percentages in which we find at least one significant classification model.

An example of the visualisation of the performance results is shown in Fig. 1b. Consider the dataset presented in Fig. 1a. This dataset is of good quality because the classes are well separated, so we expect the ML algorithms to perform very well on this data. In the permutation chart, we can see the true performance results (shown by diamonds) and all the performance results after permutations (shown by circles). Each performance result after permutation is located depending on the correlation between the original labeling and the permuted one [18]. We can notice that the true performance is high (equal to or close to 1) as expected, and the results after each permutation are lower than the true results (what is also expected if the dataset is of good quality). The lowest performance at different percentage levels is marked with a red dashed horizontal line. This can be interpreted as a *baseline of randomness*. This value can sometimes be unexpectedly high and should therefore be observed (in this case, it is around 0.55).

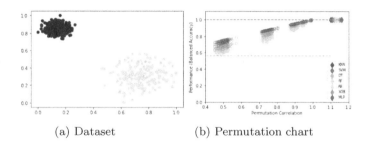

(a) Dataset   (b) Permutation chart

Fig. 1. Dataset (a) and the permutation chart (b) (Color figure online)

As can be seen in the p-value table (Table 1), all performance results are statistically significant. All classifiers at all permutation levels reject the null hypothesis (the symbol . represents the value ≤ 0.01). This means a very strong relationship exists between the observations and the labels in the original dataset.

Additionally, in the previous work [32] we proposed a scalar metric for comparing datasets. We defined a *slope* metric that corresponds to the slope of the regression line fitted to the points representing the classifier's performance scores (obtained after permutations) at different permutation levels (see Fig. 1b). Thus, we got one slope per classifier, the largest of which was defined as a measure of the quality of the dataset (in this case, the slope is approximately 0.75).

Table 1. p-value table: p-values less than or equal to the significance level 0.01 are replaced by a dot.

	50%	25%	10%	5%	1%
KNN	.	.	.	.	.
SVM	.	.	.	.	.
DT	.	.	.	.	.
RF	.	.	.	.	.
AB	.	.	.	.	.
XGB	.	.	.	.	.
MLP	.	.	.	.	.

4   Limits of Detection

In the dataset quality assessment method described in Sect. 3.2, we permute the selected percentage of the labels. However, taking 1% of the labels in a large dataset, we may not notice problems in the relationship between $\mathbf{X}$ and $\mathbf{y}$ in a minor number of instances. Since we want to detect as minor mislabelling problems as possible in the dataset, intuitively, we should permute the smallest possible number of labels. This will allow us to establish the limit of detection (LOD) of our approach. In chemistry, this term is defined as the lowest concentration of an analyte that can be reliably detected with statistical significance (for example, with 95% certainty) using a given analytical procedure [19]. Based on these considerations, this paper examines the LOD of our approach, that is, how well we can detect minor problems in datasets.

In order to investigate the limit of detection in our dataset quality evaluation method, we will perform permutation tests on a very small number of observations (for example, 100, 50, 25, 10, 5, 1), regardless of the size of the dataset. By permuting such a small fraction of the labels, we can evaluate the performance loss (if any) at a high level of detection. This allows us to assess the relevance of very small parts of the dataset and consequently assess the accuracy of the labeling of the entire dataset, i.e., to evaluate its overall quality. It is also worth noting that we will have high correlation coefficient values for a large dataset because we only change a small part of the labels.

In practice, we make one change to the algorithm presented in Sect. 3.2. We will permute the same small number of labels in each dataset instead of a percentage (in step 3).

The theoretical foundations of the above considerations can be found in our work [32], in which we explained why our method of assessing the quality of a dataset is more sensitive at low permutation percentages.

5   Experiments

In this section, we present the results of the experiments with the LOD in the permutation-based dataset quality assessment method. We also present ML techniques and performance metrics that were used in the procedure. We present two case studies conducted on the publicly available real network datasets.

5.1 ML Algorithms

In our experiments, we used a pool of well-know supervised ML methods: K Nearest Neighbours (KNN), kernel Support Vector Machine (SVM), Decision Tree (DT), Random Forest (RF), AdaBoost (AB), XGBoost (XGB), and multi-layer perceptron (MLP). The DT, RF, AB and XGB classifiers had a weight class option set to "balanced". The other hyperparameters were the default. We used the standard stratified 2-fold cross-validation (CV) with shuffling the data before splitting into batches. In other words, datasets were split into two sets (for training and testing) keeping the percentage of samples for each class, the models were then trained on one split and evaluated in the other twice, and the performance results were averaged. Data has been scaled to range $[0, 1]$. We used the Weles tool [29] to automate the generation of results.

5.2 Evaluation Metric

Our dataset quality assessment method can be used with different performance metrics [32]. For this paper, we selected a recall metric, which directly reflects the number of detected anomalies, i.e., the percentage of correctly classified positives, and which can arguably be considered especially relevant in cybersecurity research. The recall is defined as follows:

$$\text{Recall} = \frac{\text{TP}}{\text{TP} + \text{FN}} \tag{2}$$

where TP is the number of correctly predicted undesired traffic (True Positives), and FN is the number of anomalous traffic classified as normal traffic (False Negatives).

5.3 Case Studies

In this section, we present the results of the experiments on real datasets. We used publicly available datasets: inSDN and UGR16. In all experiments, we considered the following fixed number of permuted labels (instead of percentages): 100, 50, 25, 10, 5, and 1 (from each class), and we conducted 200 permutations. We focused on the binary classification problem.

Case Study 1: inSDN Dataset

The inSDN dataset is a publicly available network flow-based dataset that contains 68,424 normal (legitimate) and 275,465 attack observations captured in a Software Defined Network (SDN) environment [13]. The inSDN dataset includes attacks on the Open vSwitch (OVS) machine as well as the server-directed

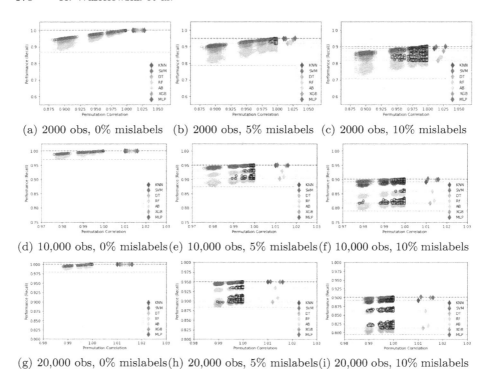

(a) 2000 obs, 0% mislabels   (b) 2000 obs, 5% mislabels   (c) 2000 obs, 10% mislabels

(d) 10,000 obs, 0% mislabels(e) 10,000 obs, 5% mislabels(f) 10,000 obs, 10% mislabels

(g) 20,000 obs, 0% mislabels(h) 20,000 obs, 5% mislabels(i) 20,000 obs, 10% mislabels

Fig. 2. Permutation charts for the inSDN datasets

attacks: DoS, probe, brute force attacks (BFA), password-guessing (R2L), web application attacks, and botnet. The inSDN dataset contains 83 traffic features.

In this scenario, we assessed the quality of the dataset against the problem of distinguishing Probe attacks from normal traffic. We created balanced datasets (prevalence[2] = 0.5) with 2000, 10,000, and 20,000 observations. We removed the following features: Timestamp, Flow ID, Src IP, Dst IP, Src Port, Dst Port, and Protocol. To the original datasets, we introduced 0%, 5% and 10% mislabels. Mislabels were injected randomly to both the normal data and attack data (in the same proportions), and were present in the training set and test set. Our goal was to capture the quality difference between original and mislabeled datasets. Using the permutation strategy described in Sect. 4, we permute a maximum of 5% (100/2000), 1% (100/10,000), and 0.5% (100/20,000) of the labels of the first, second and third dataset, respectively.

The results of the dataset quality assessment with our permutation approach is shown in Fig. 2 and Table 2. As expected, we can see that mislabeled datasets are of lower quality than the original ones. All original samples are of a good quality (even in case of the dataset with 20,000 observations and 0% mislabels we have at least one classifier with statistically significant results). However, in

---

[2] percentage of positives in the dataset.

Table 2. p-value tables for the inSDN datasets. P-values above significance level 0.01 are marked in red, lower p-values are replaced by dot.

	2000 obs 0% mislabels							2000 obs 5% mislabels							2000 obs 10% mislabels						
	100	50	25	10	5	2	1	100	50	25	10	5	2	1	100	50	25	10	5	2	1
KNN	.	.	.	.	.	.02	.02	.	.	.	.	.01	.08	.16	.	.	.	.05	.13	.18	.14
SVM	.	.	.	.	.	.02	.02	.	.	.	.	.02	.13	.15	.	.	.	.	.07	.25	.31
DT	.	.	.	.	.	.	.	.	.	.02	.18	.21	.33	.38	.	.04	.26	.51	.66	.62	.64
RF	.	.	.	.	.	.	.	.	.	.12	.66	.81	.91	.89	.	.	.10	.32	.51	.52	.56
AB	.	.	.	.	.	.	.	.	.	.01	.13	.17	.24	.32	.	.06	.26	.52	.70	.68	.68
XGB	.	.	.	.	.	.	.	.	.	.42	.86	.94	.95	.97	.	.	.05	.23	.38	.43	.41
MLP	.	.	.	.	.	.03	.01	.	.	.	.	.02	.17	.21	.	.	.	.12	.34	.74	.74

	10,000 obs 0% mislabels							10,000 obs 5% mislabels							10,000 obs 10% mislabels						
	100	50	25	10	5	2	1	100	50	25	10	5	2	1	100	50	25	10	5	2	1
KNN	.	.	.	.	.	.	.	.	.	.	.06	.15	.28	.30	.	.	.06	.17	.21	.22	.30
SVM	.	.	.	.	.	.02	.05	.	.	.	.	.02	.11	.10	.	.	.	.	.03	.15	.19
DT	.	.	.	.	.	.	.	.	.	.01	.05	.06	.10	.12	.01	.12	.35	.53	.56	.53	.55
RF	.	.	.	.	.	.	.	.	.	.	.08	.13	.10	.15	.	.	.	.05	.07	.05	.04
AB	.	.	.	.	.	.	.	.	.	.02	.03	.07	.06	.07	.	.02	.08	.20	.17	.14	.16
XGB	.	.	.	.	.	.	.	.	.	.	.01	.05	.11	.10	.	.	.01	.09	.15	.17	.19
MLP	.	.	.	.	.03	.19	.21	.	.	.	.	.03	.19	.22	.	.	.	.02	.06	.21	.26

	20,000 obs 0% mislabels							20,000 obs 5% mislabels							20,000 obs 10% mislabels						
	100	50	25	10	5	2	1	100	50	25	10	5	2	1	100	50	25	10	5	2	1
KNN	.	.	.	.	.	.	.	.	.	.10	.47	.60	.66	.69	.	.	.07	.17	.20	.23	.25
SVM	.	.	.	.	.05	.22	.24	.	.	.	.02	.09	.27	.24	.	.	.	.02	.16	.48	.48
DT	.	.	.	.	.05	.26	.27	.	.06	.26	.46	.46	.49	.56	.11	.38	.55	.68	.67	.68	.68
RF	.	.	.	.	.18	.46	.50	.	.	.05	.15	.15	.16	.18	.04	.21	.42	.55	.60	.61	.61
AB	.	.	.	.	.08	.30	.44	.	.05	.12	.28	.36	.32	.39	.14	.41	.54	.61	.73	.68	.68
XGB	.	.	.	.01	.30	.59	.65	.	.	.	.02	.13	.43	.33	.	.	.15	.63	.80	.80	.81
MLP	.	.	.	.03	.03	.57	.56	.	.	.	.	.04	.19	.24	.	.	.	.08	.27	.67	.65

the permutation charts depicted in Fig. 2, we see black circles indicating that the performance results after permutations were better than in the original dataset. In the case of mislabeled datasets, we cannot reject the hypothesis that the dataset is random as all classifiers do not have significant results when we permute 1, 2, and 5 labels. Note that if the smallest percentage were 1%, we would not be able to detect relationship problems in datasets with 10,000 and 20,000 observations having 5% mislabels (because for these datasets 1% means 100 and 200 labels, respectively, and for these permutation levels the performance results are statistically significant). Moreover, these datasets would most likely have statistically significant performance scores for 5% permutation level as well, since typically, if the results are statistically significant at some level of permutation, they're also statistically significant if more labels are permuted.

The slope analysis also confirms that the mislabeled datasets are worse than the original dataset (Table 3). The original good-quality datasets have the highest slope values, and the datasets with 10% incorrect labels have the lowest slope.

It is worth noting, however, that for all analyzed samples, we can find ML techniques which achieved true performance results above 0.9 (Table 4), and, in research practice, without the dataset quality evaluation, they could be

Table 3. The slopes computed for the inSDN consecutive normal observations and Probe/OVS attack data (samples without and with mislabels)

Dataset	0% mislabels		5% mislabels		10% mislabels	
2000 obs	0.97279	DT	0.78068	DT	0.60636	RF
10,000 obs	1.04494	AB	0.82356	DT	0.70278	AB
20,000 obs	1.04837	DT	0.85276	DT	0.63686	DT

Table 4. inSDN datasets - true performance results (recall)

	2000 obs 0% mislabels	2000 obs 5% mislabels	2000 obs 10% mislabels
KNN	1.0	0.951	0.899
SVM	1.0	0.95	0.9
DT	1.0	0.907	0.814
RF	1.0	0.921	0.852
AB	1.0	0.908	0.816
XGB	1.0	0.926	0.881
MLP	1.0	0.95	0.9
	10,000 obs 0% mislabels	10,000 obs 5% mislabels	10,000 obs 10% mislabels
KNN	1.0	0.948	0.891
SVM	1.0	0.951	0.902
DT	1.0	0.901	0.814
RF	1.0	0.93	0.854
AB	1.0	0.909	0.822
XGB	1.0	0.949	0.902
MLP	1.0	0.95	0.9
	20,000 obs 0% mislabels	20,000 obs 5% mislabels	20,000 obs 10% mislabels
KNN	1.0	0.948	0.893
SVM	1.0	0.95	0.902
DT	1.0	0.9	0.809
RF	1.0	0.936	0.864
AB	1.0	0.91	0.82
XGB	1.0	0.95	0.9
MLP	1.0	0.95	0.901

considered to be of good quality. In particular, the datasets with 5% mislabels have quite high performance results (even 0.95), and without the analysis with a method like the one we propose, they could be considered as good-quality datasets.

Case Study 2: UGR16 Dataset

Another publicly available dataset we assessed was the UGR16 dataset [20]. This dataset contains Netflow flows taken from a real Tier 3 ISP network composed of virtualized and hosted services of many companies and clients. The network traffic was captured on the border routers, so this dataset contains all the incoming and outgoing traffic from the ISP. The UGR16 dataset contains 142 features and includes attack traffic (DoS, port scanning, and botnet) against fake victims generated by 25 virtual machines that were deployed within the network.

We tested three versions of this dataset depending on whether the flows in the dataset were unidirectional or bidirectional and whether the traffic was anonymized during parsing or not (Table 5). The original dataset (V1) contains unidirectional flows that were obtained from Netflow using the nfdump tool without using the -B option which creates bidirectional flows and maintain proper ordering. After the V1 dataset was anonymized, we created two additional datasets: V2 with the -B option enabled and V3 without this option. Additionally, V2 and V3 datasets were devoid of features identifying Internet Relay Chat (IRC) flows (Src IRC Port, Dst IRC Port) that were seen to have a deep impact in the detection of the botnet in the test data. After parsing, the datasets consisted of 12,960 observations containing flows aggregated at one-minute intervals (1006 observations with attack data). These datasets were highly imbalanced with prevalence = 0.078.

Table 5. UGR16 dataset versions

Dataset	Direction	-B option	Anonymization	IRC
V1	Unidirectional	–	–	✓
V2	Bidirectional	✓	✓	–
V3	Unidirectional	–	✓	–

The results of the UGR16 dataset quality assessment with our permutation-based approach are shown in Fig. 3, Table 6, and Table 7. As you can see, the original dataset (V1) is not perfect, and the high quality of the labeling is questionable. All ML techniques do not produce significant results for 1, 2, 5, and 10 permuted labels. Additionally, enabling option -B (V2) resulted in deterioration of the quality of the dataset (the RF algorithm is an exception, although it also has statistically insignificant results). It is also worth noting that anonymization lowered the quality of the dataset which is surprising and should be investigated in the future in more detail. True performance results are presented in Table 8.

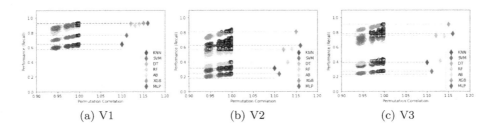

(a) V1   (b) V2   (c) V3

Fig. 3. Permutation charts for the UGR16 datasets

Table 6. p-value tables for the UGR16 datasets. P-values above significance level 0.01 are marked in red, lower p-values are replaced by dot.

	V1							V2							V3						
	100	50	25	10	5	2	1	100	50	25	10	5	2	1	100	50	25	10	5	2	1
KNN	.	.	.01	.07	.12	.13	.17	.	.07	.30	.40	.50	.56	.54	.	.04	.15	.28	.35	.46	.41
SVM	.	.	.	.15	.36	.53	.58	.	.02	.04	.12	.18	.17	.22	.	.01	.22	.62	.81	.86	.82
DT	.	.	.	.05	.18	.32	.37	.03	.26	.51	.63	.66	.70	.72	.	.	.12	.29	.42	.53	.52
RF	.	.	.	.08	.20	.24	.24	.	.	.	.02	.04	.10	.04	.	.03	.35	.64	.68	.77	.82
AB	.	.	.	.05	.21	.33	.35	.03	.09	.32	.41	.43	.54	.52	.	.04	.22	.51	.54	.65	.65
XGB	.	.	.	.16	.48	.70	.64	.	.	.17	.57	.68	.78	.83	.	.	.	.08	.20	.22	.29
MLP	.	.	.	.07	.15	.30	.31	.13	.55	.87	.96	.96	.99	.98	.	.13	.41	.53	.58	.63	.58

Table 7. The slopes computed for the UGR16 datasets

	V1		V2		V3	
Slope	1.88207	AB	1.49998	MLP	1.48212	MLP

Table 8. UGR16 datasets - true performance results (recall)

	V1	V2	V3
KNN	0.641	0.315	0.391
SVM	0.762	0.236	0.268
DT	0.917	0.565	0.753
RF	0.896	0.395	0.411
AB	0.916	0.575	0.746
XGB	0.926	0.807	0.903
MLP	0.923	0.62	0.778

6   Conclusions

Machine learning techniques require high-quality datasets. An effective method for assessing the quality of a dataset helps understand how the quality of the dataset affects the performance results and can be instrumental to solve problems related to the degradation of the model performance after the move to production. We believe that the dataset quality has to be addressed and assessed prior to any ML application.

In our previous papers [8, 32], we presented an effective method for the dataset quality assessment based on the permutation testing. The technique is based on well-known ML classifiers. In this paper, we investigated the limits of detection of this methodology, that is, how sensitive is our method to small quality problems in the dataset. For that purpose, we investigated deep permutations, that is, permutations of very small parts of the datasets. The theoretical basis and the conducted experiments prove that the method is effective. It is worth adding, however, that our method allows for the evaluation of a dataset, but does not solve the problem of building a high-quality dataset.

In future work, we aim to define the general slope metric more appropriate for assessing every dataset, which will include the solution of the detection limit. Also, we would like to leverage available metadata to describe Root Cause Analysis (RCA) of quality decrease. Moreover, we plan to improve the implementation of the proposed method to allow higher adoption in the community.

Acknowledgment. This work is partially funded by the European Union's Horizon 2020 research, innovation programme under the Marie Skłodowska-Curie grant agreement No 893146, by the Agencia Estatal de Investigación in Spain, grant No PID2020-113462RB-I00, and by the Ministry of Interior of the Czech Republic (Flow-Based Encrypted Traffic Analysis) under grant number VJ02010024. The authors would like to thank Szymon Wojciechowski for his support on the Weles tool.

References

1. Anderson, M.J.: Permutational multivariate analysis of variance (PERMANOVA), pp. 1–15. Wiley (2017). https://doi.org/10.1002/9781118445112.stat07841
2. Apruzzese, G., Laskov, P., Tastemirova, A.: SoK: the impact of unlabelled data in cyberthreat detection, May 2022. https://doi.org/10.48550/arXiv.2205.08944
3. Auer, F., Felderer, M.: Addressing data quality problems with metamorphic data relations. In: IEEE/ACM 4th International Workshop on Metamorphic Testing (MET), pp. 76–83 (2019). https://doi.org/10.1109/MET.2019.00019
4. Batarseh, F.A., Freeman, L., Huang, C.-H.: A survey on artificial intelligence assurance. J. Big Data **8**(1), 1–30 (2021). https://doi.org/10.1186/s40537-021-00445-7
5. Bergman, M., Milo, T., Novgorodov, S., Tan, W.C.: Query-oriented data cleaning with oracles. In: Proceedings of the 2015 ACM SIGMOD International Conference on Management of Data, SIGMOD 2015, pp. 1199–1214. Association for Computing Machinery, New York (2015). https://doi.org/10.1145/2723372.2737786
6. Bhatt, S., Sheth, A., Shalin, V., Zhao, J.: Knowledge graph semantic enhancement of input data for improving AI. IEEE Internet Comput. **24**(2), 66–72 (2020). https://doi.org/10.1109/MIC.2020.2979620

7. Caiafa, C.F., Zhe, S., Toshihisa, T., Pere, M.P., Solé-Casals, J.: Machine learning methods with noisy, incomplete or small datasets. Appl. Sci. **11**(9) (2021). https://doi.org/10.3390/app11094132

8. Camacho, J., Wasielewska, K.: Dataset quality assessment in autonomous networks with permutation testing. In: IEEE/IFIP Network Operations and Management Symposium (NOMS), pp. 1–4 (2022). https://doi.org/10.1109/NOMS54207.2022.9789767

9. Caviglione, L., et al.: Tight arms race: overview of current malware threats and trends in their detection. IEEE Access **9**, 5371–5396 (2021). https://doi.org/10.1109/ACCESS.2020.3048319

10. Cordeiro, F.R., Carneiro, G.: A survey on deep learning with noisy labels: how to train your model when you cannot trust on the annotations? In: 33rd SIB-GRAPI Conference on Graphics, Patterns and Images (SIBGRAPI), pp. 9–16 (2020). https://doi.org/10.1109/SIBGRAPI51738.2020.00010

11. Ding, J., Li, X.: An approach for validating quality of datasets for machine learning. In: 2018 IEEE International Conference on Big Data (Big Data), pp. 2795–2803 (2018). https://doi.org/10.1109/BigData.2018.8622640

12. Dudjak, M., Martinovic, G.: An empirical study of data intrinsic characteristics that make learning from imbalanced data difficult. Expert Syst. Appl. **182**, 115297 (2021)

13. Elsayed, M.S., Le-Khac, N.A., Jurcut, A.D.: InSDN: a novel SDN intrusion dataset. IEEE Access **8**, 165263–165284 (2020). https://doi.org/10.1109/ACCESS.2020.3022633

14. Engelen, G., Rimmer, V., Joosen, W.: Troubleshooting an intrusion detection dataset: the CICIDS2017 case study. In: 2021 IEEE Security and Privacy Workshops (SPW) (2021). https://doi.org/10.1109/SPW53761.2021.00009

15. Gupta, S., Gupta, A.: Dealing with noise problem in machine learning data-sets: a systematic review. Procedia Comput. Sci. **161**, 466–474 (2019). https://doi.org/10.1016/j.procs.2019.11.146. 5th Information Systems International Conference, Surabaya, Indonesia

16. Ibrahim, M., Helmy, Y., Elzanfaly, D.: Data quality dimensions, metrics, and improvement techniques. Future Comput. Inform. J. **6**, 25–44 (2021). https://doi.org/10.54623/fue.fcij.6.1.3

17. Joyce, R.J., Raff, E., Nicholas, C.: A framework for cluster and classifier evaluation in the absence of reference labels. In: AISec 2021. Association for Computing Machinery, New York (2021). https://doi.org/10.1145/3474369.3486867

18. Lindgren, F., Hansen, B., Karcher, W., Sjöström, M., Eriksson, L.: Model validation by permutation tests: applications to variable selection. J. Chemometr. **10**(5–6), 521–532 (1996)

19. MacDougall, D., Crummett, W.B.: Guidelines for data acquisition and data quality evaluation in environmental chemistry. Anal. Chem. **52**(14), 2242–2249 (1980). https://doi.org/10.1021/ac50064a004

20. Maciá-Fernández, G., Camacho, J., Magán-Carrión, R., García-Teodoro, P., Therón, R.: UGR'16: a new dataset for the evaluation of cyclostationarity-based network IDSs. Comput. Secur. **73**, 411–424 (2018). https://doi.org/10.1016/j.cose.2017.11.004

21. Ojala, M., Garriga, G.: Permutation tests for studying classifier performance. J. Mach. Learn. Res. **11**, 1833–1863 (2010)

22. Pesarin, F., Salmaso, L.: The permutation testing approach: a review. Statistica (Bologna) **70**(4), 481–509 (2010)

23. Pesarin, F., Salmaso, L.: A review and some new results on permutation testing for multivariate problems. Stat. Comput. **22**(2), 639–646 (2012). https://doi.org/ 10.1007/s11222-011-9261-0

24. Pin, K., Kim, J.Y., Chang, J.H., Nam, Y.: Quality evaluation of fundus images using transfer learning. In: International Conference on Computational Science and Computational Intelligence (CSCI), pp. 742–744 (2020). https://doi.org/10. 1109/CSCI51800.2020.00139

25. Sahu, A., Mao, Z., Davis, K., Goulart, A.E.: Data processing and model selection for machine learning-based network intrusion detection. In: 2020 IEEE International Workshop Technical Committee on Communications Quality and Reliability (CQR), pp. 1–6 (2020). https://doi.org/10.1109/CQR47547.2020.9101394

26. Sarker, I.H., Kayes, A.S.M., Badsha, S., Alqahtani, H., Watters, P., Ng, A.: Cybersecurity data science: an overview from machine learning perspective. J. Big Data **7**(1), 1–29 (2020). https://doi.org/10.1186/s40537-020-00318-5

27. Shaukat, K., Luo, S., Varadharajan, V., Hameed, I.A., Xu, M.: A survey on machine learning techniques for cyber security in the last decade. IEEE Access **8**, 222310–222354 (2020). https://doi.org/10.1109/ACCESS.2020.3041951

28. Soukup, D., Tisovčík, P., Hynek, K., Čejka, T.: Towards evaluating quality of datasets for network traffic domain. In: 17th International Conference on Network and Service Management (CNSM), pp. 264–268 (2021). https://doi.org/10.23919/ CNSM52442.2021.9615601

29. Stapor, K., Ksieniewicz, P., García, S., Woźniak, M.: How to design the fair experimental classifier evaluation. Appl. Soft Comput. **104**, 107219 (2021). https://doi. org/10.1016/j.asoc.2021.107219

30. Taleb, I., El Kassabi, H., Serhani, M., Dssouli, R., Bouhaddioui, C.: Big data quality: a quality dimensions evaluation, July 2016. https://doi.org/10.1109/UIC-ATC-ScalCom-CBDCom-IoP-SmartWorld.2016.0122

31. Udeshi, S., Jiang, X., Chattopadhyay, S.: Callisto: entropy-based test generation and data quality assessment for machine learning systems. In: IEEE 13th International Conference on Software Testing, Validation and Verification (ICST), Los Alamitos, CA, USA, pp. 448–453. IEEE Computer Society, October 2020. https:// doi.org/10.1109/ICST46399.2020.00060

32. Wasielewska, K., Soukup, D., Čejka, T., Camacho, J.: Dataset quality assessment with permutation testing showcased on network traffic datasets, June 2022. https://doi.org/10.36227/techrxiv.20145539.v1

33. Webb, G.I., Lee, L.K., Goethals, B., Petitjean, F.: Analyzing concept drift and shift from sample data. Data Min. Knowl. Disc. **32**(5), 1179–1199 (2018). https:// doi.org/10.1007/s10618-018-0554-1

34. Wu, M., et al.: Learning deep networks with crowdsourcing for relevance evaluation. EURASIP J. Wirel. Commun. Netw. **2020**(1), 1–11 (2020). https://doi.org/10. 1186/s13638-020-01697-2

35. Yoon, J., Arik, S., Pfister, T.: Data valuation using reinforcement learning. In Proceedings of the 37th International Conference on Machine Learning. Proceedings of Machine Learning Research, vol. 119, pp. 10842–10851 (2020). https://proceedings. mlr.press/v119/yoon20a.html

36. Zhou, Z.Q., Xiang, S., Chen, T.Y.: Metamorphic testing for software quality assessment: a study of search engines. IEEE Trans. Softw. Eng. **42**(3), 264–284 (2016). https://doi.org/10.1109/TSE.2015.2478001

Towards a General Model for Intrusion Detection: An Exploratory Study

Tommaso Zoppi(✉) [ID], Andrea Ceccarelli [ID], and Andrea Bondavalli [ID]

Department of Mathematics and Informatics, University of Florence, Viale Morgagni 65, 50142 Florence, Italy
tommaso.zoppi@unifi.it

Abstract. Exercising Machine Learning (ML) algorithms to detect intrusions is nowadays the de-facto standard for data-driven detection tasks. This activity requires the expertise of the researchers, practitioners, or employees of companies that also have to gather labeled data to learn and evaluate the model that will then be deployed into a specific system. Reducing the expertise and time required to craft intrusion detectors is a tough challenge, which in turn will have an enormous beneficial impact in the domain. This paper conducts an exploratory study that aims at understanding to which extent it is possible to build an intrusion detector that is general enough to learn the model once and then be applied to different systems with minimal to no effort. Therefore, we recap the issues that may prevent building general detectors and propose software architectures that have the potential to overcome them. Then, we perform an experimental evaluation using several binary ML classifiers and a total of 16 feature learners on 4 public attack datasets. Results show that a model learned on a dataset or a system does not generalize well as is to other datasets or systems, showing poor detection performance. Instead, building a unique model that is then tailored to a specific dataset or system may achieve good classification performance, requiring less data and far less expertise from the final user.

Keywords: Intrusion detection · General model · Transferability · Machine learning · Feature learning

1 Introduction

"*Unfortunately, we cannot claim validity of our results beyond the system/datasets used in this study*". This statement appears quite frequently when discussing threats to validity or when remarking lessons learned from an experimental study. At a first glance, it may be seen as a defensive statement, which discourages the reader from applying the proposed technique in systems other than those considered in the study. However, generalizing the results of an experimental study is together one of the main goals and at the same time one of the most difficult achievements of those studies.

In the security domain, this aspect is extremely relevant as most of the mitigations, defenses, and detection mechanisms are tightly tailored to a specific system, domain or

I. Koprinska et al. (Eds.): ECML PKDD 2022 Workshops, CCIS 1753, pp. 186–201, 2023.
https://doi.org/10.1007/978-3-031-23633-4_14

attack to defend against. More specifically, intrusion detectors are nowadays built [48] by feeding Machine Learning (ML) with performance indicators that are being continuously monitored and analyzed to spot anomalous behaviors due to ongoing attacks. Those ML algorithms are typically binary classifiers, which aim at distinguishing between normal and attack-related behavior by processing feature values. This has proven to be very effective for detecting a wide variety of attacks, and in the last two decades originated a huge amount of research papers and industrial applications [41–47] that have the potential to improve security attributes of ICT systems. However, researchers and practitioners have to craft intrusion detectors for specific systems, network interfaces and attack models, to name a few.

As a result, intrusion detectors that may have excellent detection performance for a given system will not have comparable detection performance when applied to different systems, network topologies or attack types. On the other hand, the availability of ML algorithms that are more robust, accurate and that orchestrate ensembles of ML algorithms themselves (i.e., meta-learners [14, 17]) may offer the opportunity to build intrusion detectors that generalize well to (slightly) different systems or domains.

Therefore, this paper conducts an exploratory study to understand to what extent, and under which assumptions, it is possible to craft intrusion detectors that have satisfying detection performance and generalize well to different systems. We start by listing the main threats to building general intrusion detectors according to the literature on the domain. This paves the way for proposing two software architectures that rely either on feature mapping or feature learning and that allow building intrusion detectors that are as general as possible, and can potentially be trained once and used in different systems with minimal effort. We then conduct an experimental campaign embracing 4 public attack datasets that have overlapping feature sets and that suit the evaluation of both feature mapping and feature learning architectures for intrusion detection. Results clearly show that it is not possible to build an intrusion detector that is general enough to be trained once and then be applied to other systems or datasets with no effort, achieving satisfying detection performance. Instead, it is possible to build a detector to be used as a baseline and then tailored to the specific system, requiring minimal expertise and less data with respect to creating a system/specific intrusion detector, but having comparable detection performance.

The paper is structured as follows. Section 2 summarizes related works and the main issues in building general intrusion detectors, letting Sect. 3 propose software architectures for building general intrusion detectors. Section 4 expands on our experimental campaign, whose results are elaborated in Sect. 5. Section 6 concludes the paper.

2   On Generalizing Intrusion Detectors

The traditional flow for deriving intrusion detectors [48] starts from identifying security problems and collecting data to be used for learning models. Their performance is then evaluated and compared against potential competitors, and then the detection system is deployed and put into operation. This is a consolidated flow that has been proven effective in many studies [41, 43–47].

2.1 Motivation and Novelty of this Study

However, the intrusion detector created at the end of this process is system-specific, meaning that it is meant to be effective only in a specific system, against specific attacks and under specific additional assumptions (if any).

This forces the security specialist to start almost from scratch whenever they have a new problem to deal with. Companies or research institutes often already have system monitors that can be used to gather the values of performance indicators of a system over a period of time; however, the collection process is time-consuming, and labeling monitored data has even an higher cost. That is why in recent years there were studies [2, 49] aimed at building intrusion detectors that are not system-specific and could generalize to other datasets, requiring far less data and knowledge for training, evaluating and deploying the detector. Both studies rely on two datasets with similar feature sets, learn the model (supervised in [2], unsupervised in [49]) using one dataset, and test their model on the other dataset. Authors agree that a model learned on a dataset cannot perform detection in another one with good detection performance.

In this paper, we are interested in conducting an exploratory study that spans across a wider range of software architectures that could potentially build general intrusion detectors. According to studies [2, 49], we do not expect models learned on a dataset to have excellent detection capabilities on other systems or datasets when used as they are. Instead, we explore the extent to which is it possible to tailor an existing model to a new dataset or system to perform intrusion detection satisfactorily, and the amount of knowledge that is required to perform such tailoring. Should this knowledge be small enough, this would require less expertise and save time (i.e., money) as it will allow building intrusion detectors starting from a general baseline instead of starting every time from scratch [48].

2.2 Issues in Generalizing Intrusion Detectors

Here we summarize the obstacles to building a general intrusion detector.

I1: Domain and Purpose of the System. It is widely acknowledged that modern ICT systems can be targeted by attackers [25, 26]. There is significant evidence on the risk of cyber-attacks, both in terms of the likelihood of being targeted and the cost and impact of a successful attack. The number of computer security incidents has been steadily growing over the past few years: in 2021, SonicWall [26] reported an average of 28 million cyber-attacks detected daily, with 140 000 of them being novel malware samples. Starting from 2020, the European Union Agency for Cybersecurity (ENISA) observed a spike in non-malicious incidents, most likely because the COVID-19 pandemic became a multiplier for human errors and system misconfigurations, and attributed them as the root cause for the majority of security breaches [25].

Consequently, virtually any system connected to a public (but also private) network should be willing to adopt an intrusion detector to ensure that appropriate security requirements are met. From a theoretical standpoint, a general intrusion detector should achieve satisfying detection performance when processing data from any domain, which is clearly unfeasible in practice. However, there could be small constraints to be applied and that allow building an intrusion detector with a wide (albeit not complete) range of applicability.

I2: Monitoring. Regardless of the purpose, type and domain of a system, it is not possible to conduct intrusion detection without monitoring specific attributes, areas, components or layers of the system itself. Monitoring activities collect the value of performance indicators of a system at given time-instants or when specific events occur: examples include memory usage [19, 20], the throughput of buses [20], and system calls [21]. Also, those indicators can be gathered at hardware or low-level [22], system-level [20, 21], input/sensor [24], environment [19], or even coding-level [23]. Specifically for intrusion detectors, indicators to be monitored are usually related to network usage: this reduces the uncertainty regarding where a specific indicator is going to be monitored. Unfortunately, different network monitors may provide different indicators, or similar indicators with different measure units or sampling process, which still complicates the data analysis process.

I3: Feature Extraction and Learning. The baseline upon which intrusion detectors learn how to assign the "normal" or "anomaly/attack" binary label to a data point depends on the features, which are defined as *"individual measurable properties or characteristics of a phenomenon being observed"* [17]. Feature values related to the state of the system at a given instant build a *data point*: collections of data points are typically in the form of tabular datasets. Each data point contains values for each feature engineered from monitored system indicators. Additional attributes, called meta-features, can be further extracted from the corresponding dataset during the process [18]. Not all features help in distinguishing between normal or anomalous data points, whereas some of them may just represent noise. The importance of a thorough understanding of the underlying data and their features, as well as the produced results, is stressed in [1].

Learning complex features from the training dataset is of utmost importance, especially in deep learners that exercise a backbone [16] composed of convolutional and pooling layers, and forward its outputs to the connected layers that learn how the value of those features is linked to either normal or anomalous behavior due to attacks.

I4: Availability and Quality of Data. It is of no surprise that the amount [7] and noise [9, 13] contained in training data heavily affect the model building and consequently the whole detection task. Relying on a small training data set may result in underfitting [8] the model: this means that the model was created using poor or insufficient knowledge and will not be accurate nor general. In addition, data pre-processing (or the ML algorithm itself) should minimize uncertainty due to noisy labels [9] or in the training set [13]: a noisy item should not have a major impact on the way an ML algorithm learns a model, or on the way the model is used to assign labels to novel instances.

I5: Learning Process. ML algorithms are trained using a training dataset [3], which contains data points and the associated labels describing the binary class of each point. When the model learned from the ML algorithm is not general, even small perturbations can cause classifiers with high accuracy to produce an incorrect prediction on novel samples [4]. Overfitting [8] happens when a classifier learns a model that corresponds too closely or exactly to a particular set of data, and may therefore fail to generalize to a different, albeit similar, input set.

Throughout years, ML algorithms and especially deep learners were made more and more robust to overfitting through techniques such as pruning [15], early stopping [12], batch normalization [5], dropout regularization [6], conjugate gradient [11], and weight decay [10]. Altogether, those techniques are necessary to build models which have satisfying generalization capabilities. Unfortunately, they are not sufficient, as "it is very difficult to make a detailed characterization of how well a specific hypothesis generated by a certain learning algorithm will generalize, in the absence of detailed information about the given problem instance" [14].

3   Architectures for Building Generalized Intrusion Detectors

All the issues above constitute severe obstacles in building a generalized Intrusion Detector. However, there are efforts that could be made to overcome some of them and mitigate the negative impact of other issues.

3.1   Dealing with Generalization Issues

The Domain and Purpose (I1) of the system will impact how the intrusion detector will work regardless of all the efforts we could put. Intrusions will be at least partially related to the target system: in this study, we limit the uncertainty on this aspect by assuming that an intrusion detector is a binary classifier, which raises an alert if notices something unexpected in the data flow. The data flow of performance indicators comes from Monitoring (I2) activities: each system has its own monitoring strategy we do not have control about. Whereas it is likely that network indicators will be monitored through state of the art (and usually open source) tools such as Wireshark, Nagios, Prometheus, Zabbix, CICFlowMeter or slight variations of them, we cannot reasonably assume to know how many and which indicators are going to be monitored for a given system. However, we can manage the way we Extract and Learn Features (I3) from those data, to provide the intrusion detector with a set of features of constant and predefined amount. This will require exercising a system-dependent activity that processes monitored performance indicators (PI) to extract a fixed amount of features to be fed into the intrusion detector which is therefore decoupled from the target system.

This way, it is possible to gather data from different systems or existing datasets, merge them and build training and test datasets for intrusion detection that contain far more data instances. This helps also with the issue of availability (I4) of data to make the intrusion detector learn how to distinguish between normal and attack-related data. This learning process (I5) is at this point may even be completely decoupled from the target system(s), providing the system architect with extreme freedom in choosing the binary classifier that has the best potential for building an accurate intrusion detector.

3.2 Feature Mapping and Feature Learning

Let us explore how we deal with I3 with the aid of Fig. 1. On top of the figure we find three different sample target systems, each running a monitoring strategy that gathers heterogeneous sets of performance indicators, whose cardinality may be different (size a, b, c in the figure). As a result, the intrusion detector cannot assume to know the contents and the size of the feature set. This requires crafting a *System-Dependent Feature Processing* layer that is in charge of processing performance indicators to build a feature set that contains a fixed amount of features and with known content, regardless of the size and the contents of the monitored indicators from the target system. We foresee two possible software architectures to implement this activity:

- Feature Mapping (on the left of Fig. 1): the first option creates a mapping function that processes the set of performance indicators and maps them into a pre-defined set of features of fixed length m $\{F_1, F_2, \ldots F_m\}$. Suppose you want to process performance indicators to build a set of 4 features (m $= 4$) $\{F_1 =$ protocol, $F_2 =$ packet size, $F_3 =$ packet length, $F_4 =$ header flags$\}$. The feature mapper should process performance indicators of a system or a dataset to extract those features: clearly, the mapper depends on the target system since it has to know details about performance indicators and then derive the mapping function to the defined feature set.
- Feature Learning (on the right of Fig. 1): differently, we can exercise an additional layer of ML that does not aim at classifying, but is instead directed to learn a fixed amount of features from the heterogeneous sets of performance indicators. Learned features will then be provided to the intrusion detector for the second level of learning: in other words, we are building a stacking meta-learner [27]. This approach employs a set of k ML algorithms that are trained using the specific set of performance indicators PI of a given system (and thus feature learning is system-dependent), whose output has a fixed cardinality, regardless of the size of the input indicators. The outputs of all the k ML algorithms are then assembled to build a feature set of n features $\{F_1, F_2, \ldots F_n\}$. For example, we could employ $k = 3$ ML algorithms: two binary classifiers BC1 and BC2 each of them outputting two probabilities pN (probability of data being normal) and pA (probability of data being an attack), and a deep learner DL we use as backbone, extracting the 4 features it generates after convolutional and pooling layers. This generates a set of $n = 8$ features $\{BC1\_pN, BC1\_pA, BC2\_pN, BC2\_pA, DL\_F1, DL\_F2, DL\_F3, DL\_F4\}$, which has constant size regardless of the input performance indicators.

192   T. Zoppi et al.

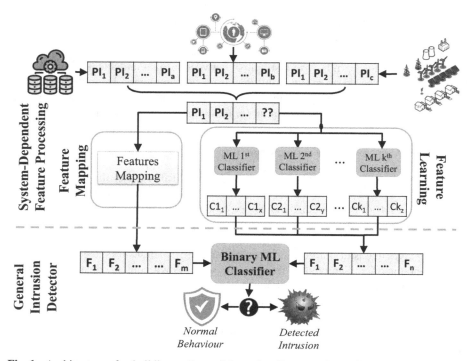

Fig. 1. Architectures for building a General Intrusion Detector. Regardless of the size of the feature set gathered from different systems (on top), exercising either Feature Mapping (on the left) or Feature Learning provides the Binary ML classifier (bottom of the figure) in charge of detecting intrusions with a feature set that has constant size.

3.3 Discussion, Advantages and Disadvantages

Those two software architectures have their strengths and weaknesses.

Feature mapping is clearly faster to execute and does not involve training ML algorithms (other than the binary classifier) which may be a time-consuming and also a complex task that involves optimizations, sensitivity analyses, and many more. On the downside, mapping performance indicators into a set of features may lead to loss of information, be very tricky and often unfeasible. For example, the NGIDS [50] dataset has only 3 features (process_id, syscall, event_id) as well as ADFANet [50] (packets, bytes, duration), whereas the CICIDS17, CICIDS18, AndMal17, and SDN20 share the same feature set of 77 network indicators. Finding a feature set that can convey most of the information contained in those datasets is not possible at all as there are no overlapping indicators between NGDIS and the other datasets. Even excluding NGDIS, ADFANet has far less indicators that other datasets and therefore it is very difficult to map all datasets into a unique feature set without losing information. It follows that this approach should be preferred whenever it is possible to tune the monitoring system to extract relevant indicators, while it is less feasible when detecting intrusions in existing datasets or in systems with non-customizable monitoring strategies.

Differently, Feature Learning is a complex process that abstracts from all those problems, which are masked by the learning process of ML algorithms used for feature learning. Moreover, it is a flexible approach since the amount and the type of feature learners can be tuned depending on the needs of the user e.g., the computational power available for intrusion detection.

In the rest of the paper we will build an experimental campaign to quantify the generalization capabilities of intrusion detectors that use either of those two architectures. Since our data baseline can be only composed of existing datasets, we will choose those that were built using the same monitoring strategy and tooling and have overlapping feature sets to make feature mapping feasible.

4 Experimental Campaign

4.1 Datasets Collection

There is a wide variety of tabular datasets related to intrusion detection, ranging from device data in Internet-of-Things (IoT) systems to network data for intrusion detection [28, 29]. Those often have heterogeneous feature sets which may not fit our exploratory study. Instead, AndMal17 [32], CICIDS17 [31], CICIDS18 [31], and SDN20 [30] were collected using the same network monitoring tool and as such fit our analysis. Table 1 summarizes the datasets considered in this study, reporting domain, name, publication year, number of data points, number of features, types, and percentages of attacks. Those datasets are quite recent (not older than 2017), and they are well-known reference datasets in the domain. Regarding the attacks logged in the datasets, (Distributed) Denial of Service and scanning attacks (e.g., probing, port scanning, reconnaissance) appear in all datasets but AndMal17. Other attacks such as malware (AndMal17, SDN20), web attacks (CICIDS17, CICIDS18), botnets (CICIDS18), spam (AndMal17) and phising (AndMal17) occur in a few datasets. Overall, these 4 datasets provide a view on most of the common attacks in the current threat landscape [25] and therefore we believe they provide a representative data baseline to experiment on. Also, the reader should notice that different datasets log system behavior under different attacks and therefore diversity among datasets is dual: both from the target system and the attack model standpoints.

Table 1. Selected datasets: name, reference, release year, size, number of features, number and percentage of attacks.

Dataset name	Ref	Year	# Data points used	# Features	# Attacks	% Attacks
AndMal17	[32]	2017	100 000	77	4	15.5
CICIDS17	[31]	2017	500 000	77	5	79.7
CICIDS18	[31]	2018	200 000	77	8	26.2
SDN20	[30]	2020	205 167	77	5	66.6

4.2 Binary Classifiers for Intrusion Detection

We then choose the candidate binary classifiers for implementing the intrusion detector. We do not aim at identifying a complete and broad set of classifiers: instead, we want to use those that were widely used in the literature and that were proven to be effective for tabular data. We ended up selecting Random Forests (RF, [35]), eXteme Gradient Boosting (XGB, [36]) and the deep learner FastAI (FAI, [37]), which has optimizations for tabular data. Random Forests are a well-known bagging ensemble of decision trees that saw a lot of applicability for intrusion detection in the last decade [33], while XGBoost has proven to outperform many classifiers including deep learners [34] for tabular data. Lastly, FastAI contains optimizations for processing tabular data and entity embedding of categorical features.

4.3 ML Algorithms to Be Used for Feature Learning

Feature learners to be used in this study can be essentially any ML algorithm: supervised, unsupervised, backbone deep learner, and so on and so forth. Since this is an exploratory study, we aim at exercising as many feature learners as possible: then, we may filter out those that learn weak features and keep only those that learn the strong ones. In our study, each feature learner learns two features, which are the probability of being a normal data point, or the probability of being an attack. Summarizing, this study employs 16 feature learners, that learn a total of 32 features (2 each):

- 10 unsupervised ML algorithms from the library PYOD [38], namely: ECOD, COPOD, FastABOD, HBOS, MCD, PCA, LOF, CBLOF, Isolation Forests, SUOD.
- 5 supervised ML algorithms from Scikit-Learn [39], different from those used for intrusion detection in the previous section: k-th Nearest Neighbors, ADABoost, Naïve Bayes, Logistic Regression, Linear Discriminant Analysis.
- A deep learner used as backbone for feature learning (FastAI), which as motivated before contains suitable optimizations to learn features from tabular data.

4.4 Experimental Setup and Methodology

Experiments are executed on a Dell Precision 5820 Tower with an Intel I9-9920X, GPU NVIDIA Quadro RTX6000 with 24 GB VRAM, 192 GB RAM, and Ubuntu 18.04, and they required approximately 6 weeks of 24 h execution.

The *Pyod*, *Scikit-Learn* and *xgboost* python packages contain all the code needed to exercise ML algorithms. We created a Python script to load datasets, orchestrate feature learners, train and evaluate intrusion detectors. The evaluation will mainly be carried out by means of evaluation metrics for binary classification i.e., confusion matrix [40] and especially using aggregated metrics as Accuracy and Matthews Correlation Coefficient (MCC). Additionally, we compute the importance that intrusion detectors assign to their features: those will help to break down the behavior of different intrusion detectors and provide insights on the way they build their models. We split each of the dataset in half (50–50 train-test split) and perform 5 series of experiments, which we explain below and partially depict in Fig. 2:

- RegularID: we exercise the ML algorithms Random Forests (RF), XGBoost (XGB), and FastAI (FAI) on all datasets separately using the 50–50 train-test split and collect metric scores. This is the usual way of training and evaluating an intrusion detector, which is entirely system-dependent (i.e., not general).
- FeatL: we exercise the 16 feature learners on the train portion of each dataset but the one used for testing, collecting their outputs. Those build a huge training set composed of data instances with homogeneous structure (i.e., each of those data points has 32 feature values), even if they come from different datasets. Those are used to train the intrusion detectors RF, XGB, FAI individually. For example, when testing the dataset AndMal17, we train the detector using the train partition of CICIDS17, CICID18 and SDN20 (i.e., without using AndMal17 at all). The resulting model is then used to detect intrusions using the test portion of AndMal17, which is completely unknown to the intrusion detector. This quantifies how well the detector generalizes to a different dataset.
- FeatL_TL: This is a process similar to FeatL, but it is not completely unrelated from the dataset used for testing. Particularly, we partially use the train partition of the dataset we want to evaluate to re-train the FeatL detector using transfer learning mechanics. This way, the binary ML classifier gets tailored using some key information about the system under test and is expected to have better classification performance than FeatL, at a cost of a less general model. We will use either 1000, 5000, 10000, 20000 data points for transfer learning, labeling the corresponding detector as FeatL_TL1, FeatL_TL5, FeatL_TL10, FeatL_TL20.
- Map: it is a process similar to FeatL, but does not execute Feature Learning. Instead, it maps directly features from different datasets to the same feature set, since the 4 datasets in this study all share the exact same feature set.
- Map_TL: it is a process similar to FeatL_TL, but does not execute Feature Learning. Instead, it maps directly features from different datasets to the same feature set, since the 4 datasets in this study all share the exact same feature set.

5   Results and Discussion

5.1   Regular, Feature Learning and Feature Mapping Intrusion Detectors

We start analyzing results with the aid of Table 2. The table reports the highest MCC achieved either by RF, XGB, or FAI for a given intrusion detector: RegularID, FeatL Map, FeatL_TL20, Map_TL20. We chose the TL20 variants of the FeatL_TL and Map_TL as they were delivering higher MCC than their counterparts which are using less data for transfer learning. It turns out evident how RF and XGB are the preferred ML algorithm for intrusion detection in most of the cases: they achieve the highest MCC on most configurations reported in the table. Also, the AndMal17 dataset is the hardest of the four to perform detection on: while for CICIDS17, CICIDS18 and SDN20 we have MCC scores over 0.90, for AndMal17 the MCC does not exceed 0.65, that corresponds to an accuracy of 92.9 and a Recall of 48.3 (i.e., more than half of the attacks, the 51.7%, are not detected by the intrusion detector).

Going into the detail of the 5 different intrusion detectors we instantiated in this study, we can observe that – as expected – RegularID has the highest MCC being specific of

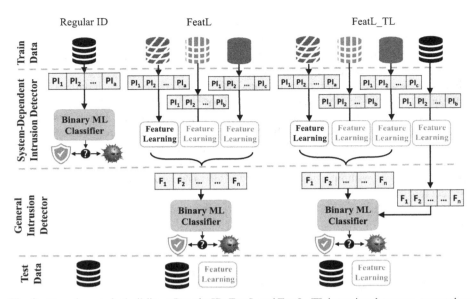

Fig. 2. Experiments for building a RegularID, FeatL and FeatL_TL intrusion detectors, separating the system-dependent from the general part of those detectors. The Map and Map_TL detectors work the same as the FeatL and FeatL_TL, but do not perform feature learning.

a dataset and with no generalization capabilities. Using only 3 datasets for training a unique model to be tested on another unknown dataset, either by mapping features (Map in Table 2) or by feature learning (FeatL in the table) generates MCC scores that are far lower than those of RegularID. Map scores are not even comparable with others, whereas FeatL scores are better than those of Map but still noticeably lower than RegularID in all datasets but SDN20, making those general detectors not applicable in a real setup due to an excessive amount of False Positives and/or False Negatives. Scores of Map_TL20 and FeatL_TL20 are clearly better than those of Map and FeatL, but still lower than those of RegularID: additionally, transfer learning limits the generalization capabilities of those detectors as it adds another system-specific training component.

Nevertheless, it is interesting to observe the impact transfer learning has on MCC scores. We discuss this aspect with the aid of Fig. 3, which also allows remarking the following important observations:

- Adopting transfer learning clearly improves capabilities of intrusion detectors: Map_TL1 has better MCC than Map, and the MCC grows the more data is used for transfer learning (i.e., Map_TL20 has better MCC than Map_TL10, which is better than Map_TL5, which outperforms Map_TL1). The same applies to FeatL and FeatL_TL.
- Transfer learning has an outstanding impact when using detectors relying on feature mapping. Map detectors have very poor scores, but improve dramatically even when only 1000 data points are used for transfer learning (Map_TL1). This can be observed in Fig. 3a and 3b looking at the two series of bars on the bottom of each bar chart.

Table 2. MCC scores of the best ML algorithm (FAI, RF, XGB) used as regular ID, FeatL, Map, FeatL_TL20, Map_TL20.

Dataset	Map		Map_TL20		FeatL		FeatL_TL20		RegularID	
AndMal17	0.023	XGB	0.251	XGB	0.313	FAI	0.453	XGB	0.647	RF
CICIDS17	0.626	XGB	0.993	XGB	0.975	FAI	0.987	RF	0.999	XGB
CICIDS18	0.260	FAI	0.853	XGB	0.890	RF	0.908	RF	0.928	XGB
SDN20	0.180	XGB	0.999	XGB	0.999	RF	0.999	RF	1.000	RF
Average MCC	**0.272**		**0.774**		**0.794**		**0.837**		**0.893**	

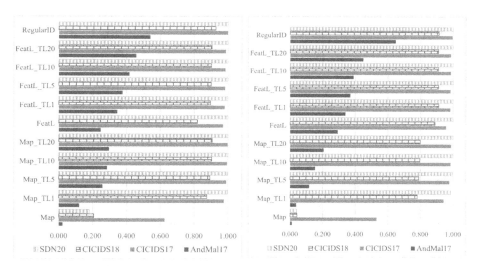

Fig. 3. a (left) and b (right). MCC scores for each of the four datasets (one bar series each). Each bar chart has 11 series of bars, one for each intrusion detector. Scores using XGB are on the left (Fig. 3a), while scores using RF are on the right (Fig. 3b).

- The FeatL detectors have overall better performance than Map and therefore their performance improvement with transfer learning is less evident than those of Map. Nevertheless, applying transfer learning brings FeatL_TL20 to achieve MCC scores that are very similar to those of RegularID scores. This is an important results because it shows how it is possible to achieve good detection performance tailoring an existing model rather than crafting an intrusion detection from scratch, saving key amount of time and thus money.

5.2 On the Contribution of Feature Learners

FeatL has better scores than Map: this is due to the feature learners, which are trained using a small portion of the novel system under test to extract features. We explain the contribution each feature learner has on the overall detection process with the aid of Table 3, which presents the importance of feature learners for FeatL and FeatL_TL20 using either RF or XGB on the CICIDS18 dataset. Importance in each row of the table sum up to 1, while each score ranges between 0 and 1: the higher, the most relevant features learned from a feature learner are for training the intrusion detector. Additionally, we report the difference in the importance of features between the FeatL_TL20 and the FeatL, which does not apply transfer learning. The importance using XGB or RF follow a similar path: the FeatL detector learns a model that is almost entirely built over features learned by KNN, which has 0.920 and 0.911 importance respectively for XGB and RF. Other feature learners have marginal to negligible contribution, making the FeatL detectors very dependent on the behavior of KNN features.

Table 3. Importance of feature learners in building the model for FeatL and FeatL_TL20 using either XGB or RF as ML algorithms for the CICIDS18 dataset.

ML Algorithm	Intrusion Detector	Unsupervised Feature Learn.										Supervised Feature Learn.					
		COPOD	ABOD	HBOS	MCD	PCA	ECOD	LOF	CBLOF	IForest	SUOD	Naïve Bayes	LDA	Logistic Reg	KNN	FAI	ADABoost
XGB	FeatL	.001	.030	.003	.002	.003	.001	.002	.003	.002	.002	.003	.002	.000	.920	.020	.003
	FeatL_TL20	.009	.012	.003	.001	.013	.007	.001	.005	.005	.007	.033	.088	.000	.455	.221	.139
	Diff	**.007**	**-.018**	**.000**	**-.002**	**.011**	**.005**	**-.002**	**.002**	**.004**	**.005**	**.030**	**.086**	**.000**	**-.465**	**.201**	**.136**
RF	FeatL	.001	.032	.004	.003	.003	.002	.002	.003	.002	.002	.003	.002	.000	.911	.021	.004
	FeatL_TL20	.010	.006	.004	.002	.011	.011	.001	.007	.007	.008	.027	.107	.000	.352	.327	.108
	Diff	**.009**	**-.026**	**.000**	**-.001**	**.008**	**.009**	**-.001**	**.004**	**.006**	**.006**	**.024**	**.105**	**.000**	**-.559**	**.306**	**.105**

Differently, the FeatL_TL20 models obtained using 20 000 data points of CICIDS18 (the system under test for building this table) for transfer learning do not rely entirely on KNN to detect intrusions. The importance of KNN features decreases a lot, favoring FAI, ADABoost and LDA features. Other feature learners, especially those unsupervised, still have very marginal contribution to the overall detection process.

Overall, it is safe to say that transfer learning makes XGB and RF learn a model that does not heavily depends on a single feature learner, but instead combines the output of different feature learners: this results in a more general model.

6   Conclusions and Future Works

In this study we proposed and experimentally evaluated two software architectures for building intrusion detectors that have good generalization capabilities. Briefly, we aimed at learning the model once and then apply it to as many datasets the user wants with minimal effort, still achieving satisfying detection performance.

Our experimental results are not fully encouraging: they tell us that no matter the intrusion detector, it will not generalize well to other datasets as is. Instead, it will be outperformed by system-specific intrusion detectors, confirming the studies [2, 49]. A non-zero amount of knowledge about the system under test is indeed required to make intrusion detectors able to detect intrusions in other datasets with satisfactory performance. Knowing only a few thousands of data points of the system under test allowed intrusion detectors reaching satisfying detection scores in our experiments, without outperforming traditional system-specific intrusion detectors. It follows that tailoring a baseline model through transfer learning has the potential to obtain satisfactorily (albeit not optimal) detection performance, requiring less data and minimal expertise from the user standpoint, which does not have to train multiple ML algorithms nor running complex performance evaluations.

Particularly, pre-processing datasets through different ML algorithms deployed as feature learners clearly builds an intrusion detector that potentially has generalization capabilities. Therefore, as future works we want to elaborate more on those detectors with respect to three dimensions of analysis, namely: i) carefully selecting feature learners to be used, ii) gathering training data from more datasets, hoping to build a detector which is more solid and as such has better generalization capabilities, and iii) performing sensitivity analyses aiming at clearly identifying the minimum amount of data which we have to gather from the system under test to train feature learners and tailor the detector to achieve satisfactory detection performance.

Acknowledgments. This work has been partially supported by the H2020 Marie Sklodowska-Curie g.a. 823788 (ADVANCE), by the Regione Toscana POR FESR 2014–2020 SPaCe, and by the NextGenerationEU programme, Italian DM737 – CUP B15F21005410003.

References

1. Sommer, R., Paxson, V.: Outside the closed world: on using machine learning for network intrusion detection. In: 2010 IEEE Symposium on Security and Privacy, pp. 305–316. IEEE, May 2010
2. Catillo, M., Del Vecchio, A., Pecchia, A., Villano, U.: Transferability of machine learning models learned from public intrusion detection datasets: the CICIDS2017 case study. Softw. Qual. J. **30**, 955–981 (2022). https://doi.org/10.1007/s11219-022-09587-0
3. Schmidhuber, J.: Deep learning in neural networks: an overview. Neural Netw. **61**, 85–117 (2015)
4. Schmidt, L., Santurkar, S., Tsipras, D., Talwar, K., Madry, A.: Adversarially robust generalization requires more data. In: Advances in Neural Information Processing Systems, vol. 31 (2018). Accessed 07 Apr 2022
5. Li, Y., Wang, N., Shi, J., Liu, J., Hou, X.: Revisiting batch normalization for practical domain adaptation, November 2016. http://arxiv.org/abs/1603.04779. Accessed 07 Apr 2022
6. Jindal, I., Nokleby, M., Chen, X.: Learning deep networks from noisy labels with dropout regularization. In: 2016 IEEE 16th International Conference on Data Mining (ICDM), pp. 967–972, December 2016. https://doi.org/10.1109/ICDM.2016.0121
7. Chen, X.W., Lin, X.: Big data deep learning: challenges and perspectives. IEEE Access **2**, 514–525 (2014)
8. Lawrence, S., Giles, C.L.: Overfitting and neural networks: conjugate gradient and backpropagation. In: Proceedings of the IEEE-INNS-ENNS International Joint Conference on Neural Networks, IJCNN 2000. Neural Computing: New Challenges and Perspectives for the New Millennium, vol. 1, pp. 114–119. IEEE, July 2000

9. Song, H., et al.: Learning from noisy labels with deep neural networks: a survey. IEEE Trans. Neural Netw. Learn. Syst. (2022, article in press). https://doi.org/10.1109/TNNLS.2022.315 2527

10. Krogh, A., Hertz, J.: A simple weight decay can improve generalization. In: Advances in Neural Information Processing Systems, vol. 4 (1991)

11. Caruana, R., Lawrence, S., Giles, C.: Overfitting in neural nets: backpropagation, conjugate gradient, and early stopping. In: Advances in Neural Information Processing Systems, vol. 13 (2000)

12. Prechelt, L.: Early stopping - but when? In: Orr, G.B., Müller, K.-R. (eds.) Neural Networks: Tricks of the trade. LNCS, vol. 1524, pp. 55–69. Springer, Heidelberg (1998). https://doi.org/10.1007/3-540-49430-8_3

13. Sietsma, J., Dow, R.J.: Creating artificial neural networks that generalize. Neural Netw. **4**(1), 67–79 (1991)

14. Kawaguchi, K., Kaelbling, L.P., Bengio, Y.: Generalization in deep learning. arXiv preprint arXiv:1710.05468 (2017)

15. Cestnik, B., Bratko, I.: On estimating probabilities in tree pruning. In: Kodratoff, Y. (ed.) Machine Learning — EWSL-91: European Working Session on Learning Porto, Portugal, March 6–8, 1991 Proceedings, pp. 138–150. Springer, Heidelberg (1991). https://doi.org/10.1007/BFb0017010

16. Gao, S.H., Cheng, M.M., Zhao, K., Zhang, X.Y., Yang, M.H., Torr, P.: Res2Net: a new multi-scale backbone architecture. IEEE Trans. Pattern Anal. Mach. Intell. **43**(2), 652–662 (2019)

17. Bishop, C.: Pattern Recognition and Machine Learning. Springer, Berlin (2006). ISBN: 0-387-31073-8

18. Rivolli, A., Garcia, L.P., Soares, C., Vanschoren, J., de Carvalho, A.C.: Meta-features for meta-learning. Knowl.-Based Sys. **240**, 108101 (2022)

19. Cotroneo, D., Natella, R., Rosiello, S.: A fault correlation approach to detect performance anomalies in Virtual Network Function chains. In: 2017 IEEE 28th International Symposium on Software Reliability Engineering (ISSRE), pp. 90–100. IEEE (2017)

20. Zoppi, T., Ceccarelli, A., Bondavalli, A.: MADneSs: a multi-layer anomaly detection framework for complex dynamic systems. IEEE Trans. Dependable Secure Comput. **18**(2), 796–809 (2019)

21. Murtaza, S.S., et al.: A host-based anomaly detection approach by representing system calls as states of kernel modules. In: 2013 IEEE 24th International Symposium on Software Reliability Engineering (ISSRE). IEEE (2013)

22. Wang, G., Zhang, L., Xu, W.: What can we learn from four years of data center hardware failures? In: 2017 47th Annual IEEE/IFIP International Conference on Dependable Systems and Networks (DSN), pp. 25–36. IEEE, June 2017

23. Li, Z., Zou, D., Xu, S., Jin, H., Zhu, Y., Chen, Z.: SySeVR: a framework for using deep learning to detect software vulnerabilities. IEEE Trans. Dependable Secure Comput. **19**(4), 2244–2258 (2022)

24. Robles-Velasco, A., Cortés, P., Muñuzuri, J., Onieva, L.: Prediction of pipe failures in water supply networks using logistic regression and support vector classification. Reliab. Eng. Syst. Saf. **196**, 106754 (2020)

25. Ardagna, C., Corbiaux, S., Sfakianakis, A., Douliger, C.: ENISA Threat Landscape 2021. https://www.enisa.europa.eu/topics/threat-risk-management/threats-and-trends. Accessed 6 May 2022

26. Connell, B.: 2022 SonicWall Threat Report. https://www.sonicwall.com/2022-cyber-threat-report/. Accessed 6 May 2022

27. Džeroski, S., Ženko, B.: Is combining classifiers with stacking better than selecting the best one? Mach. Learn. **54**(3), 255–273 (2004). https://doi.org/10.1023/B:MACH.0000015881.36452.6e

28. Khraisat, A., Gondal, I., Vamplew, P., Kamruzzaman, J.: Survey of intrusion detection systems: techniques, datasets, and challenges. Cybersecurity **2**(1) (2019). Article number: 20. https://doi.org/10.1186/s42400-019-0038-7
29. Ring, M., Wunderlich, S., Scheuring, D., Landes, D., Hotho, A.: A survey of network-based intrusion detection data sets. Comput. Secur. **86**, 147–167 (2019)
30. Elsayed, M.S., Le-Khac, N.A., Jurcut, A.D.: InSDN: a novel SDN intrusion dataset. IEEE Access **8**, 165263–165284 (2020)
31. Sharafaldin, I., et al.: Toward generating a new intrusion detection dataset and intrusion traffic characterization. In: ICISSP, pp. 108–116, January 2018
32. Lashkari, A.H., et al.: Toward developing a systematic approach to generate benchmark Android malware datasets and classification. In: 2018 International Carnahan Conference on Security Technology (ICCST), pp. 1–7. IEEE, October 2018
33. Resende, P.A.A., Drummond, A.C.: A survey of random forest based methods for intrusion detection systems. ACM Comput. Surv. (CSUR) **51**(3), 1–36 (2018)
34. Shwartz-Ziv, R., Armon, A.: Tabular data: deep learning is not all you need. Inf. Fusion **81**, 84–90 (2022)
35. Breiman, L.: Random forests. Mach. Learn. **45**(1), 5–32 (2001). https://doi.org/10.1023/A:1010933404324
36. Chen, T., et al.: XGBoost: eXtreme gradient boosting. R Package Version 0.4-2, **1**(4), 1–4 (2015)
37. Howard, J., Gugger, S.: Fastai: a layered API for deep learning. Information **11**(2), 108 (2020)
38. Zhao, Y., Nasrullah, Z., Li, Z.: PyOD: a python toolbox for scalable outlier detection. arXiv preprint arXiv:1901.01588 (2019)
39. Buitinck, L., et al.: API design for machine learning software: experiences from the scikit-learn project. arXiv preprint arXiv:1309.0238 (2013)
40. Luque, A., et al.: The impact of class imbalance in classification performance metrics based on the binary confusion matrix. Pattern Recogn. **91**, 216–231 (2019)
41. Ucci, D., Aniello, L., Baldoni, R.: Survey of machine learning techniques for malware analysis. Comput. Secur. **81**, 123–147 (2019)
42. Demetrio, L., et al.: Adversarial exemples: a survey and experimental evaluation of practical attacks on machine learning for windows malware detection. ACM Trans. Priv. Secur. (TOPS) **24**(4), 1–31 (2021)
43. Zhauniarovich, Y., Khalil, I., Yu, T., Dacier, M.: A survey on malicious domains detection through DNS data analysis. ACM Comput. Surv. (CSUR) **51**(4), 1–36 (2018)
44. Oliveira, R.A., Raga, M.M., Laranjeiro, N., Vieira, M.: An approach for benchmarking the security of web service frameworks. Future Gener. Comput. Syst. **110**, 833–848 (2020)
45. Andresini, G., Appice, A., Malerba, D.: Autoencoder-based deep metric learning for network intrusion detection. Inf. Sci. **569**, 706–727 (2021)
46. Apruzzese, G., Colajanni, M., Ferretti, L., Guido, A., Marchetti, M.: On the effectiveness of machine and deep learning for cyber security. In: 2018 10th International Conference on Cyber Conflict (CyCon), pp. 371–390. IEEE, May 2018
47. Folino, F., et al.: On learning effective ensembles of deep neural networks for intrusion detection. Inf. Fusion **72**, 48–69 (2021)
48. Arp, D., et al.: Dos and don'ts of machine learning in computer security. In: Proceedings of the USENIX Security Symposium, August 2022
49. Verkerken, M., D'hooge, L., Wauters, T., Volckaert, B., De Turck, F.: Towards model generalization for intrusion detection: unsupervised machine learning techniques. J. Netw. Syst. Manag. **30** (2022). Article number: 12. https://doi.org/10.1007/s10922-021-09615-7
50. Haider, W., Hu, J., Slay, J., Turnbull, B.P., Xie, Y.: Generating realistic intrusion detection system dataset based on fuzzy qualitative modeling. J. Netw. Comput. Appl. **87**, 185–192 (2017)

Workshop on Machine Learning for Buildings Energy Management (MLBEM 2022)

Machine Learning for Building Energy Management (MLBEM 2022)

Increased energy efficiency and decarbonization of the energy system are two primary objectives of the European Energy Union. European buildings remain predominantly inefficient, accounting for 40% of final energy consumption and 36% of the total EU CO_2 emissions. The EU targets for 2030 include reaching a 32% share of renewable energy and increasing energy efficiency by at least 32.5%. Due to the scale and complexity of current building energy systems, traditional modeling, simulation, and optimization techniques are not feasible and unable to achieve satisfactory results. To achieve the aforementioned goals, modern buildings require the capabilities of self-assessing and self-optimizing energy resources, meeting user preferences and requirements, and contributing to an overall better and sustainable energy system.

The ongoing energy transition brings the possibility of real-time energy resource management to building owners/managers and energy operators, with potential benefits for consumers, producers, and the environment. To better tap into this potential, stakeholders must be able to continuously assess the energy performance of building energy systems and appliances, identifying areas where optimization services can be applied. Implementing this assessment and optimization capability requires real-time monitoring and control of the building equipment and major energy-consuming appliances. This functionality can be effectively performed by Internet of Things (IoT) enabled sensors and devices coupled with services that can assess and optimize the energy resources in buildings.

The capability to analyze and optimize buildings' energy resources and energy-consuming equipment in useful time is not possible without employing machine learning (ML) techniques and big data infrastructures. This gives rise to ML building energy management (BEM) services that can be effective in an increasingly electrified and complex environment with energy flows between the grid, photovoltaic production, electric vehicles, storage batteries, building thermal capacity, and consideration of changing consumption patterns, occupants' comfort, and highly variable user preferences.

Machine learning is a key enabler of scalable and efficient tools for building energy assessment and for the development of services capable of dealing with the increased complexity of energy management in buildings generated by the electrification of the energy system.

Following its previous edition in 2021, MLBEM 2022 was organized as a European forum for buildings energy and ML researchers and practitioners wishing to discuss the recent developments of ML for developing BEM systems, by paying special attention to solutions rooted in techniques such as pattern mining, neural networks and deep learning, probabilistic inference, stream learning and mining, and big data analytics and visualization. The workshop aimed at filling a gap in the EU workshop panorama, providing researchers with a forum to exchange and discuss scientific contributions and open challenges, both theoretical and practical, related to the use of machine-learning approaches in building energy management. Moreover,

MLBEM 2022 aimed to highlight the latest research trends in machine learning under the context of BEM, including topics like the privacy of data, big data, deep learning, incremental and stream learning, and adversarial learning.

MLBEM 2022 received 4 submissions which were reviewed in a single-blind process, with each submission receiving at least 3 reviews. In total, 2 papers were selected for presentation at the workshop.

We hope that the workshop contributed to identifying new application areas as well as open and future research problems related to the application of machine learning in the building energy field.

Pedro M. Ferreira
Guilherme Graça

Organization

MLBEM 2022 Chairs

Pedro M. Ferreira   Universidade de Lisboa, Portugal
Guilherme Graíça   Universidade de Lisboa, Portugal

Web and Publication Chairs

Nuno Dionísio   Universidade de Lisboa, Portugal
Zygimantas Jasiunas   Universidade de Lisboa, Portugal

Program Committee

António Ruano	University of Algarve, Portugal
Bratislav Svetozarevic	Swiss Federal Laboratories for Materials Science and Technology, Switzerland
Elias Kosmatopoulos	Democritus University of Thrace and Centre for Research and Technology Hellas, Greece
Georg Jung	Vlaamse Instelling voor Technologisch Onderzoek, Belgium
Gerald Schweiger	Graz University of Technology, Austria
Iakovos Michailidis	Centre for Research and Technology Hellas, Greece
José Domingo Álvarez	University of Almería, Spain
Nuno Mateus	EDP New, Portugal
Per Heiselberg	Aalborg University, Denmark

Conv-NILM-Net, a Causal and Multi-appliance Model for Energy Source Separation

Mohamed Alami C.[1,2]([✉])[ID], Jérémie Decock[2], Rim kaddah[3], and Jesse Read[1][ID]

[1] Ecole Polytechnique, Palaiseau, France
mohamed.alami-chehboune@polytechnique.edu
[2] Accenta, Paris, France
[3] IRT SystemX, Palaiseau, France

Abstract. Non-Intrusive Load Monitoring (NILM) seeks to save energy by estimating individual appliance power usage from a single aggregate measurement. Deep neural networks have become increasingly popular in attempting to solve NILM problems. However most used models are used for Load Identification rather than online Source Separation. Among source separation models, most use a single-task learning approach in which a neural network is trained exclusively for each appliance. This strategy is computationally expensive and ignores the fact that multiple appliances can be active simultaneously and dependencies between them. The rest of models are not causal, which is important for real-time application. Inspired by Convtas-Net, a model for speech separation, we propose Conv-NILM-net, a fully convolutional framework for end-to-end NILM. Conv-NILM-net is a causal model for multi appliance source separation. Our model is tested on two real datasets REDD and UK-DALE and clearly outperforms the state of the art while keeping a significantly smaller size than the competing models.

Keywords: NILM · Single channel source separation · Deep learning

1 Introduction

In 2018, 26.1% of the total energy consumption in EU was attributed to households. This consumption mainly serves a heating purpose (78.4%). Moreover, most of the residential energy consumption is covered by natural gas (32.1%) and electricity (24.7%), while renewables account for just 19.5% [6]. However, as solar and wind generation rely on weather conditions, challenges due to intermittent generation have to be solved, and solutions for energy management such as demand response and photovoltaic (PV) battery management can play a key role in this regard. Machine Learning has proven to be a viable solution for smart home energy management [32]. These methods autonomously control heating and domestic hot water systems, which are the most relevant loads in a dwelling, helping consumers to reduce energy consumption and also improving their comfort.

Supported by Accenta.ai.

An efficient energy management system has to take into account users habits in order to anticipate their behaviour. However, comfort is hard to quantify as it remains purely subjective. We argue that in an energy management context, the users are the only ones that can offer a proper evaluation of their own comfort. Hence, a satisfactory hypothesis is to consider that their current behaviour and habits are the ones that optimise their comfort. Therefore, an efficient energy management system is one that can anticipate users habits, optimise consumption levels (for example by deciding which source to use, temperature settings etc.) while offering solutions that alter users known habits as little as possible.

Learning users' habits in a household is a hard problem mainly regarding data acquisition. The possible behaviours are diverse, if not unique, while monitoring inhabitants is not acceptable as it is a privacy infringement. From an energy provider perspective, the only available information is the household's total power consumption. A solution is therefore to decompose this consumption into the consumptions induced by each appliance in the household. The resulting disaggregated power time series can then be used as an input for a machine learning algorithm in order to learn consumption habits.

Energy disaggregation (also called non-intrusive load monitoring or NILM) is a computational technique for estimating the power demand of individual appliances from a single meter which measures the combined demand of multiple appliances. The NILM problem can be formulated as follows: Let $\bar{y}(t)$ the aggregated energy consumption measured at time t. With no loss of generality, $\bar{y}(t)$ can represent the active power (The power which is actually consumed or utilised in an AC Circuit in kW). Then $\bar{y}(t)$ can be expressed as in:

$$\bar{y}(t) = \sum_{i=1}^{C} y^{(i)}(t) + e(t) \tag{1}$$

where C is the number of appliances, $y^{(i)}$ the consumption induced by appliance i and $e(t)$ some noise. The aim is to find $y^{(i)}$ given $\bar{y}(t)$.

There exist two approaches for NILM, namely load identification and source separation. In the first case, a first step called signature detection corresponds to the activation of a given appliance then a classification algorithm classifies the appliance category. The idea behind load identification is to build appropriate features called load signatures that allow to easily distinguish the referenced appliance from others within the installation. In the latter case, separation is directly obtained while retrieving the source signal.

In order to manage a building efficiently, for example using a reinforcement learning agent, it is necessary to use a model that performs source separation while being causal. In signal processing, a causal model is a model that performs the needed task (here source separation) without looking beyond time t rather than having to look in the future as presented in Fig. 2. The model can then be used as a backend for prediction, which is necessary for energy management.

We propose Conv-NILM-net, a fully convolutional and causal neural network for end-to-end energy source separation. Conv-NILM-net is inspired from Conv-TasNet [20], a convolutional model for speech separation. The model does not require more quantities than active power and disaggregates the signal for multiple appliances at once. We evaluate it on REDD and UK-DALE datasets, compared to recent models and achieves state of the art performance. Figure 1 presents an overview of the model and Table 1 summarises the notations used throughout this paper.

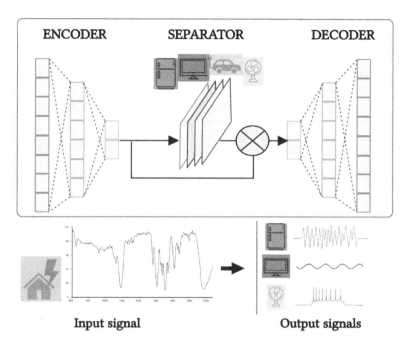

Fig. 1. Overview of Conv-NILM-net. It is composed of 2 blocs, the encoder/decoder and the separator. The encoder first projects the signal into a latent space, the separator disaggregates it into C corresponding to each appliance by learning C masks applied to input signal, then the decoder projects the C signals to the input space

2   Related Work

Most approaches in the literature are load identification approaches that predict the state of an appliance (on/off) and predict the average consumption of the given appliance during a certain period of time. Four appliance models are usually considered:

– Type I On/off devices: most appliances in households, such as bulbs and toasters;
– Type II Finite-State-Machines (FSM): the appliances in this category present states, typically in a periodical fashion. Examples are washer/dryers, refrigerators, and so on;

Table 1. Summary of notation.

$\bar{y}(t)$	Aggregated energy consumption at time t, $\bar{y}(t) \in \mathbb{R}^T$
C	Number of appliances
T	Length of a signal
$y^{(i)}(t)$	True energy consumption of appliance i at time t, $y^{(i)}(t) \in \mathbb{R}^T$
$\hat{y}^{(i)}(t)$	Predicted energy consumption of appliance i at time t, $y^{(i)}(t) \in \mathbb{R}^T$
Z	Latent space representation of the mixture signal, $Z \in \mathbb{R}^{N \times K}$
m_i	Learned mask for appliance i, $m_i \in \mathbb{R}^N$
s_i	Filtered signal from the encoder for appliance i, $s_i \in \mathbb{R}^N$
N	Number of filters in encoder-decoder
L	Length of the filters
B	Number of channels in bottleneck and the residual paths' 1×1-conv blocks
H	Number of channels in convolutional blocks
P	Kernel size in convolutional blocks
X	Number of convolutional blocks in each repeat
R	Number of repeats

- Type III Continuously Varying Devices: the power of these appliances varies over time, but not in a periodic fashion. Examples are dimmers and tools.
- Type IV Permanent Consumer Devices: these are devices with constant power but that operate 24 h, such as alarms and external power supplies.

Current NILM methods work well for two-state appliances, but it is still difficult to identify some multi-state appliances, and even more challenging with continuous-state appliances. One of the most noticeable approaches called FHMM models each appliance as a hidden markov model (HMM) [13]. The HMM of each appliance is modelled independently, each one contributing to the aggregated power. AFAMAP [15] extends FHMM by predicting combinations of appliances working states. In AFAMAP, the posterior is constrained into one state change per time step. In [26], the authors propose a hierarchical FHMM in order to stop imposing independence between appliances. The algorithm takes the active power as input and performs a clustering of the correlated signals then trains an HMM on the identified clusters called super devices. During the disaggregation step, the prediction is done using AFAMAP on the super devices then the clustering is reversed to find the original appliance.

A critical step is the construction of load signatures or features that help to uniquely identify all types of home appliances with different operation modes. Event-based techniques have been employed to identify turn-on and turn-off events using a variety of features like the active and reactive power [2,8,31], current and voltage harmonics [27,28], transient behaviour particularly during the activation and/or deactivation [3,17], current waveform characteristics [30]. Although the existing harmonic-based NILM methods achieved high load identification accuracy, their applicability is limited. The main drawback of this approach is that it requires harmonic current signatures with respect to all possible combinations of devices. Consequently, the complexity of this method increases exponentially with the number of electrical devices.

Deep Learning approaches have consistently outperformed HMM-based methods. Indeed, the number of features associated with the complexity induced by all the possible devices combinations make deep learning a natural candidate for NILM. In recent years, learning-based approaches were proposed to classify and directly estimate the power consumption of type-1 and type-2 appliances from an aggregated signal. Although FHMM-based NILM approaches are extensively used for power disaggregation, their performance is limited to the accurate approximation of appliance actual power consumption especially for type-2 (multi-state) and type-4 (always-on) appliances. Moreover, HMM-based methods have been reported to suffer from scalability and generalisation, which limits its real-world application. In contrast to classical event-based and state-based approaches, deep neural networks are capable of dealing with time complexity issues, scalability issues, and can learn very complex appliance signatures if trained with sufficient data.

Most recent NILM works employing deep neural networks used 1/6-Hz or 1/3-Hz sampled active power measurement as an input feature to train various deep neural networks. Such as long short-term memory (LSTM) networks [21,24], denoised autoencoder [1,11] and Convolutional Neural Networks (CNN) [29,33]. [11] proposed 3 different neural networks. A convolutional layer followed by an LSTM to estimate the disaggregated signal from the global one. They also used a denoising convolutional autoencoder to produce clean signals. The last neural network estimates the beginning and the end time of each appliance activation along with the mean consumption of each. [11] performs better than FHMM however their model was unable to identify multi-state appliances. To solve the multi-state appliance identification issue, [21] proposed a two-layer bidirectional LSTM based DNN model. Similarly, [29] proposed a two-step approach to identify multi-state appliances. They used a deep CNN model to identify the type of appliances and then used a k-means clustering algorithm to calculate the number of states of appliances.

Deep Learning also allowed source separation rather than load identification. This approach is more difficult but offers precise estimation of the consumption of each appliance in real time which includes continuous state appliances. [9,33] proposed sequence-to-point learning-based CNN architecture with only active power as an input feature. In [4] gated linear unit convolutional layers [5] are used to extract information from the sequences of aggregate electricity consumption. In [23], the authors used a deep recurrent neural network using multi-feature input space and post-processing. First, the mutual information method was used to select electrical parameters that had the most influence on the power consumption of each target appliance. Second, selected parameters were used to train the LSTM for each target appliance. Finally, a post-processing technique was used at the disaggregation stage to eliminate irrelevant predicted sequences, enhancing the classification and estimation accuracy of the algorithm.

In [8], the authors present WaveNILM which is a causal 1-D convolutional neural network inspired by WaveNet [22] for NILM on low-frequency data. They used various components of the complex power signal for NILM, current, active power, reactive power, and apparent power. WaveNILM, requires no significant alterations whether using one or many input signals. However, most of the existing DNNs models for NILM use a single-task learning approach in which a neural network is trained exclusively for each appliance. That is also the case for Wave-NILM. This strategy is computationally expensive and ignores the fact that multiple appliances can be active simultaneously and dependencies between them. In [7] the authors introduce UNet-NILM for multi-task appliances' state detection and power estimation, applying a multi-label learning strategy and multi-target quantile regression. The UNet-NILM is a one-dimensional CNN based on the U-Net architecture initially proposed for image segmentation [25]. However, this model is not causal like WaveNILM.

Conv-NILM-net achieves the best of both worlds as it can handle source separation for any type of appliance, for multiple appliances simultaneously, it only needs the active power (although it is possible to other types of current in the same time).

3   Conv-NILM-Net

The model aims at separating C individual power sources $y^{(i)} \in \mathbb{R}^T$, where $i \in \{1, 2, \ldots, C\}$ from a mixture of signals representing the total consumption $\bar{y}(t) = \sum_{i=1}^{C} y^{(i)}(t) + e(t)$ and T is the length of the waveform. Therefore it take as input a single channel time series corresponding to the total consumption and outputs C time series corresponding to the consumption of each individual appliance. In this section, we present and detail our proposed architecture. We will describe the overall structure before focusing on the separation module.

3.1   Overall Structure

Conv-NILM-Net is an adaptation of ConvTas-net [20]. Conv-Tasnet was originally only designed for speech separation and limited to two speakers. We propose an adaptation to energy load source separation with theoretically no limitation to the number of appliances. Our fully convolutional model is trainable end-to end and uses the aggregated active power as only input making the training easily deployable (no additional costly features needed).

Conv-NILM-net architecture consists of two parts: an encoder/decoder, and a separator. The encoder generates a multidimensional representation of the mixture signal; the separator learns masks applied to this representation to decompose the mixture signal, then the decoder translates the obtained signals from the encoded representation to the classic active power. The masks are found using a temporal convolutional network (TCN) consisting of stacked 1-D dilated convolutional blocks, which allows the network to model the long-term dependencies of the signal while maintaining a small model size.

Using encoder filters of length L, the model first segments the input total consumption into K overlapping frames $\bar{y}_k \in \mathbb{R}^L$, $k = 1, 2, \ldots, K$ each of length L with stride S. $\bar{y}_k$ is transformed into a N-dimensional representation, $Z \in \mathbb{R}^{N \times K}$:

$$Z = \mathcal{F}(w \cdot \bar{Y}) \tag{2}$$

where $Y \in \mathbb{R}^{L \times K}$ and $w \in \mathbb{R}^{N \times K}$ the N learnable basis filters of length L each. Z represents the latent space representation of the mixture series while $\mathcal{F}$ is a non-linear function. To ensure that the representation is non-negative, Conv-tasnet [20] uses the rectified linear unit (ReLU). However, this choice leads to a vanishing gradient behaviour, driving the norm of the gradients towards 0 thus making the model collapse as it eventually outputs null signals. Therefore, we replace ReLU with Leaky ReLU and only use ReLU for the last layer of the separation masks to enforce positive outputs.

The separator predicts a representation for each source by learning a mask in this latent space. It is performed by estimating C masks $m_i \in \mathbb{R}^N$. The representation of each source $s_i \in \mathbb{R}^N$, is then calculated by applying the corresponding mask m_i to the mixture representation, using element-wise multiplication:

$$s_i = Z \odot m_i \tag{3}$$

In Conv-tasnet as well as in [19], the masks were constrained such that $\sum_{i=1}^{C} m_i = 1$. This was applied based on the assumption that the encoder-decoder architecture can perfectly reconstruct the input mixture. Indeed, in their model, $e(t) = 0$, $\forall t$. This assumption cannot be made in a NILM context, it is therefore relaxed.

The input signal of each source is then reconstructed by the decoder:

$$\hat{y}^{(i)} = s_i \cdot V \tag{4}$$

where $V \in \mathbb{R}^{N \times L}$ are the decoder filters, each of length L.

3.2 Separation Module

The separator is mainly based on a temporal convolutional network (TCN) [16] and is detailed in Fig. 3. Temporal convolutions require the use of dilated convolutions which aim to increase the receptive field. Indeed, pooling or strided convolutions are usually implemented for this purpose, however they reduce the resolution. Dilated convolutions allow exponential expansions of the receptive field without loss of resolution, while achieving same computation and memory costs. These are simply implemented by defining a spacing between the values in a kernel as illustrated in Fig. 2.

In [21], the authors used LSTM [18] for NILM. This architecture can handle long sequences but suffers from the vanishing gradient issue while being computationally costly. We argue that a more efficient approach is to make use of 1D-convolutions. As illustrated in Fig. 2, convolutions for time series require future values (compared to the point of reference). During inference, these values

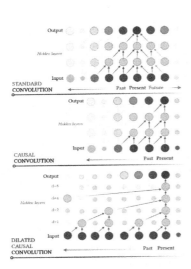

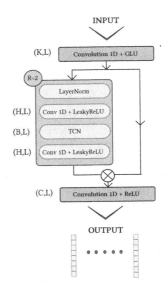

Fig. 2. Causal and dilated convolutions.

Fig. 3. Detailed representation of the separator.

are not accessible making the use of this model unpractical for prediction. This can be solved by giving a causal formulation to convolutions where the present value only depends of past ones. Moreover, the implementation is easy as it only requires an asymmetric padding.

However relevant values become sparse. As in [20], Conv-NILM-net uses dilated layers with exponentially increasing dilation rates. The dilation factors increase exponentially to ensure a sufficiently large temporal context window to take advantage of the long-range dependencies in the signal. Therefore the dilation factors increase exponentially to ensure a sufficiently large temporal context window to take advantage of the long-range dependencies in the signal. Therefore TCN consists of 1-D convolutional blocks with increasing dilation factors. Given kernels of length L and l layers, the receptive field of Conv-NILM-net is of size $RF = 2^l(L-1)$.

The output of the TCN is passed to a 1×1 conv block for mask estimation. This block also serves for dimensionality reduction and together with a nonlinear activation function estimates C mask vectors for the C target sources. The last layer of the last bloc uses a ReLU activation function to ensure the non-negativity of the outputs.

Contrary to speech separation, where simultaneous speeches are independent from one another, it is not the case in NILM context where appliance activations can be highly dependent. An elegant solution proposed in [4,10], can be to use gated linear units (GLU) [5] to replace LeakyReLU activation functions. GLU allow the model to decide itself the relative importance of the kernels by using two parallel convolutions with the first followed by a sigmoid which result is then

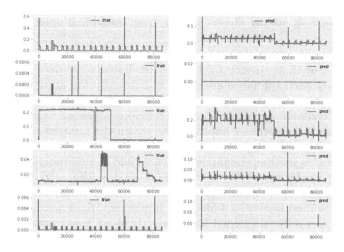

Fig. 4. Outputs of Conv-NILM-net of top 5 appliances of REDD building 1 when trained using classic MSE. We observe the presence of the artefacts although the MSE is minimized.

multiplied with the second convolution. The output of the sigmoid acts like a mask that activates depending on the input of the second convolution.

MSE, L_1, or even SI-SNR [20] losses are often used for NILM or source separation problems. The MSE takes the average squared error on all time steps for all disaggregated signals (i.e. appliances). We found that taking the mean on appliances is detrimental to the learning process as the error is distributed over all appliances. Therefore, the signals get mixed and artefacts of most consuming appliances appear on the remaining ones as illustrated in Fig. 4. We therefore choose to sum the error over all appliance rather than averaging it. The window mean squared error is calculated as:

$$\text{WMSE} = \frac{1}{T} \sum_{t=0}^{T} \sum_{i=1}^{C} \left(\hat{y}^{(i)}(t) - \bar{y}^{(i)}(t) \right)^2 \tag{5}$$

4   Experimental Methodology, Results, and Discussion

4.1   Datasets and Parameters

Our experiments are done on two real-world datasets, Reference Energy Disaggregation Dataset (REDD) [14] and UK-DALE [12]. REDD records the power for 6 houses with sampling frequency 1 Hz for mains meter and 1/3 Hz for appliance-channel meters. We choose to disaggregate the five top appliances for each building. UK-DALE data set published in 2015, records the power demand from five UK houses. In each house we record both the whole-house mains power demand every six seconds as well as power demand from individual appliances every six seconds.

For REDD, we converted the disaggregated data 1 Hz using linear extrapolation and kept 1/6 Hz frequency for UK-DALE. Usually the data are normalised and the series of each appliance are scaled individually. We argue that appliance scaling is not practical as it is not possible to apply the scaling factors to the global signal available during inference. Therefore we chose to only use a min-max scaler for all appliances combined directly on the mixture power signal. In some contributions like seq2seq and seq2point [9,33], a sliding window of the aggregate power is used as the input sequence, and the midpoint of the window corresponding to the target device reading is used as the output. This preprocessing smooths the power loads and makes the target values to retrieve easier. All results presented in Sect. 4.3 for these implementations were obtained using smoothing. The results presented for Conv-NILM-NET were obtained without smoothing, making the difference in performance even more noticeable.

For UK-DALE dataset, we compare our results to UNET-NILM [7] and seq2point [9]. The constructed artificial aggregate consumption is obtained by taking the summation of selected appliances plus additional one appliance (Television in this setting). For UNET-NILM, the authors used a quantile filter to smooth the signal. This is not required for Conv-NILM-Net.

In our implementation for Conv-NILM-Net, we used for, each dataset, one day as input. This means that 1 Hz frequency, the input to Conv-NILM-net was 86400 points for REDD and 14400 for UK-DALE (1/6 Hz). The used parameters for Conv-NILM net are: $N = 32$; $L = 48$; $B = 2$; $H = P = X = 3$; $R = 2$. The meaning of each notation is made available in Table 1 where we kept the same notation as in [20]. The model was trained for 2000 epochs using 10-fold cross-validation and a batch size of 5. We used Adam optimiser with an initial learning rate $lr = 0.01$, betas $= (0.9, 0.999)$, eps $= 0.01$.

4.2 Metrics

We evaluate the performance of the framework using the mean absolute error (MAE). Estimated accuracy is also a common metric for evaluating disaggregated power.

$$\text{Est.Acc.} = 1 - \frac{\sum_{t=1}^{T}\sum_{i=1}^{C}|\hat{y}^{(i)}(t) - \bar{y}^{(i)}(t)|}{2\sum_{t=1}^{T}\sum_{i=1}^{C}\bar{y}^{(i)}(t)} \tag{6}$$

where $\hat{y}^{(i)}(t)$ is the predicted power level of appliance i at time t, and $\bar{y}^{(i)}(t)$ is the ground truth. The above expression yields total estimated accuracy; if needed, the summation over i can be removed creating an appliance-specific estimation accuracy. We also report the Signal Aggregate Error (SAE):

$$\text{SAE} = \frac{|\hat{r} - r|}{r} \tag{7}$$

Table 2. Conv-NILM-Net scaled results on top five appliances REDD dataset. Best average results are highlighted in bold.

Building	Appliance	Model								
		Conv-NILM-NET			Causal			Causal + GLU		
		MAE	Est.Acc	SAE	MAE	Est.Acc	SAE	MAE	Est.Acc	SAE
Building 1	Fridge	0.049	0.900	0.058	0.006	0.981	0.053	0.004	0.987	0.051
	Washer dryer	0.005	0.937	0.074	0.002	0.993	0.088	0.002	0.990	0.103
	Light	0.063	0.970	0.030	0.007	0.980	0.021	0.008	0.984	0.033
	Sockets	0.015	0.874	0.092	0.005	0.984	0.131	0.006	0.992	0.191
	Dishwasher	0.006	0.916	0.102	0.002	0.993	0.095	0.003	0.997	0.070
	Total	0.027	0.919	0.071	0.005	0.986	0.078	**0.004**	**0.989**	**0.054**
Building 2	Fridge	0.038	0.912	0.052	0.032	0.939	0.068	0.041	0.956	0.054
	Washer dryer	0.018	0.914	0.109	0.031	0.940	0.098	0.034	0.967	0.087
	Light	0.012	0.986	0.024	0.002	0.981	0.104	0.008	0.987	0.099
	Sockets	0.002	0.993	0.059	0.001	0.991	0.032	0.006	0.990	0.058
	Dishwasher	0.0006	0.997	0.115	0.001	0.993	0.029	0.003	0.992	0.031
	Total	**0.014**	0.960	0.0718	**0.014**	0.969	**0.066**	0.018	**0.978**	**0.066**
Building 3	Fridge	0.006	0.820	0.089	0.072	0.822	0.078	0.009	0.856	0.068
	Washer dryer	0.007	0.997	0.061	0.003	0.993	0.065	0.004	0.993	0.087
	Light	0.009	0.863	0.123	0.037	0.854	0.098	0.006	0.900	0.098
	Sockets	0.009	0.961	0.091	0.040	0.941	0.080	0.007	0.942	0.126
	Dishwasher	0.007	0.960	0.085	0.032	0.940	0.096	0.005	0.989	0.078
	Total	**0.006**	0.920	0.90	0.037	0.910	**0.083**	**0.006**	**0.936**	0.091
Building 4	Fridge	0.003	0.961	0.054	0.007	0.982	0.021	0.050	0.930	0.043
	Washer dryer	0.002	0.947	0.105	0.016	0.933	0.087	0.031	0.954	0.056
	Light	0.002	0.936	0.076	0.019	0.940	0.055	0.002	0.901	0.080
	Sockets	0.001	0.981	0.098	0.008	0.980	0.016	0.006	0.937	0.024
	Dishwasher	0.0006	0.994	0.132	0.002	0.995	0.098	0.020	0.892	0.069
	Total	**0.002**	0.964	0.093	0.011	**0.966**	0.055	0.022	0.923	**0.054**
Building 5	Fridge	0.003	0.883	0.005	0.005	0.880	0.004	0.005	0.991	0.093
	Washer dryer	0.003	0.992	0.001	0.0009	0.993	0.001	0.003	0.983	0.012
	Light	0.0006	0.999	0.0001	0.0001	0.999	0.002	0.002	0.977	0.10
	Sockets	0.0006	0.966	0.002	0.002	0.97	0.005	0.007	0.931	0.037
	Dishwasher	0.0008	0.913	0.004	0.004	0.91	0.002	0.010	0.990	0.078
	Total	**0.002**	0.950	**0.002**	**0.002**	0.95	**0.002**	0.005	**0.974**	0.064

where $\hat{r}$ and r represent the predicted total energy consumption of an appliance and the ground truth one. SAE measures the total error in the energy within a period, which is accurate for reporting daily power consumption even if its consumption is inaccurate in every time point.

4.3 Results on REDD

Table 2 presents the results obtained on REDD dataset for five building. For each building with disaggregated the top five appliances and reported the MAE, estimated accuracy ans SAE. We tested 3 versions on Conv-NILM-net. We observe that the causal+GLU tend to perform better on average but its results are very close to the causal implementation while increasing the number of parameters dramatically. We therefore tend to prefer the causal version of our model.

Table 3. MAE results for Building 1 of REDD dataset.

Model	Fridge	Microwave	Dishwasher
seq2point	28.104	28.199	20.048
seq2seq	30.63	33.272	19.449
GLU-Res [4]	21.97	25.202	33.37
CNN-DI [34]	26.801	19.455	17.665
Conv-NILM-NET	14.67	9.67	3.56
Conv-NILM-NET (causal)	14.21	8.51	3.29
Conv-NILM-NET (GLU, causal)	15.02	9.76	3.31

Table 4. Experimental results (MAE) in the UK-DALE dataset.

Appliance	Model					
	1D-CNN	UNET-NILM	Seq2point	Ours	Ours (causal)	Ours (causal + GLU)
Kettle	20.390	16.003	2.16	1.85	1.9	2.5
Freezer	18.583	15.124	8.136	5.32	5.01	6.1
Dish washer	9.884	6.764	3.49	2.42	2.01	2.55
Washing machine	15.758	11.506	4.063	2.3	2.15	2.39
Microwave	9.690	6.475	1.305	0.902	0.91	1.05
Total	14.86	11.174	3.831	2.56	2.40	2.918

Table 3 compares the performance of Conv-NILM-net with state of the art models on 3 appliances that appear on REDD dataset. These appliances were selected as they are the only one presented in [34]. We therefore were limited to these appliance to compare our framework. We observe that our models outperform the state of the art by a margin. It decreases the MAE by 45% for the fridge, 51% for the microwave and even by 80% for the dishwasher. The best performing model is the causal model. In the appendix we present some outputs of the model for buildings 1 to 4 from REDD. These were obtained when disaggregating the top 5 appliances detailed in the same order as in Table 2.

4.4   Results on UK-DALE

Table 4 compares the MAE of our model on UK-DALE dataset with UNET-NILM and seq2point. Our model outperforms the state of the art on the selected appliances. The causal model performs the best again while the total average is decreased by 33% compared to seq2pont.

Table 5 compares the size of Conv-NILM-net with state of the art models in terms of number of parameters. We observe that the fully convolution architecture of our model along with its particular architecture (encoder/decoder + separator) allow to obtain state of the art results with a model of approximately 40K parameters. This also possible because, contrary to other models, we use

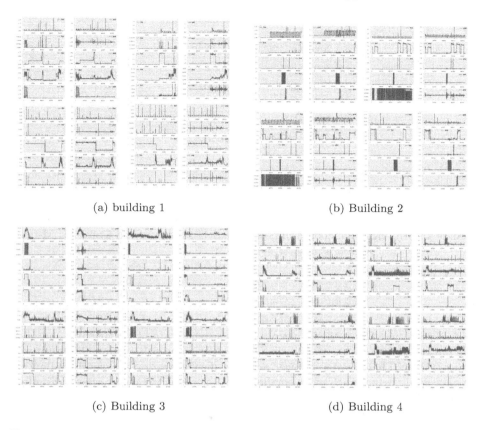

(a) building 1   (b) Building 2

(c) Building 3   (d) Building 4

Fig. 5. Selected results on top five appliances of first 4 building of REDD dataset. For each building the appliances are presented in the same order as in Table 2. The left panels correspond to the disaggregated target signals and the right panels presents the predicted output from Conv-NILM-net.

a unique loss for only one task. For instance UNET-NILM uses two separate loss functions, one to detect activation and an other to regress the average consumption while Seq2point [9] uses bidirectional residual networks which are very deep. It is also valuable to notice that models like UNET-NILM are specialized on individual appliances, meaning that in one needs to disaggregate 5 appliances, it requires 5 models, multiplying the number of parameters.

Table 5. Number of parameters

Models	# parameters
seq2point	29.2M
seq2seq	29.8M
GLU-Res	1.2M
CNN-DI	738K
Conv-NILM-net	41088

Finally, Fig. 5 presents some results on top five appliances of first 4 building of REDD dataset. For each building the appliances are presented in the same order as in Table 2. The left panels corresponds to the disaggregated target signals and the right panels presents the predicted output from Conv-NILM-net.

5   Conclusion

In this work, we presented Conv-NILM-net, an adaptation of Convtas-net to non intrusive load monitoring. We tested our model on two real world dataset and showed that Conv-NILM-net outperforms the state of the art by a margin. We presented 2 alternate models, one being causal and other using Gated Linear Units (GLU). These models allowed accurate disaggregation of several appliances at once while being much more smaller than their existing counterparts. Finally, the causal model allows consumption prediction and is ideal as input to an energy management system or a reinforcement learning model. In future work, we will use causal conv-NILM-net as a prediction model and test it in a reinforcement learning context. We will also test the GLU augmented model to verify if this implementation effectively takes into account appliances inter-dependencies and helps achieve better consumption predictions.

References

1. Bonfigli, R., Felicetti, A., Principi, E., Fagiani, M., Squartini, S., Piazza, F.: Denoising autoencoders for non-intrusive load monitoring: improvements and comparative evaluation. Energy Build. **158**, 1461–1474 (2018)
2. Bonfigli, R., Principi, E., Fagiani, M., Severini, M., Squartini, S., Piazza, F.: Non-intrusive load monitoring by using active and reactive power in additive factorial hidden Markov models. Appl. Energy **208**, 1590–1607 (2017)
3. Chang, H.-H.: Load identification of non-intrusive load-monitoring system in smart home. WSEAS Trans. Syst. **9**, 498–510 (2010)
4. Chen, K., Wang, Q., He, Z., Chen, K., Hu, J., He, J.: Convolutional sequence to sequence non-intrusive load monitoring. J. Eng. **2018**(17), 1860–1864 (2018)
5. Dauphin, Y.N., Fan, A., Auli, M., Grangier, D.: Language modeling with gated convolutional networks (2016)
6. EUROSTAT: Energy consumption in households (2018)

7. Faustine, A., Pereira, L., Bousbiat, H., Kulkarni, S.: UNet-NILM: a deep neural network for multi-tasks appliances state detection and power estimation in NILM. In: Proceedings of the 5th International Workshop on Non-Intrusive Load Monitoring, NILM 2020, pp. 84–88. Association for Computing Machinery, New York (2020)
8. Harell, A., Makonin, S., Bajić, I.V.: WaveNILM: a causal neural network for power disaggregation from the complex power signal (2019)
9. Jia, Z., Yang, L., Zhang, Z., Liu, H., Kong, F.: Sequence to point learning based on bidirectional dilated residual network for non intrusive load monitoring. Int. J. Electr. Power Energy Syst. **129**, 106837 (2021)
10. Kadioglu, B., Horgan, M., Liu, X., Pons, J., Darcy, D., Kumar, V.: An empirical study of Conv-TasNet (2020)
11. Kelly, J., Knottenbelt, W.: Neural NILM. In: Proceedings of the 2nd ACM International Conference on Embedded Systems for Energy-Efficient Built Environments. ACM, November 2015
12. Kelly, J., Knottenbelt, W.: The UK-DALE dataset, domestic appliance-level electricity demand and whole-house demand from five UK homes. Sci. Data **2**(150007), 1–14 (2015)
13. Kim, H., Marwah, M., Arlitt, M., Lyon, G., Han, J.: Unsupervised disaggregation of low frequency power measurements, pp. 747–758 (2011)
14. Kolter, J., Johnson, M.: REDD: a public data set for energy disaggregation research. Artif. Intell. **25** (2011)
15. Kolter, J.Z., Jaakkola, T.: Approximate inference in additive factorial HMMs with application to energy disaggregation. In: Lawrence, N.D., Girolami, M. (eds.) Proceedings of the Fifteenth International Conference on Artificial Intelligence and Statistics, Volume 22 of Proceedings of Machine Learning Research, La Palma, Canary Islands, 21–23 April 2012, pp. 1472–1482. PMLR (2012)
16. Lea, C., Vidal, R., Reiter, A., Hager, G.D.: Temporal convolutional networks: a unified approach to action segmentation. In: Hua, G., Jégou, H. (eds.) ECCV 2016. LNCS, vol. 9915, pp. 47–54. Springer, Cham (2016). https://doi.org/10.1007/978-3-319-49409-8_7
17. Li, J., Yang, H.: The investigation of residential load identification technologies. In: 2012 Asia-Pacific Power and Energy Engineering Conference, pp. 1–4 (2012)
18. Lindemann, B., Müller, T., Vietz, H., Jazdi, N., Weyrich, M.: A survey on long short-term memory networks for time series prediction. Procedia CIRP **99**, 650–655 (2021). 14th CIRP Conference on Intelligent Computation in Manufacturing Engineering, 15–17 July 2020
19. Luo, Y., Mesgarani, N.: TasNet: time-domain audio separation network for real-time, single-channel speech separation (2017)
20. Luo, Y., Mesgarani, N.: Conv-TasNet: surpassing ideal time–frequency magnitude masking for speech separation. IEEE/ACM Trans. Audio Speech Lang. Process. **27**(8), 1256–1266 (2019)
21. Mauch, L., Yang, B.: A new approach for supervised power disaggregation by using a deep recurrent LSTM network. In: 2015 IEEE Global Conference on Signal and Information Processing (GlobalSIP), pp. 63–67 (2015)
22. van den Oord, A., et al.: WaveNet: a generative model for raw audio (2016)
23. Rafiq, H., Shi, X., Zhang, H., Li, H., Ochani, M.K.: A deep recurrent neural network for non-intrusive load monitoring based on multi-feature input space and post-processing. Energies **13**(9), 2195 (2020)

24. Rafiq, H., Zhang, H., Li, H., Ochani, M.K.: Regularized LSTM based deep learning model: first step towards real-time non-intrusive load monitoring. In: 2018 IEEE International Conference on Smart Energy Grid Engineering (SEGE), pp. 234–239 (2018)
25. Ronneberger, O., Fischer, P., Brox, T.: U-Net: convolutional networks for biomedical image segmentation. In: Navab, N., Hornegger, J., Wells, W.M., Frangi, A.F. (eds.) MICCAI 2015. LNCS, vol. 9351, pp. 234–241. Springer, Cham (2015). https://doi.org/10.1007/978-3-319-24574-4_28
26. Schirmer, P.A., Mporas, I., Paraskevas, M.: Energy disaggregation using elastic matching algorithms. Entropy **22**(1), 71 (2020)
27. Semwal, S., Shah, G., Prasad, R.S.: Identification residential appliance using NIALM, December 2014
28. Shao, H., Marwah, M., Ramakrishnan, N.: A temporal motif mining approach to unsupervised energy disaggregation. In: Proceedings of the 27th AAAI Conference on Artificial Intelligence, AAAI 2013, January 2013
29. Zhang, Y., Yin, B., Cong, Y., Du, Z.: Multi-state household appliance identification based on convolutional neural networks and clustering. Energies **13**, 792 (2020)
30. Srinivasan, D., Ng, W.S., Liew, A.C.: Neural-network-based signature recognition for harmonic source identification. IEEE Trans. Power Deliv. **21**(1), 398–405 (2006)
31. Valenti, M., Bonfigli, R., Principi, E., Squartini, S.: Exploiting the reactive power in deep neural models for non-intrusive load monitoring. In: 2018 International Joint Conference on Neural Networks (IJCNN), pp. 1–8 (2018)
32. Liang, Y., Qin, S., Zhang, M., Shen, C., Jiang, T., Guan, X.: A review of deep reinforcement learning for smart building energy management. IEEE Internet Things J. **8**(15), 12046–12063 (2021)
33. Zhang, C., Zhong, M., Wang, Z., Goddard, N., Sutton, C.: Sequence-to-point learning with neural networks for nonintrusive load monitoring (2016)
34. Zhang, Y., Yang, G., Ma, S.: Non-intrusive load monitoring based on convolutional neural network with differential input. Procedia CIRP **83**, 670–674 (2019). 11th CIRP Conference on Industrial Product-Service Systems

Domestic Hot Water Forecasting for Individual Housing with Deep Learning

Paul Compagnon[1]([✉]), Aurore Lomet[2], Marina Reyboz[1],
and Martial Mermillod[3]

[1] Univ. Grenoble Alpes, CEA, List, 38000 Grenoble, France
`{paul.compagnon,marina.reyboz}@cea.fr`
[2] CEA, LIST, 91191 Gif-sur-Yvette, France
`aurore.lomet@cea.fr`
[3] LPNC Univ. Grenoble Alpes & CNRS, 38000 Grenoble, France
`martial.mermillod@univ-grenoble-alpes.fr`

Abstract. The energy sharing used to heat water represents around 15% in European houses. To improve energy efficiency, smart heating systems could benefit from accurate domestic hot water consumption forecasting in order to adapt their heating profile. However, forecasting the hot water consumption for a single accommodation can be difficult since the data are generally highly non smooth and present large variations from day to day. We propose to tackle this issue with three deep learning approaches, Recurrent Neural Networks, 1-Dimensional Convolutional Neural Networks and Multi-Head Attention to perform one day ahead prediction of hot water consumption for an individual residence. Moreover, similarly as in the transformer architecture, we experiment enriching the last two approaches with various forms of position encoding to include the order of the sequence in the data. The experimented models achieved satisfying performances in term of MSE on an individual residence dataset, showing that this approach is promising to conceive building energy management systems based on deep forecasting models.

Keywords: Time series forecasting · Domestic hot water · Deep learning · Convolutional Neural Networks · Multi-Head Attention

1 Introduction

In 2020, the average energy sharing used in an European house to heat water was around 15% [1]. Most of the time, water is heated before being used by a water heating system which priority is to insure user comfort by providing enough hot water at any time. The system can heat too much water in advance leading to energy waste [2]. This is even more true if the system is alimented by a heat pump which performance depends on a large number of external factors such as the weather. These considerations highlight the need for accurate forecasting models of hot water consumption, that would allow to heat up just the right amount of water at the best moment improving the building energy efficiency.

I. Koprinska et al. (Eds.): ECML PKDD 2022 Workshops, CCIS 1753, pp. 223–235, 2023.
https://doi.org/10.1007/978-3-031-23633-4_16

However, Domestic Hot Water (DHW) forecast for individual residences can be difficult due to the consumption being very sporadic and highly variable from days to days [3]. To solve this problem, we explore the use of deep learning models. Indeed, we propose to compare three deep learning approaches adapted to sequence processing to forecast individual hot water consumption: Recurrent Neural Networks (RNN), Convolutional Neural Networks (CNN) and Multi-Head Attention (MHA). Unlike RNN, CNN and MHA do not explicitly take into account the temporal dependencies in the data (they both consider a sequence as an unordered matrix). One way to correct this is to use position encoding as in the whole transformer architecture [4]. A position encoding will be added to a representation in order to drag it in a specific direction in the feature space, the same for elements at the same position in different sequences. We compare CNN and MHA equipped with 3 different position encoding: fixed as in [4], learned as in [5] and produced by a RNN. In a similar way as in [6], we also propose a version where the days and hours are embedded the same way instead of being one hot encoded. Another aspect of the proposed models is that they are constituted of a few layers unlike recent approaches proposed for time series forecasting [7] and this has two upsides. Firstly, they can be trained on a small number of samples and therefore be put into production quickly with data coming from a single accommodation. Secondly, they can also more easily be embedded inside a heating system with small computation power preserving the privacy of data. We test those architectures on a dataset recorded on a real system installed in an individual accommodation.

The remaining of the paper is organized as follows. Section 2 overviews the state of the art of water consumption forecasting with a focus on deep learning approaches. Section 3 describes the components of the employed deep architectures and specifically the different position encodings experimented. Section 4 presents the individual consumption dataset we used, the experimental setup and the achieved results. Finally, Sect. 5 concludes this paper and presents some perspectives of this work.

2   Related Work

In this section, we give an overview of the different approaches used in the literature to forecast water consumption. First, a large number of papers seek to forecast water consumption at a large scale, for neighborhood, cities or even entire regions [8–10]. Candelieri et al. [11] proposed to use several Support Vector Machine (SVM) models to forecast the water demand in a distribution network with a 24h delay. Each model takes as input the first six hours of the day and forecast one different time slot of one hour of consumption. Moreover, the authors employ time series clustering to determine several consumption profiles and train different SVM models accordingly. Mu et al. [12] proposed to use a Long-Short term memory network (LSTM) [13] to forecast the water demand of a city at a one-hour or 24h delay. They found that their approach got better results than AutoRegressive Integrated Moving Average modeling (ARIMA), which combines an autoregressive part consisting of a weighted sum of the previous times steps and a moving average part to model the error, SVM and random forests models. This was particularly true when performing high resolution predictions (e.g. a prediction every few minutes) on data with abrupt changes. They also highlighted the upside of LSTM to allow to output a sequence of predictions. Finally, in a recent paper, Karamaziotis et al. [14] compared ARIMA models, Optimized Theta (a form of exponential smoothing model), Ensemble methods and neural networks to forecast the water consumption of in European capital cities with a forecast horizon of several months. They concluded, based on various metrics, that ARIMA models seem the best approach in several prediction scenarii. From these papers, we can conclude that various machine learning models can be considered to forecast the water consumption with ARIMA models seemingly achieving the best performances.

However, individual residences present an additional difficulty since the consumption is generally non smooth and irregular compared to apartment building. Moreover, large variations across days could happen more frequently (for examples, all the inhabitants of the house leave for several days). This assumption was observed experimentally by Maltais et al. [3] who proposed to use neural networks to predict the DHW consumption of residential buildings with different sizes. They observed that the prediction performances were better when increasing size of the systems. They attributed this difference to the smallest ones presenting too much variations in their consumption and they were consequently the worst predicted. Overall, the problem of small or individual residences has been less tackled by the literature and the employed approaches generally fall into two categories. The first one is once again ARMA modeling [15]. This approach have been used by Lomet et al. [16] to perform DHW load prediction for a single family accommodation. After studying the data, notably the autocorrelograms, they decided to take into account the weekly periodicity (the seasonality of the time series) and the consumption of the two previous days to build their model. Gelažanskas et al. [17] also analyzed the effect of seasonality to improve regression performances. They likewise found that a SARIMA (Seasonal ARIMA) model taking into account daily and weekly consumption patterns performed better. The second type of approaches is deep learning. Barteczko-Hibbert et al. [18] experimented using Multi-Layer Perceptron (MLP) to predict the temperature of the drawn hot water to optimize the heating system. They trained the network on a particular heating profile and tested on another one and found that the model generalized better if it was trained on two different heating profiles instead of one. In another publication, Gelažanskas et al. [19] tackled the issue of hot water forecasting with an auto regressive neural network taking as input data from the previous hours, data from seven days before and external variables, in an autoregressive manner. They showed the importance of external variables to improve predictions. Regarding the type of approaches, the last two papers did not employed specific deep learning models for sequences such as LSTM mentioned above. Gelažanskas et al. took into account the seasonality of the data but with a MLP architecture.

If ARIMA models have proven their efficiency to model hot water consumption, more results seem needed with neural networks to conclude. However, neural networks have also been found to perform better than ARIMA in various conditions which are realized for individual housing profiles: when the needed resolution of the prediction is high and when the data present gaps [12] or high variability [20]. Moreover, ARIMA models are linear unlike neural networks than can model non-linear relationships which has proven to be useful to forecast hot water consumption [21]. As a consequence, ARIMA models seem less adapted to this task. Additionally, pure deep learning models present several upsides compared to classical machine learning or hybrid models: firstly they do not require feature engineering, secondly they can be trained end to end with a single objective and allow to simply combine different types of layers and differentiable processings, finally they have a very low inference time making them suited for real time systems. Based on these observations, in this paper, we propose to employ deep learning architectures to build lightweight forecast models for individual homes that can be easily embedded inside heat pump control systems. We focus on architectures specifically adapted for time series processing and we will now present them.

3   Proposed Architectures

In this section, we describe the different neural network components that will constitute the tested deep architectures for DHW forecasting.

3.1   Recurrent Neural Networks

Recurrent Neural Networks (RNN) are the primary component to deal with sequences and time series. A simple RNN's equation is as follows:

$$h_t = f(W_i x_t + b_i + W_h h_{t-1} + b_h), \tag{1}$$

where $x_t \in \mathbb{R}^n$ defines a sequential input, f is a non linear activation function, most of the time hyperbolic tangent or sigmoid and W_i, W_h, b_i and b_h are parameters of the models to be learned. The output $h_t \in \mathbb{R}^m$ defines a sequence with the same length as the input sequence and is reinjected each time with along the new input. This way, the RNN is able to learn temporal correlations inside the sequence.

However, vanilla RNN as the one described above actually do not work when sequence become too long. Due to a phenomenon called vanishing gradient, they are in fact not able to learn long-term dependencies in the sequence [22]. To work around this issue, gated RNN such as LSTM [13] and later Gated Recurrent Units (GRU) [23] have been developed. These neural networks emulate a memory thanks to a system of gates that let pass new information and forget old one.

3.2   One-Dimensional Convolutional Neural Networks

One-dimensional Convolutional Neural Networks (1DCNN) are a variant of CNN that has been employed to perform signal processing tasks and time series forecasting [24–26]. They are actually close to the old Time-Delay neural networks

[27]. One great upside of 1DCNN compared to their 2D counterparts is their lower time complexity: they are therefore well suited to build compact embedded architectures with few layers [28].

1DCNN uses convolutional filters that move only in the time direction on all the features at the same time, with a kernel size determining the number of convoluted timesteps. This way, they can detect local temporal correlations in the data. The locality can be extended by adding more layers. Similarly as with 2D CNN, after one or several convolution layers, a pooling layer is called. In our experiments, we used average pooling instead of the classical maximum pooling as we found it achieved better results.

3.3 Multi-Head Attention

Multi-Head attention (MHA) [4] is the central component of the transformer neural network architecture that is primarily used for natural language processing tasks. Transformer architectures can also be used for time series forecasting [7,29], by they are very deep and would require much more data to be properly trained as well as a lot of computation power. Therefore, in this paper, we will not make use of a whole transformer model but only some of its components to build an *ad hoc* architecture: position encodings (see below) and thus Multi-Head Attention.

Attention is a differentiable mechanism that allows to make a query on a discrete set to get a result as a weighted sum of the elements of the set. Formally, consider three matrices Q, K and V, respectively the query, the keys and the values, attention is computed the following way:

$$\text{Attention}(Q, K, V) = \text{softmax}\left(\frac{QK^T}{\sqrt{m}}\right) V, \tag{2}$$

where m is the number of features of K used here to scale the softmax. In practice, self-attention is used meaning that Q, K and V are the same matrix, in our case, a sequence. To make Multi-Head Attention, for the desired number of heads, Q, K and V are each projected in a different (learnable) space before Eq. 2 is applied. Then, the results are concatenated and projected again.

The output of the MHA being a sequence, we need a mechanism to obtain a vector to be then projected into a single value. We explored three way to perform this operation: with a RNN, using a average pooling similarly as with CNN and simply taking the last value of the sequence. After several tests, we finally decided to use an average pooling as with 1DCNN.

3.4 Position Encodings

Along MHA, position encoding (or embeddings) in another component of the transformer architecture [4]. It is used to introduce information about the order in the data since the transformer will see the sequence as a whole and not timesteps by timesteps as for a RNN. A similar idea was introduced in [5] for

CNN with learned embedding. For both architectures, we start by projecting the input a time t inside a first representation space for dimensionality reduction before adding the position encodings associated with time t:

$$r_t = Wx_t + e_t, \tag{3}$$

where $r_t, e_t \in \mathbb{R}^m$ and W are learnable parameters. We detailed below the two types of positional encoding previously mentioned along with two others.

Fixed Position Embedding. This approach is used in [4] and relies on fixed predefined codes to be added to the representations. Those codes are computed the following way for timestep t and feature index i:

$$e_t(2i) = \sin\left(\frac{t}{10000^{2i/m}}\right), \tag{4}$$

$$e_t(2i+1) = \cos\left(\frac{t}{10000^{2i/m}}\right). \tag{5}$$

With this position embedding, each position is uniquely represented by trigonometric functions with different frequencies.

Learned Position Embedding. This approach was proposed by Gehring et al. [5] for CNN. Here, each timestep t is embedded in a feature space of the same dimensionality as:

$$e_t = W_t t, \tag{6}$$

where W_t are learnable parameters.

Generated by a RNN. Recurrent networks take into account the temporal dependencies of the data by design since the timesteps of the sequence are input one after the other. We explore the possibility of including the temporal information of the data inside the MHA and CNN architectures by directly adding the output sequence of a RNN to the input embedding:

$$e_t = \text{RNN}(x)_t. \tag{7}$$

In this paper, the RNN is implemented by a single layer of GRU.

Enriched Learned Position Embedding. In a similar way as [6], one can add multiple different embeddings corresponding to different categories. Along with position, we propose to use learned embedding for the day of the week and the hour of the day instead of one-hot encoded features:

$$e_t = W_t t + W_d d + W_h h, \tag{8}$$

$$r_t = \frac{Wx_t + e_t}{||Wx_t + e_t||_2}, \tag{9}$$

where W_d and W_h are learnable parameters and d and h are respectively the day of week and the hour of the day. The representation r_t is normalized after the sum to preserve its scale. We shall compare experimentally those four approaches in the next section.

4   Experiments

4.1   Dataset

This dataset was recorded by the Fraunhofer Institute for Solar Energy Systems ISE on a sensor equipped heating system of an individual residence. The system contains an heat pump to supply energy and a water tank to heat up water. In addition to drinking water, the hot water is used in the floor heating of the house. The dataset contains several months of recorded data sampled at one minute. Various measurement types for each component of the heating system are available: supply an return temperatures of the water, water flow, power and energy. The system is alimented by a heat pump for which we also have the energy and power measurements. Finally, ambient temperature has also been recorded.

The raw dataset contains more than 100 features. After removing the columns that were missing to much values, there are 93 features left. We also add 24 features for the hour of the day one-hot encoded, 7 features for the day of the week one-hot encoded, 1 feature indicating if it is the weekend and another one for the holidays for a total of 126 features. A simple interpolation was realized to complete the remaining few holes in the dataset.

4.2   Experimental Setup

We used sequences of length 72, sampled at one value every twenty minutes (equivalent to a day of data). We tested different downsampling values and found that this value was sufficient. The input sequence used to predict the DHW consumption at time t is constituted of the sequence from time t-48 h to t-24 h concatenated on the feature dimension with the sequence from time t-7 days to t-6 days. This allows to take into account potential weekly periodicity in the data, as most approaches from the state of the art. The water flow to predict is accumulated during a day to smooth the values to output since the hot water consumption in the dataset is very sporadic, as expected for an individual house. We give here more details about the training process and the hyperparameters. The experiments were conducted with 2 months of data from which 3 disjoint sets were created: 1 month for the training set, 10 days for validation and 20 days for test. One value every 30 min was predicted. We used a starting learning rate of 0.001 divided by 10 every 25 epochs without improvement. The training is stopped once the loss on the validation set has not decreased during 500 epochs. The batch size is 128. Finally, the features were scaled between 0 and 1 to ease the training for the neural networks.

The position encoding approaches are compared with constant architectures. Those architectures were found after hyperparameter search. The dimensions for each architecture are reported in Table 1, in addition the kernel size used for the CNN is 3. The dimension of the position encoding thus corresponds to the dense layer sizes.

Table 1. Architecture dimension summary

Architecture type	Dense layer size	Specific layer size/filters	Output
GRU/LSTM	80	20	1
1DCNN	100	[8, 16]	1
MHA	64	32	1

The models are trained with the Mean Squared Error loss (MSE) and regularized with weight decay (factor 10^{-4} and dropout (probability 0.5). We trained each version of each model 10 times and saved the best trained model regarding validation to perform a test.

We compare the results of the deep learning models with an ARIMA model. We generally followed the results of the study by Lomet et al. [16] to select the coefficients but adapted it to our data since the sampling is notably different by using the validation set. The autoregressive and moving average orders were set to 336 (one week of data sampled at 30 min to have the same rate of prediction) with all coefficients set to zero except for $\{p_{46}, ..., p_{50}, p_{332}, ..., p_{336}, q_{47}, q_{48}, q_{49}\}$. Similarly as for deep learning models and [16], the prediction only depends on data from 24 h and one week before the prediction. We restrained the coefficients in order to avoid overfitting, especially for the moving average ones. No differentiation was performed following a study using the augmented Dickey-Fuller test and the seasonal orders were as well set to zero. The remaining exogenous variables were embedded through a principal components analysis in order to reduce their dimension to 6. The results are obtained by sliding along the validation set and making a one-step ahead prediction each time.

4.3   Results

We present in this section our results on the ISE dataset. The standard regression scores MSE and Mean Absolute Error (MAE) are reported. It is sometimes advised in the literature [30] to report Mean Average Percentage Error. However, this score explodes when the value to predict is zero which is often the case here, during the night for example. That is why we reported MAE instead.

The validation results for the version without position encodings are presented on Table 2. The best average MSE and MAE are achieved by GRU with 0.0033 and 0.0329 of MSE and MAE respectively. However, the best models overall where produced with the LSTM with 0.0028 and 0.0288 of MSE and MAE respectively. The 1DCNN and MHA architectures achieved results around ten

Table 2. Validation results on ISE dataset for models without position encoding, average of 10 runs and best values

Algorithms	Position encoding	Average MSE	Average MAE	Best MSE	Best MAE
GRU	None	**0.0033** ± 0.0002	**0.0329** ± 0.0015	0.0030	0.0310
LSTM	None	0.0037 ± 0.0006	0.0337 ± 0.0026	**0.0028**	**0.0288**
1DCNN	None	0.0336 ± 0.0074	0.1413 ± 0.0169	0.0221	0.1145
MHA	None	0.0353 ± 0.0085	0.1323 ± 0.0295	0.0245	0.1051
ARIMA	None	–	–	0.1044	0.2741

Table 3. Validation results on ISE dataset for CNN with position encoding, average of 10 runs and best values

Algorithms	Position encoding	Average MSE	Average MAE	Best MSE	Best MAE
1DCNN	Fixed	**0.0084** ± 0.0023	**0.0632** ± 0.0120	**0.0052**	**0.0463**
1DCNN	Learned	0.0185 ± 0.0029	0.1002 ± 0.0114	0.0104	0.0720
1DCNN	RNN	0.0272 ± 0.0067	0.1213 ± 0.0183	0.0175	0.0938
1DCNN	Enriched	0.0277 ± 0.0087	0.1269 ± 0.0201	0.0175	0.0996

Table 4. Validation results on ISE dataset for MHA with position encoding, average of 10 runs and best values

Algorithms	Position encoding	Average MSE	Average MAE	Best MSE	Best MAE
MHA	Fixed	**0.0067** ± 0.0015	**0.0533** ± 0.0072	**0.0045**	0.0420
MHA	Learned	0.0123 ± 0.0009	0.0723 ± 0.0024	0.0111	0.0697
MHA	RNN	0.0111 ± 0.0041	0.0692 ± 0.0148	0.0060	0.0490
MHA	Enriched	0.0132 ± 0.0074	0.0708 ± 0.0255	0.0047	**0.0407**

Table 5. Test results on ISE dataset

Algorithms	PE	MSE	MAE
GRU	None	0.0032	0.0352
LSTM	None	0.0046	0.0409
1DCNN	Fixed	0.0074	0.0917
MHA	Fixed	0.0030	0.0328

times inferior to the RNN architectures showing that information about the temporal order of the vectors seems necessary for this task on this dataset. ARIMA also seem to achieve lower results on this dataset. This observation is further confirmed in Table 3 and Table 4 which respectively present the validation results for 1DCNN and MHA with position encodings. Indeed, both approaches achieved better results with all forms of position encodings than without. However, the performance improvement is clearly better for MHA than for the 1DCNN: the best MSE scores achieved, 0.0045, is the closest we could achieve from the RNNs

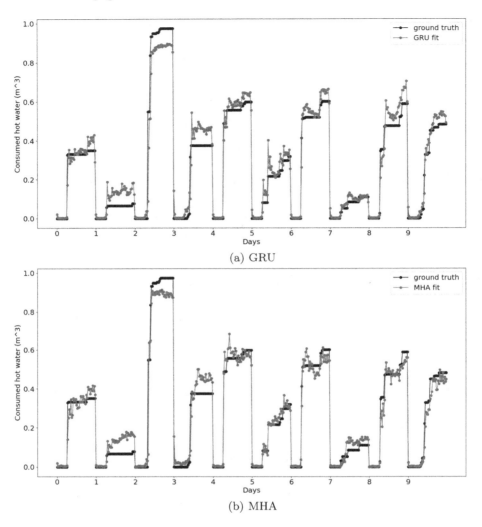

(a) GRU

(b) MHA

Fig. 1. Comparison between the fits and the true water consumption

performances. In both cases also, fixed position encoding led to the best results
with the enriched version being close second for MHA for the best iterations.
We suppose that the low quantity of data favors the fixed version since nothing
more needs to be learn. Finally, for MHA and 1DCNN, we remark than standard
deviations are higher than for GRU and LSTM. We make the assumption that
for these architectures, on this dataset, the initialization is a crucial factor to
achieve the best performances.

We now present test results on Table 5, obtained each time from the best
trained model from the validation phase. We observe that GRU and MHA with
fixed position encoding achieved the best results with the later being slightly
better with 0.0030 and 0.0328 of MSE and MAE respectively. The model based

on LSTM seems to generalize a bit less well than GRU, with an MSE of 0.0046 even though it achieved a better validation MSE than GRU. Figure 1 shows the comparison between the obtained fit for both models and the groundtruth for the 10 first days of the test set. We see that the consumption of days 1 and 3 is overestimated by both models whereas it is underestimated for day 2, though less by MHA than GRU. An interesting day is day 5 whose gaps are correctly predicted by MHA unlike GRU, the inverse is observed for day 7. Those gaps, that constitute the major difficulties of individual housing datasets, are therefore possible to predict with neural networks, though not always easily.

The 1DCNN architecture achieves lower results as expected from the validation. We make the assumption that the local temporal correlations in the sequence bring too less information to the model due notably to the presence of large plateau observed in the groundtruth curves (see blue curves on Fig. 1). Extending the range of possible correlations would require to increase the depth of the network and thus to train it with more data, threatening the use of the model in an embedded environment.

5   Conclusion and Perspectives

We proposed in this paper to use deep learning to tackle the issue of hot water consumption for individual housing. Neural networks are especially recommended when the data are variable and present abrupt variations [12,20] which is the case when dealing with individual house consumption profiles. We compared three deep learning approaches adapted to time series forecasting: RNN, 1DCNN and MHA, the last two being equipped with various form of position encodings [4] to improve their sequence processing ability. One objective was to conceive lightweight models able to be embedded in an energy management system to preserve the privacy of the data and to avoid wasting energy with computationally greedy models. We experimented the three approaches on a dataset recorded in a real individual housing. We achieved the best results with GRU and MHA with fixed position encoding architectures and demonstrated the ability of the models to correctly predict in some cases the gaps in the consumption on this dataset.

In the future, we plan to test those architectures on more datasets, notably on datasets containing less features since the inclusion of multiple sensors in a heating system also costs energy resource. We plan as well to integrate those models in real energy management system to see if the prediction they produce can effectively reduce the energy consumption.

Acknowledgment. This paper has been written as part of the Artificial Intelligence for Heat Pumps project financed by the French national Agency for Research (ANR) (ANR-19-P3IA-0003). This work has been partially supported by MIAI@Grenoble Alpes. The authors would like to thank Fraunhofer ISE and especially Lilli Frison and Simon Gölzhaeuser for providing their dataset. They also would like to thank Olivier Antoni, Romain Bailly, Yanis Basso-Bert and Marielle Malfante for constructive discussions on Transformers.

References

1. Eurostat. Energy, transport and environment statistics. European Commission (2020)
2. Lin, B., Li, S., Xiao, Y.: Optimal and learning-based demand response mechanism for electric water heater system. Energies **10**(11), 1722 (2017)
3. Maltais, L.-G., Gosselin, L.: Predictability analysis of domestic hot water consumption with neural networks: From single units to large residential buildings. Energy **229**, 120658 (2021)
4. Vaswani, A., et al.: Attention is all you need. Advances in neural information processing systems. In: 30th Proceedings of the Conference on Advances in Neural Information Processing Systems (NIPS 2017) (2017)
5. Gehring, J., Auli, M., Grangier, D., Yarats, D., Dauphin, Y.N.: Convolutional sequence to sequence learning. In: International Conference on Machine Learning, pp. 1243–1252. PMLR (2017)
6. Devlin, J., Chang, M.-W., Lee, K., Toutanova, K.: BERT: pre-training of deep bidirectional transformers for language understanding. arXiv preprint arXiv:1810.04805 (2018)
7. Lim, B., O Arik, S., Loeff, N., Pfister, T.: Temporal fusion transformers for interpretable multi-horizon time series forecasting. arXiv preprint arXiv:1912.09363 (2019)
8. Pacchin, E., Gagliardi, F., Alvisi, S., Franchini, M.: A comparison of short-term water demand forecasting models. Water Resour. Manage **33**(4), 1481–1497 (2019)
9. Shan, W., Han, H., Hou, B., Diao, K.: Hybrid model for short-term water demand forecasting based on error correction using chaotic time series. Water **12**(6), 1683 (2020)
10. Molin Ribeiro, M.H.D., et al.: Seasonal-trend and multiobjective ensemble learning model for water consumption forecasting. In: 2021 International Joint Conference on Neural Networks (IJCNN), pp. 1–8. IEEE (2021)
11. Candelieri, A., et al.: Tuning hyperparameters of a SVM-based water demand forecasting system through parallel global optimization. Comput. Oper. Res. **106**, 202–209 (2019)
12. Li, M., Zheng, F., Tao, R., Zhang, Q., Kapelan, Z.: Hourly and daily urban water demand predictions using a long short-term memory based model. J. Water Resour. Plan. Manag. **146**(9), 05020017 (2020)
13. Hochreiter, S., Schmidhuber, J.: Long short-term memory. Neural Comput. **9**(8), 1735–1780 (1997)
14. Karamaziotis, P.I., Raptis, A., Nikolopoulos, K., Litsiou, K., Assimakopoulos, M.: An empirical investigation of water consumption forecasting methods. Int. J. Forecast **36**(2), 588–606 (2020)
15. Box, G.E.P., Jenkins, G.M., Reinsel, G.C., Ljung, G.M.: Time Series Analysis: Forecasting and Control. John Wiley & Sons, New York (2015)
16. Lomet, A., Suard, F., Chèze, D.: Statistical modeling for real domestic hot water consumption forecasting. Energy Procedia **70**, 379–387 (2015)
17. Gelažanskas, L., Gamage, K.A.A.: Forecasting hot water consumption in residential houses. Energies **8**(11), 12702–12717 (2015)
18. Barteczko-Hibbert, C., Gillott, M., Kendall, G.: An artificial neural network for predicting domestic hot water characteristics. Int. J. Low-Carbon Technol. **4**(2), 112–119 (2009)

19. Gelažanskas, L., Gamage, K.A.A.: Forecasting hot water consumption in dwellings using artificial neural networks. In: 2015 IEEE 5th International Conference on Power Engineering, Energy and Electrical Drives (POWERENG), pp. 410–415. IEEE (2015)

20. Guo, G., Liu, S., Yipeng, W., Li, J., Zhou, R., Zhu, X.: Short-term water demand forecast based on deep learning method. J. Water Resour. Plan. Manag. **144**(12), 04018076 (2018)

21. Braun, M., Bernard, T., Piller, O., Sedehizade, F.: 24-hours demand forecasting based on SARIMA and support vector machines. Procedia Eng. **89**, 926–933 (2014)

22. Bengio, Y., Simard, P., Frasconi, P.: Learning long-term dependencies with gradient descent is difficult. IEEE Trans. Neural Netw. **5**(2), 157–166 (1994)

23. Cho, K., et al.: Learning phrase representations using RNN encoder-decoder for statistical machine translation. arXiv preprint arXiv:1406.1078 (2014)

24. Shengdong, D., Li, T., Yang, Y., Horng, S.-J.: Deep air quality forecasting using hybrid deep learning framework. IEEE Trans. Knowl. Data Eng. **33**(6), 2412–2424 (2019)

25. Lang, C., Steinborn, F., Steffens, O., Lang, E.W.: Applying a 1D-CNN network to electricity load forecasting. In: Valenzuela, O., Rojas, F., Herrera, L.J., Pomares, H., Rojas, I. (eds.) ITISE 2019. CS, pp. 205–218. Springer, Cham (2020). https://doi.org/10.1007/978-3-030-56219-9_14

26. Bailly, R., Malfante, M., Allier, C., Ghenim, L., Mars, J.: Deep anomaly detection using self-supervised learning: application to time series of cellular data. In: 3rd International Conference on Advances in Signal Processing and Artificial Intelligence (2021)

27. Waibel, A., Hanazawa, T., Hinton, G., Shikano, K., Lang, K.J.: Phoneme recognition using time-delay neural networks. IEEE Trans. Acoust Speech Signal Process. **37**(3), 328–339 (1989)

28. Kiranyaz, S., Avci, O., Abdeljaber, D., Ince, T., Gabbouj, M., Inman, D.J.: 1D convolutional neural networks and applications: a survey. Mech. Syst. Signal Process. **151**, 107398 (2021)

29. Li, S.: Enhancing the locality and breaking the memory bottleneck of transformer on time series forecasting. In: 32nd Proceedings of the Conference on Advances in Neural Information Processing Systems (2019)

30. Wei, N., Li, C., Peng, X., Zeng, F., Xinqian, L.: Conventional models and artificial intelligence-based models for energy consumption forecasting: a review. J. Petrol. Sci. Eng. **181**, 106187 (2019)

Workshop on Machine Learning for Pharma and Healthcare Applications (PharML 2022)

Machine Learning for Pharma and Healthcare Applications (PharML 2022)

Advances in machine learning and artificial intelligence could empower us to enhance our understanding of the mechanisms of disease and to create more efficacious therapies for patients. The drug development cycle entails many steps where large amounts of valuable data are collected in the context of clinical trials. Working on this data provides us with potential treatment targets, new biomarkers, and other information that enables us to identify which patients will benefit most from a given treatment. Additionally, safety and efficacy information is collected. After a drug enters the market, further data is generated and collected in the form of electronic medical records, disease registries, health insurance claims, surveys, digital devices, and sensors, among others. In recent years the availability of healthcare data in large quantities, as well as in diverse data modalities and data sources, has introduced new opportunities but also challenges. In addition, the use of the previously mentioned data sources has steadily increased. Using machine learning-based methodologies could help extract knowledge and enable learning from these increasingly heterogeneous data sources. The use of these innovative methods has shown the potential to revolutionize medical practice and enable us to develop personalized medicines.

This workshop invited experts from both industry and academia to share their research and experience in using artificial intelligence and machine learning methods in pharmaceutical research and development. The contents of the workshop were organized around five main thematic areas:

- Machine learning for survival analysis
- Causal inference and learning
- Domain adaptation
- Multimodal and data fusion
- Applied machine learning

Two keynote speakers, from industry and academia, were invited to present their work and to discuss current and future trends in their fields of research:

- Mihaela van der Schaar is the John Humphrey Plummer Professor of Machine Learning, Artificial Intelligence and Medicine at the University of Cambridge and a Fellow at The Alan Turing Institute in London. In addition to leading the van der Schaar Lab, Mihaela is founder and director of the Cambridge Centre for AI in Medicine. Title of the talk: "Machine Learning Meets Pharmacology: Integrating Expert Models into Deep Learning".
- Marius Garmhausen is a Principal Data Scientist at Roche in Basel, where he leads the early concept product family in the Personalized Healthcare cluster of excellence. In his work, Marius focuses on machine learning on multi-modal data across clinical trials and real-world data (RWD) to create new personalized healthcare products. Title of the talk: "Using RWD to improve trial inclusion criteria and systematically investigate mutation-treatment interactions in cancer patients".

The program also included four spotlight presentations and a poster session, which together incorporated all accepted manuscripts in the form of research abstracts or long papers. PharML 2022 received 11 submissions, and double-blind peer-review process was performed to select the manuscripts. Each submission was reviewed by at least two members of the Program Committee.

The original call for papers, workshop program, and other additional details can be found on the "PharML 2022" website (https://sites.google.com/view/pharml2022).

Lee Cooper

Naghmeh Ghazaleh

Jonas Richiardi

Damian Roqueiro

Diego Saldana

Konstantinos Sechidis

Organization

Workshop Chairs

Lee Cooper	Northwestern University, USA
Naghmeh Ghazaleh	Roche, Switzerland
Jonas Richiardi	Lausanne University Hospital and University of Lausanne, Switzerland
Damian Roqueiro	Roche, Switzerland
Diego Saldana	Novartis, Switzerland
Konstantinos Sechidis	Novartis, Switzerland

Program Committee

Mohamed Amgad Tageldin	Northwestern University, USA
Jaume Banùs Cobo	Lausanne University Hospital and University of Lausanne, Switzerland
Matias Callara	Roche, Switzerland
Valeria De Luca	Novartis, Switzerland
Tommaso Di Noto	Lausanne University Hospital and University of Lausanne, Switzerland
Robin Dunn	Novartis, USA
Christophe Freyre	Novartis, Switzerland
Marius Garmhausen	Roche, Switzerland
Costa Georgantas	Lausanne University Hospital and University of Lausanne, Switzerland
Lasse Hansen	Aarhus University, Denmark
Michael Mitchley	Roche, Switzerland
Matteo Manica	IBM, Switzerland
Joseph Mellor	University of Edinburgh, UK
Pooya Mobadersany	Janssen, USA
Nikolaos Nikolaou	University College London, UK
Marilena Oita	Novartis, Switzerland
Jon Parkinson	University of Manchester, UK
Konstantinos Pliakos	KU Leuven, Belgium
Jonathan Rafael-Patino	Lausanne University Hospital and University of Lausanne, Switzerland

Cameron Shand   University College London, UK
Grigorios Tsoumakas   Aristotle University of Thessaloniki, Greece
Lukas A. Widmer   Novartis, Switzerland

Detecting Drift in Healthcare AI Models Based on Data Availability

Ylenia Rotalinti[1]([⊠]), Allan Tucker[1], Michael Lonergan[2], Puja Myles[2],
and Richard Branson[2]

[1] Department of Computer Science, Brunel University London, London, UK
{ylenia.rotalinti3,allan.tucker}@brunel.ac.uk
[2] Medicines and Healthcare Products Regulatory Agency, London, UK
{michael.lonergan,puja.myles,richard.branson}@mhra.gov.uk

Abstract. There is an increasing interest in the use of AI in healthcare due to its potential for diagnosis or disease prediction. However, healthcare data is not static and is likely to change over time leading a non-adaptive model to poor decision-making. The need of a drift detector in the overall learning framework is therefore essential to guarantee reliable products on the market. Most drift detection algorithms consider that ground truth labels are available immediately after prediction since these methods often work by monitoring the model performance. However, especially in real-world clinical contexts, this is not always the case as collecting labels is often more time consuming as requiring experts' input. This paper investigates methodologies to address drift detection depending on which information is available during the monitoring process. We explore the topic within a regulatory standpoint, showing challenges and approaches to monitoring algorithms in healthcare with subsequent batch updates of data. This paper explores three different aspects of drift detection: drift based on performance (when labels are available), drift based on model structure (indicating causes of drift) and drift based on change in underlying data characteristics (distribution and correlation) when labels are not available.

Keywords: Concept drift · Healthcare regulation · COVID-19

1 Introduction

Many real-world learning algorithms address tasks where knowledge about a domain is collected over an extended period. The underlying characteristics of data are likely to change over time leading to poor predictions and decision outcomes. This phenomenon is known as concept drift [1,2]. Depending on the context, this scenario could happen for several reasons. For example, changes in health data can occur due to the launch on the market of new technologies which improve measurement accuracy or change in sampling strategies. However, changes might also be seen in populations and behaviours that may be harder

I. Koprinska et al. (Eds.): ECML PKDD 2022 Workshops, CCIS 1753, pp. 243–258, 2023.
https://doi.org/10.1007/978-3-031-23633-4_17

to forecast. The COVID-19 pandemic embodies a clear example. The national lockdowns fundamentally changed the assumptions and parameters of machine learning or statistical models developed previously using limited data from the early pandemic period.

Recently, learning in non-stationarity scenarios [3] has been extensively studied. In such evolving environments, where the properties of the data change over time, a non-adaptive model is bound to become obsolete in time. For this reason, several research studies highlighted the necessity to integrate a concept drift detector into the overall learning framework.

This is of vital importance to health regulators who are responsible for approving AI software. For example, after deploying a product on the market, a detector could be used to track significant changes in how the system is working. Depending on which information is available during the monitoring process, different approaches can be considered to detect concept drift. The largest group of drift detectors constantly checks a model's performance to evaluate possible degradations. However, the main challenge is that these methods require rapid feedback on the predictions based on ground truth labels which are not always immediately available. Particularly in clinical studies, outcomes in the form of disease labels might come at a later stage than the required model evaluation leading to the infeasibility of any drift detection relying on ground truth labels.

In 2021 [4], the UK's Medicines and Healthcare products Regulatory Agency (MHRA) highlighted the necessity of a rigorous programme to regulate software and AI product as it already is for all other medical devices. To be approved for the market, AI models must satisfy medical device regulators, with appropriate evidence, that they are safe and fit for the intended purpose. To ensure patient safety, it is necessary to understand if the algorithm has significantly changed since it was approved either due to the change in the actual algorithm logic or because of data drift (which could mean that the model is out-of-date in light of new data). If it has, both manufacturers and regulators need to know whether it remains safe and fit for purpose and if instructions on use have to be modified. This paper investigates methodologies to address concept drift detection in the context of 'AI as medical device' (AIaMD) regulation.

Here, a framework has been designed based on three different forms of drift detection. Firstly, the scenario where ground truth labels are available at the time of the analysis has been considered. We present a performance-based approach that keeps track of the learner performance metrics on new incoming data and detects changes through a non-parametric statistical test. The second layer of the framework aims to more deeply investigate the reasons and the causes of why a concept drift may happen. A structure-based detection approach is designed to monitor changes in the structure within a model as it is trained on upcoming data. Finally, we investigate the most challenging scenario where only unlabelled data are available during the monitoring process. A new family of methods that deal with concept drift detection in unsupervised settings has been proposed. We designed a framework that uses distance measures to estimate the similarity between data distributions and correlations in two different time windows. Concept drift is then detected if the two distributions are significantly distant. The main advantage of this approach is that it can be applied to both labelled and unlabelled datasets since this method only considers the distribution of data points. For this reason, it could address the issue of the lag between actual concept drift and labelled data becoming available.

2   Related Work

One of the most-referenced concept drift detection algorithms is the Drift Detection Method (DDM) [5]. DDM analyses the error rate of the streaming data classifier to detect changes. It was the first algorithm to define the warning level and drift level for concept drift detection. Other methods have modified DDM to enhance its performance for solving diverse tasks. For example, Early Drift Detection Method (EDDM) [6] extends DDM by tracking the distance between two consecutive misclassifications rather than the error rate.

Another popular family of drift detectors (Window-based detectors) split the data stream into windows based on data size or time interval in a sliding manner. These methods monitor the performance of the most recent observations introduced to the learner and compare it with the performance of a reference window. ADaptive WINdowing (ADWIN) and its extension (ADWIN2) [7] are among the most popular methods that use the windowing technique to detect drifts.

Ackerman et al. [8] proposed a method that utilizes feature space rules, called *data slices*, for identifying drifts in model performance based on changes in the underlying data, without assuming the availability of actual labels on new data. A data slice is a rule indicating value ranges for numeric features, sets of discrete values for categorical ones, or combinations of the above. Given a classifier model that returns predictions on a data set D, [9] present an algorithm to find a set of slices where the classification error rate of the model is higher than the average over D; such slices are called *weak slices*. Drift between data sets D_1, D_2 is detected by extracting a set of weak slices on D_1, and measuring differences between this set and the rules when mapped to D_2.

The purpose of this work differs from the methods mentioned above since the aim is to explore concept drift in the context how regulators can realistically detect drift in approved AI models that are available for public use, based on different availability of new incoming data. The project involved case studies on multiple batch releases of primary care data from the UK's Clinical Practice Research Datalink (CPRD) [10]. The CPRD is a real-world research service supporting retrospective and prospective public health and clinical studies. It collects anonymised patient data from a network of GP practices across the UK [11] and provides researches access to high-quality anonymised and synthetic health data that can be used for training purposes or to improve machine learning workflows.

In contrast to the stream learning context, where a sequence of data elements with associated timestamps are collected, the experimental methods described in this paper have been designed to deal with a *batch learning scenario*. Indeed, primary care data are often delivered in batches (potentially different in size). For example, the CPRD releases their data in monthly batches [12]. The framework is also flexible enough to detect drift based on any performance metric depending on the precise use of the software.

This work involved a case study using data on COVID-19 risks factors from the CPRD and an artificial dataset with well-known drifts for validation purposes.

3   Methods

3.1   Methodology

As highlighted in the introduction section, we assume a batch learning scenario. Contrary to online learning which deals with streaming of data, primary care data are often released in blocks of data at regular intervals time. Therefore, in the first step of our analysis, the data is divided into batches representing different blocks of time to simulate such a scenario, Fig. 1. The batch size (e.g. monthly, annual) is domain-dependant. More details about the chosen granularity are given in the following sections.

The next paragraphs describe the three different aspects of drift detection according to the proposed framework: drift based on performance, drift based on model structures and drift based on changes in data distribution and correlation. The code implemented to run the experiments has been made publicly available. For privacy reasons, only the simulated dataset has been shared[1].

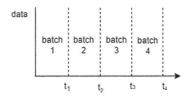

Fig. 1. Batch of data representing different CPRD releases of data. The batch size (e.g. monthly, annual) is domain-dependant.

Performance-Based Detection. We designed a customized performance-based drift detection approach to simulate post-market surveillance of a new AI product on the market to assess its compliance with the legislative requirements over time. Figure 2 summarizes the key steps of the algorithm. The first batch of data is selected and s samples are generated through bootstrapping techniques (in Fig. 2, we set $s = 4$ for explanatory purposes). Each sample is used to train

---

[1] https://github.com/yleniarotalinti/drift-detection.

a machine learning model which is then tested on subsequent data batches computing performance metrics (represented by colored circles in Fig. 2(a)). Thus, for each test set, s values (i.e. a distribution) of any given performance metric are obtained (using the s models initially generated through bootstrapping techniques). We name the first batch of data on which the models are tested as the *control set*. The performances achieved by the models on the control set represent the essential requirements a medical device must meet to be released on the market ensuring its safety and quality. The following batch in time is defined as the *next test set*. To assess concept drift, the performance distributions achieved on both selected batches of data are compared through a non-parametric statistical test i.e. the Wilcoxon Rank test, Fig. 2(b). If the distributions are significantly different, a drift is detected as the data on which the model was initially trained may be no more representative of the domain. The model is updated with the new batch of data available and a new control set is fixed, Fig. 2(c). On the other hand, if no concept drift was detected, the model is retained as is and the control set is kept for comparison with the next test set, Fig. 2(d).

The statistical significance of the test i.e. the alpha value is used to quantify the severity of the change alert triggered. Acceptable shift bounds have to be agreed upon on a case-by-case basis at the time of the initial regulatory submission depending on the nature of the outcome being predicted.

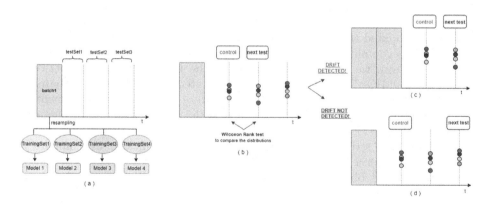

Fig. 2. Performance-based drift detection approach. a) Samples are generated using bootstrapping techniques from the first batch. They are used to train machine learning models. b) Each model is tested on subsequent batches computing a performance metric (represented by coloured circles). The distributions of the metrics obtained on the *control set* and the *next test set* are compared through the Wilcoxon-rank test. c) If the distributions are significantly different, the model is updated. d) Otherwise, the model is retained as it is.

Structure-Based Detection. In the context of AI as medical devices regulation, products may have additional complexities to consider due to different levels of transparency and interpretability that can complicate assessing significant changes. What is more, it can be challenging to determine the impact of change on the product. This is a crucial aspect to consider as there is a regulatory requirement to assess whether a positive risk-benefit ratio is maintained in the event of a significant change occurring. Understanding the nature and the reason for the change in AIaMD would provide manufacturers additional tools for quantifying, risk assessing and justifying shifts within their quality processes.

Especially in the healthcare domain, to ensure patients' safety and avoid the deployment of algorithms that take decisions for the wrong reasons, transparency and explainability are key requirements for AI models. Therefore, we designed a methodology to conduct an in-depth investigation of the reasons and the nature of changes by monitoring structural changes of a model over time. Exploring how the importance of feature changes as a model is trained on upcoming data can help to understand reasons for drift and improve domain interpretability.

The framework designed is shown in Fig. 3. Given n batches of data $B = [b_1, \ldots, b_n]$ involving m variables, a random forest classifier R_{b1} is trained on the first batch of data $b1$. Then, the feature importance ranking within the model R_{b1} is computed by obtaining a weights vector $W_{b1} = [w_{b1,1}, \ldots, w_{b1,m}]$ where each element scores how *useful* a feature is at predicting the target variable. We name R_{b1} and W_{b1} as reference model and reference weights vector. Then, we consider the next batch of data, and we train a model R_{b2} from scratch on the previous training set updated with the new data. By considering R_{b2}, a different vector of weights W_{b2} is computed. To quantify how the feature importance has changed due to new data, we measure d_{1-2} which is the Euclidean distance between vectors W_{b1} and W_{b2}. The same procedure is repeated for all the available batches of data resulting in a vector of distances $D = [d_{1-2}, \ldots, d_{1-n}]$. Each element of the vector represents how much the structure of the reference model has changed as new data is considered.

To assess if a structural change is statistically significant, we compare a distance value with a distribution of distances that simulate a stable scenario. The distribution is obtained by computing distances between a model trained on the whole dataset and 100 models trained on the 50% of the data randomly sampled.

Unsupervised-Based Detection. Most drift detection methods, as performance-based and structure-based approaches, assume that ground truth labels are available along with covariates since these methods work by monitoring the prediction results of a model. However, this is not always the case in several real-world scenarios. For instance, in medical studies, the real clinical outcome might be available at a much later stage than the actual prediction as it requires experts intervention. In this situation, performance drift detection methods are not applicable.

To cover the lag between the labels made available, an unsupervised drift detection approach can be considered. The framework designed is similar to

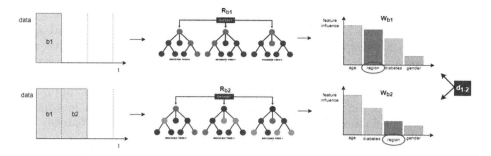

Fig. 3. Structure-based drift detection approach.

the *structure-based detection* approach described in the previous paragraph. But instead of comparing feature rankings, we measure distances from the reference point (calculated from the batch last used for training the model) in terms of correlation matrices and feature distributions (Fig. 4).

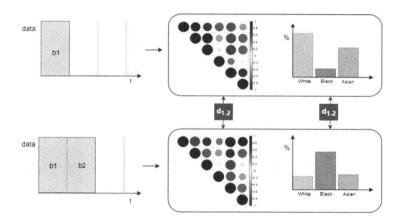

Fig. 4. Unsupervised-based drift detection approach.

3.2 Datasets

The proposed framework was assessed on two different case studies. An artificial dataset was simulated from Agrawal's data generator [17] to capture a well-known gradual drift. We generated 60 000 instances which were then converted into batches of 5 000 consecutive data points. The location of the centre of the drift (in terms of the number of instances) is 30 000 and the width is 10 000.

In addition, a high-fidelity synthetic data based on anonymized real UK primary care data generated from the CPRD Aurum database was used for the second case study. The case study involved the prediction of deaths during the COVID-19 pandemic in the UK. The dataset focuses on patients presenting to primary care with symptoms indicative of COVID-19 and includes data on socio-demographic and risk factors. Data was split into 14 monthly batches based on the temporal variable representing the date of the latest COVID event recorded. This situation embodies a case study on a new disease with presumably many sources of instability including key changes in policy (e.g. the national lockdowns [18] and the vaccination programme [19]). Expected drifts within batches are summarized in Table 1.

Table 1. Expected drifts in UK COVID-19 data.

Batch	Drift expected	Note
2020/03	FALSE	
2020/04	TRUE	First national lockdown
2020/05	TRUE	First national lockdown
2020/06	FALSE	
2020/07	FALSE	
2020/08	FALSE	
2020/09	FALSE	
2020/10	FALSE	
2020/11	FALSE	
2020/12	FALSE	
2021/01	TRUE	Second national lockdown
2021/02	TRUE	Second national lockdown
2021/03	FALSE	
2021/04	TRUE	50% of over 65 s got both doses of vaccine

4   Results

Several experiments have been carried out to investigate drift detection methods in different real-world scenarios where the choice of one approach over another can be driven by the availability of the data at the time of the analysis. If the ground truth labels are available, performance-based or structure-based approaches can be explored. On the other hand, if the true class of the instances is available just in a later stage of the analysis, an unsupervised-drift detection approach can be used to cover this lag.

4.1   Simulated Data Results

Firstly, the framework was tested on the artificial dataset from the AGRAWAL generator where a gradual drift was simulated. Figure 5 shows the results obtained when the performance-based detection approach is evaluated on model accuracy. Vertical dashed lines represent change detected ordered by drift severity. It appears clear that the algorithm correctly identifies the gradual drift simulated at the 30 000th instance.

Then, we explore the remaining drift detection approaches. The results are presented in Fig. 6. The vertical red line represents the centre of the hand-coded drift and the dashed lines denote its bounds. Figure 6(a) shows the impact of an outdated model on the area under the precision-recall curve as new batches of data are introduced over time for testing performance. A random forest model is trained on the first batch of data and then evaluated over the subsequent batches. Notice how the existence of an incremental drift causes a slow deterioration of the assessed performance. In the post-market surveillance phase of a healthcare AI product, these changes need to be identified. In this scenario, a model must be re-assessed to check its compliance with the essential requirement that was approved in the first place.

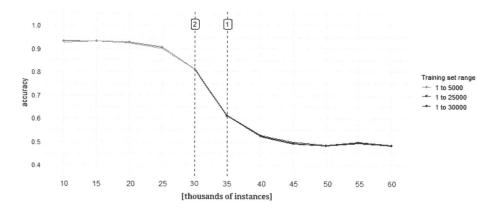

Fig. 5. Performance-based detection approach on simulated data. Vertical dashed lines represent changes detected ordered by drift severity. Colour changes represent different models based on updates when drifts are detected. The algorithm correctly identifies the gradual simulated drift.

Structure changes within the model have been investigated by implementing the framework described in the previous section. The plot in Fig. 6(b) shows the distance in terms of features' importance from the reference as new batches of data become available. Note how the measure increases drastically immediately after the drift indicating that a change in the data has occurred and the model needs to be re-assessed.

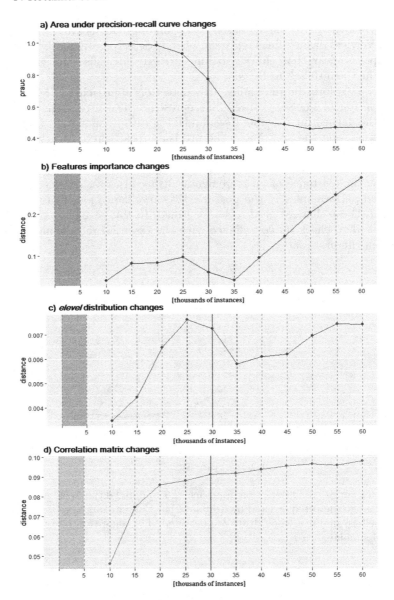

Fig. 6. Results on simulated data. a) Area under the precision-recall curve over time of a model trained on the first batch of data. b) Feature importance changes. c) Distribution of the feature *elevel* changes. d) Correlation matrix changes.

Evolving features' importance has been then explored closely. A summary of the results obtained (on the most meaningful models) is shown in Fig. 7. It is worth noticing how the importance of the variable *elevel*, which represents the education level, increases in the ranking of the features after the drift occurred, becoming the most influential one as we train a model on the whole dataset. This result is confirmed by looking at the perturbation functions used [17] to induce concept drift. The stream configuration considered to generate the initial concept includes variables *age* and *salary* that are indeed the most influential features in the first place. The new concept is simulated through a perturbation function which, instead of the variable *salary*, considers *elevel*. This results in an increasing importance of the variable elevel in the model as new batches are considered in the training set.

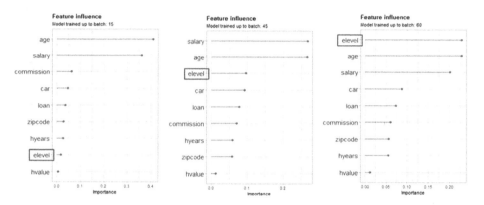

Fig. 7. Evolving features influence on simulated data as a model is trained also on upcoming data.

As highlighted in the previous sections, these methods assume the availability of the ground truth labels immediately after their prediction. As this is not always the case in several healthcare scenarios, we explore an unsupervised drift detection approach to investigate whether a change can be identified within unlabelled data. Firstly, for the reasons discussed earlier, the distribution of the variable *elevel* has been monitored as new batches of data become available. Figure 6(c) plots the distance in terms of the variable distribution from the first batch of data. The metric shows a spike close to the location of the drift and then stabilises. The trend of the changes within the correlation matrix shown in Fig. 6(d) seems also to follow a similar pattern, suggesting a change in the data.

In general, we found that the detection of change in an unsupervised scenario was a more complicated task to address because significant change in underlying distributions and correlations are more difficult to validate. On the other hand, frameworks that assume the availability of ground truth labels seem to be more capable of detecting drifts.

4.2 COVID Results

The designed performance-based detection approach has been tested with random forest models on COVID data from the CPRD. Figure 8 presents the results of the accuracies obtained. Here models are updated using all historical data when a drift is detected. Drifts are detected mainly within the first batches and then in the last ones (though they are found throughout most batches likely due to the unstable nature of the pandemic data). This result can be interpreted as the correct identification of the changes due to the national lockdowns forced by the UK government in April-May 2020 and January-February 2021 [18].

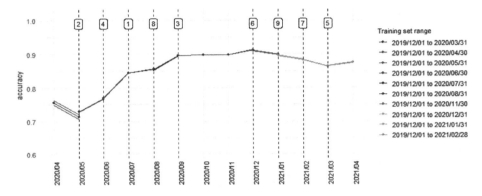

Fig. 8. Performance-based detection approach on Covid data. Vertical dashed lines represent changes detected ordered by drift severity. Colour changes represent different models based on updates when drifts are detected. Changes highlighted could represent national lockdowns forced by UK government in April-May 2020 and January-February 2021.

We then explore how the lack of ground truth labels during the monitoring process impacts drift detection. For the following results we do not apply any updates, even when drift is detected. This enables us to see how drift moves away from the original model. Similar to what was noticed in the simulated data, Fig. 10(a) shows the deterioration of the model trained on the first batch of data over time. Features importance changes over time, presented in Fig. 10(b), reveal an increasing dissimilarity from the reference point as more batches are considered. In particular, a spike in the proximity of the *batch 2020/01* suggests a correct detection of drift.

By closely monitoring the predictors importance ranking as new data become available (Fig. 9), the variable *region* was noted as its influence over time dropped significantly. This outcome could be interpreted as a consequence of the spread of the virus within the UK. This circumstance results in a decrease of the relevance of the regional information within the prediction model. For this reason, the distribution of this feature has been explored further. As can be seen in Fig. 10(c), after a stable initial phase, the metric slowly increases and reaches a *plateau* in the final batches. More interesting is the trend of the changes in the correlation matrix presented in Fig. 10(d). In the plot, we can identify three different regions: an initial peak (indicating immediate changing correlational structures), a stable phase and an increment that stabilises in the final batches. The changes in correlation structure seems to coincide with or predict expected drifts in the early and late batches.

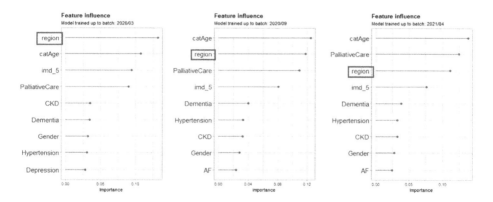

Fig. 9. Features importance ranking in Covid data as new batches become available.

As was for the artificial data, the detection of drifts resulted in more challenges in an unsupervised scenario compared to when ground truth labels are available (because the validation of a model is not possible). Nevertheless, we found that tracking changes in the distribution of relevant features and in correlations within data could provide clues about drifts until labelled data become available.

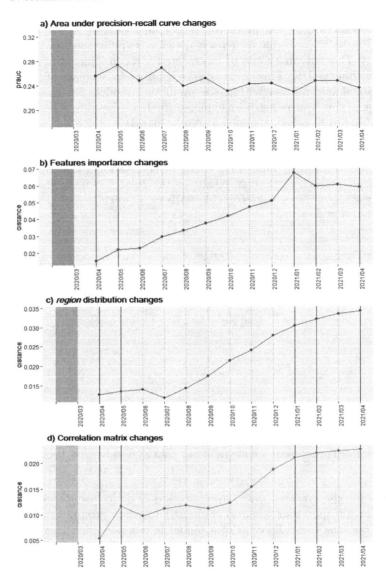

Fig. 10. Results on Covid-19 data. a) Area under the precision-recall curve over time of a model trained on the first batch of data. b) Feature importance changes. c) Distribution of the feature *region* changes. d) Correlation matrix changes.

5   Conclusions

Artificial intelligence has an increasingly prominent role within health systems. Applications of AI can range from screening, to diagnosis, and to the management of chronic conditions. However, there are also many risks to consider. For example, as the underlying characteristics of healthcare data are likely to change over time, a non-adaptive model is bound to become out-of-date leading to poor predictions. Therefore, methods for identifying changes in the data are necessary to ensure satisfactory outcomes.

Most existing drift detectors work by monitoring model performance assuming that ground truth labels are available along with covariates. Nevertheless, this is not often the case in clinical studies as the real outcome might be available at a later stage because it requires expert intervention. This paper discusses the topic in the context of how regulators can realistically detect changes in approved AI models based on the availability of new incoming data. Our proposed performance-based drift detection method can be used to detect any deterioration in performance of AIaMD products on the market. However, a detection of drift alone is unlikley to be a sufficient indication for the need for regulatory intervention as it depends on the nature of the change. Our proposed method for structure-based detection would allow AIaMD manufacturers and regulators to determine whether there has been a structural change to the model over time that may be of concern We proposed a framework to investigate drift detection by monitoring different aspects such as model performance, model structure and data underlying characteristics. The results highlight the challenges to address drift detection in an unsupervised scenario but show how tracking changes of relevant features distribution and correlation within data could provide indications about drifts until ground truth labels become available.

Acknowledgements. This project has been made possible by a grant from the £3.7 million Regulators' Pioneer Fund launched by the Department for Business, Energy and Industrial Strategy (BEIS). The fund enables UK regulators and local authorities to help create a UK regulatory environment that unleashes innovation and makes the UK the best place to start and grow a business.

This work represents research and is not a settled regulatory position or policy of the Medicines and Healthcare products Regulatory Agency (MHRA).

References

1. Hoens, T.R., Polikar, R., Chawla, N.V.: Learning from streaming data with concept drift and imbalance: an overview. Prog. Artif. Intell. **1**(1), 89–101 (2012)
2. Gama, J., Žliobaitė, I., Bifet, A., Pechenizkiy, M., Bouchachia, A.: A survey on concept drift adaptation. ACM Comput. Surv. **46**(4), 1–37 (2014)
3. Ditzler, G., Roveri, M., Alippi, C., Polikar, R.: Learning in nonstationary environments: a survey. IEEE Comput. Intell. Mag. **10**(4), 12–25 (2015)
4. Software and AI as a Medical Device Change Programme. https://www.gov.uk/government/publications/software-and-ai-as-a-medical-device-change-programme. Accessed 6 May 2022
5. Gama, J., Medas, P., Castillo, G., Rodrigues, P.: Learning with Drift detection. In: Bazzan, A.L.C., Labidi, S. (eds.) SBIA 2004. LNCS (LNAI), vol. 3171, pp. 286–295. Springer, Heidelberg (2004). https://doi.org/10.1007/978-3-540-28645-5_29
6. Baena-Garcıa, M., et al.: Early drift detection method. In: Fourth International Workshop on Knowledge Discovery from Data Streams (2006)

7. Bifet, A., Gavalda, R.: Learning from time-changing data with adaptive windowing. In: Proceedings of the 2007 SIAM International Conference on Data Mining. SIAM (2007)
8. Ackerman, S., Dube, P., Farchi, E., Raz, O., Zalmanovici, M.: Machine learning model drift detection via weak data slices. In: 2021 IEEE/ACM Third International Workshop on Deep Learning for Testing and Testing for Deep Learning (DeepTest). IEEE (2021)
9. Ackerman, S., Raz, O., Zalmanovici, M.: FreaAI: automated extraction of data slices to test machine learning models. In: Shehory, O., Farchi, E., Barash, G. (eds.) EDSMLS 2020. CCIS, vol. 1272, pp. 67–83. Springer, Cham (2020). https://doi.org/10.1007/978-3-030-62144-5_6
10. Clinical Practice Research Datalink. https://www.cprd.com. Accessed 1 June 2022
11. Wolf, A., et al.: Data resource profile: clinical practice research Datalink (CPRD) aurum. Int. J. Epidemiol. 48(6), 1740–1740g (2019)
12. Synthetic data from clinical practice research datalink. https://cprd.com/synthetic-data. Accessed 5 June 2022
13. Wares, S., Isaacs, J., Elyan, E.: Data stream mining: methods and challenges for handling concept drift. SN Appl. Sci. 1(11), 1–19 (2019). https://doi.org/10.1007/s42452-019-1433-0
14. Duda, R.O., Hart, P.E., Stork, D.G.: Pattern Classification. John Wiley & Sons, New York (2006)
15. Ramírez-Gallego, S., Krawczyk, B., García, S., Woźniak, M., Herrera, F.: A survey on data preprocessing for data stream mining: current status and future directions. Neurocomputing 239, 39–57 (2017)
16. Lu, J., Liu, A., Dong, F., Gu, F., Gama, J., Zhang, G.: Learning under concept drift: A review. IEEE Trans. Knowl. Data Eng. 31(12), 2346–2363 (2018)
17. Agrawal, R., Imielinski, T., Swami, A.: Database mining: a performance perspective. IEEE Trans. Knowl. Data Eng. 5(6), 914–925 (1993)
18. Coronavirus: a history of English lockdown laws. https://commonslibrary.parliament.uk/research-briefings. Accessed 7 June 2022
19. COVID-19 Vaccinations Archive. https://www.england.nhs.uk/statistics/statistical-work-areas/covid-19-vaccinations. Accessed 7 June 2022

Assessing Different Feature Selection Methods Applied to a Bulk RNA Sequencing Dataset with Regard to Biomedical Relevance

Damir Zhakparov[1,2(✉)], Kathleen Moriarty[1], Nonhlanhla Lunjani[1,3],
Marco Schmid[4], Carol Hlela[5], Michael Levin[6], Avumile Mankahla[7],
SOS-ALL Consortium, Cezmi Akdis[1], Liam O'Mahony[1,3],
Katja Baerenfaller[1,2], and Damian Roqueiro[2,8]

[1] Swiss Institute of Allergy and Asthma Research, University of Zurich, Davos,
Switzerland
damir.zhakparov@uzh.ch, katja.baerenfaller@siaf.uzh.ch
[2] SIB Swiss Institute of Bioinformatics, Lausanne, Switzerland
[3] APC Microbiome Ireland, University College Cork, Cork, Ireland
[4] University of Applied Sciences of the Grisons, Chur, Switzerland
[5] Department of Dermatology, University of Cape Town, Cape Town, South Africa
[6] Department of Paediatrics, University of Cape Town, Cape Town, South Africa
[7] Department of Medicine and Pharmacology, Walter Sisulu University, Umtata,
South Africa
[8] Department of Biosystems Science and Engineering, ETH Zurich,
Zurich, Switzerland
damian.roqueiro@bsse.ethz.ch

Abstract. High throughput RNA sequencing (RNA-Seq) allows for the profiling of thousands of transcripts in multiple samples. For the analysis of the generated RNA-Seq datasets, standard and well-established methods exist, which are however limited by (i) the high dimensionality of the data with most of the expression profiles being uninformative, and (ii) by an imbalanced sample-to-feature ratio. This complicates downstream analyses of these data, and the implementation of methods such as Machine Learning (ML) classification. Therefore, the selection of those features that carry the essential information is important. The standard method of informative feature selection is gene expression (DGE) analysis, which is often conducted in a univariate fashion, and ignores interactions between expression profiles. ML-based feature selection methods, on the other hand, are capable of addressing these shortcomings. Here, we have applied five different ML-based feature selection methods, and conventional DGE analysis to a high-dimensional bulk RNA-Seq dataset of PBMCs of healthy children and of children affected with Atopic Dermatitis (AD), and evaluated the resulting feature lists. The similarities between the feature lists were assessed with three similarity coefficients. The selected genetic features were subjected to a Gene Ontology (GO) functional enrichment analysis, and the significantly enriched GO terms

---

K. Baerenfaller and D. Roqueiro—These authors share last authorship.

© The Author(s), under exclusive license to Springer Nature Switzerland AG 2023
I. Koprinska et al. (Eds.): ECML PKDD 2022 Workshops, CCIS 1753, pp. 259–274, 2023.
https://doi.org/10.1007/978-3-031-23633-4_18

were evaluated applying a semantic similarity analysis combined with binary cut clustering. In addition, comparisons with consensus gene lists associated with AD were performed, and the previous identification of the selected features in related studies was assessed. We found that genetic features selected with ML-based methods, in general, were of higher biomedical relevance. We argue that ML-based feature selection followed by a careful evaluation of the selected feature sets extend the possibilities of precision medicine to discover biomarkers.

Keywords: Atopic dermatitis · Feature selection · RNA sequencing · Functional analysis · Semantic similarity

1   Introduction

Atopic Dermatitis (AD) is an allergic skin disorder that is characterized by skin rash, skin irritation and itchiness, accompanied by skin lesions in severe cases [14, 21]. AD is complex in nature due to the interplay of various factors including genetic predisposition, immune response dysregulation, epithelial barrier dysfunction, and environmental factors. Ethnicity also seems to play a role as the prevalence of asthma, allergies and AD, and the severity of disease, is higher in individuals of African ancestry compared to the population with European ancestry [5, 6, 12, 13, 16]. In addition, clinical markers that are used to describe the characteristics of AD are quite different depending on ethnicity [18, 27, 30]. It is therefore of critical importance for the identification of potential biomarkers of AD in African-ancestry populations to take into account genetics in addition to the environmental exposure.

The advancement of high-throughput RNA-Seq technologies now allows to profile the expression of thousands of gene targets in a number of samples. While the perspectives of gaining biomedically relevant insights from these data are promising, several challenges need to be met in analysing the resulting high data volume [2]. First, such datasets in general have an imbalanced sample to feature ratio, as the number of quantified transcripts greatly exceeds the number of samples. Second, only a limited number of transcripts carry the information that is necessary to discriminate between different experimental conditions, while the majority of transcripts introduce noise into the data [8]. The standard method of biomarker identification in RNA-Seq data is through differential gene expression (DGE) analysis applying classical statistics. However, depending on the experimental setup, the DGE frameworks often do not provide a robust method to select relevant targets in such a high-dimensional space [3]. Most of these methods are univariate in nature, do not account for possible interactions between genes and are prone to a certain number of false positives [8]. This poses a serious limitation, as feature selection in high-dimensional biological datasets plays a central role in subsequent downstream analysis and biological interpretation [3]. Machine learning (ML)-based feature selection provides a useful alternative that can properly and robustly deal with these issues. This can, for example, be achieved through the identification of interactions between features or highly correlated features, which is expected when two or more genes belong to the same pathway. However, it needs to be considered that every feature selection method will perform distinctively on different datasets and that no feature selection method is superior in every situation. Therefore, it is essential to compare the performance of different methods on a particular dataset before drawing any conclusions.

To this end, we have performed an extensive feature selection procedure on bulk RNA-Seq data that were acquired from peripheral blood mononuclear cells (PBMCs) of South African children living in an urban environment who either suffered from AD or were healthy. Our aim was to robustly identify transcript biomarkers that were predictive of AD diagnosis. To identify suitable methods we performed extensive feature selection using conventional differential expression analysis and five different ML-based methods. For each ML-based method, the best performing model was selected based on a 10-fold cross-validation (CV) accuracy score. The similarities between all ML-selected lists and the DGE output were assessed using three similarity coefficients (Jaccard index, Sørensen–Dice index and Overlap). The ability of each method to capture relevant genes in the context of immune processes related to AD was then assessed by analysing the resulting gene lists with Gene Ontology (GO) functional gene enrichment analyses, semantic similarity analysis and the Genevestigator search engine [9]. In addition, the selected feature lists were compared with a consensus list of genes that were associated with a predisposition to AD identified in genome-wide association studies (GWASs).

2   Methods

2.1   Dataset

Information on patient demographics was reported previously [12]. In summary, the RNA-Seq data were acquired from PBMCs of 60 Xhosa children living in an urban area in South Africa. Of these children, 31 suffered from AD (cases) while 29 were healthy (controls).

2.2   Differential Gene Expression Analysis

Differential gene expression (DGE) analysis was performed using the ARMOR workflow [15] setting cases vs. controls as contrast. Transcripts that fulfilled the following two conditions were considered as significantly changing: (1) false discovery rate (FDR) < 0.05 and (2) fold change > 1.5.

2.3   Feature Selection with ML-Based Algorithms

Recursive feature elimination (RFE) has been proposed as a robust algorithm to select relevant features [11]. Here, it was combined with Logistic Regression (RFE-LR) and Random Forest (RFE-RF) to determine the importance of features, i.e. gene transcripts. Although Logistic Regression and Random Forest could have been used directly to rank features, we found that without RFE, the final rankings given by these methods were not sufficiently reliable. To account for the inherent randomness of RFE, the feature selection procedure was repeated 10 times and the union of the feature lists selected in each iteration was considered. The additional three ML-based algorithms used for feature selection were: Univariate feature selection based on the logit function (Univariate), LASSO Regression (Lasso), and BORUTA (boruta) [10]. Both RFE methods and Lasso were implemented using the scikit-learn Python library [17]. For Univariate, we used the scikit-learn GenericUnivariateSelect module with the logit function import from the statmodels library [22], and for boruta we used the BorutaPy Python library [10]. To make the results of the different ML-based feature selection methods comparable and independent from the integral algorithm-specific methods, permutation importance was applied to determine the innate feature importance. Parameters of the feature selection methods are listed in Table 1. Due to the fact that the number of cases and controls in the data were balanced, the accuracy score was used as a performance metric. Stratified cross-validation was implemented to maintain the same ratio of cases versus controls in the training and test splits.

Table 1. Hyperparameters used to run the ML-based feature selection methods

Method	Parameters
RFE-RF	RandomForestClassifier(n_estimators = 100, n_features_to_select = 10%, step = 1000)
RFE-LR	LogisticRegression(max_iter 500, n_features_to_select = 10%, step = 1000)
Lasso	Lasso(penalty = l1, solver = 'liblinear', alpha = 1)
Univariate	GenericUnivariateSelect(score_func = logit())
boruta	estimator = RandomForestClassifier(n_estimators = 100)

2.4   Similarity Coefficients

Jaccard index (J), Sørensen–Dice index (SDI) and Overlap coefficient (OC) were used to assess the pairwise similarity between gene lists. Calculations were performed using the R package tmod, and the heatmap was plotted with the R package GeneOverlap [23,24,29].

Jaccard Index. It is calculated as:

$$J(U,V) = \frac{|U \cap V|}{|U \cup V|},\tag{1}$$

where U and V are two gene sets. The Jaccard index can take a value in the range $[0,1]$, where $J(U,V) = 1$ means that U and V are identical.

Sørensen–Dice Index. The SDI was calculated as:

$$SDI(U, V) = 2\frac{|U \cap V|}{|U| + |V|},\tag{2}$$

where U and V are two gene sets, and $|U|$ and $|V|$ are the cardinalities of sets U and V, respectively.

Overlap (Szymkiewicz-Simpson) Coefficient. The OC was calculated as:

$$OC(U, V) = \frac{|U \cap V|}{min(|U|, |V|)},\tag{3}$$

where U and V are two gene sets, and $min(|U|, |V|)$ is the size of the smallest set.

2.5   Functional Analysis

GO category functional enrichment analyses were performed using the cluster-Profiler R package [31] setting option "BP" to include the biological process (BP) enrichment terms. The resulting p-value was adjusted using the FDR method, and GO categories with FDR < 0.05 were considered significantly enriched. The Genevestigator software tool [9] was used to identify perturbation studies associated with AD, allergy and other allergic disorders. The mRNA-Seq Gene Level Homo Sapiens (ref. Ensemble 97) dataset was selected for the analyses with p-value < 0.01 and no fold-change filtering. Due to the allowed input gene list size restriction of 400 items, `RFE-RF`, `RFE-LR` and `Univariate` selected feature lists were restricted to the top 400 features with the highest mean feature importance scores.

2.6   Semantic Similarity of GO Terms

The semantic similarity between lists containing enriched GO categories was calculated using the method proposed by Wang et al. (2007) [28]. In brief, every GO term could be represented as a Directed Acyclic Graph (DAG):

$$DAG_A = (A, T_A, E_A),\tag{4}$$

where A is a GO Term, T_A is a set of all terms in DAG_A including all ancestor terms and the term A itself, and E_A are all the edges connecting the nodes in DAG_A. The semantic value (SV) of a term A is then defined by:

$$SV(A) = \sum_{t \in T_A} S_A(t),\tag{5}$$

where, $S_A(t)$ is an S-score of a child term t in the DAG_A. The S-score is then defined as:

$$S_A(t) = \begin{cases} 1, \text{ if } t = A \\ max\{w_e \times S_A(t')|t' \in \text{children of } (t)\}, \text{ if } t \neq A, \end{cases}\tag{6}$$

where w_e is the semantic contribution value for the edge e that links t to t'. Thus, the semantic similarity of two GO terms A and B is defined by [28]:

$$S_{GO}(A, B) = \frac{\sum_{t \in T_A \cap T_B} S_A(t) + S_B(t)}{SV(A) + SV(B)}. \tag{7}$$

The semantic similarity between lists of enriched GO terms and the subsequent clustering of similar terms using the binary cut method were calculated using the simplifyEnrichment package [7].

2.7 GWAS

Reported and adjacent genes of the susceptibility loci from GWAS studies performed on multiracial populations (n = 35) and black populations (n = 19) were retrieved from the studies by Tamari et al. (2014) [26], and Daya et al. (2019) [5].

3   Results

3.1 Differential Gene Expression Analysis

We first performed DGE analysis on the data, as this represents a standard approach to identify potential biomarker genes in transcriptomics datasets. The DGE analysis was done using the ARMOR workflow that implements EdgeR [15]. Of the 20,099 genes in the initial RNA-Seq data, 14,016 entered the statistical assessment comparing the conditions AD versus healthy control (HC), followed by multiple testing adjustment using FDR correction. In total, we identified 82 differentially expressed genes (DEGs) with a fold change of at least 1.5 and an FDR smaller than 0.05. In these 82 transcripts, 54 were over-expressed in AD patients and 28 over-expressed in HC subjects (Fig. 1).

3.2 Feature Selection with Machine Learning

The procedure to perform feature selection using the five ML-based methods, recursive feature elimination with random forest as the estimator (RFE-RF), recursive feature elimination with logistic regression (RFE-LR), BORUTA feature selection (boruta), LASSO regression (Lasso), and univariate feature selection (Univariate), was:

- the initial data were split into a training (90%) and a hold-out test (10%) set
- the training set was used to optimize the hyperparameters of the respective feature selection method in a 10-fold cross-validation (CV) procedure
- the performance of each method was estimated based on the mean 10-fold CV score
- permutation feature importance was calculated and ranked according to importance from highest to lowest

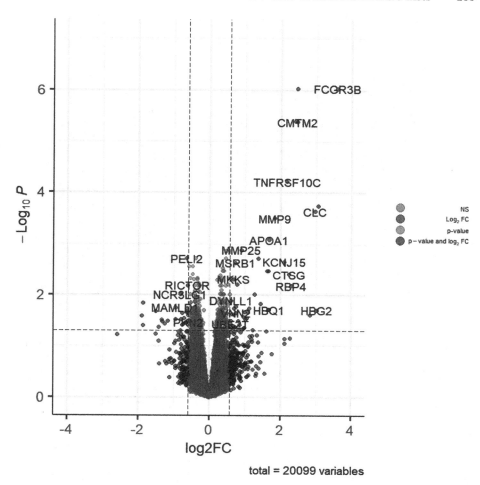

Fig. 1. Volcano plot with the results of DGE analysis comparing Atopic Dermatitis (AD) versus healthy controls (HCs) (grey: not statistically significant, green: fold change > 1.5, blue: FDR < 0.05, red: fold change > 1.5 and FDR < 0.05. (Color figure online)

- the median feature importance rank over several data splits was calculated for every feature in every list

The performance of every ML-based feature selection method was assessed by the mean accuracy score over the 10-fold CV (Fig. 2). The best performing method was `Lasso` with 276 genetic features selected, followed by `boruta` with a minor difference in performance, but with only 35 selected features. The `Univariate` method resulted in 3,727 selected features, while the two recursive feature elimination selection procedures `RFE-LR` and `RFE-RF` were ranked the lowest and resulted in 9,192 and 9,270 selected features, respectively.

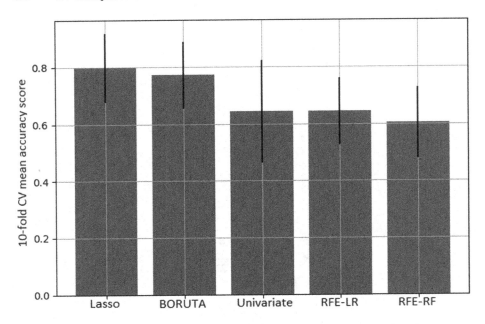

Fig. 2. Ten-fold cross-validation performance of the ML feature selection methods: LASSO regresion (`Lasso`), BORUTA (`boruta`), univariate feature selection based on the logit function (`Univariate`), recursive feature elimination with logistic regression estimator (`RFE-LR`), and recursive feature elimination with random forest estimator (`RFE-RF`). The y-axis shows the mean accuracy score with standard error.

However, while the `Univariate` feature selection method had a higher mean accuracy score than the two recursive feature elimination procedures, its standard error was higher. The overlap between the lists of features selected by the different ML-based methods consisted of only 3 genes (ENSG00000188163 (FAM166A), ENSG00000206177 (HBM), ENSG00000284491 (THSD8)), of which ENSG00000188163 was also in the list of features identified in the DGE analysis.

To study the similarity between the gene lists we calculated the pairwise Jaccard, Sørensen–Dice and Overlap similarity scores (Fig. 3). The overall Jaccard index in all pairwise comparisons was lower than 0.4, with the highest scores in the comparisons of `RFE-LR` vs. `Univariate` (0.35), and `RFE-LR` vs. `RFE-RF` (0.32) (Fig. 3A). These scores were to be expected given the similarity of the approaches and the high number of selected features in these lists. The SDI scores showed similar results to the J values and were generally lower than 0.2, again with the exception of the pairwise comparisons between the large feature lists (Fig. 3B). The result was considerably different for the OC, as this similarity score takes the different size of the datasets into account (Fig. 3C). In general, the OC was higher than 0.3. While the highest score of 1 was again observed in the compar-

ison of the two largest lists RFE-LR vs. RFE-RF (1.0), the second-highest value
was achieved in the comparison of Lasso vs. Univariate (0.93).

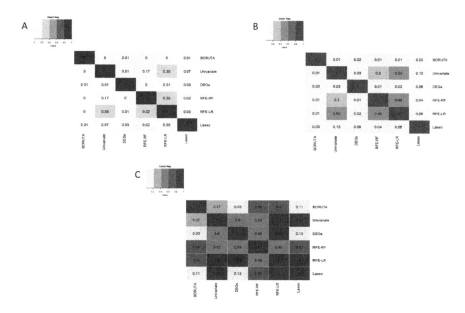

Fig. 3. Analysis of the overlap between gene lists selected by the different ML-based
feature selection methods and by DGE analysis. The heatmaps represent similarity
scores calculated with the Jaccard index (A), the Sørensen–Dice index (B), and the
Overlap coefficient (C). The similarity scores for each pairwise comparison are indicated
and color-encoded according to the respective color key.

3.3 Functional Analyses

To evaluate the biomedical relevance of the different feature lists selected by
the different approaches in the biomedical context, we performed a GO term
functional enrichment analysis applying an FDR significance threshold smaller
than 0.05 (Table 2). The list of features selected with RFE-LR resulted in the
highest number of enriched GO terms and the highest number of GO child
terms of the parent term *'immune system process'*. However, the feature list
from Lasso showed the highest percent (72.2%) of enriched GO terms assigned
to this category, followed by the RFE-RF feature list. The highest fraction of
GO child terms of the parent term *'biological process involved in interspecies
interaction between organisms'* was found in the DEGs. The Univariate gene
list resulted in the second-highest number of significantly enriched GO terms.
While most of these were not involved in immune- or defense-related processes,

Table 2. Enrichment of GO BP terms. For each list of selected features, the total number of significantly enriched GO terms is indicated along with the percentage of these terms that are related to the parent nodes GO:0002376 *'immune system process'* and GO:0044419 *'biological process involved in interspecies interaction between organisms'*.

Gene list	Total enriched	GO:0002376	GO:0044419
boruta	0	0	0
Lasso	54	72.2%	1.85%
RFE-RF	8	37.5%	0
RFE-LR	709	10.7%	0.85%
Univariate	202	3.96%	0.5%
DEG	24	4.17%	29.2%

the most significantly over-represented category in this feature list was *'T cell receptor complex'* (FDR = 1.54e–14).

To assess the overlap between the different lists of enriched GO terms, the semantic similarity (S_{GO}) was calculated between lists of significantly enriched GO terms in the union of all lists using the method from Wang et al., (2007) [28], followed by a binary cut clustering [7]. All GO terms that passed the significance threshold formed 7 distinct clusters (Fig. 4). The cluster containing the highest number of GO terms was cluster 1 with 345 GO terms that were related to general organism development. Most of the terms were significantly enriched in the RFE-LR and Univariate selected feature lists. Cluster 2 contained 87 GO terms related to cell migration, transport and signaling. Cluster 3 mainly comprised GO terms related to immune processes such as T and B cell activation and immune regulation and had 213 enriched GO terms. In this cluster, most of the terms were significantly enriched in the RFE-LR, Lasso and Univariate feature lists. Cluster 4 contained 34 enriched GO terms related to extracellular membrane organization. Clusters 5 and 7 contained 23 and 25 GO terms, respectively, and were related to metabolic processes. Interestingly, cluster 6 contained 17 GO terms that were associated with antigen presentation and processing, Major Histocompatibility Complex (MHC) assembly and were only significantly enriched in the Lasso feature selection list.

Assuming that selected features have been previously identified in experiments related to AD, we conducted a gene search in a compendium-wide analysis across perturbations using the Genevestigator search engine. The threshold for perturbation terms to be considered significant was set to FDR < 0.01 with no

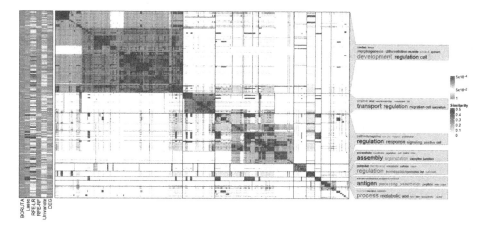

Fig. 4. Heatmap of S_{GO} scores of most (794) significant GO BP terms in all of the lists clustered with the binary cut method. At the left, the methods and the respective adjusted p-values for the over-representation of a given GO BP term are indicated. The color encoding shows the S_{GO} scores. On the right side, the word clouds demonstrate the most common keywords for every cluster. Clusters that are not annotated with a world cloud did not contain a sufficiently high number of enriched GO terms.

limitations for the fold-change (Table 3). The number of perturbations related to AD were most highly over-represented in the feature list selected by `Lasso` followed by `RFE-RF`. Furthermore, the perturbation terms psoriasis, allergy and asthma were over-represented in the `Lasso` feature list. While the feature lists selected by `boruta`, `RFE-LR`, `Univariate`, and `DGE` analysis did not show an over-representation of AD terms, at the same time terms related to asthma were over-represented in these lists, and in the case of the `boruta` and `RFE-LR` feature lists, the terms related to allergy were also over-represented.

3.4 GWAS

Consensus lists of genes that are associated with a disease with a genetic component are often based on the results of genome-wide association studies (GWASs). As genetic factors play an important role in the individual predisposition to allergic diseases, [1,4], we established a GWAS list based on two different cohorts [5,26]. The GWAS gene list contained a total of 53 genes, of which 51 were also represented in the RNA-Seq dataset. Assessing the overlap between the GWAS selected features with the different feature selection lists revealed no significant over-representation (Table 4). Interestingly, the gene that was contained in all the overlaps was ENSG00000148344 (Prostaglandin E synthase, PTGES).

Table 3. Genevestigator Perturbation analysis on the selected feature lists. For each gene list, the total number of retrieved significant perturbation terms, and the number of terms related to the categories AD, psoriasis, allergy, and asthma are given together with the p-value of the hypergeometric test assessing the probability of retrieving this number of terms in the 6,124 perturbations contained in the HS_mRNASeq_HUMAN_GL-0 dataset.

Gene list	Total studies	AD	Psoriasis	Allergy	Asthma
boruta	2121	20, 0.11	17, 0.55	21, 6.17e−04	94, 5.88e−04
Lasso	1531	29, 2.38e−08	26, 2.21e−05	15, 8.28e−03	86, 6.25e−08
RFE-RF	2170	26, 1.76e−03	18, 0.48	19, 7.57e−03	89, 0.11
RFE-LR	2182	24, 0.011	18, 0.49	19, 8.1e−03	105, 3.25e−06
Univariate	1943	12, 0.81	12, 0.9	15, 0.068	88, 4.84e−04
DEG	1256	7, 0.84	7, 0.9	10, 0.12	67, 2.65e−05

Table 4. Overlap of the 51 GWAS selected features with lists of ML-based methods and DEG. The p-values were computed using the hypergemetic test

Gene list	Overlap GWAS	p-value
boruta	0\35	1.0
Lasso	1\276	0.51
RFE-RF	23\9265	0.61
RFE-LR	28\9192	0.12
Univariate	7\3727	0.86
DEG	1\82	0.19

4   Discussion

Selection of informative features in bulk RNA-Seq datasets remains a major challenge requiring an efficient solution as a variety of subsequent steps in data analysis workflows heavily depend on a biologically meaningful selection of transcripts. To select informative features, we have employed informative feature searches and compared the results to a standard differential gene expression approach. To validate and assess the performance of different feature selection methods we 1) applied a standard statistical approach to identify DEGs, 2) employed five different ML feature selection methods and compared their predictive performance based on a 10-fold CV accuracy score, 3) performed functional analyses to see whether biomedically meaningful pathways in the context of AD were over-represented in the different selected feature lists, 4) determined the previous identification of the selected features in transcriptomics studies investigating AD, psoriasis, asthma, or allergy and 5) assessed the overlap of the feature lists with a consensus GWAS-derived gene list.

In the ML-based feature selection we found that the mean 10-fold CV accuracy of the 5 applied feature selection methods was more than 60%. The method with the highest mean accuracy score was Lasso, which identified 276 features, drastically reducing the feature space. Both RFE methods resulted in more than 9,000 selected features, while a standard univariate feature selection method selected 3,727 features. The high number of selected features might be the reason why these three methods achieved lower mean accuracy scores due to overfitting. Interestingly, the `boruta` method managed to achieve a mean accuracy score close to the best performer with a set of only 35 selected features. This might indicate that a small number of genes are enough to distinguish between AD and HC in this RNA-Seq dataset.

The discrepancy in the number of selected features by the different feature selection methods poses a considerable challenge in comparing the different feature lists, as both the Jaccard index and the Sørensen–Dice index are not informative when lists with differing lengths are compared [20]. Calculating the Jaccard index, Sørensen–Dice index and Overlap coefficient to compare the different lists, revealed that the Overlap coefficient was the method performing best, as it is sensitive to the sizes of the compared lists.

While information on the overlap between lists can be useful in assessing whether there might be a subset of consensus features that are relevant for the respective study design, there is no indication on the biological relevance of the overlap, especially when the list sizes are considerably different. Following the assumption that GO BP categories assigned to selected features should be over-represented for terms that are related to the scientific question if the features are relevant for the respective study design, a GO enrichment analysis was performed. Calculating a semantic similarity measure between the retrieved GO term lists followed by clustering revealed interesting differences for the feature lists. Cluster 3 mainly comprised GO terms related to immune processes, which were enriched in the `RFE-LR`, `Lasso` and `Univariate` feature lists. In addition, the `Lasso` feature list was the only feature list that had GO terms of cluster 6 over-represented, which were associated with antigen presentation and processing. Corresponding with this, the `Lasso` and `RFE-RF` feature lists contained the highest fraction of terms related to the parent GO term *'immune system process'*. The Lasso method therefore managed to select features that are specific to immune processes, followed by `RFE-RF`, while the feature lists selected by the other methods retrieved more general GO BP terms. Searching the Genevestigator software tool [9] for studies in which the selected features were previously associated with study designs testing for AD, psoriasis, allergy, and asthma, we again found that the Lasso feature list showed the highest over-representation for AD, followed by the `RFE-RF` feature list. In contrast, the GWAS consensus list had no over-represented overlap with any of the selected feature lists. This corresponds with the notion that not only genetic, but also several environmental factors are determinants of allergic diseases [19,25].

5   Conclusion and Future Perspectives

Feature selection in high-dimensional datasets is a cornerstone of a robust downstream analysis. In the present study we have performed an extensive feature selection procedure to find informative features in a bulk RNA-Seq dataset using five different ML-based methods and DGE analysis. In summary, the selection of features that are specifically associated with AD and are therefore expected to be biomedically relevant in our study design was largest using the Lasso method followed by `RFE-RF`. Comparing the performance of these two ML-based selection methods, Lasso had the highest mean accuracy score, while RFE-RF had the lowest. The overlap between the Lasso and `RFE-RF` lists, as determined by the OC, gave an intermediate value of 0.62. The finding that `RFE-RF` was the second-best performer with regard to selecting features with biomedical relevance was therefore not evident by the performance parameters or the similarity scores. This emphasizes the value of our approach in taking available biological information into account to evaluate the performance of different feature selection methods. However, there are some limitations to our approach that might interfere with its general applicability. First, taking into account the peculiarities of biomedical datasets with the expected considerable person-to-person variance, the sample size is rather small for ML standards. Second, the results from the ML-based feature selection is expected to differ dependent on the choice of ML algorithm. In addition, each transcriptomics dataset is different with regard to the contribution of the experimental variable to the variance in the data, which will influence the ability of the different methods to identify informative features. It is therefore generally recommended to employ a number of different methods, followed by an evaluation of the feature lists, taking into account publicly available biological data and gene annotations.

References

1. Arabkhazaeli, A., et al.: The association between a genetic risk score for allergy and the risk of developing allergies in childhood-Results of the WHISTLER cohort. Pediatr. Allergy Immunol. **29**(1), 72–77 (2018)
2. Arowolo, M.O., Adebiyi, M.O., Aremu, C., Adebiyi, A.A.: A survey of dimension reduction and classification methods for RNA-SEQ data on malaria vector. J. Big Data **8**, 50 (2021)
3. Cilia, N., Stefano, C.D., Fontanella, F., Raimondo, S., di Freca, A.S.: An experimental comparison of feature-selection and classification methods for microarray datasets. Information **10**, 109 (2019)
4. Clark, H., et al.: Differential associations of allergic disease genetic variants with developmental profiles of eczema, wheeze and rhinitis. Clin. Exp. Allergy **49**(11), 1475–1486 (2019)
5. Daya, M., Barnes, K.C.: African American ancestry contribution to asthma and atopic dermatitis. Ann. Allergy Asthma Immunol. **122**, 456–462 (2019)
6. Fischer, A.H., Shin, D.B., Margolis, D.J., Takeshita, J.: Racial and ethnic differences in health care utilization for childhood eczema: an analysis of the 2001–2013 medical expenditure panel surveys. J. Am. Acad. Dermatol. **77**(6), 1060–1067 (2017)
7. Gu, Z., Hübschmann, D.: Simplify enrichment: a bioconductor package for clustering and visualizing functional enrichment results. Genom. Proteom. Bioinform. (2022)

8. Han, H.: A novel feature selection for RNA-SEQ analysis. Comput. Biol. Chem. **71**, 245–257 (2017)
9. Hruz, T., et al.: Genevestigator v3: a reference expression database for the meta-analysis of transcriptomes. Adv. Bioinform. **2008**, 420747 (2008)
10. Kursa, M.B., Rudnicki, W.R.: Feature selection with the Boruta package. J. Stat. Softw. **36**, 1–13 (2010)
11. Li, L., Ching, W.K., Liu, Z.P.: Robust biomarker screening from gene expression data by stable machine learning-recursive feature elimination methods. Comput. Biol. Chem. **100**, 107747 (2022)
12. Lunjani, N., et al.: Environment-dependent alterations of immune mediators in urban and rural south African children with atopic dermatitis. Allergy **77**(2), 569–581 (2022)
13. Narla, S., Hsu, D.Y., Thyssen, J.P., Silverberg, J.I.: Predictors of hospitalization, length of stay, and costs of care among adult and pediatric inpatients with atopic dermatitis in the United States. Dermatitis **29**(1), 22–31 (2018)
14. Nutten, S.: Atopic dermatitis: global epidemiology and risk factors. Ann. Nutr. Metab. **66**, 8–16 (2015)
15. Orjuela, S., Huang, R., Hembach, K.M., Robinson, M.D., Soneson, C.: ARMOR: an A utomated R eproducible MO dular Workflow for preprocessing and differential analysis of R NA-seq data. G3: Genes Genomes Gene. **9**(7), 2089–2096 (2019)
16. Pearce, N., et al.: Worldwide trends in the prevalence of asthma symptoms: phase III of the International Study of Asthma and Allergies in Childhood (ISAAC). Thorax **62**(9), 758–766 (2007)
17. Pedregosa, F., et al.: Scikit-learn: machine learning in python. JMLR **12**, 2825–2830 (2011)
18. Quanjer, P.H., et al.: Multi-ethnic reference values for spirometry for the 3–95-yr age range: the global lung function 2012 equations. Eur. Respir. J. **240**(6), 1324–1243 (2012)
19. Roduit, C., Frei, R., von Mutius, E., Lauener, R.: Environmental Influences on the Immune System. In: Esser, C. (ed.), Springer, Vienna (2016). https://doi.org/10.1007/978-3-7091-1890-0
20. Salvatore, S., et al.: Beware the Jaccard: the choice of similarity measure is important and non-trivial in genomic colocalisation analysis. Brief. Bioinform. **21**(5), 1523–1530 (2020)
21. Schmidt, A.D., Strong, C.G.: Current understanding of epigenetics in atopic dermatitis. Exp. Dermatol. **30**, 1150–1155 (2021)
22. Seabold, S., Perktold, J.: Statsmodels: Econometric and statistical modeling with Python. In: Proceedings of the 9th Python in Science Conference. vol. 57, pp. 10–25080. Austin, TX (2010)
23. Shen, L., of Medicine at Mount Sinai, I.S.: GeneOverlap: Test and Visualize Gene Overlaps (2021), R package version 1.30.0
24. Shen, L.: GeneOverlap: An R Package to Test and Visualize Gene Overlaps. R Package 3 (2014)
25. Strachan, D.P.: Hay fever, hygiene, and household size. BMJ **299**(6710), 1259 (1989)
26. Tamari, M., Hirota, T.: Genome-wide association studies of atopic dermatitis. J. Dermatol. **41**, 213–220 (2014)
27. Vergara, C., et al.: African ancestry is a risk factor for asthma and high total IgE levels in African admixed populations. Genet. Epidemiol. **37**(4), 393–401 (2013)
28. Wang, J.Z., Du, Z., Payattakool, R., Yu, P.S., Chen, C.F.: A new method to measure the semantic similarity of GO terms. Bioinformatics **23**(10), 1274–1281 (2007)

29. Weiner 3rd, J., Domaszewska, T.: tmod: an R package for general and multivariate enrichment analysis. Peer J Preprints **4** (2016)
30. Wilson, D., Berardesca, E., Maibach, H.: In vitro transepidermal water loss: differences between black and white human skin. Br. J. Dermatol. **119**(5), 647–652 (1988)
31. Yu, G., Wang, L.G., Han, Y., He, Q.Y.: clusterProfiler: an R package for comparing biological themes among gene clusters. Omics: J. Integrat. Biol. **16**(5), 284–287 (2012)

Predicting Drug Treatment for Hospitalized Patients with Heart Failure

Linyi Zhou[1,2] and Ioanna Miliou[2(✉)] ⓘ

[1] Karolinska Institute, Stockholm, Sweden
linyi.zhou@stud.ki.se
[2] Stockholm University, Stockholm, Sweden
ioanna.miliou@dsv.su.se

Abstract. Heart failure and acute heart failure, the sudden onset or worsening of symptoms related to heart failure, are leading causes of hospital admission in the elderly. Treatment of heart failure is a complex problem that needs to consider a combination of factors such as clinical manifestation and comorbidities of the patient. Machine learning approaches exploiting patient data may potentially improve heart failure patients disease management. However, there is a lack of treatment prediction models for heart failure patients. Hence, in this study, we propose a workflow to stratify patients based on clinical features and predict the drug treatment for hospitalized patients with heart failure. Initially, we train the k-medoids and DBSCAN clustering methods on an extract from the MIMIC III dataset. Subsequently, we carry out a multi-label treatment prediction by assigning new patients to the pre-defined clusters. The empirical evaluation shows that k-medoids and DBSCAN successfully identify patient subgroups, with different treatments in each subgroup. DSBCAN outperforms k-medoids in patient stratification, yet the performance for treatment prediction is similar for both algorithms. Therefore, our work supports that clustering algorithms, specifically DBSCAN, have the potential to successfully perform patient profiling and predict individualized drug treatment for patients with heart failure.

Keywords: Drug treatment prediction · Heart failure · Acute heart failure · Machine learning · Clustering

1   Introduction

Heart failure (HF) is a heterogeneous clinical syndrome resulting from a structural or functional abnormality of the heart, leading to signs and symptoms such as dyspnea, orthopnea, and pulmonary congestion [17]. The prevalence of HF varies among different regions and increases with age. Approximately 6.2 million adults in the United States suffered from HF between 2013 and 2016 [33]. Additionally, at present, the prevalence of diagnosed HF appears to be 1 to

I. Koprinska et al. (Eds.): ECML PKDD 2022 Workshops, CCIS 1753, pp. 275–290, 2023.
https://doi.org/10.1007/978-3-031-23633-4_19

2% in adults in Europe and more than 10% in elderly, aged 70 years and above [20]. Given the aging population, an increasing number of individuals affected by HF is expected in the near future.

Acute heart failure (AHF) is generally described as the sudden onset or worsening of symptoms caused by HF, and it is a leading cause of hospital admission in patients aged 65 and above [20]. AHF is a syndrome with a high disease burden. The in-hospital mortality was about 9.6% in the United Kingdom, based on the 2016 National Heart Failure Audit data, and, in general, the one-year mortality ranges from 20 to 36% in developed nations [1,17]. Treatment of AHF is a complex issue since it is usually based on a combination of factors, including the severity of congestion, hypoperfusion, and other comorbidities in patients [9]. In fact, implementation of treatment guidelines is relatively poor in HF and AHF due to the existence of other conditions, for instance, renal diseases, leading to sub-optimal therapeutic doses or low utilization of drugs recommended by the guidelines [25]. Moreover, polypharmacy, the use of multiple medications, is common in patients with AHF [35] and can therefore complicate the problem by inducing adverse events and drug interactions [15].

Machine learning (ML) is a promising tool that could enable researchers and healthcare professionals to address the complexity of HF and AHF treatment. Given its ability to leverage information from multiple datasets and identify novel relationships in the data, it achieves higher predictive performance against current conventional approaches for several clinical prediction tasks, such as diagnosis, clinical procedures, and medication prescription [11,24].

Recent studies explored electronic health records (EHRs) to assess treatment outcomes in HF patients with ML models and establish associations between biomarkers and the outcome [18,36]. EHRs are a rich data source that could be useful to train ML models for estimating drug treatments. EHRs contain patient information from hospital visits, surgeries and procedures, radiology and laboratory tests, and prescription records. The data can be in various forms ranging from text, images, and signals like electrocardiograms [2]. Furthermore, longitudinal profiles of the patients in EHRs can be promising in stratifying patients and developing tailored management plans based on clinical characteristics [4].

Related Work. ML techniques have been widely adopted for predicting cardiovascular diseases to aid patient management using data from clinical settings [6]. Our work draws upon established guidelines in HF and AHF, and a variety of existing studies that leverage supervised and unsupervised ML models in predicting diagnosis and prognosis of AHF. However, such advances in prediction models, leveraging information from EHRs, focused mainly on the prediction of the onset of the syndrome [5,21] and adverse events [18,26,27,29,31] via a supervised approach. In a recent study, Li et al. [18] applied multivariate logistic regression analysis in predicting in-hospital mortality of patients admitted to intensive-care units exploiting the MIMIC III database. The authors manually screened HF-relevant features from the EHRs and XGBoost and LASSO regression models were used to further filter the features.

Unsupervised ML models have not been adequately explored for treatment prediction for HF and AHF patients. In a previous study, Panahiazar et al.

[22] focused on therapy recommendation for HF patients using two different approaches, both supervised and unsupervised. They developed a multidimensional patient similarity assessment technique that predicted a medication plan for new patients based on EHR data. However, to the best of our knowledge, this is the only published study that leverages unsupervised methods for treatment prediction while the majority of previous studies focus mainly on patient profiling. Harada et al. [10] deployed k-means clustering to group patients with HF with preserved ejection fraction. Parameters measuring cardiac functions and signs and symptoms of HF were used to cluster patients into four clusters. The authors also acknowledged that clustering algorithms have the potential to guide individualized treatment selection. Shah et al. [28] addressed the problem of readmission and mortality via phenomapping in AHF. Patient information was used as phenotypic features and three pheno-groups were identified via clustering. The pheno-groups presented differential risk profiles which gave improved discrimination compared to clinical features. Nonetheless, the profiling process in these studies was not associated with AHF treatment.

In other domains like depression, clustering was also used for treatment prediction. Wang et al. [34] applied hierarchical clustering to identify patient subgroups in major depressive disorder and perform classification for treatment prediction. Therefore, they revealed that clustering is indeed a feasible method in identifying treatment-sensitive patient groups and adjusting medication treatment, and thus the solution to better therapy choices and consequently improve clinical outcomes for HF and AHF patients.

However, despite the ML-based solutions mentioned above, little emphasis has been given to treatment prediction for HF and AHF patients via an ML approach.

Contributions. The main focus of this paper is to propose a workflow that uses clustering methods to profile AHF patients, based on data from EHRs, to identify potentially treatment-sensitive patient subgroups, and to predict individual drug treatment. The main contributions are summarized below:

1. We propose a workflow for drug treatment prediction for HF and AHF patients using machine learning methods;
2. We identify patient subgroups (clusters) with different profiles from untagged patient data using clustering algorithms;
3. We predict individual drug treatment for new patients using the previously defined clusters;
4. We benchmark two common clustering algorithms (k-medoids and DBSCAN) as parts of our workflow using an extract from the MIMIC-III database.

2 Drug Treatment Prediction for Heart Failure

We propose a workflow for stratifying patients based on clinical features and predicting the drug treatment for hospitalized patients with HF and AHF. The workflow comprises five steps: (1) feature extraction, (2) feature selection, (3) clustering, (4) clusters visualization, and (5) treatment prediction.

2.1 Problem Formulation

The problem studied in this paper can be formulated as a multi-label prediction problem for individual drug treatment for hospitalized patients with heart failure, where the labels indicate the drugs that will be administered to a patient with HF and AHF.

Given a set of p patients diagnosed with HF and AHF, we define $\mathcal{D}$ to be a collection of electronic health records (EHRs), with $|\mathcal{D}| = p$. We define $\mathcal{R}$ to be a collection of clinical features and $\mathcal{T}$ to be a collection of treatment labels. For each patient w, $\mathcal{D}_w \in \mathcal{D}$ describes her heath record that comprises $\mathcal{R}_w \in \mathcal{R}$ and $\mathcal{T}_w \in \mathcal{T}$. Each $\mathcal{R}_w$ describes a set of demographic information, vital signs, lab tests, and comorbidities, of the wth patient over the hospitalization period and contains n features of mixed nature. We perform feature selection on $\mathcal{R}$, resulting in $\mathcal{R}'$, with $|\mathcal{R}'_w| = n$. Each $\mathcal{T}_w$ describes a set of relevant drugs, of the wth patient and contains q binary features, with $|\mathcal{T}_w| = q$.

The first objective of this paper is to identify patient subgroups with similar characteristics in $\mathcal{D}$, using $\mathcal{R}$. More concretely, we want to define a mapping function $f : \mathcal{D} \rightarrow \mathcal{C}$, where $\mathcal{C}$ is a clustering of $\mathcal{D}$, consisting of a set of c clusters. Subsequently, each cluster $i \in \mathcal{C}$ will be annotated with the prescription rate of each drug treatment $m \in \mathcal{T}$. The second objective of this paper is, given an EHR of a new patient w', to assign her to the adequate patient cluster i based on $\mathcal{R}_{w'}$, and to predict the set of drug treatments $\mathcal{T}'_w$ that corresponds to the cluster ($\mathcal{T}_{w'} = \mathcal{T}_i$). Next, we define the five steps of our workflow in more detail.

2.2 Feature Extraction

Initially, based on the primary diagnosis of each patient, we only selected patients diagnosed with HF and AHF. Patients without a hospitalized record were excluded from the study.

For each patient w, based on clinical guidelines and previous studies [9,18,20,37], n clinical features were extracted from four main domains: demographic information, vital signs, laboratory test results, and comorbidities. All vital signs were extracted within the first 24 h of the patient admission, and all laboratory readings were averaged across the readings during the entire hospital stay following methods proposed by Li et al. [18].

Missing values are common in EHRs. Features containing more than 25% of missing values were removed. Subsequently, for normally distributed continuous features, the mean was used to replace missing values, and for those with asymmetrical distribution, the median was used. Missing values for categorical data were replaced with the mode. In addition, min-max normalization was performed on the data so that all features had values between 0 to 1.

As for the treatment labels, generic names of relevant drugs were extracted and sorted according to their drug classes. Finally, only q drug classes were selected, the ones that are indicated for HF or have potential benefits for HF patients (based on the literature [20,35]).

2.3 Feature Selection

Given the relatively large number of features, a feature selection was performed to choose a subset of the original features. K-medoids with Manhattan distance was used as the algorithm for the feature selection since it is compatible with mixed data types. Sequential backward elimination combined with silhouette score was utilized for feature selection [19]. The silhouette score was used as a fit criterion since it provides the goodness of the clustering [12]. The greater the silhouette score, the better the clustering result. The silhouette score was calculated after the deletion of each feature, and the feature with the lowest silhouette score was removed. Then the process was repeated until the number of features reached 20. The complete sequential backward elimination process was repeated 12 times for a different number of clusters, k, between 3 and 14, resulting in 12 potentially different sets of 20 features. Subsequently, the occurrences of individual features in the 12 sets were calculated to identify a common pool of features and further reduce the number of selected features. Depending on the actual occurrence of the features, a cut-off percentage was set to keep only the features with an occurrence higher than the cut-off point.

The feature selection was performed using k-medoids and the selected features were used to train both k-medoids and DBSCAN. The reason for this choice was that, by design, the feature selection process was repeated for different numbers of clusters. Since DBSCAN does not allow the specification of the numbers of clusters, the repetition was practically impossible with DBSCAN.

2.4 Clustering Algorithms

To investigate patient grouping for different treatments we used the following clustering algorithms:

– **K-medoids.** K-medoids clustering is a partitioning algorithm that fits p observations into k classes. Unlike the k-means clustering which is one of the most commonly used algorithms, k-medoids chooses actual data points as centers and associates each point to the closest center, making it appropriate for mixed data types [3]. We used the Manhattan distance as the distance metric since it is preferred over the Euclidean distance for high-dimensional data yielding more robust clustering results. K-medoids clustering with Manhattan distance requires the specification of the clusters number prior to clustering. To determine the appropriate number of clusters, k, the silhouette scores against different k values ranging from 3 to 14 were computed. The cluster number with the highest silhouette score and the best visualization was chosen.
– **DBSCAN.** Density-Based Spatial Clustering of Applications with Noise (DBSCAN) is a density-based algorithm built based on the idea that a cluster should occupy a continuous region of high point density exceeding a pre-defined threshold [7]. Gower distance [8] which applies different metrics for computing distances in continuous and categorical features was used to ensure DBSCAN was compatible with mixed data types. If the feature is continuous, Manhattan

distance is used. Meanwhile, if the feature is categorical, the Dice coefficient is applied [8]. For DBSCAN, we needed to determine two parameters. The first parameter, ϵ, is used to define the maximum distance between two points to be considered as neighboring points. The other parameter, $minPts$, states the minimum number of points in the neighborhood for a point to be considered as a core point. We selected the combination of ϵ and $minPts$ values that resulted in the highest silhouette score and the best visualization result.

2.5   Clustering Visualization

To visualize the clustering results with high-dimensional data we used the T-distributed stochastic neighbor embedding (t-SNE) dimensionality reduction method [32]. T-SNE transforms high dimensional Euclidean distances between data points into conditional probabilities that represent similarities, and then it uses Student's t distribution to compute the similarity between two points in the low-dimensional space. For this study, the dataset was converted into two-dimensional (2D) space and visualized using scatter plots. The goodness of visualization was based on manual scrutiny. The parameters for T-SNE were set to the default values. T-SNE was used only for the visualization of the clustering results and was not involved in the clustering process.

2.6   Treatment Prediction

Since our study aims to predict drug treatments based on patient subgroups, the likelihood or probability of a drug being prescribed was associated with the prescription rate of that drug in different clusters in the training set. The probability of each drug m being prescribed, Pr_m, for $m = 1, ..., q$ was computed based on the prescription data from the training set. In the clusters derived by k-medoids and DBSCAN, a threshold was set for each drug, and if the prescription probability of the drug m in cluster i was above the threshold Pr_m, then the final probability remained the same, otherwise it was set to 0:

$$\forall i \in \mathcal{C} : Pr_{mi} = \begin{cases} Pr_{mi}, & \text{if} \quad Pr_{mi} \geq Pr_m \\ 0, & \text{if} \quad Pr_{mi} < Pr_m. \end{cases} \tag{1}$$

Finally, the prescription probability of each drug in the test set was also derived by assigning the patients in the test set to the clusters determined by the training set. Thus, each patient inherited the drugs (along with their prescription probability) of the cluster it was assigned to and these were the predicted drug treatments for this patient.

3   Empirical Evaluation

3.1   Data Description

We used the Medical Information Mart for Intensive Care III (MIMIC III) for this study, which is an open single-centered EHR database that contains de-identified data on 46,520 patients who were admitted to intensive care units of the Beth Israel Deaconess Medical Center in Boston, US, from 2001 to 2012 [13]. The EHRs in MIMIC III comprise comprehensive patient information encompassing demographics, diagnosis using the ICD-9 code, laboratory tests, prescriptions, procedures, radiology results, notes and summaries by healthcare professionals and mortality information of the patients.

Patient Selection. In this study, we included all patients admitted from 2001 to 2012 with a primary diagnosis of AHF and HF, identified by ICD-9 codes. Diagnosis of HF were selected since hospitalization already implied an exacerbation of the disease, ergo AHF. Out of 13591 patients found to have a diagnosis or history of HF, 1352 patients with a primary diagnosis of HF were included.

Feature Extraction. We extracted 47 relevant clinical features regarding demographic information, vital signs, laboratory test results, and comorbidities, which are presented in Table 1. The extraction of the vital signs and comorbidities requires additional steps, such as unit conversion, and thus it was performed using an open code repository to support the reproducibility of the study [14,23]. In the MIMIC III database, patients older than 89 are recorded as '300' for data protection purposes [13]. Hence, *admission age* above 300 in the extracted data was replaced with 90. *Ethnicity groups* were re-classified as 'White', 'Black', 'Others', and 'Unknown'. For instance, patients with the ethnicity of 'White - Russian' and 'White - Eastern European' were grouped into the 'White' ethnic group. Notably, *LVEF* was extracted from plain text, both in numeric form (e.g. LVEF $< 30\%$, LVEF $= 30$–40%) and ordinal form (e.g. normal, moderate). Consequently, all LVEF values were transformed based on the American College of Cardiology (ACC) classification into a numeric scale from 0 to 4 [16], with 0 being hyperdynamic and 4 being severely impaired. In addition, the features that contained more than 25% of missing values, which were *NT-proBNP* and *lactate*, were removed. In the domain of comorbidities, *uncomplicated diabetes* and *complicated diabetes* were merged into one class, *diabetes*. After the preprocessing phase we obtained 45 features in total.

Feature Selection. Backward elimination for feature selection was deployed to keep 12 sets of 20 features with the best silhouette score based on the patients in the training set via k-medoids clustering with Manhattan distance. To reduce the final number of the features, we set the cut-off percentage to 75%, and as a result, features with an occurrence higher than 9 were kept for the clustering. Nine features were selected, namely *body temperature, ethnicity - white, respiratory rate (RR), red blood cells (RBC), admission age, LVEF, mean blood pressure (BP), chronic pulmonary, and diabetes*, ordered from high to low occurrence.

Treatment Labels Selection. As for the treatment labels, we selected a total of 18 drug classes, either indicated for HF or with potential benefits for HF patients, which are shown in Table 1. The treatment classes were not used for the clustering but for the model evaluation and treatment prediction. In our study population, the most prescribed medications were *antiplatelet and anticoagulant drugs* (n $= 1283$, 94.9%) and *diuretics* (n $= 1248$, 92.31%). On the other hand, *anti-anginal* drugs (n = 8, 0.59%) and *vasopressin antagonists* (n = 4, 0.29%) were the least prescribed in AHF patients.

Table 1. Features and drug classes (treatment labels) in the MIMIC III database relevant to HF and AHF

Domain	Feature
Demographic information	Admission age, sex, ethnicity
Vital signs	Body temperature, diastolic blood pressure (DBP), heart rate (HR), mean blood pressure (BP), respiration rate (RR), systolic blood pressure (SBP), saturation pulse oxygen (SPO2), and urine output
Laboratory test results	Anion gap, basophils, bicarbonate, chloride, glucose (blood), hematocrit, International normalized ratio (INR), lactate, left ventricular ejection fraction (LVEF), lymphocytes, mean corpuscular hemoglobin concentration (MCHC), mean corpuscular volume (MCV), magnesium, neutrophils, N-terminal pro b-type natriuretic peptide (NT-proBNP), partial pressure of carbon dioxide (pCO2), pH, prothrombin time (PT), platelet count, potassium, red blood cell distribution width (RDW), red blood cells (RBC), sodium, urea nitrogen, and white blood cells
Comorbidities	Blood loss anemia, cardiac arrhythmia, chronic pulmonary conditions, deficiency anemia, depression, diabetes (complicated and uncomplicated), hypertension, obesity, psychoses, renal failure
Drug Classes (Treatment Labels)	ACEi/ARB, alpha-adrenergic agonist, anti-anginal drugs, anti-diabetic, anti-arrhythmic, antiplatelet and anticoagulant drugs, beta blocker, calcium channel blocker, carbonic anhydrase inhibitor, digoxin, diuretic, erythropoietin, inotrope/vasodilator, MRA, recombinant human B-type natriuretic peptide, statin, vasopressin antagonist, and vasopressor

3.2 Setup

In our study population (n = 1352), patients were randomly divided into a training set (n = 946, 70%) and a test set (n = 406, 30%). The experiment has been repeated three times to guarantee the robustness of the results. There was no statistically significant variation found in these patient characteristics except in one of the repeats, sodium level was lower in the test set (p = 0.035). In terms of the drug treatment, there was no significant difference between the training and test sets. All our code to support the reproducibility of the study is publicly available at the GitHub repo[1].

3.3 Evaluation

This section presents the evaluation metrics for the performance of the clustering process and that of the treatment prediction, the latter being the main aim of this study.

---

[1] https://github.com/linyi234/patient-clustering.git

Clustering Performance. Initially, to assess the quality of the obtained clusters we used the Silhouette score, a useful metric that quantifies the goodness of the clustering [12]. Additionally, we adapted a cross-validation approach proposed by Tarekegn et al. [30] for algorithm evaluation on multi-label datasets. Root Mean Square Error (RMSE) and Mean Absolute Error (MAE) combined with an 10-fold cross-validation procedure were deployed. Unlike silhouette scores, RMSE and MAE factored in the strength of the algorithms to predict treatment labels for the validation data in the cross-validation process.

The training set was randomly partitioned into 10 folds where each fold took a turn to be used for validation and the remaining folds for training. For each cross-validation fold $j = 1, ..., l$, where $l = 10$, we computed two error scores per cluster and validation fold, $RMSE_{ij}$ (Eq. 2) and MAE_{ij} (Eq. 3), as follows:

$$RMSE_{ij} = \sqrt{\frac{\sum_{m=1}^{q}(\hat{y}_{mi} - y_{mi})^2}{q}} \tag{2}$$

$$MAE_{ij} = \frac{1}{q}\sum_{m=1}^{q}|\hat{y}_{mi} - y_{mi}|, \tag{3}$$

where y_{mi} is the probability that a patient from the training folds, assigned to cluster i, has the mth treatment label, and $\hat{y}_{mi}$ is the probability that a patient from the validation fold, assigned to cluster i, has the mth treatment label.

When the loop was completed and every fold was taken as the validation fold, the average RMSE for the ith cluster could be computed by averaging RMSE$_{ij}$ values from all 10 folds in that cluster. RMSE was obtained as shown in Eq. 4. MAE was also obtained in a similar fashion as RMSE. The smaller the RMSE or MAE, the more stable and better the outputs of the clustering algorithm.

$$RMSE = \frac{1}{c}\sum_{i=1}^{c}RMSE_i,$$

$$\text{where} \quad RMSE_i = \frac{1}{l}\sum_{j=1}^{l}RMSE_{ij} \tag{4}$$

Treatment Prediction. To assess the prediction accuracy for the drug treatment of each patient, after setting the threshold Pr_m for each drug m, we computed the adjusted RMSE and MAE over all the clusters, summing the adjusted RMSE and MAE of each cluster. The computation of the adjusted RMSE is shown below in Eq. 5. The adjusted MAE is computed in a similar manner.

$$adjusted\ RMSE = \frac{1}{c}\sum_{i=1}^{c}adjusted\ RMSE_i,$$

$$\text{where} \quad adjusted\ RMSE_i = \sqrt{\frac{\sum_{m=1}^{q}(\hat{y'}_{mi} - y'_{mi})^2}{q}} \tag{5}$$

where y'_{mi} is the probability that a patient from the training set, assigned to cluster i, has the mth treatment label, after the threshold was applied, and $\hat{y}'_{mi}$ is the probability that a patient from the test set, assigned to cluster i, has the mth treatment label, after the threshold was applied.

3.4 Results

Clustering. Comparing the two clustering algorithms, we observed that DBSCAN outperformed k-medoids based on the silhouette score, as reported in Table 2. For k-medoids, $k = 6$ was chosen as the optimal number of clusters and yielded a silhouette score of 0.269. Overall, k-medoids did not seem to provide the optimal clustering results based on silhouette score, but also based on the visualization results (Fig. 1). On the other hand, DBSCAN returned a higher silhouette score of 0.433 when $\epsilon = 0.12$ and $minPts = 5$. Additionally, the clustering visualization also revealed that DBSCAN resulted in clearly defined clusters (Fig. 1).

Table 2. Evaluation metrics results of clustering.

	Silhouette score	RMSE*	MAE*
K-medoids	0.269	0.104	0.078
DBSCAN	0.433	0.134	0.099

* Average of three experiments

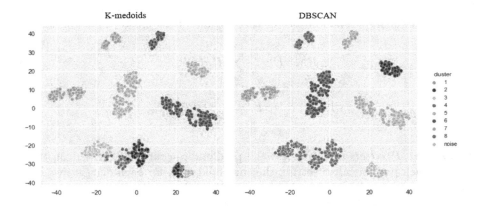

Fig. 1. 2D visualization of the clustering results on the training set.

Additional assessment of the clustering with regards to the treatment labels, includes the RMSE and MAE scores (reported in Table 2). A low RMSE value implies a high similarity between the training and the validation sets and a low MAE value reveals a good prediction of the labels in the clusters. We observed that k-medoids had slightly better performance, yielding an RMSE value of 0.104 and a MAE of 0.078 while DBSCAN yielded an RMSE of 0.134 and a MAE of 0.099. Therefore, the results suggested that k-medoids was slightly better in predicting the treatment occurrence in the dataset. Nonetheless, given a much higher silhouette score and clearly demarcated clusters, DBSCAN was deemed as the better model for patient profiling.

K-medoids resulted in 6 clusters and the selected patient characteristics for each cluster are shown in Table 3. Cluster 1 exhibited younger patients diagnosed with chronic pulmonary conditions and diabetes. Cluster 2 patients were characterized by a high LVEF level and high RBC (red blood cells) counts. In cluster 3, patients had the lowest LVEF level, highest mean BP, and no other comorbidities. Cluster 4 patients were characterized by older age, medium level of LVEF, and a higher proportion of White ethnic group. Cluster 5 was composed of patients with an absence of lung conditions and a presence of diabetes, which was the direct opposite of cluster 6 where patients had diabetes but no chronic lung conditions.

Table 3. Patient characteristics in k-medoids clusters. Data are median (interquartile range), or mean ± SD or percentage of positive cases depending on data types. Eth-W: white ethnicity; ChPul: chronic pulmonary.

	Admission age	Body temp.	LVEF	Mean BP	RBC	RR	Eth-W	ChPul	Diabetes
Cluster 1 (n = 161)	72 (63-80)	36.5 ± 0.49	3 (1-4)	75.8 ± 10.5	3.64 ± 0.71	20.0 ± 3.5	65.8%	100%	100%
Cluster 2 (n = 109)	72 (63-80)	36.5 ± 0.58	4 (4-4)	74.0 ± 10.0	3.97 ± 0.64	21.0 ± 4.1	72.5%	0	0
Cluster 3 (n = 112)	78 (66-87)	36.7 ± 0.51	1 (1-1)	76.6 ± 11.0	3.56 ± 0.54	20.5 ± 4.2	78.6%	0	0
Cluster 4 (n = 68)	84 (77-88)	36.5 ± 0.47	3 (3-3)	72.9 ± 10.2	3.68 ± 0.51	19.8 ± 3.5	82.4%	0	0
Cluster 5 (n = 263)	74 (65-82)	36.6 ± 0.54	3 (1-4)	74.2 ± 10.8	3.57 ± 0.52	20.1 ± 3.9	71.1%	0	100%
Cluster 6 (n = 233)	78 (65-85)	36.5 ± 0.51	2 (1-4)	73.2 ± 9.9	3.69 ± 0.62	20.5 ± 4.0	74.2%	100%	0

Patient characteristics in DBSCAN clusters are shown in Table 4. Cluster 1 was characterized by people with relatively high LVEF and low mean BP and previous diagnosis of lung conditions and diabetes. Patients in cluster 2 were non-Caucasians with diabetes and a relatively low number of RBCs. Cluster 3 consisted of younger non-Caucasian patients with the highest mean BP and no other comorbidities. Clusters 4 and 5 were composed of people with oldest age in which the latter group had milder LVEF dysfunction and a history of pulmonary diseases. Cluster 6 patients exhibited lower RBC counts, a history of diabetes and moderately high LVEF. Lastly, Clusters 7 and 8 were non-Caucasians with the youngest age, moderately high mean BP and chronic lung conditions, differentiated by the presence of diabetes. In addition, body temperature and RR were relatively similar across all clusters.

Table 4. Patient characteristics in DBSCAN clusters. Data are median (interquartile range), or mean ± SD or percentage of positive cases depending on data types. Eth-W: white ethnicity; ChPul: chronic pulmonary.

	Admission age	Body temp.	LVEF	Mean BP	RBC	RR	Eth-W	ChPul	Diabetes
Cluster 1 (n = 106)	76(67-81)	36.5 ± 0.5	3 (1-4)	73.8 ± 9.5	3.61 ± 0.64	20.1 ± 3.50	100%	100%	100%
Cluster 2 (n = 75)	71(60-77)	36.7 ± 0.5	3 (1-3)	77.3 ± 12.5	3.58 ± 0.48	20.2 ± 3.95	0	0	100%
Cluster 3 (n = 65)	67(52-77)	36.6 ± 0.5	3 (2-4)	81.6 ± 12.2	3.78 ± 0.72	20.5 ± 3.76	0	0	0
Cluster 4 (n = 223)	80(69-87)	36.6 ± 0.5	3 (3-3)	72.6 ± 8.7	3.72 ± 0.55	20.6 ± 4.08	100%	0	0
Cluster 5 (n = 173)	80(71-86)	36.5 ± 0.5	2 (1-3)	71.5 ± 8.6	3.65 ± 0.59	20.8 ± 4.10	100%	100%	0
Cluster 6 (n = 187)	76(67-84)	36.6 ± 0.6	3 (3-4)	72.9 ± 9.7	3.56 ± 0.52	20.1 ± 3.79	100%	0	100%
Cluster 7 (n = 60)	65(55-79)	36.5 ± 0.5	3 (2-4)	77.9 ± 11.2	3.81 ± 0.68	19.7 ± 3.44	0	100%	0
Cluster 8 (n = 54)	67(57-77)	36.5 ± 0.5	3 (2-4)	79.0 ± 10.6	3.73 ± 0.83	19.7 ± 3.44	0	100%	100%

Treatment Prediction. To assess the clustering quality with regards to new unseen data, data points from the test set were assigned to the clusters defined by the training set. Patients from the test set seemed to be well assigned to clusters both in k-medoids and DBSCAN based on the visualization results (Fig. 2). Out of 406 patients in the test set, only one patient was categorized as noise by DBSCAN, which is found close to cluster 2 in Fig. 2. It can be concluded that the clustering of new points to existing clusters was accurate in both algorithms.

Subsequently, prescription probability of each drug in the test set was derived. Each patient in the test set inherited the prescription probability of the drugs in the cluster it was assigned to. Individualized thresholds, which were the average prescription rates of each drug in the training set were also applied. To assess the treatment prediction accuracy, after setting the threshold for each drug, we calculated the adjusted RMSE and MAE scores, that revealed that the difference in the two algorithms was insignificant (Table 5). The adjusted RMSE scores were 0.041 and 0.046 and the adjusted MAE were 0.023 and 0.026 for k-medoids and DBSCAN, respectively. It may be concluded that both algorithms had similar performance for treatment prediction.

Table 5. Evaluation metrics results of treatment prediction.

	Adj. RMSE*	Adj. MAE*
K-medoids	0.041	0.023
DBSCAN	0.046	0.026

* Average of three experiments

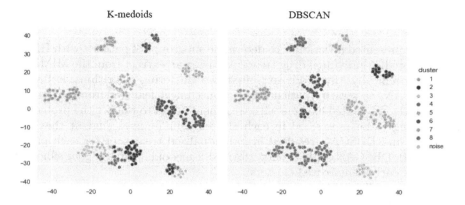

Fig. 2. 2D visualization of the clustering results on the test set.

The final predicted prescription likelihood per cluster is shown in Fig. 3A for k-medoids and Fig. 3B for DBSCAN. Color codes were also used to indicate the different levels of the likelihood a drug is being prescribed. For k-medoids, cluster 1 has the greatest number of drugs prescribed (n = 11), followed by cluster 5 (n = 10), cluster 2 (n = 8), and cluster 3 (n = 7). Clusters 4 and cluster 6 have the least number of drugs (n = 4). As seen from Fig. 2, there was an overlap of clusters 2, 3, and 4. Nonetheless, these clusters only had one drug in common, which was *anti-arrhythmic drug*, implying that patient subgroups derived by k-medoids may not be the most appropriate for treatment prediction. On the other hand, DBSCAN resulted in eight clusters, in which cluster 6 had the most number of drugs prescribed (n = 12), and after that followed cluster 1 and cluster 8 (n = 10), cluster 2 (n = 9), and cluster 7 (n = 7), cluster 5 (n = 6) lastly, clusters 3 and 4 (n = 5). Notably, there was no cluster that had the same medication combination in k-medoids and DBSCAN.

A. K-medoids

Cluster	ACEi/ARB	Alpha-adrenergic agonist	Anti-anginal	Anti-diabetic	Anti-arrhythmic	Anti-coagulant	Beta blocker	Calcium channel blocker	Carbonic anhydrase inhibitor	Digoxin	Diuretic	EPO	Inotrope/vasodilator	MRA	rBNP	Statin	Vasopressin antagonist	Vasopressor	Prescription Percentage
1	62%	0	1%	98%	0	95%	89%	38%	9%	0	94%	0	55%	0	0	80%	1%	0	0
2	77%	0	0	0	46%	0	89%	0	0	50%	94%	0	0	30%	12%	0	0	53%	0-20%
3	0	15%	0	0	34%	96%	88%	47%	8%	0	0	0	54%	0	0	0	0	0	20%-40%
4	65%	0	1%	0	40%	0	0	0	0	0	0	0	0	0	10%	0	0	0	40%-60%
5	65%	8%	0	97%	0	96%	92%	33%	0	0	0	13%	60%	0	9%	75%	0	0	60%-80%
6	0	1%	0	0	0	0	0	11%	0	93%	0	0	19%	0	0	0	0	0	80%-100%

B. DBSCAN

Cluster	ACEi/ARB	Alpha-adrenergic agonist	Anti-anginal	Anti-diabetic	Anti-arrhythmic	Anti-coagulant	Beta blocker	Calcium channel blocker	Carbonic anhydrase inhibitor	Digoxin	Diuretic	EPO	Inotrope/vasodilator	MRA	rBNP	Statin	Vasopressin antagonist	Vasopressor	Prescription Percentage
1	0	0	1%	99%	0	95%	0	36%	9%	0	95%	0	57%	0	0	79%	1%	37%	0
2	72%	9%	0	97%	0	97%	92%	43%	0	0	0	15%	71%	0	0	75%	0	0	0-20%
3	71%	15%	0	0	0	91%	0	0	0	0	92%	0	0	22%	0	0	0	0	20%-40%
4	0	0	0	0	43%	95%	0	0	32%	0	0	0	0	0	10%	0	0	39%	40%-60%
5	0	0	2%	0	30%	95%	0	10%	0	0	95%	0	0	21%	0	0	0	0	60%-80%
6	62%	8%	0	97%	0	96%	93%	0	0	0	93%	12%	55%	17%	10%	76%	0	35%	80%-100%
7	65%	10%	0	0	0	0	0	12%	28%	0	12%	0	0	13%	0	0	0	38%	
8	70%	0	0	96%	0	0	94%	41%	9%	30%	0	9%	0	17%	13%	81%	0	0	

Fig. 3. Treatment prescription likelihood for each cluster.

4 Conclusions

This study presented a workflow to determine subgroups of patients with HF and AHF and predict individual drug treatment using an extract from the MIMIC III dataset. Specifically, this study exploited two clustering algorithms, k-medoids and DBSCAN, to stratify patients based on clinical features from EHRs, and subsequently, associated clusters with treatment labels to predict the probability of each drug to be prescribed in each cluster. Our findings suggest that both k-medoids and DBSCAN resulted in individualized treatment for each patient cluster, with DBSCAN slightly outperformed k-medoids with a higher silhouette score and clearly demarcated clusters.

Having established the potential of clustering in treatment prediction, further research is encouraged. The results and the generalizability of this study will need to be verified in a larger sample size and different patient cohorts. Furthermore, temporal relation needs to be established between the clinical features and the treatment labels. Data that are obtained after a drug is prescribed should not be included in the clustering process. In addition, imputation methods could be explored to include relevant features with a large number of missing values, such as NT-proBNP. Finally, the unstructured data from the EHRs may be utilized to retrieve important information such as medication history, chief complaint, and text reports of echocardiogram in relation to AHF.

In conclusion, the work that we presented here shed new light on predicting personalized treatment for patients with AHF via ML models. It has also been one of the first attempts to use treatment labels for clustering evaluation in the field of HF and AHF. Moreover, this study raises the possibility that clustering is a viable option to identify distinguished and treatment-sensitive patient profiles to guide clinical decision. The workflow could be easily extended to predict the treatment for patients with other diseases and health conditions.

References

1. Ahmed, A., et al.: Incident heart failure hospitalization and subsequent mortality in chronic heart failure: a propensity-matched study. J. Cardiac Fail. **14**(3), 211–218 (2008)
2. Awan, S.E., Sohel, F., Sanfilippo, F.M., Bennamoun, M., Dwivedi, G.: Machine learning in heart failure: ready for prime time. Curr. Opin. Cardiol. **33**(2), 190–195 (2018)
3. Budiaji, W., Leisch, F.: Simple K-medoids partitioning algorithm for mixed variable data. Algorithms **12**(9), 177 (2019)
4. Chen, R., et al.: Patient stratification using electronic health records from a chronic disease management program. IEEE J. Biomed. Health Inform. (2016)
5. Choi, E., Schuetz, A., Stewart, W.F., Sun, J.: Using recurrent neural network models for early detection of heart failure onset. J. Am. Med. Inform. Assoc. **24**(2), 361–370 (2017)
6. Damen, J.A., et al.: Prediction models for cardiovascular disease risk in the general population: systematic review. BMJ **353** (2016)

7. Ester, M., Kriegel, H.P., Sander, J., Xu, X.: A density-based algorithm for discovering clusters in large spatial databases with noise. In: KDD, vol. 96, no. 34, pp. 226–231 (1996)
8. Gower, J.C.: A general coefficient of similarity and some of its properties. Biometrics **27**(4), 857–871 (1971)
9. Gupta, A.K., Tomasoni, D., Sidhu, K., Metra, M., Ezekowitz, J.A.: Evidence-based management of acute heart failure. Can. J. Cardiol. **37**(4), 621–631 (2021)
10. Harada, D., Asanoi, H., Noto, T., Takagawa, J.: Different pathophysiology and outcomes of heart failure with preserved ejection fraction stratified by K-means clustering. Front. Cardiovasc. Med. **7**, 607760 (2020)
11. Harutyunyan, H., Khachatrian, H., Kale, D.C., Ver Steeg, G., Galstyan, A.: Multitask learning and benchmarking with clinical time series data. Sci. Data **6**(1), 1–18 (2019)
12. Hruschka, E., Covoes, T.: Feature selection for cluster analysis: an approach based on the simplified silhouette criterion. In: International Conference on CIMCA-IAWTIC 2006, vol. 1, pp. 32–38 (2005)
13. Johnson, A.E., et al.: MIMIC-III, a freely accessible critical care database. Sci. Data **3**(1), 160035 (2016)
14. Johnson, A.E., Stone, D.J., Celi, L.A., Pollard, T.J.: The MIMIC code repository: enabling reproducibility in critical care research. J. Am. Med. Inform. Assoc. JAMIA **25**(1), 32–39 (2018)
15. Kim, J., Parish, A.L.: Polypharmacy and medication management in older adults. Nurs. Clin. North Am. **52**(3), 457–468 (2017)
16. Kosaraju, A., Goyal, A., Grigorova, Y., Makaryus, A.N.: Left Ventricular Ejection Fraction. In: StatPearls. StatPearls Publishing, Treasure Island (2022)
17. Kurmani, S., Squire, I.: Acute heart failure: definition, classification and epidemiology. Curr. Heart Fail. Rep. **14**(5), 385–392 (2017). https://doi.org/10.1007/s11897-017-0351-y
18. Li, F., Xin, H., Zhang, J., Fu, M., Zhou, J., Lian, Z.: Prediction model of in-hospital mortality in intensive care unit patients with heart failure: machine learning-based, retrospective analysis of the MIMIC-III database. BMJ Open **11**(7), e044779 (2021)
19. Marill, T., Green, D.M.: On the effectiveness of receptors in recognition systems. IEEE Trans. Inf. Theory **9**, 11–17 (1963)
20. McDonagh, T.A., et al.: 2021 ESC guidelines for the diagnosis and treatment of acute and chronic heart failure: developed by the task force for the diagnosis and treatment of acute and chronic heart failure of the European society of cardiology (ESC) with the special contribution of the heart failure association (HFA) of the ESC. Eur. Heart J. **42**(36), 3599–3726 (2021)
21. Ng, K., Steinhubl, S.R., deFilippi, C., Dey, S., Stewart, W.F.: Early detection of heart failure using electronic health records: practical implications for time before diagnosis, data diversity, data quantity, and data density. Circ. Cardiovasc. Qual. Outcomes **9**(6), 649–658 (2016)
22. Panahiazar, M., Taslimitehrani, V., Pereira, N.L., Pathak, J.: Using EHRs for heart failure therapy recommendation using multidimensional patient similarity analytics. Stud. Health Technol. Inform. **210**, 369 (2015)
23. Pollard, T., et al.: MIT-LCP/Mimic-Code: Mimic-III V1.4 (2017)
24. Purushotham, S., Meng, C., Che, Z., Liu, Y.: Benchmarking deep learning models on large healthcare datasets. J. Biomed. Inform. **83**, 112–134 (2018)

25. Rosano, G.M., et al.: Patient profiling in heart failure for tailoring medical therapy. A consensus document of the heart failure association of the European society of cardiology. Eur. J. Heart Fail. **23**(6), 872–881 (2021)
26. Sarijaloo, F., Park, J., Zhong, X., Wokhlu, A.: Predicting 90 day acute heart failure readmission and death using machine learning-supported decision analysis. Clin. Cardiol. **44**(2), 230–237 (2021)
27. Sax, D.R., et al.: Use of machine learning to develop a risk-stratification tool for emergency department patients with acute heart failure. Ann. Emerg. Med. **77**(2), 237–248 (2021)
28. Shah, S.J., et al.: Phenomapping for novel classification of heart failure with preserved ejection fraction. Circulation **131**(3), 269–279 (2015)
29. Tan, B.Y., Gu, J.Y., Wei, H.Y., Chen, L., Yan, S.L., Deng, N.: Electronic medical record-based model to predict the risk of 90-day readmission for patients with heart failure. BMC Med. Inform. Decis. Mak. **19**(1), 193 (2019)
30. Tarekegn, A.N., Michalak, K., Giacobini, M.: Cross-validation approach to evaluate clustering algorithms: an experimental study using multi-label datasets. SN Comput. Sci. **1**(5), 1–9 (2020). https://doi.org/10.1007/s42979-020-00283-z
31. Taslimitehrani, V., Dong, G., Pereira, N.L., Panahiazar, M., Pathak, J.: Developing EHR-driven heart failure risk prediction models using CPXR(Log) with the probabilistic loss function. J. Biomed. Inform. **60**, 260–269 (2016)
32. van der Maaten, L.J.P., Hinton, G.E.: Visualizing high-dimensional data using t-SNE. J. Mach. Learn. Res. **9**(Nov), 2579–2605 (2008)
33. Virani, S.S., et al.: Heart disease and stroke statistics-2020 update: a report from the American heart association. Circulation **141**(9), e139–e596 (2020)
34. Wang, X., et al.: Predicting treatment selections for individuals with major depressive disorder according to functional connectivity subgroups. Brain Connect. 0153 (2021)
35. Yancy, C.W., et al.: 2013 ACCF/AHA guideline for the management of heart failure: a report of the american college of cardiology foundation/American heart association task force on practice guidelines. Circulation **128**(16), 1810–1852 (2013)
36. Zheng, B., Zhang, J., Yoon, S.W., Lam, S.S., Khasawneh, M., Poranki, S.: Predictive modeling of hospital readmissions using metaheuristics and data mining. Expert Syst. Appl. **42**(20), 7110–7120 (2015)
37. Čerlinskaitė, K., Javanainen, T., Cinotti, R., Mebazaa, A.: Acute heart failure management. Korean Circ. J. **48**(6), 463 (2018)

A Workflow for Generating Patient Counterfactuals in Lung Transplant Recipients

Franco Rugolon(✉)[iD], Maria Bampa[iD], and Panagiotis Papapetrou[iD]

Department of Computer and Systems Sciences, Stockholm University,
Stockholm, Sweden
franco.rugolon@dsv.su.se

Abstract. Lung transplantation is a critical procedure performed in end-stage pulmonary patients. The number of lung transplantations performed in the USA in the last decade has been rising, but the survival rate is still lower than that of other solid organ transplantations. First, this study aims to employ machine learning models to predict patient survival after lung transplantation. Additionally, the aim is to generate counterfactual explanations based on these predictions to help clinicians and patients understand the changes needed to increase the probability of survival after the transplantation and better comply with normative requirements. We use data derived from the UNOS database, particularly the lung transplantations performed in the USA between 2019 and 2021. We formulate the problem and define two data representations, with the first being a representation that describes only the lung recipients and the second the recipients and donors. We propose an explainable ML workflow for predicting patient survival after lung transplantation. We evaluate the workflow based on various performance metrics, using five classification models and two counterfactual generation methods. Finally, we demonstrate the potential of explainable ML for resource allocation, predicting patient mortality, and generating explainable predictions for lung transplantation.

Keywords: Lung transplantation · Machine learning · Feature selection · Explainability · Counterfactuals

1 Introduction

Lung transplantation is a surgical procedure performed in end-stage pulmonary patients [18]. While it is often the only viable way to save a patient's life, lung transplantation is a complex high-risk procedure that can result in many complications, with a higher mortality rate (11.2% in the USA [20]) than that of heart (7.9% [6]) and liver (7.4% [15]) transplantations. Improving the allocation process is vital, as it can result in lower waiting times, improved transplant equity, and patient care. Nonetheless, the allocation process may vary from country

I. Koprinska et al. (Eds.): ECML PKDD 2022 Workshops, CCIS 1753, pp. 291–306, 2023.
https://doi.org/10.1007/978-3-031-23633-4_20

to country [11,13]. Moreover, the shortage and non-efficient use of the available organs and the cost of the operation can pose a considerable burden to the healthcare system, hence the need for a proper allocation of the available transplants to facilitate better and less costly care arises.

Given the increased availability of Electronic Health Records (EHRs) that contain longitudinal information on patient history, transplant medicine can benefit from Machine Learning (ML) applications [7,19] that can be used for informed clinical decision-making. ML methods have the capability to extract patterns from large amounts of complex data and build predictive models for various tasks in transplant medicine or provide patient phenotypes for risk assessment. The amount of variables that can be considered while training an ML model is higher than what can be viewed by clinicians, resulting in potentially higher predictive performance and hence better efficiency with regard to the allocation policies. To be more concrete, for transplant medicine, ML could determine which patients are at a higher risk of death based on historical data and demographics and can generate accurate prognostic information for informed transplant decision-making, both at the bedside and during the allocation process [1,23].

Although ML models have shown great success, for example, in predicting patient mortality risk or generating accurate prognostic information on the outcome of a chosen treatment, the lack of interpretability is a key factor that limits a wider adoption of ML in healthcare. New regulations, such as the GDPR and the AI act, require the models that are applied to be explainable [12,21] so that it is possible for humans to understand why the models suggest certain decisions. Some models are explainable by design, while some others, i.e., "black-box models", are not. The application of explainability techniques allows the users to understand why an ML model has taken a certain decision, even if the model is not explainable by nature. One such technique is the formulation of *counterfactual explanations* on a given example [8]. Simply put, given an ML model trained for a particular prediction task, a counterfactual refers to the changes (on the feature configuration) that need to be enacted to a given data example in order to change the decision taken by the ML model on that example [22]. Counterfactuals not only highlight the features that contribute most to the decision of the models but also suggest what feature changes can change the decision of the classifiers, being more useful to clinicians in the decision-making process.

Related Work. A number of ML-based studies has focused on lung transplantation formulating the prediction task as the probability of a patient experiencing transplant rejection [2,3,5,9,11]. Transplant rejection can have a high impact on life expectancy and quality of life of the recipient [17], however, in this work we differentiate the task by focusing on survival prediction *after* lung transplantation. Moreover, most studies employ data from a single hospital [11] or a small region including a few [11], making it harder to generalize the results to a wider population. In our study, we use a national-level database comprising all transplantations performed in the United States. Furthermore, earlier works used a single ML model for the prediction task, such as Support Vector Machines [2,3], deep learning architectures [5,9], or archetypal analysis [14], while in our paper we benchmark the performance of several ML models. Finally, dimensionality reduction techniques have also been applied as a feature pre-processing step [17] for the same problem; alternatively, the most relevant features for the prediction task are chosen based on medical knowledge [11].

Furthermore, there have been some attempts on ML and counterfactuals in organ transplantation. Berrevoets et al. [4] utilize not only patient data but also donor data to devise improved allocation policies for the available organs. In their work, they use counterfactuals to evaluate the benefit of a transplant recipient patient when coupled with a specific organ donor. This is achieved by generating a semi-synthetic database of organs for donation and proposing different donor-recipient couplings, and subsequently evaluating the survival probability of the recipient. Similarly, in the work by Xu et al. [24] the goal is to generate better patient-donor couplings than the ones generated following the policies that are currently in effect. The authors propose the use of counterfactuals to generate all possible couplings between donors and recipients and then evaluate the allocation policies on all couplings. An improvement in the transplantation outcomes is noted compared to the currently applicable allocation policies, both in terms of survival after the transplantation and reduced deaths while on the waiting list.

To the best of our knowledge, there is a scarcity of studies regarding survival prediction of lung transplantation patients in the literature, as well as a lack of a workflow for employing explainable ML techniques for the same task.

Contributions. The main goal of this paper is to propose a workflow that allows the formulation of predictions on the survival of patients after lung transplantation, based on data from EHRs, and to formulate explanations for these predictions using counterfactuals, hence providing clinicians with suggestions on how to increase the patient's survival probability after the transplantation. The main contributions of this paper are summarized as follows:

1. We propose an explainable ML-based workflow for predicting patient survival after lung transplantation, based on data from EHRs. The workflow consists of three main steps: (1) a pre-processing pipeline for clinical data variables, in order to use them in an ML process, (2) the employment of ML models for survival prediction on the patients that received lung transplants, and (3) the generation of counterfactuals to explain the model predictions;
2. We provide an extensive experimental evaluation of the performance of five classification models with respect to different performance metrics, and of two counterfactual generation methods, based on performance metrics and on the flexibility of use in a clinical setting;
3. We demonstrate our workflow on an extract of a real-world dataset, the United Network for Organ Sharing (UNOS) database, which is a national-level database that collects data on every transplant performed in the United States[1].

---

[1] https://unos.org/data/.

2   Explaining Survival of Lung Transplantation Patients Using Counterfactuals

In this section, we first provide the problem formulation followed by the description of the three steps of our proposed workflow for solving these two problems. More concretely, our workflow consists of three phases: (a) feature transformation and selection, (b) survival prediction, and (c) counterfactual generation. Figure 1 depicts a graphical representation of these three phases.

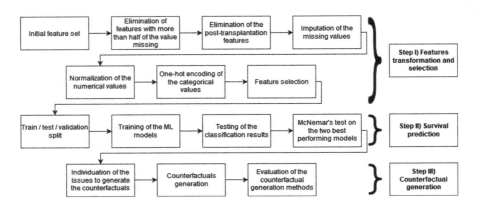

Fig. 1. A visual representation of the three phases of our proposed workflow.

2.1   Problem Formulation

Let us consider a set of EHRs related to organ transplantation denoted as $\mathcal{E} = \{p^1, \ldots, p^n\}$ of in total n patients, over a time window $T = [t_s, t_e]$ (measured in, e.g., days) ending at time point t_e (e.g., the day of transplantation), spanning a period of $w = t_e - t_s$ time points (days) before t_e. Each sample (e.g., patient) p^i in $\mathcal{E}$ is described by a *feature sequence*. A feature sequence is an ordered set of features, denoted as $x^i = \{e_1, \ldots, e_{m_i}\}$, for each patient p^i. We assume that each patient p^i is described by m_i features.

In this paper, we consider two types of feature representations, i.e., $\{\mathcal{F}^1, \mathcal{F}^2\}$, where $\mathcal{F}^1$ includes features describing a patient that will undergo lung transplantation and $\mathcal{F}^2$ includes features describing both the patient as well as the respective lung donor. In other words, $\mathcal{F}^1 \subset \mathcal{F}^2$. Both feature sets $\{\mathcal{F}^1, \mathcal{F}^2\}$ include categorical and numerical descriptors, such as sequential codes indicating different combinations of types and locations of malignancies.

Let $\mathcal{T}$ be the set of survival times of the patients, such that each patient p^i in $\mathcal{E}$ is coupled with a target survival time $t_i \in \mathcal{T}$. A patient's survival time is measured in days, starting from the time of transplantation t_e. Using the above formulation, our workflow solves the following two problems.

Problem 1. **Survival Prediction.** Given a set of EHRs $\mathcal{E}$ and the corresponding set of survival days $\mathcal{T}$, we want to learn a function $f(\cdot)$ that predicts the survival time of a patient having undergone lung transplantation. We simplify the problem to a classification problem on a class label set $\mathcal{Y}$, by assuming that if $t_i \geq \alpha$ then $y_i = 1$ (e.g., patient p_i survived) and if $t_i < \alpha$ then $y_i = 0$ (e.g., patient p_i has died), with $y_i \in \mathcal{Y}$ and $\alpha \in \mathbb{N}^+$ being a predefined threshold.

For our study, we set $\alpha = 180$, meaning that our goal is to predict whether a patient will survive for at least 180 days after transplantation.

Problem 2. **Counterfactual Generation.** Given a classifier $f(\cdot)$ trained for solving Problem 1 on a set of EHRs $\mathcal{E}$, and a survival prediction $y = f(x^i)$ for patient p^i, we want to generate a counterfactual explanation $x^{i\prime}$ such that the decision of f is swapped to another target class y' (i.e., to the opposite class, since our classification problem is binary) and the difference between x^i and $x^{i\prime}$ is minimized according to a given cost function $\delta(\cdot)$, as shown in Eq. 1,

$$x^{i\prime} = argmin_{x^{i*}}\{\delta(x^i, x^{i*})|f(x^i) = y \wedge f(x^{i*}) = y'\} \tag{1}$$

In other words, given a trained classifier f that is trained on a set of EHRs $\mathcal{E}$ we want to find the smallest change to the feature set x^i such that for patient p^i the prediction changes from $y = 0$ (deceased) to $y' = 1$ (survival). The cost function $\delta(\cdot)$ can be defined in various ways, e.g., the L1 or L2 norm of the pairwise differences of the feature values.

2.2   Step I: Feature Transformation and Selection

We first remove features from $\mathcal{F}^1$ and $\mathcal{F}^2$ with more than $\beta\%$ of missing values. In our case, we set $\beta = 50\%$ but any value can be applied. For each remaining categorical feature, we apply a one-hot encoding transformation, which introduces a new binary variable per feature, and as a result, increases the dimensionality of the feature space. Moreover, for each remaining numerical feature, normalization is applied, which in our case is min-max, but without loss of generality, any normalization can be applied.

Next, our goal is to reduce the number of features in a way that leaves the most important characteristics of the data as intact as possible. We utilize the Random Forest (RF) feature importance method. Only the features with an importance score higher than the average importance of all the features in the training set are selected. This results in a new set of features, denoted as $\hat{\mathcal{F}}^1$ and $\hat{\mathcal{F}}^2$, respectively. The selection of the most important features is only performed on the training set, so as to not introduce a bias towards the validation or test set. The same sets of features are used for both validation and test sets.

2.3   Step II: Survival Prediction

The second step of our workflow is to train a classifier for survival prediction on the reduced feature sets, i.e., $f(\hat{\mathcal{F}}^1)$, $f(\hat{\mathcal{F}}^2)$. The objective of the classifier is to learn the binary prediction problem described in Problem 1 given $\alpha = 180$.

In this paper, we employ five classifiers, namely, Decision Trees (DT), RF, K-Nearest Neighbors (KNN), Support Vector Machines (SVM), and a Multilayer Perceptron (MLP). The choice of the classifiers to be evaluated was made based on the most common classifiers employed in the related papers [2,3,5,9,11], but without loss of generality, any classifier can be applied for this step. After training, the performance of the two best classifiers is compared for both feature sets using the McNemar test to investigate if the performance difference was due to chance or to an actual difference in the classifiers.

2.4 Step III: Counterfactual Generation

In the last part of the workflow, the aim is to generate and evaluate counterfactual explanations based on the learned classification models. First, the two best-performing classification models from Step II are selected to produce the predictions for both features sets $\hat{\mathcal{F}}^1$ and $\hat{\mathcal{F}}^2$. A set of instances predicted to have a negative outcome by both classifiers are given to the counterfactual generation methods. The two selected methods are DiCE-ML [16] and the method developed by Dandl [8]. The method developed by Dandl is based on a loss function that tries to minimize four objectives: the difference between the prediction for the proposed counterfactual and the desired prediction, the difference between the proposed counterfactual and the original instance, the number of changed features, and the distance between the proposed counterfactual explanation and the nearest point in the original dataset [8]. To obtain counterfactuals that satisfy these four objectives, the authors used the Non-dominated Sorting Genetic Algorithm [10]. On the other hand, DiCE-ML is based on a loss function that tries to minimize three objectives: generating counterfactual examples that are diverse (that have a non-null distance between them), that have a low distance from the original sample, and that change as few features as possible from the original sample. In addition to this, DiCE-ML allows the user to define constraints both on the range of values that each feature can assume and on the features that can be changed to generate the proposed counterfactual explanations. DiCE-ML can accept different algorithms to generate the counterfactuals, both model-agnostic (Randomized Search, Genetic Search and Tree Search) and gradient-based (for differentiable models) [16]. Since the method developed by Dandl uses a genetic algorithm to generate the counterfactuals, the genetic option was selected for DiCE-ML as well, to obtain a fair comparison between the two different methods. A set of counterfactuals (in our case, five) are generated for each instance, suggesting an alternative feature configuration that results in a positive classification (patient survived) for the original patient that was predicted as negative (patient deceased).

3 Experimental Evaluation

3.1 Dataset

In this work, we derive our datasets from the UNOS database[2]. The UNOS database collects data about all transplantations that have been reported to the Organ Procurement and Transplantation Network (OPTN) since 1987, and it includes information about the transplantation of various organs, such as heart, lungs, liver, and kidney. The data is organized in records; each record collects data about a single transplantation, including both patient and donor-related information. Each record is composed of features, for example, related to the patient's admission to the waiting list, the transplantation time, or information related to the period between these two events.

In this work, we use a set of features related to lung transplantation that can be derived from patients and their donors. Table 1 shows a summary of the categories in which these features can be divided. Both types of representations, $\hat{\mathcal{F}}^1$ and $\hat{\mathcal{F}}^2$, include the patients' demographics, that include features like the age and the country of residence, features relative to the patient at the moment of the addition to the waiting list, like the academic level of the patient or their weight and Body Mass Index (BMI) at that moment, features relative to what happened between the addition to the waiting list and the transplantation, like the eventual onset of malignancies, and features related to the moment of the transplantation, like the level of creatinine in the serum or the use of life support devices at the moment of the transplant. In addition to these features, $\hat{\mathcal{F}}^2$ also includes features relative to the level of mismatch between the patient and the donor's major histocompatibility complex (HLA), features relative to the terminal hospitalization of a deceased donor, like the number of transfusions that the donor received, or the use of particular drugs, features relative to pathologies that the donor could present, like Hepatitis B, HIV, or any malignancies, and features related to the death of the donor, like the cause and circumstances of the death. If a patient has been transplanted for an acute problem, there will be no data regarding the waiting list period, and if a patient died waiting for the transplantation, or had to be removed from the waiting list due to worsening conditions, there will be no data related to the donor or to the period after the transplantation.

Table 1. A summary of the features included in the two feature sets $\hat{\mathcal{F}}^1$ and $\hat{\mathcal{F}}^2$, used to train the ML methods.

Feature set	Type of features	Demographics	Waiting list addition	Waiting list period	Transplantation moment	Donor-recipient mismatch	Donor terminal hospitalization	Donor pathologies	Donor death
$\hat{\mathcal{F}}^1$	Categorical	5	58	3	47	0	0	0	0
	Numerical	7	20	12	23	0	0	0	0
$\hat{\mathcal{F}}^2$	Categorical	9	58	3	51	5	17	29	13
	Numerical	7	20	12	23	0	24	0	0

[2] https://unos.org/data/.

3.2   Setup

We split the datasets into training, validation, and test sets, with proportions of 70:15:15 respectively. As we are dealing with an imbalanced problem, the split is performed in a stratified fashion to maintain the proportion of patients that survive or die. Table 2 shows a summary of the class distribution of the patients included in the three different sets for both $\hat{\mathcal{F}}^1$ and $\hat{\mathcal{F}}^2$.

Table 2. A summary of the number of patients classified as surviving at least $(y = 1)$ or less than $(y = 0)$ 180 days for the training, validation, and test sets, respectively, as well as for the whole dataset.

Dataset	$y = 0$	$y = 1$
Training set	1335	3619
Validation set	307	755
Test set	280	782
Total	1992	5156

To decrease the bias towards the specific training-validation-test split, we employ nested cross-validation while training and setting the hyperparameters of the chosen classifiers. The optimal combination of hyperparameters for each classifier is selected through a grid search, using the validation set. After the best set of hyperparameters is selected for each classifier, the actual classification task was performed on the test set, both for patient-related data only and for patient and donor-related data. The performance of the proposed workflow has been evaluated using the following benchmarked classification algorithms with the respective fine-tuned hyperparameters:

- **DT**: with a maximum depth of 3, the minimum number of samples required to split an internal node equal to 2, impurity measure equal to entropy, for both $\hat{\mathcal{F}}^1$ and $\hat{\mathcal{F}}^2$;
- **RF**: maximum depth of the tree equal to 82 and 52, number of trees in the forest equal to 60 and 220 for $\hat{\mathcal{F}}^1$ and $\hat{\mathcal{F}}^2$ respectively, with entropy being the impurity measure, and no bootstrap samples used when building trees for both representations.
- **SVM**: RBF kernel, regularization parameter equal to 0.0001 and 0.001 and kernel coefficient for RBF set to 100 and 10 for $\hat{\mathcal{F}}^1$ and $\hat{\mathcal{F}}^2$ respectively;
- **KNN**: with the algorithm used to compute the nearest neighbours set to 'ball tree', distance metric equal to 'Manhattan', number of neighbours set to 31 and 21, and weight function used in the prediction set to distance and uniform for $\hat{\mathcal{F}}^1$ and $\hat{\mathcal{F}}^2$ respectively;
- **MLP**: with activation function for the hidden layer set to identity, L2 regularization equal to 0.0001, hidden layer size equal to 100, solver equal to 'sgd' and constant learning rate of 0.001 for $\mathcal{F}^1$ and $\mathcal{F}^2$ respectively.

3.3 Evaluation Metrics

Classification. We assess the quality of the obtained predictions in terms of F1-score and ROC-AUC. We also provide the precision and recall for both the majority (the patients surviving more than six months) and the minority class.

Counterfactuals. We evaluate the counterfactuals proposed by the two generation methods using external measures, *sparsity* and the *Local Outlier Factor*. The sparsity of the changes evaluates the number of features that were varied to generate the proposed counterfactual, while the Local Outlier Factor is a method to determine how likely a data point is to be an outlier with respect to the k closest instances in the training set. These two metrics are chosen as they reflect two medically relevant objectives: (1) we would like to impose the minimum number of changes to a patient in order to counteract a negative outcome (measured by sparsity) and (2) we want the new patient configuration to be *feasible*, i.e., as close to the data manifold of the desired class as possible (measured by LOF).

3.4 Feature Selection

Table 3 summarizes the effect of feature transformation and selection for $\mathcal{F}^1$ and $\mathcal{F}^2$. More concretely, in the second and third columns, we can see the initial number of features and the resulting ones after eliminating those with $\beta\%$ missingness. In addition, the fourth column provides the amount of features after excluding the post-lung transplantation ones. Finally, the last two columns show how the dimensionality explodes after one-hot encoding, and provide the final number of features obtained by RF feature importance (see Sect. 2.2) to train the classification models.

Table 3. A table summarizing the number of features for both patient-related data only and for patient and donor-related data after each preprocessing step.

	Number of patients	Initial features	After eliminating the features with more than half of the values missing	After eliminating the post transplantation features	After one-hot encoding the categorical features	After performing feature selection
$\mathcal{F}^1$	7078	546	318	175	8182	789
$\mathcal{F}^2$	7078	546	318	271	17508	1558

Figure 2 depicts the 20 most important features as obtained by RF for $\mathcal{F}^1$ (left) and $\mathcal{F}^2$ (right). The year in which the patient was added to the waiting list, namely $LISTYR$, and the year in which the transplantation was performed, TX_YEAR, are the two first most important features for the $\mathcal{F}^1$ (patient-related data). Similarly, for $\mathcal{F}^2$ (patient-donor related data), the most important features are the transplantation year, TX_YEAR, and the year in which the patient was added to the waiting list for the transplantation, $LISTYR$, but the order of these two features is inverted when compared with the most important features for patient-related data only. However, as observed in the right figure, only three donor-related features are considered, namely $WGT\_KG\_DON\_CALC$, which refers to the calculated donor weight, AGE_DON, which refers to the age of the donor, and $PCO2\_DON$, which refers to the quantity of CO2 in the blood of the donor at the moment of the death. As it can be observed from the resulting feature importance conducted for $\mathcal{F}^1$ and $\mathcal{F}^2$ (with the task being to determine if the patient will survive more than six months after the transplantation), the features in $\hat{\mathcal{F}}^2$ have relatively lower importance when compared to those in $\hat{\mathcal{F}}^1$.

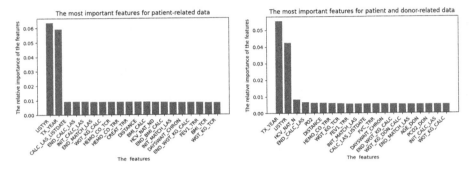

Fig. 2. Left: Twenty most important features for $\mathcal{F}^1$ (patient-related data) and their importance scores; Right: Twenty most important features for $\mathcal{F}^2$ (patient and donor-related data) and their importance scores.

3.5   Survival Prediction

The results obtained by the best combination of hyperparameters for each model are depicted in Table 4 for the $\hat{\mathcal{F}}^1$ representation (patient data) and in Table 5 for the $\hat{\mathcal{F}}^2$ representation (patient-donor data), using macro-averaging for both minority and majority class. Additionally, in both cases, we used 5-fold cross-validation for testing, which ensured that the results of the tests were not due to the way in which the data was split.

Additionally, we provide the performance metrics of all the classifiers for the majority and the minority classes can be seen in Table 6 for data relative to $\hat{\mathcal{F}}^1$ and in Table 7 for data relative to $\hat{\mathcal{F}}^2$.

Regarding the $\hat{\mathcal{F}}^1$ representation, we observe in Table 4 and Table 6 the resulting evaluation metrics for all the benchmarked algorithms on this dataset. In this case, the best performing model is the DT with an AUC of 0.82 and an F1 score equal to 0.83 and following that the RF with an AUC of 0.76 and an F1 score of 0.78. A McNemar's test was performed on the predictions made by the two best-performing models on the whole test set, to see if the difference in performance between them was statistically significant. The resulting McNemar's statistic value is 25.0000, which corresponds to a p-value of 0.0020. Since the p-value for statistically significant differences is usually set at 0.05, and the resulting p-value

Table 4. A summary of the macro-average scores for each metric on the test set on the $\hat{\mathcal{F}}^1$ feature set.

Model	Precision	Recall	F1 score	ROC-AUC
Decision tree	0.8495	0.8205	**0.8332**	**0.8205**
Support vector machine	0.8211	0.7170	0.7456	0.7170
Random forest	0.8375	0.7533	0.7808	0.7533
K-nearest neighbors	0.7224	0.5212	0.4721	0.5212
Multilayer perceptron	0.8138	0.7374	0.7623	0.7374

Table 5. A summary of the macro-average scores for each metric on the test set on the $\hat{\mathcal{F}}^2$ feature set.

Model	Precision	Recall	F1 score	ROC-AUC
Decision tree	0.8445	0.8185	**0.8301**	**0.8185**
Support vector machine	0.8006	0.7160	0.7411	0.7160
Random forest	0.8609	0.6970	0.7300	0.6970
K-nearest neighbors	0.6799	0.5263	0.4858	0.5263
Multilayer perceptron	0.7535	0.6902	0.7095	0.6902

Table 6. Left: The average scores for each metric on $\hat{\mathcal{F}}^1$ for the minority class; Right: The average scores for each metric on $\hat{\mathcal{F}}^1$ for the majority class.

Model	Precision	Recall	F1 score	Model	Precision	Recall	F1 score
Decision tree	0.8008	0.7036	**0.7490**	Decision tree	0.8983	0.9373	**0.9174**
Support vector machine	0.8061	0.4750	0.5978	Support vector machine	0.8361	0.9591	0.8934
Random forest	0.8191	0.5500	0.6581	Random forest	0.8558	0.9565	0.9034
K-nearest neighbors	0.7000	0.0500	0.0933	K-nearest neighbors	0.7447	0.9923	0.8509
Multilayer perceptron	0.7789	0.5286	0.6298	Multilayer perceptron	0.8486	0.9463	0.8948

Table 7. Left: The average scores for each metric on $\hat{\mathcal{F}}^2$ for the minority class; Right: The average scores for each metric on $\hat{\mathcal{F}}^2$ for the majority class.

Model	Precision	Recall	F1 score	Model	Precision	Recall	F1 score
Decision tree	0.7912	0.7036	**0.7448**	Decision tree	0.8979	0.9335	**0.9154**
Support vector machine	0.7640	0.4857	0.5939	Support vector machine	0.8371	0.9463	0.8884
Random forest	0.8984	0.4107	0.5637	Random forest	0.8233	0.9834	0.8963
K-nearest neighbors	0.6129	0.0679	0.1222	K-nearest neighbors	0.7468	0.9847	0.8494
Multilayer perceptron	0.6809	0.4571	0.5470	Multilayer perceptron	0.8261	0.9233	0.8720

is lower, the null hypothesis can be rejected, and the difference between the two classifiers can be considered statistically significant.

In the case of the $\hat{\mathcal{F}}^2$ representation the results are depicted in Table 5 and Table 7, where we observe the best performing models to be a DT and the SVM with AUC 0.82 and 0.72 and F1 score 0.83 and 0.74, respectively. The McNemar's test was again performed on the predictions provided by the two best-performing models, yielding statistical significance. More concretely, the resulting McNemar's statistic value is 42.0000 and the corresponding p-value is 0.0002. Comparing the two representations $\hat{\mathcal{F}}^1$ and $\hat{\mathcal{F}}^2$ on the two statistically best-performing models, we notice that the results from $\hat{\mathcal{F}}^1$ representation outperform the results from $\hat{\mathcal{F}}^2$ indicating that although additional curated features were included in the process, they did not improve the classification performance. To produce the counterfactuals we choose to proceed with the RF for $\hat{\mathcal{F}}^1$ and DT for $\hat{\mathcal{F}}^2$. In the first case, we chose to use the Random Forest to produce the counterfactual explanations in order to provide the reader with a complete view of the possibility of producing explanations based on the predictions of two different ML models.

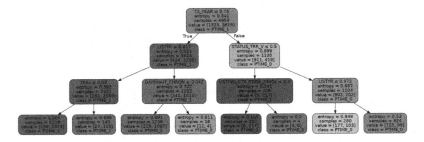

Fig. 3. A visual representation of the best performing DT on patient and donor-related data. We observe that six main features are taken into consideration for the classification task.

Additionally, we provide a graphical representation of the DT generated for the $\hat{\mathcal{F}}^2$ representation, visible in Fig. 3. It should be noted that the specific Decision Tree used in this experiment is actually a very simple model, with a maximum depth (the maximum number of consecutive splits from the root node to the leaf nodes) of three, and still, it performed well both on the training and on the test set. This motivated us to further investigate the results. As it can be seen from examining the figure, the model in question takes into consideration six features to classify the patients into the two classes, $PTIME\_1$, representing survival after the first six months from the transplantation, and $PTIME\_0$, representing non-survival at six months. The features taken into consideration by the model are as follows, indicating:

1. TX_YEAR: the year in which the patient received the transplantation.
2. $LIST\_YR$: the year in which the patient was added to the waiting list for the transplantation.
3. $STATUS\_TRR$: the status of the form for the admission of the patient at the moment in which they received the transplantation. In particular, the value V, which is taken into consideration by the Decision Tree, indicates that the form has been validated.

4. $TBILI$: the amount of total bilirubin in the serum at the moment of the transplantation.
5. $DAYSWAIT\_CHRON$: the total number of days on the waiting list.
6. $LISTING\_CTR\_CODE$: an encrypted identifier of the centre in which the patient has been admitted to the waiting list. Since the identifier is encrypted, it is not possible to find the specific centre that is considered to be relevant by this Decision Tree.

The improvement in medical care over the years accounts for the high importance of the first two features in the decision process, but it is interesting that, even in just a three-year span, these features are by far the most important.

3.6   Counterfactual Generation

In the last step, we aim to generate counterfactual explanations for a set of six patients that were predicted to have a negative class label, using the classification models presented in Sect. 3.5. We generate the counterfactuals utilizing both DiCE-ML and the method as presented by Dandl et al. [8].

For $\hat{\mathcal{F}}^1$ representation, we choose to utilize the predictions of the RF model to generate counterfactuals. The number and percentage of features changed to generate the candidate counterfactuals for each patient of interest is depicted in Table 8 (first two columns). It can be noticed in the table that this method changes nearly 10% of the features in the $\hat{\mathcal{F}}^1$ feature set in order to generate a candidate counterfactual. The number of counterfactuals classified as outliers according to the LOF score using this method is provided in Table 9 (first two columns), with 95% and 97% confidence. DiCE-ML, on the other hand, allows the user to choose which features will be varied to generate the candidate counterfactuals. To this end, we utilize this method and vary only the two most important features as presented during the feature selection phase (TX_YEAR, $LISTYR$), together with the four quantitative variables that were considered by the Decision Tree ($TX\_YEAR, LISTYR, TBILI, DAYSWAIT\_CHRON$). The number of outliers generated using DiCE-ML is provided in Table 10.

Regarding the $\hat{\mathcal{F}}^2$ representation, the DT model was chosen to generate the counterfactuals. In the last two columns of Table 8, we present the number and percentage of features changed to generate the candidate counterfactuals for each data sample of interest using the method by Dandl. We observe that in this case, nearly 8% of the features are changed on average, to generate the candidate counterfactuals. In the last two columns of Table 9, we provide the number of outliers generated by this method to provide explanations for each data sample of interest, with two different levels of confidence. Additionally, the number of outliers identified by the LOF score on the candidate counterfactuals generated by DiCE-ML for the $\hat{\mathcal{F}}^2$ representation, can be seen in Table 10. When considering 10, 15 or 20 neighbours to define if a proposed counterfactual is an outlier, shifting the focus to be less local and more global, all the proposed counterfactuals, generated with both methods, are indicated as outliers. We observe that the counterfactuals provided by DICE-ML give fewer outliers in general, both for $\hat{\mathcal{F}}^1$ and $\hat{\mathcal{F}}^2$. This behaviour can be attributed to the fact that the method allows for a selection of features that can be varied when generating the counterfactual explanations. This can potentially benefit medical applications, as the medical professional would be able to restrict the pool of available features to be changed during the process.

Table 8. A summary of the number and percentage of features changed in each proposed counterfactual explanation on $\hat{\mathcal{F}}^1$ and on $\hat{\mathcal{F}}^2$ using the method by Dandl.

Data samples of interest	Average number of features changed on $\hat{\mathcal{F}}^1$	Average percentage of features changed on $\hat{\mathcal{F}}^1$	Average number of features changed on $\hat{\mathcal{F}}^2$	Average percentage of features changed on $\hat{\mathcal{F}}^2$
2	80.67	10.22%	139.00	8.92%
3	81.67	10.35%	134.50	8.63%
7	72.83	9.23%	122.33	7.85%
13	73.33	9.29%	121.17	7.78%
18	82.00	10.39%	123.17	7.91%

Table 9. A summary of the number of counterfactuals classified as outliers according to the LOF score on counterfactuals generated using the method by Dandl on the same data samples in $\hat{\mathcal{F}}^1$ and $\hat{\mathcal{F}}^2$, considering the 5 nearest neighbours, with two levels of confidence.

Data samples of interest	Confidence 95% on $\hat{\mathcal{F}}^1$	Confidence 97% on $\hat{\mathcal{F}}^1$	Confidence 95% on $\hat{\mathcal{F}}^2$	Confidence 97% on $\hat{\mathcal{F}}^2$
2	6	4	6	5
3	6	3	4	4
7	0	0	0	0
13	1	0	0	0
18	1	0	2	1

Table 10. A summary of the number of outliers for each data sample of interest according to the LOF score on the same data samples for $\hat{\mathcal{F}}^1$ and $\hat{\mathcal{F}}^2$, on counterfactuals generated using DiCE-ML, using the 5 nearest data samples from the training set.

Data sample	Outliers in $\hat{\mathcal{F}}^1$ (two features changed)	Outliers in $\hat{\mathcal{F}}^1$ (four features changed)	Outliers in $\hat{\mathcal{F}}^2$ (two features changed)	Outliers in $\hat{\mathcal{F}}^2$ (four features changed)
2	0	0	0	0
3	4	6	0	0
7	0	0	0	0
13	0	0	0	0
18	0	0	0	0

4   Conclusion

To conclude, in this paper we proposed a workflow for employing ML models to predict the survival of patients after a lung transplant, possibly increasing the efficiency of the allocation policies. We showed that the selection of features used to train the ML models influences the outcome of the predictions, with the performance of the ML models decreasing when donor-related data are included in the feature set. We demonstrated how counterfactuals can be used as a method to provide explainability for opaque ML models, with the added value of being able to suggest changes that the patients could enact before the operation, in order to increase their probability of survival. Future research can experiment with different ML models and different patient populations, and, most importantly, can work closely with clinicians, to select the features to be changed to generate the counterfactual explanations and validate the results.

Acknowledgements. This work was supported in part by the Health Resources and Services Administration contract 234-2005-370011C, the Digital Futures EXTREMUM project on "Explainable and Ethical Machine Learning for Knowledge Discovery from Medical Data Sources", as well as by the Horizon2020 ASME project on "Using Artificial Intelligence for Predicting the Treatment Outcome of Melanoma Patients".

References

1. Balch, J.A., et al.: Machine learning applications in solid organ transplantation and related complications. Front. Immunol. 3707 (2021). https://doi.org/10.3389/fimmu.2021.739728
2. Barbosa Jr, E.J.M., et al.: Machine learning algorithms utilizing quantitative CT features may predict eventual onset of bronchiolitis obliterans syndrome after lung transplantation. Acad. Radiol. **25**(9), 1201–1212 (2018). https://doi.org/10.1016/j.acra.2018.01.013
3. Berra, G., et al.: Association between the renin-angiotensin system and chronic lung allograft dysfunction. Eur. Respir. J. **58**(4) (2021). https://doi.org/10.1183/13993003.02975-2020
4. Berrevoets, J., Alaa, A., Qian, Z., Jordon, J., Gimson, A.E.S., van der Schaar, M.: Learning queueing policies for organ transplantation allocation using interpretable counterfactual survival analysis. In: Meila, M., Zhang, T. (eds.) Proceedings of the 38th International Conference on Machine Learning. Proceedings of Machine Learning Research, vol. 139, pp. 792–802. PMLR (2021)
5. Cantu, E., et al.: Preprocurement in situ donor lung tissue gene expression classifies primary graft dysfunction risk. Am. J. Respir. Crit. Care Med. **202**(7), 1046–1048 (2020). https://doi.org/10.1164/rccm.201912-2436LE
6. Colvin, M., et al.: OPTN/SRTR 2019 annual data report: heart. Am. J. Transplant. **21**(S2), 356–440 (2021). https://doi.org/10.1111/ajt.16492
7. Connor, K.L., O'Sullivan, E.D., Marson, L.P., Wigmore, S.J., Harrison, E.M.: The future role of machine learning in clinical transplantation. Transplantation **105**(4), 723–735 (2021). https://doi.org/10.1097/TP.0000000000003424
8. Dandl, S., Molnar, C., Binder, M., Bischl, B.: Multi-objective counterfactual explanations. In: Bäck, T., et al. (eds.) PPSN 2020. LNCS, vol. 12269, pp. 448–469. Springer, Cham (2020). https://doi.org/10.1007/978-3-030-58112-1_31

9. Davis, H., Glass, C., Davis, R., Glass, M., Pavlisko, E.: Detecting acute cellular rejection in lung transplant biopsies by artificial intelligence: a novel deep learning approach. J. Heart Lung Transplant. **39**(4), S501–S502 (2020). https://doi.org/10.1016/j.healun.2020.01.100
10. Deb, K., Pratap, A., Agarwal, S., Meyarivan, T.: A fast and elitist multiobjective genetic algorithm: NSGA-II. IEEE Trans. Evol. Comput. **6**(2), 182–197 (2002). https://doi.org/10.1109/4235.996017
11. Dueñas-Jurado, J., et al.: New models for donor-recipient matching in lung transplantations. PLoS ONE **16**(6), e0252148 (2021). https://doi.org/10.1371/journal.pone.0252148
12. Goodman, B., Flaxman, S.: European union regulations on algorithmic decision-making and a "right to explanation". AI Mag. **38**(3), 50–57 (2017). https://doi.org/10.1609/aimag.v38i3.2741
13. Gottlieb, J.: Lung allocation. J. Thorac. Dis. **9**(8), 2670 (2017). https://doi.org/10.21037/jtd.2017.07.83
14. Halloran, K., et al.: Molecular phenotyping of rejection-related changes in mucosal biopsies from lung transplants. Am. J. Transplant. **20**(4), 954–966 (2020). https://doi.org/10.1111/ajt.15685
15. Kwong, A.J., et al.: OPTN/SRTR 2019 annual data report: liver. Am. J. Transplant. **21**(S2), 208–315 (2021). https://doi.org/10.1111/ajt.16494
16. Mothilal, R.K., Sharma, A., Tan, C.: Explaining machine learning classifiers through diverse counterfactual explanations. In: Proceedings of the 2020 Conference on Fairness, Accountability, and Transparency, pp. 607–617 (2020). https://doi.org/10.1145/3351095.3372850
17. Oztekin, A., Al-Ebbini, L., Sevkli, Z., Delen, D.: A decision analytic approach to predicting quality of life for lung transplant recipients: a hybrid genetic algorithms-based methodology. Eur. J. Oper. Res. **266**(2), 639–651 (2018). https://doi.org/10.1016/j.ejor.2017.09.034
18. Shahmoradi, L., Abtahi, H., Amini, S., Gholamzadeh, M.: Systematic review of using medical informatics in lung transplantation studies. Int. J. Med. Inform. **136**, 104096 (2020). https://doi.org/10.1016/j.ijmedinf.2020.104096
19. Spann, A., et al.: Applying machine learning in liver disease and transplantation: a comprehensive review. Hepatology **71**(3), 1093–1105 (2020). https://doi.org/10.1002/hep.31103
20. Valapour, M., et al.: OPTN/SRTR 2019 annual data report: lung. Am. J. Transplant. **21**(S2), 441–520 (2021). https://doi.org/10.1111/ajt.16495
21. Vitali, F.: A survey on methods and metrics for the assessment of explainability under the proposed AI act. In: Legal Knowledge and Information Systems: JURIX 2021: The Thirty-fourth Annual Conference, Vilnius, Lithuania, 8–10 December 2021, vol. 346, p. 235. IOS Press (2022). https://doi.org/10.3233/FAIA210342
22. Wachter, S., Mittelstadt, B., Russell, C.: Counterfactual explanations without opening the black box: automated decisions and the GDPR. Harv. J. Law Technol. **31**(2), 841 (2018)
23. Watson, D.S., et al.: Clinical applications of machine learning algorithms: beyond the black box. BMJ **364** (2019). https://doi.org/10.1136/bmj.l886
24. Xu, C., Alaa, A., Bica, I., Ershoff, B., Cannesson, M., van der Schaar, M.: Learning matching representations for individualized organ transplantation allocation. In: Banerjee, A., Fukumizu, K. (eds.) Proceedings of the 24th International Conference on Artificial Intelligence and Statistics. Proceedings of Machine Learning Research, vol. 130, pp. 2134–2142. PMLR (2021)

Few-Shot Learning for Identification of COVID-19 Symptoms Using Generative Pre-trained Transformer Language Models

Keyuan Jiang[1]([✉]) [ID], Minghao Zhu[2], and Gordon R. Bernard[3]

[1] Purdue University Northwest, Hammond, IN 46323, USA
kjiang@pnw.edu
[2] Tongji University, Shanghai, China
[3] Vanderbilt University, Nashville, TN 37232, USA
gordon.bernard@vumc.org

Abstract. Since the onset of the COVID-19 pandemic, social media users have shared their personal experiences related to the viral infection. Their posts contain rich information of symptoms that may provide useful hints to advancing the knowledge body of medical research and supplement the discoveries from clinical settings. Identification of symptom expressions in social media text is challenging, partially due to lack of annotated data. In this study, we investigate utilizing few-shot learning with generative pre-trained transformer language models to identify COVID-19 symptoms in Twitter posts. The results of our approach show that large language models are promising in more accurately identifying symptom expressions in Twitter posts with small amount of annotation effort, and our method can be applied to other medical and health applications where abundant of unlabeled data is available.

Keywords: Generative pre-trained transformer · Pre-trained language model · Few-shot learning · COVID-19 symptoms · Twitter

1 Introduction

The outbreak of COVID-19 pandemic, which has infected hundreds of millions of people and led to million deaths world-wide, was caused by a novel coronavirus. At the onset of the pandemic, healthcare givers were having difficulties in accurately diagnosing the infectious and deadly disease, due to its symptoms similar to flu and cold, lack of understanding and knowledge of this new disease, and insufficient supply of testing kits. Healthcare workers were learning to understand the new disease while busy treating and caring for those infected.

Interestingly, this pandemic took place at the digital age when people can freely share their personal experiences about the infection online. As such, symptomatic experiences of those infected were posted on social media, including Twitter. Although social media users do not post their experiences in a systematic and consistent manner, the diverse information of COVID-19 symptoms reported by social media users may provide useful

© The Author(s), under exclusive license to Springer Nature Switzerland AG 2023
I. Koprinska et al. (Eds.): ECML PKDD 2022 Workshops, CCIS 1753, pp. 307–316, 2023.
https://doi.org/10.1007/978-3-031-23633-4_21

hints and potentially supplement what was being discovered clinically. The sheer amount of social media posts related to COVID-19 caught attention of the research community. Chen et al. [1] started collecting COVID-19 related tweets from January 28, 2020, and has accumulated over 2 billion tweet IDs that are shared publicly – Twitter Developer Policy does not allow redistribution of the Twitter data except the IDs. Utilizing a corpus of 22.5 million COVID-19 related tweets, Müller et al. [2] pre-trained the COVID-Twitter-BERT (CT-BERT) language model, based upon Google's Bidirectional Encoder Representations from Transformers (BERT) language model. CT-BERT was intended for downstream natural language processing (NLP) tasks in the COVID-19 domain.

Tweet: My Experience:. . Day 1: Body aches and cold chills. (Tested for Covid19/positive). Day 2: Minor Body Aches, no chills. Day 3: No aches, but loss of sense of smell and taste. Day 4 thru Day 11: No sense of smell or taste. Day 12: Regained both smell and taste.

Symptoms: aches, chills, aches, loss of sense of smell and taste, and no sense of smell or taste.

Fig. 1. An example tweet showing symptomatic experience of the user.

COVID-19-related Twitter posts can contain relevant information pertaining to the infection of the Twitter users. In Fig. 1., the Twitter user mentioned several symptoms (e.g., *aches, chills, no sense of smell or taste*), and identical symptoms more than once but on different days (e.g., *ache*). The user also expressed the concept of *loss of sense of smell and taste* in two different ways – the second way is *no sense of smell or taste*. Furthermore, the same user used negation to indicate both having a symptom (e.g., ***no sense of smell or taste***) and not experiencing a symptom (e.g., ***no chills***).

Processing and analyzing Twitter data are of particular challenge, because Twitter data are known for their noisiness, and Twitter text does not follow grammatical rules, as well as containing misspelled terms and having incomplete sentences [3]. Conventional methods of identifying symptoms in formal writing will hardly perform satisfactorily. Several efforts have been made to manually identify COVID-19 symptoms in Twitter text through annotation, a laborious process requiring domain experts. Guo et al. [4] annotated a corpus of 30732 tweets with the help of n-grams and discovered 36 symptoms related to COVID-19. Krittanawong et al. [5] analyzed a collection of 14698 tweets for common COVID-19 symptoms. Assisted with semiautomatic filtering, Sarker et al. [6] manually went through 7495 tweets posted by 203 unique users who were tested positive and discovered 1002 symptoms using 668 unique expression. Jiang et al. [7] manually identified COVID-19 symptoms along with the day information from a corpus of about 700 personal experience tweets.

Given the significant cost and effort of annotating a large number of Tweets and lack of available labeled instances, we propose to utilize few-shot learning with generative pre-trained language models for identification of symptoms from COVID-19 related personal experience tweets. Large language models based on generative pre-trained transformer (GPT), such as GPT-2 [8], GPT-3 [9], and GPT-NeoX-20B [10] which are trained on massive unlabeled data, have demonstrated their power of achieving improved results in natural language understanding (NLU) tasks with fewer or no labeled examples. Using a small number of annotated instances well suits many applications of machine learning in biomedical and healthcare fields, where annotated data are scarce and cost of annotation can be potentially prohibitive to generate large corpora of labeled data for supervised learning. In the case of COVID-19-related social media posts, there is abundance of unlabeled instances, which are continually being generated by their users, and annotating a large corpus of posts can be impractical and requires significant resources of domain expert.

In addition to the unique characteristics of Twitter data, a COVID-19-related tweet may mention multiple symptoms, as shown in the example above. Not only Twitter users describe the symptom concepts with layman's terms, but also they express the same single symptom concept with various expressions. To tackle these challenges, we consider our task of identifying symptoms in tweets to be extractive question answering (EQA) with possible multiple answers, unlike common question answering tasks in which a single answer is desired.

2   Method

The pipeline of our data processing and analysis is shown in Fig. 2. We start with collecting COVID-19-related tweets which in turn are preprocessed. The preprocessed tweets are fed to a classifier to predict personal experience tweets. The predicted tweets are screened initially for possible symptoms and any tweets containing no symptoms are excluded. A collection of 699 tweets is chosen, and they are annotated for testing. Two publicly available language models trained with massive amount of unlabeled text data are utilized to perform few-shot learning for our task of identifying COVID-19 symptoms.

2.1   Pre-trained Language Models

Many large language models require a fee to use, and even with small scale tasks, the cost of using them can be significant. Two freely available large language models were considered for this research: GPT-2 (small and medium) [11] and GPT-NeoX-20B [10]. The small version of GPT-2 comprises 117 million parameters, and the medium version is made up of 345 million parameters. The GPT-NeoX-20B has 20 billion parameters, 57 times larger than the GPT-2 medium model and more than 170 times larger than the GPT-2 small version.

A team at OpenAI designed and trained the GPT-2 language model to demonstrate that language models are able to perform down-stream tasks in a zero-shot setting without any modification of parameters or architecture for the NLP applications where only minimal or no supervised data are available for training. The model was constructed from the original GPT, a transformer-based model with generative pre-training [8]. The language model has 4 different sizes, and our study focuses on two smaller models: the small one with 117 million parameters, 12 layers and 768 dimensions, and the medium one with 345 million parameters, 24 layers and 1024 dimensions. The context size of the model is 1024 tokens. The model was trained with a subset of Common Crawl dataset (https://commoncrawl.org) which is made up of Web scrapes, with slightly over 8 million documents with a size of 40 GB of text.

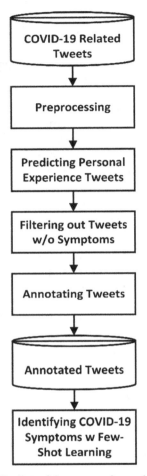

Fig. 2. Pipeline of data processing and analysis.

Developed by EleutherAI, GPT-NeoX-20B is an open-source autoregressive language model with 20 billion parameters [10]. The architecture of the model is based upon Google's BERT architecture, with 44 layers, a hidden dimension size of 6144, and 64 heads. The model is a powerful few-shot learner and achieved state-of-the-art (SoTA) performance in many few-shot learning tasks. The released pre-trained model was learned with the Pile dataset [12] which consists of 825 gibibyte (GiB. 1 GiB $= 2^{30}$ bytes) of curated raw text data from 22 data sources including PubMed Central and NIH Exporter, both of which pertain to the domain of this research.

In this study, we utilize the models as pre-trained with no modification of their parameters and architecture.

2.2 Prompt Design

One of the key components in few-shot learning, which uses a small number of annotated examples as input for training, involves the design of prompts, as few-shot learning is performed by reformulating tasks as natural language "prompts" [13]. A few examples are used to train the language models, and each example fed to the language models consists of the input text and answer.

Task: List the symptoms of COVID-19 in following tweets

Tweet: My Experience:. . Day 1: Body aches and cold chills. (Tested for Covid19/positive). Day 2: Minor Body Aches, no chills. Day 3: No aches, but loss of sense of smell and taste. Day 4 thru Day 11: No sense of smell or taste. Day 12: Regained both smell and taste.
Symptoms: {'aches', 'chills', 'Aches', 'loss of sense of smell and taste', 'No sense of smell or taste'}

[... zero or more examples ...]

Tweet: It's Day 22 of my personal battle with Covid19. To all intents & purposes I am better. I'm back at work, I'm able to function. But its still here, I still have a temperature, a slight cough, a ringing in my ears. Will this thing ever leave? #Covid19UK
Symptoms:

Fig. 3. An illustration of few-shot learning prompting. Each example consists of the text of a tweet and an order set of spans (symptoms). In this study, the number of examples can be 1, 5, 10 or 15, depending upon the number of examples needed for few-shot learning.

In our case as well as other NLP applications in the medical and health domain, we need to take into consideration the uniqueness of the text and task in question. First, the text of a single tweet may mention multiple symptoms or the same symptom multiple times on different days. Association of symptoms with the day information can help understand how the disease progresses over time. This requires the answer to be an ordered set of symptoms (or token spans). In addition, social media users frequently express medical and/or health concepts with layman's terms. Jiang et al. [7] observed in their study that Twitter users creatively came up with more than 60 different expressions to describe each common health concept of *fever*, *breathing difficulty*, and *loss of smell and/or taste* respectively. As such, we do not attempt to normalize the health concepts from various expressions. Instead, we consider the match of token spans when measuring the model performance.

Shown in Fig. 3 is our prompting template which includes one or more examples to train the language model. The trained language model is used to predict the answer(s) to the last tweet fed to the model.

2.3 Language Model Testing

To test the performance of the language model in identifying COVID-19 symptoms from tweet text, we choose to use 1 example (shot), 5 examples (shots) and 10 examples (shots) for all models, but also use 15 shots for GPT-NeoX-20B. This is due to the input token size limitation of each model: 1024 for GPT-2 and 4096 for GPT-NeoX-20B.

We randomly select the desired number of examples for training with a fixed seed to ensure that each set of examples is identical for each model. A collection of 100 tweets is used for testing using 10-fold cross-validation – that is, each time a fold is used for training and 9 other folds are used for testing. The averages of the testing performance are computed.

2.4 Data

A collection of 12 million COVID-19 related tweets was gathered from twitter.com using a homemade crawler which was devised in compliance with the Twitter crawling policy. The rationale of using a homemade crawler is to overcome the limits of Twitter APIs, such as the tweets posted within last 7 days and the number of queries within a time window. The time span of our study tweets is from 11 March 2020 to 23 April 2020, and the tweets were collected in May 2020. We used the following keywords for querying the Twitter posts: *covid19*, *COVID-19*, *coronavirus*, *Wuhan pneumonia*, and *nCoV*, which were frequently mentioned for the new disease at the time of collection.

The collected tweets were preprocessed to remove duplicates, re-tweets and non-English tweets. For COVID-19 symptoms, tweets with personal experience are of special interest in this study. We applied a transformer language model-based method [14] to predict personal experience tweets – this step helps filter out many irrelevant noisy tweets. The method was developed by Zhu et al. [14] to predict personal experience tweets pertaining to medication effects, by first updating the pre-trained Robustly Optimized BERT Pretraining Approach (RoBERTa) [15] language model with a corpus of 10 million unlabeled tweets related to medication effects, and later fine-tuning the model with annotated tweets. The RoBERTa-based language model, developed by Facebook, is made up of a structure of 12 layers, 768 hidden neurons, 12 self-attention heads and 110M parameters, and was pre-trained with over 160GB uncompressed texts [15]. The model was later fine-tuned with 12K annotated tweets. Zhu's method achieved accuracy of 0.877, precision of 0.734, recall of 0.775, and F1 score of 0.754 on the medication effect tweets. Due to lack of publicly available corpora of annotated COVID-19 symptom tweets because the Twitter Developer Policy does not permit redistribution of Tweet text, we decided to transfer Zhu's method from predicting medication-effect personal experience tweets to predicting COVID-19 symptom personal experience tweets without retraining the model. This *transfer learning* appears adequate and valid in that both are in medical domain and the relationship between a medication and its effects resembles the relationship between a disease (COVID-19) and its symptoms.

We used MetaMap Lite [16], a software tool developed by the U.S. Library of Medicine to initially screen the personal COVID-19 experience tweets for symptoms. This step is not to identify all the symptoms, but to ensure that each tweet contains at least a symptom which is identified the MetaMap Lite, helping further filter out irrelevant tweets. Any concepts mapped to the semantic type of *sosy* (sign and symptom) by MetaMap Lite are considered as symptoms. The outcome is a corpus of 11K tweets which were further processed with regular expressions to only include those mentioned any symptoms from day 1 to day 14 for the reason that COVID-19 symptoms typically develop between 1 and 14 days after exposure [17]. The final result is a corpus of 699 tweets which was manually annotated to identify all the token spans that describe the symptom concepts. MetaMap Lite does normalize the medical concepts but misses many symptom token spans due to the occurrences of layman's terms in the tweet text. Our manual process identifies symptoms in a more accurate manner.

3 Results

Shown in Table 1 are the performance measures (precision, recall, and F1 score) of running the GPT language models on our COVID-19-related tweets. GPT-2 models investigated allows for an input size of 1024 for all the input text (task description, examples and prompts) whereas the input size for GPT-NeoX-20B is 4096, significantly larger than GPT-2. As such, we were only able to test up to 10 shots on GPT-2 models, but up to 15 shots on the GPT-NeoX-20B model.

Table 1. Results of identifying COVID-19 symptoms from Twitter data using generative pre-trained transformer (GPT) language models.

Model	Shot	Precision	Recall	F1 Score
GPT-2-125M	1-shot	0.020	0.145	0.035
	5-shot	0.027	0.150	0.046
	10-shot	0.025	0.147	0.042
GPT-2-345M	1-shot	0.047	0.166	0.073
	5-shot	0.083	0.148	0.106
	10-shot	0.102	0.156	0.123
GPT-NeoX-20B	1-shot	0.430	0.526	0.473
	5-shot	0.594	0.615	0.604
	10-shot	0.575	**0.666**	0.617
	15-shot	**0.605**	0.650	**0.627**

Illustrated in Fig. 4 are the graphical views of performance measures by model. They show a consistent pattern such that larger models perform better than the smaller models and more training example generate better predictions.

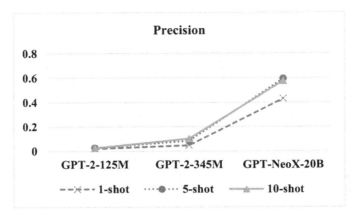

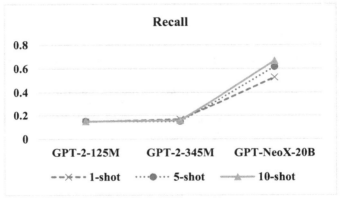

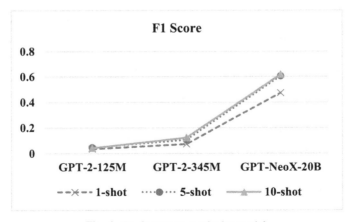

Fig. 4. Performance results by model.

4   Discussions

As can be seen in the results, the performance of our task tends to be in proportional to the number of examples (shots) used for learning. The more examples, the better performance it achieves. Five or more examples are a good choice for few-shot learning. In addition, the larger the number of parameters of the language model, the better the performance – the GPT-NeoX-20B model we tested is significantly larger than both GPT-2 models and outperforms the GPT-2 models. Also, the GPT-2-345M model which is made up of more parameters achieves better results than the small model of GPT-2 which has 117 million parameters. The GPT-NeoX-20B language model shows promising results in our task, making it possible to accurately identify COVID-19 symptoms from Twitter posts.

There exist limitations in this study. First, the few-shot learning approach does not seem to handle negation correctly, partially due to the confusing ways of how symptom concepts are expressed by the Twitter users. For examples, *no smell or taste* is not negation, but is to describe the concept of *loss of smell or taste*. Another limitation that impacts our method performance comes from the layman's terms of expressing symptom concepts by Twitter users. A commonly found instance is that many users use *temperature* or even *temp* to describe the concept of *fever* (e.g., *I have temp today*). One more limitation is the limited power of our computation resource which prevents us from testing a larger corpus of annotated tweets which would generate more convincing performance outcomes.

The study data used in this work were gathered from Twitter posts, which inherently have limitations. First, Twitter users who were capable of posting are those more likely to experience non-life-threatening symptoms – for example, they were not those on a ventilator. Therefore, symptoms reported are mostly mild. Second, due to the disparity of the age groups of Twitter users, symptoms experienced by those who do not use Twitter are unlikely to be included in the data.

Our future directions of this research include testing the few-shot learning approach on larger pre-trained language models with more powerful computational resources.

5   Conclusion

In this study, we investigated utilizing few-shot learning with generative pre-trained transformer (GPT) language models, GPT-2 and GPT-NeoX-20B, without modifying model parameters and architecture. We carefully designed prompts for few-shot learning by considering the uniqueness of our task in the medical/health domain. Our results demonstrate that 5 or more examples are appropriately needed for tackling our task using few-shot learning, and larger language models tend to outperform small language models in our task. It is conceivable that our few-shot learning method can be applied to other NLP tasks in medical/health domain, where there is scarce of annotated examples and which are similar to identifying disease symptoms studied in this work.

References

1. Chen, E., Lerman, K., Ferrara, E.: Tracking social media discourse about the covid-19 pandemic: development of a public coronavirus twitter data set. JMIR Public Health Surveill. **6**(2), e19273 (2020)
2. Müller, M., Salathé, M., Kummervold, P.E.: COVID-Twitter-BERT: A natural language processing model to analyse covid-19 content on twitter. arXiv preprint arXiv:2005.07503 (2020)
3. Wijeratne, S., et al.: Feature engineering for Twitter-based applications. In Feature Engineering for Machine Learning and Data Analytics, pp. 359–393 (2018)
4. Guo, J.W., Radloff, C.L., Wawrzynski, S.E., Cloyes, K.G.: Mining twitter to explore the emergence of COVID-19 symptoms. Public Health Nurs. **37**(6), 934–940 (2020)
5. Krittanawong, C., Narasimhan, B., Virk, H.U.H., Narasimhan, H., Wang, Z., Tang, W.W.: Insights from Twitter about novel COVID-19 symptoms. Eur. Heart J. Digital Health **1**(1), 4–5 (2020)
6. Sarker, A., Lakamana, S., HoggBremer, W., Xie, A., AlGaradi, M.A., Yang, Y.C.: Self-reported COVID-19 symptoms on Twitter: an analysis and a research resource. J. Am. Med. Inform. Assoc. **27**(8), 1310–1315 (2020)
7. Jiang, K., Zhu, M., Bernard, G.R.: Discovery of COVID-19 symptomatic experience reported by twitter users. Stud. Health Technol. Inform. **294**, 664–668 (2022)
8. Radford, A., Narasimhan, K., Salimans, T., Sutskever, I.: Improving language understanding by generative pre-training (2018)
9. Brown, T., et al.: Language models are few-shot learners. Adv. Neural. Inf. Process. Syst. **33**, 1877–1901 (2020)
10. Black, S., et al.: GPT-NeoX-20b: an open-source autoregressive language model. arXiv preprint arXiv:2204.06745 (2022)
11. Radford, A., Wu, J., Child, R., Luan, D., Amodei, D., Sutskever, I.: Language models are unsupervised multitask learners. OpenAI blog **1**(8), 9 (2018)
12. Gao, L., et al.: The pile: an 800gb dataset of diverse text for language modeling. arXiv preprint arXiv:2101.00027 (2020)
13. Logan IV, R.L., Balažević, I., Wallace, E., Petroni, F., Singh, S., Riedel, S.: Cutting down on prompts and parameters: simple few-shot learning with language models. arXiv preprint arXiv:2106.13353 (2021)
14. Zhu, M., Song, Y., Jin, G., Jiang, K.: Identifying personal experience tweets of medication effects using pre-trained RoBERTa language model and its updating. In Proceedings of the 11th International Workshop on Health Text Mining and Information Analysis, pp. 127–137 (2020)
15. Liu, Y., et al.: RoBERTa: A robustly optimized BERT pretraining approach. arXiv preprint arXiv:1907.11692 (2019)
16. Demner-Fushman, D., Rogers, W.J., Aronson, A.R.: MetaMap lite: an evaluation of a new Java implementation of MetaMap. J. Am. Med. Inform. Assoc. **24**(4), 841–844 (2017)
17. World Health Organization: Diagnostic testing for SARS-CoV-2 (2020). https://apps.who.int/iris/bitstream/handle/10665/334254/WHO-2019-nCoV-laboratory-2020.6-eng.pdf

A Light-Weight Deep Residual Network for Classification of Abnormal Heart Rhythms on Tiny Devices

Rohan Banerjee$^{(\boxtimes)}$ and Avik Ghose

TCS Research, Tata Consultancy Services, Kolkata, India
{rohan.banerjee,avik.ghose}@tcs.com

Abstract. An automatic classification of abnormal heart rhythms using electrocardiogram (ECG) signals has been a popular research area in medicine. In spite of reporting good accuracy, the available deep learning-based algorithms are resource-hungry and can not be effectively used for continuous patient monitoring on portable devices. In this paper, we propose an optimized light-weight algorithm for real-time classification of normal sinus rhythm, Atrial Fibrillation (AF), and other abnormal heart rhythms using single-lead ECG on resource-constrained low-powered tiny edge devices. A deep Residual Network (ResNet) architecture with attention mechanism is proposed as the baseline model which is duly compressed using a set of collaborative optimization techniques. Results show that the baseline model outperforms the state-of-the art algorithms on the open-access PhysioNet Challenge 2017 database. The optimized model is successfully deployed on a commercial microcontroller for real-time ECG analysis with a minimum impact on performance.

Keywords: TinyML · Healthcare · Convolutional Neural Networks · ECG classification

1 Introduction

Cardiovascular diseases are the key reason behind significant mortality and morbidity, causing 32% of all global deaths every year. They are often asymptomatic in early stages. Many patients seek medical attention in an advanced stage of a cardiac disease, which not only requires a prolonged hospital stay or a possible surgery but also reduces the chance of recovery. AI-driven on-device health monitoring systems are thus increasingly gaining attentions in recent times as part of preventive healthcare.

Automated decision-support systems are clinically appreciated in cardiology for analysis of electrocardiogram (ECG) or echocardiogram. An ECG represents the electrical activities of the heart in a graphical format by placing a set of electrodes on human-body near the chest. ECG is clinically used for diagnosis of abnormal heart rhythms like Atrial Fibrillation (AF) and other types of arrhythmias which are the early signs of a stroke or a cardiac arrest. However, it is not

I. Koprinska et al. (Eds.): ECML PKDD 2022 Workshops, CCIS 1753, pp. 317–331, 2023.
https://doi.org/10.1007/978-3-031-23633-4_22

practically feasible to manually analyze the large volume of continuous ECG data for detection of intermittent disease episodes. An automatic diagnosis from ECG using machine learning techniques has become a popular area of research. Several such algorithms are already available in literature that reported clinical-grade accuracy in detecting AF and other types of abnormalities. The traditional approaches extract relevant features from ECG which are used to train supervised machine learning algorithms like Support Vector Machine (SVM) or AdaBoost for classification [4]. The recent deep learning approaches have reportedly outperformed the traditional machine learning approaches. Convolutional Neural Network (CNN) has drawn a lot of attentions in recent days. Raw ECG data or the peak to peak intervals time-series extracted from ECG can directly be applied to a CNN structure for automatic feature extraction and classification [12,20]. Recurrent Neural Network (RNN) and Long Short-Term Memory (LSTM) networks have also been explored in literature for classification of AF via temporal modeling of ECG [2,18].

Residual Network (ResNet) is a CNN-based powerful deep learning architecture popularly used in recent days for ECG classification. ResNets are easy to optimize and very deep networks can be trained without gradient dissipation. Zhou et al. [13] proposed a ResNet architecture for classification of heartbeats from 2-lead ECG. Park et al. [15] proposed SE-ResNet, a modified residual network with an additional squeeze-and-excitation block, which outperformed the baseline ResNet model. Han et al. [8] used a multi-lead ResNet (ML-ResNet) architecture having three residual blocks along with a feature fusion module to detect and locate myocardial infarction using 12-lead ECG recordings.

Deep learning algorithms are resource-hungry and the models are large in size. A deep network is typically trained on a powerful desktop server using accelerated computing hardware like a graphics processing unit (GPU) or a tensor processing unit (TPU). However, a highly optimized model can run on smaller IoT and edge devices to make inferences. In recent times, there have been plenty of interests in edge-AI and TinyML aiming to optimize large deep learning models for effectively deploying on ultra low-powered tiny edge devices and microcontrollers. Such devices can remain active for several weeks without replacing the battery. The processing is entirely done on a personal device without sending the data to the cloud, which preserves the user's privacy. Lack of standardization in hardware, limited memory space, and lower processing capacity are some of the key challenges of the microcontrollers. Hence, a standard deep learning model needs significant optimization before porting. TinyML can be particularly important in digital healthcare for low-cost unobtrusive patient monitoring. In this paper, we propose a lightweight deep neural network that entirely runs on low-powered microcontroller for detection of AF and other abnormal rhythms using single-lead ECG. The application can be used for 24 × 7 cardiac rhythm monitoring and real-time detection of intermittent abnormal rhythms on stand-alone wearable devices in order to generate timely alerts. Major contributions of our paper are:

– A baseline deep residual network (ResNet) architecture with attention mechanism is proposed for classification of normal, AF, and other abnormal rhythms using single-lead ECG.

- The baseline network is optimized to a much smaller model for commercial edge devices and microcontrollers with a minimum impact on accuracy.
- A prototype system is designed for real-time ECG classification.

Our proposed baseline ECG classifier is detailed in Sect. 2. Section 3 provides a broad overview of the model optimization technique. Experimental dataset and results are discussed in Sect. 4 and 5 followed by a conclusion in Sect. 6.

2   Proposed Network Architecture for ECG Classification

We define a CNN-based deep ResNet architecture with attention mechanism as our baseline network for detection of normal sinus rhythms, AF, and other abnormal rhythms. Subsequently, the baseline model is optimized for microcontrollers.

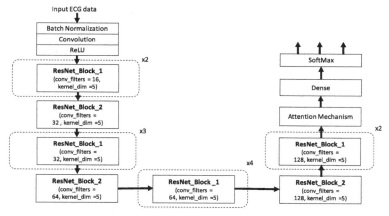

(a) Proposed network architecture

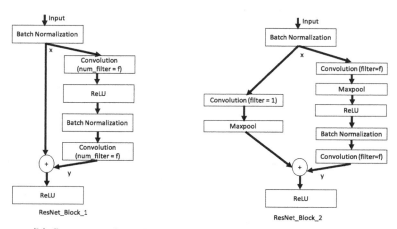

(b) Structure of two ResNet blocks in the proposed architecture

Fig. 1. Proposed ResNet architecture of the baseline model for ECG classification

Till date, most of the microcontrollers can handle only a limited number of deep network architectures. Hence, we restrict the architecture as well as the number of trainable parameters in the baseline model so that it can be effectively optimized without compromising the performance. CNNs can automatically extract features from the input using a set of convolution filters and are popularly used in image classification and computer vision applications. The convolution filters are also capable of extracting discriminating non-linear features from 1D signals. Hence, CNNs have been successfully applied in literature for analysis of biomedical signals like ECG. A multi-layer CNN can extract more detailed features from the input compared to a shallow network. However, deep CNNs are difficult to optimize and they cause vanishing gradient during training which prevents the weights to update. The ResNet architecture is designed to resolve the problem by applying identify mapping through skip connections. The skip connections skip few layers from training and connects directly to the output. This acts as a regularization term to skip certain layers in a deep architecture that do not have a positive impact in the performance.

Figure 1(a) shows the network architecture of our baseline model. The architecture comprises two residual blocks, *ResNet_ Block_ 1* and *ResNet_ Block_ 2*, as shown in Fig. 1(b). The *ResNet_ Block_ 1* takes a tensor x as input and applies to a set of weight layers, $\mathcal{F}$, comprising a pair of convolution layers having number of filters $= f$ to produce the tensor y, where $y = \mathcal{F}(x)$. There is a Rectified Linear Unit (ReLU) activation layer and a batch normalization layer in between the two convolution layers. The input tensor x is added with y and the tensor $\mathcal{F}(x) + x$ is applied to another ReLU layer to yield the output tensor which has the same dimension of the input tensor x. The structure of *ResNet_ Block_ 2* is similar to *ResNet_ Block_ 1*. However, it has few more layers for feature dimensionality reduction. There is a maxpool layer after the first convolution layer in the weight layers $\mathcal{F}$. Instead of identity connection, the input tensor x passes through a convolution layer having a single filter followed by a maxpool layer to reduce its dimension before adding with the output of the weight layers.

Single-lead ECG data having a fixed duration of 35 s and sampled 100 Hz are applied to the proposed network as input (i.e. input dimension $= 3500 \times 1 \times 1$). As shown in Fig. 1(a), the input data is first applied to a batch normalization layer, a convolution layer having 16 filters, and a ReLU activation layer. Next comes 2, 3, 4, 2 numbers of grouped *ResNet_ Block_ 1* with number of filters, $f = \{16, 32, 64, 128\}$ respectively, as shown in Fig. 1(a). In between two groups of *ResNet_ Block_ 1*, where the number of filters is increased, a *ResNet_ Block_ 2* is applied to reduce the dimension of the features. The final feature map is reshaped and applied to the attention layer to pay more focus on key locations in the input. This helps in extraction of relevant features from the complex feature map that have a critical role in classification. The feature attention mechanism proposed in [14] is used in our architecture to calculate the attention weights as output using *tanh* and *softmax* functions. The output of the attention layer is flattened and applied to a fully connected layer having 64 nodes and ReLU activation function followed by a final softmax layer for classifying normal, AF, and other abnormal rhythms. The convolution operations are done by applying zero-padding to the input. The kernel dimension is selected as 5×1 throughout the architecture with a stride length of 1. The pooling window for maxpool operations in the *ResNet_Block_2* is taken as 2×1.

2.1 Depthwise Separable Convolution

The convolution operations in the ResNet blocks are performed using depthwise separable convolution algorithm proposed in the MobileNets architecture [9]. In depthwise separable convolution, we first perform a depthwise spatial convolution on each input channel separately followed by a pointwise convolution that mixes the resulting output channels. It is an efficient way of performing the convolution task with fewer mathematical operations which also results in a lesser number of trainable parameters. Let us consider, we have a 1D input data, having dimension of $lx1$ and c input channels, upon which we want to perform the convolution operation with kernel dimension of $kx1$ and p output channels. It takes $l * k * c * p$ number of mathematical operations along with $k * c * p$ trainable parameters to perform the standard convolution operation.

In depthwise separable convolution, it takes $l * k * c$ operations and $k * c$ trainable parameters to perform depthwise convolution for the input channels. An additional $l*c*p$ operations are needed to perform a pointwise convolution for all output channels which requires $c*p$ trainable parameters. Hence, in depthwise separable convolution, the total number of mathematical operations is $l*c*(k+p)$ and the number of trainable parameters is $c * (k + p)$. In comparison to the standard convolution, the number of operations and trainable parameters are both reduced by a factor of $k * p/(k + p)$. The resulting model requires less memory space to store. It also ensures a faster model inference on resource-constrained edge devices due to lesser mathematical operations.

2.2 Training of the Proposed Network

The baseline network is trained end-to-end to minimize the categorical cross-entropy loss using an Adam optimizer. The training is done for 200 epochs setting a learning rate of 0.0005. The mini-batch size is taken as 64. The network is implemented in Python 3.8.10 using TensorFlow 2.6.0 library. Initial weights of the convolution and the dense layers are set using Xavier initialization [7] which ensures that the variance of the activations are the same across every layer. The bias terms are initialized by zeros. The training is done on a computer having Intel® Xeon(R) 16-core processor, 64 GB of RAM, and an NVidia GeForce GTX 1080 Ti graphics processing unit. A detailed description of our experimental dataset is provided in Sect. 4.

3 Model Optimization for Edge Devices

The baseline neural network has a model size of 1.8 MB, which needs to be significantly compressed in order to run on low-powered commercial microcontrollers having a RAM size of few hundred kilobytes. In this paper, we propose a pipeline for collaborative optimization by combining multiple compression approaches that produces a much smaller and faster model. By encompassing various optimization techniques, we can achieve the best balance of target characteristics such as inference speed, model size, and accuracy. The following set of optimizations are applied.

- First, the baseline model is compressed by applying weight pruning.
- Weight clustering is done on the pruned model preserving model sparsity.
- Finally, an integer-only model is obtained from the pruned and clustered model by applying quantization aware training for deployment.

The above-mentioned optimizations are lossy, causing a performance drop in every stage. Hence, the error in the resulting model after every optimization is compensated by applying a retraining for fine-tuning the performance. The retraining is done at a learning rate smaller than the baseline model. In each stage of optimization, while compression the model we set a criteria of the maximum allowable performance drop as 1% in the resulting model compared to the input model. A detailed description of different optimization techniques used in our method are provided below. Section 5.2 shows a quantitative evaluation of the optimized model on a public database.

3.1 Magnitude-Based Weight Pruning

Significant amount of weights in a large neural networks are of very small values. They generally have a minimum impact on overall model performance. Magnitude-based weight pruning is a popular optimization technique that introduces sparsity to different layers in the network by eliminating few elements. This is done by gradually zeroing out some of the low-magnitude weights based on their L2-norm. Sparse models are easy to compress, and occupy less memory space in the target device. The amount of sparsity is introduced to the baseline model in an iterative manner, and the corresponding impact on overall performance is noted. Being critical feature extraction layers, the attention mechanism, the final dense layer, and the final softmax layer are skipped from pruning. We start by adding 10% of sparsity to the selected layer of the baseline model and gradually increase the amount using a polynomial decay function, and eventually stop at 40% of sparsity. In every step, the sparse model is retrained for 20 epochs using an Adam optimizer at a learning rate of 0.00005 to fine-tune the performance.

3.2 Weight Clustering

The pruned model is further compressed by weight clustering that reduces the number of unique weight values in the model. The weights in a particular layer are divided into N different clusters using K-Means algorithm. All weight values in a cluster are represented by the corresponding cluster centroid. A lesser number of clusters can create a more compressed model, but with a negative impact on model accuracy. In our approach, the weight values in each layer of the pruned model are divided into 24 clusters to get the optimum performance. The cluster centroids are initialized by K-Means++ algorithm. The resulting model is fine-tuned by retraining for 20 epochs at a learning rate of 0.00003 using an Adam optimizer and the performance is noted. Similar to weight pruning, the critical layers are again skipped from clustering.

3.3 Quantization Aware Training

Many microcontrollers do not have direct hardware support for floating point arithmetic. One of the easiest ways to reduce the size of a large neural network is to lower the precision of the model weights. In quantization aware training, the weights are reduced from 32-bit floating points to 8-bit integers, which results in an approximately 4x smaller model. Integer-based models also have an improved CPU latency on microcontrollers. Lowering the precision from floating points can have a negative impact on accuracy. Hence, the model is again fine-tuned via retraining to mitigate the quantization error via backpropagation of the error. The following scale is defined to map the weight values in the floating point range to the values in the quantized range in each layer.

$$scale = \frac{f_{max} - f_{min}}{q_{max} - q_{min}}$$

Here, f_{max} and f_{min} represent the maximum and minimum values in floating point precision, q_{max} and q_{min} represent the maximum and minimum values in the quantized range.

The *TensorFlow Lite* library is used for model optimization in a compressed *TFLite* format, and the deployable microcontroller equivalent C++ libraries are created using *TensorFlow Lite for Microcontrollers* [5]. The final model has a size of 144 KB which is around 12x smaller and 8x faster than the baseline model. Training of the baseline model, optimization, and converting to the equivalent *TFLite* model is done on a desktop. The optimized light-weight model is tested on two target hardware. The initial proof of concept is done on Raspberry Pi 3 Model B+ and the final deployment is done on Arduino Nano 33 BLE sense [1]. Raspberry Pi is a Linux-based tiny single board computer which is popularly used in edge computing. It has Cortex-A53 (ARMv8) 64-bit processor at a clock speed of 1.4 GHz and 1 GB of RAM. Arduino Nano 33 is a microcontroller-based development board highly recommended for TinyML applications. It has an operating voltage of 3.3 V. It comes with an ARM Cortex-M4 processor at a clock speed of 64 MHz. It has 256 KB of RAM and 1 MB of flash memory which is enough to store and load our optimized model of 144 KB to make inferences.

4   Dataset Description

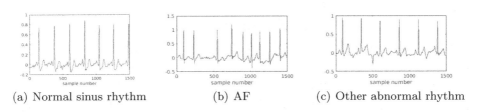

(a) Normal sinus rhythm   (b) AF   (c) Other abnormal rhythm

Fig. 2. Sample ECG waveform from the PhysioNet Challenge 2017 database

The PhysioNet Challenge 2017 training database [3] is used for training and evaluation of the proposed network. It is a large publicly available annotated database having 8528 single-lead ECG segments. It has four target labels. In the highly imbalanced database, 5124 recordings are normal sinus rhythms, 771 recordings are AF, 2557 recordings are other types of abnormal rhythms, and remaining 46 recordings are too noisy to annotate. The original signals are sampled 300 Hz. The noisy recordings are omitted from our study because of the small amount of available data. Figure 2 shows sample waveform corresponding to different class labels. Single-lead ECGs are in general noisier than standard 12-lead data and hence the classification is more challenging. 80% of all data from the database is randomly selected to form our training set and the remaining portion is kept as the test set. Tuning of various network hyper-parameters of the baseline model is done in a random search manner applying 5-fold cross validation on the training data. Training of the final baseline model and retraining during optimization are done on the entire training data before final evaluation on the test set.

4.1   Data Preprocessing

Duration of the original recordings varies from 9 s to 61 s with a mean duration of 32.5 s. A longer data contains more important disease markers, but the high computational latency compromises the real-time classification performance in the target platform. The input data duration is selected as 35 s in our network. The shorter recordings in the database are appended on time-axis to get the desired length of input, whereas the longer recordings are truncated into multiple independent segments. It is strongly enforced that multiple segments obtained from the original recording are not mixed up in the training and test sets and also during cross validation analysis. The original signals are down-sampled 100 Hz for reducing the computational load of the network. In order to improve the diversity of the training set for a generalized performance, we incorporate various data augmentation techniques like addition of white Gaussian noise, band-pass filtering, baseline shift etc. to extend the amount of data in the training set.

5   Experimental Results

Our experimental results can be broadly divided into three subsections, as mentioned below.

5.1   Performance of the Baseline ECG Classifier

The classification performance is reported in terms of F1-score of detecting normal ($F1_{norm}$), AF ($F1_{af}$), and other abnormal rhythms ($F1_{oth}$). We also report the overall F1-score ($F1_{chal}$), the metric provided in the PhysioNet Challenge 2017 [3] to form the leader-board. The metric measures the mean F1-scores for all three target classes.

$$F1_{chal} = \frac{F1_{norm} + F1_{af} + F1_{oth}}{3}$$

Table 1 summarizes the average classification performance in terms of F1-scores by applying 5-fold cross validation on the training set and also reports the performance achieved on the test set when the network is trained on the entire training set. Here, we compare the proposed baseline ResNet architecture with a plain CNN architecture having similar structure in terms of different layers including the attention mechanism but without having any skip connection.

Table 1. Classification performance of the baseline ResNet in comparison with a plain CNN model having a similar architecture on the PhysioNet Challenge 2017 database

Architecture	Average F1-scores in a 5-fold cross validation on the training set	Performance on the test set
Plain CNN structure without Skip connections	$F1_{norm} = 0.95$	$F1_{norm} = 0.95$
	$F1_{af} = 0.80$	$F1_{af} = 0.76$
	$F1_{oth} = 0.92$	$F1_{oth} = 0.89$
	$F1_{chal} = 0.89$	$F1_{chal} = 0.87$
Proposed baseline ResNet	$F1_{norm} = 0.97$	$F1_{norm} = 0.96$
	$F1_{af} = 0.87$	$F1_{af} = 0.84$
	$F1_{oth} = 0.94$	$F1_{oth} = 0.93$
	$F1_{chal} = 0.93$	$F1_{chal} = 0.91$

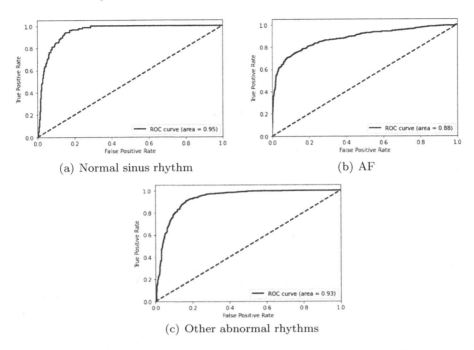

(a) Normal sinus rhythm   (b) AF

(c) Other abnormal rhythms

Fig. 3. ROC curves for all three target classes on the test set of the PhysioNet database

Although both networks are quite similar in terms of overall architecture and number of trainable parameters, the ResNet architecture provides a much better classification performance due to the skip connections that ensure a better feature learning in a deep architecture. The improvement achieved by the ResNet architecture over the plain CNN model can be particularly seen in detection of AF which is the minority class in the database. Figure 3 shows the receiver operating characteristic (ROC) curves of the baseline ResNet model and the corresponding area under the curve (AUC) values for all three target classes on the test set. Table 2 shows that the proposed baseline ResNet outperforms a number of popular prior approaches reported their accuracy on the PhysioNet Challenge 2017 database using deep architectures like ResNet, CNN, Bi-LSTM, and neural architecture search (NAS). For performance comparison, we have considered the performance reported by the prior arts on the publicly available training part of the PhysioNet Challenge 2017 data.

Table 2. Comparison of the proposed baseline ResNet model with prior approaches reported on the PhysioNet Challenge 2017 database

Authors	Brief description of the methodology	Reported performance in $F1_{chal}$
Warrick *et al.* [19]	The approach used a combination of CNNs and a sequence of long short-term Memory units, with pooling, dropout and normalization techniques to design the classifier	Overall F1-score = 0.83
Plesinger *et al.* [16]	The authors used two machine learning methods in parallel, a bagged tree ensemble (BTE) process and a CNN connected to a shallow neural network. The two classifiers are combined for final prediction	Overall F1-score = 0.83
Shi *et al.* [17]	The authors proposed discriminant canonical correlation analysis-based feature fusion, which integrates traditional features extracted by expert knowledge and deep learning features extracted by the residual network and gated recurrent unit network for classification	Overall F1-score = 0.88
Najmeh Fayyazifar [6]	A neural architecture search (NAS) algorithm was designed to discover an accurate classifier using CNN and RNN operations	Overall F1-score = 0.82
Jiang *et al.* [11]	A hybrid attention-based deep learning network was proposed using residual network and bidirectional long short-term memory to obtain fusion features containing local and global information and improve the interpretability of the model through the attention mechanism	Overall F1-score = 0.88 using cross validation
Proposed approach	**Residual network with attention mechanism**	**Overall F1-score = 0.93 using cross validation, = 0.91 on the test set**

5.2 Classification Performance of the Optimized Model

A compressed deep learning model is small enough to run on resource-constrained target hardware, but the performance is often compromised compared to the baseline model. A trade-off between model size and classification performance needs to be maintained during optimization. Figure 4(a) shows the impact of weight-pruning on the test set by gradually increasing the amount of sparsity in the baseline model. In the plot, the model performance is shown in terms of the challenge metric ($F1_{chal}$). It can be observed that there is a significant drop in classification performance only when the amount of sparsity is more than 40%. Hence, we can safely add 40% of sparsity to the model. In Fig. 4(b), we show the impact of weight clustering on the pruned model. We start with 64 clusters in each layer to divide the weights. In spite of producing good classification performance, it causes no compression at all. Subsequently, we reduce the number of clusters. The optimum performance with a reduced model size is achieved when 24 clusters are used. In Table 3, we summarize the impact of proposed collaborative optimization in various stages in terms of model size and overall F1-score ($F1_{chal}$) on the test set. The baseline model has a size of 1.758 MB which can not be deployed on the target microcontroller having a RAM size of 256 KB and 1 MB of flash memory. Apart from loading the model, the RAM should have available memory space for storing the input ECG data and various intermediate variables to make an inference. In stage 1, the compressed model size gets reduced to 632 KB after magnitude-based weight pruning. In stage 2, the pruned model is further reduced to 416 KB after weight clustering. The final model size becomes 144 KB after quantization aware training which is around 12× smaller than the baseline model. The final model reports an overall F1-score ($F1_{chal}$) of 0.885 on the test set which still outperforms the prior approaches discussed in Table 2, but with a much smaller model size.

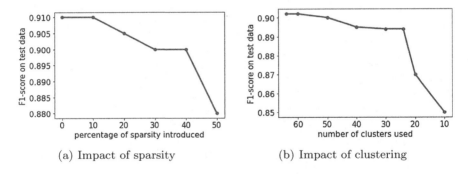

(a) Impact of sparsity   (b) Impact of clustering

Fig. 4. Effect of weight pruning and clustering to create the optimized model

5.3   Deployment on Target Microcontroller

The optimized model is used to design an end-to-end prototype system for on-device cardiac monitoring using commercially available components. MAX86150, an integrated ECG-PPG breakout board [10] is used for recording of ECG. The board has an operating voltage of 3.3 V and has three leads with disposable electrodes for attachment to the human body for recording of ECG data as analogue voltage. It communicates with an Arduino Nano 33 BLE Sense microcontroller via the I2C interface which hosts the optimized deep learning model trained and evaluated on the PhysioNet Challenge database. The recorded data is sampled 100 Hz and the continuous data-stream is sent to the microcontroller for making an inference on every 35 s of accumulated data. A five-point moving average

Table 3. Stage-wise impact of collaborative optimization on the baseline model

Stage	Optimization technique	Overall F1-score ($F1_{chal}$) on the test set	Resultant model size
0	Baseline model (no optimization)	0.910	1.758 MB
1	After weight-pruning by adding 40% of sparsity in each layer	0.902	632 KB
2	After weight clustering via 24 clusters in each layer	0.894	416 KB
3	After quantization aware training (final model)	0.885	144 KB

filter is applied to the input data for noise cleaning. *TensorFlow Lite for Microcontrollers* is used to convert the TensorFlow model into the equivalent C++ libraries for Arduino. Since *TensorFlow Lite* has a limited number of supported APIs for deep learning models, few layers of our model (e.g. attention mechanism, batch normalization) were rewritten and slightly modified to maintain the desired performance on the target platform. Figure 5(a) shows an image of our prototype system. A sample waveform recorded by the ECG breakout board is shown in Fig. 5(b). Real-time performance of the prototype system is evaluated on a small population of 10 consenting subjects including normal subjects, subjects having chronic AF, and other types of arrhythmias like bradycardia, tachycardia etc. Our system achieves a classification accuracy of 90% on the small test population, where it only fails to detect one subject having AF. Average inference latency for a 35 s long ECG window is measured as 243 milliseconds on the Arduino Nano board.

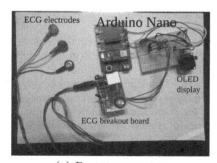

(a) Prototype system

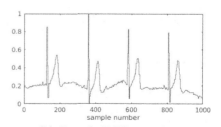

(b) Sample ECG waveform

Fig. 5. Prototype system for on-device ECG classification using MAX86150 ECG-PPG breakout and Arduino Nano BLE 33 Sense

6   Conclusion

Edge-AI and TinyML have become the latest trend in machine learning. In spite of deployment challenges, such applications can ensure very low latency, reduced power consumption, increased security, and privacy which is particularly important in healthcare applications dealing with sensitive patient information. In this paper, we propose a light-weight deep neural network for classifying abnormal heart rhythms using single-lead ECG. A novel ResNet architecture is proposed as the baseline model which is successfully evaluated on a large public database. Subsequently, the baseline model is optimized to realize a system for real-time ECG analysis using a commercially available microcontroller. Experimental results show that the baseline model as well as the optimized model outperform a number of relevant prior approaches. However, the present model can only detect a limited number of cardiac abnormalities, as all non-AF but abnormal heart rhythms are classified under one category of other abnormal rhythms. There are more than 30 types of different arrhythmias in medical dictionary. It remains to be explored how the model performs to individually detect different arrhythmias on available databases. The real-time performance of the deployed model is only evaluated on a very small population. We are planning to extend our study on a larger cohort along with measuring the actual power consumption by the system during continuous patient monitoring.

References

1. Arduino.cc. Arduino nano 33 ble sense - product reference manual (abx00031). https://docs.arduino.cc/hardware/nano-33-ble-sense
2. Banerjee, R., Ghose, A., Khandelwal, S.: A novel recurrent neural network architecture for classification of atrial fibrillation using single-lead ECG. In: 2019 27th European Signal Processing Conference (EUSIPCO), pp. 1–5. IEEE (2019)
3. Clifford, G.D., et al.: AF classification from a short single lead ECG recording: The physionet/computing in cardiology challenge 2017. In: 2017 Computing in Cardiology (CinC), pp. 1–4. IEEE (2017)
4. Datta, S., et al.: Identifying normal, AF and other abnormal ECG rhythms using a cascaded binary classifier. In: 2017 Computing in cardiology (Cinc), pp. 1–4. IEEE (2017)
5. David, R., et al.: Tensorflow lite micro: Embedded machine learning on tinyml systems. arXiv preprint (2020). arXiv:2010.08678
6. Fayyazifar, N.: An accurate CNN architecture for atrial fibrillation detection using neural architecture search. In: 2020 28th European Signal Processing Conference (EUSIPCO), pp. 1135–1139. IEEE (2021)
7. Glorot, X., Bengio, Y.: Understanding the difficulty of training deep feedforward neural networks. In: Proceedings of the Thirteenth International Conference on Artificial Intelligence and Statistics, pp. 249–256 (2010)
8. Han, C., Shi, L.: Ml-resnet: A novel network to detect and locate myocardial infarction using 12 leads ECG. Computer methods and programs in biomedicine **185**, 105138 (2020)
9. Howard, A.G., et al.: Mobilenets: Efficient convolutional neural networks for mobile vision applications (2017). arXiv preprint arXiv:1704.04861

10. Integrated, M.: Integrated photoplethysmogram and electrocardiogram bio-sensor module for mobile health. https://www.maximintegrated.com/en/products/interface/signal-integrity/MAX86150.html
11. Jiang, M., et al.: Hadln: Hybrid attention-based deep learning network for automated arrhythmia classification. Front. Physiol. **12** (2021)
12. Li, D., Zhang, J., Zhang, Q., Wei, X.: Classification of ECG signals based on 1d convolution neural network. In: 2017 IEEE 19th International Conference on e-Health Networking, Applications and Services (Healthcom), pp. 1–6. IEEE (2017)
13. Li, Z., Zhou, D., Wan, L., Li, J., Mou, W.: Heartbeat classification using deep residual convolutional neural network from 2-lead electrocardiogram. J. Electrocardiol. **58**, 105–112 (2020)
14. Liu, F., et al.: An attention-based hybrid ISTM-CNN model for arrhythmias classification. In: 2019 International Joint Conference on Neural Networks (IJCNN), pp. 1–8. IEEE (2019)
15. Park, J., Kim, J.K., Jung, S., Gil, Y., Choi, J.I., Son, H.S.: ECG-signal multi-classification model based on squeeze-and-excitation residual neural networks. Appl. Sci. **10**(18), 6495 (2020)
16. Plesinger, F., Nejedly, P., Viscor, I., Halamek, J., Jurak, P.: Parallel use of a convolutional neural network and bagged tree ensemble for the classification of holter ECG. Physiol. Measur. **39**(9), 094002 (2018)
17. Shi, J., Chen, C., Liu, H., Wang, Y., Shu, M., Zhu, Q.: Automated atrial fibrillation detection based on feature fusion using discriminant canonical correlation analysis. Comput. Math. Methods Med. **2021** (2021)
18. Sun, L., Wang, Y., He, J., Li, H., Peng, D., Wang, Y.: A stacked ISTM for atrial fibrillation prediction based on multivariate ECGs. Health Inf. Sci. Syst. **8**(1), 1–7 (2020)
19. Warrick, P., Homsi, M.N.: Cardiac arrhythmia detection from ECG combining convolutional and long short-term memory networks. In: 2017 Computing in Cardiology (CinC), pp. 1–4. IEEE (2017)
20. Zhai, X., Tin, C.: Automated ECG classification using dual heartbeat coupling based on convolutional neural network. IEEE Access **6**, 27465–27472 (2018)

Workshop on Data Analysis in Life Science (DALS 2022)

1st Workshop on Data Analysis in Life Science (DALS 2022)

In the last decades, thanks to continuous and radical improvements in bio-technologies, we have witnessed a significant increase in the volume of data available for investigation regarding life science and health care environments. This is equally evident for human genomics as well as for viruses and microorganisms; for instance, during two and a half years of the COVID-19 pandemic, more than 10 million SARS-CoV-2 sequences have been collected and are actively being studied to understand the genetic mechanisms of viruses and the relationship with the infected host. As data generation nowadays is much simpler and less expensive than in the past, we could claim that, in this new century, biologists and clinicians have moved their focus from data generation to data analysis. This paradigm shift allows providing answers and insights to complex life science questions. Moreover, life science data require (a) the use of particular algorithms in some steps of the analysis (e.g., alignment to identify mutations) and (b) the development of ad hoc machine learning/deep learning methods.

In such a scenario, the data science community plays a fundamental role in analyzing biological, genomics, and health care data to pave the ground for personalized medicine. This kind of data needs to be properly managed, integrated, and analyzed by employing statistical inference tools as well as machine learning, data mining, and deep learning methods. Many data scientists actively work with bio-data aiming at different goals, including patient stratification, personalized medicine, drug design, and treatment development. Furthermore, analyzing and mining publicly available databases have already proven to be paramount for biological and clinical knowledge discovery.

The first international Workshop on Data Analysis in Life Science aimed at gathering researchers with expertise in data management and analysis, machine learning, and knowledge discovery applied to bioinformatics and life science problems to share their experience and foster discussion about improving data-driven personalized medicine, genetic data management, and health care system advancement. It also aimed to share cutting-edge data science methodologies and their applications to build a strong research community in the area of data analysis in life science.

DALS 2022 was held online in conjunction with the European Conference on Machine Learning and Principles and Practice of Knowledge Discovery in Databases (ECML PKDD 2022). The workshop papers were selected through a peer-review process in which each submitted paper was assigned to three members of the Program Committee. Based on the evaluation, a total of two papers were accepted for presentation. Moreover, Anna Bernasconi from Politecnico di Milano, Italy, accepted our invitation to give a keynote talk entitled "Data analysis for unveiling the SARS-CoV-2 evolution".

The organizers would like to thank the authors, keynote speakers, and Program Committee members for their contributions to the workshop.

October 2022

Gaia Ceddia
Arif Canakoglu
Pietro Pinoli
Sara Pido

Organization

Organizing Committee

Gaia Ceddia	Barcelona Supercomputing Center, Spain
Arif Canakoglu	Fondazione IRCCS Ca' Granda Ospedale Maggiore Policlinico, Italy
Pietro Pinoli	Politecnico di Milano, Italy
Sara Pido	Politecnico di Milano, Italy

Program Committee

Rosario Piro	Politecnico di Milano, Italy
Stefano Perna	National University of Singapore, Singapore
Tommaso Alfonsi	Politecnico di Milano, Italy
Ruba Al Khalafi	Politecnico di Milano, Italy
Luca Nanni	University of Lausanne, Switzerland
Giuseppe Agapito	Universitá Magna Græcia, Italy
Colin Logie	Radboud University, The Netherlands
Matteo Chiara	Universitá di Milano, Italy
Marco Masseroli	Politecnico di Milano, Italy
Stefano Ceri	Politecnico di Milano, Italy
Giulio Pavesi	Università di Milano, Italy
Sergio Doria-Belenguer	Barcelona Supercomputing Center, Spain
Alexandros Xenos	Barcelona Supercomputing Center, Spain
Katarina Mihajlovic	Barcelona Supercomputing Center, Spain
Milana Raickovic	Barcelona Supercomputing Center, Spain
Alberto Zanella	Policlinico di Milano, Italy
Luigi Vivano	Policlinico di Milano, Italy
Gaetano Vivano	Policlinico di Milano, Italy
Anirban Bhattacharyya	Mayo Clinic, USA
Laure Berti-Equille	French Institute of Research for Sustainable Development, France
Dongyu Liu	Massachusetts Institute of Technology, USA

DALS 2022 Keynote Talk

Data Analysis for Unveiling the SARS-CoV-2 Evolution

Anna Bernasconi

Politecnico di Milano, Italy

Abstract. The COVID-19 epidemic has brought enormous attention to the genetics of viral infection and the corresponding disease. In this seminar, I will provide a viral genomic primer. Then, I will discuss the potential of big data in this domain, especially when millions of SARS-CoV-2 sequences are available on open databases. I will present a collection of current analysis problems, focusing on viral evolution, monitoring of variants, and the categorization of their effects. Finally, I will hint at open problems that should attract the interest of data scientists.

Biography

Anna Bernasconi is a postdoctoral researcher with the Dipartimento di Elettronica, Informazione e Bioingegneria at Politecnico di Milano and a visiting researcher at Universitat Politècnica de València. Her research areas are Bioinformatics, Databases, and Data Science, where she applies conceptual modeling, data integration, and semantic web technologies to biological and genomic data. Starting from a Ph.D. thesis on the modeling and integration of data and metadata of human genomic datasets, she has then extended her expertise to the fastly growing field of viral genomics, particularly relevant since the COVID-19 pandemic outbreak. She is active in the conceptual modeling and database communities, with several paper presentations and the organization of tutorials and workshops.

I-CONVEX: Fast and Accurate *de Novo* Transcriptome Recovery from Long Reads

Sina Baharlouei[1(✉)], Meisam Razaviyayn[1], Elizabeth Tseng[2], and David Tse[3]

[1] University of Southern California, Los Angeles, CA, USA
baharlou@usc.edu
[2] Pacific Biosciences, Menlo Park, CA, USA
[3] Stanford University, Stanford, CA, USA

Abstract. Long-read sequencing technologies demonstrate high potential for *de novo* discovery of complex transcript isoforms, but high error rates pose a significant challenge. Existing error correction methods rely on clustering reads based on isoform-level alignment and cannot be efficiently scaled. We propose a new method, I-CONVEX, that performs fast, alignment-free isoform clustering with almost linear computational complexity, and leads to better consensus accuracy on simulated, synthetic, and real datasets.

Keywords: Isoform recovery · Sequencing · Long reads

1 Introduction

Alternative splicing is the process by which a single gene can create different alternative spliced forms (isoforms) by using different combinations of exons. The process of identifying isoforms is called transcriptome sequencing. Transcriptome sequencing methods fall into two categories: genome-guided and *de novo*. Genome-guided methods align reads back to the reference genome to identify the exon boundaries. This alignment information is often combined with reference annotations to assemble the transcripts. *De novo* transcriptome sequencing, on the other hand, uses information from the reads alone and does not rely on a reference genome. The *de novo* approach is not biased by the reference genome/annotation and thus can be used in applications with the mutated genome, such as cancer, or when a high-quality reference genome is not available.

Most transcripts are 1–10 kb long, and different isoforms can share the same subset of exons. Thus, accurate characterization of the exon connectivities using short reads (100–250 bp) is computationally challenging and in some cases, even statistically impossible [1–4]. In contrast, the transcriptome sequencing problem through long reads is statistically identifiable (Supplementary Note 1). However, such a task is computationally challenging due to higher error rates of long reads. To deal with the high error rate, various transcriptome sequencing pipelines [5–7] have been developed [5–8] and used to discover novel isoforms [9], cancer fusion genes [10], and genotypes of immune genes [11].

© The Author(s), under exclusive license to Springer Nature Switzerland AG 2023
I. Koprinska et al. (Eds.): ECML PKDD 2022 Workshops, CCIS 1753, pp. 339–363, 2023.
https://doi.org/10.1007/978-3-031-23633-4_23

Figure 1a illustrates the process of full-length transcriptome sequencing. Each long read covers a transcript completely, with substitution, insertion, and deletion errors distributed randomly. The number of reads covering each transcript depends on its abundance in the sequencing library. We define the *de novo* transcriptome recovery as the problem of using the full-length reads with random errors to estimate the sequence of the transcripts and their abundances. One solution to this problem is to cluster the reads based on their similarity, assuming that each cluster contains reads coming from the same isoform and within-cluster differences solely come from sequencing errors. The software ICE [5], which is based on this clustering viewpoint, performs pairwise alignment among the reads to construct a similarity graph and then uses this graph to cluster the reads. While optimal clustering algorithms often require solving mathematically non-convex and computationally intractable problems, heuristic clustering algorithms such as maximal decomposition can be used in practice [5]. Unfortunately, these heuristics often provide no statistical guarantee for the final clusters. In addition, computing similarity graphs relies on aligners which are subject to parameterization and sensitivity/specificity tradeoffs. Another software based on this clustering viewpoint is IsoCon [8]. IsoCon first creates a nearest neighbor graph based on the pairwise edit distance of the reads, then it successively removes and denoises nodes with the largest number of neighbors. This procedure is continued until all the reads are clustered. While IsoCon demonstrates significantly better recall and precision compared to ICE, it is not scalable to large-scale datasets with millions of long reads.

In contrast to ICE and IsoCon, our method I-CONVEX does not require read-to-read alignment. I-CONVEX consists of two subprograms: scalable pre-clustering of reads (Fig. 1b), and alignment-free isoform recovery via convexification (Fig. 1c). We first describe the alignment-free isoform recovery step (Fig. 1c), which is the core module of I-CONVEX and is based on the following observation: When the list of transcripts is known, estimating the abundances is a convex problem and can be done efficiently using convex optimization approaches such as the EM algorithm [12, 13]. However, the list of transcripts is not known in *de novo* transcriptome recovery *a priori,* which makes the problem non-convex. A convex reformulation of the problem could be obtained by assuming that all sequences are possibly transcripts (with many of the sequences having zero abundances). However, this reformulation would grow exponentially with sequence lengths. To overcome this exponential increase, we first reduce the size of the problem by partitioning the reads into a small number of equivalence classes that share the same (short) prefixes, then we estimate their aggregate abundances (Fig. 1c). Many of the equivalence classes would have near-zero abundances that are then "pruned". Keeping only the classes with sufficiently large abundance estimates, we further partition, or "branch" them by extending the prefixes one base at a time until a maximum length threshold is reached. At each step of the algorithm, the abundance of each equivalent class can be estimated using the EM algorithm with added sparsity regularization (Supplementary Note 2). The computational complexity of the algorithm grows linearly with the number of reads. This alignment-free isoform recovery step can fully utilize multiple computational cores by processing the reads in parallel (Sect. 3). The parallelization is achieved without losing any statistical accuracy as the parallel version, and the single-core version returns exactly the same output.

To scale I-CONVEX to millions of reads, the first step of I-CONVEX performs a fast pre-clustering algorithm on the input reads by constructing a "conservative" similarity graph (Fig. 1b). The nodes in this graph correspond to the reads, and an edge shows a similarity level higher than a certain threshold. A low threshold is chosen to capture any potential similarity among the reads. Thus, each connected component (pre-cluster) in this graph contains all the reads coming from a group of similar transcripts. To obtain the similarity graph, we use a locality sensitive hashing (LSH) method based on the Jaccard similarity [14–16] between k-mer signatures. This idea has been used before in Mash [15] and MHAP [16]. However, to make the computational complexity of the algorithm linear in the number of reads, we adopt the idea of banding technique [17] (Supplementary Note 3). In this pipeline, the resulting similarity graph may contain a large number of false positive edges since k-mer sharing amongst non-homologous transcripts is frequent. To reduce the number of false positives, we trained a convolutional neural network to validate and correct the similarity of read pairs. Then, the obtained pre-clusters are processed in parallel by the clustering via convexification step (Fig. 1c).

2   Results

In this section, we introduce artificial and real datasets used to evaluate I-CONVEX and other state-of-the-art approaches for de novo transcriptome recovery. Next, we demonstrate the results on the dataset to compare the quality of recovered isoforms and the efficiency of methods.

2.1   Introducing Datasets

Simulated Datasets. To create the simulated datasets in Fig. 2 with 200K, 400K, and 1M number of reads, we have selected the 500 transcriptomes from the GENCODE dataset. Then, the transcript abundances are randomly drawn from a log-normal distribution and normalized. Supplementary Figure 3 shows the histogram of the transcript abundances for the dataset with 200K reads. The reads are sampled based on the independent identical error model. The three datasets and ground-truth transcripts are publicly available at https://doi.org/10.5281/zenodo.4019965.

SIRV Datasets. The Lexogen SIRV dataset is a synthetic RNA spike-in control and consists of four sequencing runs. Four libraries were constructed from the Lexogen SIRV E0 (two technical replicates), E1, and E2, respectively. Each library was sequenced on the PacBio RS II platform. In Supplementary Figure 3 and Supplementary Figure 4 the sequence lengths and the ground-truth transcript abundances are demonstrated. The dataset is publicly available at https://www.lexogen.com/sirvs.

FMR1 Dataset. The FMR1 Iso-Seq dataset consists of amplicon FMR1 cDNA from three premutation and three control brain samples. Each individual was prepped independently and sequenced on three SMRT Cells on the PacBio RS II platform. The methodology of generating FMR1 dataset is described in Tseng et al. (2017) [22]. The data is publicly available at https://zenodo.org/record/185011#.XU3fKpNKiqQ.

Sequel II Dataset. The Universal Human Reference (UHR) Iso-Seq dataset consisted of two SMRT Cell 8M runs. The cDNA library is a whole transcriptome Iso-Seq library generated using the Clontech SMARTer cDNA kit followed by SMRT bell library preparation. Data is publicly available and can be downloaded from https://downloads.pacbcl oud.com/public/dataset/UHR_IsoSeq/.

Generated Dataset for Training Convolutional Neural Network. To train the convolutional neural network validating the similarity of candidate similar read pairs, we have generated a balanced dataset of 50000 similar and 50000 dissimilar read pairs from a set of simulated transcripts. Two reads are labeled as similar if they are generated from a single transcript by adding insertion, deletion and substitutions. A naïve idea to simulate transcripts is to create completely random sequences consisting of {A, C, G, T}; however, in practice, it is highly probable that different transcripts have common sub-strings (exons). Thus, in our training data, we first generate a pool of 400 exons $(e_1, e_2, ..., e_{400})$. Each exon is a sequence of {A, C, G, T} with length 20. Each simulated transcript is generated by concatenating 20 exons $\{e_{i_1}, e_{i_2}, ..., e_{i_{20}}\}$ picked from the pool in order $(i_1 < i_2 < ... < i_{20})$. We repeated this procedure to simulate 100 transcripts. To generate a similar pair, we choose a transcript and generate two reads by adding insertions, deletions, and shifts in the beginning and the end of the selected transcript. The insertion and deletion errors are i.i.d with 2% probability. The length of the shift is a random variable, uniformly chosen from 0 to 5. To generate a dissimilar pair, we do the same, except that the reads are generated by perturbing two different transcripts. Compared to the scenario where the transcripts are simulated completely at random, this approach leads to a more powerful convolutional neural network with higher accuracy on real datasets.

2.2 Evaluation of I-CONVEX

We compare the performance and efficiency of I-CONVEX against IsoCon and ICE on simulated and real datasets in Fig. 2. Aside from the capability of algorithms to recover high quality transcripts, we have investigated how scalable they are based on their required execution time on simulated and real dataset. As can be seen in Fig. 2a, I-CONVEX can efficiently scale to large size datasets with over a million reads. For such datasets, we set a limit of 48 h for each method to be executed on the dataset. IsoCon and ICE cannot complete the task of transcript recovery within 48 h for the liver and 1M artificial datasets. The resources allocated to all three methods are the same (128 CPU cores and 180 GB of Memory). Figure 2b and Fig. 2d compare the recall, precision, and F-score for I-CONVEX, ICE, and IsoCon on SIRV and simulated datasets. For these datasets, the ground-truth transcripts are available. Recall measures the percentage of ground-truth transcripts recovered with accuracy of more than 98%. On the other hand, precision measures what proportion of recovered transcripts (output of methods) have high quality (more than 98% similarity to at least one of the ground truth transcripts). To evaluate the recall and precision of different methods simultaneously, we use F-score which is the harmonic mean of recall and precision. In contrast to ICE and IsoCon, the number of false positives in I-CONVEX output decreases as the read depth increase. Thus, the F-score of I-CONVEX is enhanced by increasing the number of reads, while the other two methods suffer from low F-scores when we increase the sequencing coverage. We further evaluate I-CONVEX on the Sequel II dataset containing approximately 7 million reads. The only existing approaches that can be executed on this large-scale dataset, is IsoSeq3 (a successor of ICE in the PacBio SMRTAnalysis software suite). Since the actual transcriptome is not available, we use SQANTI2 [18] to the predicted transcriptome by two methods. SQANTI2 outputs the number and percentage of full-splice matches (perfect matches to a reference transcript), incomplete-splice matches (possible degraded matches to a reference transcript), and novel transcriptome (which are not high-quality transcripts with high probability) in the predicted transcripts. As depicted in Fig. 2c, I-CONVEX generates fewer transcripts (high precision) compared to the IsoSeq3, while the majority of them are either full-splice matches or incomplete-splice matches.

3   Methods

3.1   Estimating Abundances of Transcripts

In this section, we show how I-CONVEX isoform recovery module estimates the abundances of isoforms given the set of reads.

Computing Abundances. The likelihood of observing the set of reads $R = \{r_1, r_2, \ldots, r_n\}$ from a given set of transcripts $T = \{t_1, t_2, \ldots, t_n\}$ with abundances $\rho = \{\rho_1, \ldots, \rho_m\}$ can be computed as [12]

$$P(R; \rho, T) = \prod_{i=1}^{n} P(r_i; \rho, T) = \prod_{i=1}^{n} \left(\sum_{j=1}^{m} \alpha_{ij} \rho_j \right),$$

where α_{ij} is the probability of observing the read r_i from transcript t_j. We compute α_{ij} parameters using banded dynamic programming [20], taking $\mathcal{O}(w|t_i|)$ operations, where w is the width of the band and is a constant much smaller than the length of the transcript and the read. Therefore, the maximum likelihood estimation of ρ is given by

$$\hat{\rho}_{ML} = \underset{\rho}{argmax} \sum_{i=1}^{n} log \left(\sum_{j=1}^{m} \alpha_{ij} \rho_j \right) \quad \text{subject to} \quad \rho \geq 0, \quad \sum_{j=1}^{m} \rho_j = 1$$

which can be solved through Expectation Maximization (EM) algorithm iteration [12]:

$$\rho_j \leftarrow \frac{1}{n} \sum_{i=1}^{n} \frac{\alpha_{ij}\rho_j}{\sum_{k=1}^{m} \alpha_{ik}\rho_k} \quad \forall j = 1, \ldots, m.$$

Sparsification of the Abundance Vector Estimation. The abundance of the sequences in the *Isoform Recovery via Convexification step* in I-CONVEX is a sparse vector. Hence, Isoform recovery via convexification step (Fig. 1c) estimates the abundance vector through l_q-norm regularization for imposing sparsity by solving

$$\hat{\rho}_{ML} = \underset{\rho}{argmax} \sum_{i=1}^{n} \log \left(\sum_{j=1}^{m} \alpha_{ij}\rho_j \right) \quad \text{subject to} \quad \rho \geq 0, \quad \sum_{j=1}^{m} \rho_j^q = 1,$$

where q is some positive constant less than 1. In our experiments, we observe that setting the value of q close to one, e.g. $\frac{1}{q} = 1.03$, reduces the number of false positives while does not decrease the number of true positives. This modified optimization problem can be solved through the following iterative procedure (Supplementary Note 2):

$$\rho_j \leftarrow \left(\frac{1}{n} \sum_{i=1}^{n} \frac{\alpha_{ij}\rho_j}{\sum_{k=1}^{m} \alpha_{ik}\rho_k} \right)^{\frac{1}{q}} \quad \forall j = 1, \ldots, m. \tag{1}$$

Parallelization. Isoform recovery via convexification step (Fig. 1c) partitions the reads evenly among the cores before running the algorithm. Each core keeps a copy of the estimated prefixes and abundances while it computes the parameters α_{ij} for its own reads. Let us assume that the set of reads $R = \{r_1, \ldots, r_n\}$ is partitioned into subsets $R_1, \ldots, R_c$ with c being the number of computational cores. At each iteration of the algorithm, each core l computes local alues

$$\rho_j^l \leftarrow \frac{1}{n} \sum_{i \in R_l} \frac{\alpha_{ij}\rho_j}{\sum_{k=1}^{m} \alpha_{ik}\rho_k} \quad \forall j = 1, \ldots, m, \tag{2}$$

and then the consensus abundance value is obtained by

$$\rho_j \leftarrow \left(\sum_{l=1}^{c} \rho_j^l \right)^{\frac{1}{q}} \quad \forall j = 1, \ldots, m. \tag{3}$$

The above two steps (2, 3) are equivalent to (1) and return the exact same values for abundances.

3.2 Pre-clustering

To reduce the time and memory complexity of the isoform recovery via convexification procedure, we propose a fast pre-clustering algorithm (Fig. 1b) consisting of three main steps:

1. Fast mapping of reads to buckets based on MinHash and Locality Sensitive Hashing (LSH) algorithms. The more similar a pair of reads, the higher the probability of mapping them to the same bucket is.
2. Validating similar candidate pairs with a trained convolutional neural to eliminate false positive pairs obtained from the previous step.
3. Pre-clustering the similarity graph whose vertices are reads and edges show the similarity between the reads.

Each of these steps is explained in details below:

Fast Mapping of Reads to Buckets. To measure the proximity of read pairs, a widely used idea is to compute the Jaccard similarity of their k-mer set [16, 17]. The k-mer set of a given read is the set of all of its consecutive subsequences with length k. As an example "GCTACCT" consists of {"GCTA", "CTAC", "TACC", "ACCT"} 4-mers. For a given dataset containing N reads with the average length of L, it takes $O(NL)$ operations to obtain the k-mer representation of all the reads. For convenience, each k-mer is hashed to a 32-bit integer number. Having the k-mer set of all the reads in the dataset, we form a representation matrix M with its columns representing different reads and different rows representing different k-mers (that appear in at least one read). Each entry M_{ij} equals to 1 if and only if the i-th k-mer appears in the j-th read, and 0 otherwise. Since computing the Jaccard similarity of read pairs is computationally expensive, we compress the reads using MinHash signatures, which are unbiased estimators of Jaccard similarity (Supplementary Theorem 2 in Supplementary Note 3). Thus, instead of exact computation of Jaccard similarity of all read pairs, we can estimate them by finding the Hamming similarity of their MinHash signatures. $h << L$ MinHash functions are applied to the representation matrix M to obtain a MinHash signature with length h for each read. Choosing a larger value for h, , corresponds to a smaller variance of the Jaccard estimator (Supplementary Theorem 3 in Supplementary Note 3). Hence a signature matrix S with N columns and h rows can be formed such that S_{ij} represents the i-th element of the MinHash code corresponding to the j-th read in the dataset. To compute S_{ij}, let $\mathcal{P}_i = \{i_1, i_2, ..., i_t\}$ be a permutation of $\{1, 2, ..., t\}$ corresponding to the i-th MinHash function, where t is the number of rows in M. Let i_{min} be the smallest integer such that $M[i_{min}][j] = 1$. Then, the MinHash value of the j-th read with respect to the permutation P_i equals i_{min}.

Computing the similarity of two MinHash signatures rather than the original k-mer sets is significantly more efficient. However, even after hashing long reads to MinHash signatures, calculating the similarity of all $\binom{N}{2}$ pairs of MinHash signatures is still a computationally expensive task. To avoid pairwise comparison of all reads, we adopt the locality sensitive hashing (LSH) algorithm. The corresponding MinHash signature of each read is divided into b bands with size $d\,(h = bd)$. Accordingly, the first d rows of the signature matrix form the first band. The second d rows of the signature matrix correspond to the second band, and so on. If two columns (which correspond to two different reads) are equal in all rows of at least one of these bands, they will be mapped to the same bucket, and we call them a **candidate similar pair** (Fig. 1b). Assume s is the true Jaccard similarity of S_1 and S_2. Since MinHash is an unbiased estimator of the Jaccard similarity, the probability that S_1 and S_2 are equal in each row is s. Thus, the probability of being equal in all d rows of a band is s^d. Hence S_1 and S_2 will be mapped to the same bucket with the probability $p = 1 - (1 - s^d)^b$. d and b can be seen as two hyper-parameters that control the false positive and false negative rates. Increasing d leads to the decrease in the value of p. Thus, the number of pairs mapped to the same bucket is decreased; and true positive and false positive rates are reduced simultaneously (Supplementary Figure 2). The same logic implies that by increasing the number of bands (b), p will be increased. Therefore, both true positive and false positive rates will be increased. To avoid low true positive rate, we choose small values for d and b, and then we eliminate the false similar candidate pairs using a trained convolutional neural network. In the implementation we tried (b, d) = (1, 10) and b, d = (2, 12) and the one with the best performance is chosen.

Validating Candidate Similar Pairs via Convolutional Neural Networks. To validate the candidate pairs obtained by applying LSH on the dataset of reads, we designed a Convolutional Neural Network (CNN), which takes a pair of sequences and generates the output one if the sequences are similar and zero otherwise (Fig. 1b). Supplementary Table 1 depicts the architecture of the designed convolutional neural network in detail. The training data consists of 100000 pairs of the reads, where half of them are similar, and the rest are dissimilar (The details of the training dataset is available in Supplementary Note 4). We optimize the following objective function applying an Adam optimizer with the step-size $\alpha = 10^{-4}$ and the momentum $\beta_1 = 0.9$:

$$\ell l(y, \hat{y}) = \sum_{i=1}^{n} (\hat{y}_i - y_i)^2$$

Pre-clustering the Similarity Graph. The similarity graph among the reads is an undirected graph in which a vertex represents a read in the dataset. We connect two vertices with an edge if and only if their corresponding reads are detected as a similar pair by the convolutional neural network introduced in the previous step. Ideally, if the LSH algorithm combined with the validation phase by the designed CNN can detect all the similar pairs without producing any false edges, each connected component of the similarity graph corresponds to one cluster. However, due to the existence of false positives in the graph, each connected component may contain more than one actual cluster. In practice, there is typically a large connected component containing 10% to 40% of the nodes. For this specific component, we run a fast greedy community detection algorithm [21] to find the pre-clusters it contains.

Partitioning the reads into pre-clusters has several advantages over running the "iso-form recovery via convexification" module on the entire dataset. First, this module can be executed on different pre-clusters independently and in parallel. Hence, the amount of memory per task, and the entire time needed for the transcriptome recovery will be decreased profoundly as a result of parallelization. Second, the time complexity of the convexification stage is dependent on the product of the number of transcripts and the number of reads. Since the number of transcripts in each pre-cluster is much smaller than the total number of transcripts, pre-clustering significantly improves the computational complexity of "isoform recovery via convexification" step.

Determining Maximum Length Threshold of Transcripts in Isoform Recovery Module. To apply the isoform recovery module on a given pre-cluster, we add the base-pair 'A' to the end of the pre-cluster reads to reach the longest read within the pre-cluster. This makes all the reads of the same length. Then, we apply the isoform recovery module depicted in Fig. 1C to these equal size reads. To remove extra 'A' characters from the end of the obtained transcripts, we consider the original reads (without additional 'A' characters) assigned to each one of them. The extra 'A' characters are removed from the end of the transcript by determining the last character based on the majority vote on the last entries of the original reads assigned to the transcript.

Code Availability. The I-CONVEX package is available online at https://github.com/ sinaBaharlouei/I-CONVEX. We have provided the basic instructions to run I-CONVEX in Supplementary Note 5.

4 Discussion

From a broader viewpoint, I-CONVEX solves a clustering problem over finite-alphabet sequences. The ability of I-CONVEX for fast and accurate clustering of the sequences can be beneficial in various other applications. For example, the read or k-mer denoising problems can be viewed as a clustering problem where reads/k-mers from identical sequences belong to the same cluster. As another example, the reconstruction of antibody repertoire, which is an important step in immunology and drug development, can be viewed as a clustering problem [19] and the idea behind I-CONVEX could lead to linear time algorithms for this purpose.

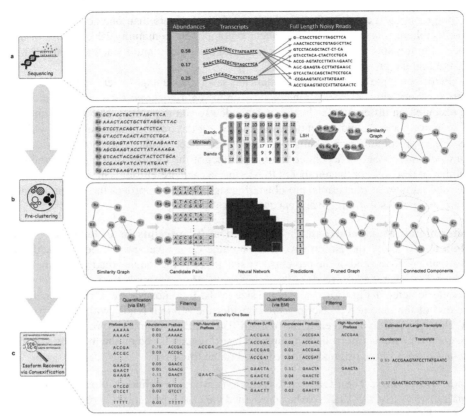

Fig. 1. I-CONVEX algorithm workflow: (**a**) *Sequencing full-length transcriptome using long reads*. The reads cover the full transcripts and the number of reads from each transcript is proportional to its abundance in the sequencing library. Different error types such as insertion, deletion, and substitution may occur in the reads. The reads are the input to I-CONVEX. (**b**) *Pre-clustering stage*: First, we use MinHash to obtain the signature matrix. Then, the signature matrix is divided into several bands (e.g., two bands with size 3). Two reads are in the same bucket if they are equal in all rows of a band (e.g. R4, R5). Next, a similarity graph is formed by connecting reads that are in the same bucket. The edges of this graph are then validated with a neural network to reduce the number of false positive edges (red edges). Each connected component of the similarity graph leads to one pre-cluster. (**c**) An example run of *Clustering via Convexification*. First, the list of all possible short prefixes is considered (e.g. $4^5 = 1024$ prefixes of length $\mathbf{L = 5}$ ranging from 'AAAAA' to 'TTTTT'). The abundances of these prefixes are then estimated by aligning them to the reads and solving a maximum likelihood estimation problem through the (sparse) expectation maximization (EM) algorithm [13, 14] (See Sect. 3). I-Convex only keeps the prefixes with the abundance higher than a specified threshold. Then each length $\mathbf{L}$ prefix 'XXXXX' is replaced by four extended prefixes 'XXXXXA', 'XXXXXC', 'XXXXXG', and 'XXXXXT'. Using the previous alignment of the prefixes to the reads, the abundance of these length $L + 1$ prefixes are estimated and the list is filtered and extended to obtain a list of prefixes of length $L + 2$. This procedure continues until the complete recovery of all transcripts.

(a)

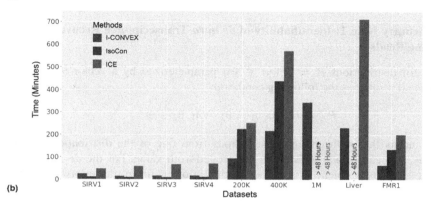

(b)

Method		SIRV1			SIRV2			SIRV3			SIRV4		
		Recall	Precision	F-score	Recall	Precision	F-score	Recall	Precision	F-score	Recall	Precision	F-score
	I-CONVEX	95.65%	27.61%	0.42	95.65%	21.29%	0.34	95.65%	16.25%	0.27	88.40%	15.13%	0.25
	ICE	97.10%	7.46%	0.13	95.65%	5.11%	0.09	94.20%	9.48%	0.17	79.71%	7.23%	0.13
	IsoCon	95.65%	14.60%	0.25	97.10%	11.71%	0.20	97.10%	9.43%	0.17	92.75%	9.07%	0.16

(c)

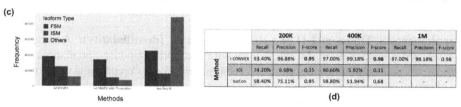

Method		200K			400K			1M		
		Recall	Precision	F-score	Recall	Precision	F-score	Recall	Precision	F-score
	I-CONVEX	93.40%	96.88%	0.95	97.00%	99.18%	0.98	97.00%	98.18%	0.98
	ICE	74.20%	8.68%	0.15	80.60%	5.92%	0.11	-		
	IsoCon	98.40%	75.11%	0.85	98.80%	51.94%	0.68	-		

(d)

Fig. 2. Performance Comparison of I-CONVEX, ICE, and IsoCon. (a) Running time of I-CONVEX, ICE, and IsoCon for real and simulated read datasets. The insertion/deletion/substitution error is generated according to the identical independent error model. All the methods have the same amount of memory (180 GB) and computational resources (16 cores per cluster). ICE and IsoCon could not complete the denoising task within 48 h for the 1M dataset. In addition, IsoCon cannot complete the denoising task for the Liver dataset within 48 h. (b, d) Comparison of the recall, precision, and F-score performed on several simulated datasets with known ground-truth. Recall measures the ratio of the actual transcripts detected with an accuracy of larger than 98%. Precision measures the number of recovered ground truth transcripts divided by the total number of estimated transcripts. While the recall of three methods is close to each other, I-CONVEX demonstrates a better performance in terms of precision. (c) The frequency of Full Splice Matches (FSM) and Incomplete Splice Matches (ISM) obtained by running Iso-Seq 3 and I-CONVEX on the Sequel II dataset. The "I-CONVEX + Truncation" means pre-clusters with size 1 are thrown away. We could not get the result of IsoCon and ICE on this dataset after waiting for more than 48 h.

Appendix

Supplementary Note 1: Identifiability of *de novo* Transcriptome Recovery from Long Reads

A family of distributions $P = \{P_\theta | \theta \in \Theta\}$ parameterized by a vector θ is called identifiable if it satisfies the following condition:

$$P_{\theta_1} = P_{\theta_2} \Rightarrow \theta_1 = \theta_2 \quad \forall \theta_1, \theta_2 \in \Theta,$$

This means that with enough observations from one of the distributions inside the family, one can decide which θ is the ground-truth value. For the *de novo* transcriptome recovery problem, θ is defined as the set of unknown transcripts/sequences $S = \{s_1, s_2, ..., s_m\}$ and their corresponding abundances $\rho = \{\rho_1, \rho_2, ..., \rho_m\}$. For a given read r, we define $P_\theta(r)$ as the probability of observing r, given $\theta = (S, \rho)$. We assume that a read generated from a sequence by adding insertion, deletion, or substitution errors through an i.i.d. process which does not depend on the location of the error. For simplicity, let δ_s, δ_i, and δ_d be the probability of observing a substitution, insertion, or deletion error at each location of the sequence respectively. In Theorem 1, we prove that the problem of *de novo* transcriptome recovery is identifiable.

Supplementary Theorem 1 (Long-Read Sequencing Identifiability): Assume that the set of sequences $S = \{s_1, s_2, ..., s_m\}$ with the corresponding abundances $\rho = \{\rho_1, \rho_2, ..., \rho_m\}$ is unknown. Suppose that for any read r, $P_{S,\rho}(r)$ represents the probability of observing read r given that it is generated from a sequence in S with the abundance vector ρ. Then, given $P_{S,\rho}(r)$ for all reads r, both S and ρ can be exactly recovered when substitution error parameter $\delta_s \neq \frac{3}{4}$.

Proof: Each read r with non-zero $P(r)$ can be obtained by adding insertions, deletions, and substitutions to one or several sequences in S. Without loss of generality, we can model the transcriptome recovery problem as denoising the reads obtained by applying three noise channels to the set of sequences in S sequentially (Supplementary Figure 1). In this model, $P_1(r)$ is the distribution of reads after the substitution channel; and $P_2(r)$ is the distribution of reads after applying the deletion channel (and before the insertion channel). Lastly, $P(r)$ is the final probability distribution observed after applying the insertion noise. If we prove that the transcriptome recovery is identifiable under each one of these three channels (insertion, deletion, and substitution) individually, then the entire problem is identifiable. This is because of the fact that using the given probability of observing reads $P(r)$, we can recover $P_2(r)$ by denoising the effect of the insertion channel. Then, with the same argument, we can recover $P_1(r)$ by denoising the effect of the deletion channel. Finally, we can find the vector ρ by denoising the effect of the substitution channel on the probability vector P_1. Thus, it suffices to show that $P_2(r)$, $P_1(r)$, and ρ can be recovered sequentially given $P(r)$. In what follows, we show each one of these three channels is identifiable.

Supplementary Figure 1. Each channel affects the probability vector of reads from the previous step. To prove the identifiability of the transcriptome recovery problem, it suffices to denoise the effect of the channels sequentially from last to first.

Identifiability Under the Substitution Channel: For the substitution channel, we can observe that a read r with length L can only be generated from a sequence of size L, since the substitution does not change the sequence length. Thus, for estimating the abundances of the sequence with size L, we can only focus on the set of reads with size L. It means that without loss of generality we can assume that the set of reads and sequences are all of size L. Moreover, without loss of generality, assume that S consists of all 4^L possible transcripts with size L with possibly zero abundances. Thus, the problem is reduced to recovering vector ρ, given the $P(r)$ and S. Let $\delta_s = \delta$ be the substitution error rate. Then the probability of observing the read r_i can be written as follows:

$$P(r_i) = \sum_{j=1}^{n} \rho_j P(r_i|s_j) = \sum_{j=1}^{n} \rho_j \left(\frac{\delta}{3}\right)^{d(r_i,s_j)} (1-\delta)^{L-d(r_i,s_j)}$$

Here $d(r_i, s_j)$ is the number of mismatches between r_i and s_j. This relationship can be written in a matrix form. For example, when $L = 1$, let the abundances of 'A', 'C', 'G', and 'T' be ρ_1, ρ_2, ρ_3 and ρ_4 respectively. Then, the probability of observing each {'A', 'C', 'G', 'T'} can be obtained by the following equation:

$$\begin{bmatrix} P(r_1) \\ P(r_2) \\ P(r_3) \\ P(r_4) \end{bmatrix} = A \begin{bmatrix} \rho_1 \\ \rho_2 \\ \rho_3 \\ \rho_4 \end{bmatrix}$$

where

$$A = \begin{bmatrix} 1-\delta & \delta/3 & \delta/3 & \delta/3 \\ \delta/3 & 1-\delta & \delta/3 & \delta/3 \\ \delta/3 & \delta/3 & 1-\delta & \delta/3 \\ \delta/3 & \delta/3 & \delta/3 & 1-\delta \end{bmatrix}$$

Thus, the identifiability problem in this case reduces to showing the invertibility of this matrix. Notice that the determinant of this matrix can be computed as

$$
\begin{vmatrix}
1-\delta & \delta/3 & \delta/3 & \delta/3 \\
\delta/3 & 1-\delta & \delta/3 & \delta/3 \\
\delta/3 & \delta/3 & 1-\delta & \delta/3 \\
\delta/3 & \delta/3 & \delta/3 & 1-\delta
\end{vmatrix}
$$

$$
= (1-\delta)\begin{vmatrix} 1-\delta & \delta/3 & \delta/3 \\ \delta/3 & 1-\delta & \delta/3 \\ \delta/3 & \delta/3 & 1-\delta \end{vmatrix} - \frac{\delta}{3}\begin{vmatrix} \delta/3 & \delta/3 & \delta/3 \\ \delta/3 & 1-\delta & \delta/3 \\ \delta/3 & \delta/3 & 1-\delta \end{vmatrix}
$$

$$
+ \frac{\delta}{3}\begin{vmatrix} \delta/3 & 1-\delta & \delta/3 \\ \delta/3 & \delta/3 & \delta/3 \\ \delta/3 & \delta/3 & 1-\delta \end{vmatrix} - \frac{\delta}{3}\begin{vmatrix} \delta/3 & 1-\delta & \delta/3 \\ \delta/3 & \delta/3 & 1-\delta \\ \delta/3 & \delta/3 & \delta/3 \end{vmatrix}
$$

$$
= (1-\delta)\begin{vmatrix} 1-\delta & \delta/3 & \delta/3 \\ \delta/3 & 1-\delta & \delta/3 \\ \delta/3 & \delta/3 & 1-\delta \end{vmatrix} - \delta\begin{vmatrix} \delta/3 & \delta/3 & \delta/3 \\ \delta/3 & 1-\delta & \delta/3 \\ \delta/3 & \delta/3 & 1-\delta \end{vmatrix}
$$

$$
= (1-\delta)\left(\frac{8}{27}\delta^3 + \frac{3}{2}\delta^2 - 2\delta + 1\right) - \delta\left(\frac{16}{27}\delta^3 - \frac{8}{9}\delta^2 + \frac{\delta}{3}\right)
$$

$$
= \frac{24}{27}\delta^4 + \frac{14}{27}\delta^3 + \frac{7}{3}\delta^2 - 3\delta + 1,
$$

where the second equality is due to the effect of permuting rows on the determinant of the matrix. One can easily check that this polynomial is non-zero for all $\delta \in [0, 1]$ except $\delta = \frac{3}{4}$, which implies the invertibility of the matrix for all $\delta \in [0, 1]$ except $\delta = \frac{3}{4}$.

Now, let us consider the case of general length $L > 1$. Assume that we order the set of all possible sequences with size L (all $m = 4^L$ possible sequences) according to the order of sequences in base 4. In this case, the probability transition relation can be written as

$$
\begin{bmatrix} P(r_1) \\ P(r_2) \\ \dots \\ P(r_m) \end{bmatrix} = \underbrace{A \otimes \dots \otimes A}_{L \text{ times}} \begin{bmatrix} \rho_1 \\ \rho_2 \\ \dots \\ \rho_m \end{bmatrix}
$$

where the Kronecker product of two matrices $A_{(m \times n)}$ and $B_{(p \times q)}$ is a matrix $C_{((m \times p) \times (n \times q))}$, defined as:

$$
C = A \otimes B = \begin{bmatrix} a_{11}B & a_{12}B & \dots & a_{1n}B \\ a_{21}B & a_{22}B & \dots & a_{2n}B \\ \dots & \dots & \dots & \dots \\ a_{m1}B & a_{m2}B & \dots & a_{mn}B \end{bmatrix}
$$

The Kronecker product of L matrices is invertible if and only if each one of them is invertible [23]. We have already shown that A is an invertible matrix when $\delta_s \neq \frac{3}{4}$. Thus, $A \otimes A \otimes \dots \otimes A$ is invertible as well, which shows the problem is identifiable when the substitution channel is applied.

Insertion Channel: Let R be the support of P ($R = \{r : P(r) > 0\}$). We define the operator $\leq$ on a pair of reads as follows: $r_1 \leq r_2$ if r_2 can be obtained by inserting zero or more bases to r_1 in different locations. It is easy to observe that $(R, \leq)$ forms a partially ordered set (poset). Since it satisfies the reflexivity, anti-symmetry, and transitivity. We have the following observations:

- If $r' \leq r$ and $r \neq r'$, then $|r'| < |r|$.
- R has at least one minimal element.
- Any minimal element of R belongs to S.

To see the correctness of the first observation, assume that $r' \leq r$, which means r is obtained by adding zero or more characters to r. However, since $r' \neq r$, the number of added characters cannot be zero. Thus at least one character is added to r' to obtain r. This means that $|r'| \leq |r|$.

To prove the second observation, assume that r_{min} is an element of R with the minimum length (it is not necessarily unique). Indeed, such an element exists, because $|r| \geq 1$ for all $r \in R$. We claim that r_{min} is a minimal element. We prove by contradiction. Assume that r_{min} is not a minimal element. Thus, there exists an element $r' \neq r_{min}$ in R such that $r' \leq r_{min}$. According to the first observation $|r| < |r_{min}|$, which contradicts the fact that r_{min} is an element with the minimum length in R.

Finally, we prove that a minimal element of R belongs to S. We prove by contradiction. Assume that r_{min} is a minimal element that does not belong to S. Thus, there exists an element $s \in S$, such that $s \leq r_{min}$. Clearly $r = s$ belongs to R, since $P(r) \geq P(r|s) = \rho_s(1 - \delta_i)^{|s|} > 0$. Therefore, s is an element in R which is not equal to r_{min} and $s \leq r_{min}$ which contradicts with the fact that r_{min} is a minimal element in R.

Now, we prove the identifiability of the transcriptome recovery problem under the insertion channel by induction on the size of S.

For $|S| = 1$, according to the third observation, the minimal member of R belongs to S, and its abundance is clearly 1.

Based on the induction hypothesis, assume that the problem is identifiable when $|S| = m$. We want to prove it is identifiable, when $|S| = m + 1$. Based on the third observation, any minimal element r_{min} of R belongs to S. Set $S' = S - \{r_{min}\}$ and update the probability vector of the reads accordingly: $P'(r) = P(r) - P(r|r_{min})\rho_{r_{min}}$. For updating the probability vector of reads we need to estimate $\rho_{r_{min}}$ exactly. Since r_{min} is the minimal element, it can be only obtained from a sequence with the exact same structure. Hence, $P(r_{min}) = \rho_{r_{min}}(1 - \delta)^{|r_{min}|}$, which means $\rho_{r_{min}} = \frac{P(r_{min})}{(1-\delta)^{|r_{min}|}}$. According to the assumption of induction, since $|S'| = m$. we can recover S' using P'. Thus, $S = S' \cup \{r_{min}\}$, which means we can recover S exactly.

Deletion Channel: The argument is similar to the insertion channel. The only difference is that the operator $\leq$ is defined for a pair of reads $r_1 \leq r_2$ if r_2 can be obtained by deleting some elements of r_1. Moreover, the minimal element of R is the longest read in this case.

Supplementary Note 2: Sparse EM Algorithm Inside the Isoform Recovery via Convexification

As discussed in Sect. 3, the maximum likelihood estimator of the abundance vector given the set of transcripts and reads can be written as:

$$\hat{\rho}_{ML} = \underset{\rho}{\text{argmax}} \sum_{i=1}^{n} log\left(\sum_{j=1}^{m} \alpha_{ij}\rho_j\right) \quad \text{subject to} \quad \rho \geq 0, \quad \sum_{j=1}^{m} \rho_j = 1$$

Or equivalently:

$$\hat{\rho}_{ML} = \underset{\rho}{\text{argmin}} \sum_{i=1}^{n} -log\left(\sum_{j=1}^{m} \alpha_{ij}\rho_j\right) \quad \text{subject to} \quad \rho \geq 0, \quad \sum_{j=1}^{m} \rho_j = 1$$

Applying the Expectation Maximization (EM) algorithm, at each iteration, we minimize a tight local upper bound of the above objective function:

$$\rho^{t+1} = \underset{\rho}{\text{argmin}} - \sum_{i=1}^{n}\sum_{j=1}^{m} \frac{\alpha_{ij}\rho_j^t}{\sum_{j'=1}^{m}\alpha_{ij'}\rho_{j'}^t} log\left(\frac{\rho_j}{\rho_j^t}\right)$$
$$- \sum_{i=1}^{n} log\left(\sum_{j=1}^{m} \alpha_{ij}\rho_j\right) \quad \text{subject to} \quad \rho \geq 0, \quad \sum_{j=1}^{m} \rho_j = 1$$

The Lagrangian function of the above problem can be written as:

$$L(\rho, \lambda) = - \sum_{i=1}^{n}\sum_{j=1}^{m} \frac{\alpha_{ij}\rho_j^t}{\sum_{j'=1}^{m}\alpha_{ij'}\rho_{j'}^t} log\left(\frac{\rho_j}{\rho_j^t}\right) - \sum_{i=1}^{n} log\left(\sum_{j=1}^{m}\alpha_{ij}\rho_j\right) + \lambda\left(\sum_{j=1}^{m}\rho_j - 1\right)$$

And the dual problem takes the form of:

$$\max_{\lambda} \min_{\rho} L(\rho, \lambda)$$

Since the Lagrangian function is convex in ρ, and the constraints are linear, the strong duality holds [24]. Thus, by setting the gradient of L with respect to ρ to 0, we have:

$$- \sum_{i=1}^{n} \frac{\alpha_{ik}\rho_k^t}{\sum_{j'=1}^{m}\alpha_{ij'}\rho_{j'}^t}\frac{1}{\rho_k} + \lambda^* = 0, \quad \forall k = 1,\ldots,m.$$

Which means:

$$\rho_k^{t+1} = \frac{1}{\lambda^*} \sum_{i=1}^{n} \frac{\alpha_{ik}\rho_k^t}{\sum_{j'=1}^{m}\alpha_{ij'}\rho_{j'}^t} \quad \forall k = 1,\ldots,m.$$

Since $\sum_{j=1}^{m} \rho_j^{t+1} = 1$, we have:

$$1 = \sum_{k=1}^{m} \rho_k^{t+1} = \sum_{k=1}^{m} \frac{1}{\lambda^*} \sum_{i=1}^{n} \frac{\alpha_{ik}\rho_k^t}{\sum_{j'=1}^{m}\alpha_{ij'}\rho_{j'}^t} = \frac{1}{\lambda^*} \sum_{i=1}^{n} \frac{\sum_{k=1}^{m}\alpha_{ik}\rho_k^t}{\sum_{j'=1}^{m}\alpha_{ij'}\rho_{j'}^t} = \frac{n}{\lambda^*}$$

Therefore $\lambda^* = n$, and

$$\rho_k^{t+1} = \frac{1}{n} \sum_{i=1}^{n} \frac{\alpha_{ik}\rho_k^t}{\sum_{j'=1}^{m} \alpha_{ij'}\rho_{j'}^t} \quad \forall k = 1, \ldots, m.$$

This update rule is similar to the one used by Express [12] to obtain the abundance vector.

Sparsification. One naïve approach to impose sparsity to the estimated abundances in the above problem is to use the ℓ_1 regularizer [25]. However, the abundances are non-negative and their summation is equal to 1. Therefore, the ℓ_1 regularizer does not change the objective function at all. Thus, instead of using ℓ_1 regularizer, we apply the ℓq regularizer to the objective function with $0 < q < 1$. Using this regularizer, the above problem can be written as

$$\rho^{t+1} = \underset{\rho}{\operatorname{argmin}} - \sum_{i=1}^{n} \sum_{j=1}^{m} \frac{\alpha_{ij}\rho_j^t}{\sum_{j'=1}^{m} \alpha_{ij'}\rho_{j'}^t} \log\left(\frac{\rho_j}{\rho_j^t}\right)$$
$$- \sum_{i=1}^{n} \log\left(\sum_{j=1}^{m} \alpha_{ij}\rho_j\right) \quad \text{subject to} \quad \rho \geq 0, \quad \rho_q \leq 1$$

Thus, the Lagrangian function for the sparse EM takes the following form:

$$L(\rho, \lambda) = -\sum_{i=1}^{n} \sum_{j=1}^{m} \frac{\alpha_{ij}\rho_j^t}{\sum_{j'=1}^{m} \alpha_{ij'}\rho_{j'}^t} \log\left(\frac{\rho_j}{\rho_j^t}\right) - \sum_{i=1}^{n} \log\left(\sum_{j=1}^{m} \alpha_{ij}\rho_j\right) + \lambda\left(\left(\sum_{j=1}^{m} \rho_j^q\right)^{\frac{1}{q}} - 1\right)$$

Again, by writing the optimality condition for the dual problem, we have

$$\nabla L_\rho(\rho, \lambda) = 0 \Rightarrow$$

$$-\sum_{i=1}^{n} \frac{\alpha_{ik}\rho_k^t}{\sum_{j'=1}^{m} \alpha_{ij'}\rho_{j'}^t} \frac{1}{\rho_k^{t+1}} + \lambda^* q \left(\rho_k^{t+1}\right)^{q-1} \left(\left(\rho_1^{t+1}\right)^q + \cdots + \left(\rho_m^{t+1}\right)^q\right)^{\frac{1}{q}-1} = 0, \quad \forall k = 1, \ldots, m.$$

Moreover, according to the complementary slackness, we have:

$$\lambda^* \left[\left(\sum_{j=1}^{m} \left(\rho_j^{t+1}\right)^q\right)^{\frac{1}{q}} - 1\right] = 0$$

It is easy to observe that $\lambda^* \neq 0$, otherwise the last two equalities have no solution. Thus, similar to the previous case, we can conclude that $\lambda^* = n$, and we have the following closed-form update rule:

$$\rho_k^{t+1} = \left(\frac{1}{n} \sum_{i=1}^{n} \frac{\alpha_{ik}\rho_k^t}{\sum_{j'=1}^{m} \alpha_{ij'}\rho_{j'}^t}\right)^{\frac{1}{q}}, \quad \forall k = 1, \ldots, m.$$

We refer to $\frac{1}{q}$ as the sparsity power. This hyper-parameter is set to 1.03 in the implementation of *Isoform Recovery via Convexification* module. As we increase the sparsity power, the abundance vector is sparser, and thus the number of recovered isoforms is smaller at the end. Sparsification of EM can help to remove false positive isoforms further. However, we should avoid setting it to very large numbers as it may lead to the removal of true positives.

Supplementary Note 3: Further Analysis of MinHash and Locality Sensitive Hashing Algorithms

Definition 1: Suppose that S_1 and S_2 are k-mer sets of two given sequences. The Jaccard similarity of S_1 and S_2 is defined as

$$J(S_1, S_2) = \frac{|S_1 \cap S_2|}{|S_1 \cup S_2|}$$

Definition 2: Given a set of sequences $S_1, \ldots, S_m$ and the set of k-mers $S'_1, \ldots, S'_{N'}$, we say a matrix $M \in \{0, 1\}^{N' \times m}$ is a representation matrix if it satisfies the following property: The element in row i and column j equals 1 if and only if the i-th k-mer appears in j-th sequence, and 0 otherwise.

Definition 3: Assume the representation matrix M has N' rows and m columns, and let $\mathcal{P} = \{i_1, i_2, \ldots, i_{N'}\}$ be a permutation of set $\{1, 2, \ldots, N'\}$, and column c in M corresponds to a sequence S. Then the MinHash signature of S with respect to $\mathcal{P}$ is defined as $\text{MinHash}_{\mathcal{P}}(c) = i_j$ where j is the smallest number in $\{1, 2, \ldots, N'\}$ such that $M[i_j][c] = 1$.

Example: Assume that $S_1 = \text{ACCAGTC}$ and $S_2 = \text{ACCGTCA}$. The set of 3-mers that appears at least once in S_1 or S_2 is {ACC, CCA, CAG, AGT, GTC, CCG, CGT, TCA}. Let $\mathcal{P} = \{7, 5, 2, 3, 1, 4, 6\}$ be a random permutation of 3-mer indices. Since 5 is the first 3-mer index in $\mathcal{P}$ such that its corresponding 3-mer appears in S_1, thus, the MinHash signature of S_1 with respect to $\mathcal{P}$ is 5. With the same logic, we can observe that the MinHash signature of S_2 with respect to $\mathcal{P}$ is 7.

Supplementary Theorem 2: Let $J(S_1, S_2)$ be the Jaccard similarity between two given sequences S_1 and S_2, and $\mathcal{P}_1, \ldots, \mathcal{P}_h$ are h distinct randomly generated permutations of set $\{1, 2, \ldots, N'\}$. For each sequence, a vector of MinHash signatures with length h is computed with respect to permutations $\mathcal{P}_1, \ldots, \mathcal{P}_h$. Then, $\frac{\text{\#Matches between signature vectors of } S_1 \text{ and } S_2}{h}$ is an unbiased estimator of the Jaccard similarity of S_1 and S_2.

Proof: Let c_1 and c_2 be the indices of columns in M corresponding to S_1 and S_2. Let R_1 denote the set of rows in which c_1 and c_2 both have the value 1, and R_2 be the set of rows in which exactly one of c_1 and c_2 is 1. Fix a permutation $\mathcal{P} = \{i_1, i_2, \ldots, i_{N'}\}$, and let j be the smallest index such that at least one of $M[i_j][c_1]$ or $M[i_j][c_2]$ is 1. Thus $i_j \in R_1 \cup R_2$. Moreover, $\text{MinHash}_{\mathcal{P}}(c_1) = \text{MinHash}_{\mathcal{P}}(c_2) = i_j$ if and only if $i_j \in R_1$.

Hence $Pr[\text{MinHash}_{\mathcal{P}}(c_1) = \text{MinHash}_{\mathcal{P}}(c_2)] = \frac{|R_1|}{|R_1|+|R_2|}$ which is equal to the Jaccard similarity of S_1 and S_2. Thus, we have

$$\mathbb{E}\left[\frac{\#\text{Matches between signature vectors of } S_1 \text{ and } S_2}{h}\right]$$
$$= \frac{\sum_{k=1}^{h} Pr\left[\text{MinHash}_{\mathcal{P}_k}(c_1)=\text{MinHash}_{\mathcal{P}_k}(c_2)\right]}{h}$$
$$= \frac{hJ(S_1,S_2)}{h} = J(S_1, S_2),$$

which means the estimator is unbiased.

Supplementary Theorem 3: The variance of the estimator proposed in Theorem 2 is equal to $\frac{J(S_1,S_2)-J^2(S_1,S_2)}{h}$.

Proof: Since the probability of match between two MinHash signatures for each permutation $\mathcal{P}_k$ equals to $J(S_1, S_2)$, thus #Matches between signature vectors of S_1 and S_2 follows a binomial distribution with h trials (number of permutations) and $p = J(S_1, S_2)$. Thus its variance equals $hp(1 - p)$. Therefore,

$$\text{Var}\left[\frac{\#\text{Matches between two signatures}}{h}\right] = \frac{\text{Var}\left[\#\text{Matches between two signatures}\right]}{h^2}$$
$$= \frac{hJ(S_1, S_2)(1 - J(S_1, S_2))}{h^2}$$
$$= \frac{J(S_1, S_2)(1 - J(S_1, S_2))}{h}$$

To obtain the MinHash signatures of reads in a given dataset, we need $O(NL)$ operations to form k-mer set of sequences, and $O(hNL)$ operations to obtain MinHash signatures of reads, where N is the number of reads, L is the average length of the sequences, and h is the length of MinHash signatures.

Choosing the Hyper-parameters of the Locality Sensitive Hashing Algorithm
Hashing the reads using MinHash reduces the computational complexity of comparison significantly, since comparing the MinHash signature of two given reads needs $O(h)$, while computing the edit distance of two reads requires $O(L^2)$ operations (L can be varied from 400 to $10k$, while h can be selected as a constant number typically less than 100). Still, comparing the MinHash signatures of all $O(N^2)$ pairs of sequences is inefficient for large-scale datasets consisting of millions of sequences. LSH algorithm copes with this issue by dividing the h entries of the MinHash signature into b bands of size d ($h = bd$). If two sequences are equal in all rows of at least one of the bands, they are considered as a candidate similar pair. For the default hyper-parameters of I-CONVEX ($d = 1, b = 10, k = 15$) the probability of considering two sequences as similar for different values of their Jaccard similarity is depicted in Supplementary Figure 2. We have selected the default values of hyper-parameters such that the probability of having a false negative is small. However, this leads to a higher rate of false positives as well. As we mentioned in Sect. 3, we validate the obtained candidate pairs by a designed convolutional neural network to remove the false positive edges in our similarity graph.

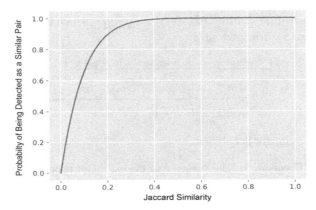

Supplementary Figure 2. The Probability of considering a pair of sequences as similar when d = 1 and b = 10 for different values of Jaccard similarity of the pair.

Supplementary Note 4: Architecture of Convolutional Neural Network

To validate the similarity of candidate pair obtained from Locality Sensitive Hashing Algorithm we trained a convolutional neural network with the training data described in Results section. In this supplementary, we explain the architecture of the convolutional neural network.

Architecture. To train the convolutional neural network that validates the similarity of candidate pairs, for each pair in the generated training dataset (which can be similar or dissimilar), both reads are one-hot encoded first (Each letter corresponds to a 4×1 array). Since the length of each read in the generated dataset is 400, we obtain two arrays of size 4×400 after one-hot encoding of the reads. Then, we concatenate these two arrays row-wise to obtain an 8×400 array. These 8×400 arrays are the input data to the convolutional neural network with the layers depicted in Table 1.

Table 1. Structure of the convolutional neural network designed to validate the similarity of candidate pairs.

Layer	Input	Filter Size	Filters	Stride	Activation
Convolution 1	8X400	8X8	32	1	Relu
Max Pool 1	8X400X32	2X2	-	2	-
Convolution 2	8X100X32	5X5	64	1	Relu
Max Pool 2	8X100X64	2X2	-	2	-
Fully connected 1	4X50X64		50		Relu
Fully connected 2	50		1		Linear

The final value after passing each 8×400 input from the convolutional neural network is a scalar representing the predicted value. This scalar ranges between -1 and 1, representing the similarity of a given pair. To compute the loss, let y_i and $\hat{y}_i$ be the predicted value, and the true label corresponding to the i-th candidate pair. We use ℓl_2 loss defined as follows:

$$\ell l(y, \hat{y}) = \sum_{i=1}^{n} (\hat{y}_i - y_i)^2$$

To optimize the weight parameters in the network, an Adam optimizer is applied to the ℓl_2 loss.

Validation of Candidate Similar Pairs: To validate a given candidate similar pair by the trained convolutional neural network, first each read is trimmed to a sequence with length 400 (if the length of a read is less than400, we add enough base 'A' to the end of the sequence to reach the length of400). Each one of the two trimmed reads is one-hot encoded to get an array of size 4×400. By concatenating them, an array with the size 8×400 is obtained. Then, it will be passed through the convolutional neural network, and it gives a number within the range of $[-1, +1]$. If the number is greater than0, we consider them as a similar pair.

Supplementary Note 5: I-CONVEX Pipeline

To run I-CONVEX on a given genome reads dataset, first move the fasta file to the Clustering folder and rename it to ***reads.fasta***. Then execute the following commands in order to obtain **pre-clusters**:

Pre-clustering

```
ClusteringReads/Clustering$ python SplitFile.py
ClusteringReads/Clustering$ chmod 777 commands.sh
ClusteringReads/Clustering$ ./commands.sh
```

The result is a Cluster folder containing subfolders, each of which represents a pre-cluster. Now, the following commands run the *clustering via convexification* module on pre-clusters:

Clustering via Convexification

```
ClusteringReads/Clustering$  python  CreateConvexScript.py
8
ClusteringReads/Clustering$ ./run_convex.sh
ClusteringReads/Clustering$ python CollectTranscripts.py
```

The last command stores the final collected transcripts on the ***final_transcripts.fasta*** file.

360   S. Baharlouei et al.

To run all parts of the algorithm step by step, or change the hyper-parameters such as k, d, and b, follow the advanced version instructions on https://github.com/sinaBaharlouei/I-CONVEX.

Supplementary Figures: Distribution of Sequence Lengths in Synthetic and Real Datasets

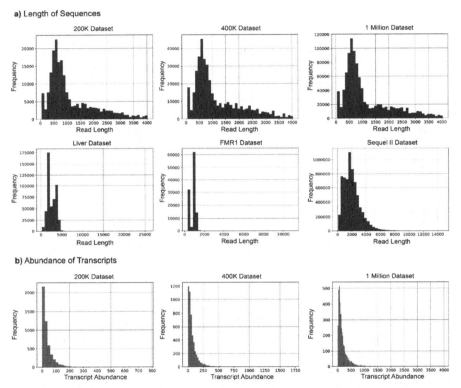

Supplementary Figure 3. Distribution of the Read Lengths and Transcript Abundances for the simulated and real datasets.

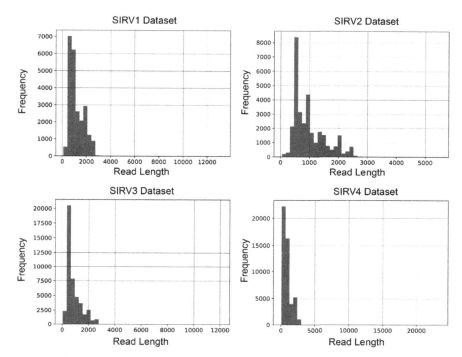

Supplementary Figure 4. Histograms of sequence length of four SIRV datasets.

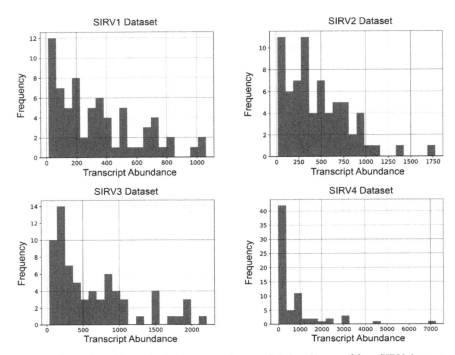

Supplementary Figure 5. Histograms of transcript abundances of four SIRV datasets.

References

1. Steijger, T., et al.: Assessment of transcript reconstruction methods for RNA-seq. Nat. Meth. **10**, 1177–1184 (2013)
2. Kannan, S., Hui, J., Mazooji, K., Pachter, L., Tse, D.: Shannon: an information-optimal de Novo RNA-Seq assembler. Preprint at https://www.biorxiv.org/content/10.1101/039230v1 (2016)
3. Mortazavi, A., Williams, B.A., McCue, K., Schaeffer, L., Wold, B.: Mapping and quantifying mammalian transcriptomes by RNA-Seq. Nat. Meth. **5**, 621–628 (2008)
4. Wang, Z., Gerstein, M., Snyder, M.: RNA-Seq: a revolutionary tool for transcriptomics. Nat. Rev. Genet. **10**, 57–63 (2009)
5. Gordon, S.P., et al.: Widespread polycistronic transcripts in fungi revealed by single-molecule mRNA sequencing. PLoS ONE **10**, e0132628 (2015)
6. Wang, B., et al.: Unveiling the complexity of the maize transcriptome by single-molecule long-read sequencing. Nat. Commun. **7**, 11708 (2016)
7. Hwang, B., Lee, J.H., Bang, D.: Single-cell RNA sequencing technologies and bioinformatics pipelines. Exp. Mol. Med. **50**, 96 (2018)
8. Sahlin, K., Tomaszkiewicz, M., Makova, K.D., Medvedev, P.: Deciphering highly similar multigene family transcripts from Iso-Seq data with IsoCon. Nat. Commun. **9**, 4601 (2018)
9. Abdel-Ghany, S.E., et al.: A survey of the sorghum transcriptome using single-molecule long reads. Nat. Commun. **7**, 11706 (2016)
10. Weirather, J.L., et al.: Characterization of fusion genes and the significantly expressed fusion isoforms in breast cancer by hybrid sequencing. Nucleic Acids Res. **43**, e116 (2015)

11. Westbrook, C.J., et al.: No assembly required: full-length MHC class I allele discovery by PacBio circular consensus sequencing. Hum. Immunol. **76**, 891–896 (2015)
12. Roberts, A., Pachter, L.: Streaming fragment assignment for real-time analysis of sequencing experiments. Nat. Meth. **10**, 71–73 (2013)
13. Trapnell, C., et al.: Transcript assembly and quantification by RNA-Seq reveals unannotated transcripts and isoform switching during cell differentiation. Nat. Biotechnol. **28**, 511–515 (2010)
14. Broder, A.Z.: On the resemblance and containment of documents. Compression Complex. Seq. **1997**, 21–29 (1997)
15. Ondov, B.D., et al.: Mash: fast genome and metagenome distance estimation using MinHash. Genome Biol. **17**, 1–14 (2016)
16. Berlin, K., et al.: Assembling large genomes with single-molecule sequencing and locality-sensitive hashing. Nat. Biotechnol. **33**, 623–630 (2015)
17. Gionis, A., Indyk, P., Motwani, R.: Similarity search in high dimensions via hashing. In: VLDB, vol. 99, no. 6 (1999)
18. Tardaguila, M., et al.: SQANTI: extensive characterization of long-read transcript sequences for quality control in full-length transcriptome identification and quantification. Genome Res. **28**, 396–411 (2016)
19. Safonova, Y., et al.: IgRepertoireConstructor: a novel algorithm for antibody repertoire construction and immunoproteogenomics analysis. Bioinformatics **31**, i53–i61 (2015)
20. Gibrat, J.F.: A short note on dynamic programming in a band. BMC Bioinf. **19**(1), 1–5 (2018)
21. Clauset, A., Newman, M.E.J., Moore, C.: Finding community structure in very large networks. Phy. Rev. E **70**, 066111 (2004)
22. Tseng, E., Tang, H., AlOlaby, R.R., Hickey, L., Tassone, F.: Altered expression of the FMR1 splicing variants landscape in premutation carriers. Biochim. Biophys. Acta **1860**, 1117–1126 (2017)
23. Steeb, W., Hardy, Y.: Matrix Calculus and Kronecker Product: A Practical Approach to Linear and Multilinear Algebra, 2nd edn. World Scientific Publishing Company, Singapore (2011
24. Bertsekas, D.P.: Nonlinear programming. J. Oper. Res. Soc. **48**, 334 (1997)
25. Tibshirani, R.: Regression shrinkage and selection via the lasso. J. R Stat. Soc. Ser. B Methodol. **58**, 267–288 (1996)

Italian Debate on Measles Vaccination: How Twitter Data Highlight Communities and Polarity

Cynthia Ifeyinwa Ugwu[2] and Sofia Casarin[1(✉)]

[1] Universita' degli Studi di Padova, Padova, Italy
sofia.casarin@studenti.unipd.it
[2] Free University of Bozen-Bolzano, Bolzano, Italy
cugwu@unibz.it

Abstract. Social media platforms such as Twitter, Facebook, and You-Tube had proven to be valuable sources of information. These platforms are a fruitful source of freely collectible public opinions. Due to the recent outbreak of the monkeypox disease, and in light of the historical pandemic that affected the whole world, we examine the issue of understanding the Italian opinion towards vaccinations of diseases that have apparently disappeared. To address this issue, we study the flow of information on the measles vaccine by looking at Twitter data. We discovered that vaccine skeptics have a higher tweeting activity, and the hashtags used by the three classes of users (pro-vaccine, anti-vaccine, and neutral) fall into three different communities, corresponding to the groups identified by opinion polarization towards the vaccine. By analyzing how hashtags are shared in different communities, we show that communication exists only in the neutral-opinion community.

Keywords: Measles · Sentiment analysis · Machine learning · Twitter

1 Introduction

Measles is an acute, viral, highly contagious airborne disease. It is spread by coughing and sneezing, close personal contact, or direct contact with infected nasal or throat secretions. It is one of the world's most contagious diseases, and as it is shown in [1], nine out of ten people who are not immune and share living space with an infected person get the disease. The virus can indeed be transmitted by an infected person from 4 day before the onset of the rash to 4 day after the rash erupts [2]. This extremely contagious disease should reach an absorbing state, *i.e.* the disease should die out as it happened for smallpox, but it is continuously provided with new susceptible individuals, *i.e.* not vaccinated children. For this reason, despite the availability of vaccines for more than 50 years, measles remains one of the leading causes of global child mortality [3].

C.I. Ugwu and S. Casarin—Contributed equally to this work.

I. Koprinska et al. (Eds.): ECML PKDD 2022 Workshops, CCIS 1753, pp. 364–375, 2023.
https://doi.org/10.1007/978-3-031-23633-4_24

Between 2020 and 2021 a worldwide vaccination campaign took place to bring an end to the SARS-CoV-2 (COVID-19) pandemic. The success of the campaign relied heavily on the actual willingness of individuals to get vaccinated. In this scenario, social media platforms such as Twitter, Facebook, and YouTube had proven to be valuable sources of information [4]. Many studies were conducted to understand the opinion, public awareness of COVID-19, and the characteristics and the status of the outbreak [4,6]. On top of that, the identification in May 2022 of clusters of monkeypox cases in several non-endemic countries with no direct travel links to an endemic area had thrown back into a state of alarm the world. In December 2017, the Italian Ministry of Health reported about 5000 measles cases, and 88% of them were not vaccinated [7]. For this reason, in December 2017 the (DDL 770) was approved and made 10 vaccines (that included meases) mandatory for children. These numbers led to our interest in understanding Italian opinion about vaccines. Having witnessed the impact of social media during the COVID-19 pandemic and the recent cases of monkeypox whose outbreak is preventable by also harnessing the power of social media, this paper analyses the Italian opinion towards measles vaccination during 2017 outbreak that can be considered atypical and similar to what is currently occurring with monkeypox. To this aim, we exploit the Twitter Streaming API to collect Italian tweets' opinions on the measles vaccine and characterize the study from several prospective: (i) qualitative, analyzing the geo-localized tweets, (ii) quantitative, building a bipartite network and the corresponding projection networks, and (iii) semantically, conducting a sentiment analysis through the use of deep learning.

The remainder of this paper is organized as follows: in Sect. 2 we describe works that make use of Twitter data. Section 3 focuses on data retrieval, preprocessing, and sentiment analysis. In Sect. 4 we built a choropleth map expressing vaccine opinion and the network. Our main results are presented in Sect. 5, while in Sect. 6 the conclusions are drawn.

2 Related Background

Twitter has been propagating billions of personal or professional posts, stories, and debates since 2006. The circadian substructure characterizing Twitter offers a constant affluent volume of data to examine the gregarious human sentiments and opinions. Enormous methods are offered to automatically extrapolate the public expressed thoughts, bringing Twitter data to be the focus of many research papers addressing different topics [5,8–10]. We built our study on four main research works, integrating and extending many of the pursued techniques to address our analysis of Italian opinion towards vaccination. Marcec *et al.* [6] conducted sentiment analysis using English-language tweets mentioning AstraZeneca/Oxford, Pfizer/BioNTech, and Moderna vaccines from 1 December 2020 to 31 March 2021. The target was to implement a tool to track the sentiment regarding SARS-CoV-2 vaccines. The results show the sentiment regarding the AstraZeneca/Oxford vaccine appears to be turning negative over time, this may boost hesitancy rates towards this specific vaccine. In [11], Cossard *et al.*, examined the extent to which the vaccination debate on Twitter is conducive to potential outreach to the vaccination hesitant. The study was centered on the Italian debate on vaccination as a general topic. Their results show how vaccination skeptics and advocates reside in their distinct echo chambers. Gargiulo *et al.* [12] investigate the flow of information on vaccine administration on the French-speaking realm of Twitter between 2016 and 2017. By analyzing the retweet networks, the authors highlight how vaccine critics and defenders tend to focus on different vaccines, leading to asymmetric behavior. As a consequence, despite the presence of a large number of pro-vaccine accounts, vaccine-critical accounts display greater craft and energy, using a wider variety of sources, and a more coordinated set of hashtags, resulting in more effective in spreading their vaccine-critical opinion.

An epidemiological overview of the Italian situation in 2017 is finally conducted by Filia *et al.* [13], who addressed the topic by collecting measles cases since 2013 and emphasizing the impact per region of the 2017 Italian measles epidemic.

3   Methodology

Considering the historical events mentioned in Sect. 1, we aim at extracting tweets from May to December 2017, with the goal of:

– mapping vaccine hesitancy through geo-located tweets;
– performing sentiment analysis based on a Deep Learning framework;
– performing a quantitative study of the interaction existing in a network composed of users and posted hashtags.

This section consists of a description of the data collection and cleansing procedure in Sects. 3.1, 3.2. Then, in Sect. 3.3 we introduce the carried out sentiment analysis, the further preprocessing of the data specific for Natural Language Processing (NLP) and the SentITA tool [14].

3.1   Data Retrieval

The Twitter API (Application Programming Interface) was accessed using the Python programming language. Despite having numerous restrictions from the SandBox Twitter Developer account, we have applied successive attempts to access as many posts as possible. We chose the tweets extraction period based on the historical events, *i.e.* the outbreak and the Lorenzin decree. We extracted tweets from May to December 2017. The tweeting activity about measles vaccination, after the first months of 2018, is indeed much less consistent. We queried the Twitter Streaming API two times for each month (one· for the first half and the other for the second half of the month) extracting 200 tweets per month. The query was performed multiple times with 28 pairs of Italian keywords (Table 1) to extract only Italian tweets. To obtain a final tweet database of 10340 tweets, we combined words/hashtags related to vaccinations with ones related to measles.

Table 1. Examples of some combinations of words/hashtags used to query the Twitter API.

1	2	3	4	5	6	7
#autismo/ #morbillo	autismo/ #morbillo	epidemia/ morbillo	morbillo/ #antivax	morbillo/ #provax	MPR/ vaccino	MPR/ epidemia

3.2 Data Preprocessing

After the initial cleaning, only the relevant information was kept: the tweet id, the date and time of creation, the username, the location, the coordinates, the mentions and retweets of other users, the hashtags, and the full text. Further cleaning was carried out to store only the tweets with a non-empty location or coordinates field. We converted to lowercase all the letters and removed mentions, hashtags, retweets, URLs, newlines, and extra spaces obtaining a total of 6279 tweets. We also decided to remove emojis. When dealing with text analysis indeed, two possible approaches can be used to deal with emojis: they can be discarded, or they can be converted to text. In our work we observed many meaningless emojis and for the sake of simplicity we decided to discard them, but future analysis will include the second approach.

Based on all tweets with a non-empty coordinates field, we selected the ones with Italian locations and applied a mapping operation to assign the corresponding region name to each location. We converted all tweets' location fields to lowercase letters and removed punctuation, parentheses, and other symbols, such as "/" and "@". The mapping operation was performed manually, adding 100 cities to a dictionary that maps cities' names in the corresponding regions' names. In this coarse mapping, we lost data, but we assumed that the remaining ones (3420 tweets) were sufficient for the following analysis.

3.3 Sentiment Analysis

Sentiment analysis of Twitter data is helpful to analyze the information in the tweets where opinions are highly unstructured, heterogeneous, and are either positive or negative, or neutral in some cases. Sentiment analysis is a text mining technique that automates the scouring of attitudes, opinions, and emotions from text through Machine Learning (ML) and NLP. It involves classifying opinions in text into categories like "positive" "negative" or "neutral". Sentiment analysis is a complex task, as accurate processing is rather hard on texts such as tweets, which are short, rich in abbreviations and intra-genre expressions, and often syntactically ill-formed. Moreover, the State of the Art presents a limited number of available tools for Italian sentiment analysis, thus making the goal more challenging. To perform a sentiment analysis of the tweets we exploited the SentITA tool [14], a ML framework that exploits a pre-trained neural network to perform sentiment classification. The model was pre-trained on manually labeled text extrapolated from the datasets available in the Evalita challenge [15]. The dataset over which the model was pre-trained is composed of 7500 positive, 7500 negative, and 88000 neutral sentences. The deep learning model is a Bidirectional LSTM-CNN (detailed in Fig. 1) that operates at the word level. The model receives in input a word embedding representation of the single words and outputs two signals s_1 and s_2 ranging between 0 and 1, one for positive sentiment detection and one for negative sentiment detection. The two signals can be triggered both by the same input sentence if this contains both positive and negative sentiments (*e.g.* "The food is very good, but the location isn't nice"). The model can handle texts of lengths up to 35 words. To classify tweets in one of the three classes, we considered the highest among the two output signals and we compared its value with a threshold τ, as described in Eq. 1.

$$sentiment = \begin{cases} \text{neutral}, & \text{if } \max(s_1, s_2) < \tau \\ \max(s_1, s_2), & \text{otherwise} \end{cases} \quad (1)$$

The sentiment expressed in the tweet is classified as neutral if both output signals s_1 ad s_2 are below the threshold, negative if s_1 is the maximum and is above the threshold, and positive if s_2 is the maximum and is above the threshold. We empirically chose the threshold $\tau = 0.25$ by observing the values returned by the SentITA algorithm.

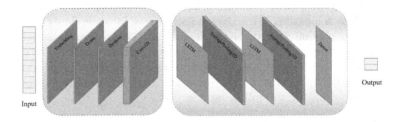

Fig. 1. Bidirectional LSTM-CNN neural network architecture.

4   Vaccine Opinion Elaboration Strategy

4.1   Vaccine Hesitancy Map

With the geolocalized tweets, we built a map of Italy to express how vaccine hesitancy about measles is distributed qualitatively among Italian regions. For each region, the overall opinion was computed using the formula in Eq. 2, which is the difference between the number of positive and negative tweets, normalized by the total number of tweets (neutral tweets included) in that region. The geographic coordinates were computed by exploiting the Geopy library [16] with the Nominatim geocoder [17], which identifies the coordinates of an address looking at the OpenStreetMap dataset. A data frame was built with the name of the regions, the associated coordinates, and the region's opinion about the measles vaccine. The results were represented in a choropleth map, Fig. 2, where the higher the color intensity, the more the opinion is polarized toward pro-vaccine.

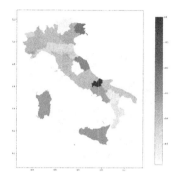

Fig. 2. Italian opinion polarization about the measles vaccine.

4.2   Network Creation

Focusing on users and hashtags, we decided to associate tweets' opinions with the user who posted the tweet and the list of hashtags contained in it. Before the creation of the network, we did some preprocessing, converting the opinion of the tweet to a number, assigning favorable (pro), contrary (con), and neutral the values 1, -1 and 0 respectively. Furthermore, we also removed the tweets for which the list of hashtags was empty. For each hashtag and user, we associated a polarity measure that follows Eq. 2, which is the mean value between the number of times a hashtag was in a favorable, contrary, or neutral tweet.

$$polarity = \frac{(1) * n_{positive} + (-1) * n_{negative} + (0) * n_{neutral}}{n_{all}}. \tag{2}$$

With all this information we were able to create a bipartite. A bipartite network has two sets of nodes, *e.g.* U and V. Nodes in the U-set connect directly only to nodes in the V-set. Hence there are no direct U-U or V-V links. Usually, rather than analysing the original bipartite graph, which is complex, performing the analysis on the projections is a common practice. Projection U is obtained by connecting two U-nodes if they link to the same V-node in the bipartite representation. Projection V is obtained in the same way. We used as sets of nodes hashtags and users. In this case, the link that connects two nodes is weighted by the number of times a user uses a particular hashtag in a tweet. From the bipartite composed of 1528 nodes and 3455 edges, we created the projection of the two sets obtaining a network for the users and for the hashtags where the weights are the number of shared neighbors.

4.3   Network Analysis

Once the two networks were built, we proceeded with the network analysis. Figure 3 gives a visual representation about the centrality of the hashtags - the bigger the name the more central the hashtag. We determined the centrality of a hashtag simply using the "most common" function of a Counter object. The visual representation is obtained with Wordcloud library.

Fig. 3. Wordcloud representation of the most used hashtags in the Hashtags Projection Network: the bigger the font, the higher the frequency of appearance.

We extracted some topological aspects of the network, *e.g.* the number of nodes and edges, the diameter, and the density of the network. We identified the number of communities, their interactions with each other and within themselves. Community detection was performed on Gephi tool [18], a visualization and exploration open-source software which implements a community detection algorithm optimizing a quality function called modularity. Despite its speed, this method can produce different results. Therefore, we run it multiple times and took the number of communities that appeared the most.

5   Experimental Results

5.1   Geographical Spread on Vaccine Opinion

The results after the sentiment analysis described in Sect. 3.3 are shown in Fig. 4.

The majority of tweets have a negative opinion ($\approx$ 44%), and only a few of them were classified as positive ($\approx$ 17%). Although these results depend on the threshold τ in Eq. 1 chosen for the final classification, they are consistent with what we expected: anti-vaccine users have a higher tweeting activity with respect to pro-vaccine users [11,12]. This yields the representation of the opinion polarization in the Italian map in Fig. 2 to have an overall negative attitude. Moreover, the results are highly biased due to an unbalance tweet count between regions (see Table 2): there are some regions like Basilicata and Molise with only 2 and 1 tweet, respectively.

For this reason, we cannot state that the information on the map represents the overall opinion of the inhabitants but we can deduce the opinion polarization

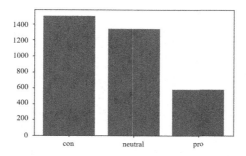

Fig. 4. Tweet's classification based on sentiment analysis.

Table 2. Number of tweets in each region and average opinion.

	Lazio	Lombardia	Toscana	Sicilia	Piemonte	Veneto	Emilia Romagna
Opinion	−0.385	−0.371	−0.389	−0.31	−0.353	−0.346	−0.451
Tot. tweets	724	523	514	441	224	214	206
	Campania	Friuli Venezia Giulia	Puglia	Liguria	Trentino Alto Adige	Sardegna	Umbria
Opinion	−0.333	−0.202	−0.407	−0.442	−0.529	−0.313	−0.581
Tot. tweets	144	89	54	52	51	48	42
	Marche	Calabria	Abruzzo	Valle d'Aosta	Basilicata	Molise	
Opinion	−0.270	−0.478	−0.391	−0.429	−0.500	0.000	
Tot. tweets	37	23	23	7	2	1	

of each region. Furthermore, from the choropleth map, we cannot compare the opinion among different regions because we don't know the percentage of people active on Twitter in 2017. Nevertheless, the opinion uncovered from the tweets seems to be polarized toward negative opinions regarding the measles vaccine, because in all regions the majority of tweets are classified as contrary or neutral, proving that anti-vaccine users tweet more frequently.

5.2   Projection Networks

The downloaded tweets were modeled through a bipartite graph, as previously mentioned in Sect. 4.2. The quantitative analysis of the Italian opinion was conducted in parallel on the two projection networks, *i.e.* the Users Projection Network and the Hashtag Projection Network. Both projection networks were initially very connected, as expected. To obtain meaningful results, we studied the distribution of the edges' weights and filtered the networks according to

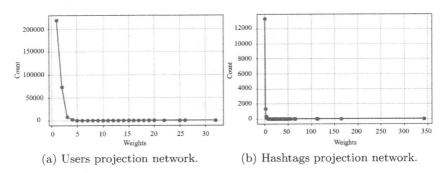

(a) Users projection network.   (b) Hashtags projection network.

Fig. 5. Distribution of the weights characterizing the edges.

the results displayed in Fig. 5. Figures 5a, 5b highlight that the majority of the edges a weight $w = 1$. To find an optimal trade-off between discarding meaningless edges and keeping as much information as possible, we chose a threshold $\tau_w = 2$ for the Users Projection Network and $\tau_w = 1$ for the Hashtags Projection Network.

Users Projection Network. The graph is composed, after the filtering operation, of 397 nodes with an average degree $deg_u = 53.5$. In the network, three groups of users can be identified (Fig. 6a): (i) pro-vaccine users (*yellow nodes*), (ii) anti-vaccine users (*purple nodes*), and (iii) users with a neutral opinion (*pink nodes*). It appears from the graph that the majority of users posting the collected tweets show a neutral or negative opinion towards the measles vaccine. Only 5.53% of users express a positive opinion in their tweets, confirming the initial hypothesis reported also by Gargiulo *et al.* in their work [12]. It emerges indeed that most of the people with negative sentiments towards vaccines are very active on Twitter, while pro-vaccine users are less cohesive and post fewer tweets. These results are confirmed also by the presence of hubs, identified through the PageRank algorithm, expressly present in the anti-vaccine group.

Hashtag Projection Network. This projection network, depicted in Fig. 6b, is composed of 2016 nodes with an average degree $deg_h = 22.4$. We computed a density of 0.11, and classified the graph as "not fully connected". The giant component indeed has 204 nodes, while the isolated components carry the remaining two nodes. This network allows deriving some interesting considerations derived from the application of the PageRank algorithm and community detection. PageRank returned the most important hashtags in the graph, annotated in Table 3 and clearly visible in Fig. 3. It is worth mentioning that "morbillo", "vaccini" and "vaccino", the three hubs of this network, are mostly used with a negative sentiment.

 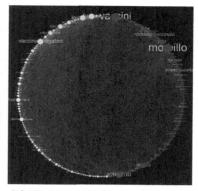

(a) Users Projection Network.   (b) Hashtags Projection Network.

Fig. 6. Gephi vizualization of the projection networks. The nodes are colored according to the community they belong.

Table 3. Most important nodes identified through PageRank in the Hashtags projection Network.

	1	2	3	4	5
Hashtags	Morbillo	Vaccini	Vaccino	Vaccini-obbligatori	Novax
PageRank	0.098	0.084	0.038	0.031	0.030
	6	7	8	9	10
Hashtags	Freevax	Iovaccino	Liberta-discelta	Mpr	Noobbligo-vaccinale
PageRank	0.028	0.026	0.024	0.023	0.022

The community detection algorithm returned three communities that interestingly correspond to the groups identified by the sentiment toward vaccination. We quantified this aspect by counting the number of pro-vaccine, anti-vaccine, and neutral opinions belonging to each community, we observed from Fig. 7 that: (i) community 0 (*pink bars*) gathers mostly neutral hashtags, community 1 (*purple bars*) is composed of many adverse hashtags, while community 2 (*yellow bars*) gathers favorable hashtags.

We finally analyzed the *communication* between different nodes in the network by (i) observing in Fig. 6b that edges (colored as the source node) are connecting particular communities, and (ii) quantifying the phenomenon by computing the percentage of edges going from one community to another. Figure 6b highlights some patterns: the neutral community strongly exchanges edges within itself (76%), and it is much less connected with the pro-vaccine community (16%) and the anti-vaccine community (8%); the pro-vaccine community exchanges edge within itself (45%) and with the neutral community (38%); the anti-vaccine

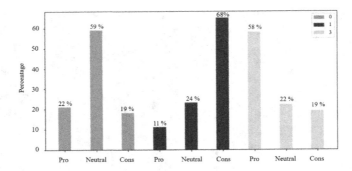

Fig. 7. Sentiment distribution of the hashtags gathered per community in the Hashtags Projection Network. (Color figure online)

community shows similar behavior to the pro-vaccine one, exchanging edges within itself (44%) and with the neutral community (37%).

6   Conclusions

In this paper, we proposed a deep analysis of the Italian opinion towards the measles vaccine, (i) to understand the potentiality of the information available on Twitter, and (ii) to bring an overview of the opinions of Italians towards vaccination. We performed a qualitative study, by exploiting sentiment analysis on tweets, and focused on a regional overview of vaccination. More precisely, we observed that all the regions are negatively polarized underling that there is a prevalence of anti-vaccination tweets. Through a quantitative study of the projection networks, we observed that the anti-vax community tweets more than the pro-vax community, as it's also stated in [11, 12]. Only a few approaches address the Italian opinion about vaccination by performing sentiment analysis, as most of the available APIs can be applied to a limited number of languages, *e.g.* English, German and French. Therefore, to the best of our knowledge, this is the first study that addresses Italian opinion on measles vaccination from a different point of view, extending previous studies with sentiment analysis. We plan to apply our analysis also to Covid19 and Monkeypox, that became worldwide everyday hot topics. This will probably overcome some of the limitations we encountered, *e.g.* lack of geolocalized tweets, lack of powerful tools for sentiment analysis applied to Italian.

References

1. Gastanaduy, P., Haber, P., Rota, P.A., Patel, M.: Epidemiology and Prevention of Vaccine-Preventable Diseases. 14th edn. (2021). Chap. 13
2. WHO Homepage, https://www.who.int/news-room/fact-sheets/detail/masles. Last accessed 16 June 2022

3. Medić, S., et al.: Epidemiological, clinical and laboratory characteristics of the measles resurgence in the Republic of Serbia in 2014–2015. Publ. Lib. Sci. (PLoS), 14(10) e0224009 (2019). https://doi.org/10.1371/journal.pone.0224009

4. Manguri, K.H., Ramadhan, R.N., Mohammed Amin, P.R.: Twitter sentiment analysis on worldwide COVID-19 outbreaks. Kurdistan J. Appl. Res. 54–65 (2020). https://doi.org/10.24017/covid.8

5. Boon-Itt, S., Skunkan, Y.: Public perception of the COVID-19 pandemic on Twitter: Sentiment analysis and topic modeling study. JMIR Public Health Surveill (2020). https://doi.org/10.2196/21978

6. Marcec, R., Likic, R.: Using Twitter for sentiment analysis towards AstraZeneca/Oxford, Pfizer/BioNTech and Moderna COVID-19 vaccines. Postgraduate Med. J. (2021). https://doi.org/10.1136/postgradmedj-2021-140685

7. Epicentro. https://www.epicentro.iss.it/morbillo/Infografica2017. Accessed 17 June 2022

8. Geetha, R., Rekha, P., Karthika, S.: Twitter opinion mining and boosting using sentiment analysis. In: International Conference on Computer, Communication, and Signal Processing (ICCCSP), pp. 1–4 (2018). https://doi.org/10.1109/ICCCSP.2018.8452838

9. Pak, A., Paroubek, P.: Twitter as a corpus for sentiment analysis and opinion mining. In: Proceedings of the Seventh International Conference on Language Resources and Evaluation (LREC'10). European Language Resources Association (ELRA), Valletta, Malta (2010)

10. Kolasani, S.V., Assaf., R.: Predicting stock movement using sentiment analysis of twitter feed with neural networks. J. Data Anal. Inf. Process. (2020). https://doi.org/10.4236/jdaip.2020.84018

11. Cossard, A., De Francisci Morales, G., Kalimeri, K., Mejova, Y., Paolotti, D., Starnini, M.: Falling into the Echo Chamber: the Italian Vaccination Debate on Twitter. In: Proceedings of the Fourteenth International AAAI Conference on Web and Social Media (ICWSM 2020)

12. Gargiulo, F., Cafiero, F., Guille-Escuret, P., Seror, V., Ward, J. K.: Asymmetric participation of defenders and critics of vaccines to debates on French-speaking Twitter. In: Sci. Rep. **10**(1) 6599 (2020). https://doi.org/10.1038/s41598-020-62880-5

13. Filia, A., Bella, A., Del Manso, M., Rota, M.C.: L'epidemia di morbillo in Italia nel 2017. In: Rivista di Immunologia e Allergologia Pediatrica (RIAP) (2018)

14. Giancarlo, N.: SentITA, a sentiment analysis tool for Italian. 2018. https://github.com/NicGian/SentITA. Accessed 6 Apr 2022

15. EVALITA. Evaluation of NLP and Speech Tools for Italian. https://www.evalita.it/evalita-2016/tasks-challenge/. Accessed 1 June 2022

16. GeoPy's Documentation. https://geopy.readthedocs.io/en/stable/. Accessed 17 June 2022

17. Nominatim. https://nominatim.org/. Aaccessed 17 June 2022

18. Gephi. https://gephi.org/. Accessed 17 June 2022

3rd Workshop and Tutorial on Streams for Predictive Maintenance (IoT-PdM 2022)

3rd Workshop and Tutorial on IoT Streams for Predictive Maintenance (IoT-PdM 2022)

The Workshop

Maintenance is a critical issue in the industrial context for preventing high costs or injuries. Various industries are moving increasingly toward digitalization and collecting "big data" to enable or improve their prediction accuracy. At the same time, the emerging technologies of Industry 4.0 have empowered data production and exchange, which has led to new concepts and methodologies exploitation of large datasets for maintenance. The intensive research effort in data-driven predictive maintenance (PdM) has produced encouraging outcomes. Therefore, the main objective of this workshop series is to raise awareness of research trends and promote interdisciplinary discussion in this field.

Data-driven PdM deals with big streaming data that include concept drift due to both changing external conditions and normal wear of the equipment. It requires combining multiple data sources, and the resulting datasets are often highly imbalanced. The knowledge about the systems is detailed, but in many scenarios there is a large diversity in both model configurations and their usage, additionally complicated by low data quality and high uncertainty in the labels. In particular, many recent advancements in supervised and unsupervised machine learning, representation learning, anomaly detection, visual analytics, and similar areas can be showcased in this domain. Therefore, the research gap between machine learning and PdM has recently increased.

This year's workshop followed the success of the two previous editions, co-located with ECML PKDD 2019 and ECML PKDD 2020. Each year, there was strong interest in the workshop, as evidenced by the number of submitted papers, active participation by many researchers and practitioners, and in-depth discussions following the presentations. The key part of the program in 2022 was eight presentations of accepted manuscripts; those were selected using a double-blind peer-review process, with each submission reviewed by at least three members of the Program Committee. The call for papers, program, and detailed description can be found on the website: https://abifet.wixsite.com/iotstream2022.

The organizers would like to thank the authors, keynote speaker, and Program Committee members for their contributions to the workshop. We hope and believe that the workshop has been a valuable resource for participants and contributed to identifying new ideas, applications, and future research papers in IoT, data streams, and predictive maintenance. The workshop provided a premier forum for sharing findings, knowledge, insights, experience, and lessons learned from practical and theoretical work in predictive maintenance from streams of data. The intrinsic interdisciplinary nature of the workshop promoted the interaction between different competencies, thus paving the way for an exciting and stimulating environment involving researchers and practitioners.

Mykola Pechenizkiy, a full professor and chair of data mining at the Department of Mathematics and Computer Science, TU Eindhoven, delivered the keynote talk on "Foundations of Trustworthy Machine Learning on Data Streams".

Trustworthy AI is broadly used as an umbrella term encompassing multiple aspects of machine learning-based solutions, including robustness, reliability, safety, security, scalability, and interpretability. Some aspects are highly important for adopting mostly autonomous solutions and others for applications involving humans in the loop in decision making. In his talk, Mykola used examples of both kinds of applications to illustrate various research challenges and related trade-offs being addressed. He also focused on the peculiarities of trustworthy AI in machine learning over evolving data streams.

The Tutorial

Today, in many industries, various AI systems, often black-box ones, predict failures based on analysing sensor data. They discover symptoms of imminent issues by detecting anomalies and deviations from typical behavior, often with impressive accuracy. However, PdM is part of a broader context. The goal is to identify the most probable causes and act to solve problems before they escalate. In complex systems, knowing that something is wrong (to detect an anomaly) is not enough; the key is to understand its reasons and potential consequences and provide alternatives (solutions/advice) to mitigate those consequences. However, this often requires complex interactions among several actors in the industrial and decision-making processes. Doing it fully automatically is unrealistic, despite recent impressive progress in AI. For example, in wind power plants, a repair requires synchronization of inventory (availability of pieces to be replaced), logistics (finding a ship to reach the installation), personnel management (availability schedule), weather predictions (suitability of conditions to perform maintenance, such as for high towers in offshore farms), and more. All these cannot be done by AI and require human expertise since the complete relevant context cannot be formalized in sufficient detail.

Recent developments in the field based on different machine learning and artificial intelligence methods are promising for fully- and semi-automated data-driven pattern recognition and knowledge creation enabled by IoT streams. Explanations of the models are necessary to create trust in prediction results for complex systems and non-stationary environments.

The tutorial, which took place during the morning session, introduced current trends and promising research directions within machine learning for PdM. This year, the focus of the tutorial was on explainable predictive maintenance (XPM). We presented some of the state-of-the-art methodologies in explainable AI (XAI) relevant to PdM problems. Further, we provided hands-on examples of applying XAI in benchmark datasets. We presented a discussion about future challenges and open issues on this topic. Two case studies related to PdM challenges, namely a metro operation and a steel factory, were presented hands-on during the tutorial.

September 2022

Sławomir Nowaczyk
Joao Gama
Albert Bifet
Sepideh Pashami
Grzegorz J. Nalepa
Rita P. Ribeiro
Bruno Veloso
Szymon Bobek
Carlos Ferreira

Organization

Workshop Chairs

Joao Gama   University of Porto, Portugal
Albert Bifet   Telecom-Paris, France, and University of
           Waikato, New Zealand
Sławomir Nowaczyk   Halmstad University, Sweden
Carlos Ferreira   University of Porto, Portugal

Tutorial Chairs

Sepideh Pashami   Halmstad University, Sweden
Grzegorz J. Nalepa   Jagiellonian University, Poland
Rita P. Almeida Ribeiro   University of Porto, Portugal
Bruno Veloso   University of Porto, Portugal
Szymon Bobek   Jagiellonian University, Poland

Program Committee

Anders Holst   RISE SICS, Sweden
Andreas Theissler   University of Applied Sciences Aalen,
           Germany
Anthony Fleury   Mines Douai, Institut Mines-Telecom, France
Carlos Ferreira   University of Porto, Portugal
David Camacho Fernandez   Universidad Politecnica de Madrid, Spain
Elaine Faria   Federal University of Uberlândia, Brazil
Enrique Alba   University of Malaga, Spain
Erik Frisk   Linkoping University, Sweden
Florent Masseglia   Inria, France
Hadi Fanaee-T   Halmstad University, Sweden
Indre Zliobaite   University of Helsinki, Finland
Jonathan De Andrade Silva   University of Mato Grosso do Sul, Brazil
Maria Pedroto   University of Porto, Portugal
Martin Atzmüller   Osnabrück University, Germany
Mykola Pechenizkiy   TU Eindonvhen, Netherlands
Paula Silva   University of Porto, Portugal
Saulo Martiello Mastelini   Universidade de São Paulo, Brazil
Thorsteinn Rögnvaldsson   Halmstad University, Sweden

Online Anomaly Explanation: A Case Study on Predictive Maintenance

Rita P. Ribeiro[1,2]([✉]) [ID], Saulo Martiello Mastelini[3] [ID], Narjes Davari[1] [ID], Ehsan Aminian[1] [ID], Bruno Veloso[1,2,4,5] [ID], and João Gama[1,2,5] [ID]

[1] INESC TEC, 4200-465 Porto, Portugal
rpribeiro@fc.up.pt
[2] Faculty of Sciences, University of Porto, 4169-007 Porto, Portugal
[3] ICMC - University of S. Paulo, 13566-590 São Carlos, Brazil
[4] University Portucalense, 4200-072 Porto, Portugal
[5] Faculty of Economics, University of Porto, 4200-464 Porto, Portugal

Abstract. Predictive Maintenance applications are increasingly complex, with interactions between many components. Black-box models are popular approaches due to their predictive accuracy and are based on deep-learning techniques. This paper presents an architecture that uses an online rule learning algorithm to explain when the black-box model predicts rare events. The system can present global explanations that model the black-box model and local explanations that describe why the black-box model predicts a failure. We evaluate the proposed system using four real-world public transport data sets, presenting illustrative examples of explanations.

Keywords: Explainable AI · Rare events · Predictive maintenance

1 Introduction

Real-world predictive maintenance applications are increasingly complex, with extensive interactions of many components. Data-driven predictive maintenance (PdM) solutions are a trendy technique in this domain, and especially the black-box models based on deep learning approaches show promising results in predictive accuracy and capability of modeling complex systems. However, the decisions made by these black-box models are often difficult for human experts to understand and make the correct decisions. The complete repair plan and maintenance actions that must be performed based on the detected symptoms of damage and wear often require complex reasoning and planning processes, involving many actors, and balancing different priorities. It is not realistic to expect this complete solution to be created automatically - there is too much context that needs to be considered. Therefore, operators, technicians, and managers require insights to understand what is happening, why, and how to react. Today's primarily black-box Machine Learning models do not provide these insights, nor do they support experts in making maintenance decisions based on detection

I. Koprinska et al. (Eds.): ECML PKDD 2022 Workshops, CCIS 1753, pp. 383–399, 2023.
https://doi.org/10.1007/978-3-031-23633-4_25

deviations. The effectiveness of the PdM system depends much more on the pertinence of the actions operators perform based on the triggered alarms than on the accuracy of the alarms themselves.

Fault detection is one of the most critical components of predictive maintenance. Nevertheless, predictive maintenance goes much behind predicting a failure. It is essential to understand the consequences and what will be the collateral damages of the failure. A critical issue in predictive maintenance applications is the design of the maintenance plan after a fault is detected or predicted. To elaborate the recovery plan, it is important to know the causes of the problem (root cause analysis), which component is affected, and the expected remain useful life of the equipment.

The contribution of this work is an explanatory layer in a deep-learning-based anomaly detection system in data-driven predictive maintenance. There are several works discussing the problem of explainability of deep learning models, for example, [6,7,10,12]. To our best knowledge, none of the works focuses on explaining deep-learning models for rare cases: the focus of this work.

In this work, we resort to real-world public transport area scenarios to present a generic system to explain the anomalies detected by black-box models. An online deep-learning, specifically Long-Short Term Memory Autoencoder (LSTM-AE), receives data reflecting the system's current state in the proposed architecture. It computes the reconstruction error as a function of the difference between the input and output. If the reconstruction error exceeds a threshold, we signal an alarm. In parallel, we learn regression rules that will explain the outputs of the black-box model.

This paper is organized as follows. The following section briefly introduces the Predictive Maintenance problem and the importance of obtaining explanations for detected faults. We also refer to existing works in the field of Explainable AI. Then, in Sect. 3, we present our case study on the public transport area. We describe the data that we used in this work. Next, in Sect. 4 we introduce our approach to obtain explanations from detected faults. In Sect. 5 we discuss our results in the four data sets that compose our case study. We conclude in Sect. 6, pointing out the generality of our approach to other similar scenarios and further research directions.

2   Background and Related Work

Maintenance is the process that deals with the health of equipment and system components to ensure their normal functioning under any circumstances. Over the years, and due to technological advances, different maintenance strategies have been developed. Nowadays, deep-learning techniques are quite popular, mostly due to their performance [17]. In a well-known PdM story, a train went into the workshop due to an alarm in the compressed air unit. They replace the wrong part in the workshop visit, and the train is back in motion. A few hours later, it was forced to return to the workshop with the same problem. This type of problem is persistent in maintenance and reinforces the need to explain fault alarms in an understandable way for everyone.

Two popular general proposed methods for explainable AI are LIME [13] and SHAP values [8]. None of these methods can be used in our context because we work in an online scenario, requiring fast explanations.

In the state-of-the-art of machine learning literature, a small set of existing interpretable models is recognized [6]: decision trees, regression rules, and linear models. These models are considered easily understandable and interpretable for humans. In [6] the authors differentiate between *global* and *local* explainability:

"A model may be completely interpretable, i.e., we are able to understand the whole logic of a model and follow the entire reasoning leading to all the different possible outcomes. In this case, we are speaking about global interpretability. Instead, we indicate with local interpretability the situation in which it is possible to understand only the reasons for a specific decision: only the single prediction/decision is interpretable."

In our case, we use online regression rules able to generate global and local interpretabilities!

3 Case Study on a Public Transport System

One of the approaches in data-driven predictive maintenance (PdM) is to learn the normal operating condition of a system such that any significant deviation from that operating condition could be spotted as a potential failure. One of the methods to attain this is by learning LSTM-AE on the normal examples of operation. The intuition is that if we give an abnormal example of operation, the reconstruction error of the LSTM-AE will be very high. Those examples are relevant from the PdM perspective and are, typically, rare.

The purpose of online anomaly detection and explanation for fault prediction is to identify and describe the occurrence of defects in the operational units of the system that result in unwanted or unacceptable behaviour of the whole system. As reported, a single on-the-road breakdown substantially outweighs the cost of a single unneeded component replacement. This work implements an anomaly detection framework based on deep learning as a reliable and robust technique that issues an alert whenever a sequence of abnormal data is detected. However, it is no longer enough to have the best experimental accuracy in the anomaly detection segment, and it is necessary to explain the obtained outputs to users to increase their confidence. To this end, in parallel with anomaly detection, the anomalies are explained based on rule learning algorithms.

In this work, a case study on the public transport system is investigated to evaluate the proposed framework. The case study includes four datasets collected from a fleet of Volvo city buses operated in traffic around a city on the west coast of Sweden between 2011 and 2014. For each bus, onboard data were collected from ten sensors, described in Table 1, where each sensor data with 1 Hz sampling rate was recorded while the engine was running in the bus, typically more than eight hours per day. We also have an off-board database containing Vehicle Service Record (VSR) information for evaluation of anomaly detection method. The

Table 1. Onboard sensors from Volvo city buses.

nr	Description	nr	Description
1	Wet Tank Air Pressure	2	Longitud Acc
3	Engine Speed	4	Fuel Rate
5	Engine Load	6	Boost Pressure
7	Engine Air Inlet Pressure	8	Accelerator Pedal Position
9	Vehicle Speed	10	Brake Pedal Position

VSR database includes repair and maintenance services, date of service, mileage, and unique part identifiers. In our case, the buses spent about 1.5 months per year in workshops on average. It can be expected that a rapid and accurate diagnosis of the part that needs repair can reduce the total downtime by 50 %.

The anomaly detection framework carries out data pre-processing, develops a network to several aggregate features obtained from sensor readings, detects abnormalities in the data stream that might be indicators of imminent faults, and uses the identified normal data in the network retraining for updating parameters. Finally, the anomaly explanation framework applies the features and anomaly score of the model as input to generate the root cause of each anomaly.

4   From Fault Detection to Anomaly Explanation

Figure 1 presents the global architecture of our system. The figure details the two layers of the system. The Detection layer is based on the reconstruction error of the LSTM-AE network. It assumes that rare and high extreme values of the reconstruction error (re) is a potential indicator of failures. The second layer receives as independent variables (X) the input features of the LSTM-AE network, and the dependent variable (y) is the corresponding reconstruction error. We learn a transparent model that learns a mapping $y = f(X)$. Both layers run online and in parallel, which means that for each observation, based on the reconstruction error, our system produces a classification regarding whether it is faulty and inputs it to AMRules, an online rule learning algorithm. This architecture allows two levels of explanations: i) Global level: the set of rules learned that explains the conditions to observe high predicted values; and ii) Local level: which rules are triggered for a particular input.

An essential characteristic of this problem is that failures are rare events. It is expected that an LSTM-AE trained with normal operating conditions would struggle to reconstruct the input when it receives an abnormal operating condition. Thus, the reconstructed error is expected to be higher for such cases.

Our goal is to obtain explanations focused on cases with high and extreme reconstruction error because that can indicate a potential failure. This particularity of having a non-uniform preference across the target variable domain and the focus being on scarcely represented values configures an Imbalanced

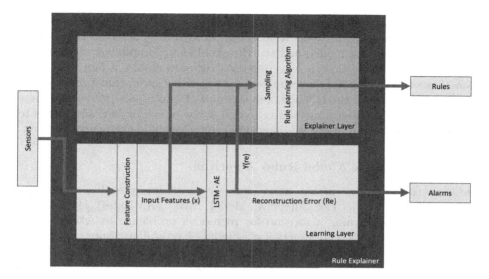

Fig. 1. Global architecture of the online anomaly explanation system. The bottom panel details the fault detection system, while the top panel details the explanation system. Both systems run online and in parallel.

domain learning problem [15]. As reported in many related studies in the area [3], standard machine learning approaches and evaluation metrics hinder the performance in the most relevant cases. They thus are not suitable to address predictive tasks from imbalanced domains. From the learning perspective, two main approaches for tackling this type of task exist: data-level and algorithm-level. This work resorted to data-level approaches applied to the rule learning algorithm and used a specific error metric to cope with imbalanced domain learning.

In the following subsections, we first describe the online anomaly detection and then explain the online rule learning algorithm, the applied sampling techniques, and the used evaluation metric to properly assess the effectiveness of our approach in an imbalanced data streams regression scenario [1].

4.1   Fault Detection Based on LSTM-AE

In the online fault detection framework, we use the normal data stream in a predetermined long-time window for initial training of the LSTM-AE network to capture the time series' temporal characteristics. The reconstruction error, the divergence between the input features and the reconstructed one, is applied to update the model parameters and compute the anomaly score for each sliding window. The root mean square of the reconstruction error RMSE_{re} for the training dataset is used to estimate a threshold value (thr_{re}) through a boxplot analysis to label data [16]. The boxplot is a consistent method to display the distribution of the dataset, which can be used to ignore extreme observations. Next, the test data is employed to examine the network performance. If the RMSE_{re}

of a time window i is larger than the threshold $(i - 1)$, then the window i is considered an anomalous observation. Then, normal data detected is passed to retrain the LSTM-AE model, and the threshold thr_{re} is updated; the learning procedure is repeated once a new test data set is available. Adaptive estimation of the threshold can follow the new data distribution in that time window. Finally, the output of the labeling step is inputted into a post-processing phase to decrease the false alarm rates. To this end, a low pass filter is implemented to remove the sudden variations and unwanted components in the network output.

4.2   The Adaptive Model Rules Algorithm

Decision rules are one of the most expressive and interpretable models for machine learning [6]. The Adaptive Model Rules (AMRules) [4] was the first stream rule learning algorithm for regression problems. In AMRules the antecedent of a rule is a conjunction of conditions on the attribute values. The consequent can be a constant (the mean of the target variable) or a linear combination of the attributes. The set of rules learned by AMRules can be ordered or unordered. They employ different prediction strategies to achieve 'optimal' prediction. In the case of ordered rules, only the first rule that covers an example is used to predict the target value. In the case of unordered rules, all rules covering the example are used for prediction, and the final prediction is decided by aggregating predictions using the mean.

Each rule in AMRules implements three prediction strategies: $i)$ the mean of the target attribute computed from the examples covered by the rule; $ii)$ a linear combination of the independent attributes; $iii)$ an adaptive strategy that chooses between the first two strategies, the one with the lower mean absolute error (MAE) in the previous examples. In this case, the MAE is computed following a fading factor strategy. We use the implementation of AMRules available in [11].

The standard AMRules algorithm learns rules to minimize the mean squared error loss function. In the predictive maintenance context, the relevant cases are failures, rare events characterized by large values of the reconstruction error. We aim to apply AMRules to predict the obtained reconstruction error as the target value from the original set of features. The most important cases that constitute potential failures have high and extreme target values. We want our model to focus on those cases, even though they are rare. The following section explains two sampling strategies to learn from rare events.

4.3   Online Sampling Strategies for Extreme Values Cases

Few approaches to learning from imbalanced data streams discuss the task of regression.

In this work, we use the approach described in [1], which resorts to Chebyshev's inequality as a heuristic to disclose the type of incoming cases (i.e., frequent or rare). It guarantees that in any probability distribution, 'nearly all' values are close to the mean. More precisely, no more than $\frac{1}{t^2}$ of the distribution's values can be more than t times standard deviations away from the mean.

This property substantiates the fact that extreme values are rare. Although conservative, the inequality can be applied to completely arbitrary distributions (unknown except for mean and variance).

Let Y be a random variable with finite expected value $\overline{y}$ and finite non-zero variance σ^2. Then, Chebyshev's inequality states that for any real number $t > 0$, we have:

$$\Pr(|y - \overline{y}| \geq t\sigma) \leq \frac{1}{t^2} \tag{1}$$

Only the case $t > 1$ is helpful in the above inequality. In cases $t < 1$, the right-hand side is greater than one, and thus the statement will be "always true" as the probability of any event cannot be greater than one. Another "always true" case of inequality is when $t = 1$. In this case, the inequality changes to a statement saying that the probability of something is less than or equal to one, which is "always true".

For $t = \frac{|y - \overline{y}|}{\sigma}$ and $t > 1$, we define *frequency* score of observation $\langle x, y \rangle$ as:

$$P(|\overline{y} - y| \geq t) = \frac{1}{\left(\frac{|y - \overline{y}|}{\sigma}\right)^2} \tag{2}$$

The above definition states that the probability of observing y far from its mean is small, and it decreases as we get farther away from the mean.

In an imbalanced data streams regression scenario, considering the mean of target values of the examples in the data stream ($\overline{y}$), examples with rare extreme target values are more likely to occur far from the mean. In contrast, examples with frequent target values are closer to the mean. So, given the mean and variance of a random variable, Chebyshev's inequality can indicate the degree of the rarity of an observation. Its low and high values imply that the observation is probably a frequent or a rare case, respectively.

Having equipped with the heuristic to discover if an example is rare or frequent, the next step is to use such knowledge in training a regression model. In [1], authors proposed ChebyUS and ChebyOS, two sampling methods described in detail next.

ChebyUS: Chebyshev-Based Under-Sampling. This is an under-sampling method that only selects an incoming example for training the model if a randomly generated number in $[0, 1]$ is greater or equal to its Chebyshev's probability. As more examples are received, the statistics (i.e., mean and variance) computed incrementally [5] and, consequently, Chebyshev's probability is more stable and accurate. At the end of the model's training phase, it is expected that the model has been trained over approximately the same portion of frequent and rare cases.

ChebyOS: Chebyshev-Based Over-Sampling. Another proposed method [1] to make a balanced data stream is to over-sample rare cases of the incoming imbalanced data stream. Since those rare cases in data streams can be discovered by their Chebyshev's probability, they can be easily over-sampled by replication. Examples that are not as far from the mean as the variance are probably frequent cases. They contribute only once in the learner's training process while the others contribute more times[1].

4.4   Evaluation

As stated before, errors over rare and relevant cases in imbalanced domains are more costly, and this means that, in this setting, it is reasonable to assign a higher weight to the errors of rare cases. With this aim, we use the relevance function $\phi : \mathcal{Y} \to [0,1]$ introduced in [14] as a weight function to each example's target in the Root Mean Square Error (RMSE). We use the proposed automatic method [14,15] based on a boxplot to obtain the relevance function that specifies values in the tail(s) of the distribution of target variable as regions of interest.

As an evaluation metric, we have used both the standard RMSE and the RMSE$_\phi$ - $\phi()$ weighted version of this function where the prediction error for each example is multiplied by the relevance value assigned to that example, as follows:

$$\text{RMSE}_\phi = \sqrt{\frac{1}{n} \sum_{i=1}^{n} \phi(y_i) \times (y_i - \hat{y}_i)^2}, \qquad (3)$$

where y_i, $\hat{y}_i$ and $\phi(y_i)$ refer to the true value, the predicted value and relevance value for i-th example in the data set, respectively.

Figure 2 depicts the summary of values associated with a numeric variable according to its distribution. In particular, based on the boxplot, we have: the inverse of Chebyshev's probability used in the under-sampling approach (ChebyUs); the computed K value used in the over-sampling approach (ChebyOs); and the relevance function $\phi()$ derived automatically from the boxplot.

5   Experimental Results

We evaluated the architecture proposed in Fig. 1 where AMRules learns a rule set in parallel with the LSTM-AE.

The components used to create the processing pipelines are available in River[2]. In all the cases, we selected the same set of hyperparameters for AMRules to provide a fair comparison. The interval between split attempts, n_{min}, was set

---

[1] The implementations of **ChebyOS** and **ChebyUS** used are available in River [11].
[2] https://riverml.xyz.

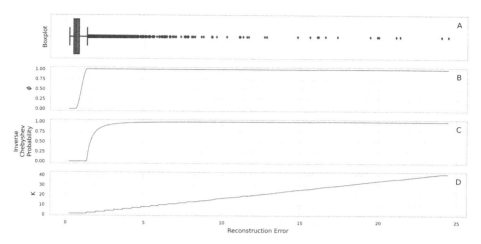

Fig. 2. A) Box plot for the target variable B) Data-points relevance C) Inverse Chebyshev probability used by the under-sampling approach D) K-value used in the over-sampling approach.

to 100. The split confidence parameter, δ, was set 0.05, and the selected prediction strategy was the target mean. As a feature splitter algorithm, we relied on the Truncated Extended Binary Search Tree (TE-BST) [9]. ADWIN [2] was the selected concept-drift detector for the AMRules models. All the remaining hyper-parameters were kept at their default values, as defined in River. All the used scripts are also publicly available, with instructions to reproduce our experiments.[3] In our experiments, we used four datasets collected from Volvo Buses. In the proposed incremental learning procedure, the LSTM-AE is initially trained by a large normal dataset (about one month) and a sliding time window with a length of three minutes is selected to extract the features. Next, test data with a length of at least three minutes (which may contain abnormal data) is inputted into the LSTM-AE model to predict normal/abnormal data. Previously, we examined many network designs for the LSTM-AE, which were consistent with the experimental datasets. Finally, we chose the network topology that leads to the best performance in the learning and prediction stages. The tuned parameters of LSTM-AE are summarised in Table 2. Then, the detected normal data can be used to retrain the model and whenever enough normal data set is available the training procedure is repeated incrementally.

We start our discussion by reporting the measured RMSE and RMSE_ϕ values when predicting the reconstruction errors of the LSTM-AE. Next, we discuss the global and local explanations obtained from our models.

---

[3] https://anonymous.4open.science/r/XPdM-AMRules/README.md.

Table 2. Parameters of the LSTM-AE.

Parameter	Value
Nodes in input layer	160
Neurons in the 1st hidden layer	120
Neurons in the 2nd hidden layer	60
Neurons in the 3rd hidden layer	30
Neurons in the Bottleneck layer	15
Dropout	20%
Learning rate	1e-3
Batch size	100
Number of epochs	300

5.1   Feature Extraction

Feature extraction aims to discover or generate distinguishable vectors to characterize the raw observation of the sensors. Feature extraction is of extreme importance in determining the accuracy of the model. The most appropriate features should be chosen from a wide range of features, so that machine training leads to precise decision-making. The feature selection transforms raw data into meaningful information which leads to performing the classification task with the least errors. Proper feature extraction can be challenging in data stream analysis due to the observations' dynamic and/or non-stationary nature. In our high-dimensional datasets, there are some insignificant and unimportant characteristics in time-series raw data whose contribution toward overfitting is almost great and the training of network with this type of feature takes more time. Therefore, In this work, we extracted statistical features, the mean, the standard deviation, the skewness, the kurtosis, and the deciles, for each sensor in a sliding time window. Note that the assumed normal distribution is divided into tenths in the computation of deciles. Thus, 13 statistical features are computed for each sensor through the feature extraction step, i.e., the dimension of the matrix extracted from this step is 10×13. Table 3 shows the statistical features in a sliding time window for 10 sensors. Finally, statistical features are fed into the LSTM-AE network and the rule learning algorithm to detect and explain the suspicious activity.

5.2   Error Measurements

We report in Table 4 the RMSE and $RMSE_\phi$ results measured while training the different regressors. The threshold $t_\phi = 0.8$ was selected to the relevance of $RMSE_\phi$, as previously reported in [1]. In other words, we are interested in the predictive performance of values whose relevance is higher than 0.8. We used sliding windows of size 1000 examples to compute the metrics.

As expected, the standard AMRules algorithm yielded the smallest values of RMSE in comparison with the AMRules with ChebyUS and ChebyOS sampling

Table 3. Statistical features extracted in a sliding time window with length n and per sensor, with the following notation: `metric.j`, where `metric` is the statistical feature and `j`$= 1, \ldots, 10$ refers to each one of the sensors indicated in Table 1.

Feature	Description	Value
`m.j`	mean	$\bar{x} = \frac{1}{n} \sum_{k=1}^{n} x_k$
`std.j`	Standard deviation	$\sigma = \sqrt{\sum_{k=1}^{n} \frac{(x_k - \bar{x})^2}{n}}$
`Skew.j`	skewness	$skew = \frac{\sum_{k=1}^{n}(x_k - \bar{x})^3}{n\sigma^3}$
`Kurt.j`	kurtosis	$kurt = \frac{\sum_{k=1}^{n}(x_k - \bar{x})^4}{n\sigma^4}$
`Decil.j-r`	decile	$decil = \frac{r}{10}(n+1)^{th}\ term, \quad r = 1, \ldots, 9$
`Quart.j-r`	quartil	$quartil = \frac{r}{4}(n+1)^{th}\ term, \quad r = 1, \ldots, 3$

Table 4. RMSE and RMSEϕ, with $t_\phi = 0.8$, for four bus data sets, according to standard AMRules, and ChebyUS and ChebyOS applied to AMRules. The bold values are the best results by bus and error metric.

Bus	RMSE			RMSE$_\phi$ $(t_\phi = 0.8)$		
	AMRules	ChebyUS + AMRules	ChebyOS + AMRules	AMRules	ChebyUS + AMRules	ChebyOS + AMRules
369	**0.3048**	1.4960	0.4171	0.8215	**0.7894**	1.2127
370	0.8497	3.2848	**0.8015**	2.4741	3.1210	**2.3349**
371	**0.6126**	2.9007	1.7285	**1.5530**	1.7574	4.5358
372	0.8796	2.2651	**0.8341**	2.5420	**2.0597**	2.3769

strategies. RMSE privileges models that produce outputs close to the mean value of the target, which is often the desideratum for regression. However, in imbalanced regression tasks, the extremes of the target variable distribution are the focus. In our case, the highest values of reconstruction error are indications of potential failures in the buses. When we look to RMSE$_\phi$, the gains of the re-sampling strategies become clear. Although our main goal was not predictive performance properly, models with smaller values of RMSE$_\phi$ ought to produce more reliable explanations for the failures.

In Table 5 we have the impacts of applying ChebyUS or ChebyOS strategies. Even though these are reference values, as time and memory measurements may slightly differ if the experiments are performed multiple times, we observe that we have reduced the amount of memory consumed by the model for both strategies. We get a negligible difference for the run time in the case of ChebyOS.

Table 5. Impacts of re-sampling strategies when measured as relative changes in the results obtained for the traditional AMRules Values smaller than one mean the re-sampling strategy was more computationally efficient than AMRules, whereas values over one imply AMRules was more the most efficient regressor.

Bus	Relative Memory			Relative Time		
	AMRules	ChebyUS + AMRules	ChebyOS + AMRules	AMRules	ChebyUS + AMRules	ChebyOS + AMRules
369	1.0	0.0210	0.4591	1.0	0.0163	0.8191
370	1.0	0.0186	0.5881	1.0	0.0174	1.0130
371	1.0	0.0679	0.5697	1.0	0.0318	0.9519
372	1.0	0.1018	0.3629	1.0	0.0511	0.9933

5.3 Global Explanations

In all the four datasets collected from Volvo Buses, AMRules without Chebyshev sampling generated large rule sets, with just a few rules predicting a large reconstruction error.

In Table 6 we present the number of rules learned for each bus and the different configurations of AMRules. After processing the available data, the rules we report in this section are the final rule sets. They reproduce the LSTM-AE network behaviour and reflect when and why LSTM-AE predict high values. They are a global explanation of the failures. Note that the threshold thr_{re} is obtained by applying the boxplot in $RMSE_{re}$ as explained in Sect. 4.1.

Table 6. The number of rules learned for each bus and for the different configurations of AMRules. We indicate the percent of rules with consequent higher than thr_{re} - the reconstruction error threshold - around parenthesis.

Bus	thr_{re}	AMRules	ChebyUS + AMRules	ChebyOS + AMRules
369	1.1124	38 (21.05%)	2 (100.0%)	21 (33.33%)
370	1.2152	61 (22.95%)	1 (100.0%)	55 (43.54%)
371	1.1246	32 (09.38%)	2 (100.0%)	30 (40.00%)
372	1.1492	40 (17.50%)	4 (75.00%)	27 (55.56%)

Below, we present two sets of unordered rules obtained as global explanations for two buses (Bus 371 and 372) using Chebyshev-based sampling with AMRules.

Global Explanation 1: Bus 371, ChebyUS+AMRules

```
Rule 0: IF Decil.6_6 <= 3.8 THEN 2.8473
Rule 1: IF Decil.7_8 > 0.6 THEN 11.0998
```

Global Explanation 2: Bus 372, ChebyOS+AMRules

```
Rule 1: IF m.3 > 640.5 AND Decil.10_7 > 51.4 AND kurt.10 > 78.7 THEN 0.7616
Rule 5: IF Decil.10_1 > 12.9 THEN 40.7956
Rule 6: IF Decil.8_9 > 10.9 THEN 39.9092
Rule 10: IF m.4 > 24.5 AND m.1 > 8.7 AND m.1 <= 10.0 THEN 1.9024
Rule 11: IF Decil.3_1 > 66.4 AND m.4 > 25.9 THEN 0.9386
```

In both cases, some rules predict large values of the reconstruction error. These rules predict potential failures and are pretty simple. In the first case, with ChebyUS+AMRules, all rules are focused on large reconstruction errors. While in the second case, ChebyOS+AMRules generates rules focused on failures and normal cases.

5.4 Local Explanations

Local explanations refer to the rules that are triggered by a given an example. When, for a specific example, the reconstruction error of the LSTM-AE exceeds a threshold, the system outputs the rule or rules that were triggered by that example. Below, we present a few examples.

Local Explanation 1: Bus 370, ChebyOS+AMRules, instance 86077, y=4.3597

```
Rule 5: IF Decil.10_4 <= 12.4 THEN 1.2838
Rule 33: IF kurt.1 > 1.0 THEN 0.7656
Rule 34: IF Decil.9_9 <= 8.2 THEN 1.4498
Rule 35: IF Decil.4_4 <= 9.7 THEN 0.8471
Rule 36: IF Decil.10_7 <= 46.4 THEN 0.9069
Rule 37: IF Decil.10_3 <= 4.2 THEN 17.2866

Final prediction: 3.7566
```

Local Explanation 2: Bus 372, ChebyUS+AMRules, instance 53813, y=4.3069

```
Rule 1: IF Decil.6_7 > 0.1 THEN 4.9463
Rule 2: IF Decil.5_3 > 0.2 THEN 2.8791

Final prediction: 3.9127
```

Local Explanation 3: Bus 372, AMRules, instance 26938, y = 48.0100

```
Rule 2: IF Skew.4 <= 1.9 and Decil.5_7 <= 693.3 and Quart.7_3 <= 10.9 THEN 1.2508
Rule 5: IF Decil.4_5 > 0.1 THEN 2.6736
Rule 7: IF Decil.9_6 <= 50.0 and m.1 <= 10.3 THEN 1.6335
Rule 11: IF Decil.9_6 <= 52.8 and m.1 <= 8.9 THEN 1.3419
Rule 12: IF Decil.4_7 <= 6.0 and m.1 <= 8.9 THEN 1.1995
Rule 15: IF Skew.10 > -0.2 and Decil.4_4 <= 8.0 THEN 0.8850
Rule 16: IF Decil.10_8 <= 15.3 THEN 0.8623

Final prediction: 1.4067
```

Local Explanation 4: Bus 372, ChebyUS+AMRules, instance 26938, y = 48.0100

```
Rule 1: IF Decil.6_7 > 0.1 THEN 5.2619
```

Local Explanation 5: Bus 372, ChebyOS+AMRules, instance 26938, y = 48.0100

```
Rule 5: IF Decil.10_1 > 12.9 THEN 40.7956
Rule 6: IF Decil.8_9 > 10.9 THEN 39.8575
Rule 9: IF Decil.10_2 <= 597.9 THEN 1.9486

Final prediction: 27.5339
```

It is worth noting that, for *Local Explanation 1* and *Local Explanation 2*, most of the rules generated for high reconstruction errors have a single condition.

The three *Local Explanations 3, 4 and 5* refer to the same instance of the Bus 372 dataset with the approaches AMRules, ChebyUS+AMRules and ChebyOS+AMRules, respectively. None of the approaches accurately predicted the reconstruction error. The rules predict reconstruction errors distant from the observed value. Rule 5 of *Local Explanation 5*, is the rule with the highest output, but the other rules attenuate its influence.

In *Local Explanation 4*, ChebyUS+AMRules triggered only one out of the four rules that compose its ruleset (cf. Table 6). Although not close to the actual reconstruction error, its output is higher than the one predicted by the standard AMRules and can indicate a failure.

Finally, the rules triggered by ChebyOS+AMRules in *Local Explanation 5*, were the most accurate among the three regressors compared for this measure. The predicted reconstruction error is much higher than the two previous models yet far from the actual observed value. The two first triggered rules alone would provide much better estimates. However, as we have chosen an unordered ruleset, the output of Rule 9 decreased the overall prediction.

The choice of an ordered ruleset could be a solution for this specific case. Alternatively, AMRules could use other strategies to aggregate predictions of individual rules. A simple solution would be using the median value rather than the arithmetic mean. As a more complex solution, one could create regression models that take the rules' predictions as inputs and output the final prediction.

The bus 372 dataset contains 89864 instances, from which only 37 have reconstruction errors above 20. Such high reconstruction errors account for only 0.04117% of the available data. Still, ChebyUS + AMRules and mainly ChebyOS + AMRules could predict high reconstruction error values.

5.5   Discussion

The case study clearly illustrates that we can identify and interpret anomalies in real-time. Overall, the rules that were obtained for the anomalies are compact, i.e. based on few conditions and, moreover, based on a restricted set of sensors. For example, in these sets of rules, sensor 2 (Longitud Acc) never appeared while others sensors appeared more often, such as sensors 4 (Fuel Rate), 9 (Vehicle Speed) and 10 (Brake Pedal Position). Also, it is worth to note that the conditions are mostly on statistical features that do not conform the average behavior of the sensor, which could be indicated by the mean or standard deviation statistics. In effect, most of the rules rely on statistical features that reflect the deviation from the average, i.e. `Kurt`, `Skew`, `Decil`, which might be in line with an indication of an evolving failure.

The proposed sampling strategy improves the learning of rules for rare cases. Comparing the two sampling strategies, ChebyUS+AMRules produces a more compact rule set without being as effective as ChebyOS+AMRules to predict normal cases. Also, ChebyOS+AMRules might take longer to train in comparison with the standard AMRules. ChebyUS+AMRules is the fastest approach.

It is important to highlight that the two learning systems, the deep learning and the rule learning system, are complementary. The LSTM-AE works in unsupervised mode using data from the normal behavior. The role of LSTM-AE is to detect non-normal data. The rule learner works in supervised mode, where the target is the reconstruction error of the LSTM-AE computed in real-time. The role is to learn a function that maps the input features to the output of the LSTM-AE. We cannot replace the LSTM-AE with the rule system because they play different roles.

6 Conclusions

With the development of the internet of things, manufacturing technology, and mass production, the methodology of maintenance scheduling and management has become an important topic in the industry. In these contexts, there is an urgent need for understanding and trust models and their results [10].

One of the common approaches taken in data-driven predictive maintenance (PdM) is to learn the normal operating condition. Any large deviation from that operating condition could be a potential failure. One of the methods to attain this is by learning LSTM-AE on the normal examples of operation. The intuition is that if we give an abnormal example of operation, the reconstruction error of the LSTM-AE will be very high. Those examples are relevant from the PdM perspective and are, typically, rare. This configures an imbalanced data stream regression problem, where only very few studies exist.

In this paper, we propose an online system able to learn in parallel an LSTM-AE trained to identify anomalies and a regression rules algorithm that models the large values of the reconstruction error of LSTM-AE. The proposed model generates global explanations in the form of a rule-set, and local explanations for any example, as the rule that triggered that example. The main contribution is that the rule learner algorithm is wrapped in a sampling schema, allowing for selection the of relevant examples. This is the main reason why the proposed framework works. We applied this methodology in a PdM scenario with data from Volvo city buses. Results showed that we could learn rules for the high values of the reconstruction error. These are the cases of interest.

The methodology we present is general enough to be applied to other online imbalanced streaming scenarios that use black-box models to predict peaks or bursts in events. We are exploring other scenarios outside PdM applications. Finally, interpretability and explainability are human-computer-interface problems. While decision rules have a high degree of understandability for computer-science people, we intend to translate the rules into a natural language to enlarge the scope of people that understand the messages.

Acknowledgments. This work was supported by the CHIST-ERA grant CHIST-ERA-19-XAI-012, and project CHIST-ERA/0004/2019 funded by FCT. This work was also supported by FAPESP grant 2021/10488-7.

References

1. Aminian, E., Ribeiro, R.P., Gama, J.: Chebyshev approaches for imbalanced data streams regression models. Data Mining Knowl. Discovery **35**(6), 2389–2466 (2021). https://doi.org/10.1007/s10618-021-00793-1
2. Bifet, A., Gavalda, R.: Learning from time-changing data with adaptive windowing. In: Proceedings of the 2007 SIAM International Conference on Data Mining, pp. 443–448. SIAM (2007)
3. Branco, P., Torgo, L., Ribeiro, R.P.: A survey of predictive modeling on imbalanced domains. ACM Comput. Surv. **49**(2), 1–50 (2016)
4. Duarte, J., Gama, J., Bifet, A.: Adaptive model rules from high-speed data streams. ACM Trans. Knowl. Discov. Data **10**(3), 1–22 (2016)
5. Finch, T.: Incremental calculation of weighted mean and variance. University of Cambridge Computing Service, Tech. rep. (2009)
6. Guidotti, R., Monreale, A., Ruggieri, S., Turini, F., Giannotti, F., Pedreschi, D.: A survey of methods for explaining black box models. ACM Comput. Surv. **51**(5), 1–42 (2019)
7. Hall, P., Gill, N.: An introduction to machine learning interpretability. O'Reilly Media, Incorporated (2019)
8. Lundberg, S.M., Lee, S.: A unified approach to interpreting model predictions. In: Guyon, I., von Luxburg, U., Bengio, S., Wallach, H.M., Fergus, R., Vishwanathan, S.V.N., Garnett, R. (eds.) Advances in Neural Information Processing Systems 30: Annual Conference on Neural Information Processing Systems 2017, pp. 4765–4774 (2017)
9. Mastelini, S.M., de Leon Ferreira, A.C.P., et al.: Using dynamical quantization to perform split attempts in online tree regressors. Pattern Recogn. Lett. 145, 37–42 (2021)
10. Molnar, C.: Interpretable machine learning. Independently published, 2 edn. (2022). https://christophm.github.io/interpretable-ml-book
11. Montiel, J., et al.: River: machine learning for streaming data in python (2020)
12. Moreira, C., Chou, Y.L., Velmurugan, M., Ouyang, C., Sindhgatta, R., Bruza, P.: An interpretable probabilistic approach for demystifying black-box predictive models. Decis. Support Syst. **150**, 113561 (2021)

13. Ribeiro, M.T., Singh, S., Guestrin, C.: "why should i trust you?": explaining the predictions of any classifier, pp. 1135–1144, KDD 2016. Association for Computing Machinery (2016)
14. Ribeiro, R.P.: Utility-based Regression, Ph. D. thesis, Dep. Computer Science, Faculty of Sciences - University of Porto (2011)
15. Ribeiro, R.P., Moniz, N.: Imbalanced regression and extreme value prediction. Mach. Learn. **109**(6), 1803–1835 (2020). https://doi.org/10.1007/s10994-020-05900-9
16. Ribeiro, R.P., Pereira, P., Gama, J.: Sequential anomalies: a study in the railway industry. Mach. Learn. **105**(1), 127–153 (2016)
17. Serradilla, O., Zugasti, E., Zurutuza, U.: Deep learning models for predictive maintenance: a survey, comparison, challenges and prospect (2020)

Fault Forecasting Using Data-Driven Modeling: A Case Study for Metro do Porto Data Set

Narjes Davari[1]([⊠]) [iD], Bruno Veloso[1,2,4] [iD], Rita P. Ribeiro[1,3] [iD],
and João Gama[1,4] [iD]

[1] INESC TEC, 4200-465 Porto, Portugal
narjes.davari@inesctec.pt
[2] University Portucalense, 4200-072 Porto, Portugal
[3] Faculty of Sciences, University of Porto, 4169-007 Porto, Portugal
[4] Faculty of Economics, University of Porto, 4200-464 Porto, Portugal

Abstract. The demand for high-performance solutions for anomaly detection and forecasting fault events is increasing in the industrial area. The detection and forecasting faults from time-series data are one critical mission in the Internet of Things (IoT) data mining. The classical fault detection approaches based on physical modelling are limited to some measurable output variables. Accurate physical modelling of vehicle dynamics requires substantial prior information about the system. On the other hand, data-driven modelling techniques accurately represent the system's dynamic from data collection. Experimental results on large-scale data sets from Metro do Porto subsystems verify that our method performs high-quality fault detection and forecasting solutions. Also, health indicator obtained from the principal component analysis of the forecasting solution is applied to predict the remaining useful life.

Keywords: Anomaly detection · Fault forecasting · System identification · Predictive maintenance

1 Introduction

Recent developments in smart manufacturing, the Internet of things (IoT), and big data have significantly increased, and with the growth of types of machinery, these systems' technical levels and complexity are enhanced. The system complexity causes new maintenance challenges. Predictive maintenance is a collection of operations that detect deviations in the physical state of equipment (signs of failure) and alerts to perform necessary maintenance work, which maximizes the equipment's service life while minimizing the risk of failure and increasing equipment availability and reliability. Failure in equipment results in unpredicted downtime and causes expensive operational and maintenance costs. Early detection of anomalies makes it possible to acquire advanced knowledge of the system's health and provides advanced maintenance possibilities through effective

I. Koprinska et al. (Eds.): ECML PKDD 2022 Workshops, CCIS 1753, pp. 400–409, 2023.
https://doi.org/10.1007/978-3-031-23633-4_26

real-time data. Thus, accurate and robust detection and prediction of anomalies are essential for detecting potential failures in industrial systems and proactive management of maintenance schedules. There are three anomaly detection methods, including model-based methods, knowledge-based methods, and data-driven methods.

Fault forecast, which tries to predict faults before they cause failure, is consequently crucial to ensuring the safety and reliability of equipment. Production forecasting for predictive maintenance purposes results from analyzing various data sets. Time-series data are the most common data type in the amount of data collected in different areas of Industry 4.0. Time-series data are referred to as observations sequentially recorded over time.

Time series sensor data from air compressor subsystems are used to detect real-time variations in the system's performance that may be symptomatic of a future failure in a metro train. Thus sensor-based condition monitoring can be necessary for the reliability of Metro train systems and improve safety. However, there is a demand for effective and robust techniques to detect and predict such variations in the time series data stream. In this paper, sensor data from some sensors installed on the inputs and outputs of an air compressor are used for anomaly detection and prediction. The focus is on unsupervised data-driven methods based on system identification, and the idea is to mathematical model system dynamics by using sensor data in normal operating conditions and assess whether new observations belong to the model.

The system identification is developed in the automatic control community [2]. Many accomplishments were achieved with linear system identification, and data-driven modelling became an enabler in current design methodologies. System identification allows users to create mathematical models of a dynamic system based on input and output signal measurements. In this case, a linear dynamic model is fitted to the observed changes in quantities, and new observations then evaluate the model. The main difference with machine learning (ML) techniques is that the system identification techniques deliver a parametric model. However, the ML prediction for a new input is supplied as a function of the data points used for the model's "training". Moreover, while ML approaches are more adaptable since they do not need the user to specify a structure, they have additional restrictions (e.g. computational effort) [5]. We review the most relevant and most recent works. Basseville et al. [1] address the problem of detecting faults in a linear dynamical system. They describe and analyze new fault detection algorithms based on recent stochastic subspace-based identification methods and the local statistical approach to the design of detection algorithms. Wei et al. [7] proposed a method for fault detection and isolation in three-bladed wind turbines with a horizontal axis. They built a dynamic model based on the closed-loop identification technique for a wind turbine. The fault detection issue is investigated based on the residuals generated by dual Kalman filters. Yang et al. [8] proposed a data-driven fault detection and isolation (FDI) method for distributed homogeneous systems. They developed the fault detection method according to the one-step identification of the stable kernel representation and evaluated the proposed method by numerical examples.

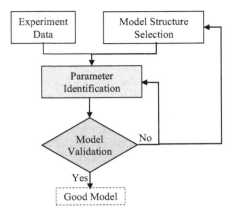

Fig. 1. System identification loop [4]

The main contribution of this work is the presentation of a state-space model (SSM) of an air compressor system using a system identification methodology based on the subspace identification method. Then SSM is applied to provide fault detection and forecasting. Also, the features of forecasted output are inserted into PCA for health indicator computation and RUL prediction.

The remainder of the paper is structured as follows: Sect. 2 reviews the system identification theory; next, the problem of dynamic modelling of compressor in the metro do Porto case study is investigated in Sect. 3; Sect. 4 demonstrate the experimental results for fault detection, forecasting, and RUL prediction. Finally, Sect. 5 give a conclusion of the work.

2   System Identification Theory

The system identification technique, a parametric model, creates a model using measured input-output data and is characterized by three main components: the data, a set of candidate models, and an estimation method. Also, a validation technique, which establishes confidence in the estimated model, should be included in these components [4]. It is critical to understand that no model can be a perfect representation of the actual system under consideration. The system identification loop is shown in Fig. 1. This model forecasts the system's future behaviour with new inputs. This section presents a highly organized, unified picture of data-driven modelling by quickly presenting these four components.

The Data: This system identification model requires data at the beginning of the process to build the model and at the end of the process to evaluate the model.

Model Structure: The identification of the data-driven model was accomplished in two steps. A closed-form subspace identification approach was used to establish state-space models with different orders. The subspace system identification approach has three main steps: diminish the effects of inputs on state sequence, reconstruct the state sequence, and estimate the model. The subspace identification method based on prediction error methods provides a good alternative to non-linear optimization [3]. In the second step, the parameters of the state-space models can be addressed as an optimization problem of a cost function. In practice, several models are trained, and the identification procedure essentially becomes the process of evaluating and selecting among the created models. The quality of the resultant model is greatly influenced by the quality of the signals to be monitored, the configuration of the input, and the collection of data using proper sampling techniques.

The subspace method aims to approximate the system's state sequence and then uses this approximate state to estimate the system matrices; it uses the numerical algorithms for subspace state-space system identification (N4SID), canonical variable analysis methods, and the orthogonal decomposition method. The SSM has the following structure:

$$\dot{\mathbf{x}}(t) = f(\mathbf{x}(t), \mathbf{u}(t), \mathbf{w}(t)), \tag{1}$$

$$\mathbf{y}(t) = g(\mathbf{x}(t)) + \mathbf{r}(t), \tag{2}$$

where $\mathbf{x}$, $\mathbf{u}$, and $\mathbf{y}$ are system state, the control input, and the measured output, respectively. $f(\cdot)$ is a nonlinear function that describes the system's dynamic behaviour, and $g(\cdot)$ is a nonlinear function of the state. $\mathbf{w}$ and $\mathbf{r}$ are the input noise and measurement noise due to uncertainty in the sensors' control input and output measurements, respectively.

An estimation from the parameters of the model is archived by minimizing the following cost function [6]:

$$\mathbf{J}(\theta) = \sum_{k=1}^{N} (\mathbf{y}(t) - \hat{\mathbf{y}}(t, \theta))^2, \tag{3}$$

where $y(t_k)$ is the measured outputs vector at time t_k and $\hat{y}(t_k, \theta)$ is the vector of corresponding simulated values at the same time instant, and θ used as a vector of candidate parameters.

3   Dynamic Modelling of Compressor in Our Case Study

A comprehensive model of the compressor is needed to identify the compressor's dynamic. The model should also be precise and sufficient to forecast the system's future behaviour under operational situations. SSM as a first-order differential equation is used to describe the dynamic behaviour of the compressor system. In the modelling procedure, a large part of the input-output normal dataset is applied for the model training and estimation of parameters. The subspace system identification technique estimates a linear time-varying SSM based on a data-driven which is a linearization of Eqs. (1) and (2). The model has the following structure:

$$\mathbf{x}(k+1) = A\mathbf{x}(k) + B\mathbf{u}(k) + K\mathbf{e}(k), \tag{4}$$

$$\mathbf{y}(k) = C\mathbf{x}(k) + D\mathbf{u}(k) + \mathbf{e}(k), \tag{5}$$

where $\mathbf{A}$ is a state matrix and determines the system's dynamics, B, C, D, and K are input, output, feed-forward, and disturbance matrices. The state variable $\mathbf{x}$ can be computed from input/output data, and they are not measured during an experiment. We should mention that θ in equation (3) is $\mathbf{A}, \mathbf{B}, \mathbf{C}, \mathbf{D}, \mathbf{K}$.

In our case study, the compressor is one of the main components in a train in which several sensors are positioned on input and output to monitor system behaviour. In this case, we considered two control inputs, "TP2", "COMP" and "TP3" as the output of the system. The real control inputs and real output are inputted to system identification method (see Fig. 2). "TP2" sensor measures the pressure on the compressor and "COMP" sensor distinguishes the different working modes of the compressor: active ("1") means the compressor is without load or turned off when there is no admission of air on the compressor, and inactive ("0") means the compressor is under load. "TP3" sensor measures the pressure generated at the pneumatic panel. Figure 3 shows control inputs and measured output over time. To obtain the parameters of the model, a large normal input and output dataset (similar to what is shown in Fig. 3) is applied for training the model and also the number of required states to identify the system (order of the model) is important to obtain a model that shows the right dynamic of the system. An algebraic method using the input-output data is performed to obtain the system's order and then check whether this value is sufficient to represent the system.

$$n = rank(\mathbf{Y}^T \mathbf{U}^\perp) \tag{6}$$

where n is the order of the system, $\mathbf{Y}$ and $\mathbf{U}^\perp$ are the output data matrix and the orthogonal matrix from input data, respectively. In this case study, the minimum order of the model is obtained "2". The extracted second-order SSM with estimated parameters for the compressor system is shown in Eqs. 7 and 8.

$$\mathbf{x}(k+1) = \begin{bmatrix} -0.006216 & 0.04267 \\ 0.03569 & -0.3455 \end{bmatrix} \mathbf{x}(k) + \begin{bmatrix} -1.77e-5 & 4.302e-5 \\ -1.313e-5 & -0.001 \end{bmatrix} \mathbf{u}(k)$$
$$+ \begin{bmatrix} -0.005799 \\ -0.04791 \end{bmatrix} \mathbf{e}(k), \tag{7}$$

$$\mathbf{y}(k) = \begin{bmatrix} -179.6 & -0.186 \end{bmatrix} \mathbf{x}(k) + \begin{bmatrix} 0 \end{bmatrix} \mathbf{u}(k) + \mathbf{e}(k) \tag{8}$$

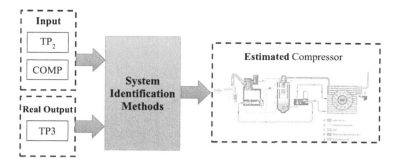

Fig. 2. Inputs and output of system identification algorithm.

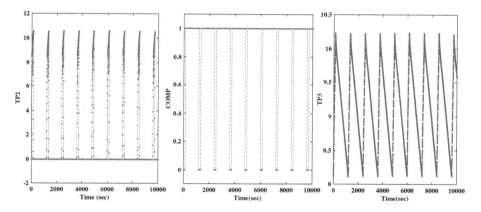

Fig. 3. The control inputs, a) TP2, b) COMP, the measured output, c) TP3.

In Fig. 4 the real output and estimated output ("TP3") by the extracted SSM is shown. In this comparison the fit percentage between real and estimated value is about 80%. It is clear that the extracted model based on data driven has high accuracy.

4   Experimental Results

In this section, we want to use the extracted SSM to detect and forecast faulty data. In this way, some data with abnormal behaviour is inputted into the model for the evaluation of SSM, and its response is investigated. Figure 5 shows a time window with a length of one day that contains both normal and abnormal data. At the beginning of the window, the estimated output by SSM follows actual normal output and abnormal parts of data (high-frequency part and constant part) can not follow by the extracted model (see blue curve).

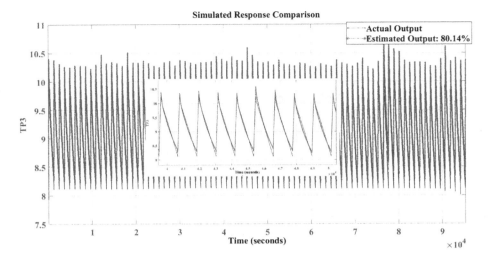

Fig. 4. Comparison of real output and estimated output.

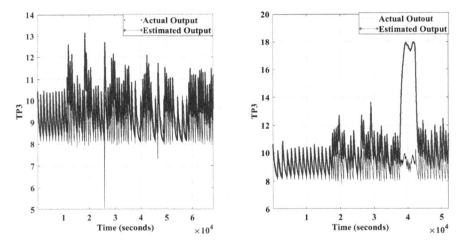

Fig. 5. A time window contains normal and abnormal data for actual and estimated output ("TP3").

In the prediction phase, output and input measurements are applied to project a future response. Figure 6 shows the 3600-step predicted response by the SSM. The number of "step" represents the number of time samples between the time point of each actual output measurement and the time point of the resulting predicted response. The predicted output show prediction from an abnormality in 3600-step (second) before being seen in the system output, and then we can conclude the model can predict abnormal data at least one hour in advance.

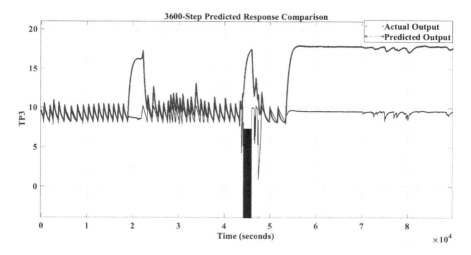

Fig. 6. 3600-step predicted response by the extracted SSM.

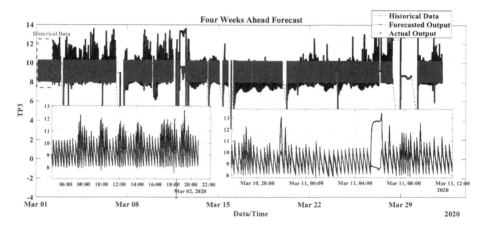

Fig. 7. Four-weeks ahead the forecasted output of compressor.

In the forecast phase, see Fig. 7, a prediction into the future output in a time range beyond the last instant of measured data is performed. Among the most widely used approaches for time series forecasting, we use the autoregressive integrated moving average (ARIMA) model and past measured data and future inputs are applied to the model. We can observe in the Figure the initial chunk of data "Historical Data" used to train the model. The blue line is the actual output, and the black line is the output of the ARIMA. Looking at the predicted output, the ARIMA model highlights the abnormal behaviour and failure of the APU with values out of range in normal operation mode.

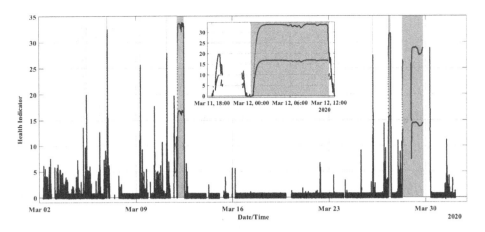

Fig. 8. Health Indicator over time, the pink rectangles are failure reports.

On the other hand, the prediction of the remaining useful life (RUL) of the monitored compressor in the time domain through the extracted SSM model is crucial. The statistical features (i.e., mean, standard deviation, skewness, kurtosis, and decile) obtained from the forecasted output are used to construct the health indicator (HI) to indicate the degradation of the system components. HI is used to predict the RUL of the compressor. In order to reduce the computational time and determine the principal components of features, principal component analysis (PCA) is performed. PCA applies the orthogonal linear transformation on the features so that the data with the most considerable variance becomes the first coordinate variance (principal component 1), the following most significant variance lies as the second coordinate (principal component 2), and so on. As the first principal component (PC1) consists of 90% of the variability of the forecasted output has been chosen as the HI. Figure 8 represents the preliminary result of the obtained HI for about one month. The rectangles highlighted with pink show failures reported by the maintenance workshop. It can be observed from the zoomed window that HI exhibits a regular expected trend. If we consider a threshold value over 5, It can be observed that the predicted HI trend reaches the threshold value on the 11th of March at 18:30.

5   Conclusion

In this study, the dynamic of a compressor is modelled based on data-driven system identification. Data-driven modelling approaches generate an accurate description of the dynamics of the system from a set of data. Experimental outcomes on large-scale data sets from Metro do Porto subsystems confirm that the extracted model performs high-quality fault detection and forecasting. Also, a health indicator was constructed in order to predict the RUL of the compressor. Different statistical features were computed from the forecasted output obtained from the compressor system's model. Principal component analysis was performed, and the first principal components from the input feature were considered a health indicator.

Acknowledgements. This work was supported by the CHIST-ERA grant CHIST-ERA-19-XAI-012, and project CHIST-ERA/0004/2019 funded by FCT.

References

1. Basseville, M., Abdelghani, M., Benveniste, A.: Subspace-based fault detection algorithms for vibration monitoring. Automatica **36**(1), 101–109 (2000)
2. Ding, S.X., Zhang, P., Naik, A., Ding, E.L., Huang, B.: Subspace method aided data-driven design of fault detection and isolation systems. J. Process Control **19**(9), 1496–1510 (2009)
3. Keyvaani, H., Mohammadi, A., Pariz, N.: Identification of modal series model of nonlinear systems based on subspace algorithms. J. Appl. Sci. **10**(11), 909–914 (2010)
4. Ljung, L.: System identification. In: Rayner, P.W.J., Kingsbury, N.G. (eds) Signal Analysis and Prediction. Applied and Numerical Harmonic Analysis, pp. 163–173. Springer, Boston (1998). https://doi.org/10.1007/978-1-4612-1768-8_11
5. Ljung, L., Andersson, C., Tiels, K., Schön, T.B.: Deep learning and system identification. IFAC-PapersOnLine **53**(2), 1175–1181 (2020)
6. Vicente, B.A.H., James, S.S., Anderson, S.R.: Linear system identification versus physical modeling of lateral-longitudinal vehicle dynamics. IEEE Trans. Control Syst. Technol. **29**(3), 1380–1387 (2020)
7. Wei, X., Verhaegen, M., van Engelen, T.: Sensor fault detection and isolation for wind turbines based on subspace identification and kalman filter techniques. Int. J. Adapt. Control Signal Process. **24**(8), 687–707 (2010)
8. Yang, X., Gao, J., Huang, B.: Data-driven design of fault detection and isolation method for distributed homogeneous systems. J. Franklin Inst. **358**(9), 4929–4949 (2021)

An Online Data-Driven Predictive Maintenance Approach for Railway Switches

Emanuel Sousa Tomé[1,2]($\boxtimes$) ![ORCID], Rita P. Ribeiro[1,2]![ORCID], Bruno Veloso[2,3,4]![ORCID], and João Gama[2,3]![ORCID]

[1] Faculty of Sciences, University of Porto, 4169-007 Porto, Portugal
{emanuel.tome,rpribeiro}@fc.up.pt
[2] INESC TEC, 4200-465 Porto, Portugal
[3] Faculty of Economics, University of Porto, 4200-464 Porto, Portugal
jgama@fep.up.pt
[4] University Portucalense, 4200-072 Porto, Portugal

Abstract. An online data-driven predictive maintenance approach for railway switches using data logs obtained from the interlocking system of the railway infrastructure is proposed in this paper. The proposed approach is detailed described and consists of a two-phase process: anomaly detection and remaining useful life prediction. The approach is applied to and validated in a real case study, the Metro do Porto, from which seven months of data is available. The approach has been revealed to be satisfactory in detecting anomalies. The results open the possibilities for further studies and validation with a more extensive dataset on the remaining useful life prediction.

Keywords: Predictive maintenance · Remaining useful life · Online learning · Log Data · Railway switches

1 Introduction

The infrastructure systems such as the railways' infrastructures are vital elements in modern societies, driving social and economic development. Due to the growing service demands, rapid deterioration provoked by extensive usage, and little maintenance due to budget restrictions, the need for infrastructure maintenance is continuously growing [2]. Moreover, the way decisions are taken in the industry has been changing due to the increasing availability of data [18]. Due to these reasons, there is a considerable need for modern tools to assist asset managers in taking maintenance decisions effectively and efficiently.

In this context, predictive maintenance, which uses Machine Learning and Artificial Intelligence tools for modelling system behaviour, discovering trends, and predicting failures [6], emerges as a promising technology to increase the safety and reliability of infrastructure systems. ML models can be used not only for fault detection but also for fault prediction, such as the estimation of the

© The Author(s), under exclusive license to Springer Nature Switzerland AG 2023
I. Koprinska et al. (Eds.): ECML PKDD 2022 Workshops, CCIS 1753, pp. 410–422, 2023.
https://doi.org/10.1007/978-3-031-23633-4_27

Remaining Useful Life (RUL). RUL can be defined as the time left before the machinery loses its operation ability [14]. Usually, techniques for estimating the RUL are classified into physics-based, data-driven and hybrid approaches [14]. The physics-based approach requires the development of a behavioural model of the failure mechanism, for example, through finite element analysis. However, these models can be very expensive since they could require a great amount of engineering time [17]. Data-driven models are usually based on historical data and do not require an analytical model. Therefore, in this work, we follow a data-driven approach.

Given the significant impacts of the malfunction of railway switches on railway operation [2,11,15], this topic has been receiving increasing attention over the last years. However, the PdM approaches for railway infrastructures found in the literature usually require the installation of complementary sensory systems, which turns the proposed strategies expensive and not saleable to the whole network [2]. Moreover, it is not always obvious what and how should be instrumented. In many cases, expensive and time-consuming physics-based models are necessary to decide what and how to instrument and interpret the obtained results.

In this work, we propose a two-stage PdM approach that uses only data logs available from the normal operation of the railway infrastructure, particularly for railway switches. The first phase consists of an anomaly detector and the second phase correspond to the Remaining Useful Life (RUL) prediction. We apply the developed approach to a real case study, the Metro do Porto, from which seven months of data is available.

The paper is organised as follows. An overview of the related work is provided in Sect. 2. The third section describes the case study of Metro do Porto as well as the proposed approach for anomaly detection and prediction of the RUL of railway switches using log data. Section 4 presents the obtained experimental results, and Sect. 5 the achieved conclusions and future works.

2   Related Work

Railway switches are considered critical track elements on the railway network [2,12] since their failure significantly affects train operation and safety [1,3]. A railway switch, also known as a point machine, allows different train routes by driving the switchblade from one position to the opposite position [3].

Several data-driven approaches for anomaly detection in railway switches have been proposed over the last few years. Many studies use traditional ML for anomaly detection, such as Support Vector Machines and tree-based algorithms. Asada et al. [3] proposed an approach for fault detection and diagnosis of railway point machines using electrical active power collected from electrical current and electrical voltage sensors. Wavelet transforms are used for feature extraction and a support vector machine for classification. Vileiniskis et al. [19] presented a methodology based on a one-class support vector machine with the similarity measure of edit distance with real penalties, using measurements of current drawn by the motor of the railway point machine. Lee et al. [13] proposed a sound analysis to detect and diagnose faults in railway point machines. The Mel-frequency cepstral coefficients from audio signals are used as features, and then a support vector machine is used for classification.

Deep learning has also been applied for anomaly detection in railway switches. Bian et al. [4] proposed a degradation detection method based on self-organising feature maps and support vector machines. The methodology was demonstrated using a field-monitoring dataset of 52 days of power data. Alessi et al. [1] studied the correlation between environment, field layout and the point system behaviour. Moreover, a comparison between fleet-based and asset-based approaches using Self-Organising Maps is presented. The used dataset entails six months of data from 20-point systems and consists of the direct current and voltage of the electric motor during a manoeuvre as well as contextual information such as the direction of movement and the final position. Guo et al. [10] proposed an unsupervised fault-detection method for railway turnouts using current signals. The proposed fault-detection algorithm is based on deep autoencoders, addressing issues such as unlabelled field data, unknown multiple nodes, and small nodes' modelling.

Interpretable ML tools have also been explored in the context of failure detection of railway switches. Allah Bukhsh et al. [2] proposed a practical solution approach for the efficient maintenance planning of railway switches using historical data of visual inspections, condition state and maintenance records. Tree-based algorithms (decision trees, random forests, and gradient boosted trees) are used for data classification and feature importance analysis, as well as a Local Interpretable Model-Agnostic Explanations (LIME), are also presented.

With regards to RUL prediction, assuming an exponential model for the degradation of point machines, Guclu et al. [9] used an Auto Regressive Moving Average (ARMA) model to predict the future states of railway switches. The ARMA model is trained on data obtained from force sensors installed on the railway turnout system and the RUL is defined as the number of predictions made from the current health state to the final state. Eker et al. [8] proposed a Simple State Based Prognostic (SSBP) method to detect and forecast the health condition of the electromechanical system of a railway switch. The method consists of three phases: clustering, clustering evaluation and RUL prediction using the transition probabilities between health states. Later, Eker et al. [7] improved their work by proposing a new state-based prognostic method using state duration information. Letot et al. [15] estimated the RUL of a railway switch using Monte Carlo simulations on stochastic processes. Several random degradation paths are simulated until they reach a given threshold value and the reliability function is obtained from the collection of hitting times of the threshold. The RUL is then computed from the reliability function. Bohm [5] proposed an approach that uses Artificial Neural Networks and Support Vector Machines to predict the RUL in the form of classes. The developed approach uses measurement data of the electrical power consumption of switch engines.

3   Case Study: Railway Network of Metro Do Porto

3.1   Problem Definition

This paper aims to develop a data-driven predictive maintenance system that issues an alert whenever a railway switch system of a train network is predicted to suffer a failure. These systems are critical components of the railway network. In the case of failure, they can provoke a derailing of a train or deny the possibility of changing the train between lines to keep the regular train operation. The railway switches can be described by an automaton containing three states: "Point Moving", "Points Left", and "Points Right". This study focuses on the behaviour of several signal devices installed on the railway switches that indicate a specific device's current state. The experimental data set used in this paper was collected from July to December 2021 are logged 1 Hz frequency by an embedded device. We want to explore the observation and frequency of anomalous sequences of states to identify imminent failures. Furthermore, we explore these failure sequences to predict the remaining useful life of the equipment installed on the railway tracks.

3.2   Proposed Approach

The proposed approach in this paper can be divided into five stages and its flowchart is schematically represented in Fig. 1. The proposed approach should generally apply to any railway switch from which data logs obtained from the interlocking railway system are available. The first stage is the pre-processing phase, where the dataset is pre-processed to encode all the possible states that the railway switch machine can have. Since the behaviour of a railway switch machine can be described as an automaton, the second stage of the approach is verifying whether the sequence of states is admissible. If an unexpected sequence takes place, that abnormal sequence is stored. In a third stage, using a sliding window approach, the number of anomalous sequences inside the window is computed. If the number of abnormal sequences inside the sliding window is more significant than a pre-defined threshold, an alarm should be triggered (fourth stage of the approach). Finally, in stage five of the approach, if an alarm was triggered in stage four, the equipment's Remaining Useful Life (RUL) is estimated using a machine learning (ML) model. Note that all these stages can be done online simultaneously with the data stream.

Anomaly Detection. One of the goals of this work is to propose an approach for anomaly detection in railway switches using log data obtained from the interlocking railway system. As stated before, the railway switches can be described as an automaton containing three states: "Point Moving", "Points Left", and "Points Right" (see Fig. 2). These are the acceptable states, represented in white in Fig. 2. The "Undefined Position" state is an abnormal state that occurs when

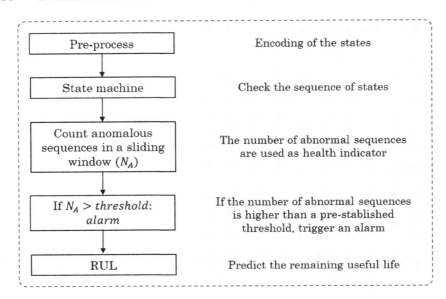

Fig. 1. Flowchart of our approach.

the moving time is greater than 17 s, represented in grey in Fig. 2. Therefore, the first stage of our approach is to encode the possible states as:

- 1 - "Point Moving"
- 2 - "Points Left"
- 3 - "Points Right"
- 4 - "Undefined Position"

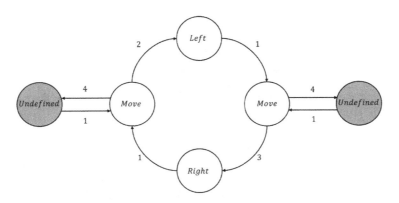

Fig. 2. Set of movements of the point machine and possible reached states: normal (white) and abnormal (grey). (Color figure online)

The second stage of the approach consists in evaluating the sequence of states. Normal sequences are sequences as "1213" or "1312"; that is, when there is a "Points Moving" state followed by a "Points Left" or "Points Right" state, they should be followed by a "Points Moving" state and then by "Points Right" or "Points Left", respectively. Examples of anomalous sequences are "1212", "1313", "11" or "14". Moreover, since a switch of the railroad usually takes up to six seconds, when a movement takes more than that amount of time, it is also considered an anomalous sequence/event. Then the number of abnormal sequences in a sliding window is computed. An alarm is triggered if the number of anomalous sequences in the window exceeds a predetermined threshold. This procedure is schematically illustrated in Phase 1 of Fig. 3.

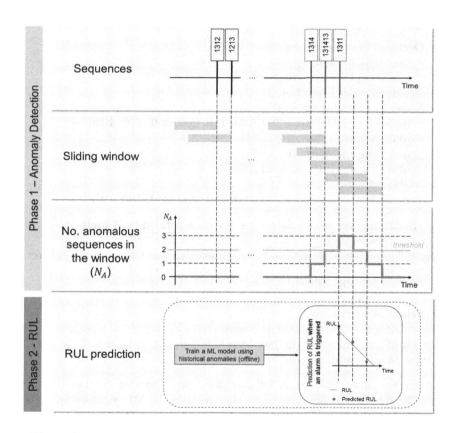

Fig. 3. Schematic diagram of the two phases that compose our approach.

Remaining Useful Life (RUL). After an anomaly is detected, the Remaining Useful Life (RUL) is predicted using a machine learning (ML) model, as depicted in phase 2 of the flowchart of Fig. 3. For that purpose, a pipeline with three components is trained on a historical dataset of anomalies. The components of the pipeline are a min-max scaler, a feature selector and an ML model. As a feature selector, we used SelectFromModel available on Scikit-Learn [16] with a random forest being the features selected based on the feature importances. Regarding the ML model, the performance of four algorithms is evaluated with regard to the regression task. The hyperparameters are set using a grid search procedure with a time-based cross-validation approach using the history of each anomaly as a fold (see Fig. 4) optimised for the Exponential Transformed Accuracy. The algorithms and their respective search space are:

- Feature Selector:
  - feature importance threshold: [0.025, 0.05, 0.075, 0.1]
- ML algorithms:
  - Linear Regression:
    * No search performed.
  - Decision Tree Regressor:
    * max depth: [3, 5, 7, 10]
    * min samples split: [10, 5, 2]
    * min samples leaf: [3, 4, 11, 20]
  - Random Forest Regressor:
    * number of estimators: [50, 100, 150, 200, 250, 500, 1000]
    * max depth: [3, 5, 7, 10]
    * min samples split: [10, 5, 2]
    * min samples leaf: [3, 4, 11, 20]
  - XGB regressor:
    * number of estimators: [50, 100, 150, 200, 250, 500, 1000]

The remaining hyperparameters are the ones defined by default in the Scikit-learn python package [16].

The ML pipeline is trained in the dataset with the following 20 features:

- 6 bins used for anomaly detection;
- sum of the 6 bins;
- time since last anomaly;
- number of movements since last anomaly;
- number of movements in the last hour, 2 h, 3 h, 6 h, 12 h, 24 h, 2 days, 4 days, 7 days, 14 days and 30 days.

An incremental approach is followed for the estimation of the RUL. More specifically, we use the previous anomalies to train an ML pipeline and when a new anomaly is triggered by the anomaly detector, the RUL is estimated using the previously trained ML pipeline. After the anomaly, the process is restarted. That is, the ML pipeline is retrained using data from all past anomalies and when a new alarm is triggered, the RUL is predicted using the ML pipeline.

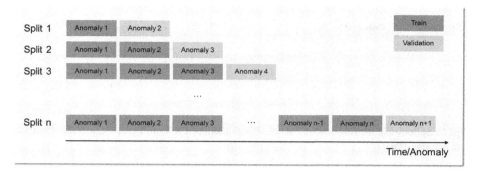

Fig. 4. Time-based cross-validation. In blue, anomalies are used for training; in yellow, the anomalies are used for validation. (Color figure online)

4 Experimental Evaluation

4.1 Data Description

The experimental dataset used in this work was collected from June to December 2021, and it consists of a log dataset with the following attributes:

- Time - timestamp of the log entry.
- Site - Geographical localization of the railway switch.
- Object - The code name of the railway switch.
- EventText - Description of the occurrence that took place.

The dataset comprises logs from 154 railway switches distributed across six Metro do Porto's railway network lines. The railway switch with the lower number of logs has 56 logs, and the railway switch with the higher number of logs has 93424 entries. The median number of logs is 3046.5, and the first and third quartiles are 401 and 24433 logs.

4.2 Evaluation of the Anomaly Detection Approach

Figure 5 represents examples of alarms which are considered True Positive (TP), False Positive (FP) and False Positive * (FP*). An Alarm is considered a TP if it occurs up to 60 min before the anomaly (ground truth). If the alarm occurs within 10 min after the anomaly (ground truth), it is considered an FP*. The FP* is not used to compute metrics such as precision or recall. In other words, these alarms do not count as FP. However, if an anomaly (ground truth) does not have an alarm in the TP zone, it is still considered as a False Negative (FN) even if there is an alarm in the FP* zone. If the alarm occurs outside these two time windows before and after the anomaly (ground truth), it is considered an FP. If there is not an alarm in the TP zone, it is considered a FN. It should also be noted that the anomalies (ground truth) are not presented in the dataset,

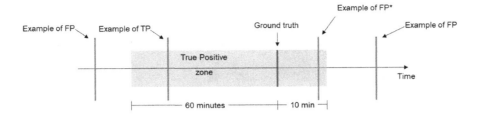

Fig. 5. Schematic representation of what is considered a True Positive, a False Positive and a False Positive*.

but it was provided by the asset manager and refers to interventions that had to take place on the railway switch machines.

In Table 1 are presented the anomalies that took place in the machine AGC463 during the period analyzed. In the same Table, one can also notice that all the anomalies were detected and the delay in time that those anomalies were detected. For example, a delay of −29.45 min was obtained for the first anomaly, meaning that the anomaly was flagged by the proposed approach 29.45 min before it happened. In the same way, the second anomaly listed in Table 1 was detected with a delay of 2.75 min, meaning that that anomaly was not detected in time. Therefore, for this anomaly there is one FP* and one FN.

Table 1. Anomalies in machine AGC463 and delays in the detection of them by the proposed approach.

Timestamp (ground truth)	Detected	Timestamp Detected	Delay (minutes)
06-07-2021 22:50:00	True	06-07-2021 22:20:33	−29.45
07-07-2021 23:47:00	False	07-07-2021 23:49:45	2.75
12-07-2021 07:53:00	True	12-07-2021 07:18:06	−34.9
13-07-2021 06:14:00	True	13-07-2021 06:13:34	−0.43
06-10-2021 15:04:00	False	06-10-2021 15:04:47	0.78
06-10-2021 17:25:00	True	06-10-2021 17:03:17	−21.72

In order to evaluate the proposed anomaly detection approach, the metrics Precision, Recall, and F1-score are used:

$$Precision = \frac{TP}{TP + FP} \tag{1}$$

$$Recall = \frac{TP}{TP + FN} \tag{2}$$

$$F1 = \frac{2 \times Precision \times Recall}{Precision + Recall} \tag{3}$$

In Table 2 are summarised the obtained metrics for all the railway switches machines that had anomalies over the analysed period. One can notice that the performance of the approach can vary a lot with the machine. In general, there are few FN. However, regarding the FP, the performance is not uniform for all machines. Machines such as AGC458 and AGC459 have a high number of FP. If all machines are considered, a precision of 0.25 and a recall of 0.792 were obtained. Without consideration of machines AGC458 and AGC459, there is a slight improvement in precision and F1-score. Even though, further sensitivity analysis to the hyperparameters is envisaged in order to improve the obtained results.

Table 2. Obtained metrics for the considered machines with anomalies.

Machine	TP	FP	FN	FP*	Precison	Recall	F1
AGC463	4	2	2	2	0.667	0.667	0.667
AGE405	2	1	0	0	0.667	1.000	0.800
AGS414	0	6	2	2	0.000	0.000	NaN
AGS417	3	4	0	0	0.429	1.000	0.600
AGS418	3	4	0	0	0.429	1.000	0.600
AGP401	0	1	1	1	0.000	0.000	NaN
AGS402	2	1	0	0	0.667	1.000	0.800
AGS401	2	1	0	0	0.667	1.000	0.800
AGC458	1	15	0	0	0.062	1.000	0.118
AGC459	1	15	0	0	0.062	1.000	0.118
AGC462	1	7	0	0	0.125	1.000	0.222
All	19	57	5	5	0.250	0.792	0.380
All \ {AGC458, AGC459}	17	27	5	5	0.386	0.773	0.515

4.3 Evaluation of Remaining Useful Life (RUL) Prediction Approach

In this section, the RUL prediction results for the machine AGC463 are presented. The first 3 anomalies were used for training the first ML pipeline. Therefore, the hyperparameters were defined by means of a grid search using time-based cross-validation. For instance, in the first pipeline, two splits were used: split one with anomaly 1 for training and anomaly 2 for validation; split two, with anomalies 1 and 2 for training and anomaly 3 for validation (see Fig. 4). As objective loss, the Exponential Transformed Accuracy 1 (ETA1) was used (Eq. 4). Compared to other loss functions such as root mean square error (RMSE), ETA1 has the advantage of having different hazard severity for under and over-estimation of RUL. In other words, an over-estimation of RUL will be more penalised than an under-estimation of RUL.

$$\text{ETA1} = \begin{cases} \exp(-\frac{ER}{13}) - 1, & \text{if ER} < 0 \\ \exp(\frac{ER}{10}) - 1, & \text{if ER} \geq 0 \end{cases}, \text{ER} = \hat{y} - y \qquad (4)$$

Table 3 and Fig. 6 present the true RUL and the predicted RUL for all the anomalies triggered by the anomaly detector of phase 1 of the approach proposed in this work, including the false positives such as the one with the alarm with the timestamp 2021-09-22 18:34:27 (see Table 3). With exception of the alarm number 5, the obtained RUL predictions for all the alarms are poor. This may be due to several reasons. Since the used dataset is small, the available anomalies could have different sources and causes. Therefore, the obtained poor results might be to a lack of representation of all possible types of anomalies in the training dataset. The fact that the last anomaly has the best results in terms of the quality of the predictions seems to agree with this. However, further studies with more data for this machine and/or using data from anomalies of other machines should be considered to re-evaluate the developed approach.

Table 3. RUL and predicted RUL (in minutes) for each of the alarms triggered by the anomaly detector.

Alarm no	Timestamp	Type	RUL (min)	RUL prediction (min)
1	2021-07-13 06:13:34	TP	0.43	2.08
2	2021-09-06 16:59:11	FP	30.00 (inf)	3.18
3	2021-09-22 18:34:27	FP	30.00 (inf)	3.07
4	2021-10-06 15:04:47	FP*	0.00	3.05
5	2021-10-06 17:03:17	TP	21.72	17.52

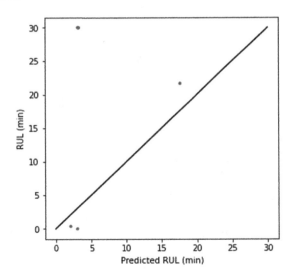

Fig. 6. Obtained results for Remaining Useful Life (RUL) prediction.

5 Conclusions

This work presented an approach for predictive maintenance of railway switches. The proposed approach was applied to a real case study, the Metro do Porto, from which seven months of log data obtained from the interlocking system is available. The proposed approach consists of a two-phased methodology, where the first stage consists of an anomaly detector and the second stage consists of the prediction of RUL after an anomaly is triggered. The proposed approach works in an online manner.

The results obtained for the anomaly detector (phase 1) were generally satisfactory. However, the algorithm's performance is not uniform for all the machines considered. There are machines with a good performance and others where a high rate of False Positive was obtained. This may be because different machines have different usage histories, are subject to different environmental conditions, and therefore have other root causes for the anomaly. Regarding the results obtained for the prediction of the RUL (phase 2), only preliminary results were obtained. However, it should be pointed out that a small data set is available and where it is not guaranteed that all anomalies have the same type of root cause.

As further developments, we intend to do a sensitivity analysis of the different hyperparameters of the proposed approach as well as to apply the proposed approach to more data when available.

Acknowledgements. This work was supported by the CHIST-ERA grant CHIST-ERA-19-XAI-012, and project CHIST-ERA/0004/2019 funded by FCT. This paper is also a result of the project Safe Cities - Inovação para Construir Cidades Seguras, with the reference POCI-01-0247-FEDER-041435, co-funded by the European Regional Development Fund (ERDF), through the Operational Programme for Competitiveness and Internationalization (COMPETE 2020), under the PORTUGAL 2020 Partnership Agreement.

References

1. Alessi, A., La-cascia, P., Lamoureux, B., Pugnaloni, M., Dersin, P.: Health assessment of railway turnouts?: a case study. Proceed. Third European Conf. Prognostics Health Manage. Soc. **2007**, 5–8 (2016)
2. Allah Bukhsh, Z., Saeed, A., Stipanovic, I., Doree, A.G.: Predictive maintenance using tree-based classification techniques: a case of railway switches. Transp. Res. Part C: Emerging Technol. **101**(January), 35–54 (2019). https://doi.org/10.1016/j.trc.2019.02.001
3. Asada, T., Roberts, C., Koseki, T.: An algorithm for improved performance of railway condition monitoring equipment: Alternating-current point machine case study. Transp. Res. Part C: Emerging Technol. **30**, 81–92 (2013). https://doi.org/10.1016/j.trc.2013.01.008
4. Bian, C., Yang, S., Huang, T., Xu, Q., Liu, J., Zio, E.: Degradation detection method for railway point machines. arXiv, pp. 1–25 (2018)
5. Böhm, T.: Remaining useful life prediction for railway switch engines using classification techniques. International Journal of Prognostics and Health Management 8(Special Issue 7) (2017)

6. Davari, N., Veloso, B., de Assis Costa, G., Pereira, P.M., Ribeiro, R.P., Gama, J.: A survey on data-driven predictive maintenance for the railway industry. Sensors **21**(17), 1–22 (2021). https://doi.org/10.3390/s21175739

7. Eker, O.F., Camci, F.: State-based prognostics with state duration information. Qual. Reliab. Eng. Int. **29**(4), 465–476 (2013). https://doi.org/10.1002/qre.1393

8. Eker, O.F., Camci, F., Guclu, A., Yilboga, H., Sevkli, M., Baskan, S.: A simple state-based prognostic model for railway turnout systems. IEEE Trans. Industr. Electron. **58**(5), 1718–1726 (2011). https://doi.org/10.1109/TIE.2010.2051399

9. Guclu, A., Yilboga, H., Eker, O.F., Camci, F., Jennions, I.: Prognostics with autoregressive moving average for railway turnouts. Annual Conf. Prognost. Health Manage. Soc. PHM **2010**, 1–6 (2010)

10. Guo, Z., Wan, Y., Ye, H.: An unsupervised fault-detection method for railway turnouts. IEEE Trans. Instrum. Meas. **69**(11), 8881–8901 (2020). https://doi.org/10.1109/TIM.2020.2998863

11. Hamadache, M., Dutta, S., Olaby, O., Ambur, R., Stewart, E., Dixon, R.: On the fault detection and diagnosis of railway switch and crossing systems: an overview. Applied Sciences (Switzerland) **9**(23), 5129 (2019). https://doi.org/10.3390/app9235129

12. Jin, W., et al.: Development and evaluation of health monitoring techniques for railway point machines. In: 2015 IEEE Conference on Prognostics and Health Management: Enhancing Safety, Efficiency, Availability, and Effectiveness of Systems Through PHAf Technology and Application, PHM 2015 (2015). https://doi.org/10.1109/ICPHM.2015.7245016

13. Lee, J., Choi, H., Park, D., Chung, Y., Kim, H.Y., Yoon, S.: Fault detection and diagnosis of railway point machines by sound analysis. Sensors (Switzerland) **16**(4), 549 (2016). https://doi.org/10.3390/s16040549

14. Lei, Y., Li, N., Guo, L., Li, N., Yan, T., Lin, J.: Machinery health prognostics: a systematic review from data acquisition to RUL prediction. Mech. Syst. Signal Process. **104**, 799–834 (2018). https://doi.org/10.1016/j.ymssp.2017.11.016

15. Letot, C., et al.: A data driven degradation-based model for the maintenance of turnouts: A case study. IFAC-PapersOnLine **28**(21), 958–963 (2015). https://doi.org/10.1016/j.ifacol.2015.09.650

16. Pedregosa, F., et al.: Scikit-learn: Machine Learning in Python. J. Mach. Learn. Res. **12**, 2825–2830 (2011)

17. Sousa Tomé, E.: Smart structural health monitoring applied to management and conservation of bridges, Ph. D. thesis, University of Porto (2019)

18. Susto, G.A., Schirru, A., Pampuri, S., McLoone, S., Beghi, A.: Machine learning for predictive maintenance: a multiple classifier approach. IEEE Trans. Industr. Inf. **11**(3), 812–820 (2015). https://doi.org/10.1109/TII.2014.2349359

19. Vileiniskis, M., Remenyte-Prescott, R., Rama, D.: A fault detection method for railway point systems. Proceed. Institut. Mech. Eng. Part F: J. Rail Rapid Transit **230**(3), 852–865 (2016). https://doi.org/10.1177/0954409714567487

curr2vib: Modality Embedding Translation for Broken-Rotor Bar Detection

Amirhossein Berenji$^{(\boxtimes)}$ ⓘ, Zahra Taghiyarrenani ⓘ, and Sławomir Nowaczyk ⓘ

Center for Applied Intelligence Systems Research, Halmstad University,
Halmstad, Sweden
amirhossein.berenji@hh.se

Abstract. Recently and due to the advances in sensor technology and Internet-of-Things, the operation of machinery can be monitored, using a higher number of sources and modalities. In this study, we demonstrate that Multi-Modal Translation is capable of transferring knowledge from a modality with higher level of applicability (more usefulness to solve an specific task) but lower level of accessibility (how easy and affordable it is to collect information from this modality) to another one with higher level of accessibility but lower level of applicability. Unlike the fusion of multiple modalities which requires all of the modalities to be available during the deployment stage, our proposed method depends only on the more accessible one; which results in the reduction of the costs regarding instrumentation equipment. The presented case study demonstrates that by the employment of the proposed method we are capable of replacing five acceleration sensors with three current sensors, while the classification accuracy is also increased by more than 1%.

Keywords: Induction motor · Broken rotor bar · Fault diagnosis · Predictive maintenance · Contrastive pre-training · Multi-modal latent translation

1 Introduction

Induction motors, mainly due to their affordable operational and maintenance costs alongside their reliability, are the most frequently used type of motors for industrial use cases [21]. The significance of their use in comparison to other equipment can be better understood by their share in energy consumption; they are estimated to consume up to 68% of the total energy in industrial sector, worldwide [2]. Therefore, optimizing the uptime of induction motors is of vital importance. Various faults can be expected to occur over the lifetime of this type of machinery. In particular, Broken Rotor Bar (BRB) problem – which is a partial crack, or a complete breakage, of the rotor bar – is categorized as one of the major faults of rotors [9]. Such an occurrence brings up different consequences, from increased power consumption [14] to unbalanced current in

© The Author(s), under exclusive license to Springer Nature Switzerland AG 2023
I. Koprinska et al. (Eds.): ECML PKDD 2022 Workshops, CCIS 1753, pp. 423–437, 2023.
https://doi.org/10.1007/978-3-031-23633-4_28

remaining rotor bars [9]. BRB can be detected by monitoring and analyzing a wide range of physical properties, with motor current and machinery vibrations considered to be among the most effective ones [7].

In recent years, enabled by the developments in the field of Internet-of-Things (IoT), we have witnessed an exponential growth in the amount of information that is being collected [18]. It has transformed the predictive maintenance (PdM) field, since the IoT is now the tool to collect, process and distribute large amounts of streaming data. The growth in the available information is not limited to the volume of data, but it also includes the variety of information being collected, in terms of different sources and sensor types [13,18].

On the one hand, employing more modalities to solve any given problem is likely to improve the performance due to the inherent increase in the amount of available information. However, it is not always cost efficient, as the multi-source data is likely to include notable level of redundancy, potentially making the investment into additional equipment questionable. It has been shown that fusion of the data from different sources is not always helpful and extraction of high level features from key sources is often more important [18]. Moreover, multiple modalities are likely to vary from both accessibility (how easy it is to collect an arbitrary modality) and applicability (how useful this modality is to implement the in-hand task) point of view; therefore it can be logical to transfer knowledge from more applicable modality to more accessible modality to optimize the accessibility-applicability trade-off.

The contribution of this paper is an extension of our previous study [23], where we have compared vibrations against phase currents for BRB detection, and demonstrated that the former offer higher level of classification accuracy. Unfortunately, due to higher price and stricter requirements of proper sensors installation, vibrations is a less accessible modality in production environments. Building on these results, in this paper we demonstrate the possibility of employing modality embedding translation techniques to transfer knowledge from source (vibrations) to target (currents) modality in fault diagnosis case studies. We establish the effectiveness of this approach by showing that transferring the knowledge from vibrations to currents leads to increase in BRB detection accuracy.

Remaining of this paper is organized as follow: in Sect. 2, a number of previous studies preserving similarities to the present study are discussed. Afterwards, in Sect. 3, we introduce the proposed methods used in this study in details. Consecutively, in Sect. 4, experimental setups to evaluate the effectiveness of the proposed method is reported. Finally, yet importantly in Sect. 5 results from Sect. 4 is discussed and conclusions of this study is provided.

2   Related Works

2.1   Intelligent BRB Detection

Application of intelligent methods for detection and severity assessment of BRB problem have been studied in depth. For example, in [3], Empirical Mode Decomposition combined with an Adaptive Linear Network, alongside Feed Forward

Neural Network are employed to diagnose various types of defects in motor (including the BRB problem) based on motor current signal. Similarly, in [20], Wavelet Packet Decomposition is used to extract highly abstract set of features from stator current signals. The extracted feature set is next provided to a Multi-Layered Perceptron to classify the number of broken rotor bars in the induction motor. Besides stator current, machinery vibrations is also a great source of information for intelligent BRB detection. In [17], Sparse Representation is utilized to extract features from vibrations signals and these features are then used to evaluate the machinery health state, from BRB problem point of view. Likewise, in [19] the feature set extracted by Wavelet Discrete Transform is employed alongside K-Nearest Neighbors to not only detect complete BRB problem, but also to classify the severity of partial BRB. The methodology presented in that study is applicable to different levels of loading condition. Moreover, they had also considered the noise robustness of the proposed method.

Similar to the referenced studies, in this study we employ frequency domain signals of both vibrations three-phase currents to diagnose a squirrel cage induction motor, according to BRB problem.

2.2 Contrastive Representation Learning

When it comes to supervised learning of deep classification networks, cross-entropy loss is the most frequently used loss function [10]; alternatively, we may consider extraction of a feature set with optimum separability of classes as the objective of a learning process. A set of strategies known as Contrastive Representation Learning (CRL) are concerned with the construction of feature space, where different classes are sufficiently separable. CRL can be defined as learning by comparing the data [12]. Taking advantage of CRL strategies, one can be able to unlock higher level of classification accuracy, when compared with conventional baselines. For example, in [23], one step CRL-based pre-training turned out to be noticeably more effective for BRB classification. Moreover, the application of CRL-based pre-training is not limited to only classification tasks; in [15] contrastive pre-training is employed to learn de-noised sequence representations in both language and language-vision domains, based on self-supervised approaches. Similarly in [26], contrastive pre-training is utilized for event extraction in an unsupervised manner.

In our previous work [23], we showed that the application of CRL-based pre-training is an effective approach to overcome loading variation problem; therefore, in the presented work we also use this technique.

2.3 Multi-source Fault Diagnosis

With the advances in IoT and sensors technology, information from more diverse sources is available. This has resulted in the application of Multi-Modal, or Multi-Source, techniques to PdM use cases. For instance, in [25], the traditional fusion of Multi-Source information is replaced by considering multiple sensors as different channels of the input fed to a Convolutional Neural Network. This network is used to diagnose bearing faults, given time-domain vibration signals collected from three different locations. Moreover, in [1] a novel Hybrid Deep Neural Network is used to firstly extract two sets of features, temporal and spatial, respectively using Long Short Term Memory (LSTM) and Convolutional Neural Network (CNN) branches; subsequently, a fully-connected network is employed to fusion these two sets of features. The proposed architecture is used for remaining useful life estimation problem. Although fusion is beneficial in most cases, however, it is not always the best approach to take; mainly because of redundancy in multi-source datasets, or the added noise that comes from additional sensors. Therefore, a set of techniques is concerned with the maximization of the similarity over the representations derived from different modalities, or sources. As an example, in [16] a Deep Coupling Autoencoder is used to derive a joint representation from vibration and acoustic emission signals to capture the correlation between these two different modalities. The referenced methodology is shown to provide superior performance in comparison with traditional approaches, in bearing and gearbox fault diagnosis case studies.

Multi-Modal Translation, defined as the task to transfer or translate knowledge from a source modality to a target one [22], enables one to learn a mapping from a source modality to a target one. Multi-Modal Translation includes variety of applications, such as Image Captioning [8] (generation of a textual representation from an image) and Multi-Modal Speech synthesis [22] (generating audio given its textual representation). It is worth mentioning that Multi-Modal translation where the target modality is high-dimensional can get extremely challenging; one way to respond to this challenge is translating to a low-dimensional representation of the target modality containing higher level of semantic information in comparison with the input belonging to the source modality [27]. Taking this approach also saves the need to re-learn the latent space representation from its reconstructed version; making the implementation of consequent tasks, such as classification, easier.

3   Method

We propose a method that is based on Hybrid Classification, i.e., utilizing contrastive pre-training to derive the low-dimensional representation of the target modality. That embedding is then reconstructed, using a Pseudo-Autoencoder for Modality Embedding Translation, directly from the source modality. The whole process of extraction of low-dimensional representation and implementation of the modality embedding translation is demonstrated in Fig. 1. Finally, in Sect. 3.3, we present the Centered Kernel Alignment which we use to highlight the similarity of representations learned by different networks.

3.1   Hybrid Classification

Siamese neural networks are one way to implement a contrastive pre-training. As the name suggests, a Siamese network is made of two exactly identical networks;

not only using the same architecture, but also sharing parameters. During its training process, the network is fed with positive pairs (both instances belong to same class) and negative pairs (instances belong to different classes). It is trained to aggregate all the observations sharing a class in the same region of the latent feature space it reconstructs (embedding); and simultaneously, to project observations from different classes to separate regions. Different options are available to train a Siamese network, including Contrastive Loss, defined as:

$$ContrastiveLoss = (1 - Y)D_w^2 + (Y)\frac{1}{2}(\max\{0, m - D_w\})^2, \qquad (1)$$

where Y is the label of a given pair, either 0 (for negative pairs) or 1 (for positive pairs), D_w is the similarity of the embedding of the observations in a pair and the m is the margin used to set a base value for the desired distance between negative pairs.

As mentioned earlier, access to a low-dimensional representation of the target modality is essential for the modality embedding translation task. In our previous work, we demonstrated that the application of contrastive pre-training is capable of improving the classification accuracy [23]. We use the same approach here, by first training a hybrid classifier and then re-using the low-dimensional representation created this way to train a Pseudo-AE network. Training the hybrid classifier involves two steps; first, we train a feature extractor network using contrastive learning approaches; second, a softmax layer is added to the feature extractor and the whole network is trained as a classifier. It is noteworthy that we divide the training dataset into two distinct portions, Contrastive and Regular. They are used during pre-training and actual training, respectively. The process of training the hybrid classifier and extracting the representation (embedding) is demonstrated in the Fig. 1a.

3.2 Pseudo-AE for Modality Embedding Translation

Modality embedding translation is implementable using different methods, including an Autoencoder-like network, pseudo-AE for short. Such a network can be used to learn a mapping from source modality to a lower dimensional representation of the target modality. Autoencoders are networks capable of reconstructing a given input at its output, with the constraint of learning a lower dimensional representation of the input in its bottle-neck. Similarly, a pseudo-AE can be defined as a network capable of reconstructing an arbitrary but somehow related representation from a given input. Taking such an approach, we are able to reconstruct a representation, originally extracted from target modality, using only the source modality. A pseudo-AE can be trained using a similarity maximizing loss function, such as a Mean Squared Error.

In our previous work [23], we showed that vibrations offer a significantly higher classification performance, compared to current. On the other hand, the collection of multi-point vibrations from an induction motor is far more challenging compared with three-phase currents; in most cases, it requires invasive

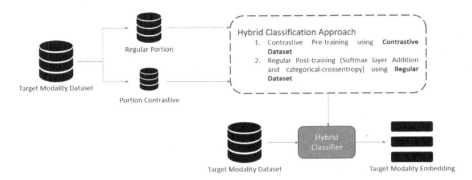

(a) Training procedure for creating the Hybrid Classifier.

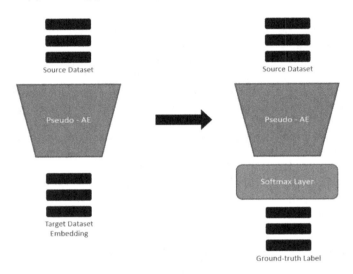

(b) Pseudo-AE Training and Post-training Procedure

Fig. 1. Visual demonstration of the proposed method

measurements which do not suit practical online monitoring use cases. Moreover, current sensors are likely to be more affordable in comparison with their vibration counterparts. Last but not least, in the case study presented here, by taking advantage of the modality embedding translation technique, we would be able to decrease the number of required sensors from 5 (number of vibrometers) to 3 (number of current sensors), resulting in a more affordable technical infrastructures for data collection and storage.

To perform the modality embedding translation, we assume that we have access to synchronously measured signals from both modalities. Moreover, we also assume that we have access to the corresponding superior (task-specific) embeddings of the target modality (vibrations), for every observation of the source modality. In Sect. 3.1, we have explained the procedure used to extract such superior embedding.

Using the Pseudo-AE network, we are able to learn a mapping from three phase currents FFT spectra towards the latent space of vibrations embedding. Having access to such a mapping, we will be able to reconstruct the corresponding vibration embedding, given an arbitrary observation in the three-phase current spectra. Once the mapping is learned, we are adding a softmax layer on top of the Pseudo-AE network and post-training it – utilizing Categorical Cross-Entropy loss function. This way, the network can be used for induction motor health state diagnosis, from BRB point of view, based only on the currents input data. Having the currents to vibrations embedding mapping learned sufficiently well, we are able to improve the performance of current-only dependent BRB detection classifier beyond what is possible by learning directly from raw data.

3.3   CKA for Representation Similarity Comparison

The effectiveness of a network in the fulfillment of a modality translation task, can be done by comparing the representations learned by the network at each layer. In the modality embedding translation task, an ideal translator should have representations similar to the ones from the source modality network in the early layers, while the final layers should be more similar to those of a network trained on the target modality. This way, we can make sure that a mapping from the source modality to the desired subspace of the target modality is learned well.

A number of techniques from a field known as Representational Similarity can be used to capture and quantify the similarity between two arbitrary embeddings. Among various proposed metrics, all possess different advantages and disadvantages; however, Centered Kernel Alignment (CKA) is considered as the current state of the art [4]. CKA not only enables measuring similarity between representations derived by different layers of the same network, but is also capable of quantifying the similarity between representations at different layers of different networks [11].

CKA mainly relies on the idea that the similarity of two sets of representations can be measured by calculating the similarity between every pair of examples in each set separably and comparing the similarity structures. Consider X and Y as two matrices including representations derived from n examples. Dot product can be used to evaluate the level of similarity between the representations, as demonstrated in the Eq. 2:

$$\langle vec(XX^T), vec(YY^T) \rangle = tr(XX^TYY^T) = \|Y^TX\|_F^2 \qquad (2)$$

Assuming that X and Y are centered, it implies Eq. 3:

$$\frac{1}{(n-1)^2} tr(XX^TYY^T) = \|cov(X^T, Y^T)\|_F^2 \qquad (3)$$

By employment of the Hilbert-Schmidt Independence Criterion [6], Eqs. 2 and 3 can be generalized to inner products from kernel Hilbert spaces; moreover, squared Forbenius norm of the cross-covariance matrix turns into the squared Hilbert-Schmidt norm of the cross-covariance operator [11]. Considering $K_{i_j} = k(x_i, y_j)$ and $L_{i_j} = l(x_i, y_j)$ where k and l are two kernels, empirical estimator of HSIC can be defined as:

$$HSIC(K, L) = \frac{1}{(n-1)^2} tr(KHLH), \tag{4}$$

where H is the centering matrix $H_n = I_n - \frac{1}{n}11^T$. A normalization step can make it invariant to isotropic scaling $S(X, Y) \neq S(\alpha X, \beta Y)$ for all $\alpha, \beta \in \mathbb{R}^+$. Normalized HSIC is known as Centered Kernel Alignment:

$$CKA(K, L) = \frac{HSIC(K, L)}{\sqrt{HSIC(K, K)HSIC(L, L)}}) \tag{5}$$

In this work, we employ CKA to compare the representations derived by the vibration embedding modality translator network, given corresponding current observation (curr2vib for short). This way, we would be able to investigate the goodness of the mapping learned by modality latent space translator in transforming input from the source modality (currents frequency spectra) to the latent space originally derived from the target modality (vibrations frequency spectra).

4   Experiments

Three different experiments are carried out in this study. This section starts with introducing the dataset and the pre-processing procedure. Next, in Sect. 4.2, we present results of training hybrid classifiers directly on the raw data of different modalities. This is followed, in Sect. 4.3, with the demonstration of improvements provided by training the Pseudo-AE model. Last but not least, in Sect. 4.4, we employ CKA to compare the similarity of representations derived from different networks and modalities.

4.1   Dataset and Pre-processing Procedure

Data is the essential ingredient of every data-driven study and ours is not an exception. We took advantage of the experimental dataset for detecting and diagnosing rotor broken bar in a three-phase induction motor [24] to carry out our case study. This dataset provides us with both electrical (phase voltages and currents) and mechanical (multi point vibrations) signals. Five different states from BRB problem point of view (from zero to four broken rotor bars), over eight different levels of mechanical torque as loading conditions are available in this dataset. In this study, we consider four distinct levels of mechanical torque to consider the various loading condition, corresponding to 12.5%, 50%, 62.5% and 100% of nominal load. The classification problem we take into account in this study is to predict the number of broken rotor bars (from zero to four ones), over a balanced training and testing dataset, from both loading conditions and number of broken rotor bars.

The original time-domain signals are split into shorter ones, using 1024 and 6667 points-long windows for vibrations and currents signals, respectively. Moreover, Fast Fourier Transform (FFT) is employed to map time domain signals to frequency domain signals, resulting in 512 and 3333 points long vibrations and currents signals, in frequency domains. The 5 point vibration signals collected from different location and three phase currents are then concatenated horizontally to form 2560 and 9999 points long signals for vibrations and currents modalities.

The whole dataset is randomly split into training (75%) and testing (25%) sets. In addition to that, min-max scaling is used to normalize the feature space. The fact that by the application of min-max scaling every frequency components in frequency spectrum is regarded as an individual feature, makes this scaling strategy an optimal choice for the problem in hand.

4.2 Hybrid Classification by Contrastive Pre-training

As mentioned in Sect. 3.1, we employ contrastive pre-training to train a hybrid vibrations classifier. This classification network is used to extract a 64-dimensional representation of the original vibrations input (2560 long space); we believe it is a reasonable size to compress the original 2560-dimensional space. The referenced low dimensional representations are derived from the last layer of the classification network, excluding the softmax layer (since this layer is expected to contain the feature set with the highest level of abstraction). This latent subspace would be later used to learn a mapping from currents to the vibrations embedding latent subspace. This process is discussed in more detail in Sect. 4.3.

To train the hybrid vibration classification network, we start with splitting the training vibrations dataset into regular and contrastive portions, with a ratio of 25% contrastive to regular. Afterwards, 10 pairs are created per observation in the contrastive portion of the training dataset, consisting of five positive and five negative ones. These pairs are used to conduct a contrastive pre-training process for the feature extractor of the hybrid vibration classification network. The feature extractor utilizes a multi-layered perceptron architecture with 2560-1280-640-580-512-256-128-64 neurons per layer. All the layers use hyperbolic tangent as the activation function. During the contrastive pre-training Contrastive Loss is used as the loss function, number of epochs is 100 and learning rate is 0.00001. It is worth mentioning that, the choice of learning rate and epoch, not only for this specific experiment but also for all the experiments carried out in this paper, is done to 1) keep training process properly smooth by using relatively low learning rate and 2) achieving the best possible model parameters by the employment of surpass number of epochs. Having the pre-training process finished, a softmax layer is added to the feature extractor to form a classification network and the remaining 75% portion of the training data is used to post-train the classification network. During the post-training process Categorical Cross-entropy – as the most frequent choice of loss function in multi-class classification problems– is used as the loss function, number of epochs is 400 and learning rate is 0.000001.

Having the whole network post-trained, the latent space required to conduct the modality embedding translation process is now extractable. This can be done by extracting the representations available in the last layer of the classification network before softmax layer, corresponding to all the vibrations observations available in the training dataset.

Similarly, a hybrid classifier utilizing currents as the input is implemented, also using hyperbolic tangent as the activation function and following 9999-7500-6000-4500-3000-1500-750-500-250-50 architecture. For the contrastive pre-training of this network, four pairs are created per each observation in the contrastive portion. Moreover, the choices of hyperparameters such as loss function, number of epochs and learning rate for both contrastive pre-training and categorical cross-entropy post-training are kept the same as the ones used for hybrid vibrations classifier. To account for the randomness, experiments are conducted 5 times and mean of the classification accuracy is used as the metric to evaluate the performance, as it is the most frequent metric to evalueate the performance of a classifier in balanced classification problems. Results regarding the classification performance of hybrid classifiers on the testing dataset are shown in the first two rows of Table 1. As it is clearly observable, both modalities are offering +90% accuracy in classification of the BRB detection problem. Additionally, vibrations are offering significantly higher performance in comparison with current.

Table 1. Average (AVG) and Standard Deviation (STD) of classification accuracy of each network.

Network	AVG	STD
Currents	0.9096	0.0070
Vibrations	0.9769	0.0033
curr2vib	0.9204	0.0041

4.3   Modality Embedding Translation Using Pseudo-AE

Different approaches are available for Modality Embedding Translation; in this study, we employ a Pseudo-AE network, utilizing a Multi-Layered Perceptron with the architecture of 9999-6000-3000-750-250-150-50-64. In the proposed architecture, the last layer before the output is kept to a lower-dimensional compared with the output to preserve the constraint of learning the lowest dimensional representation in the middle layers of network. Moreover, in all the neurons of this network, hyperbolic tangent is used as the activation function. Besides, Logarithmic Mean Squared Error, 100 and 0.0000001 are used as the loss function, number of epochs and learning rate during the Seq2Seq reconstruction training of the Pseudo-AE network. Once the mapping from current to vibrations embedding is learned, we need a post-training process to make a classification network out of the Pseudo-AE network. This is done by addition of a softmax layer to the Pseudo-AE network and employment of Categorical Cross-entropy as the loss function of the whole classification network. Categorical Cross-Entropy is chosen, as it is the most frequent option to use for multi-class classification tasks. Moreover, 0.0000001 and 2000 are employed as the learning rate and number of epochs for the implementation of the post-training process. It is worth mentioning that the whole training dataset is employed to learn the mapping from current to vibrations embedding, however, similar to the Sect. 3.1 only 75% of the training dataset is used during the post-training process.

In the final row of Table 1, the performance of the proposed method (curr2vib) is presented. When compared with the performance of current-based hybrid classifier, we managed to increase the classification performance by more than 1% due to taking advantage of the modality embedding translation technique and the vibrations embedding. Moreover, lower STD of the curr2vib classifier in comparison with hybrid current classifier demonstrates the higher level of stability of this approach.

4.4   Using CKA to Evaluate the Effectiveness of Pseudo-AE to Translate Modality Embedding

Comparison of the representations learned by neural networks at different layers can be used to quantify the similarities between the set of features learned at each layer. In particular, in this study we employ CKA – current state of the art tool to investigate the similarities between representations learned by different networks at different layers – to evaluate the effectiveness of our proposed method in the extraction of features similar to the target modality, given the source modality as the input. Representations extracted for these comparisons are derived from observations included in the testing dataset. Moreover, we employed the implementations[1] provided by authors of [11].

Using the heatmaps present in Fig. 2, we are able to compare the similarity of the representations learned by different models, pairwise. The color which has filled the cells of these heatmaps is an indicator of the similarity scores, measured using CKA technique. In the Fig. 2a, the similarity between representations extracted from Vibrations Classifier and Currents Classifier is demonstrated. As it is expected, representations at the initial layers are not similar, since the two networks are fed with information belonging to different modalities as input. Moreover, significant increase in the similarities of the representations is observed among those extracted from fourth and further layers; clearly, in these layers both networks are able to extract related, highly-abstract feature sets. Besides that, in Fig. 2b, representations extracted from Currents Classifier, and curr2vib Classifier are compared. Unlike the previous figure, in this figure, a noticeable level of similarity is found between first three layers of the networks; this makes intuitive sense, as they are fed with identical inputs. Moreover, we experience significant reduction in the similarity from the fourth layer, showing that the features learned by

---

[1] https://cka-similarity.github.io/.

two networks in these layers differ, which is the reason for the gap between these two networks in the classification of BRB problem.

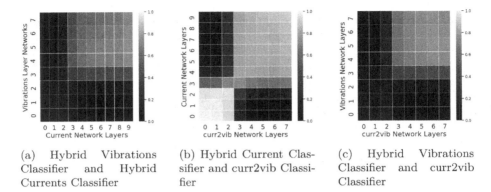

(a) Hybrid Vibrations Classifier and Hybrid Currents Classifier

(b) Hybrid Current Classifier and curr2vib Classifier

(c) Hybrid Vibrations Classifier and curr2vib Classifier

Fig. 2. Plots of CKA values of pairwise comparisons of the three networks.

Last but not least, in Fig. 2c, representations from Hybrid Vibrations Classifier and curr2vib Classifier are compared. Again, as in Fig. 2a, the initial layers are not similar as the inputs belong to different modalities. Moreover, significant increase in the similarities is noticeable from the fourth layers to the end of the networks; this increase happens in the similar region where the Fig. 2b experienced the drop in the similarity, demonstrating that the transformation of the representations available in the fourth layer to the rest of the network extracted by the curr2vib Classifier is making them more similar to the ones extracted by the Hybrid Vibrations Classifier. Being more similar to the representations extracted from Hybrid Vibrations Classifier, rather than the ones extracted from Hybrid Currents Classifier, can be considered as the reason behind the improvement in the classification performance.

5   Discussion and Conclusion

Comparison of the similarity of the representations learned by source-only based classifier (currents classifier), target-only based classifier (vibrations classifier) and Multi-Modal Embedding Translation classifier (curr2vib classifier), showed that the proposed method is capable of learning, using only the weaker source modality, representations similar to those coming from the stronger target modality. Therefore, this approach exploits some of the principles underlying Knowledge Distillation; a set of techniques and approaches to transfer what a superior model (teacher), or ensemble of them, has learned, to an inferior one (student) [5]. Knowledge Distillation is mainly concerned with improving the performance of a model with the help of another model. According to the above definition, vibration classifier is the teacher model and the curr2vib is the student model; Moreover, as the teacher model in this study is kept non-trainable during the knowledge transfer process, curr2vib utilizes an offline distillation scheme.

This study applies Modality Embedding Translation – as a Multi-Modal approach – to transfer knowledge from source modality (with high classification performance but expensive to collect) to the target one (cheaper, but with lower performance). As shown in the case study investigated, employment of such strategy is capable of improving the performance, when compared against conventional approaches learning on raw data in target modality separately. Although both modalities are required during the training process, in the deployment stage only the target modality is needed; therefore this approach is considerably more affordable in comparison with sensor fusion. Using the proposed strategy, we are able to replace expensive instrumentation pieces of equipment with more affordable ones while the performance is kept within acceptable range. One limitation is that the implementation of the proposed method requires having access to synchronously measured signals from both modalities, which can be hard to provide. Although measuring signals from both modalities simultaneously tends to reduce the data collection time, however, it is not always cost efficient to record both modalities at the same time, as it would require data acquisition equipment with higher capacities. The future works on this topic can be directed towards development of strategies to eliminate this constraint.

Acknowledgments. This work was partially supported by Vinnova and by CHIST-ERA grant CHIST-ERA-19-XAI-012 funded by Swedish Research Council.

References

1. Al-Dulaimi, A., Zabihi, S., Asif, A., Mohammadi, A.: A multimodal and hybrid deep neural network model for remaining useful life estimation. Comput. Ind. **108**, 186–196 (2019)
2. Beleiu, H.G., Maier, V., Pavel, S.G., Birou, I., Pică, C.S., Dărab, P.C.: Harmonics consequences on drive systems with induction motor. Appl. Sci. **10**(4), 1528 (2020)
3. Camarena-Martinez, D., Valtierra-Rodriguez, M., Garcia-Perez, A., Osornio-Rios, R.A., Romero-Troncoso, R.d.J.: Empirical mode decomposition and neural networks on FPGA for fault diagnosis in induction motors. Sci. World J. **2014**(1971), 908140 (2014)
4. Csiszárik, A., Kőrösi-Szabó, P., Matszangosz, Á., Papp, G., Varga, D.: Similarity and matching of neural network representations. Adv. Neural. Inf. Process. Syst. **34**, 5656–5668 (2021)
5. Gou, J., Yu, B., Maybank, S.J., Tao, D.: Knowledge distillation: a survey. Int. J. Comput. Vision **129**(6), 1789–1819 (2021)
6. Gretton, A., Bousquet, O., Smola, A., Schölkopf, B.: Measuring statistical dependence with Hilbert-Schmidt norms. In: Jain, S., Simon, H.U., Tomita, E. (eds.) ALT 2005. LNCS (LNAI), vol. 3734, pp. 63–77. Springer, Heidelberg (2005). https://doi.org/10.1007/11564089_7

7. Gritli, Y., Di Tommaso, A., Filippetti, F., Miceli, R., Rossi, C., Chatti, A.: Investigation of motor current signature and vibration analysis for diagnosing rotor broken bars in double cage induction motors. In: International Symposium on Power Electronics Power Electronics, Electrical Drives, Automation and Motion, pp. 1360–1365. IEEE (2012)
8. Hossain, M.Z., Sohel, F., Shiratuddin, M.F., Laga, H.: A comprehensive survey of deep learning for image captioning. ACM Compu. Surv. **51**(6), 1–36 (2019)
9. Kanović, Ž., Matić, D., Jeličić, Z., Rapaić, M., Jakovljević, B., Kapetina, M.: Induction motor broken rotor bar detection using vibration analysis-a case study. In: 2013 9th IEEE International Symposium on Diagnostics for Electric Machines, Power Electronics and Drives (SDEMPED), pp. 64–68. IEEE (2013)
10. Khosla, P., et al.: Supervised contrastive learning. Adv. Neural. Inf. Process. Syst. **33**, 18661–18673 (2020)
11. Kornblith, S., Norouzi, M., Lee, H., Hinton, G.: Similarity of neural network representations revisited. In: International Conference on Machine Learning, pp. 3519–3529. PMLR (2019)
12. Le-Khac, P.H., Healy, G., Smeaton, A.F.: Contrastive representation learning: a framework and review. IEEE Access **8**, 193907–193934 (2020). https://doi.org/10.1109/ACCESS.2020.3031549
13. Lei, Y., Yang, B., Jiang, X., Jia, F., Li, N., Nandi, A.K.: Applications of machine learning to machine fault diagnosis: a review and roadmap. Mech. Syst. Signal Process. **138**, 106587 (2020)
14. Lizarraga-Morales, R.A., Rodriguez-Donate, C., Cabal-Yepez, E., Lopez-Ramirez, M., Ledesma-Carrillo, L.M., Ferrucho-Alvarez, E.R.: Novel FPGA-based methodology for early broken rotor bar detection and classification through homogeneity estimation. IEEE Trans. Instrum. Meas. **66**(7), 1760–1769 (2017)
15. Luo, F., Yang, P., Li, S., Ren, X., Sun, X.: CAPT: contrastive pre-training for learning denoised sequence representations. arXiv preprint arXiv:2010.06351 (2020)
16. Ma, M., Sun, C., Chen, X.: Deep coupling autoencoder for fault diagnosis with multimodal sensory data. IEEE Trans. Industr. Inf. **14**(3), 1137–1145 (2018)
17. Morales-Perez, C., Rangel-Magdaleno, J., Peregrina-Barreto, H., Amezquita-Sanchez, J.P., Valtierra-Rodriguez, M.: Incipient broken rotor bar detection in induction motors using vibration signals and the orthogonal matching pursuit algorithm. IEEE Trans. Instrum. Meas. **67**(9), 2058–2068 (2018)
18. Ran, Y., Zhou, X., Lin, P., Wen, Y., Deng, R.: A survey of predictive maintenance: Systems, purposes and approaches. arXiv preprint arXiv:1912.07383 (2019)
19. Rangel-Magdaleno, J., Peregrina-Barreto, H., Ramirez-Cortes, J., Morales-Caporal, R., Cruz-Vega, I.: Vibration analysis of partially damaged rotor bar in induction motor under different load condition using dwt. Shock Vibrat. **2016**, 3530464 (2016)
20. Sadeghian, A., Ye, Z., Wu, B.: Online detection of broken rotor bars in induction motors by wavelet packet decomposition and artificial neural networks. IEEE Trans. Instrum. Meas. **58**(7), 2253–2263 (2009)
21. Spyropoulos, D., Mitronikas, E., Dermatas, E.: Broken rotor bar fault diagnosis in induction motors using a goertzel algorithm. In: 2018 XIII International Conference on Electrical Machines (ICEM), pp. 1782–1788. IEEE (2018)
22. Summaira, J., Li, X., Shoib, A.M., Abdul, J.: A review on methods and applications in multimodal deep learning. arXiv preprint arXiv:2202.09195 (2022)
23. Taghiyarrenani, Z., Berenji, A.: An analysis of vibrations and currents for broken rotor bar detection in three-phase induction motors. In: PHM Society European Conference, vol. 7, pp. 43–48 (2022)

24. Treml, A.E., Flauzino, R.A., Suetake, M., Maciejewski, N.A.R.: Experimental database for detecting and diagnosing rotor broken bar in a three-phase induction motor. In; IEEE DataPort (2020)
25. Wang, J., Wang, D., Wang, X.: Fault diagnosis of industrial robots based on multi-sensor information fusion and 1d convolutional neural network. In: 2020 39th Chinese Control Conference (CCC), pp. 3087–3091. IEEE (2020)
26. Wang, Z., et al.: CLEVE: contrastive pre-training for event extraction. In: Proceedings of the 59th Annual Meeting of the Association for Computational Linguistics and the 11th International Joint Conference on Natural Language Processing (Volume 1: Long Papers), pp. 6283–6297. Association for Computational Linguistics, August 2021. https://doi.org/10.18653/v1/2021.acl-long.491, https://aclanthology.org/2021.acl-long.491
27. Zhu, J.Y., et al.: Toward multimodal image-to-image translation. In: 30th Proceedings of the Conference on Advances in Neural Information Processing Systems (2017)

Incorporating Physics-Based Models into Data Driven Approaches for Air Leak Detection in City Buses

Yuantao Fan$^{(\boxtimes)}$ (ID), Hamid Sarmadi (ID), and Sławomir Nowaczyk (ID)

Center for Applied Intelligent System Research, Halmstad University,
Halmstad, Sweden
{yuantao.fan,hamid.sarmadi,slawomir.nowaczyk}@hh.se

Abstract. In this work-in-progress paper two types of physics-based models, for accessing elastic and non-elastic air leakage processes, were evaluated and compared with conventional statistical methods to detect air leaks in city buses, via a data-driven approach. We have access to data streamed from a pressure sensor located in the air tanks of a few city buses, during their daily operations. The air tank in these buses supplies compressed air to drive various components, e.g. air brake, suspension, doors, gearbox, etc. We fitted three physics-based models only to the leakage segments extracted from the air pressure signal and used fitted model parameters as expert features for detecting air leaks. Furthermore, statistical moments of these fitted parameters, over predetermined time intervals, were compared to conventional statistical features on raw pressure values, under a classification setting in discriminating samples before and after the repair of air leak problems. The result of this exploratory study, on six air leak cases, shows that the fitted parameters of the physics-based models are useful for discriminating samples with air leak faults from the fault-free samples, which were observed right after the repair was performed to deal with the air leak problem. The comparison based on ANOVA F-score shows that the proposed features based on fitted parameters of physics-based models outrank the conventional features. It is observed that features of a non-elastic leakage model perform the best.

Keywords: Fault detection · Air leaks · Elastic air leakage model ·
Non-elastic air leakage model · Physics-informed machine learning ·
Explainable predictive maintenance

1 Introduction

Predictive maintenance enables a cost-effective approach for maintaining industrial equipment and helps ensure high operational performance as well as adherence to safety requirements. Different aspects of monitoring and analysis, such as fault detection, identification or estimation of remaining useful life, can be

© The Author(s), under exclusive license to Springer Nature Switzerland AG 2023
I. Koprinska et al. (Eds.): ECML PKDD 2022 Workshops, CCIS 1753, pp. 438–450, 2023.
https://doi.org/10.1007/978-3-031-23633-4_29

done using data-driven techniques that leverage historical data of the equipment. Approaches based on Machine Learning (ML) algorithms have shown promising performance and were adopted by many industrial applications. Lately, deep neural networks have became very popular among researchers, however, industrial adoption is somewhat slower; one disadvantage of this approach is that it needs a great amount of training data (i.e., it is not very data-efficient), with a representative population including both normal operation data as well as fault and failure cases. Furthermore, inferences and predictions made with deep learning methods often lack interpretability and explanations of the decisions made.

Recently, a new trend has been developing to make ML methods more effective and data-efficient: to take advantage of models inspired by physics knowledge [9–11]. Physics-based models aim to calculate physical parameters from sensor data or outputs of ML models. These calculated parameters are employed to reduce workload on the ML model while increasing its explainability. This trend builds on decades-long desire to infuse data-driven reasoning with existing (often partial) domain knowledge, as opposed to requiring computers to learn completely from scratch. As a consequence of higher explainability, it is also easier to use physics-based ML models for enforcing, for example, policies or regulatory laws [7]. The calculated physics-based parameters can reduce the complexity of the problem for the ML-based method and hence improve the efficiency of the whole prognosis system. Another advantage is capability to do prognosis over an extended period of time, which might not be possible with purely ML-based methods when training samples come from a limited length of observation [8].

In the literature, several different approaches to combining ML and physics-based models have been proposed. One example is reducing the dimensions of the output space through orthogonal decomposition [9]. Another common approach is generating extra inputs for the learning method (i.e., virtual sensors) based on the values of other inputs [2,3,5]. A common theme among many works is the usage of recurrent neural networks (RNNs), including LSTM, which makes it possible to directly use the differential equations prevalent in physics-based modeling [10].

The case study presented in this paper focuses on detecting leak-related faults in a vehicle air system. The vehicle air supply, and the corresponding distribution system, were designed to provide compressed air to drive various components, e.g., air brakes, suspension, doors, gearbox, etc. The air pressure is regulated within a predefined range which is of crucial importance for the driver since without compressed air the vehicle will not operate. Air leaks in the system, depending on the severity, may render a lower operation efficiency, and, in the worst case, compromise the braking system, and thus jeopardize overall safety. The specific case presented in this study is based on a commercial fleet of buses, of the same model, driving in city and intercity traffic. Previous work on predicting air compressor failures in the same fleet by incorporating expert knowledge, using the charging rate of the air pressure as an expert feature, for predicting air compressor failures, is available in [4]. The air leak events (the time of the occurrences, the types of the leakage, and any additional relevant details) were inferred from the vehicle service record. The six air leak cases included in this study have occurred in four buses, during their daily operation. Repairs were performed in a workshop to deal with the air leak problems. It is crucial to point out that the information is quite limited, and details such root cause or fault mode are approximate at best – there is no guarantee that all six cases exhibit similar symptoms. We have acquired sensor data of three months for each of these cases, around the repair date, for analysis. Naturally, we label the samples prior to the repair as faulty, and samples following the repair as healthy, or fault-free.

In this study, we have investigated the use of two types of physics-based model, namely elastic and non-elastic air leakage models. They are used to generate expert features suitable for detecting air leaks. The general idea is to fit these physical models to the pressure data, during the leakage periods, and estimate the model parameters that correspond to current physical properties. One particular challenge is that we do not have access to the exact system schematic design, nor did a dedicated simulator for the underlying physical process of the air system is available. In earlier work those were typically considered prerequisites for using physics-based techniques. The nature of the six air leaks were also not available, such as the exact location or type of the air leak. Therefore, it is not known a priori which physics-based model (e.g., elastic or non-elastic leakage) they correspond to. Finally, the number of the air leak cases available is not sufficient to train an effective machine learning model for fault detection or prognosis.

The contribution of this exploratory study is to evaluate and compare the usefulness of two relevant physics-based leakage models in detecting real air leak cases for city buses. The fitted parameters of the physics-based models are used as expert features, and the performance of these features is evaluated for discriminating faulty samples from fault-free ones. The results show that, in three out of the six cases, the fitted parameters are useful for the fault detection task. Furthermore, it is shown that the statistical features computed using the fitted parameters of the physics-based models outperform the conventional statistical features computed directly from the raw sensor data.

2   Background

The air system on-board buses in this fleet consist of the supply system, the control system, the distribution network, and the end-use components that consume the air for different purposes. A conceptual diagram of the air system in the city buses investigated in this study was illustrated in Fig. 1. Compressed air flow was generated from the air compressor, and afterward regulated, dry filtered, and supplied to the air tank, which serves as a reservoir to store and facilitates the air supply when needed. The air pressure was maintained within a certain range, normally from 10 to 12 bars, to ensure the air demand of the end-use components was always met. Whenever the air pressure dropped below the

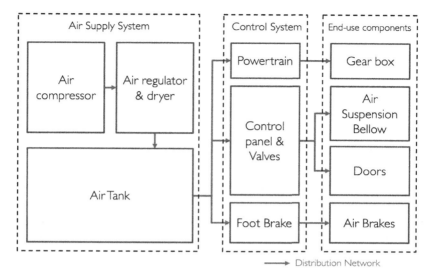

Fig. 1. A conceptual diagram of the air system in this study

bottom threshold, the compressor started charging the air into the system until the upper bound of the pressure level is reached. Through the control system (e.g., foot brake, valves, buttons, etc.), the operator determines the usage of the air, to activate different end-use components, e.g., air brake, doors, suspension bellows, gearbox, etc.

The only observation directly available for monitoring the air system behavior is the *Wet Tank Air Pressure* (WTAP), collected via a pressure sensor placed in the air tank. This data stream was accessed through the vehicle CAN network. The brake pedal position and selected gear were available as the control signals. The availability of the control signals varies over different time periods and buses in the fleet. Unfortunately, the signal indicating the door operation was not available for these buses. On the other hand, it can be derived, at least with some level of approximation, from the GPS signal and the vehicle speed. Figure 2 shows the pressure signal in the air tank, and the associated activation of the end-use components, derived from the control signals.

Air leaks may occur at various locations within the air system; the leakage mechanism and the cause of it may vary. In this work, we focus on the six air leak cases: i) bus A had leaks in the pipe and in the air bellow; ii) bus B had its air regulator replaced due to malfunctioning once it was unable to meet the operation requirements; iii) after 14 weeks, bus B had reports of leaks in the air bellows; iv) the fleet operator reported that there was a compressed air leak in Bus C, and the bus would not start; v) After ten months, bus C was reported to exhibit leaks in the air bellows; vi) oil and water were found to have leaked into the air tank through other components in bus D. In this study, we focus on the two-month period before and after the repair event, and on the air

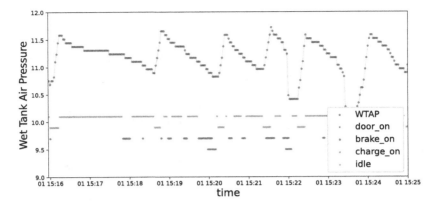

Fig. 2. Wet Tank Air Pressure (WTAP) and the corresponding activities of different vehicle components (represented as horizontal bars of various colors). (Color figure online)

leakage faults. Samples prior to the repair event were labeled as faulty, and the subsequent samples after the repair event were labeled as fault-free, i.e., healthy.

3   Method

In this study, since the exact model of the faults is unknown, we analyze three physics-based models: one non-elastic leakage model, and two variants of elastic leakage models.

The first step in the proposed approach is to identify the portions of the data where the system behaves in as simple as possible way. Particularly in the case of vehicle air system, different components use the air in very different fashion, and the specific often depend, in quite complex manner, on external circumstances. Those internal control processes are too complex to model here, and they often use inputs that are not available in the data collected from CAN network. Therefore, we have decided to identify segments where none of the end-usage components are active. In a perfect world, this means WTAP signal should remain constant during those periods – any change in value can be attributed to a leak. Moreover, the parameters of any such potential leak are going to be the most clearly visible, and easiest to estimate. Therefore, the model parameters were estimated during such "leakage segments" extracted from the air pressure signal, and statistical features of the fitted parameters were adopted as expert features for air leak detection.

3.1   Physics-Based Air Leakage Models

We take advantage of a formula inspired by the physics of leakage. The formula of the leak rate [6] of a vessel is defined by:

$$R = -V\frac{\mathrm{d}P_v}{\mathrm{d}t}, \tag{1}$$

where R is the leak rate, V is the volume of the vessel, P_v is the pressure inside the vessel, and t represents time. Also, assuming the leak is big enough to have a non-molecular flow the leak rate can be approximated [1] as:

$$R = L(P_v - P_o),\tag{2}$$

where L is called "leak size" and is proportional to the area of the leak, and P_o is the pressure outside of the leakage. Equating the two formulas leads to:

$$-V\frac{dP_v}{dt} = L(P_v - P_o).\tag{3}$$

Solving the differential equation and assuming L, P_o and V are constant, we obtain:

$$P_v = k\left[\exp\left(-\frac{L}{V}t\right)\right] + \frac{LP_o}{V}.\tag{4}$$

Since there might be also elastic leaks (e.g., in the seals of the vessel), we simulate them by assuming that P_o can be higher than its actual value. Therefore, we can re-parameterize the formula to account for a general leak:

$$P_v = k\left[\exp\left(-at\right)\right] + b\tag{5}$$

This way one can fit the data to our physics-inspired model simply by estimating the three parameters: a, b, and k.

An alternative way of modeling elastic leaks is to make the leak size pressure-dependent. For this purpose, we define:

$$L = \alpha(P_v - P_o)^2\tag{6}$$

This leads to the following solution to Eq. 3:

$$P_v = \frac{1}{\frac{\alpha}{V}t + C} + P_o,\tag{7}$$

where C is a constant. After re-parametrization we get:

$$P_v = \frac{1}{mt + n} + P_o.\tag{8}$$

To summarize, in this study we investigate the use of a non-elastic leakage model (Eq. 4) and two elastic leakage models (Eqs. 5 and 8) for detecting air leak events.

3.2 Fitting Model Parameters

Conceptually, the *Wet Tank Air Pressure* signal is affected by all components within the air system: i) during the charging period the compressor charges the air into the air tank and raises the pressure; ii) during the air releasing period the end-use components use the air; iii) and as one would expect, during the period when none of the components are activated, the pressure changes only due to air leakage. The air pressure segments without any components in use were extracted for analysis.

The pressure values are denoted as $x^i_{v,t}$, where i indicates the i-th segment $S^{i,\tau}_{v,t}$ it associates to, v and t corresponds to the vehicle and time the value being collected, and τ denotes a set of the time indices (e.g. $\tau = \{t_1, t_2, ..., t_n\}$) of the corresponding leakage segment. All pressure values of the leak segments $S^{i,\tau}_{V,T}$ of vehicle V over the period T are denoted as $X_{V,T}$. In this study, T is selected to be one day period. The parameters θ^i of the physics-based model f_{θ^i} are fitted over each segment $S^{i,\tau}_{v,t}$, minimizing squared errors between real pressure values and model prediction:

$$\underset{\theta^i}{\mathrm{argmin}} \left\| \left(\sum_{t \in \tau} f_{\theta^i}(t) - x^i_{v,t} \right) \right\|^2 \tag{9}$$

Fitted model parameters of all segments $S^{i,\tau}_{V,T}$ over time interval T of bus V were denoted as $\Theta_{V,T}$. For the non-elastic leakage model (Eq. 4), $\{k, \frac{L}{V}\}$ are the model parameters; for the elastic leakage model, $\{k, a, b\}$ are the parameters for model Eq. 5, and $\{m, n\}$ for model Eq. 8.

3.3 Computing Statistical Features

A conventional data-driven approach for fault detection would take statistical features of the raw sensor readings as the input to train a model. In this study, we investigate the usefulness of the fitted parameter of the three physics-based models, denoted as $\Gamma(\Theta_{v,t})$, and we compare them against the statistical features computed on raw sensor readings $\Gamma(X_{v,t})$.

For fitted parameters $\Theta_{V,T}$ of the physics-models and the raw pressure values $X_{V,T}$ collected from one bus V over one day period T, a set of statistical features $\Gamma(\cdot)$ were computed, including the arithmetic mean μ, the standard deviation σ, the 3rd and 4th standardized moments (Skewness $\frac{\mu_3}{\sigma_3}$ and Kurtosis $\frac{\mu_4}{\sigma_4}$), percentiles (the 10-th, 25-th, 50-th, 75-th, 90-th were selected), the entropy, and the root mean squared (RMS) values $\frac{1}{|T|}\sum_{t \in T}(x_t)^2$ (where $|\cdot|$ denotes the cardinality).

ANOVA F-test was conducted, and the F-score was used for ranking different types of features. In addition, machine learning models were trained with the two types of the features, i.e., $\Gamma(\Theta_{v,t})$ and $\Gamma(X_{v,t})$, and the area under the ROC curve were used for comparing the performance in discriminating the faulty samples (prior to air leak repair event) from the healthy sample (after repair was performed and the fault was dealt with).

4   Results

The results section is organized as follows: i) illustration of fitted physics-based models on the WTAP air leak segments; ii) visual inspection of fitted parameters of the physics-based models using box plot, focusing on two air leak cases; iii) comparing histograms of fitted parameters between the healthy and the faulty populations; iv) the ranking of the features with ANOVA F-score, and comparison of the area under the ROC curve.

Figure 3 shows three example air leak segments and the corresponding fit of the three selected model equations. Since the sensor has a relatively low resolution, the pressure values are quantized into the levels shown. The two elastic models (Eq. 5 and Eq. 8) skew in different directions, while the non-elastic model behaves, in all three example segments, similarly to a linear model. For the elastic leakage model (Eq. 5), the parameter k and a corresponds to the leakage speed of the air pressure, while b corresponds to the offset of the segments; for the elastic leakage model (Eq. 8), m and n corresponds to the change in curvature of the fitted model; the fitting of parameters k and $\frac{L}{V}$ of the non-elastic leakage model (Eq. 4), which has a stronger constrain in the offset term compared to the model Eq. 5, leads to the term $\frac{LP_0}{V}$ dominating over the exponential decreasing term; therefore the fitted model behaves similarly to a linear model.

Table 1 shows a set of box plots summarizing the fitted parameters $\Theta_{v,t}$ (of the three selected model equations, in rows) for the two air leak cases (in columns). The vertical solid lines mark the time of the repair action performed to fix the air leak fault. It can be observed that there is a clear distinction in the parameters b of model Eq. 5, as well as m and n of model Eq. 4, between the faulty and healthy time periods in "Air Leak Case 2" (left column). It is also visible, in the right column, that there are obvious distinctions in the fitted

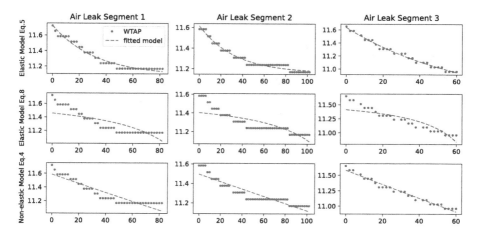

Fig. 3. Visual demonstration of the fitted parameters of three different physics-based models on three example air leak segments.

parameter $\frac{L}{V}$ of model Eq. 8 and both parameters (m and n) of model Eq. 4 between the "before" and "after" the repair. Moreover, there are differences (albeit not obvious) in the model parameters (k and b of model Eq. 5) between healthy and faulty samples.

Table 2 illustrates the difference in the distribution of selected statistical features $\Gamma(\Theta_{v,t})$ between healthy and faulty population. As is shown, there are obvious distinctions between the distribution of the mean, the RMS, and the three percentiles values of model parameter k of model Eq. 5, and $\frac{L}{V}$ of model Eq. 4.

Figure 4 shows the ranking result of the ANOVA F-test (based on healthy and faulty samples of all six cases), comparing conventional statistical features $\Gamma(X_{v,t})$ on the raw data and the statistical features $\Gamma(\Theta_{v,t})$ of physics-inspired parameters, for all three model equations. The experiment was conducted with 6-fold cross-validation, in a leave-one-out setting, i.e. one failure case (and its corresponding three months of data) out of the six cases was left out of the training set non-repeatedly in each of the 6-fold cross-validation experiments; the error bars are generated correspondingly with the leave-one-out experiments. It is clear that overall, across all six air leak cases, most of the fitted parameters of the elastic model (Eq. 5) outrank the conventional features. Four fitted parameters of model Eq. 4 were placed in the top five features, while the fitted parameters of model Eq. 8 scored five features in the top 10 features. These results convincingly demonstrate the advantage of physics-inspired features over the raw sensor readings.

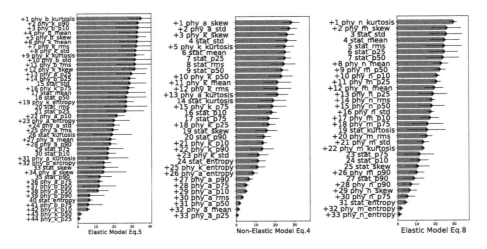

Fig. 4. Comparison of ANOVA F-score between features

Table 1. Illustration of evolution over time of the physics-based model parameters for two example air leak cases; the vertical solid lines mark the time of the air leak repair.

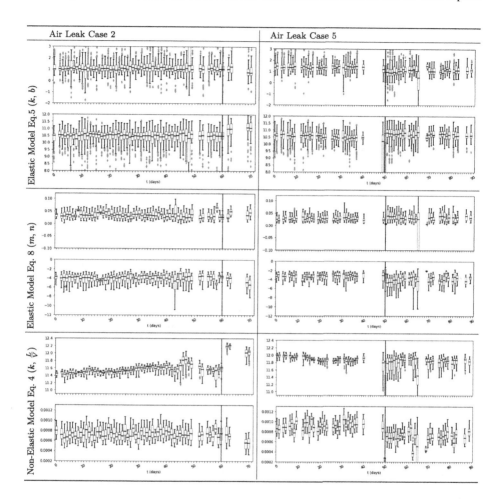

Table 2. PDF comparison of fitted parameters between "before" (red) and "after" (blue) air leak faults being treated in workshop (from case 5)

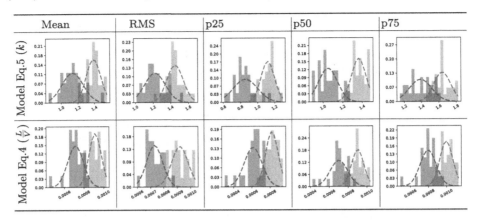

Table 3. Performance (AUC) comparison between using different features for discriminating faulty samples from fault-free samples, on all failures cases with 6-fold cross-validation.

	$\Gamma(\Theta)$			$\Gamma(X)$
	Model Eq. 5	Model Eq. 4	Model Eq. 8	WTAP
KNN	65.80 ± 10.37	63.00 ± 3.78	58.05 ± 5.71	46.94 ± 10.91
MLP	58.77 ± 10.95	68.78 ± 8.89	60.05 ± 7.23	40.07 ± 15.10

The preliminary result, presented in Table 3, of training and testing conventional machine learning models (k-Nearest-Neighbour (kNN) and multi-layer perception (MLP) classifier), with 6-fold cross-validation, shows that using the conventional features $\Gamma(X_{v,t})$ is not better than random guesses. The experiment was conducted in the same way as the result presented in Fig. 4. On the other hand, using the statistical features $\Gamma(\Theta_{v,t})$ on fitted parameters of the three physical models scored 65.80 ± 10.37 (model Eq. 5 with kNN), 68.78 ± 8.89 (model Eq. 4 with MLP), and 60.05 ± 7.23 (model Eq. 8 with MLP).

5 Conclusion and Future Work

In this study, we are exploring the use of physics-based air leakage models in generating useful features for detecting air leaks in city buses. We have compared the proposed physics-model-based features against the conventional ones and showed a clear advantage of the proposed features. With the visual inspection of all box plots, we conclude that, in three out of the six air leak cases, there is a visible difference in the distribution of fitted parameters $\Theta_{v,t}$ between samples before and after the repair treated to the air leak faults. Although the box plot and histogram showed that there is a visual difference in the distribution of the features between the two classes (in half of the cases), the AUC indicated further efforts can be made to improve the performance, e.g. finding a proper learning setting for detecting the air leaks; further development on improving the fitting of physics-based air leak models by imposing relevant constraints for model fitting; exploring the vehicle service records for more air leak cases.

In this paper, only the detection of air leak faults was addressed and pressure values only during the idle state were used to estimate physical parameters. However, the air system is rather complicated, and the air pressure in the wet tank is affected by the usage of the end-use components. Therefore, a wider scope of this work is to consider the impact of all end-use components in the air system: design a comprehensive model that takes into account all possible operational states, i.e., activation associated with all end-use components, with respect to their physical process; utilizing fitted parameters of the physical models not only for detecting faults but also for fault isolation and identification, based on exploring the interpretability of the models; incorporating the fitted parameters into a data-driven fault detection and prognostic framework, utilizing deep learning methods for higher prediction performance.

Acknowledgments. This work was partially supported by Vinnova, Knowledge Foundation and by CHIST-ERA grant CHIST-ERA-19-XAI-012 funded by Swedish Research Council.

References

1. Davy, J.: Calculations for leak rates of hermetic packages. IEEE Trans. Parts Hybrids Pack. **11**(3), 177–189 (1975). https://doi.org/10.1109/TPHP.1975.1135069,
2. Desai, A., Guo, Y., Sheng, S., Sheng, S., Phillips, C., Williams, L.: Prognosis of wind turbine gearbox bearing failures using SCADA and Modeled Data. Ann. Conf. the PHM Soc. **12**(1), 10–10 (2020). https://doi.org/10.36001/phmconf.2020.v12i1.1292,https://papers.phmsociety.org/index.php/phmconf/article/view/1292,
3. El Mir, H., Perinpanayagam, S.: Certification approach for physics informed machine learning and its application in landing gear life assessment. In: 2021 IEEE/AIAA 40th Digital Avionics Systems Conference (DASC), pp. 1–6, October 2021. https://doi.org/10.1109/DASC52595.2021.9594374. ISSN: 2155-7209
4. Fan, Y., Nowaczyk, S., Rögnvaldsson, T.S.: Incorporating expert knowledge into a self-organized approach for predicting compressor faults in a city bus fleet, pp. 58–67 (2015)
5. Gálvez, A., Seneviratne, D., Galar, D.: Hybrid model development for HVAC system in transportation. Technologies **9**(1), 18 (2021)
6. Lees, F.: Lees' Loss Prevention in the Process Industries: Hazard Identification, Assessment and Control. Elsevier Science & Technology, Oxford (2012). http://ebookcentral.proquest.com/lib/halmstad/detail.action?docID=1031883
7. von Rueden, L., et al.: Informed machine learning - a taxonomy and survey of integrating prior knowledge into learning systems. IEEE Trans. Knowl. Data Eng. (99), 1–1 (2021). https://doi.org/10.1109/TKDE.2021.3079836

8. Sepe, M., et al.: A physics-informed machine learning framework for predictive maintenance applied to turbomachinery assets. J. Glob. Power Propul. Soc. **2021**(May), 1–15 (2021). https://doi.org/10.33737/jgpps/134845,https://journal.gpps.global/A-physics-informed-machine-learning-framework-for-predictive-maintenance-applied,134845,0,2.html, publisher: Global Power and Propulsion Society

9. Swischuk, R., Mainini, L., Peherstorfer, B., Willcox, K.: Projection-based model reduction: Formulations for physics-based machine learning. Comput. Fluids **179**, 704–717 (2019). https://doi.org/10.1016/j.compfluid.2018.07.021,https://www.sciencedirect.com/science/article/pii/S0045793018304250

10. Willard, J., Jia, X., Xu, S., Steinbach, M., Kumar, V.: Integrating scientific knowledge with machine learning for engineering and environmental systems. ACM Compu. Surv. (CSUR) **55**(4) (2021)

11. Yucesan, Y.A., Viana, F.: A hybrid model for main bearing fatigue prognosis based on physics and machine learning. In: AIAA SciTech 2020 Forum. AIAA SciTech Forum, American Institute of Aeronautics and Astronautics, January 2020. https://doi.org/10.2514/6.2020-1412,https://arc.aiaa.org/doi/10.2514/6.2020-1412

Towards Geometry-Preserving Domain Adaptation for Fault Identification

Zahra Taghiyarrenani[(✉)], Sławomir Nowaczyk, Sepideh Pashami,
and Mohamed-Rafik Bouguelia

Center for Applied Intelligent Systems Research, Halmstad University,
Halmstad, Sweden
{zahra.taghiyarrenani,slawomir.nowaczyk,sepideh.pashami,
mohamed-rafik.bouguelia}@hh.se

Abstract. In most industries, the working conditions of equipment vary significantly from one site to another, from one time of a year to another, and so on. This variation poses a severe challenge for data-driven fault identification methods: it introduces a change in the data distribution. This contradicts the underlying assumption of most machine learning methods, namely that training and test samples follow the same distribution. Domain Adaptation (DA) methods aim to address this problem by minimizing the distribution distance between training (source) and test (target) samples.

However, in the area of predictive maintenance, this idea is complicated by the fact that different classes – fault categories – also vary across domains. Most of the state-of-the-art DA methods assume that the data in the target domain is complete, i.e., that we have access to examples from all the possible classes or faulty categories during adaptation. In reality, this is often very difficult to guarantee.

Therefore, there is a need for a domain adaptation method that is able to align the source and target domains even in cases of having access to an incomplete set of test data. This paper presents our work in progress as we propose an approach for such a setting based on maintaining the geometry information of source samples during the adaptation. This way, the model can capture the relationships between different fault categories and preserve them in the constructed domain-invariant feature space, even in situations where some classes are entirely missing. This paper examines this idea using artificial data sets to demonstrate the effectiveness of geometry-preserving transformation. We have also started investigations on real-world predictive maintenance datasets, such as CWRU.

Keywords: Predictive maintenance · Fault identification · Domain adaptation · Geometry

1   Introduction

In recent years, data-driven fault identification methods have attracted increasing research attention for different applications, including rotating machinery, gearbox, wind turbines, and more [9]. These methods are generally based on

I. Koprinska et al. (Eds.): ECML PKDD 2022 Workshops, CCIS 1753, pp. 451–460, 2023.
https://doi.org/10.1007/978-3-031-23633-4_30

machine learning and learn predictive models from provided training samples. Those models are used to classify new, previously unseen data. However, the generalization ability of the models to predict the label of the test samples is inherently connected to the assumption that training and test samples are generated by independent and identically distributed random variables. In a predictive maintenance setting, this corresponds to equipment operating under the same conditions and consequently generating data of the same distribution.

However, in a real industrial setting, the variation in working conditions is inevitable. The most common setup is that fault identification methods are created by the equipment manufacturer in their lab setting and then deployed at customer installation, often in a different part of the world. This means that the data from these two situations will inherently differ. We call each of these settings and the corresponding data distributions, "domains."

In this paper, we assume that the training samples belong to one domain, called source, and test samples belong to another domain, called target. The goal is to identify a method where the model trained based on data collected by the manufacturer can be applied to the data collected by the customer. In the following text, we will, for simplicity, use "source samples" (resp. target samples) to refer to samples generated in the source (resp. target) domain.

To tackle the problem of working with the training data and test data generated from different domains (different working conditions), several cross-domain fault identification methods are reported in the literature [8]. In this work, we will focus on Domain Adaptation (DA), where the goal of is to minimize the distribution distance between the source and target domains. It is one of the methods used to solve cross-domain fault identification tasks.

Two DA settings are applied to fault identification: Full Domain Adaptation (FDA) and Limited Domain Adaptation (LDA). FDA assumes that unlabeled samples exist for all fault categories (classes) in both the source and the target domains. In practice, this means that in order to identify faults in the target domain, FDA techniques must wait until the occurrence of all of the faults in the customer installation; only then can they collect enough samples to perform domain adaptation. In contrast, LDA techniques can adapt corresponding source and target samples even if there are no (unlabeled) samples for some fault categories. As an extreme example, the ultimate goal is to be able to perform DA based on healthy target samples only; before any faults are recorded at the customer installation and when the faulty samples come only from the lab experiments.

The main idea of this work is to adapt source and target domains while preserving the geometry of the data; Keeping the data's geometry helps transfer knowledge about missing classes to the target domain. This promises to capture the transformation between source and target domains without requiring the complete correspondence between all the classes or fault categories. To this end, a new loss function is proposed to adapt the source and target domains while preserving the distance between different samples and consequently preserving the distance between fault categories. The results of the proposed idea on artificial data sets show the effectiveness of preserving the initial geometry and the adaptation of corresponding faults in the source and target domains.

2   Related Works

DA techniques have been applied successfully in several applications, including predictive maintenance and specifically for fault identification [8]. The core idea of DA is to minimize the distance between the data distribution in source and target domains. They do the minimization either explicitly using distribution distance measurements such as MMD [3], or implicitly using adversarial training methods [5]. Most papers presented in the literature solve the FDA problem. Regarding the LDA setting, Liu ZH, et al. in [4] proposed a method for the LDA setting. They assume that in the target domain, only healthy samples are available. Their method learns functions that map the healthy category to each faulty category in the source domain. Those functions are then applied to healthy samples in the target domain to generate fake faulty samples. Finally, a cross-domain classifier is trained using real source samples and fake target samples. The proposed method in [7] solves the problem in the LDA setting with any number of missing fault categories in the target domain. They adapt the target sample toward source samples while preserving the relationship between source samples to prevent them from distortion. However, the model is not trained for missing categories; thus, they will be placed randomly in the constructed domain-invariant feature space.

3   Problem Formulation

The proposed method is designed with the following assumptions in mind:

- Training and test samples are generated from two domains corresponding to different working conditions. In particular, there is only one source domain and one target domain.
- The (potential) fault categories are the same for source and target domains.
- Samples from the source domain are labeled and correspond to all the possible fault categories.
- Samples from the target domain are unlabeled.

More formally, the above assumptions can be stated as follows. Considering source domain as $D_s = \{(x_s, y_s)\}$ and target domain as $D_t = \{(x_t, y_t)\}$, the label space of source and target domain are equal to each other, i.e. $C_t = C_s$.

The label space of the available target samples during adaptation is $C'_t \subseteq C_t$. If $C'_t = C_t = C_s$, the problem is a full domain adaptation(FDA); and if $C'_t \subset C_t$, the problem is limited domain adaptation(LDA).

The need for maintaining the relationships within fault categories in the source domain is particularly important for the LDA setting. If we were to simply map C_s into our available C'_t categories, the "surplus" source samples from $C_s \setminus C'_t$ cannot be matched to any available samples from the target domain. Since they lose their relationship with other samples, they are very likely to cause a negative impact on adaptation [1]. Therefore, to utilize them and extract information in the target domain, a geometry preserver keeps the relationship between samples in the new representation and original representation space consistent. Consequently, the source samples from C'_t categories will be adapted to target samples from C'_t as much as possible, while source samples from $C_s \setminus C'_t$ categories will be mapped into areas of space that are not occupied by any D'_t samples – based on maintaining their relationships to other C_s classes.

More specifically, the overall goal is to utilize geometry information during DA, to solve the problem of LDA. However, we first show the effectiveness of preserving geometry in the FDA setting. Notably, for the FDA setting, we construct a shared feature representation for both source and target domains in which they are aligned.

4   Proposed Method

In this section, we describe how to employ a new method to maintain the geometric information of the samples while adapting the source and target samples in the FDA settings. To this end, source and target samples are mapped to a new domain-invariant feature representation. In the new feature representation, the source and target samples are indistinguishable, and all pairwise distances are maintained. This idea is implemented using a neural network, illustrated in Fig. 1.

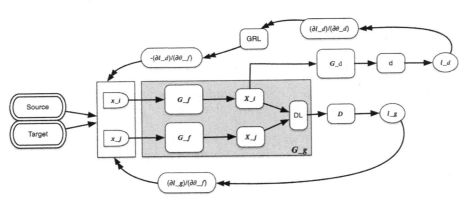

Fig. 1. Proposed method

At first, we generate all pairwise samples in each of the source and target domains, e.g., (x^i, x^j) along with two labels; The first label is the distance between x^i and x^j. The second label is the domain to which x^i belongs. Similarly, the network has two inputs and two outputs; So, it takes pairwise samples (x^i, x^j) as input and predicts the distance of the inputs in the new feature space and the domain to which x^i belongs.

There is a component as *feature extractor*, G_f; The output of the feature extractor is the new feature space. There are two copies of G_f in the network with completely the same parameters. Each of the inputs feeds into one of them. So, they will be generated in the new feature space. We call them X^i and X^j.

X^i and X^j feed into a Distance Layer(DL) that calculates the distance between X^i and X^j.

We want to train the feature extractor so that the distance between x^i and x^j is equal to the distance between X^i and X^j. So, the output of the Distance Layer for the pairwise inputs (x^i, x^j), which we call D, must be equal to the first provided label of (x^i, x^j). We call this part of the network as *Geometry Preserver*, G_g. The geometry preserver is shown in gray color in Fig. 1.

On the other hand, the output of the first feature extractor is fed into a component called *Domain Regressor*, G_d. The domain regressor predicts the domain of the first input, x^i, which is shown by d. The responsibility of G_d is to align the source and target domains. So, it is trained in such a way that it can't distinguish source and target samples. In continue, we will discuss the details of the proposed method.

Feature extractor and domain regressor follow the same notation as [2]. Feature extractor $G_f(., \theta_f)$ learns a function (parameterized by θ_f) that maps input samples to the new feature spaces. Geometry preserver $G_g(.,.,\theta_f)$ controls the output of G_f by adding a loss function. The purpose of the geometry preserver is to preserve the relationship between pair samples after mapping them to the new feature space. To this end, we adopt a Siamese-like neural network configuration to implement G_g [6]. A Siamese-like network contains two identical subnetworks with shared parameters. So, we have configured the G_g using two copies of the feature extractor followed by a Distance Layer (DL). DL calculates the distance between the outputs of two G_f.

To give an example, let us assume that x^1 and x^2 are two samples belonging to the same domain, either source or target. Then $G_f(x^1) = X^1$ and $G_f(x^2) = X^2$ are the same samples, but transformed into the new feature space. Moreover, $G_g(x^1, x^2; \theta_f) = dis_{new}(x^1, x^2)$ is the distance of $G_f(x^1)$ and $G_f(x^2)$, and the parameters θ_f are optimized to make sure that this distance is as close as possible to $dis_{original}(x^1, x^2) = \|x^1, x^2\|$ (the distance between these samples in the original space).

Accordingly, given n_s source samples and n_t target samples, training G_g for both source and target samples lead to the following optimization problem:

$$\min_{\theta_f} \quad [\frac{1}{n_s^2 + n_t^2}(\sum_{i=1}^{n_s}\sum_{j=1}^{n_s} l_g^{(i,j)}(\theta_f) + \sum_{i=1}^{n_t}\sum_{j=1}^{n_t} l_g^{(i,j)}(\theta_f)) + \lambda R(\theta_f)], \qquad (1)$$

where l_g is the loss function of the geometry preserver and $R(\theta_f)$ is a regularizer weighted with the λ. In order to adapt source and target domains, we use a domain regularizer that is proposed by [2], as $R(\theta_f)$. Similar to [2], we call domain regularizer as G_d with parameters θ_d that is a domain regressor layer. $G_d(., \theta_d)$ learns a logistic regressor that model the probability that x^i is from the source or target domain. However, we only adapt the samples from shared classes; therefore, we define an array I so that $I_i = 1$ if x^i is a target sample or it is a source sample belonging to the shared classes, otherwise $I_i = 0$.

Considering the loss function of G_d as l_d, the regularizer will be calculated as follow [2]:

$$R(\theta_f) = \max_{\theta_f,\theta_d} \ [\frac{-1}{n_s+n_t}(\sum_{i=1}^{n_s+n_t} I_i l_d^i(\theta_f,\theta_d))]. \tag{2}$$

So, using Eqs. 1 and 2, the complete optimization objective will be:

$$E(\theta_d,\theta_f) = \ [\frac{1}{n_s^2+n_t^2}(\sum_{i=1}^{n_s}\sum_{j=1}^{n_s} l_g^{(i,j)}(\theta_f) + \sum_{i=1}^{n_t}\sum_{j=1}^{n_t} l_g^{(i,j)}(\theta_f)) - \lambda(\frac{1}{n_s+n_t}(\sum_{i=1}^{n_s+n_t} l_d^i(\theta_f,\theta_d)))].$$
$$\tag{3}$$

A gradient reversal layer(GRL) [2] is used between the feature extractor and the domain regressor. GRL act as an identity function in forward propagation. But during back-propagation, it changed the sign of the gradient. So, the following gradient updates, to find the saddle point θ_f and θ_d can be done using stochastic gradient descent (SGD).

$$\theta_f \leftarrow \theta_f - \mu(\frac{\partial l_g^{(i,j)}}{\partial \theta_f} - \frac{\partial l_d^{(i)}}{\partial \theta_f}), \qquad \theta_d \leftarrow \theta_d - \mu(\frac{\partial l_d^{(i)}}{\partial \theta_d}) \tag{4}$$

where μ is the learning rate. As a result, the trained feature extractor maps both source and target samples into a new feature representation in which different domains are not distinguishable while the geometry of data within each domain is preserved. In the constructed feature space, the labeled source samples can be used as training samples to learn a predictive model to predict the label of unlabeled target samples.

5 Experiments

As this paper is a work-in-progress, we only demonstrate the efficiency of our proposed method using synthetic data. We first conduct a set of experiments in FDA setting and then in the LDA setting. For all experiments, the following configurations are fixed; We describe each layer in the neural network as (size of neurons, activation function); the feature extractor consists of 3 dense layers as (15, relu),(15, relu), (2, linear); the new feature space is constructed in the last layer of the feature extractor. We have deliberately chosen the size of the last layer of the feature extractor equal to two in order to compare the original and constructed feature spaces visually and intuitively. Domain regressor is shaped with two dense layers as (15, relu), (1, sigmoid). In both subnetworks, *Batch Normalization* is used. The loss functions of geometry preserver and domain regressor are *mean square error(MSE)* and *binary-cross-entropy*, respectively. *Euclidean* distance is used to calculate dis_{new} and $dis_{original}$ (the pairwise distances of the samples in the original and new feature spaces, respectively).

5.1 FDA Setting

In this section, we study the behavior of the proposed idea in an FDA setting.

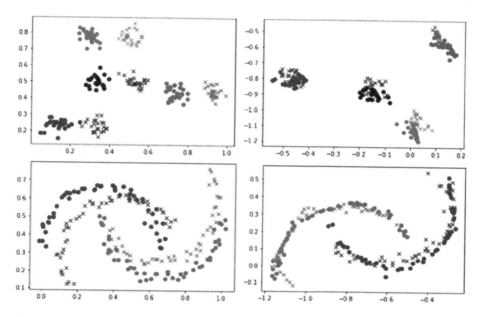

Fig. 2. Two toy data sets are presented in the first column. The markers ∘ and ×
denote the samples from source and target, respectively. Different colors show different
categories. The results of domain adaptation are shown in the second column. (Color
figure online)

Figure 2 shows the results comparing the source and target samples in their
original (on the left) and new or constructed (on the right) feature spaces. The
two rows of Fig. 2 correspond to two different artificial data sets. For the first
problem, on the top, the transformation to generate target samples is a shift
(translation) of all the source samples by 0.2 to the left. In the second one, all
source samples are rotated 30° with respect to point (0.5, 0.5).

It can be seen that in both cases, the source and target samples in the
new feature space are not only adapted to each other but also their geometry is
preserved. As a consequence, the method keeps the relationship between different
categories. This is a clear advantage of our proposed method over existing state-
of-the-art approaches. Methods that only aim for adaptation generally distort
the within-domain relationships. Accordingly, this approach provides a promising
result; in the next subsection, we extend this functionality for an adaptation in
an LDA setting.

In Fig. 3, we present the training loss per epoch for the first problem example.
GP-loss, *DR-loss* and *loss* are the loss of geometry preserver, domain regressor
and total loss of the network, respectively. It can be seen that the loss amount
gets steady around 0.6; that means the saddle points to optimize the objective
function are obtained.

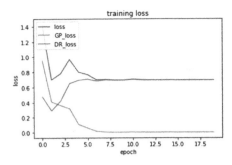

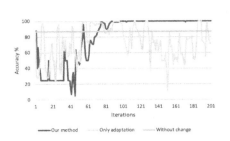

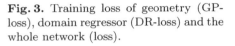

Fig. 3. Training loss of geometry (GP-loss), domain regressor (DR-loss) and the whole network (loss).

Fig. 4. Accuracy of the target label set prediction using 1-NN classifier.

In the next experiment, we evaluate how well the DA approach supports fault identification tasks. To this end, we use source and target samples in the new space as training and test samples. We use a K-nearest-neighbor classifier with $k = 1$ to predict the label of target samples. Thus, in each iteration of training the model, we construct a 1-NN classifier and predict the target labels. The obtained accuracy per iteration is shown in Fig. 4 as *Our method*. In order to show the training procedure, in each iteration, 10% of all samples are used (since when using all of the data in an epoch, the training converges already in the first iteration). In addition, in order to show the effect of the geometry preserver, we compare the result of our method against a neural network that only adapts source and target with an adversarial method; i.e., we omit the effect of the geometry preserver from the network; the corresponding results are shown in Fig. 4 as *Only adaptation*. It can also be seen that by using the geometry preserver, the network will converge faster than the alternative. Besides, we use the source and target samples in their original space as training and test samples and predict the label set of target samples using a 1-NN classifier; The results are also shown in Fig. 4 as *Without change* (It is the results in the original space, i.e., without adaptation.). By comparing the results, the effectiveness of the proposed method to adapt domains is self-evident.

Table 1. Classification results on 4 adaptation problem.

Rotation degree	Our method	Only adaptation	Without change
15	$1.0 + 0.0$	$0.865 + 0.0541$	$1.0 + 0.0$
30	$0.997 + 0.0064$	$0.804 + 0.0709$	$0.91 + 0.0$
45	$0.875 + 0.1891$	$0.692 + 0.0957$	$0.55 + 0.0$
60	$0.875 + 0.0532$	$0.563 + 0.1391$	$0.39 + 0.0$

Finally, we perform a similar analysis as above in a more complex dataset, by creating four versions of the 2D moon data set by rotating it by 15, 30, 45, and 60 °C. A case of the source and target samples with a rotation degree equal to 30 can be seen in the left bottom of Fig. 2. For each of these problems, a 1-NN classifier in the constructed new feature space is used to predict the label set of the target samples. We repeat this experiment for our method, only adaptation (omitting the effect of geometry preserver) and without adaptation (applying 1-NN classifier in the original space). The results, in terms of the mean and standard deviation, calculated after the 10 times run, are shown in Table 1.

5.2 LDA Setting

We examine two cases of LDA: one-missing and two-missing target classes during the training. The first row of the Fig. 5 demonstrates a one-missing class scenario. Figure 5a indicates that we do not have access to the training samples for class 3 (red samples). Nevertheless, in the constructed space shown in Fig. 5b, we can observe that the test samples of class 3 are aligned with their counterparts from the source domain. In other words, our method compensates for the absence of samples of class 3 in the target domain by preserving the geometry information while adapting domains.

Likewise, Fig. 5c shows the 2-missing scenario where we do not have access to any samples of classes 2 and 3. The results shown in Fig. 5d shows that the proposed method is capable of achieving the right adaptation, not only for the available classes, but also for the missing ones.

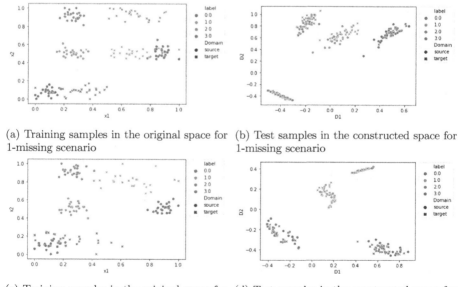

(a) Training samples in the original space for 1-missing scenario

(b) Test samples in the constructed space for 1-missing scenario

(c) Training samples in the original space for 2-missing scenario

(d) Test samples in the constructed space for 2-missing scenario

Fig. 5. Two LDA scenarios, with 1-class-missing scenario in top row and 2-class-missing in the second row. (Color figure online)

6 Conclusion

In this paper, we propose a new method for limited domain adaptation, leveraging geometry information of both the source and target domains. We present, as a work-in-progress one, results in the FDA setting confirming that the relationships between samples are preserved in the new feature space. After that, we provide the results for LDA settings on toy datasets. According to the results, maintaining geometry information within domains allows for the use of source samples to compensate for the missing classes in the target domain. As the next step, we plan to use this method to solve real-world problems, in particular identifying faults in an industrial system. In other words, by utilizing this method, there is no need to wait for all types of faults to occur in a system before developing a predictive model, but rather use data from other systems.

Acknowledgements. This research has been funded in part by the Knowledge Foundation and by Vinnova, Strategic Vehicle Research and Innovation programme.

References

1. Cao, Z., You, K., Long, M., Wang, J., Yang, Q.: Learning to transfer examples for partial domain adaptation. In: Proceedings of the IEEE/CVF Conference on Computer Vision and Pattern Recognition, pp. 2985–2994 (2019)
2. Ganin, Y., et al.: Domain-adversarial training of neural networks. J. Mach. Learn. Res. **17**(1), 2030–2096 (2016)
3. Han, T., Liu, C., Yang, W., Jiang, D.: Deep transfer network with joint distribution adaptation: a new intelligent fault diagnosis framework for industry application. ISA Trans. **97**, 269–281 (2020)
4. Li, X., Zhang, W., Ding, Q.: Cross-domain fault diagnosis of rolling element bearings using deep generative neural networks. IEEE Trans. Industr. Electron. **66**(7), 5525–5534 (2018)
5. Liu, Z.H., Lu, B.L., Wei, H.L., Chen, L., Li, X.H., Rätsch, M.: Deep adversarial domain adaptation model for bearing fault diagnosis. IEEE Trans. Syst. Man Cybern. Syst. **51**(7), 4217–4226 (2019)
6. Pai, G., Talmon, R., Bronstein, A., Kimmel, R.: Dimal: deep isometric manifold learning using sparse geodesic sampling. In: 2019 IEEE Winter Conference on Applications of Computer Vision (WACV), pp. 819–828. IEEE (2019)
7. Wang, Q., Michau, G., Fink, O.: Missing-class-robust domain adaptation by unilateral alignment. IEEE Trans. Industr. Electron. **68**(1), 663–671 (2020)
8. Yan, R., Shen, F., Sun, C., Chen, X.: Knowledge transfer for rotary machine fault diagnosis. IEEE Sens. J. **20**(15), 8374–8393 (2019)
9. Zhang, W., Yang, D., Wang, H.: Data-driven methods for predictive maintenance of industrial equipment: a survey. IEEE Syst. J. **13**(3), 2213–2227 (2019)

A Systematic Approach for Tracking the Evolution of XAI as a Field of Research

Samaneh Jamshidi [ID], Sławomir Nowaczyk[(✉)] [ID], Hadi Fanaee-T [ID], and Mahmoud Rahat [ID]

Center for Applied Intelligent Systems Research (CAISR), Halmstad University, Halmstad, Sweden
{samaneh.jamshidi,slawomir.nowaczyk,hadi.fanaee-t,mahmoud.rahat}@hh.se

Abstract. The increasing use of AI methods in various applications has raised concerns about their explainability and transparency. Many solutions have been developed within the last few years to either explain the model itself or the decisions provided by the model. However, the number of contributions in the field of eXplainable AI (XAI) is increasing at such a high pace that it is almost impossible for a newcomer to identify key ideas, track the field's evolution, or find promising new research directions.

Typically, survey papers serve as a starting point, providing a feasible entry point into a research area. However, this is not trivial for some fields with exponential growth in the literature, such as XAI. For instance, we analyzed 23 surveys in the XAI domain published within the last three years and surprisingly found no common conceptualization among them. This makes XAI one of the most challenging research areas to enter. To address this problem, we propose a systematic approach that enables newcomers to identify the principal ideas and track their evolution. The proposed method includes automating the retrieval of relevant papers, extracting their semantic relationship, and creating a temporal graph of ideas by post-analysis of citation graphs.

The main outcome of our method is Field's Evolution Graph (FEG), which can be used to find the core idea of each approach in this field, see how a given concept has developed and evolved over time, observe how different notions interact with each other, and perceive how a new paradigm emerges through combining multiple ideas. As for demonstration, we show that FEG successfully identifies the field's key articles, such as LIME or Grad-CAM, and maps out their evolution and relationships.

Keywords: Field's evolution · XAI · Explainable AI

1 Introduction

In recent years, the usage of Machine Learning (ML) and Artificial Intelligence (AI) techniques has increased greatly, especially as these methods are becoming more and more popular across all aspects of life. From the efficiency and performance standpoint, new algorithms and architectures are being continuously

I. Koprinska et al. (Eds.): ECML PKDD 2022 Workshops, CCIS 1753, pp. 461–476, 2023.
https://doi.org/10.1007/978-3-031-23633-4_31

proposed, providing essentially day-by-day improvements. In particular, the last decade brought the Deep Learning (DL) revolution; powered by hardware developments and enormous labeled datasets, these new models outperform, in many tasks, not only classical ML approaches but also human experts.

However, much of the new power of ML methods come at the cost of creating models of very high complexity. While traditional methods, such as (shallow) decision trees or linear regression, give the users a good understanding of how they make their decisions, the more complex methods are opaque. Often known as black boxes, they are not explainable by themselves. Although many such black box models achieve high performance, the lack of transparency that comes with it makes it so that they are not suitable in every setting. Given the desire to take advantage of new developments enabled by AI in many domains, this drawback is sometimes a deal-breaker, especially in safety-critical settings. In a domain like healthcare, it is not easy to trust a model and accept its decision without knowing the reasons for the decisions made [28]; ultimately, it is the human clinician who is responsible for the treatment, and they can only use AI-based decision support systems that provide relevant medical evidence. Prognostics and Health Management (PHM) is another interesting topic because of its high operating, maintenance, and downtime cost. So predictive remaining useful life and predictive maintenance are critical industry issues. Using AI and ML algorithms is increasing in this area, like in other areas, but lack of transparency, interpretability, understanding, and interpretation is one of the main challenges. Companies and factories cannot rely on decisions that they do not know the reasons for and can not understand why. Not only is this lack of trust related to bias and lack of representation of the training datasets, but it also includes adversarial attacks [14,19,34]. As an example, authors in [27] show that it is easy to produce meaningless images, unrecognizable to humans, but such that the DNNs classify them with 99.99% confidence. On the other hand, the right explanation methods can help to significantly improve the model performance or design a better architecture, as demonstrated in [52]. Generally, there are two main motivations to develop methods that make black box models explainable: 1) understanding the reasons behind a decision to make the model trustable; 2) having a better view of a model and its weakness, with the aim of debugging.

It is for those reasons that XAI is today one of the most popular and heavily researched topics in AI. It is clear that the challenges are real, but significant progress has been made in the last couple of years, in part due to cross- and inter-disciplinary collaborations. This is readily visible in the rapid growth of the number of publications within the field. For instance, more than 5500 research articles (400 for survey papers) are returned by a Google Scholar search just by using the phrase "explainable artificial intelligence" – within the year 2021 alone (Fig. 1).

This explosion in popularity, however, creates unique challenges in terms of understanding the current landscape, identifying common trends, comparing solutions, and finding overlaps and gaps in state-of-the-art. This is an especially frustrating obstacle for newcomers into the field – which poses a danger

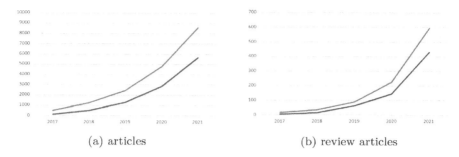

(a) articles   (b) review articles

Fig. 1. The statistics appeared in Google Scholar for the number of articles and review articles published per year from 2017 to 2021, based on the search for **blue lines:** the phrase "explainable artificial intelligence" and **orange lines:** the phrase "explainable artificial intelligence" OR "explainable machine learning" OR "understanding artificial intelligence" OR "understanding machine learning", by year (Color figure online)

of creating narrow, hermetic, splintered societies; spelling disaster for the field, which, by its very natures, requires broad and interdisciplinary collaborations and perspectives. Among the survey articles in the area, some focus on the XAI for rather specific topics, including medical [28,47] or natural language processing [12]. Although domain-specific review articles have advantages, their biggest problem is missing out on the ideas that have been successful on other data or in other domains and could be applied to that specific domain. Also, among the survey articles, there are many conflicts on how to categorize the methods in the XAI field. In addition, there is no agreement on the most important articles in the field; since there are so many articles, the vast majority are only cited by a very small number of review articles.

To tackle the challenges explained above, we propose a systematic and universal approach that enables newcomers to identify the fields' main ideas and track their evolution. The remainder of the paper is organized as follows. Section 2 gives an overview of related work. Section 3 presents the proposed method. Section 4 is dedicated to experimenting with details. Section 5 demonstrates the results. Finally, Sect. 6 concludes the paper.

2   Related Work

In many domains, the number of published scientific papers rapidly increases every year, and some researchers have suggested automating survey generation via AI solutions. This is typically framed as a multi-document summarization, a subset of natural language processing. Abstractive [25] and extractive [48] summarizations are among the most common approaches. The idea of using citation graphs or citation links for analyzing the relations between papers has also been explored before [1,9,50]. One common approach is leveraging citation sentences to pinpoint important aspects of the papers. For instance, [33,45] exploit a template-based framework and composes a template-tree. The latter crawls citation index databases such as PubMed and Semantic Scholar and analyses the citation graph. However, more advanced methods to process the citation graphs are still to be developed. For instance, it is not clear if all the citations in a paper are relevant and reliable or if they share the same level of importance in the context.

Although text summarization-based approaches have been relatively good at producing a summary of related works, they are not able to make semantic relationships between the papers or identify the evolution of the key ideas.

3   Proposed Method: Field's Evolution Graph (FEG)

Our fundamental goal in this paper is to understand the "evolution" of XAI as a field of research. We are particularly interested in identifying the key concepts and ideas that shaped further development. We aim to express these by finding a graph of relations between papers in XAI, allowing us to identify influences and concepts that have been developed and improved over time, discover groups and communities related to key ideas, etc.

The sheer volume of papers in the field makes this task infeasible if attempted manually. Therefore, we are proposing an approach that allows us to (partially) automate the task.

The key focus of our approach is analyzing the citations among papers since in the scientific world bibliographic references are the most reliable source of information about inspirations, extensions, development, and improvement of ideas. Therefore, we first extract a graph network of paper relations, second, we identify the important edges, and third, we analyze the resulting structure to uncover the thread of the evolution of key concepts in the XAI field. The key challenge, and the main focus of this section, is the discovery of different types of edges and identifying how they indicate the evolution of ideas within the field.

Algorithm 1. Field's Evolution Graph

1: Select a list of survey papers in the XAI field.
2: Extract their references using Semantic Scholar API.
3: Calculate the repetition of extracted references among those surveys (**repetition rate**).
4: Pick those papers of step 3 that are cited by at least 25% of the survey list (**Influential papers**).
5: Rank them based on publication year, citation number, and repetition rate.
6: Draw a graph of citations between papers of the previous step.
7: Remove unnecessary links from the graph.

3.1   Identification of Influential Papers

At first, we need a number of important and influential papers in this field. The most obvious approach would be to start with highly-cited papers. However, citations alone do not provide accurate and reliable results for several reasons. First, the number of citations depends on the year of the publication, as well as the venue, and does not necessarily accurately reflect the true importance of the contribution. More importantly, many articles belong to more than one domain, i.e., not only XAI, and their citation may be due to importance for other domains. Finally, some of the important papers just focus on a specific issue or data and, despite their importance in this area, will be referenced by a smaller number of articles. Therefore, there is a need to use other features to identify these articles.

Instead, we propose a different approach to obtaining such papers, namely, by exploring the existing surveys. This is feasible in an exploding area like XAI due to the available number of review articles published every year. We select a number of recent survey articles, based on popularity; then, we extract their references (by using Semantic Scholar API), and calculate the repetition of each paper among those survey articles. Papers with a high repetition count, i.e., those included in many surveys, are likely to be the most influential and important ones in the field. Thus, three features, including citation rate, repetition count in surveys, and publication year, have been used in identifying key articles.

3.2   Citation Importance

The next step is to find the relations between the papers we have identified as key papers, revealing a structure within the XAI field. In particular, we aim to discover how different methods have evolved in this area over time. We would like to track the evolution and incremental improvements of an idea, starting from the original paper. We also want to show how the combinations of existing methods are effective in shaping new methods and identify when it happens. Finally, we want to group the methods by revealing the different approaches in XAI in an automatic way.

The starting point is to analyze citations since they are the most direct measure of influence across papers. By considering key articles as nodes and references' status as edges, a graph of the relationships between these articles is formed. A directed graph can show these relations perfectly.

Articles refer to each other in different ways, and those references can have different meanings. For example, depending on the section (such as background, method, experiments, results, etc.) where a citation occurs, the importance and influence across papers vary greatly. Looking back at our goal, we do not consider all these types of citations. In particular, citations referring to the methodological relationships are the most important for our purpose – since it is the methodology where new ideas and solutions are formed. There are many ways of assessing citations. One of them is to do it by hand, which is time-consuming and costly, especially in a large number of articles. The automatic alternative is Semantic Scholar, which provides high-quality citation data via API [16]. It indexes published peer-reviewed scientific literature across various disciplines, currently covering more than 187 million research papers. Semantic Scholar integrates a set of query and analytics features, several of which have been identified as useful for our study. It offers an API to pull data regarding individual records, references list, and citation data for each indexed paper. It also classifies paper references into different reference types: background, results, methods, or without a label. However, since the whole procedure is processed automatically, the accuracy of citation data does not seem perfect, and some errors are expected, thus, some manual post-processing is required.

3.3   Visualization of FEG

Visualization is a useful and efficient way in many fields, especially in analysis. It gives a higher chance of discovering insights when interacting with data. Graphs, on the other hand, are a good tool for showing the connections between the components of a set. Following the directed edges from one node to another provides useful information about the type and manner of connection between two nodes. We use FEG plots to show the relevance of articles. Although there are various methods for examining and analyzing graphs, we have used graph visualization and analysis manually at this stage of the work.

4   Experiment

We conduct a relatively small-scale experiment where we evaluate the feasibility of the proposed approach before scaling it up.

The first step toward obtaining the list of key articles in the XAI field is to analyze recent surveys. Therefore, we started from a list of 23 review articles published between 2018 and 2021. We then analyzed all the references present in those review articles, obtaining an initial list of more than 1800 potentially interesting papers. Next, we ranked the articles in this list using the three important features: publication year, citation number, and repetition rate (i.e., how many selected review articles referred to that article). There are two significant findings regarding this list:

- There is a *very* long tail of papers that were only cited by one of the selected survey papers – more than 1400 papers were only cited once among the 23 surveys. Almost 900 of them are published before 2018, which means that all of those papers were published before all the surveys, but they have been only noticed by one of them.
- Only 9 papers were cited by half (or more) of the surveys and 8 of them were published before 2018. This means that the consensus among the surveys about important papers is virtually non-existent. An extremely small ratio (half a percent) of articles has been agreed upon by the majority of review articles.

The above observations show that using these surveys for finding influential and important articles in the field is problematic, to say the least. It is very likely that, by relying on input from a handful of such papers, a new reader would get a very biased and incomplete picture of the field.

Instead, we believe that some of these issues can be diminished, even if not completely removed, by aggregating data from multiple surveys.

5 Results

Figure 2 shows the FEG plot for all the connections of selected articles: a subset of key articles: those which are referenced by at least 25% of the reviews [2–8, 10, 11, 13, 15, 17, 18, 20–24, 26, 27, 29–32, 35–44, 46, 49, 51–55].

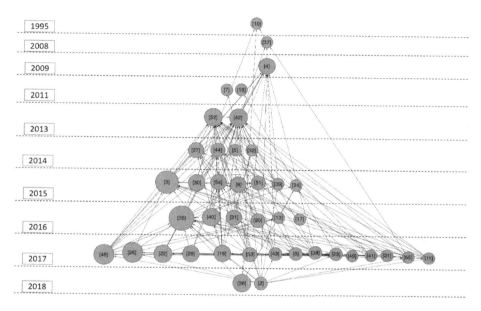

Fig. 2. FEG plot: links between extracted key articles (only those referenced by at least 25% of selected review articles). The directed edge from node A to node B means article A cites article B. The radius of each circle indicates the number of review articles referencing this paper. The vertical axis refers to the time (the upper, the older)

As discussed above, not all the links between articles are actually meaningful. For the purpose of tracking the evolution of the XAI field, we want to focus on methods that significantly influenced each other. To this end, we used semantic Scholar to label the links. A total of 158 links were found among the articles, out of which 92 included methodologies, 12 included results, and 91 included backgrounds (note that some links include multiple tags). Finally, 32 of the links are unlabeled. For our work, links with the methodology label are the most important; a bit less than 60% of the links have this label. Accordingly, in Fig. 3,

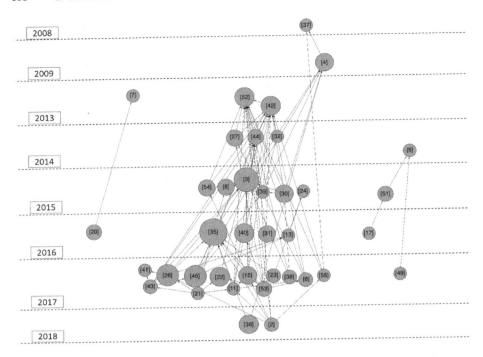

Fig. 3. FEG plot: links and labeled methods based on Semantic Scholar result, between extracted key articles referenced by at least 25% of selected review articles.

we keep the edges labeled "methodology" for further consideration and remove the rest.

One can immediately notice in Fig. 3 that there are two (small) disconnected sub-graphs, and a large part remains connected. Those two sub-graphs can be representative of two different types of methods in this field. By analyzing the articles of these two groups, it can be seen that one of those represents methods related to providing prototypical examples as an explanation, while the other is related to the use of image captioning as an explanation. Those findings are discussed in more detail in the following subsections.

5.1   Example-Based Methods

One of the key ideas we found from FEG plots is example-based methods. The best example of this category is the work of [7] who propose to select a few instances from the dataset; those that are a good representative of data can be a way to make a better understanding dataset. These kinds of methods, known as prototype methods, are usually used as a preprocessing part. This method suggests that the desired prototype or representative of class C should cover as many training data of class C as possible while covering as few training data as possible of classes other than C. In addition, it should be sparse. An interpretable representative of a dataset must not only contain examples of each class, but it is also necessary to provide some criticism samples. The criticism can explain what is not captured by prototypes. For instance, [20] develop the maximum mean discrepancy criticism (MMD-critic) method for prototype Selection and criticism motivated by the Bayesian model criticism framework.

5.2   NLP-Based Approaches

The second class of ideas we can infer from FEG plot are natural language processing (NLP) based techniques. These methods provide a solution to explain the model decisions. The main application is creating a text to describe an image, known as image captioning. The four papers forming the rightmost sub-graph in Fig. 3 are examples of this class. Being able to describe the image from the extracted features can also be approached to make the feature production model understandable.

Inspired by attention-based models, [51] introduced a method to describe an image. Unlike other models in image captioning, which use object detectors or represent images as a single feature vector from the top layer of a pre-trained convolutional network, their model learns hidden alignments from scratch. This model extracts features used by the encoder from the lower convolutional layer instead of the fully connected layer. This way, the decoder can be more focused on the parts of the image that are important. The learned attention in the decoder can be used as a solution to visualize the model generation process and make this model interpretable. In other words, by using those attention, one can show which parts of the image are the most important contributors to producing each word; this provides an understanding of how the model works.

On the other hand, [17] discusses that a textual description of an image should not only describe that image correctly but should also be class discrimination. Explanations produced by this model are not only conditioned on the images but also conditioned on the respective classes. The authors used a discriminative loss function to encourage captioning sentences to correspond primarily to features that are class-specific. Although this model produces sentences that are discriminative as well as descriptive, it is not able to show which part of the image is related to the features mentioned in the sentences. Moreover, it is possible that some features do not appear in an image and just come to the sentences based on being class discriminative.

5.3   Feature Importance Techniques

The largest group of ideas belongs to feature importance techniques, specified in the FEG plot as a sub-graph formed in Fig. 3 contains a number of articles that are all linked together. Disentangling those relations is going to be more challenging and requires a more in-depth analysis than Sects. 5.1 and 5.2. First, however, it is important to notice that almost all articles in this group use feature importance to explain either the model as a whole or individual decision. They have taken different approaches to do so; however, it is clear that they are all related.

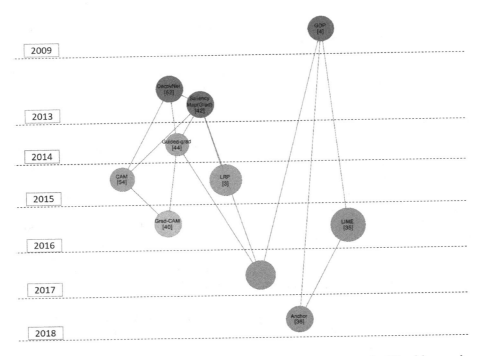

Fig. 4. FEG plot of the articles in features importance approach. The blue nodes belong to the model-specific approach, and the red nodes belong to the model-agnostic approach. The gray node represents a paper that does not fit either category; notably, it is linked to both aforementioned approaches. (Color figure online)

By subjective visual analysis, one can notice that papers [52] and [42], together with [4], form important "hubs". So there are two main approaches in between, which we will discuss in the following, and how the formation, expansion, and evolution of methods in these two.

By focusing on these, and the papers that cite them and ignoring the rest, one can obtain the FEG plot presented in Fig. 4. We thus now focus on analyzing this group of papers.

Model-Specific. One way to explain a model and its decisions are to show which features play the most critical role in output generation. Some methods are proposed on specific models to show the influential features of making a decision, which we will discuss. In 2013, [52] proposed a method to visualize the convolutional layers. They used a multi-layer DeconvNet to map the activities of each layer to the input of that layer. By doing so and displaying it in the original pixel space, one can identify the parts of the input that have the most impact on that layer. Doing this for the last layer can provide a strong visualization of the input that shows the important pixels for each decision. One of the problems with this method is that the max-pooling operator is non-invertible.

The authors, therefore, approximated the inverse of this operation by producing Max Locations Switches to record the location of maximum value within each pooling area to solve this problem.

As the name implies, this method is applied to convolution layers. Following this, another method was presented by [42] to obtain the class saliency map from the gradient of the score of class $c(Y_c)$, with respect to the input image I. It can be shown that except for the RELU layer, DeconvNet effectively corresponds to the gradient backpropagation through a ConvNet. Gradient backpropagation applies to visualize the class score neurons in the final fully-connected layer. It means this method can be applied not only to a convolutional layer but also to any other type of layer. In this sense, it is seen as a generalization of [52]. In more details, this method obtains the class saliency map from the gradient of the score of class $c(Y_c$, with respect to the input image I, by taking the magnitude of it and a maximum along all its channels. If the values of the derivation of Y_c w.r.t the I is close to zero, it means that small changes in that part of the image have no effect on determining that output class. The values which are high in magnitude mean that small changes in that pixels can have a major impact on the result of score class c. Note that for obtaining that gradient, instead of back-propagating on the loss, it should be backpropagation on the score Y_c.

Later, [44] offered another improvement in [52] by eliminating the need for switches and replacing max-pooling layers with convolution' and proposed a combination of methods in [52] and [42]. The difference between' deconvolution' [52] and backpropagation [42] is handling backpropagation through the rectified linear (ReLU) non-linearity. While deconvolution computes gradient based on the top gradient signal, backpropagation computes this based on negative entries of the bottom data. In the case of the ReLU non-linearity, this amounts to setting to zero certain entries based on the top gradient in deconvolution and bottom data in backpropagation. [44] combined them and zerosout the negative gradients during backpropagation. This method, called guided Backprop or guided-grad, often produces more visually appealing and less noisy results and can be used even without' switches' (Max Location).

Class Activation Maps (CAM) is also trying to understand which pixels of an image have more contribution to the final output of the model [54]. This method replaced fully connected layers at the very end of the model with the Global Average Pooling (GAP) layer. This layer averages the activations of each feature map and concatenates them as a vector and a weighted sum of this vector is fed to the final soft-max loss layer. According to [42, 52], each unit is expected to be activated by some visual patterns. Thus, the most relevant part of an input image (to a particular class) is identified by up-sampling CAM to the size of the image.

Although the output of the CAM is class discriminative, the network must be fine-tuned in this method. Also, fully-connected layers are replaced, so it is not applicable to all networks. Grad-CAM [40] as a combination of the saliency map [42] and CAM [54] was introduced to deal with these limitations. Grad-CAM calculates gradients of any class score with respect to the activations maps of the final convolutional layer. Then, similar to CAM, score importance is obtained by averaging the gradients across each feature map. Grad-CAM can only produce coarse-grained visualizations, therefore the authors have also combined guided-grad [44] with Grad-CAM(via element-wise multiplication) and propose Guided Grad-CAM which is able to highlight fine-gradient details.

Model-Agnostic. Although the methods described in the previous approach apply to a wide range of neural networks, they are all model-specific. However, several feature importance-based methods are model-agnostic and therefore can be applied to different models (the left part of Fig. 4).

In particular, [4] proposed a procedure to understand the decisions for every single instance by obtaining local explanation vectors based on Gaussian Process Classification (GDP). Local gradients, as explanation vectors, determine how a data sample should be changed to change its predictive label and find the most influential features in the decision of the model for a particular instance. This technique can be applied to any classification method.

LIME [35] is also a well-known method to generate a local explanation of any black-box model. This method uses local surrogate interpretable models to approximate the prediction of the model. Its main idea is that train an accurate black-box model and then explain the model based on the simple and easy-to-understand model such as linear or logistic regression locally. LIME generates some neighborhoods of the instance that has to be explained, labels them by the black-box model, and weights them based on their vicinity to the original instance. Finally, an interpretable model applies to these weighted instances and their predicted labels to create the explanations.

6   Conclusion

We propose a systematic solution for newcomers who are interested to enter a new research area but face information overload due to the intractable number of publications. Our solution is able to efficiently identify the key group of ideas and track their evolution. This is essential in fields such as XAI that are evolving at an extremely high pace. We show how FEG can be used to uncover different key concepts in XAI, their temporal evolution, and how these ideas relate to each other. For example, the FEG created using our approach identifies three different branches within XAI: the example-based approaches, the natural language-based approaches, and the feature importance-based approaches. FEG can also show how these ideas are formed and how mature they are. For instance, we can see how the guided-grad idea [44] evolved from the DeconvNet idea [52] or how the grad-CAM idea [40] is formed by combining CAM [54] and Guided-grad [44].

This paper is a work-in-progress. We ran the experiments on a limited number of articles in the field, removed irrelevant citations based on Semantic Scholar labeling, and analyzed the remaining graph manually. Nevertheless, we believe already these results are going to be of interest. However, at larger scales, the complete process can be automated by natural language and graph processing techniques. Another direction is the identification of the key papers in a more automatic way by using metrics and statistics in (social) network analysis. These methods can provide some important information on the relation between nodes and can also identify the important and influential nodes automatically.

Acknowledgments. This work was supported by CHIST-ERA grant CHIST-ERA-19-XAI-012 funded by Swedish Research Council.

References

1. Abu-Jbara, A., Radev, D.: Coherent citation-based summarization of scientific papers. In: Proceedings of the 49th Annual Meeting of the Association for Computational Linguistics: Human Language Technologies, pp. 500–509 (2011)
2. Adebayo, J., Gilmer, J., Muelly, M., Goodfellow, I., Hardt, M., Kim, B.: Sanity checks for saliency maps. In: Advances in Neural Information Processing Systems, vol. 31 (2018)
3. Bach, S., Binder, A., Montavon, G., Klauschen, F., Müller, K.R., Samek, W.: On pixel-wise explanations for non-linear classifier decisions by layer-wise relevance propagation. PLoS ONE **10**(7), e0130140 (2015)
4. Baehrens, D., Schroeter, T., Harmeling, S., Kawanabe, M., Hansen, K., Müller, K.R.: How to explain individual classification decisions. J. Mach. Learn. Res. **11**, 1803–1831 (2010)
5. Bahdanau, D., Cho, K., Bengio, Y.: Neural machine translation by jointly learning to align and translate. arXiv preprint arXiv:1409.0473 (2014)
6. Bau, D., Zhou, B., Khosla, A., Oliva, A., Torralba, A.: Network dissection: quantifying interpretability of deep visual representations. In: Proceedings of the IEEE Conference on Computer Vision And Pattern Recognition, pp. 6541–6549 (2017)
7. Bien, J., Tibshirani, R.: Prototype selection for interpretable classification. Ann. Appl. Statist. **5**(4), 2403–2424 (2011)
8. Caruana, R., Lou, Y., Gehrke, J., Koch, P., Sturm, M., Elhadad, N.: Intelligible models for healthcare: Predicting pneumonia risk and hospital 30-day readmission. In: Proceedings of the 21th ACM SIGKDD International Conference on Knowledge Discovery and Data Mining, pp. 1721–1730 (2015)
9. Chen, J., Zhuge, H.: Automatic generation of related work through summarizing citations. Concurr. Comput. Pract. Exp. **31**(3), e4261 (2019)
10. Craven, M., Shavlik, J.: Extracting tree-structured representations of trained networks. In: Advances in Neural Information Processing Systems, vol. 8 (1995)
11. Dabkowski, P., Gal, Y.: Real time image saliency for black box classifiers. In: Advances in Neural Information Processing Systems, vol. 30 (2017)
12. Danilevsky, M., Qian, K., Aharonov, R., Katsis, Y., Kawas, B., Sen, P.: A survey of the state of explainable ai for natural language processing. arXiv preprint arXiv:2010.00711 (2020)
13. Datta, A., Sen, S., Zick, Y.: Algorithmic transparency via quantitative input influence: theory and experiments with learning systems. In: 2016 IEEE Symposium on Security and Privacy (SP), pp. 598–617. IEEE (2016)
14. Fink, O., Wang, Q., Svensen, M., Dersin, P., Lee, W.J., Ducoffe, M.: Potential, challenges and future directions for deep learning in prognostics and health management applications. Eng. Appl. Artif. Intell. **92**, 103678 (2020)

15. Fong, R.C., Vedaldi, A.: Interpretable explanations of black boxes by meaningful perturbation. In: Proceedings of the IEEE International Conference on Computer Vision, pp. 3429–3437 (2017)

16. Hannousse, A.: Searching relevant papers for software engineering secondary studies: semantic scholar coverage and identification role. IET Softw. **15**(1), 126–146 (2021)

17. Hendricks, L.A., Akata, Z., Rohrbach, M., Donahue, J., Schiele, B., Darrell, T.: Generating visual explanations. In: Leibe, B., Matas, J., Sebe, N., Welling, M. (eds.) ECCV 2016. LNCS, vol. 9908, pp. 3–19. Springer, Cham (2016). https://doi.org/10.1007/978-3-319-46493-0_1

18. Huysmans, J., Dejaeger, K., Mues, C., Vanthienen, J., Baesens, B.: An empirical evaluation of the comprehensibility of decision table, tree and rule based predictive models. Decis. Support Syst. **51**(1), 141–154 (2011)

19. Kan, M.S., Tan, A.C., Mathew, J.: A review on prognostic techniques for non-stationary and non-linear rotating systems. Mech. Syst. Signal Process. **62**, 1–20 (2015)

20. Kim, B., Khanna, R., Koyejo, O.O.: Examples are not enough, learn to criticize! criticism for interpretability. In: Advances in Neural Information Processing Systems, vol. 29 (2016)

21. Kim, B., Wattenberg, M., Gilmer, J., Cai, C., Wexler, J., Viegas, F., et al.: Interpretability beyond feature attribution: Quantitative testing with concept activation vectors (TCAV). In: International Conference on Machine Learning, pp. 2668–2677. PMLR (2018)

22. Koh, P.W., Liang, P.: Understanding black-box predictions via influence functions. In: International Conference on Machine Learning, pp. 1885–1894. PMLR (2017)

23. Lakkaraju, H., Kamar, E., Caruana, R., Leskovec, J.: Interpretable and explorable approximations of black box models. arXiv preprint arXiv:1707.01154 (2017)

24. Letham, B., Rudin, C., McCormick, T.H., Madigan, D.: Interpretable classifiers using rules and Bayesian analysis: building a better stroke prediction model. Ann. Appl. Statist. **9**(3), 1350–1371 (2015)

25. Li, W., Xiao, X., Liu, J., Wu, H., Wang, H., Du, J.: Leveraging graph to improve abstractive multi-document summarization. arXiv preprint arXiv:2005.10043 (2020)

26. Lundberg, S.M., Lee, S.I.: A unified approach to interpreting model predictions. Advances in Neural Information Processing Systems, vol. 30 (2017)

27. Mahendran, A., Vedaldi, A.: Understanding deep image representations by inverting them. In: Proceedings of the IEEE Conference on Computer Vision and Pattern Recognition, pp. 5188–5196 (2015)

28. Markus, A.F., Kors, J.A., Rijnbeek, P.R.: The role of explainability in creating trustworthy artificial intelligence for health care: a comprehensive survey of the terminology, design choices, and evaluation strategies. J. Biomed. Inform. **113**, 103655 (2021)

29. Miller, T.: Explanation in artificial intelligence: insights from the social sciences. Artif. Intell. **267**, 1–38 (2019)

30. Montavon, G., Lapuschkin, S., Binder, A., Samek, W., Müller, K.R.: Explaining nonlinear classification decisions with deep Taylor decomposition. Pattern Recogn. **65**, 211–222 (2017)

31. Nguyen, A., Dosovitskiy, A., Yosinski, J., Brox, T., Clune, J.: Synthesizing the preferred inputs for neurons in neural networks via deep generator networks. In: Advances in Neural Information Processing Systems, vol. 29 (2016)

32. Nguyen, A., Yosinski, J., Clune, J.: Deep neural networks are easily fooled: high confidence predictions for unrecognizable images. In: Proceedings of the IEEE Conference on Computer Vision and Pattern Recognition, pp. 427–436 (2015)
33. Nikiforovskaya, A., Kapralov, N., Vlasova, A., Shpynov, O., Shpilman, A.: Automatic generation of reviews of scientific papers. In: 2020 19th IEEE International Conference on Machine Learning and Applications (ICMLA), pp. 314–319. IEEE (2020)
34. Rezaeianjouybari, B., Shang, Y.: Deep learning for prognostics and health management: state of the art, challenges, and opportunities. Measurement **163**, 107929 (2020)
35. Ribeiro, M.T., Singh, S., Guestrin, C.: "why should i trust you?" Explaining the predictions of any classifier. In: Proceedings of the 22nd ACM SIGKDD International Conference on Knowledge Discovery and Data Mining, pp. 1135–1144 (2016)
36. Ribeiro, M.T., Singh, S., Guestrin, C.: Anchors: High-precision model-agnostic explanations. In: Proceedings of the AAAI Conference on Artificial Intelligence, vol. 32 (2018)
37. Robnik-Šikonja, M., Kononenko, I.: Explaining classifications for individual instances. IEEE Trans. Knowl. Data Eng. **20**(5), 589–600 (2008)
38. Ross, A.S., Hughes, M.C., Doshi-Velez, F.: Right for the right reasons: training differentiable models by constraining their explanations. arXiv preprint arXiv:1703.03717 (2017)
39. Samek, W., Binder, A., Montavon, G., Lapuschkin, S., Müller, K.R.: Evaluating the visualization of what a deep neural network has learned. IEEE Trans. Neural Netw. Learn. Syst. **28**(11), 2660–2673 (2016)
40. Selvaraju, R.R., Cogswell, M., Das, A., Vedantam, R., Parikh, D., Batra, D.: Grad-cam: Visual explanations from deep networks via gradient-based localization. In: Proceedings of the IEEE International Conference on Computer Vision, pp. 618–626 (2017)
41. Shrikumar, A., Greenside, P., Kundaje, A.: Learning important features through propagating activation differences. In: International Conference on Machine Learning, pp. 3145–3153. PMLR (2017)
42. Simonyan, K., Vedaldi, A., Zisserman, A.: Deep inside convolutional networks: visualising image classification models and saliency maps. In: Workshop at International Conference on Learning Representations. Citeseer (2014)
43. Smilkov, D., Thorat, N., Kim, B., Viégas, F., Wattenberg, M.: Smoothgrad: removing noise by adding noise. arXiv preprint arXiv:1706.03825 (2017)
44. Springenberg, J.T., Dosovitskiy, A., Brox, T., Riedmiller, M.: Striving for simplicity: the all convolutional net. arXiv preprint arXiv:1412.6806 (2014)
45. Sun, X., Zhuge, H.: Automatic generation of survey paper based on template tree. In: 2019 15th International Conference on Semantics, Knowledge and Grids (SKG), pp. 89–96. IEEE (2019)
46. Sundararajan, M., Taly, A., Yan, Q.: Axiomatic attribution for deep networks. In: International Conference on Machine Learning, pp. 3319–3328. PMLR (2017)
47. Tjoa, E., Guan, C.: A survey on explainable artificial intelligence (XAI): toward medical XAI. IEEE Trans. Neural Netw. Learn. Syst. **32**(11), 4793–4813 (2020)
48. Tohalino, J.V., Amancio, D.R.: Extractive multi-document summarization using multilayer networks. Physica A **503**, 526–539 (2018)
49. Vaswani, A., et al.: Attention is all you need. In: Advances in Neural Information Processing Systems, vol. 30 (2017)
50. Wang, J., Zhang, C., Zhang, M., Deng, S.: Citationas: a tool of automatic survey generation based on citation content. J. Data Inf. Sci. **3**(2), 20–37 (2018)

51. Xu, K., et al.: Show, attend and tell: Neural image caption generation with visual attention. In: International Conference on Machine Learning, pp. 2048–2057. PMLR (2015)
52. Zeiler, M.D., Fergus, R.: Visualizing and understanding convolutional networks. In: Fleet, D., Pajdla, T., Schiele, B., Tuytelaars, T. (eds.) ECCV 2014. LNCS, vol. 8689, pp. 818–833. Springer, Cham (2014). https://doi.org/10.1007/978-3-319-10590-1_53
53. Zhang, Q., Wu, Y.N., Zhu, S.C.: Interpretable convolutional neural networks. In: Proceedings of the IEEE Conference on Computer Vision and Pattern Recognition, pp. 8827–8836 (2018)
54. Zhou, B., Khosla, A., Lapedriza, A., Oliva, A., Torralba, A.: Learning deep features for discriminative localization. In: Proceedings of the IEEE Conference on Computer Vision and Pattern Recognition, pp. 2921–2929 (2016)
55. Zintgraf, L.M., Cohen, T.S., Adel, T., Welling, M.: Visualizing deep neural network decisions: prediction difference analysis. arXiv preprint arXiv:1702.04595 (2017)

Frequent Generalized Subgraph Mining via Graph Edit Distances

Richard Palme and Pascal Welke[(✉)] [ⓘ]

University of Bonn, Bonn, Germany
`welke@cs.uni-bonn.de`

Abstract. In this work, we propose a method for computing generalized frequent subgraph patterns which is based on the graph edit distance. Graph data is often equipped with semantic information in form of an ontology, for example when dealing with linked data or knowledge graphs. Previous work suggests to exploit this semantic information in order to compute frequent generalized patterns, i.e. patterns for which the total frequency of all more specific patterns exceeds the frequency threshold. However, the problem of computing the frequency of a generalized pattern has not yet been fully addressed.

1 Introduction

Nowadays, an ever-increasing amount of graph data is collected, often in form of linked data or knowledge graphs. Linked data, and especially knowledge graphs, often come with an ontology, which provides background knowledge about the entities and entity relations that appear in the dataset. Naturally, the question arises if it is possible to exploit the semantic information given by an ontology, in order to improve the performance of data mining methods on graph data.

A common graph data mining task is to generate the set of frequent subgraphs of a graph database. The frequent subgraph mining problem (FSM) has many applications, ranging from database compression [9] to machine learning [6]. To improve the results of FSM, the semantic information provided by a label hierarchy or taxonomy can be used as background knowledge.

As an example, suppose the graphs in a database contain vertex labels such as "donkey", "rabbit", "carrot" or "cabbage", and suppose these four vertex labels do not appear frequently in the database. If there is a label hierarchy which tells us that "donkey" and "rabbit" are herbivores, while "carrot" and "cabbage" are vegetables, then we can exploit this semantic information in order to find frequently occurring patterns in the database, such as "herbivore eats vegetable". These patterns are called generalized patterns. The problem of frequent generalized subgraph mining has a long history [4,10] and recently gained more traction, again [7,12,14].

Definition 1 (Frequent Generalized Subgraph Mining (FGSM)). *We say that there is a generalized subgraph isomorphism (GSGI) between two graphs*

I. Koprinska et al. (Eds.): ECML PKDD 2022 Workshops, CCIS 1753, pp. 477–483, 2023.
https://doi.org/10.1007/978-3-031-23633-4_32

H and G if G contains a subgraph H′ (up to isomorphism) s.t. H′ can be constructed from H by replacing any label of H by a more specific label w.r.t. the label hierarchy. Here, the root in the label hierarchy is the most general label. A graph H is a frequent generalized subgraph w.r.t. a graph database D if there are at least t graphs $G_1, \ldots, G_t$ in D s.t. there is a GSGI between H and G_i for any $i = 1, \ldots t$. The FGSM problem is then to compute the set of all frequent generalized subgraphs of D.

In order to determine the frequency of a generalized pattern, we need an algorithm for solving the generalized subgraph isomorphism problem (GSGI). Unfortunately, to our knowledge, no previous work gives an algorithm for the GSGI problem. A naive solution to GSGI solves a subgraph isomorphism (SGI) problem with input H′ and G for every specialization H′ of H. Since the number of specializations of H is exponential in the size of H, this solution is not a feasible method for solving GSGI.

In this work we reduce GSGI to the graph edit distance problem (GED), thereby solving GSGI by a single computation of a specific GED between two graphs. Subsequently, we use a heuristic solver for GED within a frequent subgraph mining framework to enumerate frequent generalized subgraphs of arbitrary labeled graph databases.

2   Reduction of Generalized Subgraph Isomorphism (GSGI) to Graph Edit Distance (GED)

The graph edit distance (GED) is a measure for the dissimilarity between two labeled graphs [15]. Two graphs H and G are interpreted to be dissimilar w.r.t. GED if, for any sequence of edit operations that transforms H into G, the cost incurred by the sequence of edit operations is high. We remark that, like SGI and GSGI, GED is NP-hard. In fact, this follows immediately from Eq. (1) below. However, there exist efficient heuristics to compute GED in practice [1–3].

Definition 2 (Graph Edit Distance). *Let H and G be labeled graphs, let Σ be a finite label alphabet, and let ε be a symbol which is not an element of Σ. Denoting $\Sigma \cup \{\varepsilon\}$ by Σ_ε, we call a function*

$$c \colon \Sigma_\varepsilon \times \Sigma_\varepsilon \to [0, \infty)$$

an edit cost function if

$$\forall \alpha \in \Sigma_\varepsilon \colon c(\alpha, \alpha) = 0.$$

An edit cost function assigns an edit cost to each edit operation. Table 1 contains a comprehensive list of all considered edit operations and their associated edit costs. An edit path π between H and G is a finite sequence of edit operations $(o_i)_{i=1}^k$ that transforms H into a graph $\pi(H)$ that is isomorphic to G. The cost incurred by π is defined as

$$c(\pi) := \sum_{i=1}^k c(o_i),$$

Table 1. Edit operations and their associated edit costs. Deleting an edge $\{u, v\}$ does not delete u or v, and inserting an edge $\{u, v\}$ is only possible if u and v have been previously inserted or are vertices of H.

Edit operation	Edit cost
Insert an isolated vertex with label $\alpha \in \Sigma$	$c(\varepsilon, \alpha)$
Delete an isolated vertex u	$c(\lambda(u), \varepsilon)$
Substitute the label of a vertex u by $\alpha \in \Sigma$	$c(\lambda(u), \alpha)$
Insert an edge with label $\alpha \in \Sigma$	$c(\varepsilon, \alpha)$
Delete an edge e	$c(\lambda(e), \varepsilon)$
Substitute the label of an edge e by $\alpha \in \Sigma$	$c(\lambda(e), \alpha)$

where $c(o_i)$ denotes the edit cost of the edit operation o_i. We denote the set of edit paths between H and G by $\Pi(H, G)$, and define the graph edit distance between H and G as follows:

$$GED(H, G) := \min_{\pi \in \Pi(H,G)} c(\pi).$$

The GED can be used to solve the subgraph isomorphism problem (SGI) by imposing the following three constraints on the edit cost function:

$$\forall \beta \in \Sigma_\varepsilon : c(\varepsilon, \beta) = 0 \qquad \text{(free insertions)}$$
$$\forall \alpha \in \Sigma : c(\alpha, \varepsilon) > 0 \qquad \text{(paid deletions)}$$
$$\forall \alpha, \beta \in \Sigma : c(\alpha, \beta) > 0 \iff \alpha \neq \beta \qquad \text{(paid substitutions)}$$

We call the graph edit distance between two graphs the subgraph edit distance (SGED), if the edit cost function obeys these three constraints. For any two graphs H and G, we get

$$H \preceq G \iff \text{SGED}(H, G) = 0, \qquad (1)$$

where $H \preceq G$ is a shorthand for H being subgraph isomorphic to G. Thus, the SGI problem can be solved using the SGED problem.

Assuming the edit cost function obeys the triangle inequality in addition to the three constraints above, we get

$$H' \preceq H \implies \text{SGED}(H', G) \leq \text{SGED}(H', H) + \text{SGED}(H, G) = \text{SGED}(H, G).$$

In other words, SGED is monotone in its first argument. Many algorithms for frequent subgraph mining rely on the monotonicity of SGI in its first argument, and SGED also being monotone in its first argument ensures that SGED can be used as a drop-in replacement for SGI in many pattern mining algorithms.

To solve the generalized subgraph isomorphism problem (GSGI), we impose the following four constraints on the edit cost function:

$$\forall \beta \in \Sigma_\varepsilon : c(\varepsilon, \beta) = 0 \qquad \text{(free insertions)}$$
$$\forall \alpha \in \Sigma : c(\alpha, \varepsilon) > 0 \qquad \text{(paid deletions)}$$
$$\forall \alpha, \beta \in \Sigma : c(\alpha, \beta) > 0 \iff \alpha \neq \beta \text{ and } \alpha \text{ is not more general than } \beta$$
$$\text{(paid substitutions)}$$
$$\forall \alpha, \beta \in \Sigma : c(\alpha, \beta) = 0 \iff \alpha = \beta \text{ or } \alpha \text{ is more general than } \beta$$
$$\text{(free specializations)}$$

With these constraints, we get

$$\mathrm{GSGI}(H, G) = \text{true} \iff \mathrm{GED}(H, G) = 0.$$

Thus, the GSGI problem can be solved using the GED problem with an edit cost function that satisfies the four constraints given above. We can then use this solution to the GSGI problem in order to solve the frequent generalized subgraph mining problem (FGSM). Alternatively, we can impose the following four constraints on the edit cost function c for some $M > 0$ large enough:

$$\forall \beta \in \Sigma_\varepsilon : c(\varepsilon, \beta) \ll M \qquad \text{(cheap insertions)}$$
$$\forall \alpha \in \Sigma : c(\alpha, \varepsilon) = M \qquad \text{(forbidden deletions)}$$
$$\forall \alpha, \beta \in \Sigma : c(\alpha, \beta) = M \iff \alpha \neq \beta \text{ and } \alpha \text{ is not more general than } \beta$$
$$\text{(forbidden substitutions)}$$
$$\forall \alpha, \beta \in \Sigma : c(\alpha, \beta) \ll M \iff \alpha = \beta \text{ or } \alpha \text{ is more general than } \beta$$
$$\text{(cheap generalizations)}$$

Then we get
$$\mathrm{GSGI}(H, G) = \text{true} \iff \mathrm{GED}(H, G) < M.$$

3 Application to Generalized Subgraph Mining

The four constraints for the generalized subgraph edit distance leave us the freedom to choose insertion costs and specialization costs as we wish. We can use this freedom in order to infuse additional background knowledge into the GED computation. As an example, suppose a label hierarchy has been computed by a hierarchical clustering of all vertex labels. Then each leaf node in the cluster hierarchy corresponds to a label, and each non-leaf node corresponds to a generalized label which does not appear in the database. Since the cluster hierarchy is a dendrogram, for any generalized label α, we know the distance $d(\alpha, \beta)$ between α and any label β which is more specific than α.

We can infuse these distances into the GED computation as follows: We set the cost $c(\alpha, \beta)$ of substituting a generalized label α by a more specific label β to $d(\alpha, \beta)$, while the remaining edit costs are chosen s.t. the four constraints

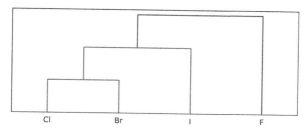

Fig. 1. A section of the dendrogram created by clustering chemical elements. The chosen section of the dendrogram shows a cluster which only contains halogens.

above are satisfied. Using these edit costs, the collection of graph edit distances between a generalized pattern H and all graphs G in the database yields an interestingness measure for H. Large values for $GED(H, G)$ indicate that H is a rather specific pattern, while smaller values indicate that H is a rather general pattern. Since generalized patterns are arguably interesting if they are both frequent and specific, infusing label distances into the GED computation yields a method for ranking the frequent generalized subgraphs. We note that the mere *frequency* of generalized patterns can not be used for ranking them, since maximally general patterns have the highest frequency but are not interesting.

In most cases, label hierarchies do not specify label distances. However, for any generalized label α, we can always set the distance $d(\alpha, \beta)$ between α and any more specific label β to the length of the unique path between α and β in the hierarchy tree.

We implemented a frequent generalized subgraph miner by making use of the C++ library GEDLIB [3] to compute graph edit distances. We tested our method on the MUTAG [5] and PTC-MR datasets [8], which contain graphs representations of chemical compounds, in the format of Morris et al. [13].

To compute a label hierarchy on chemical elements, we use the inter-cluster distance between clusters of chemical elements given by Leal et al. [11]. This inter-cluster distance has the property that many of the resulting clusters correspond to common groups of elements. Figure 1 shows a small part of the dendrogram which is the result of hierarchical clustering when using this distance. Our preliminary experiments confirm that FGSM can uncover frequent patterns that are not found by frequent subgraph mining. An example of our findings is illustrated in Fig. 2.

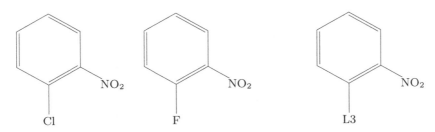

Fig. 2. The two molecules on the left appear as subgraphs in the MUTAG database, while the graph on the right is a generalized pattern. Both molecules are infrequent for a relative frequency threshold of 5%, while the generalized pattern is frequent w.r.t. the same frequency threshold.

4   Conclusion

Frequent generalized subgraph mining is a variant of graph mining which exploits the semantic information provided by a label hierarchy. In this work, we propose a method for solving FGSM by using graph edit distance computations. Our method imposes constraints on the edit cost function in order to encode the background knowledge given by the label hierarchy. Since these constraints do not fully determine the edit cost function, we are free to choose the values for a subset of the edit costs. We have seen that this freedom of choice can be exploited to achieve additional goals. For example, we were able to assign an interestingness measure to each frequent generalized subgraph by choosing the values for selected substitution costs.

As an outlook, we note that edit cost functions are not restricted to model label hierarchies, and thus graph edit distances are a powerful tool for including domain knowledge beyond label hierarchies into graph mining procedures. While we don't include extensive experiments in this article, the source code of our mining algorithm is available at https://github.com/RichardPalme/fasm.

References

1. Bause, F., Schubert, E., Kriege, N.M.: EmbAssi: embedding assignment costs for similarity search in large graph databases. Data Mining Knowl. Disc. **36**, 1–28 (2022). https://doi.org/10.1007/s10618-022-00850-3
2. Blumenthal, D.B., Boria, N., Gamper, J., Bougleux, S., Brun, L.: Comparing heuristics for graph edit distance computation. VLDB J. **29**(1), 419–458 (2019). https://doi.org/10.1007/s00778-019-00544-1
3. Blumenthal, D.B., Bougleux, S., Gamper, J., Brun, L.: GEDLIB: A C++ library for graph edit distance computation. In: Conte, D., Ramel, J.-Y., Foggia, P. (eds.) GbRPR 2019. LNCS, vol. 11510, pp. 14–24. Springer, Cham (2019). https://doi.org/10.1007/978-3-030-20081-7_2
4. Cakmak, A., Özsoyoglu, G.: Taxonomy-superimposed graph mining. In: International Conference on Extending Database Technology, ACM International Conference Proceeding Series, vol. 261, pp. 217–228. ACM (2008). https://doi.org/10.1145/1353343.1353372

5. Debnath, A.K., de Compadre, R.L.L., Debnath, G., Shusterman, A.J., Hansch, C.: Structure-activity relationship of mutagenic aromatic and heteroaromatic nitro compounds correlation with molecular orbital energies and hydrophobicity. J. Med. Chem. **34**(2), 786–797 (1991). https://doi.org/10.1021/jm00106a046
6. Deshpande, M., Kuramochi, M., Wale, N., Karypis, G.: Frequent substructure-based approaches for classifying chemical compounds. IEEE Trans. Knowl. Data Eng. **17**(8), 1036–1050 (2005). https://doi.org/10.1109/TKDE.2005.127
7. Faci, A., Lesot, M.-J., Laudy, C.: cgSpan: Pattern mining in conceptual graphs. In: Rutkowski, L., Scherer, R., Korytkowski, M., Pedrycz, W., Tadeusiewicz, R., Zurada, J.M. (eds.) ICAISC 2021. LNCS (LNAI), vol. 12855, pp. 149–158. Springer, Cham (2021). https://doi.org/10.1007/978-3-030-87897-9_14
8. Helma, C., King, R.D., Kramer, S., Srinivasan, A.: The predictive toxicology challenge 2000–2001. Bioinformatics **17**(1), 107–108 (2001). https://doi.org/10.1093/bioinformatics/17.1.107
9. Holder, L.B., Cook, D.J., Djoko, S.: Substucture discovery in the SUBDUE system. In: AAAI Workshop on Knowledge Discovery in Databases, pp. 169–180. AAAI Press (1994)
10. Inokuchi, A.: Mining generalized substructures from a set of labeled graphs. In: IEEE International Conference on Data Mining, pp. 415–418. IEEE Computer Society (2004). https://doi.org/10.1109/ICDM.2004.10041
11. Leal, W., Restrepo, G., Bernal, A.: A network study of chemical elements: from binary compounds to chemical trends. MATCH Commun. Math. Comput. Chem. **68**, 417–442 (2012)
12. Martin, T., Fuentes, V., Valtchev, P., Diallo, A.B., Lacroix, R.: Generalized graph pattern discovery in linked data with data properties and a domain ontology. In: Symposium on Applied Computing, pp. 1890–1899. ACM (2022). https://doi.org/10.1145/3477314.3507301
13. Morris, C., et al.: Tudataset: a collection of benchmark datasets for learning with graphs. In: ICML Workshop on Graph Representation Learning and Beyond (2020)
14. Petermann, A., Micale, G., Bergami, G., Pulvirenti, A., Rahm, E.: Mining and ranking of generalized multi-dimensional frequent subgraphs. In: International Conference on Digital Information Management, pp. 236–245. IEEE (2017). https://doi.org/10.1109/ICDIM.2017.8244685
15. Sanfeliu, A., Fu, K.: A distance measure between attributed relational graphs for pattern recognition. IEEE Trans. Syst. Man Cybern. **13**(3), 353–362 (1983). https://doi.org/10.1109/TSMC.1983.6313167

Author Index

Printed in the United States
by Baker & Taylor Publisher Services